CONTEMPORARY
LATIN AMERICA

A SHORT HISTORY

CONTEMPORARY LATIN AMERICA

A SHORT HISTORY
text and readings

LEWIS HANKE
Professor of History,
University of California • Irvine

D. VAN NOSTRAND
COMPANY, INC.
PRINCETON, NEW JERSEY
TORONTO • LONDON • MELBOURNE

Van Nostrand Regional Offices: *New York, Chicago, San Francisco*

D. Van Nostrand Company, Ltd., *London*

D. Van Nostrand Company (Canada), Ltd., *Toronto*

D. Van Nostrand Australia Pty. Ltd., *Melbourne*

✓

Published simultaneously in Canada by
D. Van Nostrand Company (Canada), Ltd.

Library of Congress Catalog Card No. 68–20919

Cover design adapted from Peruvian textile, 1000 A.D.

PRINTED IN THE UNITED STATES OF AMERICA

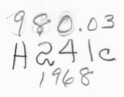

Preface

In preparing this volume I have been mindful of Geoffrey Barraclough's observation that "contemporary history" means "more than scratching about on the surface of recent events and misinterpreting the recent past in the light of current ideologies," and I have become convinced that his view of the difficulties is sound: "If it is to be of any lasting value, the analysis of contemporary events requires no less—perhaps, indeed, a good deal more—than any other kind of history; our only hope of discerning the forces actually operative in the world around us is to range them firmly against the past." [1]

Whatever may be the orientation of historians analyzing contemporary Latin America, most of them agree that colonial ideas and institutions still powerfully influence the present and are sure to affect the future.[2] Moreover, Latin America has come of age in the twentieth century, and its problems are world problems. As one writer states: "It is only if one perceives what this America conserves of its colonial nature that one can understand the kinship of its problems with those of the underdeveloped nations of the world." [3]

This volume is intended to provide enough factual material and controversial opinions to make possible intelligent consideration of the past history and present prospects of that vast region to the south that we arbitrarily label Latin America. Gone forever are the days when an author could pretend to tell all about these enormously varied nations. Their problems are too pressing, too complicated, and too susceptible of contradictory interpretations to be confidently described, "explained," and prescribed for.

My effort has been, therefore, to present in the text what appear to me to be the essential facts and the important developments. The documents, many of them written by Latin Americans, have been selected to reinforce and illuminate the text. They constitute a small but I believe representative selection from the literature available. A statement on the "Sources of Information on Contemporary Latin America" has been added to guide the reader to other writings, because, like many authors, I cherish the hope that this introduction will stimulate more study of a region and peoples of permanent concern to our citizens who, today more than ever before, need to know about the great problems facing Latin America as it struggles to enter the society of developed nations. One inescapable element in the discussion is the doubt expressed inside and outside of Latin America on how the actions of the United States bear upon this struggle as the forces representing tradition and revolt confront each other south of the Rio Grande.

Since I first visited Latin America in 1935, my principal interest has been its colonial history, particularly the struggle for justice that occurred in sixteenth-century Spanish America and the story of silver mining in Peru. But colonial experience has exerted such a powerful influence in shaping the ideas, institutions, and values of Latin Americans that one finds it difficult, at times impossible, to separate the past from the present. This book includes, moreover, not only the "facts" about Latin America but also the feelings and viewpoints of a variety of Latin Americans. They do not all feel the same way, but friendship over the years with them has deepened my knowledge of their way of life. Yet I remain a "Yankee"; that is, a descendent of Scottish and Wendish families that emigrated to New England in the eighteenth and nineteenth centuries, whose parents were born in California and Massachusetts, and who first studied Spanish in the high school of a small town in Ohio.

Many persons and many institutions over the years have helped me to travel in Latin America and to study its history. From many discussions with my colleagues there, I have learned how easy it is to misjudge events from afar, and how variegated are the patterns of life emerging in Latin America. The friends who have helped me are too numerous to list here, though I would like to pay special tribute to my students at the University of Texas and Columbia University. James Nelson Goodsell of *The Christian Science Monitor* and Dana S. Green of the National Council of the Churches of Christ made an unusual contribution by reading critically the text of the paperback volumes in the Anvil series,[4] which form the basis for this volume. The Pan American Union and the Inter-American Development Bank have been generous in allowing me to use their publications and collections. To all of those who assisted to make the work possible I offer my grateful thanks.

Acknowledgment for the book's illustrations is very especially due to the Brazilian artist Percy Lau, to Professor John W. F. Dulles, to the Pan American Union, and to Compix.

February, 1968   LEWIS HANKE

---

[1] Geoffrey Barraclough, *An Introduction to Contemporary History* (Basic Books: New York, 1965), 12, 8.

[2] For some lively discussion on this topic, see the remarks by Woodrow Borah, Charles Gibson, and Robert A. Potash, "Colonial Institutions and Contemporary Latin America," *The Hispanic American Historical Review,* XLIII (1963), 371–394.

[3] The statement is by Marcel Bataillon, as quoted in the writer's *History of Latin American Civilization,* II (Boston: Little, Brown, 1967), x.

[4] *Modern Latin America, Continent in Ferment,* 2 vols. Second edition, revised and enlarged (Princeton: Van Nostrand, 1967).

Contents

READINGS

MAPS

SOME PRELIMINARY OBSERVATIONS

- **The Winds of Change.** The 20 republics south of the Rio Grande have come of age internationally in the twentieth century. In 1899 only Brazil and Mexico were deemed sufficiently important to receive invitations to the first Hague Peace Conference. All the Latin American nations were invited to the second conference in 1907, and 18 attended. Henceforth, Latin Americans were both seen and heard at international conference tables.

Their influence grew slowly, however. They played no large part in World War I, except as sources of raw materials, but the shock of being cut off from Europe made Latin Americans realize as never before the need to develop their own industries and their own spiritual resources. During the 1920's many Latin American nations joined the League of Nations, partly as a protection against the power of the United States, and thus gained some experience in international affairs. The depression of the 1930's demonstrated how closely Latin America was tied to the economy of Europe and the U.S., and strengthened the position of those who insisted on greater industrialization.

During World War II Latin America increased its prestige and strength. By 1945 she was ready to exert a more steady and significant pressure on world affairs than ever before. She participated vigorously in the establishment of the United Nations, supplied a considerable number of elected and appointed officers to the organization, and for the first ten years Latin America's 20 votes constituted a powerful bloc in the General Assembly. When many new members were admitted beginning in 1957, Latin America lost her special power in the Assembly, but remains a force in the United Nations. In its specialized agencies on cultural and economic affairs, Latin Americans and their projects have been vital from the beginning.

Yet, the leaders and people of this vast region are more disturbed than ever before. They have entered the world scene, but are distinctly unhappy with their position in the world today. A powerful and pervasive spirit of dis-

1

enchantment is abroad in the countries south of the Rio Grande. (*See Readings 78–86.*)

● **The Wine Is Bitter.** Latin Americans are dissatisfied above all with their position in the Western Hemisphere, and with what they regard as both gross neglect and brazen interference in their internal affairs by the U.S. since 1945. Although politically their position improved somewhat in the conduct of the Organization of American States after the Charter of 1948, they compared the $36 billion distributed to Europe in the period 1945–1957 through economic and military aid with the approximately $3.5 billion sent to Latin America, and concluded that the Good Neighbor policy had definitely ended. They also noted bitterly that the U.S., though it lectured Latin Americans against the dangers of communism, gave more economic aid to communist Yugoslavia with its population of only 20 million people than to all of Latin America with a population some six or seven times as large.[1]

Castro's triumph in Cuba in 1959 changed the attitude of the United States. A new epoch began when the 21 hemisphere governments established the Inter-American Bank for Development in April, 1959, an institution which the U.S. had opposed for years. President Kennedy took an even more dramatic step when he announced the Alliance for Progress in March, 1961: "a vast effort, unparalleled in magnitude and nobility of purpose, to satisfy the basic needs of the American people for homes, work, and land, health and schools." The U.S. would contribute $20 billion toward this "vast, new ten year plan . . . to transform the nineteen sixties into an historic decade of democratic progress." [2]

The halfway mark—1965—has been passed, but few still believe that the Alliance will accomplish the objective Kennedy announced of hemispheric self-sustaining growth by the end of the 1960's. Much has been achieved, but the aims were too high, the obstacles too deep rooted, and perhaps the U.S. was not well enough prepared for such a bold effort: "No sane person would attempt to put a space ship in orbit without elaborate supporting education and research activities. Yet this is precisely what we have attempted in the more subtle and complex areas of overseas operations." [3] Though the Alliance has not been the complete success some of its fervent U.S. backers had hoped for, it has exerted one significant though not widely noted influence. The Alliance has served notice that the U.S. is interested in promoting the growth of prosperous democratic societies throughout the Americas and it has encouraged all—except Haiti—to play the development game. Now Latin-American governments—whether democratic regimes, military juntas, or something else—must at least begin to plan for agrarian reform, income taxes, and education if they wish to receive U.S. aid.

The Bay of Pigs fiasco in 1961 and U.S. unilateral intervention in the Dominican Republic in 1965 convinced many in Latin America that "gunboat diplomacy" had returned, that the worldwide concerns of the U.S. have permanently diminished their relationship with them, and that the cold war will drag them inexorably and repeatedly into unwanted controversies.

Besides these current doubts, Latin Americans have other long-standing criticisms of U.S. policy and practice. They dislike the seeming approval that the United States accords to some dictators, and they attack military aid to their countries as aid to dictators against their own peoples. They have failed to obtain price supports for the export commodities on which their economies depend, and they desire more investment of U.S. Government capital. They feel, too, that we underestimate their culture, know little about their history, and ignore their aspirations. Many of them fear that the U.S. at times is chiefly obsessed with the number of communists in Latin America, and that our policy revolves around this subject in which, until very lately, they have taken relatively little interest.

Latin Americans do not share the hope that characterizes the emerging peoples of Africa and Asia, for they won their political independence over a century ago and by now have few utopian illusions. They have achieved great economic progress but no comparable improvement in the lot of the masses who are still hungry, sick, and exploited. The enormous changes in their social and economic life have seldom been accompanied by corresponding developments in political institutions or political stability. Latin Americans are beginning to search for assistance outside the hemisphere, specifically in Europe and even in communist countries, and are hoping to find new markets for their commodity products.

The U.S. has likewise been taking a new look at Latin America, particularly since the attacks on Vice-President Nixon in 1958. The hostility which that incident dramatized has not diminished with the years or with the development of plans such as the Alliance for Progress. Students at the University of Concepción, Chile, for example, not only hurled rotten eggs at Senator Robert Kennedy in November, 1965, but they also prevented him from speaking. Now some voices in the U.S. are asking sharp questions: have the money, food, and other assistance sent to Latin America really helped those nations? Is the area always to be plagued with some dictatorial governments and unstable economies? Will the governing elites never work out a program to educate the masses of their countrymen and incorporate them as responsible participants in the national life? Will they always want aid from the U.S. at the same time that they resist accountability for how they use it, and will they still prefer to attack the U.S. rather than their own problems?

Both Latin America and the U.S. seem convinced that a new deal is needed, and that the Organization of American States must be brought into line with the present realities of the world. They differ radically, however, in their respective diagnoses of the problem and in their recommendations for improvement. A focal issue for many discussions on this topic has been the question of hemispheric unity. Beginning with Bolívar, a mystique developed in the countries of the Americas concerning their common destiny as New World nations. At Pan American conferences and elsewhere the oratory flowed copiously on this topic. (*See Readings Nos. 80–86.*)

As much as Latin Americans were profoundly disturbed by the attitude of the House of Representatives in September, 1965, which approved intervention in Latin America whenever the U.S. judged such action necessary, many in the U.S. are disquieted by the wide-spread assumption in Latin America that the U.S. is responsible for all or most of the ills of the area. Overshadowing all opinion on what caused the situation are the actual social, economic, and political strains now reaching danger points in a number of countries. As Milton Eisenhower concluded: "The crucial question is whether Latin America will plunge into the future on the heels of Castro or whether it will have the patience and wisdom to follow more slowly the procedures initiated by the Alliance. Scholars and knowledgeable journalists disagree on the probable outcome of the struggles among the internal political forces in Latin America. Some contend that only in bloodshed will desirable social changes be brought about. The Alliance for Progress, they contend, is pallid fare for people long starved for justice." [4]

The struggle for economic and social justice for the Latin American masses is no new phenomenon, however. The friar Bartolomé de las Casas and other Spaniards who fought for justice for the Indians began the struggle. From Las Casas to Simón Bolívar, from Bolívar to José Martí, all the great Latin-American reformers would have strongly supported the following statement: "Any human society, if it is to be well-ordered and productive, must lay down as a foundation this principle, namely, that every human being is a person, that is, his nature is endowed with intelligence and free will. By virtue of this, he has rights and duties of his own, flowing directly and simultaneously from his very nature, which are therefore universal, inviolable, and inalienable." And Arturo Morales-Carrión remarks: "This is one of the great ideas, if not the greatest, that has animated Latin-American civilization. It is as old as the stirring writings of Bishop las Casas on behalf of the Indians. It is as novel as the encyclical *Pacem in Terris* from which it is quoted." [5]

● **The Perils of Generalization.** Most writers on Latin America feel the urge to generalize about it. Fortunately the Yankee cliché no longer flourishes that Latin Americans all strum guitars in quaint costumes and live in hot, moist places where bananas and sin dominate the scene. But much sheer ignorance still exists. One of my colleagues in Latin American history remarked that some of his fellow faculty members couldn't be sure of spelling Ecuador correctly, or whether Chihuahua is north or south of Tierra del Fuego.

Many Latin Americans are also ignorant of other countries in the hemisphere. Few Mexicans or Chileans speak Portuguese or know Brazil, and

Brazilians reciprocate by taking only a minute interest in the affairs of Spanish America. Though air transportation and improved newspaper coverage have bettered the situation somewhat in recent years, it is still true that educated and travelled Latin Americans often know Europe or the United States better than they know the other Latin-American countries.

Writers in the twenty nations to the south of the United States have been much preoccupied with the question of what to call themselves and the lands they live in. They resent United States citizens appropriating the term "American," and yet no general description has been devised to include Portuguese-speaking Brazil, the Spanish American republics, and French-speaking Haiti except the term Latin America, at best a tolerated misnomer. Luis Alberto Sánchez, the Peruvian intellectual, wrote a book entitled *Existe América Latina?* His conclusion was Latin America does not, in fact, exist. The culture of the area, he holds, is Indian and Iberian (either Spanish or Portuguese). "Latin America" came into vogue among the newly emancipated nations during the nineteenth century as a reaction against the mother countries, and in favor of French (Latin) culture which was long dominant and still greatly attracts intellectuals in many parts of the continent. Sánchez considers that "Latin America" cannot properly be used to label an area where millions of Indians, mestizos, and Negroes live who have no connection with the "white, European, viceregal, and absolutist tradition" which he believes the term "Latin America" connotes.

Today another kind of simplification can be found among those who classify all Latin Americans as either urban or rural; this is another cliché to be resisted. Anthropologists emphasize that no less than nine distinct "types of sub-cultures" exist, ranging from the tribal Indian groups to the urban upper class.[6]

Many Latin Americans, however, feel that they have something in common, and that they are gradually creating a culture of their own. Gone forever are the days when school buildings were constructed in the form of the Parthenon because some Minister of Education loved Greek culture, and everywhere one observes a great determination among Latin Americans to develop their own way of life. Gabriela Mistral, the Chilean Nobel Prize winning poet, is said to have declared: "What unites us in Spanish America is our beautiful language and our distrust of the United States." Even this generalization does not apply to Brazil, for there Portuguese is spoken and Brazil has been friendly in the past to the United States, partly because Brazilians feel reserved toward Spanish America, especially their neighbor Argentina, which reciprocates this feeling. Yet these nations certainly have some cultural attitudes and some problems in common, and the world inclines to consider them as a unit. One experience which all Latin American countries share is the disastrous effects of earthquakes, tidal waves, floods, and other natural disasters which have destroyed so many lives and so much property there. A recent compilation of such disasters recorded since the conquest in the Americas demonstrates how severely Latin America has suffered in comparison with other areas in the Americas: Canada, 3; the U.S., 27; Latin America, 180.[7]

The greatest disaster of nature, which Latin America has just begun to understand, is the population explosion. As an example of the almost incredible growth in South America, Peru has witnessed "an increase of about 49 per cent within the past 20 years despite the fact that almost half of the newborn die before reaching the age of one." [8] Population grows at the explosive rate of about 2.5 per cent annually, while the figure for the world as a whole is about 1.6. The present Latin-American population of about 200 million is expected to reach 300 million by 1975 and almost 600 million by the year 2000, or almost twice the estimated population for the U.S. and Canada at that date. Given the present low standards in education and living conditions, thoughtful Latin Americans foresee continued economic insufficiency and social disturbance, accentuated perhaps at least for the time being by the emphasis of the Alliance for Progress on reform. Agrarian reforms, for example, have often resulted in an immediate decline in food production.

The ravages of all these natural disasters differ in intensity from region to region, so that generalizations are dangerous in this field too. In fact, general agreement on the nature of the crisis in Latin America or on the remedies to be used, is difficult to find. To an outsider, at least, it is clear that its society is in ferment and that the elite class is losing ground as middle and lower class groups press forward on economic and education fronts, at least in the cities where industrialization has advanced. But it should always be remembered that the vast and variegated region arbitrarily called "Latin America" cannot be described as if it were a solid unit or confidently summed up in brief compass. (*See Readings Nos. 1–5.*)

• **Latin America Is "Discovered" Again.** An alternation of famine and feast has characterized U.S. action toward Latin America since World War II. Up to about 1960 relatively little attention was paid to her; other parts of the post-war world had higher priority. With the coming to power of Castro all this changed suddenly. The government and the people again "discovered" Latin America. Not only was the Alliance for Progress announced in 1961, but funds became available through the Office of Education for fellowships, the Fulbright exchange program was stepped up, and professors as well as students moved back and forth more easily. The greatest boom period in the history of Latin American studies in the U.S. now began.

The U.S. Army and other government agencies now seemed to have ample funds for research activities, and one of the results was the preparation of valuable manuals and special studies, as well as such irresponsible projects as Operation Camelot. After opposing the creation of an Inter-American Development Bank for many years, U.S. officials found in 1959 that such action was entirely feasible. As another indication of the changing attitude, the editor of one of the basic studies of the area, *Social Change in Latin America Today,* has stated that the volume was ready for publication in 1957 but the publisher, the Council on Foreign Relations, did not judge it sufficiently important to bring out until 1960.[9]

Private foundations, particularly the Ford Foundation, began to support many projects with grants totalling millions of dollars and massive assistance given to university institutes of Latin American studies in the U.S., as well as support for a variety of projects in a number of Latin American countries. Spanish and Portuguese are being taught to more students in the U.S., and better taught, than ever before. Conferences on the area have been held in many colleges and universities and by many business and religious groups; and commercial publishers have learned that books on Latin America can be brought out without financial loss. Alfred A. Knopf, one of the pioneers in translating Latin American works, was bold enough to celebrate the fiftieth anniversary of his firm by starting a twenty-odd volume series of Borzoi Books on Latin America. The Rockefeller Foundation, for a long time active in agricultural and medical programs in Latin America, made it possible for the Association of American University Presses to translate and publish about one hundred substantial volumes by Latin American authors. Congress continued to produce quantities of documentation on communist penetration in Latin America, many reports of its numerous committees and individual members who visited the area to review government operations there, and some detailed studies such as the large volume on *United States Latin American Relations* prepared by universities and research organizations at the request of Senator Wayne Morse's Subcommittee on American Republics Affairs.

Canada's interest in Latin America has steadily increased during recent years. In the not-too-distant future regular courses will probably be offered on Latin America in a number of Canadian universities whether or not Canada decides to join the Organization of American States.[10]

The United Nations, the Organization of American States, and such specialized agencies as the Inter-American Development Bank have published a multitude of factual and challenging reports. Indeed, the Bank's annual Social Progress Trust Fund report has become since its first appearance in 1960 one of the basic sources of data.

European developments are notable as well. An Institute of Latin American Studies has been established in London; France and Germany are busily engaged in strengthening their university resources and economic relations in the field; and in European academic circles generally more interest in Latin America exists than ever before. Increased European interest will mean an even larger and richer literature on Latin America, and it is also likely that the Latin American nations will be less solely dependent on the United States for financial support. The official visit of President Eduardo Frei Montalva to England, France, and Italy in July, 1965, was designed to increase Europe's assistance to Chile and to emphasize Latin America's growing desire to move out from under the shadow of the United States.

Soviet Russia has become increasingly concerned with Latin America since 1945. Her Latin Americanists now participate in international conferences, keep up-to-date on publications relating to Latin America that appear outside Russia, particularly in the U.S., and Soviet interest in underdeveloped countries of the world, including Latin America, has evolved during the past decade into a major undertaking.[11] As one study states:

This is evident by the growth of periodical literature and monographic studies, academic meetings, the organization during the summer of 1960 of the Soviet Association of Friendship and Cultural Cooperation with Latin American Countries, and the founding early in 1962 of a special Institute of Latin-American Affairs at the Academy of Sciences of the USSR. The aim of the Institute is to publish works on Latin-American history, politics, economics, and culture, to coordinate Latin-American studies and research within the USSR as well as in the countries of the Soviet bloc, to establish and to maintain contacts with Latin American countries, and to train Soviet personnel qualified in Latin American affairs. The Institute plans to publish a two-volume abstract on Latin America, a volume of articles on the recent national liberation and working-class movements, a symposium on contemporary problems of Brazil, and a volume dealing with 'the success of socialist construction' in Cuba.[12]

The Japanese interest in Latin America that began before World War II has revived. Universities are adding scholars trained in Latin-American studies to their faculties, publications are brought out, and organizations are established to foster economic and cultural relations.[13] The People's Republic of China has apparently begun to concern itself with Latin America only in the political and propagandist sense, if one may judge from the list of publications available in English. The best index to the booming state of Latin-American studies and Latin American affairs generally probably is the newly established *Latin American Research Review,* an impressive periodical record of research in progress and of information useful to investigators.[14] Yet affluence can bring problems, and Latin Americanists in the U.S. are discovering political and other obstacles in their path.

Perhaps the most significant change has occurred in Latin America itself. More and more her scholars and institutions of higher education are increasing their research and are devoting their energies to an examination of their own problems. In economics notable results have been achieved; in anthropology and sociology substantial progress has been made, while the realistic study of governmental, administrative, and political processes is under way. The coming generation will profit as never before from the insights and the contributions of Latin American scholars as they turn their attention to studying their own society with the tools of modern social sciences.

[1] Donald M. Dozer, *Are We Good Neighbors? Three Decades of Inter-American Relations, 1930–1960* (Gainesville: University of Florida Press, 1956), pp. 370–371.

[2] *The New York Times,* October 22, 1960, pp. 8–9.

[3] Statement by Milton J. Esman, as quoted by William and Paul Paddock, *Hungry Nations* (Boston: Little, Brown, 1964), p. 270. See also "The Question of the Effectiveness of the Alliance for Progress, pro and con," *Congressional Digest,* XLI (Washington, D.C., 1963), pp. 67–96; John Dreier, ed., *The Alliance For Progress. Problems and Perspectives* (Baltimore: The Johns Hopkins Press, 1962). Simon Hanson has published annually critiques of the Alliance in *Inter-American Economic Affairs.* For the latest one, see Vol. XXI (1967). Víctor Alba gives a hard-hitting view in *Parásitos, mitos y sordomudos. Ensayo sobre la Alianza para el Progreso.* Suplemento a la revista *Panoramas* (Mexico, 1964), No. 11.

[4] Milton S. Eisenhower, *The Wine Is Bitter, The United States and Latin America* (Garden City, New York: Doubleday, 1963), p. 313.

[5] Morales-Carrión, "Social Change and the Church in Latin America Today," *Bulletin, Commission on Ecumenical Mission and Relations of the United Presbyterian Church in the U. S. A.,* IV, No. 1 (1964), p. 2.

[6] Charles Wagley and Marvin Harris, "A Typology of Latin American Cultures," *American Anthropologist,* 57 (1955), pp. 428–451. For some lively observations and questions on the nature of Latin America, see Maria José de Queiroz, "A América Latina no mundo moderno," *Kriterion,* XVII (Belo Horizonte, 1966), no. 64, pp. 153–161.

[7] Frédéric Montandon, "Les megaseismes en Amérique," *Revue pour l'étude des calamities* (December, 1962), No. 38, pp. 57–97.

[8] Frederick B. Pike, *The Modern History of Peru* (London: Weidenfeld and Nicholson, 1967), p. 312.

[9] Richard Adams, "Politics and Social Anthropology in Spanish America," *Human Organization,* XXIII (1964), No. 1, pp. 2–3.

[10] D. L. B. Hamlin, *The Latin Americas* (Toronto: University of Toronto Press, 1960).

[11] J. Gregory Oswald, "Contemporary Soviet Research on Latin America," *Latin American Research Review,* No. 2 (1966), pp. 77–96. See also I. R. Lavretski, "A Survey of the Hispanic American Historical Review," *Hispanic American Historical Review,* XL (1960), pp. 340–360; *Latin America in Soviet Writings, 1944–1958* (Hispanic Foundation, Library of Congress, 1959), compiled by Leo A. Okinshevich and Cecilia J. Gorokhoff. The Hispanic Foundation is preparing similar guides for the periods 1917–1944 and 1959–1964. Also useful are Warren Schiff, "An East German Survey Concerning Recent Soviet Historical Writings on Latin America," *Hispanic American Historical Review,* XL (1960), pp. 70–71; G. R. Coulthard, "Recent Marxist Interpretations of Latin American Literature," *Caribbean Quarterly,* IX (1963), No. 3, pp. 10–15.

[12] Quoted from an article by Basil Cmytryshyn and Jessie L. Gilmore, "The Monroe Doctrine: A Soviet View," by Donald M. Dozer, *The Monroe Doctrine* (New York: Knopf, 1966), p. 199.

[13] Hiroshi Saito and Yoshiro Ikushima, "Estudos sobre o Brasil e América Latina No Japão," *Sociologia,* XX (1958), pp. 222–232. As an example, see the handsomely produced volume *Andes: the Report of the University of Tokyo Scientific Expedition to the Andes in 1958* (Tokyo: Bijutsu Shuppan Sha, 1961). This well-documented study is in Japanese, with captions and references also in English.

[14] Austin: University of Texas Press. The first issue appeared in November, 1965.

RICHARD M. NIXON AND THE LATE GENERALISSIMO RAFAEL L. TRUJILLO OF THE
DOMINICAN REPUBLIC SHARE A WARM ABRAZO DURING THE FORMER U.S. VICE
PRESIDENT'S TRIP TO LATIN AMERICA IN 1960   CREDIT: UPI PHOTO

MEXICO AND THE CARIBBEAN

11

1
MEXICO

AREA: 759,530 sq. mi.

POPULATION IN MID-1966: 42,231,000

LARGEST CITIES:

Mexico City (capital): 3,118,059 (est. 1963)

Guadalajara: 977,779 (est. 1963)

Monterrey: 774,059 (est. 1963)

PRINCIPAL EXPORTS (1961): cotton, coffee, sugar, shrimp, cattle

PRESIDENT: Gustavo Díaz Ordaz, civilian, took office Dec. 1, 1964, for a 6-year term.

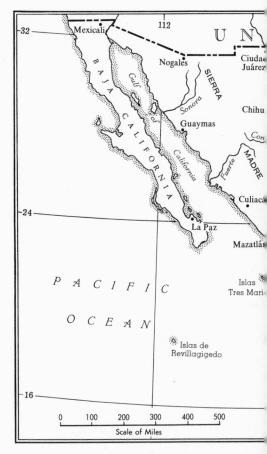

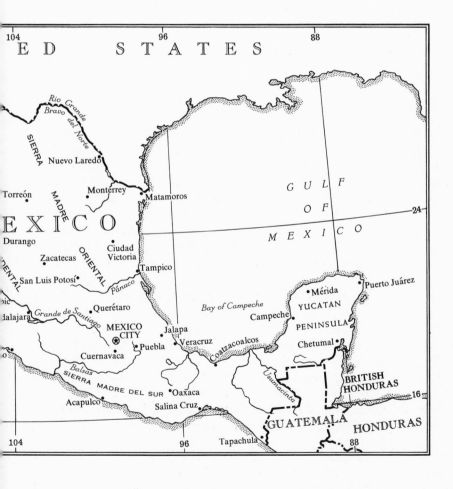

MEXICO

● **Mexico Seen from Chapultepec Hill.** For centuries the finest view of Mexico City has been from the wooded eminence on which an Aztec fort once stood. In 1521 the conquistador Ferdinand Cortez gazed from Chapultepec out upon the island-city of Tenochtitlán, then the home of perhaps 30,000 Indians ruled by Montezuma. In the 18th century the Spanish viceroys who enjoyed Chapultepec as a summer residence saw a colonial capital of 100,000 Spaniards, Indians, and mestizos. When General Winfield Scott stormed the Hill in 1847, despite the heroic resistance of the boy-cadets, to end the Mexican War, the population stood at 200,000. In 1910, as Porfirio Díaz's dictatorial regime was about to fall, Mexico City with its 400,000 inhabitants had still a provincial air. Today, visitors to historic Chapultepec Hill see below them a great metropolis of 7 million people. Moreover, the city is growing so rapidly, due to its high birthrate and the constant influx of country people, that by 1970 the population is expected to reach 8 million and by 1976 some 10 million.

The oldest city on the North American continent, the capital of Mexico is also becoming one of the most modern. Despite a spongy subsoil which makes construction difficult, its imposing skyline is dominated by the tallest building in Latin America. Many tall glass-sheathed government and private buildings rise above the impressive tree-lined Paseo de la Reforma that leads from the base of Chapultepec to downtown Mexico City. South of the city rise the dazzling new buildings of the continent's oldest university and of the adjacent residential area Pedregal, where modern architecture flourishes. Circling jets mark the location of the busy international air terminal on the eastern edge of the city.

The six-year term of President Adolfo Ruíz Cortines (1953–1958) saw a remarkable upsurge of construction, which continued under subsequent administrations, with many improvements for the federal district: modern public markets, schools, fire stations, and transportation terminals, and a model

14

penitentiary which included a guest house to make possible regular visits of the wives of prisoners. The last of the famous street markets, the Lagunilla and the Merced, were moved to spacious new quarters where the vendors occupy concrete buildings provided with running water and refrigeration.

Descending from the Hill, one begins to see evidence of the strain that the city's spectacular growth has created. One-third of its people live in squalor on the edge of the city or in downtown slums, where the families are portrayed in the books by Oscar Lewis as living "the culture of poverty." (*See Reading No. 35.*) Shanty suburbs of tin and cardboard house the thousands of country folk who have chosen to abandon rural life for even their miserable share of the capital. This flood sweeps in so inexorably that the city is hard-pressed to provide such essential services as water, electricity, paved streets, sewage disposal, transportation, and public health facilities. The newspaper *Excélsior* has described Mexico City's plight as "a catastrophic accumulation of human needs that cannot be satisfied." Meanwhile, thousands of the rural poor make their way north, legally or illegally, to the U.S. in spite of the hard conditions they sometimes meet there.

Leaving Mexico City by any of the modern highways that lead away from it, one sees raging the dramatic running battle between progress and poverty— in industrial Monterrey near the Texas border, in Guadalajara to the northwest, in Oaxaca to the south and, indeed, everywhere in this republic of 40 million people. It was estimated in 1956 that more than 60 per cent of the population were poorly fed, housed, and clothed, 40 per cent were illiterate, and 40 per cent of the children of school age did not attend school; today, these percentages have all fallen due to vigorous government action during the last 10 years, but much remains to be done. Though Indians—defined as those who speak one of the 50 distinct native languages and wear Indian clothing—now constitute only about 10 per cent of the population, many of them live as primitively as their ancestors did in the time of Montezuma. To understand the violent contrasts between luxury and poverty, especially notable in the capital city, one must turn to the background of the Revolution.

● **Pre-Revolutionary Mexico.** The essential features of the Spanish colonial regime which lasted three centuries after Cortez conquered the land has been summarized as follows: "It was a period of comparative peace—the peace of suppression, stagnation, and decay. Its outstanding characteristics were: politically—absentee absolutism resting on military and religious domination, with complete denial of local self-expression and self-training, and disregard by officials of laws that it was to their interest to disregard; economically— extraction of raw materials based on slave labor, with office-holding the universal desideratum; socially—splendor and privilege contrasted with misery and degradation; spiritually—corruption, ignorance, fanaticism, intercaste hatred." [1] Though this view of colonial Mexico is simplified and not wholly

accurate, many of the revolutionaries both in 1810 and 1910 believed that this was their whole heritage from Spain.

The fighting which brought Mexico independence from Spain in 1821 did little to alter the colonial social and economic structure. Reform did not begin until the Constitution of 1857 was framed and various laws to restrict the economic and political power of the Church were enacted. President Benito Juárez, a full-blooded Zapotec Indian, was the great figure during the next decade, but he was too busy fighting both Napoleon's puppet Emperor and the French, between 1862–1867, and also the entrenched Mexican conservatives, to implement the Constitution and the various reform laws. La Reforma ended in November, 1876, when Porfirio Díaz, under the remarkable slogan, "effective suffrage—no re-election," set up his dictatorship which endured, save for a four-year interval, for thirty-four years. The previous half-century had been a period of almost continuous instability; under Díaz the national budget was balanced, national income increased fivefold, Mexico was "prosperous" and could borrow all the money it wanted at about 5 per cent. But the overwhelming majority of Mexicans were poor; 1 per cent of the population owned most of the land, which was worked by landless peasants whose standard of living declined steadily. One economist states that agricultural wages remained constant from 1810 to 1910, but that the cost of food for agricultural workers increased 300 per cent.

The relation of the peons to the upperclass landowners was generally one of complete dependence. The typical hacienda included homes of workers, the hacienda store where they had to buy their supplies at high prices which led them into debt slavery, a chapel, a jail, a cemetery, and, sometimes, a school. The owner ordinarily lived in Mexico City or a provincial capital, and the hacienda was directed by a mayordomo who rode his territory with a gun or whip in hand to stimulate recalcitrant workers and protect himself from attack.

Díaz and his clique organized Mexico into one vast machine whose monopoly of political power was maintained by police power, the *rurales* (rural police), and the army. The Church generally preached submission to authority, whether dictator, *hacendado*, factory owner, or mine superintendent. The pastoral letter of the Archbishop of Guadalajara has been cited as typical of this viewpoint, although the message was promulgated in Revolutionary days:

> As all authority is derived from God, the Christian workman should sanctify and make sublime his obedience by serving God in the person of his bosses. In this way obedience is neither humiliating nor difficult. . . . Poor, love your humble state and your work; turn your gaze towards Heaven; there is the true wealth.[2]

Indians were considered "racially inferior" and lazy; when the Indians opposed the robbery by *hacendados* of the land they had held for centuries,

WASHERWOMEN AND CHILD

they were mercilessly repressed. Between 1883 and 1894, Díaz and his obedient Congress gave away to foreign speculators and personal friends one-fifth of the entire area of the Republic, or 134,500,000 acres of the public domain. By 1910 less than 10 per cent of the Indian communities had any land whatever, and the Indians themselves were social outcasts in their own country. When the Pan American Conference met in Mexico in 1901–1902, the dictator forbade that Indians be employed at any of the hotels housing the visitors, lest these get the idea that Mexico was an Indian country.

The *Pax Porfiriana* was a Golden Age for foreigners, whose investments were protected; Mexico became a preserve for foreign capitalism. But the massive dictatorship was beginning to crumble. The 1907 depression in the United States was felt in Mexico, and Díaz and his coterie were growing old. By 1910 the dictator was 80, two of his twenty state governors were over 80, and some past 70. Yet, the regime and its beneficiaries seemed to believe the show would never end. On September 16, 1910 the celebration of the one-hundredth anniversary of Mexico's independence and Díaz's 80th birthday was regal in style. Thousands of guests and visitors poured into the capital. Díaz, the genial host, spent $20 million of the nation's funds on fireworks, military parades, banquets, music, speeches, and carloads of champagne. The guests could see how cultured and contented the Mexican people were; the city's poor and barefoot Indians were barred from the center of the capital. When Díaz was again declared "elected" President on September 27, 1910, the storm broke and the most important event of twentieth-century Mexico began —the Revolution.

● **"Tierra y Libertad."** The tumult began with this cry of the people, "land and liberty," and for ten years Mexico was in a confused uproar, with Francisco Madero, Emiliano Zapata, Francisco "Pancho" Villa, Venustiano Carranza, and other revolutionary leaders playing their various roles on the crowded scene. The passion and the confusion of this period is excellently conveyed by the collection of remarkable photographs, with pungent captions, entitled *The Wind That Swept Mexico*.[3]

The greatest achievement was the drawing up and promulgation of the Constitution of 1917 by a convention summoned by Carranza, who had emerged by 1915 as the strongest of the revolutionary leaders. This legal basis for the Revolution, which held and still holds much the same mystical authority and practical power as the U.S. Constitution, was a product of Mexican history, forged for Mexican purposes; it principally renewed and strengthened the 1857 Constitution. It went beyond the 1857 document, however, to establish a planned agrarian and industrial system.

Article 3 made all public education secular and the primary grades compulsory, thus declaring the nation independent from the educational monopoly of the Church. Article 27 denied the ownership of land in fee simple to those given *ejido* lands, land belonged to the nation, including all subsoil minerals and petroleum, which could be exploited only by Mexican nationals or foreigners who agreed "to consider themselves as nationals" and not to invoke the protection of their governments. This vital article also aimed to restore to the Mexican people the lands alienated by previous laws, especially those of Díaz. Article 123 has been termed the "Magna Carta" of Mexican labor; it recognized labor's right to organize, to bargain collectively, and to strike. Labor was also promised the eight-hour day, the end of child labor, control of wages, equal pay for equal work, and responsibility of the employer in cases of occupational accidents and diseases.

The Constitution of 1917 in effect declared war on all the most powerful groups of the past: the clergy, the *hacendados,* and employers. It also gave stern warning to the United States, Great Britain, and other foreign states whose citizens had exploited Mexican land, oil fields, and mines. Its pronouncements have influenced the course of events in Chile, Colombia, and other Latin American republic with similar problems in later years.

Under Carranza the Revolution got under way although he exhibited little pride in the constitution he had theoretically fathered and did little to implement it; his generals devoted themselves to fattening on the public purse. Carranza had that honest revolutionist Zapata shot. He carried on a continuous debate with President Woodrow Wilson, who had recognized his government in October, 1915, despite the loud cries of U.S. landowners, oil companies, and churchmen against "godless and socialistic Mexico." Opposition to Carranza mounted on all sides when the country saw that he intended to name his successor. He saw that his time was up, filled a twenty-car train with sacks of bullion and other loot, and set out for Veracruz with it. One of his previous supporters arranged an attack on the train, but he escaped into the mountains only to be trapped and murdered there by one of his own officers. With his death in May, 1920, the first and most violent phase of the Mexican Revolution ended.

Considering Mexico's stability and independence today, one must remember how dearly they were bought. The pent-up forces which exploded in the Revolution in 1910 involved so much turbulence with murders, riots, clashes of armies, assassinations, and other bloody deeds occurring daily as to produce a veritable cataclysm. In 1920, after ten years of strife, the country's population had not only not increased for the first time in its history, but also the census registered a net loss of almost a million people. The Mexican scholar Daniel Cosío Villegas sums up the results of the upheaval in these words:

> the landowner class, which held 60 to 70 per cent of the country's entire wealth, disappeared; large professional groups—the executive and political personnel, the army, the body of university professors—were almost completely replaced; new social classes with a decisive political power emerged in the brand new collective owner of the land, the industrial worker, a popular army, and a new upper middle class so new, so tender, so fragile that not one of the thousand

millionaires we have in Mexico has had his wealth over 20 or 30 years . . . not one of the great newspapers survived. Only two of about 50 banks continued under the new regime.[4]

● **The Era of Obregón and Calles.** Comparative peace returned to Mexico when General Álvaro Obregón came to power in 1920. He was the first President to give a strong impetus to the social revolution by encouraging trade union organization, a modest program of land distribution, and education. José Vasconcelos, Minister of Education, undertook, with imagination and creative optimism, the gigantic task of teaching the Mexican masses. Vasconcelos, respecting both the European and Indian past, printed Spanish translations of Plato and Aristotle, and established a thousand rural schools on a new pattern, calling each one *La Casa del Pueblo* (The House of the People) and designing it to serve the entire life of the village as a permanent educational mission with a program of the three R's, music, painting, sports, theater, and practical instruction in sanitation and scientific agriculture.

Under Vasconcelos, too, the artists of Mexico were encouraged to paint murals on the walls of public buildings and thus to carry their interpretations of Mexico's epic struggle to the people. New World art must be popular art, declared José Clemente Orozco. (*See Reading No. 30.*) Diego Rivera and David Siqueiros were other great names in this movement; they organized an artists' union and stood on their scaffolds with conspicuous pistols to prove that they too belonged to the Revolution. Vasconcelos also launched Carlos Chávez on his distinguished musical career by commissioning a ballet. Although he later turned conservative, his individual attitude toward Mexican affairs persisted until his death in 1959.

Obregón's political troubles were many. He was recognized by the United States only late in 1923; difficulties with the Church led him to expel the apostolic delegate, and he retained army support only by creating many new generals and overlooking their flagrant pilfering. When his minister of war lost 80,000 pesos in one sitting at the gaming tables, Obregón approved payment of the sum from the Treasury. Even so, a revolt occurred when he announced his support of Plutarco Elías Calles as his successor. But the uprising was suppressed, and he finished his presidential term in peace.

Calles was inaugurated December 1, 1924, amidst colorful ceremonies in which Indians, peasants, and industrial workers, fetched at public expense from the far corners of Mexico, mingled with several hundred U.S. labor leaders led by Samuel Gompers, the veteran President of the American Federation of Labor. The social revolution continued, not without bitter disputes concerning its direction and pace. The C.R.O.M. (*Confederación Regional Obrera Mexicana*) was given a practical monopoly over labor, road and irrigation programs were launched, the rural school program continued, and the

National Bank of Mexico was established. The army was kept under strict civilian control.

Although sorely tried by the threatened internal disintegration of the country due to conflicting ideas in the revolutionary family and by corruption in many quarters, Calles stood firm in his controversy with the United States over oil and agrarian legislation which brought the two countries close to war. Dwight W. Morrow, U.S. ambassador beginning in 1927, decisively improved relations, and the oil and land disputes were eventually resolved.

One of Calles' greatest struggles was with the Church, which openly opposed him when he began to enforce strictly the anti-clerical provisions of the Constitution; he deported foreign priests, closed Church schools and convents, and accused the hierarchy of treason. In protest, the priests withdrew from their altars on July 31, 1926, and for the first time since 1519 no public Mass was celebrated in all Mexico. For almost three years the grim struggle went on. Through it all the faithful came to pray in the empty churches, and some families with large houses smuggled in priests in lay garb to celebrate Mass behind drawn curtains—services in which the wives of leading revolutionaries, including Calles, participated. In 1929, the government reached a settlement with the Church, with some discreet assistance by Ambassador Morrow.

The tense election of 1928 brought a number of opposition candidates into the field, but Obregón won, with Calles' support, against much popular opposition. The newly elected president was killed by a young religious fanatic before he could take office, and Calles was in practical control for the next six years through men whom he named for the presidency and then dominated. This dreary period for Mexico and the Revolution has been described by Frank Tannenbaum as "debased and clouded years" in which the revolutionary leaders failed.

> They had risked their lives for the redemption of the people from poverty and serfdom . . . Their difficulty lay in the fact that they had come to power suddenly and without preparation, either morally, psychologically, politically, or even administratively. They were taken from their villages as barefooted youngsters who had slept on the floor and could barely read, and after a few years spent on the battlefields found themselves tossed in high office and great responsibility. This new world was filled with a thousand temptations they had not dreamed of: gold, women, houses, carpets, diamonds, champagne . . . It was a world of fable, and in their innocence and hunger—or greed, it does not matter—they succumbed to it. They succumbed to it because they had no moral fortitude. They had no philosophy and no faith, no system of values, no sense of the big world. The big world, especially the big city, was too much for them.[5]

In this struggle to bring political equilibrium to a country wracked by contending elements and ideas and deprived of a leader—Obregón—who had at least kept the intricate machine of Mexican political life ticking, Calles formed in 1929 an "official party"—*Partido Nacional Revolucionario* which has become the cornerstone of Mexico's political life. It bound together the numerous regional and state political organizations and bosses so that a small group might prearrange elections and write legislation before it reached the halls of Congress. The president holds office for only a single 6 year term and thus the "no re-election" slogan is kept intact, but the party maintains control in a single-party state. Yet, as Howard Cline points out, "simultaneously Mexico preserves a full roster of civil liberties—free speech, free press, free assembly. Only the right to successful revolution is limited in fact." [6] No political machinery can run itself; the man who assured the party the dominance in Mexican life that it still enjoys was the most interesting and powerful figure the Revolution produced—General Lázaro Cárdenas.

● **Cárdenas Implements the Revolution, 1934–1940.** The new president took office in December, 1934, for a six-year term by grace of Calles, but quickly ejected his protector and henchmen from the government. By June, 1935, he controlled the nation more certainly than Díaz had ever done, and, unlike the dictator, enjoyed popular support even greater than that of Juárez. The people believed in this dedicated and modest president who gave his attention to the problems of Mexico and Mexicans beyond the glittering lights of the national and state capitals.

From this position of strength Cárdenas declared that the Revolution had not yet been effected, and began to put into effect a Six-Year Plan. He transferred some 45,000,000 acres of land to villages, twice as much land as had been distributed up to 1934; he found strong support for his program from a new labor union he sponsored, the CTM (*Confederación de Trabajadores Mexicanos*) led by Vicente Lombardo Toledano; and in June, 1937, he nationalized most of the railroads. He turned the nationalized roads over to a committee of railway unions to run, which compounded the confusion but, in the opinion of most Mexicans, was preferable to foreign control. He also greatly extended the educational system, even to remote areas of the country.

It was his expropriation of the properties of seventeen foreign oil companies on March 18, 1938, that won Cárdenas the permanent title of "defender of the sovereignty of the nation"; the date became an annual occasion for celebrating Mexico's "Declaration of Economic Independence." The legal arguments involved were complicated. But the essential fact was that Mexico believed that the foreign companies had shown disrespect for Mexico and her laws, and thus could not retreat with honor. The presence of a friendly U.S. ambassador, Josephus Daniels, committed to the Good Neighbor Policy, the determination of President F. D. Roosevelt to make the policy work, and the already looming shadow of World War II all helped to make a peaceful solution possible. Mexico agreed to pay for the oil properties within ten years, and the U.S. government recognized Mexico's right of expropriation upon "adequate, effective, and prompt payment."

President Cárdenas completed his turbulent term of office and settled down to life as the conscience of the Revolution; his radical policies were hotly debated inside as well as outside of Mexico, but few anywhere questioned his integrity. He still towers above all the other revolutionary leaders.

● **The Revolution Slows Down.** In 1940 Mexico turned right, and has tended to move slowly in this direction ever since. Under Manuel Ávila Camacho (1940–1946), Mexico joined the United States against the Axis and began to develop her economy, particularly industry. The war years saw inflation, a revival of the rightist and religious movement now called *Sinarquismo,* as well as continuing educational progress and the founding of a Social Security Institute. Lombardo Toledano was ejected from his labor post and anti-Communist leaders assumed charge.

The Catholic Church regained much influence in this period. The provisions of the Constitution of 1917 severely restricting Church, economic, educational, and political activities have not been seriously invoked since 1940 when President Ávila Camacho declared publicly "I am a believer." Today Catholic churches and seminaries flourish; schools which used to function secretly do so openly, though they are named after Mexican patriots instead of saints. Yet Mexico, like Latin America generally, has a very low number of priests in relation to communicants. Protestant groups are also active throughout the Republic and claim over 2 million members. One of these groups, a U.S. organization, is translating the Bible into various Indian languages with some 180 translators at work. Mixtec, Tzeltal, and Totonac versions have been published; other translations are on the way.

Under Miguel Alemán (1946–1952) the official party was re-baptized the *Partido Revolucionario Institucional,* as if to show that the Revolution had indeed been won and was now an institution. Alemán vigorously pushed agricultural development, with technical aid from the Rockefeller Foundation; invigorated Pemex, the nationalized petroleum monopoly, and constructed an impressive University City on the edge of the capital. But his principal concern was to promote industry and, with the help of *Nacional Financiera,* a government finance corporation, some 50,000 industrial concerns of many different types had been established by 1950. Alemán and his official family became famous for the upsurge of corruption which accompanied Mexico's material advance; the *mordida* (bite) became almost as institutionalized as the Revolution itself. One observer interprets the corruption in Mexico as the essential "grease" that enables the governmental machine to operate by piecing out the inadequate salaries of the bureaucrats.[7]

Adolfo Ruíz Cortines (1952–1958) continued the policies of his two predecessors. During his presidency labor leader Fidel Velázquez built up the CTM to 1,500,000 members, and organized the Labor Unity Bloc to strengthen government control over labor and combat communist infiltration. When Adolfo López Mateos was elected president in July, 1958, his success in averting all labor strikes as Secretary of Labor was expected to stand him in good stead. Yet, in August a university student strike against city bus fare increases led to street riots in Mexico City where labor dissidents joined the students. Demetrio Vallejo, one-time Communist party member, won control of the railroad workers later in the year in a nationwide strike, pulled them out of the Unity Bloc, and in February, 1959, called another strike and forced major wage concessions. Teachers, oil workers, telephone workers, and electrical workers are also involved in this struggle for the control of approximately 2 million trade unionists. Leftists are making some headway in their effort to break the government dominance of the labor unions, which they claim serve governmental ends rather than the workers. Vallejo clearly miscalculated his power, however, in Easter Week, 1959, by calling a railroad strike which stranded thousands of vacationers; popular indignation enabled the government to crack down on the left-wing labor leaders responsible. Both the Electrical Workers Union and the Petroleum Workers Union, previously united with Vallejo in a leftist bloc, disassociated themselves from his actions and supported the government's move against the railroad strike which they said "had its roots abroad." Inflation and resentment of large industrial profits were also elements in the situation; a shift of power within the revolutionary family was also involved.

- **Mexico, the "Stabilized Revolution."** President Ruíz Cortines, in time-honored fashion, selected his successor Adolfo López Mateos during whose term of office (1958–1964) Mexico continued to prosper.

Evidence of another possible political shift was López Mateos' attack on provincial dictators such as Gonzalo Natividad Santos in San Luis Potosí, Leobardo Reynoso in Zacatecas, and Margarito Ramírez in Quintana Roo. In the early revolutionary days local strong men (*caciques*) staked out a territory and ruled over it at gunpoint with the aid of their henchmen called *pistoleros,* extorting taxes and collecting bribes systematically. López Mateos announced opposition to them during his campaign but had to move cautiously, for the official party has been sustained by these very bosses. Santos, for example, delivered his province's vote for the party for twenty years and has handpicked the governors, mayors, and congressmen from San Luis Potosí. If labor and the state bosses may not regularly be counted upon as solid supporters of the party, its future is uncertain.

Mexico under López Mateos made solid progress. He completely nationalized the electric power industry, distributed more land than any president since Cárdenas, made a determined effort to collect taxes, and reached a settlement with Washington on the century-old "Chamizal" boundary dispute.

Clearly Mexico had constructed the apparatus of a modern state, which included a civil service, a set of public banking institutions, an organization able to design and build large public works, and an administrative machinery capable of directing a complex tax system, import control, subsidies, and price control. As one American economist emphasized, Mexico "had discovered the concepts of modern entrepreneurship, including mass-production and marketing, public financing, and objective record keeping." Sometimes the world forgets that Mexico has advanced industrially by resting its economy largely on private initiative, despite its dramatic emphasis on the need to manage directly certain sectors such as the petroleum industry. The State, however, has played an important role in promoting and guiding economic development "through its agrarian policy; public investments to improve the substructure and create and improve basic industries; the supply of low-cost fuels and the establishment of domestic plants whose activities are the outgrowth of the oil industry; industrial financing; credit facilities and tax exemptions to encourage new and necessary industries; and the adoption of a custom's tariff appropriate to the advancement of Mexico's industrialization." [8] Perhaps most important of all, López Mateos tried to recapture in 1959 something of the early revolutionary spirit of dedication to the education of the people by establishing the National Free Textbook Commission which has distributed over 100 million textbooks to elementary pupils throughout the nation.

Mexico stands out in Latin America as a very paragon of political stability, and this equilibrium is all the more noteworthy because it is not the peace-of-the-grave type of "stability" that flourished in the Dominican Republic before Trujillo was assassinated or that prevails today in General Stroessner's Paraguay or General Somoza's Nicaragua. Mexico's stability derives from a rough sort of balance of political and economic forces. (*See Reading No. 33.*) Mexico's presidents must respond to the pressures of her dynamic businessmen as well as to the influence of labor, agriculture, the intellectuals, the politicians, the Catholic Church, the North and the South, the countryside as well as the city. Keeping the balance has been a major concern of every president, but thus far by skillful maneuvering it has succeeded. The "Revolutionary Family" has thus far been able to dominate, and President Gustavo Díaz Ordaz (1964–1970) was chosen in the traditional way, despite some public opposition by such political veterans as the late Ramón Beteta and the novelist Carlos Fuentes, who has one of his characters in *Where the Air Is Clear* say:

> I agree that our 'one party' is better than the so-called opposition parties. But what I reject is the sleep our one party has imposed on Mexican politics, preventing the birth of political movements which could solve our problems and make good use of elements which have lapsed into somnolence and indifference; good elements that have never associated with either the clerical reaction or the Soviet reaction. Must the party go on accepting a *status quo* that gives no

solution at all? Which is the same as saying to the Mexican masses, You're quite well off as you are. Don't think, don't speak. We know what's best for you. Just lie quiet. Isn't that precisely what Porfirio Diaz said? [9]

Though some observers point out that the Mexican "one-party" rule under the present system of checks and balances is more like the U.S. political system than it seems, the Mexican President in some respects exerts more power over the individual states than the president of the United States. If President Díaz Ordaz wanted legislative action in a certain state, he would not send a representative, hat in hand, to request politely a change in the national interest, as President Kennedy did when Maryland's racial laws insulted ambassadors from African states journeying from New York to Washington.

The Revolution gave the modern State somewhat the same authoritarian and interventionist character as the royal government had in the colonial period. Today the State is the most important element in Mexican life: trade unions, employer's associations, Indian affairs, cultural matters, the economy of the country—all depend upon the State.

● **How Much Improvement?** Anthropologists report that important changes are occurring in Mexico, not only in the federal district which constitutes less than a thousandth part of the republic but houses one-seventh of the population and produces through its many activities 70 per cent of the national revenue, but also in the country generally. More and more rural people sleep on beds instead of on the ground, wear shoes, use store-bought clothes, travel by bus instead of on foot or by burro. In towns and cities their phonographs are being replaced by radios and TV's, and cotton is losing out to nylon. Woolworth and Sears Roebuck subsidiaries flourish in Mexico City, and even the quick lunch has begun to replace the traditional midday meal at home followed by the siesta.

Nevertheless, the great mass of peasants continue to work in their tiny subsistence holdings with century-old back-breaking methods. And 60 per cent of all Mexicans are ill-fed, ill-housed, and ill-clothed. Despite the distribution of free textbooks to elementary school children one child in three does not go to school for lack of teachers and buildings.

The powerful study *Five Families* by the anthropologist Oscar Lewis describes somberly the grinding poverty of the poor in Mexico City's slums and the problems of even the more economically secure families. The English-reading public is no longer given an idyllic picture of contented Mexican peasants serenely at harmony with their world. Throughout Mexico many people use tools and techniques that have remained largely the same since the days of Montezuma. According to Lewis these folk "have taken many new traits of modern life. They now have Coca-Cola, aspirin, radios, sewing machines, phonographs, poolrooms, flashlights, clocks, steel plows, and some labor-saving devices. They also have a greater desire to attend school, to eat better, to dress better, and to spend more. But in many ways their world view is still much closer to sixteenth-century Spain and to pre-Hispanic Mexico than to the modern scientific world. They are still guided by superstition and primitive beliefs; sorcery, magic, evil winds, and spirits still dominate their thinking. It is clear that, for the most part, they have taken on only the more superficial aspect and values of modern life. . . ." [10]

Mexico is forging ahead, of this there can be no doubt, and her leaders recognize the need for a balance between agriculture and industry. The Mexican economy has developed more rapidly and more uniformly than that of any other Latin-American country; many Mexicans are sure they have found the formula for balanced growth which will soon take Mexico out of the category of "under-developed country." But the enthusiastic reports of progress must be weighed against the acute analysis of the facts worked out by her growing body of trained economists. Mrs. Ifigenia M. de Navarrete of the University of Mexico, for example, has made "a very important contribution to the literature on income distribution" by her acute analysis of what happened in Mexico between 1950 and 1957. The national product increased by 148 per cent, from 38.8 million pesos to 94.4 million pesos, but the position of the low income groups worsened considerably. Rapid economic development took place, but income distribution became more unequal.[11]

The Revolution thus did not change everything in Mexico, where historical forces run deep. Alexander von Humboldt noted in 1800 the fearful differences in the living conditions among the people; today, even the physical location of the wealthy remains the same. The Spanish viceroys of the eighteenth century used the lovely hills of Chapultepec, then outside the city, as their summer residence; many upper-class families live there today, even though some of the new economic royalists build luxurious homes in the Pedregal district south of the capital where the black basalt rock from ancient lava flows provides a handsome setting. These favored few live in much the same spirit as did the *científicos* under Porfirio Díaz. They appear to have little concern for their fellows; their gifts go, if they are made at all, to the Church, and the absence of philanthropic foundations is striking. One Mexican has bluntly described the 1000 or more millionaires who have made their fortunes during Mexico's great upsurge of the last two decades in these terms: "Many of our Independence heroes were gentlemen of wealth; all over Latin America the upper middle class that came into existence during the second half of the nineteenth century was often cultured, generous, and progressive; but the rich man today is unforgivable, in whatever light he is considered." [12] It may be noted, too, that even some radicals live well in Mexico. The Communist-painter David Alfaro Siqueiros was noted for his luxurious home and expensive sports cars.[13]

● **Has the Revolution Ended?** Most Mexicans and many foreigners hold strong opinions on this subject.[14] The purpose of the Revolution was never closely defined, hence a consideration of the extent to which it has succeeded and failed leads to political polemics.

Those who believe that the democratic level of a country is indicated by the quality of the men willing to serve it point to Agustín Yáñez, recently governor of Jalisco for six years and now Minister of Education, as an example of an admirably competent public servant. Called Mexico's greatest living novelist, he gave himself wholeheartedly to the many pressing problems of his powerful and turbulent state, listened to the people, persuaded *políticos* and others not to carry pistols, and when asked to comment on his role as Governor said: "Government calls for the essential quality of the novelist: imagination."

When Madero criticized Díaz in 1910, the novelist Federico Gamboa considered him mentally deranged, for who in his right mind would oppose the dictator? [15] The Revolution brought on "respect for human life and freedom of thought," and in 1945 Jesús Silva Herzog declared: "there are no political prisoners in any part of the national territory; everyone can express his ideas, whatever they may be, without danger; one can attack the government, one can even attack the President anywhere; one can write against the authorities; nothing will happen to the writer, the orator, the agitator." [16] Today considerable freedom of expression exists in Mexico, and the country's problems are ventilated vociferously every day in the press. But this freedom is not unlimited. Siqueiros, the Communist painter, and others have been jailed for remarks and actions which the government considered to be in violation of Mexican law. Some observers point out that government control of newsprint means that no attacks on the President or his close friends and no more than mild criticism of government policies appear in the newspapers. The government permits the publication of *Política,* one of the most strident left-wing weeklies in the continent, but its editor, Víctor Rico Galán, was arrested in the fall of 1966 when the government sharply cracked down on subversion.[17] (*See Reading No. 34.*)

Even though discussion of the Revolution leads to no generally accepted conclusion, it is now the subject of historical investigation. Bibliographies are being compiled, documents published, generals' memoirs collected, and a new day is dawning for those who study the history of modern Mexico. However Mexicans may interpret their Revolution, they are "proud that it antedates the Russian upheaval by some years, that its methods and ideals were indigenous; no German exiles provided its philosophy; no technician in revolution told them how to do it." [18] Soviet historians who forget this are sharply reminded of the facts.[19] Moreover, the "ideals of the Revolution" are a goal rather than a doctrine, to which even the Chamber of Commerce and the Association of Manufacturers proclaim their devotion.

The Revolution, Mexicans feel, helps to relate their country to the world. Mexico's situation is so like that of many other countries in Latin America, Africa, and the Orient that the poet-diplomat Octavio Paz believes this creates a special bond between them: "We have ceased to be an inert material which the strong could use as they wished. We were objects before, but now we have begun to be the agents of historical changes, and our acts and our omissions affect the great powers." [20]

● **Mexico and the United States.** Most of Mexico's international trade is with the U.S., and the millions of tourists who have gone south since World War II for recreation and stimulation provided Mexico with an important source of foreign exchange which now brings in half as much as Mexico derives from all her exports. Available tourist rooms doubled between 1954 and 1962, 80 per cent of all tourists in recent years have been from the U.S., and the government expected foreign tourists to spend, beginning in 1966, over a billion dollars annually. U.S. private investment comes to almost $700 millions, about the same dollar investment as at the beginning of the Revolution, but now U.S. investments represent a much larger percentage of total foreign investments than in the earlier period. The nature of the investment has also changed radically; mining, railroads, and oil have yielded first place to manufacturing. Many of the large business enterprises are in U.S. hands, a predominance which has been characterized by a Mexican group as "a serious menace to the integrity of the nation and to the freedom of the country to project its own economic development." [21]

Opposition to U.S. investment unites many diverse elements—Nationalists, small manufacturers, intellectuals, and industrialists—but Alfredo Navarrete, Jr., Director of Economic Investigations for the powerful government investment agency Nacional Financiera, argued that Mexico must not only foster greater investment by Mexicans but also attract foreign funds available in the great insurance companies of the world. He feels that Mexico's economy needs more capital, and that the country is sufficiently strong to use foreign capital without danger. [22]

This confident proposal, based on Mexico's needs and Mexico's capabilities, is a far cry from the 1941 pronouncements of such economists as Eduardo Villaseñor who predicted that the United States must export private capital to Latin America, "You may even have to give your capital away," he said, "lest you become a modern Midas and witness the decline and fall of the United States in the midst of a golden age of plenty—with all your gold interred somewhere in the Union." [23]

"Mexico has one international problem; it is a permanent one, serious and sometimes grave," asserts one of Mexico's outstanding figures, and this problem arises because Mexico borders on the United States, "the most powerful nation of the earth in modern times; and this country is imperialistic, an economic phenomenon which results from its formidable financial and industrial development." [24] (*See Reading No. 39.*)

Relations between the two countries have markedly improved, however, since 1940. Mexicans now have greater confidence in their own strength, and increased contact has brought greater understanding in many areas. Friction over treatment of the agricultural workers who streamed yearly across the border to perform "stoop-labor" in the fields of California, Texas, and other states notably diminished in the years before it was largely abolished in 1965 by Congress. According to L. B. Simpson, this remarkable migration may prove to have been—despite the abuses practiced on some of the workers while in the United States—"the most effective program in international education that could be devised." [25] The Mexicans were excellent workmen, naturally courteous, and helped to dispel the ignorance and prejudice existing in some U.S. circles. The Mexicans returned with more than $35 million annually in savings, automobiles, clothing, refrigerators; they also had new techniques and new ideas, and a generally friendly attitude to the United States. At any rate, the problem is no longer a danger to Mexican-U.S. relations.

President López Mateos characterized the peaceful resolution of the Chamizal dispute with the U.S. as the most important achievement of his administration. President Díaz Ordaz started his administration in 1964 by reaching an agreement with the U.S. to control the salinity of the Colorado River water that had been damaging Mexican crops.

Intellectuals oriented toward Europe and small industrialists who fear competition from the great U.S. firms maintain the traditional suspicion or at least reserve toward the United States. And many Mexicans view with apprehension what they call the "cocacolonization" of Mexican culture, by which they mean a wide variety of cultural influences from the north that range from "Santa Claus to psychoanalysis." Mexico feels the economic and social influence of the U.S., but she has become more capable of resisting it or at least using it in her own way. Her own deep and richly variegated culture exists more strongly than ever before. In fact, Mexico has never had as interesting and lively a development in art, letters, philosophy, and science as today.

● **Mexican Culture Today.** Nineteenth-century Mexicans tended to depreciate their own achievements, to believe them innately inferior to those of Europe. Beginning with the Revolution, Mexicans began to change their views. Wars disillusioned many with respect to Europe and a new national sense of their own culture, distinct from that of Europe, was born. "And in turning its back on Europe, Mexico has availed itself of the ideas of nationalism . . . a European concept." [26] This movement quickly came to be the dominant voice in art, literature, music, philosophy. Book stores, art galleries, and historical museums sprang up, and cultural missions were dispatched to the provinces to shed light there. "Mexican character" was probed; the one most powerful and persistent theme in this upsurge of national spirit was the inquiry into what it means to be a Mexican in the contemporary world.[27] Mexican culture is heterogeneous and defies neat categorization, but one notable characteristic has been an intense concern with itself, at times almost amounting to an obsession. (*See Reading No. 36.*)

A trend away from "Mexicanism" toward a more universalistic approach is now in progress. The Spanish intellectuals, who brought their knowledge and skills to Mexico after Franco triumphed in Spain, helped to bring the thought of the world to Mexico. That extraordinary publishing house, the *Fondo de Cultura Económica,* has aided cultural development in Mexico by providing excellent translations of substantial foreign books in many fields and by publishing the work of many Mexican writers. The legitimate theater in Mexico City has also been a cosmopolitan influence in recent years. In 1950 there were only three theaters; by 1958 thirty were in full swing. Some are small and intimate; the *Teatro de los Insurgentes* seats 1,200 and is one of the most perfectly equipped in Latin America, and the government-built Cultural Unity Center in Chapultepec Park holds 18,000. In recent years some of the finest plays of other countries have been produced. The percentage of foreign importations has been so high that the intense Nationalists have raised their ancient banner with a new motto: "Mexican theaters for Mexican authors." [28]

Since about 1956 a lively polemic has been under way with Communists and Nationalists shouting the long-popular slogan "Mexico for Mexicans!" Many friends of Moscow are to be found among the intellectuals but few are Communists, though membership in the Party would not be particularly frowned upon. These friends have convinced some of the Nationalists that all writing and painting that does not directly concern itself with the Mexican peasant, wet-back, or Indian is therefore anti-Mexican and subservient to base Yanqui interests. Rockefeller grants to young Mexican scholars have been attacked as corrupting the intelligent and encouraging the mediocre. According to one Spanish-American observer, a "fifth-column" among the Mexican intellectuals works assiduously to keep alive all possible points of friction between the two countries and thus serve the world-wide strategy of communism. "The communists have meticulously investigated every action of North Americans in Mexico . . . They have counted how many Marines disembarked from the ship *Buffalo* in 1913 and how many months General Sedgwick spent in Matamoros in 1866 . . . They seek new historical, economical, and sentimental arguments against the events of 1847." [29]

U.S. visa regulations and their administration still alienate intellectuals: Frank Wardlaw of the University of Texas Press publicly deplored the way in which Jaime García Terrés, a Mexican intellectual, was subjected to humiliation by U.S. immigration authorities. Wardlaw, a leading figure in the campaign to translate Latin-American books for English-speaking audiences, called for a reappraisal of visa procedures to make possible a freer exchange of ideas.[30] In the *Revista de Literatura Mexicana* and elsewhere, Emanuel Carballo, Octavio Paz, Jorge Portilla, and others have decried chauvinistic nationalism in any field and brilliantly defended the right of Mexicans to complete freedom of artistic expression and to acceptance of influences from abroad. They believe that the Mexican creative spirit should flower in any field it wishes and its products be made known to the world. Mexico now moves confidently on the world scene. She organizes a "Year of Mexican-Philippine Friendship" which involved much travelling of intellectuals to and from Manila in 1964; her Nuclear Energy Commission announces that Mexico is capable of making an atomic bomb but chooses instead to take the lead in the effort to have Latin America declared a nuclear-free zone, and is proud of her cultural projection in Latin America.

Art exhibits are sent to New York, Paris, and Stockholm; a young but able and dedicated ballet group performed in Russia, and the symphony orchestra has had highly successful European tours. Members of the so-called "third generation" of music composers, such as Raúl Cosío, do not feel that they must draw exclusively upon Mexico's rich treasury of folk music for their themes.[31] Orozco early in his career mocked at those who allowed politics to dominate their art: the young painter José Luis Cuevas expressed his feeling thus: "What I want in my country's art are broad highways leading out to the rest of the world, rather than narrow trails connecting one adobe village with another." (*See Reading No. 37.*) And Cuevas has already made his mark, for he has been described as "one of the most sophisticated of artists. . . . Not even Hieronymous Bosch has managed to make horror more elegant." [32] Mexico has also produced the writer Alfonso Reyes (died in 1959), judged by many inside and outside Mexico to be the most complete, the most universal Mexican. Reyes taught his countrymen to prize their own arts while remaining fully aware of other cultures. Mexico remains faithful to her Indian past—there is no public monument to Cortez in the republic whereas an imposing one to Cuauhtémoc stands in the capital—but her face is turned toward the world. (*See Reading No. 37.*)

Writers and researchers of Mexico today are frankly and steadfastly examining the realities of Mexican life and judging them with critical power. In 1937 Eyler N. Simpson observed that the Mexican investigator who actually went out into the field to look for facts about his own country was so rare as to be a curiosity. "I could name on the fingers of one hand the research monographs dealing with modern social problems published by Mexican students in the last decade." [33] Now Lucio Mendieta y Núñez directs an active Institute of Social Investigations at the University, which issues solid studies regularly; professional reviews such as *El Trimestre Económico,* and *Revista Mexicana de Sociología* attract competent writers, while *Problemas Agrícolas e Indus-*

triales de México provides a forum for active debate on Mexican needs. The latter publication frequently translates serious studies on Mexico, often by U.S. professors, and then invites leading Mexican scholars to comment. The result is a lively and valuable contribution to the clarification of ideas on important topics. Monographs such as José Iturriaga's *La estructura social y cultural de México* bring penetration and sophistication to the study of Mexican society. Another sign of Mexico's maturity was the refusal of Mexican courts to ban Oscar Lewis' book *The Children of Sánchez,* which had been formally denounced as obscene and anti-Mexican by the venerable Sociedad Mexicana de Geografía e Estadística.[34]

The development of a universal view of the world rooted in Mexican experience, and the determination to look squarely at the social facts of Mexican life may prove to be the greatest revolution of them all—a revolution testifying powerfully to the vigor and independence of the people of Mexico today.

● **From Marble Palace to Anthropological Museum.** Just as one may climb Chapultepec Hill to gain visual perspective on the great city of Mexico, so one may stand amidst the dramatic new buildings of the oldest university of the Western Hemisphere and find another meaningful perspective on the present and future of the Republic.

When Porfirio Díaz wished to impress the world with the impressive culture Mexico had attained under his rule, he began to build in 1900 a marble Palace of Fine Arts in the center of the capital—grandiose, expensive, with a colored glass stage curtain made by Tiffany of New York and complicated stage machinery from Germany. The guide book describes part of the ornate interior in these terms: "The dressing rooms of the stage artists are palatial boudoirs. There is a fine café and bar, a vast cellar filled with thousands of bottles of choice wines and liqueurs, a smoking room, and reception rooms, and *salons* that would grace a castle in Spain." [35] Today, the Palace remains a monument to the strange period in which it was built when its grandeur bore little relation to the lives and needs of most Mexicans. The marble edifice was so poorly suited to the subsoil conditions of Mexico City that it began to sink into the spongy ground before it was half-completed. The only Indian seen by the top-hatted gentlemen and bejeweled ladies who attended functions there was a melancholy, squatting basalt figure from an eighteenth-century excavation, known as the *Indio Triste* (Sad Indian).

When Mexicans half a century later wished to erect a gigantic symbol of their position they constructed a University City on the hard black lava flow of great antiquity called the Pedregal. Modern, enormous in size (its stadium alone holds about 100,000 persons, more than any university stadium in the United States), exultant in spirit, the Ciudad Universitaria dramatizes "Mexico's modernity, her technology, her resources and her power." [36]

The construction of the university was a colossal undertaking, accomplished in a remarkably short time. Many of the architects and engineers in Mexico were mobilized for the task; some construction elsewhere was halted to make men and materials available for this great effort to stimulate national pride and develop Mexico's technical and industrial resources so that future constructions might be erected by modern means.

The University City does not, in fact, provide a particularly convenient campus for its 70,000 students and professors; communication on foot between the widely scattered buildings is laborious. Although the medical school might well be near the hospitals, it was moved to University City 10 miles south of the capital to enlarge the total effect.

Harwell Harris, an American architect, applauded the University City as a splendid example "of the dynamic function of architecture—of an architecture's power to embody the spirit of a nation in a symbol that her citizens recognize and that arouses them to further expressions of it," but he also wondered if some of the new architectural forms transplanted from Europe and adapted here—the thin vaults, the cantilevers, the stilts used to support some buildings—might not represent a possible new "colonialism." [37]

Mexicans also question and criticize the university, for neither persons nor institutions escape the rapier wit of Mexico's writers and cartoonists. They point out that these splendid buildings were erected at the expense of the poorer and smaller provincial universities and that within the stunningly decorated library's walls too few books are provided for the students. But they are proud of the great undertaking and rejoice that university teaching has become, at last, a full-time profession. They see the flamboyance and variety of architectural styles brought together here and some yet unsolved problems as truly symbolic of the transitional state of Mexican culture.

Further evidence of Mexican pride in its culture was the opening in 1965 of the National Museum of Anthropology in Chapultepec Park. This was another crash program: forty specialists worked with the architect Pedro Ramírez Vásquez to create it in 20 months, while teams of archaeologists and technicians designed the galleries which display the artifacts of the various ancient cultures of pre-Cortez Mexico. The result was "one of the most beautiful buildings in the Americas and [it] may very well be the finest museum in the world. . . . A museum filled with life. No single bit of it suggests a past embalmed, or exhumed." [38] The Mexican school children and other visitors are brought face to face here with the grandeur and rich variety of Mexico's Indian past. The presentation is so remarkable that Sir Philip Hendy wrote: "in museography Mexico is now ahead of the U.S. by perhaps a generation and of the United Kingdom perhaps by a century." [39] And this remarkable presentation of the rise and fall of more than 30 Indian cultures in Mexico may become an inspiration for other nations striving to enter the modern world, for one Peruvian visitor remarked: "As a Latin American, this magnificent place tells me how Mexico has arrived. She has integrated past with present.

She has made her Indian cultures and peoples part of the modern nation. How different from my country where our people are mainly Indian, but where 400 years of European rule have failed to bring them into modern times." [40]

The small army, though it has more generals than either the U.S. or Soviet Russia, has become the instrument of civilian thinking and direction, and there has been no successful revolt for many years. Mexican governments have enforced discipline; in fact, some observers believe that the optimistic views earlier expressed on the state of civil liberties in Mexico should be revised. They feel that the former subtle control of press, speech, and assembly is today more overt; the press is not wholly trusted, the president may not be attacked, and the single party keeps dissidents in line. The Revolution, which started out with the cry of *"Tierra y Libertad,"* they hold, has not only ended, but reversed itself. Large landholdings have come back, especially in the irrigated areas, though they are farmed much more scientifically than under the dictatorship of Porfirio Díaz. The Socialist state which emerged from the Revolution laid the foundation for full-scale modern capitalism.

How much truth there is in these and other controversial opinions now held in and about Mexico will appear in perspective only in the future. Meanwhile, it is clear that the "people" for whom the Revolution was fought have not been forgotten although their condition still requires great improvement. Most important of all, the Mexican nation has experienced a profound social revolution and has passed beyond it to achieve a special and Mexican kind of stability which gives it a unique position in Latin America. Octavio Paz, one of the wisest interpreters of contemporary Mexico, has written:

The Mexican Revolution forced us to come out of ourselves and to face up to history, assigned to us the task of inventing our own future and our own institutions. The Mexican Revolution has died without having resolved our contradictions. After the Second World War we are realizing that this self-creation which our reality demands of us is identical with that which a similar reality demands of others. We live, like the rest of the planet, in a decisive and mortal era, orphans of the past and with an uncharted future. Universal History is now a common task, and our labyrinth, the labyrinth of all mankind.[41]

[1] Ernest Gruening, *Mexico and Its Heritage* (New York: Century, 1928), p. 27.

[2] As quoted by Clarence Senior, *Land Reform and Democracy* (Gainesville: University of Florida Press, 1958), p. 19.

[3] Anita Brenner and George R. Leighton, *The Wind that Swept Mexico. The History of the Mexican Revolution, 1910–1942* (New York: Harpers, 1943).

[4] *Change in Latin America. The Mexican and Cuban Revolutions* (Lincoln: The University of Nebraska, 1961), p. 13.

[5] Tannenbaum, *Mexico: The Struggle for Peace and Bread* (New York: Knopf, 1950), pp. 69–70.

[6] Cline, *The United States and Mexico* (Cambridge: Harvard University Press, 1953), p. 198.

[7] Philip B. Taylor, Jr., in the *American Political Science Review,* LVII (1963), p. 73.

[8] Raymond Vernon, *The Dilemma of Mexico's Development* (Cambridge: Harvard University Press, 1963), pp. 2–3; *Comercio Exterior de México,* VII, No. 5 (1961), p. 14.

⁹ As quoted by Joseph C. Goulden, Mexico: PRI's False Front Democracy (New York: The Alicia Patterson Fund, 1966). For a detailed, recent interpretation of the "Revolutionary Family," see Frank Brandenburg, The Making of Modern Mexico (Englewood Cliffs, New Jersey: Prentice-Hall, 1964), pp. 1–18.

¹⁰ Oscar Lewis, Five Families. Mexican Case Studies in the Culture of Poverty (New York: Random House, 1959), pp. 7–10. For a wide-ranging collection of opinions on Lewis' work, see the analysis by John Paddock who devotes the entire No. 6 issue (144 pages) of Mesamerican Notes (Mexico City: Department of Anthropology, University of the Americas, 1965) to the subject. See also Julio César Olivé Negrete and Beatriz Barba de Piña Chán, "Estudio de las clases sociales en la ciudad de México," Anales del Instituto Nacional de Antropología e Historia, XIV, No. 43 (Mexico, 1961), pp. 219–262, for a detailed study of the lives of 200 lower class workers and the effects of their work on their families and their attitudes.

¹¹ F. M. Andic, "Economic Development and Economic Inequality: The Case of Mexico," Caribbean Studies, I (1962), pp. 28–34. According to Enrique Suárez del Real, 80 per cent of the people of Mexico live on a diet which does not provide the minimum requirements of proteins and calories for the average worker, "El problema alimenticio en México," Revista Mexicana de Sociología, XXIV (1962), pp. 367–381. For a comparison, including much statistical material, see Anselmo Marino Flores, "Los problemas sociales de México en 1900 y 1950," Journal of Inter-American Studies, IV (1962), No. 2, pp. 157–185.

Heriberto Jara has always insisted that the prosperity of a country should not be measured by the number of skyscrapers or automobiles: "In Mexico, we have an average of 5,000 barefoot persons for each automobile," Stanley R. Ross, Ed., Is The Mexican Revolution Dead? (New York: Knopf, 1966).

¹² Cosío Villegas, Change in Latin America, pp. 8–9.

¹³ Robert F. Scott, Mexican Government in Transition, revised ed. (Urbana: University of Illinois Press, 1964), p. 85.

¹⁴ For a representative selection of opinions, see Ross, ed., Is the Mexican Revolution Dead?

¹⁵ Gamboa, Diario, II, pp. 169, 189.

¹⁶ Jesús Silva Herzog, Un ensayo sobre la revolución mejicana, in Benjamin Keen, ed., Readings in Latin American Civilization (Boston: Houghton Mifflin, 1955), p. 364.

¹⁷ Joseph C. Goulden, Mexican Subversion: The Hammer Falls (New York: The Alicia Patterson Fund, 1966).

¹⁸ Gladys Delmas, "Mexico from the South," The Atlantic (March, 1964), p. 94. This article appears in a special supplement on "Mexico Today," which gives an excellent general view of Mexico's art, economics, ideas, literature, and politics.

¹⁹ Juan Ortega y Medina, Historiografía soviética iberoamericanista, 1945–1960 (Mexico: Universidad Nacional Antónoma de México, 1961), pp. 123 ff.; J. Gregory Oswald, "México en la historiografía soviética," Historia Mexicana, XIV (1965), No. 56, pp. 691–706.

²⁰ Paz, The Labyrinth of Solitude (Austin: University of Texas Press, 1961), p. 193.

²¹ Quoted by Oscar Lewis, "Mexico desde 1940," Investigación Económica, XVII (Mexico City, 1958), No. 70, p. 207.

²² Navarrete, "Una política de inversiones extranjeras," Comercio Exterior, VII (Mexico City, August, 1958), No. 8, pp. 421–424.

²³ Villaseñor, "Inter-American Trade and Financial Problems," in Walter H. C. Laves, ed., Inter-American Solidarity (Chicago: University of Chicago Press, 1941), pp. 93–94.

²⁴ Jesús Silva Herzog, "Meditaciones sobre México," Cuadernos Americanos, XXXV (Sept.–Oct. 1947), p. 34.

²⁵ Simpson, Many Mexicos, third ed. (Berkeley: University of California Press, 1952), pp. 312–313.

²⁶ Samuel Ramos, Profile of Man and Culture in Mexico (Austin: University of Texas Press, 1962), p. 96.

²⁷ John L. Phelan, "México y lo Mexicano," Hispanic American Historical Review, XXXVI (1956), pp. 309–318.

[28] Allan Lewis, "The Theater in Mexico," *The Texas Quarterly*, II (1959), No. 1, p. 145.

[29] Alberto Baeza Flores, "Marx y Engels contra México," *Política*, III (Caracas, 1964), No. 35, pp. 59–75. Mexican journalists on the whole give a most unflattering picture of the U.S., according to the analysis by John C. Merrill, "The United States as seen from Mexico," *Journal of Inter-American Studies*, V (1963), No. 1, pp. 53–66.

[30] See the letter by Wardlaw to *Harper's* (January, 1965).

[31] Horacio Flores Sánchez, *"Los compositores rebeldes se presentan con su música,"* in "México en la cultura," No. 506, *Novedades* (Mexico City, Nov. 24, 1958). Carlos Chávez as early as 1930 published a book on music and electricity, calling attention to the new technical resources made available to music by 20th century technology, even while he was composing "proletarian music" for the masses, Gilbert Chase, "The Artist," in John J. Johnson, ed., *Continuity and Change in Latin America* (Stanford: Stanford University Press, 1964), p. 124.

[32] John Canady, "Growing up with José Luis Cuevas," *The New York Times* (May 23, 1965), section X, p. 17. For a statement on the evolution of 20th century Mexican art from its revolutionary concern for the masses to the present middle class orientation, see Virginia B. Derr, "The Rise of a Middle Class Tradition in Mexican Art," *Journal of Inter-American Studies*, III (1961), No. 3, pp. 385–409.

[33] Simpson, *The Ejido—Mexico's Way Out* (Chapel Hill: University of North Carolina Press, 1937), p. 579.

[34] "La justicia en defensa de la libertad de expresión," *La Gaceta* (Mexico City: Fondo de Cultura Económica, April, 1965).

[35] *Terry's Guide to Mexico* (Boston: Houghton Mifflin, 1935), pp. 327–328.

[36] Harwell Hamilton Harris, "Regionalism and Nationalism in Architecture," *The Texas Quarterly* (1958), No. 1, p. 123.

[37] *Ibid.*, p. 123.

[38] John Canady, "A Dramatic Symbol of the New Mexico," *The New York Times* (April 11, 1965), section X, p. 17.

[39] *Ibid.*, p. 17.

[40] John D. Harbron, *The Mexican Model* (Toronto: Canadian Institute of International Affairs, 1966), p. 1.

[41] Paz, *Labyrinth of Solitude*, pp. 172–173.

2
CENTRAL
AMERICA

Guatemala

AREA: 42,040 sq. mi.
POPULATION IN MID-1966: 4,575,000
LARGEST CITY:
Guatemala City (capital): 439,081
(est. 1963)
PRINCIPAL EXPORTS (1960): coffee,
bananas, cotton
PRESIDENT: Julio César Méndez
Montenegro, civilian, took office
July 1, 1966, for a 6-year term.

El Salvador

AREA: 8,083 sq. mi.
POPULATION IN MID-1966: 3,011,000
LARGEST CITY:
San Salvador (capital): 281,122
(est. 1963)
PRINCIPAL EXPORTS (1960): coffee,
cotton, textile yarns and fibers
PRESIDENT: Fidel Sánchez Hernández,
military, took office July 1, 1967,
for a 5-year term.

Panama

AREA: 29,208 sq. mi.
POPULATION IN MID-1966: 1,287,000
LARGEST CITY:
Panama City (capital): 318,536
(est. 1964)
PRINCIPAL EXPORTS (1961): bananas,
shrimp, sugar
PRESIDENT: Marco Aurelio Robles,
civilian, took office Oct. 1, 1964,
for a 4-year term.

Nicaragua

AREA: 53,668 sq. mi.
POPULATION IN MID-1966: 1,715,000
LARGEST CITY:
Managua (capital): 234,600
(est. 1963)
PRINCIPAL EXPORTS (1961): cotton,
coffee, gold
PRESIDENT: Anastasio Somoza Debayle,
military, took office May 1, 1967,
for a 5-year term.

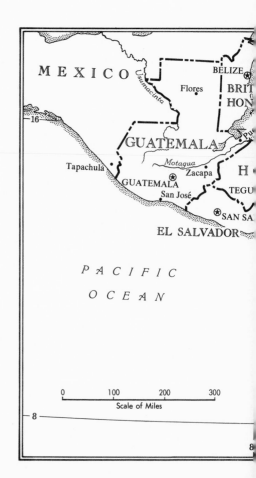

Costa Rica

AREA: 19,653 sq. mi.

POPULATION IN MID-1966: 1,491,000

LARGEST CITY:
San José (capital): 322,208
(metropolitan area, 1963)

PRINCIPAL EXPORTS (1960): coffee,
bananas, cacao

PRESIDENT: José Joaquín Trejos
Fernández, civilian, took office
May 8, 1966, for a 4-year term.

Honduras

AREA: 43,277 sq. mi.

POPULATION IN MID-1966: 2,363,000

LARGEST CITY:
Tegucigalpa (capital): 134,075
(est. 1961)

PRINCIPAL EXPORTS (1960): bananas,
coffee, wood

PRESIDENT: Osvaldo López Arellano,
military, seized power October 5,
1963; took office as constitutional
president, June 6, 1965, for a
6-year term.

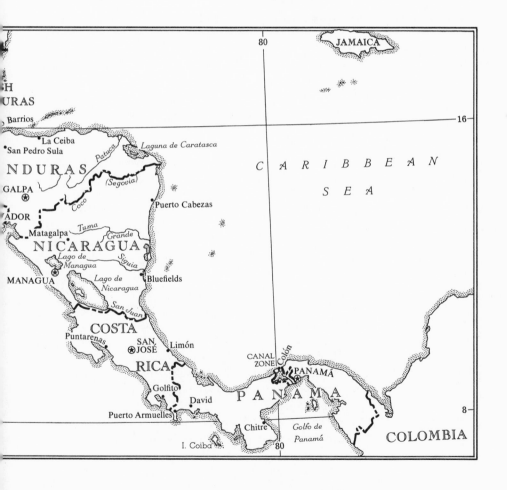

CENTRAL
AMERICA

● **Sub-Continent in Crisis.** The tapering land mass separating Mexico from South America has always been one of the least-known areas in the new world. Relatively few visitors go there and some diplomats are inclined to regard appointment there like an assignment to Siberia. Central America catches the world's attention only when one of its volcanoes erupts, when communism is believed to be about to take over one of its republics, or when an archaeological expedition uncovers another ancient city.

The 14 million people who live in this sub-continent have much in common, despite many dissimilarities. All six countries—Guatemala, El Salvador, Honduras, Nicaragua, Costa Rica, and Panama—were a part of the vast Spanish empire which endured for three centuries. When independence came in 1821, except to Panama, the people equally lacked political experience, a fact which helps to explain their 19th century tribulations. Another tremendous obstacle to development of commerce and a sense of unity was the difficult terrain, which helps to account for the fragmentation of the region and the bitter hostility that marks the relations of several of the nations. With the coming of the 20th century some parts of Latin America developed steadily but, except for Costa Rica, Central America lagged behind.

Although there are some rugged mountains and high plateaus, much of the area is tropical and subject to heavy rainfall. In the lowlands some sections are deluged with 15 feet per year, and even the higher regions average 6 feet annually. Thus land communications remain an enormous problem. In Honduras and Panama bananas constitute the principal export crop but in the other countries coffee is the significant crop, except Nicaragua, where cotton is dominant, and Costa Rica, where bananas share honors with coffee. Little manufacturing is done in the area and a middle class scarcely exists.

The social complexion of the area is far from uniform. Costa Rica's citizens are largely of European stock, while more than half of the Guatemalans are Indians. Negroes are concentrated in the hot, coastal areas; mulattoes, mestizos, and other racial combinations are found almost everywhere. Nearly 70 per cent live in rural areas where the family group holds sway under a patriarchal system. A few hundred families in each country own most of the land and live in leisure and security; the vast majority suffer a life of drudgery.

Little attention or money has been devoted to education. The Catholic Church exerts relatively little influence. More than half of the people are illiterate and, despite potential wealth, the republics of Central America exist in a state of poverty. Government efforts to develop national industries and control exchange have increased in recent years but have sometimes been ill-planned and inflationary. Economic productivity has increased only slightly, and the wealthy families tend to invest in real estate or in foreign enterprises.

Given these unfavorable circumstances, it is not surprising that political instability characterizes much of the region and that dictators flourish. At almost any given moment at least one Central American government is convinced that another one is plotting against it, often with reason. When the presidents of the republics met with President Kennedy in San José, Costa Rica, in 1963, Luis Somoza of Nicaragua feared an attack on his life and 70 agents guarded his every move. The support given by the U.S. to some dictators in Central America has drawn severe criticism. *The Christian Science Monitor* editorialized: "One potential liberator has served as spokesman for all when he said: 'I didn't especially enjoy being carried to jail in a jeep with a sign on it, Gift of the People of the United States to the People of Nicaragua.' " [1]

Guatemala

When General Jorge Ubico was overthrown in 1944, one of the most ruthless dictators left the scene. Since seizing power in 1931 Ubico had accomplished few material improvements. He expanded the gravely inadequate educational system, built a few roads which could be used only in dry season, and managed to maintain a mere semblance of economic prosperity thanks to an agreement permitting the free entry of coffee into the United States. The peace of the grave established by this dictator was definitely a poor prelude to the hoped for development of Guatemalan life.

Juan José Arévalo, who had been in exile for years lecturing at Argentine universities, began his term as President (1945–1951) by undertaking a fundamental social revolution: he abolished forced labor and promulgated an advanced Labor Code, laid plans for the breakup of large landholdings, created a Social Security Institute, reorganized the army to diminish its power, and made several educational improvements. Under his stimulus the Indians began to participate in government. His ambivalent attitude toward communism caused some criticism; he declared against it, but the Party organized swiftly and strongly during his regime.

When Colonel Jacobo Arbenz took the presidential oath in 1951 before 50,000 spectators in the national stadium, an impressive structure that Guatemala could ill afford, the way was paved for further communist influence in the courts, legislature, and propaganda media. Arbenz announced his objective to be the conversion of Guatemala from a dependent nation with a semi-colonial economy to an economically independent country, and the conversion of its predominantly feudal economy into a modern capitalistic one.

The principal step Arbenz took toward these distant goals was the enactment of the controversial Agrarian Reform Law of July 15, 1952, which planned the distribution of expropriated land to some three hundred thousand families. When the U.S. government supported the United Fruit Company in its opposition to the expropriation of its lands without what it regarded as just compensation, a perfect instrument to rouse anti-American feeling was at hand. Secretary of State John Foster Dulles insisted on presenting a declaration against international communism at the Tenth Inter-American Congress in Caracas in March, 1954. Guatemala denounced U.S. policy as that of "the Big Stick, tarnished dollar diplomacy, and the landing of Marines in Latin American ports." After much maneuvering and heated discussion, the declaration was passed by a vote of seventeen to one. But two of the most important countries—Argentina and Mexico—abstained and the U.S. "victory" was hollow.

Events now moved swiftly. The disclosure in May, 1954, that a shipment of arms from Poland was en route to Guatemala led Dulles to fear that a Communist coup was imminent in Guatemala, only two hours distant by air from the Panama Canal. In June, 1954, an obscure Guatemalan exile in Honduras, Colonel Carlos Castillo Armas, launched his rebel force against the Arbenz government. Neither the United Nations nor the Organization of American States was called in to avert this threat to peace, and the U.S. relied on the Central Intelligence Agency to help overthrow the Arbenz regime.[2]

Since then, Guatemalan affairs have been confused and uncertain. Castillo Armas announced a five year economic plan, revised the agrarian law, stood fast against the Catholic Church's demand for recognition as "preeminent," and acknowledged the need to incorporate the Indians into the national life. But in 1957 he was assassinated by a personal guard, a fanatic without apparent political motives. By March, 1958, his successor was inaugurated, the conservative General Miguel Ydígoras Fuentes, who had been elected "in the first relatively free and fair election in 137 years of Guatemalan history."[3] Ydígoras was forced out in 1963 by a junta headed by Colonel Enrique Peralta Azurdía, against whom a variety of political forces were arrayed, including the guerrilla leftist Marco Antonio Yon Sosa. Elections were finally held in March, 1966, when Julio César Méndez Montenegro won a plurality but not a majority. The race was therefore thrown into Congress, which on May 11 officially elected him. Méndez Montenegro was inaugurated July 1, 1966, the first government opposition candidate to win in many years and the first civilian president since Juan José Arévalo completed his term 15 years previously.

Guatemala today, despite the alarms and upheavals since dictator Ubico left, confronts its familiar basic problems: a one-crop economy, inadequate transportation, and the disparity of a few wealthy families among a largely illiterate population—all of which promises continued economic and political instability. Although the second largest and most populous (4.5 million inhabitants) of the Central American nations, Guatemala has not yet found that "benevolent dictator" Chester Lloyd Jones called for as necessary for the salvation of the country,[4] nor has a firm base been established for a democratic government.

El Salvador

Beset with essentially the same past and present problems as Guatemala, this small and most densely populated country (2.8 million inhabitants) of all Central America offers a considerable contrast to its neighbor. During 1931–1944 the country was ruled by Maximiliano Hernández Martínez, an eccentric military dictator who was a Theosophist and, ignoring the educated Salvadoreans, appealed directly to the poverty-stricken peons. He devised unusual methods of corn planting which fascinated the peons but produced little corn, invented nostrums promising relief from rheumatism, heart disease, and dysentery, and as one scheme failed he concocted an even more captivating one to keep his people interested. He was a bloody dictator, however, and put down the frequent uprisings with cruelty. He was once quoted as saying: "It is a greater crime to kill an ant than a man, for when a man dies he becomes reincarnated, while an ant dies forever." Yet a decade after his downfall a Dutch community worker in a small Salvadorean town was astonished to find this dictator so popular:

> *Campesinos* don't seem to care much about civil liberties. They prefer order and security. Martínez was a "man," according to them. He knew how to keep order and to prevent murder and other crimes with a strong hand. Now there is more danger everywhere. Besides this he carried out great works, like the Pan-American Highway and other things that gave employment. He also leased much land for low rents to poor campesinos for many years, so that they got some feeling of security.[5]

When he was forced to resign in 1944, a period of uncertainty set in with a number of men assuming, and losing, the presidency until an army officer, Oscar Osorio, gained it with a promise of "honest reconstruction." To almost everybody's surprise, he accomplished just that, diversifying agriculture, stimulating light industry, developing highways, housing, and electrical power.

Another army officer, José María Lemus, Osorio's handpicked candidate, won the fantastic election of 1956 described by *The New York Times* as "by all odds the most rancorous and confused campaign in El Salvador's recent history." Lemus promised to continue his predecessor's reforms, but in 1960 a bloodless coup overthrew him, and the elections of 1962 brought still another army officer, Julio A. Rivera to power for a five year term. His regime provided relatively responsible leadership and undertook a meaningful program of broad reform as part of the Alliance for Progress. Colonel Fidel Sánchez won the 1967 election, thanks to the backing of President Rivera and the small conservative landowning oligarchy which runs this tiny nation. He faces, as all Salvadoran presidents have, the threat of an uncertain world market for coffee and the exhaustion of the country's soil. (*See Reading No. 40.*)

On May 3, 1965, two important events occurred. One was a disastrous earthquake; the other, the passage of a minimum wage law for agricultural labor which raised the daily wage to 90 cents, but released the planters from providing two full meals a day for their workers. Even as the nation struggled to repair the damage which nature had done to their country, it had taken a decisive step away from the paternalistic past.

El Salvador has made one unique contribution to the peace of Central America. Its most far-sighted leaders have tried hard to pull together this badly divided subcontinent which has sought unity since independence. Many projects for cultural, economic, and political unification have originated in El Salvador, and most of the existing regional organizations make their headquarters in its capital city. While its neighbors often conspire against each other, El Salvador has maintained an exemplary and noteworthy neutrality that presages a growing political maturity which will much assist the peaceful settlement of the many and bitterly contested disputes among the Central American nations. Other nations have participated in the search for Central American unity, but if it ever becomes a reality El Salvador will be one of its chief architects.

Honduras

With a population of over 2 million, this is the country to which the term "banana republic" most applies. Revolutions, invasions, and civil wars have been endemic throughout its history and, in General Tiburcio Carías, Honduras produced a dictator who, in his sixteen-year presidency, exhibited all the usual traits of a paternalistic, authoritarian *caudillo*. Yet he was one of the first presidential candidates in Honduras to accept defeat in open elections (in 1928) without starting a revolution, and when he left office in 1949 he removed himself more completely from the government than anyone anticipated. His conservatism led him to oppose suffrage for women and labor organization, and under his regime democratic institutions withered. Although generally lenient with opponents, he felt that serious lawbreakers should be conspicuously discouraged: some three hundred prisoners, including political transgressors, were kept at public work in the capital while chained to heavy balls. With complete power in his hands for many years, he failed to accomplish any resounding material progress.

The years since 1949, when the dictator stepped down in favor of his friend, Juan Manuel Gálvez, have been difficult, although Gálvez (1949–1954) proved to be an unexpectedly independent president. He began some much needed transportation improvements, allotted more money to education, supported agricultural diversification to mitigate the unhealthy dependence on bananas, encouraged foreign investment, and even tried to get Hondurans to pay income taxes. Besides laboring for material improvement, Gálvez tried to foster democratic ideals and the long dormant but awakening popular desire for freedom. All his constructive efforts were undermined by the prolonged and expensive controversy with the United Fruit Company in 1954 which led to the first general labor strike in Honduran history. Communists were active, but the longstanding poverty, illiteracy, and disorganization of the workers were enough in themselves as fertile ground for agitation for better working and living conditions. Some $15 million worth of bananas ripened and rotted unpicked, but Honduran labor won a position far superior to its unorganized subservience under Carías.

A second serious blow to President Gálvez's constructive enterprises was the acrimonious and confused election of 1954, won by José Ramón Villeda Morales. He was not permitted to take office, and for two years thereafter Honduras was governed by decrees issued by the self-appointed "chief of state" Julio Lozano Díaz, who exercised dictatorial powers until forced out by a military junta in October, 1956. The junta governed reasonably well until December 19, 1957, and two days later Villeda Morales was installed as "duly elected constitutional president" for a six-year term. Until forced out in 1963 by a military cabal, Villeda Morales seems to have kept Honduras on a fairly even keel despite various uprisings and bombings from both left and right elements.

The basic economic and social ills still persist. Yet the picture is not wholly dark for, as William S. Stokes has pointed out, even under the successive dictatorships "the average Honduran is to a large extent a free agent." (*See Reading No. 41.*)

Nicaragua

Except for an American adventurer named William Walker "elected" President in 1856, and for having one of the obvious sites for a much-disputed transisthmian canal, Nicaragua in the 19th century ran the regular course for a small Caribbean country. Relentless warfare between the two political parties was endemic, and from 1893 to 1909 an unscrupulous dictator, José Santos Zelaya, held sway. The United States intervened both diplomatically and with arms, and for the period 1909–1933 dominated Nicaragua through a customs collectorship and Marine occupation which led to vigorous Latin-American criticism of "dollar diplomacy." Washington found this criticism increasingly embarrassing and Herbert Hoover withdrew the Marines in 1933.

Anastasio Somoza quickly rose to power after the Marines left; present-day Nicaragua is largely the result of his work, for good and for evil. By 1937 he had risen by strong-arm methods from army chief to president and had, according to many reports, eliminated the elusive and popular rebel leader, Augusto Sandino, by assassination. Once in power, he promoted economic development by attracting foreign capital and encouraging private enterprise. A thorough economic study by an International Bank mission in 1951–1952 produced much useful advice, and both coffee and cotton prices boomed in the 1950's. Roads and ports were improved, electrical power developed, and education increased. Indeed, by 1954 Nicaragua published the news that it had more teachers than soldiers—4,991 to 4,052—a boast that neighboring Costa Rica had been making for years. Hospitals were built, public health services expanded throughout the country, and gross national production grew from $170 million in 1951 to $310 million in 1956. Even though most of Somoza's reforms came after 1950, when he had been in complete control for a dozen years, the resulting material benefits were impressive.

His relations with his neighbors, however, particularly Costa Rica, progressively deteriorated. The Organization of American States had to be called in during December, 1948, and for a time hostility ceased. Personal friction continued between Costa Rican President José Figueres and Somoza, who believed that Costa Rica supported communist plots to kill him. As he considered himself one of the great bulwarks against communism in the Americas, this specter was particularly galling to him. He was shot on September 21, 1956, by a young Nicaraguan poet, Rigoberto López Pérez, who apparently had no other motive than a patriotic desire to eliminate the dictator. At Somoza's death his son Luis assumed the reins of government and was "elected" for the 1957–1963 presidential term, while another son, Anastasio, took charge of the National Guard.

Reaction to the death of Somoza varied strikingly. Cuba, ruled by his great friend, the dictator Fulgencio Batista, declared three days of mourning, while the Uruguayan parliament passed a resolution honoring the murderer. President Eisenhower roused the ever latent hostility to the United States in Latin America when he expressed his deepest sympathy and called the attack "dastardly." Much unnecessary ill-will was generated by this extremely solicitous attitude toward one of the most notorious Latin-American dictators. After the President's brother, Dr. Milton Eisenhower, made his "fact-finding visit" to Central America in 1958, he strongly advocated that the United States treat dictators with cold correctness, reserving warm *abrazos* for democratic leaders in Latin America.

What was the nature of Somoza's dictatorship and what did he accomplish for the country? He undoubtedly brought Nicaragua political peace and he was certainly a man of personality and acumen who gave a chaotic and backward country a measure of economic progress. Yet the new roads he built ordinarily led to or passed near one of his many ranches. His private commercial interests included distilleries, sugar mills, cotton gins, lumber, cattle, cement, soap, textiles, ice-making, a steamship line, and even a barber shop. By these means he built up a great personal fortune in a poor country. Perhaps the worst blot on his regime was its failure to prepare the people for participation in government. He made all serious decisions; his ministers were glorified clerks. He harshly suppressed democratic opposition, prohibited trade unionism, and vociferously opposed freedom of the press.

The Kennedy administration soon replaced Ambassador Thomas Whelan, political appointee and close friend of the dictator, with Aaron Brown, a career diplomat. Whelan's long term (1951–1961) left "deep anti-U.S. scars in the memories of many Nicaraguan people." [6]

René Schick Gutiérrez, a civilian, took office in 1963 for a four-year term but died in August, 1966, and one of the three vice-presidents filled in until February, 1967, when General Anastasio Somoza Debayle, Jr., easily won the election from Dr. Fernando Aguero. The army and the Somoza family continued in power.

Costa Rica

This small nation of about 1.5 million population has long considered itself in a class apart from the rest of Central America, and its leaders have no hesitation in speaking their minds on hemisphere matters. In 1954, for example, Costa Rica opposed holding the Tenth Inter-American Conference in Caracas because a dictatorship was in power in Venezuela, and refused to attend.

Costa Rica has a largely white European population, a high literacy rate, a police force instead of a standing army, and a relatively peaceful history. Her presidents have usually been civilians, and Costa Rica is well ahead of most Latin American countries in political maturity and dedication to liberty. Ever since the election of 1889 there has been a reassuring development in political stability, partly made possible by the system of widely distributed land holding. Dictators did not flourish, yet events since 1948 demonstrate that democracy is still somewhat insecure in Costa Rica. In that year, when the election of Otilio Ulate was disputed, a young agriculturist named José Figueres led an "Army of National Liberation" to put down those who opposed Ulate. Ulate proved to be an honest president (1949–1953) whose adherence to conservative fiscal policies and devotion to economic development saved Costa Rica from difficult days.

Figueres was elected to succeed Ulate, on a platform emphasizing the need for radical economic policies to make the nation more independent and to register opposition to the dictatorial regimes in the Caribbean. He won a smashing victory at the polls in a democratic election, was inaugurated in November, 1953, and quickly became one of the most controversial figures in Central American politics. He favored economic expansion through increased productivity, welcomed foreign investment but offered no privileged status, and believed that the United States should support democracy in Latin America by ending aid and encouragement to dictators whether they were duly elected or not. His greatest triumph was to negotiate a new contract with the United Fruit Company on June 4, 1954, by which Costa Rica received 35 per cent of the company's net earnings instead of 15 per cent. This contract symbolized a new and constructive step that brought positive benefits to both parties and had favorable repercussions in other banana-producing countries.

Costa Rica has been usually described in glowing terms as a model democracy, a land of peace and progress very different from her Central American neighbors. To a certain extent this is true, but sociological investigations reveal that Costa Rica has much in common with other Latin-American countries: "The class structure with emphasis on manual labor as an important factor in determining status; the notion of 'first families'; the subordination of women; the superior prestige of professional life rather than business; the great interest in politics, a politics of personalities rather than issues; the idealization of democracy; the 'easy' Catholicism; the valuing of the life of 'culture' rather than of technology; the disinclination to join clubs or civic enterprises—these are some of the features of Costa Rican life which help us to know Latin America generally." [7]

Costa Ricans are proud of their democratic traditions and indignant when corruption creeps into their political life. They recognize the ills of their country which another sociologist describes thus: "The red tile roofs of the little villages are picturesque, yet many shelter homes where half the children die of stomach trouble or malaria, where the father's earnings in the coffee groves or cane fields buy little more than beans, rice, and tortillas, where clothes are shabby and blankets inadequate for the chilly nights. The country has more teachers than soldiers, but the teachers are underpaid and in the schools there are ten times as many in the first grade as in the sixth. Literacy is as high as it is in any Latin-American country; nevertheless, the gap between the uneducated peon and the son of his wealthy employer is wider than ever before. Ticos are friendly and sociable, yet they are individualists and rarely cooperate for common ends. The girls strolling in the *retreta* (park promenade) are pretty, but they have a world of masculine prejudice and pride to conquer before they achieve a higher status. There is a great pride of family, but little concern for illegitimacy, prostitution, and venereal diseases. The soil is fertile; still many are underfed. Coffee is a 'grain of gold' to some, while it keeps others poor and dependent. Although land ownership is widespread, many of the registered properties are mere scraps of land big enough for a house, while in other cases, many land units are owned by one man." [8]

These basic problems are being confronted in Costa Rica, but some other nations in Central America—less satisfied and less complacent with their present position—appear to be moving ahead faster.

Panama

Panama was established in 1903 because of U.S. action. The great canal, after its opening in 1914, became the outstanding fact of Panamanian life. One third of all Panamanian revenue derives from the Zone, through income paid by the U.S. government for the lease of this 50-mile waterway which cost originally $366 million, and through wages paid Zone employees, or expenditures by U.S. personnel assigned to the Zone. Without the canal, the 1.2 million Panamanians would live meagerly from the sale of their bananas. Politics and economics revolve around this single fact.

At this strategic crossroad of world trade, the atomic age and the ancient life of the jungle live side by side. The rural districts are centuries away in culture from the world of the modern office buildings in the capital city and the jet planes which land in considerable numbers. In spite of widespread anti-Yankee feeling and resentment against racist and domineering attitudes displayed by U.S. officials and citizens in the Zone (*see Reading No. 42*), communism has not found fertile soil in Panama. Waves of nationalism break out in the country periodically: political passions are nowhere more intense or divisive. All the classic problems of Central American republics are present: a one-crop export (bananas), illiteracy, poverty, housing deficiencies, insufficient electric power, and unstable political institutions. Revolutionary outbursts and bloody riots have been common during the past decade or so; few of Panama's presidents have served a full term in office.

Political decisions in Panama have been made by a few powerful families, by shifting political combinations, by the national police, at times by the clamor of an aroused populace, and often by American authorities. The United States resorted to armed intervention until 1918 and since then has tried diplomatic pressure. Panama improved her position by the Treaty of 1936 by which the United States formally terminated Panama's protectorate status, agreed not to intervene, raised the annual payment for lease of the Zone from $250,000 to $430,000, and met other Panamanian demands.

Despite this treaty, relations between the two countries continued to be

uneasy. The Axis-supporter Arnulfo Arias was president for a time (1940–1941) and then returned to win the election of 1949, when the strong support of police chief José Antonio Remón more than made up for his unsavory past. But this strange combination fell apart, and for four years Remón installed and removed presidents with lightning rapidity. When he had himself legally elected president in 1952, many Panamanians had misgivings but, until his career was cut short by assassination in January, 1955, his policies were sound. Assisted by his energetic and politically conscious wife Cecilia, he achieved political tranquility for Panama, introduced higher income taxes and other realistic economic improvements, kept an eye on the communists, and won a substantial victory by negotiating a new treaty with the United States, signed and ratified in 1955 after sixteen months of difficult but generally amicable discussions. The United States agreed by this treaty to pay $1,930,000 as annual rent instead of the 1936 figure of $430,000, agreed to limit some of the Zone business activities which competed with Panamanian commerce, and agreed to abolish the hated double standard in wages by accepting for the first time the principle of one basic wage scale for all U.S. and Panamanian employees in the Zone. Panama in return made available twenty thousand acres for training and military maneuvers.

Although President Remón was assassinated before the treaty was formally approved, his influence was the dominant one in Panama's achievement of long wished for improvements in relations with the United States. And the State Department showed itself willing to negotiate with a small country although the cold war and its anxieties undoubtedly played a part, for Panama has learned to use a very effective weapon—international public opinion. Panama's position has been dramatized to the world; its delegates to youth congresses, athletic meetings, and labor conferences, all have something to say on "Yankee Imperialism" and "Racial Discrimination" in the Canal Zone.

Following the murder of Remón, Panama's situation deteriorated swiftly. Vice-President José Ramón Quizado was convicted of complicity in the crime and Second Vice-President Ricardo Arias was sworn in as president, staying in office until Ernesto de la Guardia, Jr., won the regular election in May, 1956. He was inaugurated during the excitement and bitterness that again flared up when the United States ignored Panama during the Suez crisis of 1956. Secretary Dulles chose to exclude Panama from the London Conference, which led Panama and ten communist and neutralist nations to adhere to a plan opposed to the "international control" proposed in London. Dulles reopened an old wound when he stated at a press conference that the U.S. "has rights of sovereignty over the Panama Canal" and that these rights were enjoyed by the U.S. "to the entire exclusion of the exercise by the Republic of Panama of any such sovereign rights, power, or authority." In reaction, Panama redoubled its efforts to get a treaty more satisfactory to itself and also accused Zone authorities of noncompliance with the 1955 agreement to end discrimination in wages.

Thus the two nations found themselves at loggerheads, and the Canal lay like a black shadow across Panama. Only a small hard core of Panamanians argued for the ultimate ousting of the U.S. from the Zone, but many Panamanians, in and out of official positions, feel that the United States took advantage of Panama's immaturity in 1903 in the original treaty and has continued to do so ever since. Therefore, they fight continually for renegotiations of the treaty and to assert their basic sovereignty over the zone. An American sociologist pointed out that the United States, which has met the challenge of hills and jungles with courage, skill, and intelligence, has not yet learned how to handle successfully the social challenges produced by the head-on collision of Panamanian and American cultures. The U.S. official position was that the Canal was built as a service to the shipping of the world, and not as a moneymaker for anyone; running expenses are barely met by the toll charges, and of the billion and a half dollars spent on the Canal the United States had thus far recovered about one billion.

When the students of Balboa High School in the Canal Zone raised the U.S. flag in January, 1964, without that of Panama beside it, an action contrary to the orders of the U.S. Governor, a new crisis arose. In the ensuing riots, 21 persons were killed and several hundred wounded; some $2 million in property damage accompanied the three days of clashes between Panamanians and U.S. forces in the Zone. All the old grievances were revived; the tense relations were reflected in newspaper headlines in both countries. President Johnson's announcement in December, 1964, that the U.S. was prepared to renegotiate the 1903 treaty and also to build a second, sea-level canal led to wide speculation on the future role of the present canal. (*See Reading No. 43.*) While moderate voices were heard in both countries, extremists in Panama continued to agitate and counter charges were made "that the U.S. has become the scapegoat in Panama, utilized by the wealthy oligarchy, in an unholy alliance with extremists of all types, to divert attention from economic and political inefficiency, greed, corruption, and injustice." [9]

As Panama's international position remains unclear, its internal progress appears uncertain. As one sympathetic observer puts it: "The list of needs is staggering. It includes agricultural diversification, electrification, increased tourist facilities, expanded education, improved housing and public health, light industrialization, additional road construction, and social enlightenment. It will be years before any one of these problems can be coped with satisfactorily." [10]

The Future of Central America

Political instability is likely to be a source of concern for a long time to come. Vigorous and enlightened leaders of the type of Oscar Osorio in El Salvador and the late José Antonio Remón of Panama can do much to alter the general situations of their countries. And if the United States adopts a policy of cool correctness toward dictators, future members of the Somoza dynasty may need to address themselves to more than material progress if they are to receive U.S. aid.

The Pacific lowlands of Central America offer much hope for those who believe that progress is possible. These plains were long considered an unhealthy and unattractive habitat for man, but in recent years malarial control, highway construction, and port improvements have radically changed the picture. One experienced geographer is convinced that another ten years "may see this long neglected tropical lowland converted into the economic heartland of Guatemala and Nicaragua." [11]

Some benefits may be obtained for all countries by putting into effect some of the long-cherished dreams of Central American union, at least in the economic field. The unfortunate effects of the rigid national boundaries, the small individual markets, and the confusion of tariffs which immensely complicate trade crossing so many borders may be mitigated by the pact signed in 1957 to create a free trade zone and a system of regional industries. In 1958 plans were laid for a regional university, a normal school, polytechnic school, and an agricultural school. Because since 1838 the Central American republics have gone their separate ways, all attempts at union face formidable obstacles.[12] The Central American common market idea could count on a united front to uphold coffee prices; in July, 1965, the proposal to build a tire manufacturing plant in Costa Rica was approved despite some opposition in the other countries, and other similar developments indicate modest progress.

Another constructive step is the recent attempt by the United Fruit Company to mend its social fences. Central Americans are not overly impressed with the company's claim of leaving seven dollars in each country for every dollar it takes out in profit, or by its practice of paying higher wages than local employers. More convincing changes to Central Americans would be if it fully recognized labor unions, obeyed national laws, and definitely abandoned its old swashbuckling tactics.

A final question remains and can only be posed, not answered. Will the politically and economically important people of Central America play their part? One experienced student of Central American affairs emphasizes the reluctance of the moneyed class to give up its privileged status: "In what does the reluctance consist? Unwillingness to pay taxes—both before and after the passage of tax laws—to provide schools for Indians or peasants. Aversion to giving up land, even unused land—with or without compensation—which could provide a living for hungry workers, but which if retained grants power or prestige. Hesitation to invest in new industry at home when safer investments are available abroad. Refusal to pay a living wage to a countryman who has nowhere else to go." [13] Such an experienced and sympathetic student as the late Chester Lloyd Jones raised a fundamental issue in 1934 when he stated that the major problems "continue to be as they have been in the past—little as they themselves and foreign observers have at times recognized this fact—primarily domestic and not foreign problems. Their future—economic, social, and political—turns in all but slight degree on what their peoples can do for themselves, not on influences from outside the national borders." A representative of the United States AID program in Guatemala expressed a somewhat similar view, and warned that there could be in Latin America no rapid success as there had been in Europe through the Marshall Plan:

> There the U.S. helped with the physical rebuilding of a modern but temporarily shattered society. In Latin America, the modern society exists in rare and scattered pockets only. . . .
>
> Modernization of countries such as Guatemala is dependent upon a transformation of national character, of an entire culture. We can't do it with schools and tractors and tapeworm medicine.[15]

[1] March 3, 1960.

[2] Julio Adolfo Rey, "Revolution and Liberation: A Review of Recent Literature on the Guatemala Situation," *Hispanic American Historical Review,* XXXVIII (1958), pp. 239–255; David Wise and Thomas B. Ross, *The Invisible Government* (New York: Random House, 1964), p. 165.

[3] James L. Busey, *Latin American Political Guide* (9th edition; Boulder, Colorado: The Printed Page, 1965), p. 8.

[4] Jones, "If I Were Dictator," *Guatemala Past and Present* (Minneapolis: University of Minnesota Press, 1940), pp. 339–356.

[5] Gerrit Huizer, "Some Observations in a Central American Village," *América Indígena,* XXIII (1963), pp. 211–224. The quotation appears on pp. 222–223.

[6] Busey, *Latin American Political Guide,* 9th ed., p. 11.

[7] John and Mavis Biesanz, *Costa Rican Life* (New York: Columbia University Press, 1944), p. viii. The statement quoted was made by Robert Redfield.

[8] *Ibid.,* pp. 252–253.

[9] J. Fred Rippy, "The High Cost of Appeasement," *Inter-American Economic Affairs,* XVII (1964), No. 4, p. 88. See also John Biesanz and Luke M. Smith, "Panamanian Politics," *Journal of Politics,* XIV (1952), pp. 386–402.

[10] John D. Martz, *Central America. The Crisis and the Challenge* (Chapel Hill: University of North Carolina Press, 1959), p. 318.

[11] James J. Parsons, "Cotton and Cattle in the Pacific Lowlands of Central America," *Journal of Inter-American Studies,* VII (1965), p. 158. For more information, see the January, 1966, issue of *Current History,* which is devoted to Central America.

[12] The basic study on the federation is Thomas L. Karnes, *The Failure of Union: Central America, 1824–1960* (Chapel Hill: University of North Carolina Press, 1961).

[13] Franklin D. Parker, *The Central American Republics* (London: Oxford University Press, 1964), p. 315. Another useful recent account is by Mario Rodríguez, *Central America* (Englewood Cliffs, New Jersey: Prentice-Hall, 1965).

[14] Chester Lloyd Jones, *Costa Rica and Civilization in the Caribbean* (San José, Costa Rica, 1941), p. 151.

[15] Joseph C. Goulden, *Time for the Psychiatrists?* (New York: The Alicia Patterson Fund, 1966), p. 20.

3
THE
CARIBBEAN
ISLANDS

Cuba

AREA: 44,204 sq. mi.
POPULATION IN MID-1966: 7,800,000
LARGEST CITY:
Havana (capital): 950,000
PRINCIPAL EXPORTS: sugar, tobacco
PREMIER: Fidel Castro

Haiti

AREA: 10,714 sq. mi.
POPULATION IN MID-1966: 4,485,000
LARGEST CITY:
Port-au-Prince (capital): 240,000
(est. 1960)
PRINCIPAL EXPORTS (1961): coffee,
sugar, sisal
PRESIDENT: François Duvalier, civilian,
first took office October 22, 1957.
He has now proclaimed himself
president for life.

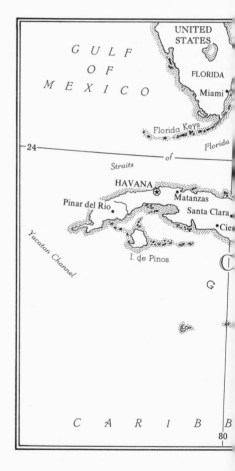

Dominican Republic

AREA: 18,703 sq. mi.
POPULATION IN MID-1966: 3,750,000
LARGEST CITY:
 Santo Domingo: 367,053 (est. 1960)
PRINCIPAL EXPORTS (1960): sugar,
 coffee, cacao beans
PRESIDENT: Joaquín Balaguer, civilian,
 took office July 1, 1966,
 for a 4-year term.

Puerto Rico

AREA: 3,325 sq. mi.
POPULATION IN MID-1966: 2,700,000
LARGEST CITY:
 San Juan (capital): 750,000
PRINCIPAL EXPORTS: sugar, rum, tobacco
GOVERNOR: Roberto Sánchez Villela

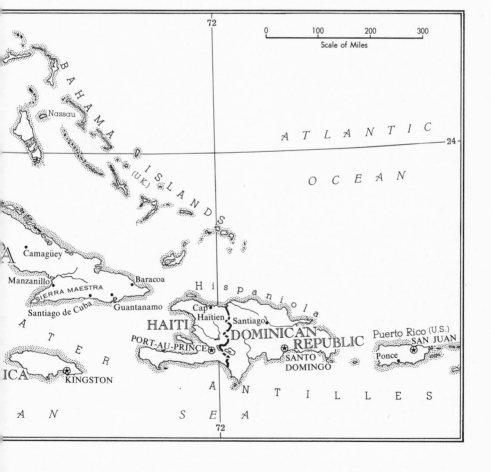

THE
CARIBBEAN
ISLANDS

● **Paradise or Poorhouse?** The development of cheap air transportation, the discovery of that effective insect destroyer DDT, and the rapid development of tourist facilities have made the Caribbean a favorite area of relaxation for tourists from other countries. Those who visit the islands, which stretch 2,000 miles from Central America eastward to the lesser Antilles, find a tropical playground which provides the beauty and in some parts the isolation of the South Sea Islands a few hours by air from the mainland. If they are inclined to call it a paradise, as did Columbus when he first landed, they may later discover the realities behind the glamour.

The Caribbean Islands did, indeed, enjoy a period of grandeur in the 17th and 18th centuries when they were among the finest prizes of empire, with European nations vying to obtain the famous "sugar islands." But they languished nearly forgotten during the 19th and early 20th centuries, and are beset with problems today. Although in the last 20 or 30 years they have begun to emerge from their backward role, they still have far to go before the millions of poor, disease-ridden, illiterate people who constitute most of the population in many of the islands achieve a reasonable standard of living. Most of them work on the land, are of Negro descent, and have very small incomes. Important changes have occurred in some of these islands in recent years, but these lands of sugar, coffee, bananas, cocoa, and tobacco hold a population with a markedly depressed standard of living. So many have left the British territories for England that race tension has been felt there, and so many Puerto Ricans have migrated to New York—though Puerto Rico enjoys a relatively higher standard of living—that Manhattan probably has more Puerto Ricans than San Juan. It was President Herbert Hoover who once, injudiciously perhaps but accurately, described the Caribbean as a poorhouse.

The possibility of at least a partial confederation of independent but cooperating communities, one observer reports, "has given way to competition between islands motivated strictly by self-interest . . . the dominant force stirring in the Caribbean is nationalism . . . and is far stronger than any ideological force emanating from Moscow, Peking, or Washington. Nationalism, the desire of the Jamaican, Puerto Rican, Cuban, or Trinidadian to determine for himself the future of his island community . . . is destructive as well as constructive, and the future of the Caribbean will depend on the way it develops." [1]

Cuba

● **Pre-Castro Cuba.** Many Americans greeted Fidel Castro's victory in 1959 with enthusiasm.[2] Today a very small room would probably hold all those U.S. citizens who completely agree on why Castro subsequently set up the first communist government in the Americas. This need not astonish anyone who knows the variety of attitudes Cuba inspired in the U.S. in the nineteenth century. Even when a number of U.S. statesmen thought the U.S. should annex Cuba, they had different and at times contradictory motives.[3] When the battleship *Maine* exploded in Havana harbor in 1898, the incident that led the U.S. to join in the war of the Cuban rebels against Spain, U.S. policies toward the island were uncertain. President McKinley wanted a free hand to impose a settlement on both Spaniards and Cubans. A strong element in Congress, however, favored recognizing the Cuban insurgents as the legal government, capable of working out their own problems.[4] During the fighting, U.S. armed forces often operated independently of the Cubans; this led some Cuban historians to claim later that they had been robbed of their victory, just as some Cubans have felt that the U.S. did not give due credit to Dr. Carlos Finlays's contribution toward the conquest of yellow fever there.[5]

● **Era of the Platt Amendment.** The generals heading the occupation forces could not agree on recommendations for the political future of the island. Leonard Wood believed in an indefinite occupation ending in annexation. James Harrison Wilson supported the idea of creating a customs union with Cuba which would bind it economically to the U.S., and then terminating the occupation quickly while retaining the island as a protectorate. General Wilson's basic thought was that establishing trade relations was more important than establishing political institutions.[6] The protectorate was established through the Platt Amendment embodied in the treaty of 1903 between the two countries. Cuba was free, but not free to make her own mistakes; the Amendment gave the U.S. the right to intervene "for the preservation of Cuban independence, the maintenance of a government adequate for the protection of life, property, and individual liberty." No one seems to have heard, or to have paid much attention to, the declaration by the sociologist William Graham Sumner in 1899 that Spain, not the U.S., had won the war over Cuba since the U.S. was now entering upon the path of imperialism which Spain had been forced to abandon.[7]

The "philanthropic American imperialism" was bitterly resented in Cuba and the deposition of President Gerardo Machado in 1933, after years of murder and oppression under what many Cubans considered virtual American protection, finally brought abrogation of the hated amendment in 1934. Mounting opposition to the corrupt and ruthless Machado and his fall in the summer of 1933 provided the first major test for the Good Neighbor Policy President Franklin D. Roosevelt had enunciated on March 4. Though Sumner Welles had helped formulate the policy in the weeks before Roosevelt's inauguration,[8] as Ambassador to Cuba he called for warships and Marines during the long and complicated Machado crisis negotiations.[9] Josephus Daniels, newly appointed ambassador to Mexico, doubted that Welles exhibited the spirit of good neighborliness and in forthright personal messages to Roosevelt opposed any show of armed force. When the revolutionary junta designated a university professor, Dr. Ramón Grau San Martín, as Provisional President, Welles decided against him, judging the new government to be "frankly communistic," "evanescent," and supported only by left-wing students and other radicals of no importance.[10] Daniels doubted that the Grau San Martín government was under Communist or radical control, felt that his group was leading a movement of intellectuals and workers on behalf of the forgotten men in Cuba, and suspected that "if our Government had shown more interest in the rights of the Cuban workers than for the profits of American investors, the Machado reign of terror would have been ended before the present uprising." [11] But Washington continued to support Welles, and Colonel Fulgencio Batista overthrew Grau San Martín. Welles favored Colonel Carlos Mendieta, a conservative leader, whom the U.S. promptly recognized.[12] He proved to be the first of several presidents who were Batista's puppets.

● **The Rule of Batista.** Cuba now passed brusquely from the era of the Platt Amendment to the age of Batista, which ended only in January, 1959. This one-time sergeant had risen to power in the confusion that followed the overthrow of Machado. Chief Clerk at army headquarters when the dictator fell, Batista organized an enlisted men's revolt which helped to overturn the provisional government that replaced Machado's regime. The sergeant-stenographer quickly consolidated his control of the army, the classic instrument of dictators. Soon almost all the higher officers owed their positions to him, and he provided substantial benefits for the enlisted men as well: he raised their pay, built excellent barracks, furnished good uniforms and excellent food, provided recreation fields, and established pension funds. He also cultivated organized labor successfully and used patronage profusely to control civilian leaders. Only some of the intellectuals and university students grumbled much against his early regime.

For seven years he ruled through other men; in 1940 he assumed the presidency himself. His four-year term was marked by good government— at least, it seemed better than any Cuba had ever had before. With sugar prices steady during World War II, Batista was able to expand public works vigorously—roads, bridges, harbor installations, and power plants. He conducted public business expeditiously, improved education somewhat, permitted relative freedom to the press, and perpetrated few political crimes despite the persistent strain of violence in Cuban politics. When he allowed Grau San Martín's election in 1944, the dictator retired to Florida with both a large fortune and the good will of many Cubans. Neither Grau San Martín, later indicted in Cuban courts for allegedly misappropriating $178 million during his administration, nor his successor Carlos Prío Socarrás (1948– 1952), was able to withstand the temptations of the presidency; there was sufficient support for Batista, or indifference, to permit him to return to seize power again in 1952 in a barracks conspiracy. Now he imposed a thorough and increasingly harsh dictatorship. He dissolved Congress indefinitely, although keeping its members on the payroll. He muzzled the press, and closed the University; groups of exiled Cubans in New York, Mexico, and elsewhere began to plot his downfall. Corruption and "institutionalized violence" became a way of life. Perhaps this explains why so politically sophisticated a liberal as the theologian Reinhold Niebuhr could write as late as 1959: "it is not clear whether the average Cuban would not be better served by our continued sovereignty over the island than under the military dictatorships which have ruled that island since its independence." [13]

● **Castro's Revolution.** In December 1956, Fidel Castro and a dozen youths landed on the eastern end of the island and from the Sierra Maestra began a dogged and ever-increasing armed rebellion, eventually attracting enough adherents to bring Batista down on January 1, 1959. He took refuge first in the Dominican Republic and then in Europe, living well on the money he had amassed while in power. Now a new age began for Cuba, and for its relations to the U.S. and the world. This was no ordinary change of government, but a political, social, and economic upheaval whose effects will be felt for generations to come.

The number of books written about Castro is probably already greater than that on the Liberator Simón Bolívar or even on the Cuban poet-patriot José Martí, whose writings have constituted a kind of Bible for Cubans. In dogmatism, fanaticism, and bulk, the Castro bibliography is comparable to the Spanish Civil War material. Many accounts of Castro and the Cuban Revolution are by writers in a high state of ideological excitement. Some apologists view Castro as a chosen instrument of the dialectic, a man sent by History to liberate the Cuban and, eventually, the Latin-American masses. On the other hand the "hard-nose" school of writers are confident the revolution was a Moscow plot from the beginning and are convinced that the fatal flaw in U.S. policy was our refusal to give wholehearted support to the Batista dictatorship. Journalists have split sharply on Castro's policies, purposes, and achievements as have professors, students, and many others who became concerned with the increasingly complex situation in the Caribbean. Some substantial and informative studies have appeared on Cuba before Castro.[14] Much remains unknown on the course of events since January, 1959 because the archives in Cuba, the United States, Russia, and other countries are not available. Moreover Castro has spoken millions of words; his pronouncements would already fill a good sized library. "His casual interviews with reporters, debates with students, interrogations of prisoners, and nearly interminable television speeches offer a rich fount of information. If you wait long enough, it seems, Castro will tell you everything." [15] As a sample of his style and approach, see his explanation of the Cuban Revolution before the United Nations (*Reading No. 45*).

In many parts of the world, except Cuba where Castro's voice prevails, a vigorous debate has developed on U.S. policy and action toward Cuba. Herbert Matthews' dispatches to *The New York Times* from the Sierra Maestra in 1958 informed the world that the rebels were still in the field, and his later writings on Castro opened the way for a host of analysts, propagandists, and reporters of almost every political persuasion. The strident attack on U.S. policy, *Listen Yankee* (1960), by the U.S. sociologist, C. Wright Mills, was widely read in various languages throughout the world. The *Declaration of Havana* in 1960 was one of the first full-length expositions by the Cuban regime of its objectives. (*See Reading No. 44.*) Theodore Draper's articles and books have provided careful analysis of Castro's ideology and actions by a writer thoroughly familiar with the history of communism; a Canadian commentator believes him to be "better prepared than the others to give balanced and articulate reasons why Castro and his revolution have moved the way they have." [16]

Castro is reported to have subsidized the American Waldo Frank to write *Cuba, Prophetic Island* in 1962; favorable reports on the new regime were also made by such left-wing French writers as Simone de Beauvoir and Jean-Paul Sartre. Extreme right-wingers such as Nathaniel Weyl traced "Castro's alleged sympathies with communism almost to his days in the cradle on his father's big estate in Oriente Province." [17] No general study of depth or importance has so far appeared anywhere in Latin America about Castro or the revolution, but there as elsewhere (three books on Castro were published in Stockholm in 1962–1963), the flood of articles and books shows no signs of abating.[18]

Many if not most of these publications deal with the reasons for Castro's rise to power. One U.S. historian, emphasizing the economic factors, considers those members of the American business community and government officials determined to protect U.S. economic interests largely responsible for the errors of the United States. This historian also believes that U.S. support for the conservative upper classes and their American allies and our opposition to sweeping economic reforms designed to improve the welfare of Cuban workers helped to perpetuate an intolerable situation in Cuba.[19] A British writer, Hugh Thomas, has a somewhat different interpretation: he considers the stagnant economy an important factor as well as the dominance of sugar and the weakness of Cuba's institutions, such as the army, the Church, the trade unions and civil service. (See Reading No. 46.) The fact that Cuba was one of the most highly developed countries in Latin America, with no Indian problem, no climatic or geographical obstacles, with immensely fertile land, suggests that poverty alone did not cause the revolution.[20] One writer with long experience in Cuba and warm feeling for the Cuban people has written: "In all of what has been written in explanation of Castro's rise, I have seen nothing about the possible effect of the hatred preached into Cuban youth from childhood up by teachers, writers, historians, orators, etc. For nearly 19 years I listened to this and cannot but wonder why this has not been discussed as a cause of the ease with which demagogue after demagogue was able to get followings, until the demagogue of them all came and capitalized on it." [21]

● **The Dragon Fighter.** "I have even wondered about the effect of the glorification of Martí as a revolutionary. Even as early as 1933 it seemed to me that every high school and university student pictured himself as a second Martí fighting for Cuban liberty against dragons real and imaginary. And there were some dragons that were real, whether imperialistic, economic, or otherwise." [21]

Cuban nationalism has shallow roots. Throughout most of Spanish America the revolutionary period beginning in 1810 has served as a continuing inspiration, but Cubans cannot draw upon such sustenance and have had to concentrate all their patriotic fervor on their struggles for independence between 1868 and 1898. Their one great hero was José Martí: "Castro's inspiration in prison was Martí, not Marx." [22]

In all the controversy on the significance of Castro, few will deny that the revolution of 1933 which overthrew Machado, "had a profound impact on the generation which produced Fidel Castro." The "generation of 1930," made up of the young professional men and students who had brought about Machado's fall, spoke of far-reaching social, economic, and political reforms. Hugh Thomas states: "The men of 1959 were undoubtedly in many cases the real sons of the men who made the revolution in 1933. Castro was to do the things that many people had been talking about before. . . . The Cuban Revolution of 1959, far from being an isolated event, was the culmination of a long series of thwarted revolutions."

● **Castro's Cuba.** The period 1959–1966 was a momentous one, with dramatic events succeeding one another so rapidly that it is still difficult to evaluate them. Every one has been and will continue to be passionately discussed in the light of the predilections and information available to the writers.

1959

January 1:	The Batista regime collapsed, as the columns of the 26th of July Movement marched into Havana.
February:	Fidel Castro became Prime Minister, and visited the U.S. in April.
June:	The Agrarian Reform Law was passed. Expropriation of land owned by U.S. citizens began. The Cuban government seized and intervened in the Texaco Oil refinery when officials of the plant refused to refine Soviet oil which had been delivered following the Soviet-Cuban Trade Agreement of February. The last two foreign-owned oil refineries were similarly seized in July.

1960

February:	The Cuban government signed a series of aid and trade agreements with the Soviet Union, providing for the purchase of one million tons of sugar a year for five years and a credit of $100 million for industrialization.
July:	Khrushchev made his "symbolic" offer of Russian rockets in case Cuba needed help against the United States.
December:	The U.S. cancelled the Cuban sugar quota, and the Russians agreed to take all the sugar Cuba had sold formerly to the United States.

1961

January 3:	President Eisenhower broke off relations with Cuba.
March:	The U.S. announced the Alliance for Progress.
April 17–19:	The U.S.-organized invasion of Cuba by Cuban exiles at the Bay of Pigs failed.
May:	Castro publicly announced the "socialist" nature of his revolution.
December:	Castro delivered his famous five hour "I am a Marxist" speech.

1962

January:	The Organization of American States formally expelled Cuba, at the insistence of the United States.

October: The confrontation between the U.S.S.R. and the U.S. over Soviet missiles secretly placed in Cuba occurred.[23]

1963

August: After a poor harvest, Castro announced that agriculture, not industry, would be the base of the Cuban economy during the 1960's.

1965 Six million tons of sugar were produced, and a crop of 10 million tons was predicted for 1970.

November: Refugee agreement was signed between the U.S. and Cuba, the first communist state ever to allow such departures.

1966

January: 82 countries sent 500 delegates to Havana to the third conference of the Afro-Asian Latin American Organization. One of its resolutions supported "wars of liberation" in Latin America.

March: Castro followed up his January 2 charge that Communist China had welshed on an agreement to supply Cuba with 250,000 tons of rice by denouncing Peking's "imperialist-type campaign against Cuba," and warned that a break between the two governments was near.

Relations between the U.S. and Cuba steadily worsened in early 1959. The brief honeymoon period quickly passed. The public trials of the "war criminals" in Havana, Cuban charges of aggressive American intentions, and the nationalization of many U.S. properties led to an increasingly tense situation. The campaign of abuse by Cuban state propaganda sources surpassed any previous anti-Yankee statements in Latin America—"Caesar Attila Nero Caligula Eisenhower, emperor of the United States and its putrid adjacent democracies"—was one of the characterizations reported by *The Christian Science Monitor*. Cuba re-established diplomatic relations with the Soviet Union on May 7, 1960 and by mid-1960 "relations between the Cuban regime and the U.S. government were past the point of accommodation." [24] The U.S. trade with Cuba of over a billion dollars in 1958 dwindled to $19.7 million in 1962; Cuba's trade with the Communistic bloc soared in the same period from $42 million to almost $1 billion.[25]

This early period was chaotic. Castro "surrounded himself with as varied a group of advisers as any national politician in memory: Centrist career politicians, Keynesian economists, ex- and would-be bureaucrats, sincere liberals, professional revolutionaries, and amateur Marxist tacticians." [26] Castro characterized the early revolutionary leadership in his "Marxist-Leninist" speech of December 1, 1961, in this way: "We were like a man with a vocation for music. But a man's vocation for music does not grant him a right to call himself a musician if he has not studied musical theory. When we started our revolutionary struggle we already had some knowledge of Marxism-Leninism and we were in sympathy with it. But, by virtue of this, we could not call ourselves Marxists-Leninists. We were apprentice revolutionaries." [27]

The Havana Hilton Hotel was re-named Havana Libre and its character changed drastically. The old crowd of tourists, movie stars, businessmen, gamblers, and gangsters disappeared. A U.S. visitor in 1962 reported "Polish instructors in mechanical engineering, a British physics professor, a Rumanian oil driller from Ploesti (whose 200 foot high rig was on display nearby), Czech agronomists, and a handful of Americans. . . . Thousands of Russian and Chinese technicians are scattered elsewhere in hotels and private homes in the swank Vedado and Miramar districts." [28] During this early period some 300,000 Cubans fled their native land for a variety of reasons. Included in this group were many professional men, middle class citizens, and others who could not accept the Castro regime with its increasing dependence on Communists and Soviet Russia. The story of this tragic exodus, mostly to the United States, has not yet been told. But the fact that several hundred thousand Cubans have abandoned their homeland and that many more will do so means that the composition of society has radically altered as Castro's revolution rolls on. The cleavage between the Cubans who remained and the exile groups is so deep that they can probably never be reconciled to each other even after Castro is gone.

● **Bay of Pigs Invasion.** The Bay of Pigs invasion in 1961, mounted by the Central Intelligence Agency for the U.S. Government, has been described as "one of the worst conceived, planned and executed military-intelligence operations in history," "a wild misjudgment," and "a disastrous adventure diplomatically, militarily,—and journalistically." [29] Cuban and American lives were lost; the C.I.A. is reported to have spent 45 million dollars on the operation. Published accounts of this fiasco, including the memoirs of advisers to President Kennedy, indicate that the Cuban-U.S. military effort will long be a source of speculation and bitterness. A reporter who has analyzed the news coverage in the U.S. concluded: "once again we are confronted with a clear case wherein it is proven that deceit and distortion are no substitutes for frankness, trustworthiness, and truthfulness." [30]

The U.S. received scant support for her hostility to Cuba from the other American Republics. Even after the missile crisis of October, 1962, Bolivia, Brazil, Chile, Mexico, and Uruguay continued diplomatic relations with Cuba and, in the early years at least, considerable sympathy and admiration were expressed throughout Latin America for Castro's courage to attempt drastic solutions, and for his success in defying the United States. As his dependence on Russia became more apparent as well as his support for guerrilla activities abroad, particularly in Venezuela, the enthusiasm of some Latin Americans cooled, but probably only a handful of dictatorships would support further military intervention by the United States.[31]

● **The Missile Crisis.** The missile crisis confrontation between Soviet Russia and the U.S. put Cuba on the world map as never before. Western Europeans now realized that they could "suddenly be placed in mortal peril by a confrontation by giants over a Caribbean island, or some other unlikely spot, in which the average Frenchman, German, or Italian and his government had not the slightest interest." Some Europeans, especially De Gaulle, were strengthened in the belief that Western Europe should develop its own nuclear power in order to control its own destiny, while for "many more it reinforced the inclination to get out from between, out of the dangerous, tiresome crunch of the superpowers and into neutralism." [32] And it was noted that the Kennedy administration did not choose to challenge the Soviet military and economic presence in Cuba, but only the threat of the medium-range missiles. Other observers emphasized the control exercised by Washington of news during the crisis. The government demonstrated its ability to protect its vital interests, at least for a short period, "but over the long haul such control would be fatal to a free press and an open society." [33]

● **King Sugar and Emerging Industrialization.** Another important struggle as the Revolution developed was between industrialization and sugar which had long dominated Cuba's economy, and was King when Castro took power.[34] Some industrialization had developed and tourism had steadily increased, but four-fifths of Cuba's export revenue in 1959 came from sugar. The dangers of mono-culture had long been recognized: José Martí, the Cuban national hero, had written in 1883: "A people commits suicide the day on which it bases its existence on a single crop." The four-year development plan for 1962–1965 aimed to achieve a minimum goal of 10 per cent annual increase in the gross national product by diversifying agriculture. Cuba's dependence on sugar was to end, and industrialization in the light and consumer goods field, with some heavy industry, was also to end Cuba's humiliating "colonial" subjection to the United States.

By mid-1963 the policy had failed. Raw materials for manufacturing had to be imported at high prices; the factories and equipment promised by the Communist bloc had fallen short in both quality and quantity; and too-rapid diversification of agriculture had led to a drop in sugar production from 6.8 million tons in 1961, the second largest crop in history, to 3.8 million tons in 1963, the smallest since World War II. A reversal in economic policy now took place and Cuba returned to sugar as its principal earner of foreign exchange. As Ernesto Ché Guevara, the Argentine-born Minister of Industry explained: "We attempted to do too much at once." [35] However, cattle ranching would be pushed also, and within 10 years might equal sugar in importance. But the romantic period of Cuban economy under the Revolution had ended and, until 1970 at least, sugar would still be King. No longer were ecstatic reports issued on agrarian triumphs by such U.S. sympathizers as C. Wright Mills, Leo Huberman, Paul Sweezy, and Paul Baran, as in 1961 and 1962.[36] More sophisticated analyses began to appear, such as the evaluations by the Chilean economist, Jacques Chonchol, and the French agronomist, René Dumont, who were sympathetic but realistic. Chonchol pointed out how the pre-Castro system of large sugar plantations had greatly facilitated their socialization: "basically the differences are not great between the large capitalist enterprise and the large socialist undertaking of the State." [37] Writing in 1962, he emphasized how much of the "analysis" of Cuba's situation had been made in terms of black or white. He deplored all doctrinaire attitudes and declared that the great question posed by the Cuban agrarian reform—the first attempt to organize a Marxist-Socialist system in a tropical land—was whether the new regime could utilize efficiently every useful person whether or not he happened to agree with a predetermined economic ideology.[38] Dumont also criticized Cuban economic thinking. In what Draper termed "one of the few indispensable works on the subject, not the least because it is written from a sympathetic rather than a hostile point of view," [39] the French expert found the greatest obstacle to Cuban development to be "the general conception of the direction of the economy." [40] Other problems appeared; the 1965 sugar crop was less than the 6 million tons of the previous year, partly because of drought, and because agricultural production lagged in general during 1965.

Some of the present agricultural methods in revolutionary Cuba, however, will have an impact on other sugar producing areas of the Caribbean. In the 1964 harvest, large cane cutting machines were used and by 1968 Cuba hopes to have 4,000 machines harvesting at least 50 per cent of the sugar crop on most of the 60 large government farms which have between 220,000 and 600,000 acres each. Jamaica, Puerto Rico, and possibly other Caribbean islands may have to mechanize to keep pace with Cuba.

● **The Cuban People Today.** What has happened to the people of Cuba during these turbulent years? The exodus of Cubans in the early years, mostly to the United States, has eliminated most of the hard-core opposition, and guerrilla warfare inside Cuba has all but disappeared. Castro appears to be in firm control. One London correspondent reported in 1963 the "widespread assessment which gives him the active, even fanatical backing of about 30 per cent of the population, with another 40 per cent varying from warm to cool— a floating vote, as it were—and the remaining 30 per cent wanting to see him gone." [41] The refugee agreement, signed in November, 1965, between Cuba and the U.S., permits 800 Cubans to leave each week, a further draining off of anti-Castro forces. Since Castro came to power in 1959, more than 375,000 Cubans have left the island for exile, over 300,000 of them going to the United States.

No one starves in Cuba today, though life is very hard, according to *The*

New York Times, but "through it all the revolution, now in its seventh year, proceeds." Few U.S. visitors have seen Cuba during the last two or three years; State Department policy, until the spring of 1966, allowed visas only to journalists, businessmen with long-standing interests in the island, or those on humanitarian missions: "The Cuban Wall, erected by the United States, still stands. Scientists in general, Latin Americanists, historians, political scientists and students are forbidden to visit Cuba and study the first full-fledged social revolution in the Western Hemisphere since Mexico's in 1910." [42] Recent events may alter U.S. policy slightly, but at best probably a trickle of U.S. citizens will be allowed to see Cuba, unless a radical reversal occurs in Washington

The President Emeritus of Princeton Theological Seminary, Dr. John A. MacKay, published in early 1964 a glowing account of advances in Cuba: "A dispassionate study of the Cuban situation must take full cognizance of such facts as the following: Until recently 700,000 Cubans were without work; today there are no unemployed in Cuba. The sick, the aged and the poor are being cared for. Crime is decreasing. One sees no vagrants or beggars on the streets. Gambling is illegal; prostitution is being fought; a very high tax has been placed on liquor. A huge park in Havana formerly used for dog races is now a field for children's games. A national campaign is under way to wipe out illiteracy. Once luxurious homes and club houses on Havana beaches, including the Batista gambling palace, are today being used to house 51,000 teen-agers from all parts of the island, boys and girls who are being given a five-year course designed to train them to become teachers among the island's mountain dwellers and peasants. The universities and professional schools are crowded with young people who are being educated at government expense for future careers. In the evening hours the corridors of the great Havana Libre are thronged with students going to and from classes in hotel rooms now used as schoolrooms." [43]

Is this too rosy a picture? Some other churchmen and other observers think so, but Washington's visa policy prevents the American public from getting fuller information based on a greater variety of more normal and more prolonged contacts. Dr. MacKay saw none of the thousands of political prisoners (Castro mentions 15,000 but exiles estimate at least 45,000). He visited no labor camps, such as the one at Guanahacabibes, nor the "re-education camps." Nor does he record any of the punishments meted out to those Cubans who dissent. No one knows for certain how much opposition to Castro now exists on the island, but the spotty reporting available brings out news such as that Cuba in 1964 traded Franco's Spain tobacco for 10,000 pairs of handcuffs.[44] Cuba also had a cultural exchange with Spain; one of the two non-communist airlines still maintaining regular service to Havana is the Spanish company, Iberia.

Several observers report that education, accompanied by indoctrination, has made great strides, although the long-standing addiction to rote learning has not been abolished even by the Revolution. The Church survives, the colored people (30 per cent of the population) feel better off, and the position of women has been transformed. Corruption has apparently been eliminated, and gangsterism has been brought under control. A great popular force seems to have been liberated.[45]

Historians would like to know what is happening to their discipline in Cuba. Castro has shown a keen awareness of its importance, beginning with his famous "History Will Absolve Me" declaration of 1953. Earlier he had said: "History is made. It is made by people, by the masses . . . The revolution is the result of a long process of struggle which began with our ancestors in 1868 and culminated today, right now, and will continue to advance." [46] Intellectuals such as José Antonio Portuondo insist there is need to revise historical studies,[47] an Instituto de Historia has been created as a part of the Academia de Ciencias, and historians from communist countries, but not as yet from the U.S., are at work in Cuba.

Thus a full and objective account is hard to obtain at present. The U.S. travel restrictions have little to do with American security: "It is merely one part of the strategy of diplomatic pressure being applied against Cuba; the aim is to help isolate Cuba from the other nations of the Western Hemisphere." [48] Is this U.S. policy wise? Walter Lippmann wrote, in 1959: "The thing we should never do in dealing with revolutionary countries, in which the world abounds, is to push them behind an iron curtain raised by ourselves. On the contrary, even when they have been seduced and subverted and are drawn across the line, the right thing is to keep the way open for their return." [49]

● **The Future of Cuba.** The forces affecting Castro and his regime are too many and too little known to permit any prediction now on Cuba's future. And historians, though they may wonder, should not predict. Yet the government, and the people of the U.S. must decide on their course of action vis-à-vis Cuba. American public opinion may today be just as dangerously misinformed about Cuban affairs as it was earlier. One American historian has written that the great majority of Americans were at first sympathetic to the revolution. It was the kind of movement they understood: "one directed against tyranny, professing desire for greater democracy, liberty, and economic freedom." [50] Contrary to the general impression abroad, public opinion in the U.S. was not alienated by seizures of American property or by the first overtures by Castro to the Soviet Union. The violent turn came when Americans realized that Castro would actually align Cuba with the Soviets and Chinese: "This seemed incredible. It was beyond American comprehension that any people could voluntarily accept satellite status, abandon democracy and political liberty, and surrender to regimentation and dictatorship. As was demonstrated by the events leading to the Bay of Pigs landing, highly placed and very well-informed Americans remained unable to credit the facts." [51]

U.S. policy continues to be to isolate Cuba as much as possible, especially from contact with Latin America. J. W. Fulbright, Chairman of the Senate Foreign Relations Committee, favors a kind of co-existence and more attention to the pressing problems in other parts of the hemisphere. (*See Reading No. 47.*) Castro has been able to reach an understanding with the Catholic Church. According to Monsignor Cesare Zacchi, representative of Pope Paul VI in Havana, "Cuba is the first socialist nation in which peaceful co-existence between the State and the Catholic Church can be qualified in very correct and precise terms, because here cooperation in work between the two can be translated into benefits for the people." [52]

Castro now enjoys fewer alternatives than ever before. His bitter denunciation of China in January, 1966, in the wake of Cuba's failure to obtain as much rice as he had expected, indicated that he had lost the help of a powerful friend in the communist world and must depend more than ever on Soviet Russia's economic aid. The two countries signed a trade agreement in February amounting to $913 million for 1966. The Soviet Union will continue to supply Cuba with such vital products as petroleum, wheat, fertilizers, a large assortment of raw materials, and agricultural and industrial equipment. Cuba will export mainly sugar, minerals, and tobacco. Cuba's debt to the communist bloc, growing steadily, was estimated at the end of 1965 to be $1 billion.

In the Americas, too, Castro appears to be losing ground. President Frei of Chile declared in July, 1965: "We wish to see Cuba reintegrated into the American family. Cuba belongs to this family by indestructible links." However, Castro's announcement at the Afro-Asian-Latin American Solidarity Organization's conference in Havana in January, 1966, of backing armed insurgency throughout Latin America will make it less likely that any hemispheric government will press for Cuba's return to "the American family." Castro also aroused strong nationalistic feelings in Chile during the serious 1966 strikes in the copper mines there when he called President Frei a "reactionary," a "liar," and a "coward."

Castro later denied he had insulted Frei or Chile, and if need be he probably can even reverse the crucial policy of aiding guerrilla warfare if enough Latin Americans are thereby alienated, just as he returned to King Sugar after desperate attempts to industrialize Cuba. Castro has made Cuba the most state-directed of all the communist countries, many old communist leaders are in disgrace or semi-retirement, and he goes far beyond orthodox communism: "Marxism-Leninism appears milk and water beside the throat-burning definition given of it in Cuba." [53] Theodore Draper has dedicated much effort to demolishing myths about the Cuban Revolution but even he believes that Castro's charismatic leadership is so powerful that he can make the nation, particularly the younger generation, follow any course he takes: "He established a mass relationship primarily with his person, not with his ideas, and so could change his ideas without changing this relationship." [54] Could he afford, or not afford, to renew commercial relations with the Western hemisphere if this were possible?

Meanwhile Cuba and the United States continue to exist in an astonishing ignorance of each other: "At the extreme poles of feeling, absolute hatred blinds the opponents. Thus American hatred of the Cuban Revolution engenders an almost universal press distortion, including a syndicated comic-strip which grotesquely caricatures Fidel Castro as a cigar-smoking animal." [55] And the Cuban leader contemptuously refers to President Lyndon B. Johnson as "that ignorant cowboy from Texas."

It is too soon to evaluate the long-range influence of Castro and his totalitarian system on the Cuban people. The pictures of stern young women in fatigue uniforms snappily marching down the streets, Castro's almost interminable speeches by radio and before massed multitudes, the intense fervor of patriotism kept at high tension—these phenomena astonish those who have not visited the island since 1958. How long can this independent, fun-loving, witty people conform to such a regimen? But in any case the clock cannot be turned back, according to one experienced reporter: "For whatever else Fidel Castro has done or not done, he has most assuredly given Cubans an unforgettable glimpse of a freer and fuller life that they might enjoy." [56]

The words written many years ago by Fernando Ortiz, the grand old man of Cuban letters, still alive and still in Havana, seem particularly apt:

Cuba is an *ajiaco* . . . the most typical and complex of stews, made from a variety of vegetables . . . and from chunks of different kinds of meat . . . the Cuban ajiaco has gone on boiling and simmering, on the open fire or on the back of the stove, clean and dirty, various as the ages which brought new human substances to be thrust into the pot by the hand of the chef, who, in this metaphor, is the ever-changing tide of history. In every era our nation has had, like the ajiaco, new, raw elements just thrown into the pot; a heterogeneous conglomeration of diverse races and cultures . . . which were stirred, mixed together, and disintegrated in the boiling of society; and down at the bottom of the stew there now rests a new mass, produced by the elements which, upon disintegrating in this historic boiling, have contributed their most durable essences to settle in a rich and tastily seasoned mixture, which has the true character of a new creation. A mixture of cuisines, of races, and of cultures. A thick broth of civilization which bubbles on the Caribbean fire.[57]

But the "new mass" no longer lies at the bottom of the stew. Perhaps that is the meaning of the Cuban Revolution. And in one fundamental way, Cuba is like most Latin American countries: its population has increased by more than a million since Batista fled in 1959. Though at one time Castro was reported to have fostered an important birth control program, on September 19, 1966, he publicly supported the position set forth by Martí, but gave it a contemporary twist in commenting on the idea of those who maintain that birth control is the solution to the population problem: "This can be said only by the capitalists and by the exploiters. No one who is aware of what man can accomplish with technology and science will ever establish a limit to the number of human beings who can exist on this earth." (*The New York Times,* Sept. 22, 1966.)

Cubans now number about 8 million, and their growing needs will strain the capacity of every government there no matter what its political character. And sugar is still King.

Haiti and the Dominican Republic

Immediately eastward from Cuba lies an island with some 8 million people, divided into two separate nations, the western third occupied by the Negro republic Haiti, and the eastern two-thirds by the Dominican Republic. The first permanent European settlement was established here in Columbus' time, named Santo Domingo, and for the first half century it was a key area in the Spanish empire. The more spectacular conquests of Mexico and Peru turned it into a poor way-station, harassed by European rivals. Eventually Spain ceded the island to France; in 1804 the French-speaking western end won its independence under the dramatic Negro leader and ex-slave Touissant L'Ouverture.

Four decades later the eastern part of the island won its freedom as the Dominican Republic. Both countries suffered almost continuous tumult, confusion, and tyranny during the 19th century. In the early years of the 20th century the U.S. imposed fiscal supervision and occupation by the Marines in both countries, fearing that anarchy in the islands would enable European powers to gain a fresh foothold in the Caribbean and that American investments would be imperiled.

When the occupation forces withdrew in 1930 from the Dominican Republic and in 1934 from Haiti, the U.S. had become disillusioned about its ability to govern the islands. Some good had doubtless been accomplished, although the methods and achievements differed somewhat in the two countries, but Dominicans and Haitians alike celebrated the end of U.S. rule as their second emancipation.

● **Haiti.** Haiti is the poorest nation in the Americas although it does not suffer from a one-crop economy. Its fundamental economic problem, to quote a 1949 United Nations investigation, "derives from the relentless pressure of a steadily growing, insufficiently educated population upon limited, vulnerable and—so far as agricultural land is concerned—alarmingly shrinking natural resources." Its four and a half million people try to scratch out a living on tiny plots of land in half the space which the 3.5 million Dominicans have next door. It has the highest birth rate in the Americas; 90 per cent of its people live in abject poverty.

It has become one of the most isolated nations in the New World. The French-speaking Haitian elite maintain cultural relations with France, while economically Haiti is closely connected with the United States. The great majority of the densely packed-in Haitians, who constitute the nation's lowest class, have no effective link with their own intellectual and social elite.

Haiti produced a remarkable group of intellectuals between 1890 and 1915: doctors, essayists, lawyers, poets, and novelists. But the nation collapsed during their generation and the subsequent anarchy led in 1915 to the occupation of Haiti by the U.S. Marines. The intellectuals opposed foreign rule, and worked to hasten its withdrawal. One of them, Jean Price-Mars, tried to bridge the chasm between the city-dwellers and the rural Haitians by publishing in 1928 *Ainsi Parla l'Oncle,* a collection of folklore essays, in which he criticized the Haitian elite for aping European culture and for denying its African origins. Through his influence and that of Jacques Roumain, anthropology became a popular pursuit of some of the elite, and "the new black intellectual and folklorist undertook a 'Return to Africa' attitude while praising unconditionally every aspect of Haitian culture that actually (or supposedly) had something to do with Africa." [58] Voodoo, the primitive popular religion, was to be understood rather than reviled or persecuted. Folklore had become a political activity.[59]

The U.S. troops withdrew in 1934, and trouble followed: "one half of the Senate was summarily discharged and intellectuals and journalists were jailed and killed . . . The government ignored the black intellectuals and was bent on favoring the mulattoes regardless of their capacity." [60] The black intellectuals found much inspiration in the study by Yale professor James G. Leyburn, *The Haitian People* (1941); his frank picture of the gulf between the elite and the masses strengthened their conviction that the black intellectual must regain political power for the benefit of the nation.

The army returned to politics. Dumarsais Estimé, the well-educated son of a peasant family who had shown great ability as minister of education, was installed as president in 1946 by troops trained by the Marines. Negro leadership returned, but not peace. Estimé was forced out in 1950, as was his successor, Paul Magloire, in 1956.

After six months of chaos Dr. François Duvalier, ardent folklorist and the blacks' candidate, won the election of 1957 over the mulattoes' candidate. He came to power with the army's support, but quickly curbed its power and now rules through his private army, the much-feared Ton Ton Macoutes. He remains dictator "by playing (and paying) off ambitious and greedy subordinates and factions; by calculated extirpation of alternative leadership; by fear, espionage and every totalitarian brutality; by suppressing civil liberties." [61] He proclaimed himself "Chief of the Revolution" and permanent president; he has expelled chiefs of mission from Chile, Great Britain, the Netherlands, Santo Domingo, and Venezuela as well as two U.S. ambassadors. Since 1945 the U.S has given well over $100 million to Haiti; Duvalier received aid totalling about one third of Haiti's budget, but he remained dissatisfied. In 1961 he cast the crucial vote to expel Cuba from the OAS but he had been willing to sell it to Castro, and the U.S. is reported to have paid dearly for it: "the story had it that Dean Rusk's expense account for the day read 'Breakfast, two dollars. Lunch with Haitian delegate, 2.8 million dollars.' " [62] But all grants to Haiti were withheld as relations deteriorated between the two countries during 1962 and 1963.

The end of one of the cruelest dictatorships in this century, when it comes, will surely bring more bloody turmoil to Haiti. Meanwhile most of Haiti's intellectuals are in exile, and many trained administrators desperately needed at home are finding useful work to do in the developing nations of Africa.

One thoughtful Haitian remarks that the revolution of 1946 led to an era of transition but that

> 85 per cent of the population, consisting of black peasants, is still undernourished and has not yet learned how to read and write. The peasants are waiting for *their* revolution. . . . If Haiti wants a decent way of life for everyone, there must be a reorientation in the ethics and behavior of her rulers. The love of folklore is not enough: what is needed is love of the people.[63]

Professor Leyburn, 25 years ago, charged that the elite did not really want any change:

> Aware that so long as conditions remain as they are Haiti will be poor and backward, they are nevertheless not ready to promote what would be a thoroughgoing social revolution. If any government should become oversolicitous for the well-being of the masses, it would soon find itself bitterly opposed by the upper class. In the long run, what will be the result of keeping things as they are? Elite who know their history can find several possible answers, no one of which appeals to them: a peasants' revolt, a Reign of Terror, intervention by a foreign power. They are on the horns of a dilemma: if as rulers they promote material welfare, they lose their present positions of security; if they do not promote a change, violent change will unseat them.[64]

● **The Dominican Republic.** When the notorious Generalissimo Rafael L. Trujillo was assassinated in May 1961 after a 31 year dictatorship whose corruption and cruelty had become a byword even in the Caribbean, a period of uncertainty followed until the Trujillo family disappeared and the OAS sanctions of 1960 were lifted. The Alliance for Progress gave the Dominican Republic top priority, and is reported to have committed over $86 million for agricultural credit loans, the construction of farm to market road systems, cattle and livestock improvement programs, low-cost housing projects, school construction and teacher training, and the cultivation of rice. Other grants were designed to facilitate imports from the U.S., to subsidize sugar prices, and to service the large foreign debt (58 million). Technical missions descended upon the land and the Peace Corps went into practically every valley and village. The U.S. seemed determined to turn the Dominican Republic into a show place of capitalism and democracy in contrast to Castro's Cuba.

The election of December, 1962, resulted in an overwhelming victory for Professor Juan Bosch, a highly respected intellectual who had long lived in exile during which he had established the Partido Revolucionario Dominicano. After the radical Constitution of April 1963 was promulgated, he began to be accused of inefficiency, of being "soft" on communism, and of even permitting communists to infiltrate his administration. He did not forbid Dominican students to visit Cuba, though he refused to establish relations with Castro. He promised the long-oppressed people much: to break up the Trujillo estates, to guarantee a minimum wage, to provide social security.[65] The new Constitution, whittling down Church influence and legalizing divorce, roused opposition in conservative circles. Bosch felt his principal task to be the re-education of the Dominican people, and that Trujillo-like methods should not be used to maintain himself in power. One observer has noted "that Bosch was not master of his household . . . and Ambassador John Bartlow Martin was not the exclusive spokesman for the U.S. within the Republic." [66]

Bosch was overthrown by a military *coup* in September, 1963, and the army installed a civilian triumvirate, whose leading member was Donald Reid Cabral, son of a Scottish immigrant, who had married into the Dominican oligarchy. The new regime was held by many Dominicans to be conservative and opposed to economic and social reform; many trained Dominicans became frustrated and left the country.[67] The austerity program Reid Cabral inaugurated alienated the middle classes, the masses, and the military so that plots again began to form. In April, 1965, Colonel Francisco Caamañò Denó rose against the Reid Cabral junta to restore Bosch, the legally elected president, to power and to enforce the 1963 Constitution. Then began an almost incredibly sorry period. Though the whole story is not yet known, the important fact is that President Lyndon Johnson sent in detachments of Marines whose presence led to many charges, in and outside the U.S., that the era of U.S. gunboat diplomacy had returned.

● **Is the Organization of American States Dead?** The Marines had landed, so it was first announced, to protect American and foreign lives, but soon the danger seemed to U.S. officials to be the possibility of a Communist take-over, another Cuba. In any case, the U.S. had not referred the problem to the OAS and had violated several solemn treaty obligations; a sharp domestic debate soon developed on the purpose of the unilateral intervention. Some asked whether 35,000 soldiers and Marines were really needed to handle the 58 Communists in the Dominican Republic whom the State Department declared such a danger. One writer pointed out that no foreigners were killed in the Dominican Republic until after the Marines arrived, and that historically there had been "a remarkable Latin-American record of foreigners' immunity in Latin American revolutions." [68] One of the most disquieting aspects of the confused situation was that the U.S., in the early days at least, seemed to be backing a right-wing military group against the supporters of the Constitutionalists, who vociferously denied they were Communists but insisted on the need for significant social changes.

The congresses of Chile and other countries passed votes of censure, and both Communists and non-Communists throughout the hemisphere and elsewhere attacked the intervention. The U.S. managed to squeeze a vote in the Council of the OAS on May 6 in favor of an OAS military force but only after six sessions and 10 days of tough "backstage" talks. The bare majority was made possible by the affirmative vote cast by the "phantom delegate" from the deposed Reid Cabral regime. Only six Latin-American nations, most of them under military rule, contributed to the force: Brazil, which supplied the bulk of the troops, other than the U.S., as well as the commander of the force, Costa Rica, El Salvador, Honduras, Nicaragua, and Paraguay. Moreover, some of the nations voting for the May 6 resolution did so to set up some form of machinery to allow a hemisphere voice in the settlement. Much opposition has been generated to the U.S. proposal to set up a permanent peace-keeping force in the OAS. Meanwhile, the U.N. and the OAS are both at work on the confused scene in the Dominican Republic and the future is unclear. The Senate has opened hearings in Washington and a great deal of dirty linen was washed, inasmuch as the American correspondents had reported fully and frankly on what they saw in the Dominican Republic. Mike Mansfield, Senate Majority Leader, praised their despatches as more accurate than information he received from official sources.

The problems of the OAS have long been discussed (*see Readings Nos. 78–85*), but the Dominican crisis has brought them to general attention as never before. Only two weeks before the intervention began, the Inter-American system had celebrated 75 years of "peace and progress." But many people in the hemisphere believe that the OAS must be radically improved if it is to endure.

The still-troubled Dominican Republic will probably be a testing ground for any future crises over intervention. Joaquín Balaguer, who had been president when Trujillo was assassinated in 1961, won a clear victory over Bosch at the polls in the election on June 1, 1966, but extremists of both right and left probably will attempt to unseat him. The withdrawal on September 20, 1966 of the last American units from the Inter-American Peace Force indicated to the world that the United States honored its word to leave as soon as possible, but President Balaguer was left without any visible prop from outside to confront the military and the police elements that make the Dominican situation so explosive. General Elías Wessin y Wessin, who ousted Bosch from the presidency in 1963, who led the fight against the rebels in

April, 1965, and who is regarded as a key figure in any projected coup against the Balaguer government, has recently announced his candidacy for the 1970 presidential elections. How long will this right-wing general be content to stay in Manhattan? Will the Dominican military and police, whose top leadership has ties which link it with the former Trujillo dictatorship, support President Balaguer? The uncertainty concerning the future actions of this leadership explains why *The Christian Science Monitor* reported that "a mood of deep anxiety" existed as the last contingents of the Inter-American Peace Force departed.

Puerto Rico

● **Operation Bootstrap.** When Nelson Rockefeller successfully campaigned for the governorship of New York in 1958 he spoke in Spanish to the Puerto Ricans in Manhattan and often had his wife and family with him at political rallies. It was clear recognition of the presence of the thousands of Puerto Ricans who have steadily migrated to the U.S. during the last 20 years. The many movie houses in upper Manhattan that show only Spanish language films is another indication of their numbers and that of the other Spanish-speaking residents of New York City, now reportedly with the sixth largest Spanish-speaking population (1,500,000) in the world. But Puerto Ricans are the largest group because they can freely enter the United States.[69]

The confusion and uncertainty in Puerto Rico after the U.S. acquired this island by the Spanish American War did not promise much. Without mineral resources, Puerto Rico presented the familiar pattern of a densely populated, underdeveloped tropical area where, of all the important indices, only the population showed sustained and uninterrupted growth. Agricultural improvements and land distribution had only limited value, for no matter how well tilled or how equitably divided, the cultivated land could not possibly support the growing population. In addition, Puerto Rico faced the problem of protecting her own cultural identity against powerful and pervasive U.S. influences, and of deciding politically whether she aimed at independence, statehood, or some other status. The island made gradual progress toward self-government during the years 1898–1952 during which it was "an unincorporated territory" of the United States.

The political tempo increased in 1938 with the creation of the Popular Democratic Party, which provided Luis Muñoz Marín with an increasingly firm political base and enabled him to undertake many economic reforms with the effective support of New Deal Governor Rexford Tugwell. During World War II Puerto Rico, strategically located at the gateway to the Caribbean and the Panama Canal, became a military bastion, with feverishly constructed military bases that brought jobs, money, trade—and attention. In 1948 Muñoz Marín took office as the first elected native governor; economic and social development continued. Temporary tax exemptions and low wages for labor attracted industry from the mainland. Public health facilities so improved that life expectancy rose from 46 years in 1940 to 61 years in 1952; education became a significant part of Puerto Rico's progress and included the development of the University of Puerto Rico.

In 1950 the U.S. Congress provided the basis for a decisive political step by "fully recognizing the principle of consent and approved that principle in the manner of a compact subject to agreement by the people of Puerto Rico." This act ushered in a period of intense political and constitutional activity which culminated in the adoption, on March 3, 1952, by a vote of 375,000 to 83,000 of a Constitution establishing the Commonwealth (Estado Libre Asociado) of Puerto Rico.

Thus began a unique experiment in American constitutional development. No taxes are collected in the island for the U.S. Treasury, and Puerto Rico has no voting representation in Congress. Puerto Ricans have been U.S. citizens since 1917; foreign relations are conducted by the Department of State. Puerto Rico, according to Muñoz Marín, neither seeks statehood nor wishes to give up its basic Latin-American way of life.[70] It cherishes its Spanish language and literature, and cultivates its cultural heritage through such institutions as the government sponsored Instituto de Cultura Puertorriqueña and its University.

The political pot bubbles while economic and cultural development proceeds, though Muñoz Marín's party still leads by a comfortable margin. The Nacionalistas, a fringe group with a very small following, which was outlawed in the 1930's, made world news in 1954 when some of their members went to Washington and shot five Congressmen. The Independentista Party, with adherents from many classes, stands for planned and nonviolent political separation. The Statehood Party, affiliated with the U.S. Republican Party, with its strength among the rising bourgeoisie, put forward a candidate for governor, Luis Ferré, a dynamic industrialist, who lost to Muñoz Marín in 1952, in 1956, and in 1960; in 1964 Ferré lost again to the candidate handpicked by Muñoz Marín, Roberto Sánchez Vilella.

A United States-Puerto Rican Commission on the Status of Puerto Rico was established in 1964 to take evidence and canvass opinions on this complicated constitutional question. Cultural matters are vitally important, as Rector Jaime Benítez of the University of Puerto Rico explained in his Testimony before the Commission on July 31, 1965. (*See Reading No. 48.*) The alternatives to the present arrangement are an improvement of the Commonwealth or departure from it by statehood or independence. Some doubt that Congress would admit Puerto Rico as a state, although Alaska's and Hawaii's achievement of statehood have raised the hopes of the Republican Statehood Party.

Independence would pose grave economic problems for the island, now one of the few areas in the Caribbean where economic development roughly parallels the growth of population, for unrestricted emigration to the U.S., which would probably cease with independence, and U.S. aid have played no small part in easing that pressure. The Commission heard a considerable variety of opinion for and against independence during the two years it studied the issues, and recommended on August 5, 1966, that the Puerto Rican people decide by plebiscite whether to continue in commonwealth status, be independent, or apply for statehood. The Commission also recommended the establishment of joint advisory groups to consider proposals for improvement or growth of the Commonwealth, or for change to statehood or independence, but gave no status preference of its own, declaring: "All three forms of political status . . . are valid and confer upon the people of Puerto Rico equal dignity with equality of status and of national citizenship."

Leaders in Washington of the Democratic and Republican parties have promised that the U.S. will quickly grant independence to the island whenever a majority of the Puerto Rican people clearly favor it. That the idea of independence is by no means dead is evidenced in the recent book[71] by the Welsh Socialist, Gordon K. Lewis, who taught in Puerto Rico for some years. "By far the best general survey of Puerto Rico ever written," [72] this substantial volume puts forward the view that the Commonwealth concept denies Puerto Rican identity and must be abandoned. Lewis considers independence the only acceptable solution with the U.S. underwriting the island's economic future (a moral duty he believes, in view of what he terms the exploitative past). (*See Reading No. 49.*)

Whether the Puerto Ricans or the U.S. Congress will also hold this view remains to be seen. Despite the Commission's hearings and impressive documentation[73] on almost every aspect of the history and life of Puerto Rico, the plebiscite it recommended ran into many legal and political obstructions before the vote was taken on July 23, 1967. Over 700,000 of the 1.1 million registered voters cast their ballots; about 60 per cent favored the Commonwealth and almost 40 per cent voted for statehood. The Independence Party officially boycotted the plebiscite.

Muñoz Marín may have taken Puerto Rico so far along Commonwealth path that it will not turn back. Perhaps, as Benítez believes, the Commonwealth idea was a triumph of intelligence over the "intelligentsia" who are wedded to theoretical propositions and emotional loyalties of the past. Much depends upon what happens now that Muñoz Marín has stepped aside and his party must maintain unity under his successor, Governor Roberto Sánchez Vilella. Despite the recent plebiscite, the future will test the strength of Puerto Rico's economic institutions and political maturity.

Its economic development has, indeed, been spectacular. Between 1940 and 1964 over a thousand new industries were brought to the island and have doubled the contribution from industrial sources to the island's income. The resulting prosperity has been reflected in rising wages ($1.15 an hour average) and one of the highest per capita incomes in the Caribbean ($800 plus for the fiscal year 1963–1964). But unless the birth rate declines, the population of almost 3 million will find it difficult to attain higher living standards. The birth rate has dropped 22 per cent since 1950, but its present population of almost 3 million still makes Puerto Rico more densely populated than any Latin-American country—764 persons for each square mile, whereas the U.S. had an average of 51 persons per square mile. Four million people are estimated for 1985. The island now enjoys an annual 10 per cent growth in national product—faster than almost any other area in the world —but even this merely enables it to hold its own.

Will industries continue to flow to Puerto Rico when their tax exemptions end? And will the migration to Manhattan flow on in spite of possible recessions in the economy of the United States? Unless the answer to both questions is affirmative, "Operation Bootstrap" will be in deep trouble. Meanwhile Puerto Rican political leaders are proud to have created the plan for a commonwealth in voluntary association with the United States. Governor Sánchez Vilella is sure that Puerto Rico has made important advances, but he does not believe it necessarily a model for other Latin-American countries:

> In Puerto Rico we have transformed a society in twenty-five years, we have achieved a dramatic social revolution in peace. We have remained an island of tranquility in a boiling sea. However, we don't pretend to export our own solution. Each country and each area has to be examined on the basis of its history, its people, its resources. Each country in our Hemisphere is, in a sense, a universe itself. But we can offer our experience.[74]

Non-Hispanic Areas

The Caribbean was the cockpit of America during the three centuries after Columbus; and the British, Dutch, and French areas there today reflect this historical fact. They are scattered over the huge Caribbean area, from British Honduras in Central America to the Guianas on the South American continent. About 4 million people live in the British territories with perhaps another million in all the other areas combined. Most of them suffer from low wages and a low standard of living. During the last twenty years smallpox, typhus, cholera, sleeping-sickness, and yellow fever have been wiped out and typhoid, tuberculosis, and malaria greatly reduced. For people under 50, illiteracy has almost disappeared in the Dutch West Indies, Martinique, and some of the British islands. Yet, the region has a high percentage of general unemployment and a shortage of technical workers. In recent years, over 100,000 British subjects have migrated to the United Kingdom, including a considerable number of the relatively few trained workers in the area.

Most of the European areas have only slight relations with their mainland Latin-American neighbors and differ from them in two respects: (1) their people are preponderantly of African stock with an appreciable percentage of Asiatics; (2) they have remained in association with the European powers but most of them have moved or are moving toward complete political autonomy without conspicuous revolution or bloodshed.

The exception was British Guiana, where Dr. Cheddi Jagan began his turbulent political career in 1946. He developed a new mass party, the People's Progressive Party (PPP), through which he strove for self-government and social revolution.[75] By 1953 the PPP was strong enough to win the first election held under universal suffrage, which led to a period of confusion and controversy as Dr. Jagan deliberately led the left-wing party to clash with the governor and other British-nominated functionaries in order to expose the constitutional limitations then in force. The party's communist affiliations and aggressive policies led Britain to suspend the constitution within a few months, and it was not restored until 1961 when the PPP again won at the polls. Now a new wave of disorders occurred, for the second PPP government was plagued with labor strikes and riots. Most serious of all Dr. Jagan's problems now was the fact that a large and predominantly Negro element left his party, which thereafter depended largely on the East Indian population for support.

PPP lost the election in December 1964, which Dr. Jagan attributed to the machinations of the Central Intelligence Agency. The high percentage of the electorate voting—96.9 per cent, the highest recorded in a British Territory—reflected the genuine fear of racial oppression or misrule which each party felt at the prospect of independence under their opponents. The conservative and national socialists managed to restore social peace and to halt the economic decline, which encouraged Britain to announce in mid-1965 that independence would be granted on May 26, 1966. Dr. Jagan boycotted the independence celebrations, just as he had managed to be absent in Moscow when Queen Elizabeth had earlier visited the country, and maintained that Washington still called the tune.

The Development Plan for 1966–1972, drawn up by the new Government with the help of a distinguished team of Western economists, will go far to improve Guyana's economy if it succeeds. It includes improved social and educational service, a road-building program, surveys to locate and exploit hydro-electric and forest potential, and the preparation of new lands for settlement.

The real problem, however, is political. Will the coalition Government be able to hold together and also convince a mistrustful half of the population that they are acting in the best interests of the nation? The Guyana Independence Act aimed at curbing autocratic rule and may do so, if regard for due legal process becomes the rule. As one observer reported: "In this England-sized territory on the continent of South America the principles of parliamentary democracy, which Britain taught the races she brought thither or found there, may receive their severest testing and, one hopes, their best vindication." [76] One of the most ominous facts to confront the new state is the population growth; the population doubled in the period 1946–1960.

Various types of constitutional arrangements exist between the non-Hispanic Caribbean areas and the European powers. Martinique and Guadeloupe are departments of France and have a relationship similar to that of any other French Department. Surinam (Dutch Guiana), like the Netherlands Antilles, has become a partner in the Kingdom of the Netherlands and since the ratification of the 1954 constitution has enjoyed autonomy in internal affairs.

Efforts to organize these widely-separated and diverse areas have failed. The "weak, colonial-minded Caribbean Organization" finally collapsed, and the long-heralded and much-publicized West Indies Federation established in 1958 dissolved in 1962. Jamaica as well as Trinidad and Tobago became independent nations a few months later, were subsequently admitted to the United Nations, and may become members of the Organization of American States in the future. The historian, Dr. Eric Williams,[77] Prime Minister of Trinidad and Tobago, is already recognized as an articulate spokesman in British Commonwealth affairs. Barbados received its independence November 30, 1966, and four other small British islands in the Windward group of the Lesser Antilles—St. Lucia, Grenada, St. Vincent, and Dominica are scheduled soon to become independent crown colonies.

The economies of all the non-Hispanic areas are basically agricultural except for the island of Trinidad which derives 35 per cent of its revenue from oil, the Netherland Antilles where oil is also the principal export, and Surinam where bauxite accounts for 80 per cent of all export receipts. Elsewhere, sugar is usually the main crop, although other products are being developed— bananas, citrus fruits, cocoa, and coffee. Since 1956 mining has assumed importance in the economy of Jamaica, British Guiana, and Surinam. The livestock and dairy industries are beginning to develop, and may be important in the future. But in most countries sugar still dominates the economy and employs the most labor.

The area as a whole is struggling to move into the industrial age to meet its new responsibilities. World War II changed the earlier attitudes of the metropolitan powers who had used it as a source of raw materials and discouraged setting up industries or even independent food production. Since 1946 representatives of the three European powers and the U.S. have encouraged both food and industrial production, development of fishing, forest products, mining, and a wide range of light industries. Technical and vocational education is now stressed, particularly in Trinidad. Everywhere facilities for visitors are being improved; the tourist "industry" will doubtless be a growing resource of all Caribbean areas. The University of the West Indies established in 1948 as an affiliate of the University of London, to make it possible to obtain higher education without leaving the British Caribbean, emphasizes quality. It is now one of the most effective means yet taken to encourage the British areas to think regionally, and since 1962 the University has been independent.

The European areas in the Caribbean, then, also participate in the ferment of Latin America. Significant economic, educational, political, and social changes are all under way—but the discreet guidance of European powers has begun to give way to local responsibility and independence.[78]

But the basic economic and social conditions in the non-Hispanic areas of the Caribbean remain, as for the rest of this great tropical region, unsatisfactory. They have undoubtedly improved significantly during the last decade or so, "but with Puerto Rico's per capital national income in the 1960s no more than half that of the poorest state of the American union, Jamaica's no more than a third of that of the United Kingdom, and many territories not half as well off as Jamaica, West Indian socio-economic aspirations remained far from satisfied." [79]

[1] Thomas Mathews, "The Caribbean Kaleidoscope," *San Juan Review* (April, 1965), pp. 17–20. This article originally appeared in *Current History* (January, 1965). See also G. Etzel Pearcy, *The West Indian Scene* (Princeton: Van Nostrand, 1965); "Social and Cultural Pluralism in the Caribbean," *Annals of the New York Academy of Sciences,* Vol. 83 (1960), art. 5, pp. 761–916.

[2] Mark Chester and Richard Schmuck, "Student Reactions to the Cuban Crisis and Public Dissent," *Public Opinion Quarterly,* XXVIII (1964), No. 3, pp. 467–482.

[3] Herminio Portell-Vilá, *Historia de Cuba en sus relaciones con los Estados Unidos y España,* 4 vols. (Havana: J. Montero, 1938–1941).

[4] David F. Healy, *The United States in Cuba, 1898–1902* (Madison: University of Wisconsin Press, 1965), pp. 10, 13, 17 ff., 81 ff.

[5] Duvon C. Corbitt, "Cuban Revisionist Interpretations of Cuba's Struggle for Independence," *HAHR,* XLIII (1963), pp. 395–404.

[6] Robert F. Smith, *The United States and Cuba. Business and Diplomacy, 1917–1960* (New Haven: College and University Press, 1960), pp. 22–23. One U.S. professor went so far as to say that "there would be no missiles of any description or range in Cuba if the U.S. actions toward Cuba since 1898 had followed and honored its professions and promises," William Appleman Williams, *The United States, Cuba, and Castro. An Essay on the Dynamics of Revolution and the Dissolution of Empire* (New York: Monthly Review Press, 1962), p. 173.

[7] William Graham Sumner, *The Conquest of the United States by Spain. A Lecture Before the Phi Beta Kappa Society of Yale University, January 16, 1899* (Boston, 1899).

[8] Charles C. Griffin, ed., "Welles to Roosevelt: a Memorandum on Inter-American Relations, 1933," *Hispanic American Historical Review,* XXXIV (1954), pp. 190–192.

[9] E. David Cronon, "Interpreting the New Good Neighbor Policy: The Cuban Crisis of 1933," *HAHR,* XLIX (1949), pp. 542, 545, 546, 548.

[10] *Ibid.,* pp. 546, 553.

[11] *Ibid.,* pp. 554–555.

[12] For detailed information on U.S.-Cuban relations in this period, based on a close examination of State Department files, see Bryce Wood, *The Making of the Good Neighbor Policy* (New York: Columbia University Press, 1961), pp. 48–117. For a general background, see the volume of documents edited by Robert F. Smith, *Background to Revolution. The Development of Modern Cuba* (New York: Knopf, 1966).

[13] Niebuhr, *The Structure of Nations and Empires* (New York, 1959), pp. 24–25.

[14] Wyatt MacGaffey and Clifford R. Barnett, *Twentieth-Century Cuba. The Background of the Castro Revolution* (Garden City: Doubleday, 1965); Robert F. Smith, *What Happened in Cuba* (New York: Twayne, 1963); Federico G. Gil, "Antecedents of the Cuban Revolution," *The Centennial Review,* VI (1962), pp. 373–392.

[15] Roberta Wohlstetter, "Cuba and Pearl Harbor: Hindsight and Foresight," *Foreign Affairs,* XLIII (1965), p. 693.

[16] John Harbron, "Cuba: Bibliography of a Revolution," *International Journal,* XVIII (Toronto, 1963), p. 319. Matthews', *The Cuban Story* (New York: Braziller, 1961), was followed by Draper's *Castro's Revolution, Myths and Realities* (New York: Praeger, 1962) and *Castroism, Theory and Practice* (New York: Praeger, 1965). *Encounter* of London has been publishing some of the liveliest controversy. See Matthews' "Dissent over Cuba" (July, 1963), to which Draper riposted, "The Confused Martyr" (August, 1964) as well as Arthur Schlesinger, Jr., "The Risks of Dissent" (*ibid.*), "Dissent Over Matthews" by Claude Constant shows how keen is the interest roused by this debate (*ibid.*).

[17] Harbron, "Cuba: Bibliography of a Revolution," p. 217.

[18] An excellent running account of current publications is given in *Caribbean Studies,* published by the Institute of Caribbean Studies of the University of Puerto Rico. See, for example, Vol. II (1963), pp. 62–65, 82–85; Vol. IV (1964), pp. 69–75. See also *Bibliografía Cubana* (Gainesville, 1964) compiled by Fermín Peraza Sarausa, the veteran Cuban bibliographer. This volume is No. 26 in Dr. Peraza's standard *Anuario Bibliográfico Cubano.* Another useful list is in Lyman M. Tondel, Jr., *The Inter-American Security System and the Cuban Crisis* (Dobbs Ferry, New York: Oceana Publications, 1964), pp. 73–97.

[19] Smith, *The United States and Cuba,* Preface, pp. 183–186.

[20] C. A. M. Hennessy, "Cuba: The Politics of Frustrated Nationalism," in Martin C. Needler, ed., *Political Systems of Latin America* (Princeton: Van Nostrand, 1964), p. 204.

[21] Personal communication to the author.

[22] Hennessy, "Cuba: The Politics of Frustrated Nationalism," p. 183.

[23] For a detailed account, see *The Cuban Crisis: A Documentary Record* (New York: Foreign Policy Association, 1963). Elaborate analyses have been made of this crisis: Richard R. Fagen, "Calculation and Emotion in Foreign Policy. The Cuban Case," *Journal of Conflict Resolution,* VI (1962), pp. 214 ff.; Klaus Knorr, "Failures in National Intelligence Estimates. The Case of the Cuban Missiles," *World Politics,* XV (1964), pp. 455–467.

For the text of ninety-four documents, without analysis or evaluation, see David L. Larson, ed., *The "Cuban Crisis" of 1962: Selected Documents and Chronology* (1963).

[24] Ronald M. Schneider, "Five Years of the Cuban Revolution," *Current History* (January, 1964).

[25] For an analysis, see Robert S. Walters, "Soviet Economic Aid to Cuba, 1959–1964", *International Affairs,* v. 42 (London, 1966), no. 1, p. 74–86.

[26] James O'Connor, "On Cuban Economy," *Political Science Quarterly,* LXXIX (1964), p. 244.

[27] *Ibid.*

[28] Samuel Shapiro, "Cuba Today: Eyewitness Report," *The Nation* (September 22, 1962), p. 146.

[29] Opinions given respectively by Tad Szulc (*The New York Times Book Review,* May 24, 1964); Theodore C. Sorensen (*The Christian Science Monitor,* July 29, 1965); Dom Bonafede, "The Press and the Cuban Fiasco," *Nieman Reports,* XV (July, 1961) No. 3, pp. 5–6.

[30] Bonafede, "The Press and the Cuban Fiasco," pp. 5–6. See also Tad Szulc and Karl E. Meyer, *The Cuban Invasion. The Chronicle of a Disaster* (New York: Ballantine, 1962); Haynes Johnson, *The Bay of Pigs* (New York: Norton, 1964); David Wise and Thomas B. Ross, *The Invisible Government* (New York: Random House, 1964). The figure on the C.I.A. expenditure comes from an Associated Press dispatch.

[31] For an analysis, see David D. Burks, *Cuba Under Castro* (New York: Foreign Policy Association, 1964), pp. 21–29 and Boris Goldenberg, *The Cuban Revolution and Latin America* (New York: Praeger, 1965). See also Ernst Halperin, *Castro and Latin American Communism* and *The Ideology of Castroism and Its Impact on the Communist Parties of Latin America,* both studies being published in 1963 by the Center for International Studies, Massachusetts Institute of Technology. For a representative

non-communist statement in the early period, see *Política,* No. 10 (Caracas, June, 1960), pp. 5–7. On education, see Joseph S. Roucek, "Pro-Communist Revolution in Cuban Education," *Journal of Inter-American Studies,* VI (1964, pp. 323–335.

[32] John Paton Davies, Jr., *Foreign and Other Affairs* (New York: Norton, 1964), pp. 150–151.

[33] For a sophisticated analysis, see Ben H. Bagdikian, "Press, Independence and the Cuban Crisis," *Columbia Journalism Review,* I (Winter, 1963), No. 4, p. 8.

[34] For a remarkably complete historical picture see Roland T. Ely, *Cuando reinaba su majestad el azúcar* (Buenos Aires: Sudamericana, 1963).

[35] Guevara, "The Cuban Economy. Its Past, and Its Present Importance," *International Affairs,* XL (1964), pp. 589–599.

[36] Draper, *Castroism. Theory and Practice,* p. 163.

[37] Jacques Chonchol, "Análisis crítico de la reforma agraria cubana," *El trimestre económico,* XXX (1963), pp. 69–143.

[38] *Ibid.,* p. 143.

[39] Draper, *Castroism. Theory and Practice,* p. 162.

[40] *Ibid.,* p. 165.

[41] Edwin Tetlow of the *Daily Telegraph,* as quoted by Burks, *Cuba Under Castro,* p. 14.

[42] *The New York Times,* March 3, 1965.

[43] MacKay, "Cuba Revisited," *The Christian Century* (Feb. 12, 1964), pp. 200–203. A Canadian ecclesiastic Leslie Dewart, author of *Christianity and the Revolution,* debated with a Cuban priest. See "Cuba and the Church: an Exchange of Views," *Commonweal* (March 13, 1964), pp. 716–719.

[44] Alistair Reid, "Report on Spain," *The New Yorker* (July 10, 1965), p. 59.

[45] Dudley Seers, *et al., Cuba: The Revolution Within* (Chapel Hill: University of North Carolina Press, 1964).

[46] As recorded by Foreign Broadcast Information Service. Daily Report, Supplement (March 29, 1962), No. 5, p. 27.

[47] Portuondo, "Hacia una nueva historia de Cuba," *Cuba socialista,* III (1963), No. 24, pp. 24–39. See also his "Los intelectuales y la Revolución," *ibid.,* IV (1964), No. 34, pp. 51–64, and Antonio Núñez Jiménez, "La naciente Academia de Ciencias de Cuba," *ibid., IV* (1964), No. 32, pp. 22–37.

[48] *Commonweal* (Sept. 27, 1963), p. 4.

[49] As quoted by Matthews, *The Cuban Story,* p. 249.

[50] Ernest R. May, *The American Foreign Policy* (New York: Braziller, 1963), p. 15.

[51] *Ibid.*

[52] Mario Menéndez Rodríguez, "Cuban Catholic Church Clarifies its Stand on the Cuban Revolution," *CIF Reports,* V (Cuernavaca, Mexico: Nov. 1, 1966), No. 21, p. 1. See also Leslie Dewart, *Christianity and the Revolution. The Lessons of Cuba* (New York: Herder and Herder, 1963).

[53] Hugh Thomas, *The New York Times Book Review* (July 11, 1965), p. 3.

[54] Draper, *Castroism. Theory and Practice,* p. 127.

[55] Gordon K. Lewis, *Puerto Rico: Freedom and Power in the Caribbean* (New York: The Monthly Press, 1963), p. 538.

[56] Edwin Tetlow, *Eye on Cuba* (New York: Harcourt, Brace and World, 1966).

[57] Ortiz, "Los factores humanos de la cubanidad," *Revista Bimestre Cubana,* XLV (1940), pp. 165–169. An "Homenaje a Fernando Ortiz" appeared in *La Gaceta de Cuba,* IV (January, February, 1965).

[58] Rémy Bastien, "The Role of the Intellectual in Haitian Plural Society," *Annals of the New York Academy of Sciences,* Vol. 83, art. 5 (1960), pp. 843–849. The quotation is on p. 846.

[59] For a recent interpretation of the voodoo as a force of "tremendous flexibility and adaptability" which will continue to be significant in Haitian life, see *Religion and Politics in Haiti. Two essays by Harold Courlander and Rémy Bastien.* Preface by Richard P. Schaedel (Washington, D.C.: Institute for Cross-Cultural Research, 1966).

[60] Bastien, "The Role of the Intellectual," p. 847. See for this troubled period

Colbert Bonhomme, *Révolution et Contre-Révolution en Haiti de 1946 a 1957* (Port-au-Prince, 1957).

[61] Robert Debs Heinl, Jr., "Haiti. A Case Study in Freedom," *The New Republic* (May 16, 1964), pp. 18–19.

[62] Rayford W. Logan and Martin C. Needler, "Haiti," in *Political Systems of Latin America,* Martin C. Needler, ed. (Princeton: Van Nostrand, 1964), p. 161.

[63] Bastien, "The Role of the Intellectual in Haitian Society," p. 849.

[64] James G. Leyburn, *The Haitian People* (New Haven: Yale University Press, 1941), p. 289.

[65] Mathews, "The Caribbean Kaleidoscope," p. 17.

[66] Mathews, "The Caribbean Kaleidoscope," p. 17. Dr. Bosch defended himself in a moving address, "Conferencia del Dr. Juan Bosch," *Ciscla Instituto Sobre la República Dominicana Contemporánea* (San Germán: Inter-American University, 1964), pp. 54–67. English and Spanish versions are given. See also the remarks of James Nelson Goodsell, Latin American editor of *The Christian Science Monitor, ibid.,* pp. 21–24. Another useful report by Ciscla is *The Caribbean in Crisis* (San Germán: Inter-American University of Puerto Rico, 1966).

[67] L. Orlando Haza, "La recuperación económica dominicana, un modelo de frustración," *Foro Internacional,* V (Mexico, 1964), No. 1, pp. 38–52.

[68] Letter of Bryce Wood to *The New York Times,* June 13, 1965.

[69] Dan Wakefield, *Island in the City; Puerto Ricans in New York* (New York: Corinth Books, 1959).

[70] Muñoz Marín, *Address before the Inter-American Press Association,* October 16, 1957. Mimeographed.

[71] Lewis, *Puerto Rico: Freedom and Power in the Caribbean* (New York: Monthly Review Press, 1963).

[72] Review of Lewis' book by Frank Otto Gatell, *American Historical Review,* LXX (1965), p. 831. Another substantial review is by Thomas Mathews, *Caribbean Studies,* IV (1964), no. 1, pp. 24–37.

[73] See the *Selected Background Studies Prepared for the United States—Puerto Rico Commission on the Status of Puerto Rico* (Washington: Government Printing Office, 1966).

[74] Address at the Commencement Exercises of the City College of New York, June 16, 1965.

[75] *The First Institute on British Guiana* (San Germán: Ciscla, The Inter-American University of Puerto Rico, 1965), pp. 47–48.

[76] B. A. N. Collins, "Independence for Guyana," *World Today,* XX (June, 1966), p. 268. See also Ernst Halperin, "Racism and Communism in British Guiana," *Journal of Inter-American Studies,* VII (1965), pp. 95–134.

[77] His latest work is *History of the People of Trinidad and Tobago* (London: Deutsch, 1962). For an analysis of the breakup of the West Indies Federation, see Amitai Etzioni, *Political Unification* (New York: Holt, Rinehart, Winston, 1965), Chap. V.

[78] For up-to-date information on the complicated and changing Caribbean scene, see *Politics and Economics in the Caribbean. A Contemporary Analysis of the Dutch, French, and British Caribbean,* edited by T. G. Mathews, *et al.* (Río Piedras: Institute of Caribbean Studies, University of Puerto Rico, 1966).

[79] D. A. G. Waddell, *The West Indies and the Guianas* (Princeton: D. Van Nostrand Co., 1967), p. 122.

4
COLOMBIA

AREA: 439,513 sq. mi.

POPULATION IN MID-1966: 18,617,000

LARGEST CITIES:

Bogotá (capital): 1,680,758 (1964)

Cali: 812,810 (est. 1964)

Medellín: 776,970 (est. 1964)

Barranquilla: 521,070 (est. 1964)

PRINCIPAL EXPORTS (1960): coffee, petroleum, bananas

PRESIDENT: Carlos Lleras Restrepo, civilian, took office August 7, 1966, for a 4-year term.

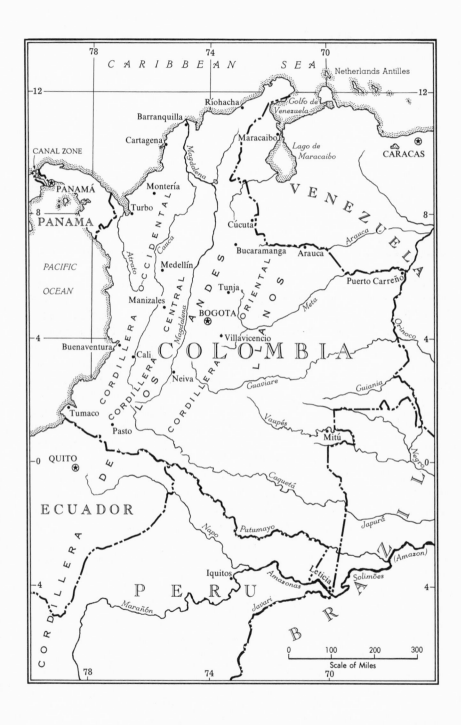

COLOMBIA

● **"Forty Years of Democratic Progress."** When the left-wing political leader Jorge Eliécer Gaitán was assassinated in Bogotá on April 9, 1948, Colombians and the world generally could hardly believe what they read in the newspapers. The fact that the Ninth Inter-American Conference was in session there, with General Marshall leading the U.S. delegation, meant that the story of the nation-wide outbreak of rioting and looting was carried to the world in all its dreadful detail. Destruction and looting became widespread, particularly in the heart of Bogotá where howling mobs broke into liquor and hardware stores and raced through the streets armed with dynamite, machetes, torches, and gasoline. Immense physical damage was wrought and some 1,200 persons were killed. Severe damage was done both to the social fabric of the nation and to the widely held idea that Colombia represented Latin American democracy at its best: a cultivated country that produced poets and philologists of distinction, whose National Library was a model, whose journalists were true men of letters, whose man on the street in Bogotá spoke the purest Castilian in the continent, perhaps better Spanish than his counterpart in Madrid. The Instituto Caro y Cuervo in Bogotá is, indeed, one of the most respected linguistic centers in the Spanish-speaking world, and Colombians' concern with language may be illustrated by the story, perhaps apocryphal, that the day of the attack on Pearl Harbor a leading Bogotá newspaper carried as a lead story: "How we ought to use the gerund." [1]

The immediate reaction in Colombia and elsewhere that the 1948 uprising was wholly the work of the Communists has given way slowly to the view that the party did indeed take advantage of a disturbed situation, but that basically the bloody events constituted a social upheaval, not a palace revolt in the time-honored Latin American pattern. It was belatedly recognized that during the previous so-called "forty years of democratic progress" popular democracy had, in fact, failed to materialize and was largely a myth, or at least it was confined to an oligarchy of wealth and Great Families, to an upper class described as "white, privileged, and competent." (*See Reading No. 5.*) When General Gustavo Rojas Pinilla seized power from the Conservative President Laureano Gómez in June, 1953, a further blow to Colombian pride was struck, for dictatorships in Colombia have been infrequent, unpopular, and brief. The General was toppled from power only after four years of rule. During those tumultuous years anti-Protestant activity intensified, and the country endured a kind of civil war. Gravest of all indications of the weakening of the ties of society in Colombia was the death after 1948 of an estimated 300,000 people in the undeclared guerrilla wars which flared up in some parts of the republic between the Liberals and Conservatives, with bandit elements taking their toll in the general uproar.

What was wrong with the nation? Inasmuch as Colombia has a highly-educated minority—Bogotá has been called the "Athens of South America" —much attention has been given during recent years to answering this question. In trying to understand the desperate times Colombia has experienced, many writers and foreign observers have emphasized her difficult geography, her one-crop economy, the individualism of Colombians, and the gulf between the powerful, educated minority and the mass of the poor. They also suggest that historians have drawn a false picture of Colombia, that they have seen mostly the visible America and not the invisible masses so graphically described by Germán Arciniegas, one of Colombia's most brilliant writers.[2]

● **Geography, Crops, and Transportation.**   Even in a continent famous for its physical contrasts, Colombia is unique. Its rugged, broken topography has an extraordinary diversity of climates, vegetation, and agricultural crops. Here in juxtaposition are desert wastes, rain forests, temperate valleys, wind-swept barren plains, and snowy peaks. The Chocó area in northwest Colombia, through which the Pan American highway will join with the Panama stretch, consists of thousands of square miles of nearly impenetrable jungle. This unknown land is reported to have 100 mountains more than 8,000 feet high. Down their slopes run some 200 torrential rivers that rise and drop 5 or 6 feet in a few hours, night after night. In eastern Colombia the warm and wet piedmont plains stretch unbroken toward the Orinoco and Amazon rivers. One of Colombia's best-known novels, *La Vorágine* by José Eustacio Rivera, is laid in this Amazonian region. These lowlands occupy more than two-thirds of Colombia's 440,000 square miles but contain less than 2 per cent of its 17 million people.

The Andean highland zone is the Colombia that counts, the Colombia where 6 million bags of coffee are grown annually to account for one-fifth of the world's coffee production and 80 per cent of Colombia's foreign revenue, the Colombia of hillside farms, of oil and orchids, of textile mills and cities. Here live 78 per cent of the country's population, and here are the three largest cities—Bogotá (elevation 8,700 feet), Medellín (5,100 feet), and Cali (3,300 feet).

With the opening of the railroad from the Magdalena River to Medellín in the 1880's, the volcanic slopes of Antioquia began to produce for world markets the famous mild Colombian coffee. The proud and frugal "Antioqueños," with their aggressive colonizing genius and high birth rate—families of 15 and 20 are not uncommon even today in upper class as well as poor families—have been the most important single force behind the economic growth and development of the country since 1900. Their family-size farms produce more than three-fourths of Colombia's coffee crop. Medellín is today a bustling city of over half a million people; many of the largest banks, industries, especially textiles, and transportation companies are located there and many a modern capitalist started penniless there. The Antioqueños through initiative and hard work have produced a relatively democratic society based upon industry and upon many small landholdings. The Antioqueños have become such a powerful force in Colombian life, especially since many have migrated and have become leading citizens of such provinces as Caldas and Tolima, that one U.S. economist has concluded that their strength lies not in the economic advantages they enjoy—a larger market, greater access to technical knowledge, greater capital—but in their entrepreneurial spirit: "they may be thought of as a different breed of men." [3]

Another important region is the Cauca valley, in southwestern Colombia, an extraordinarily attractive area which once held great cattle and sugar estates but is gradually diversifying its agriculture as the floods that plague it are brought under control. The ambitious Cauca Valley Development project, a 20-year plan modeled on TVA, includes power, flood control, irrigation, reclamation, reforestation, and mineral and industrial development.

Colombian transport was mainly limited to river navigation for more than three centuries following the Spanish conquest. The lower Magdalena, navigable for 615 miles from its mouth on the Caribbean to the rapids at La Dorada, had been the lifeline linking the interior with the coast and the outside world. From various river ports, railroads, aerial cables, and truck roads have been built to the principal highland centers. The trip from the coast to Bogotá still requires five to seven days on a river boat, depending on the season, and another day by rail or road. This situation has been greatly improved now that the new railroad running from Santa Marta on the Caribbean along the Magdalena River to La Dorada has been completed, though it is still under-utilized. The new Paz del Río blast furnace and steel mill (capacity 122,000 tons) dramatically illustrate Colombia's basic transportation problem. Built in isolated highlands at an elevation of almost 9,000 feet, 150 miles north of Bogotá and even farther from other large consuming centers, it is ideally located for raw materials, since iron ore, coal, and limestone are in ample supply nearby. But Paz del Río steel delivered in Colombia is sometimes more costly than imported steel because of transportation and

COFFEE-BEAN GATHERERS

manufacturing costs. Only a high protective tariff, at the expense of the Colombian consumer, can make the project "economic." Yet it has a symbolic role in Colombia, eager to demonstrate its maturity by industrialization. "For those who believe that a national steel industry is justifiable at any price, Paz del Río is indeed a new El Dorado; for others, perhaps, the ailing steel mill . . . is a grotesque and costly monument to misguided nationalism." [4]

Colombia was the first country in the Americas to establish a regular air service when SCADTA was inaugurated in 1919 with German pilots and capital. It quickly expanded its service throughout the country and to adjacent countries. In 1940 it merged with a Pan-American Airways subsidiary to form AVIANCA which held a monopoly until the end of the war when numerous competitive companies began to flourish. Much cargo that would move by land in other countries goes by air in Colombia; ironically her superior air service has delayed the development of an adequate overland transport system. The 30 minute jet flight between Bogotá and Medellín costs little more than the 24-hour truck trip over a tortuous mountain road.

Air service meant political as well as economic changes. Provincial barriers crumbled, or seemed to, the press found a national audience, and for the first time political and social integration appeared possible.

● **The Colombian People.** The conquistadores virtually annihilated the warlike Indians along the Caribbean coast, and found it necessary to import slaves from Senegal and the Congo in the seventeenth and eighteenth centuries. Cartagena became a Negro center, made noteworthy by the Jesuit Alonso de Sandoval's advocacy of Christian treatment for the Negro slaves and for his proposal, about 1630, that a School of African Studies be set up to forward the work of the missionaries. One of his disciples was another Jesuit, Pedro Claver, Colombia's only saint. Today the descendants of the slaves, a small percentage of the population, are concentrated in the hot coastal areas. About half the population of Colombia have mixed Indian-Spanish blood, about one-quarter are white, and the balance are mulattoes. In attempting to characterize the Colombians, most observers, native and foreign, emphasize the strong influence of the wide geographical differences already described. Psychological traits have developed in the various regions: "The Antioqueño is traditionalist, regionalist, conquering, intrepid, and neurotic. . . . The Narinense is sober, highly industrious and hospitable, passionate in his religious and political beliefs, obstinate to excess. . . . The Costeño is expansive, conceited, and vehement." [5]

The temper of the politically conscious minority has been described as "anarchistic," deriving from its Hispanic inheritance, and "every Colombian is a political party." Simón Bolívar, the revolutionary hero of Colombia, declared: "To form a stable government, one must have as a national base a general spirit whose object is to incline everyone uniformly toward two

points: moderation of the general will, and limitation of public authority."
It is doubtful that such a spirit has ever existed in Colombia to any great
extent.

Luis López de Mesa, one of Colombia's brilliant intellects, developed the
idea that Colombia represented the true synthesis of all Latin America. This
dream was rudely interrupted by the turmoil and trouble of Colombia's postwar years.

● **"The Salutary Change."** For almost a century after Bogotá banished the
Viceroy and proclaimed the Act of Independence in 1813, Colombia suffered
a long period of intermittent anarchy. She experienced ten revolutions of national scope, some seventy more limited uprisings, and in 1899–1902 a bloody
civil conflict called "The War of the Thousand Days," in which the country's
economy was gravely damaged and some 100,000 men are said to have died.

The twentieth century brought spectacular changes beginning with the loss
of Panama in 1903, which embittered Colombian-U.S. relations for a generation. The Conservative Party assumed control of the country and kept it
until 1930. Meanwhile, World War I brought the impact of at least temporary new markets and, following the Russian Revolution of 1917, the old
social order was disturbed by the spread of proletarian doctrines which in
turn led to the growth of labor unionism. Foreign money poured into Colombia during the 1920's. The $25,000,000 of U.S. "conscience money" paid
to heal the breach over Panama was devoted to the building of ports, highways, and railroads. Foreign oil companies invested some $45,000,000. A
veritable tidal wave of $200,000,000 was loaned by U.S. bankers to the Co-
lombian government, departments, and municipalities for an expansion of
coffee production, development of textile industries, and other improvements.
Corruption and inflation came in its wake.

When the worldwide depression of 1929 reached Colombia in the form
of low coffee prices, the Conservatives were discredited and their split made
it possible for the Liberals to come into office peacefully after half a century
of Conservative domination. Alfonso López, a wealthy patrician, served as
Liberal President 1934–1938, and worked for a reform program that included land laws, improvement of the status and conditions of workers,
recognition that public assistance is a function of the state, and a firmly
imposed progressive tax on income and utilities. For the first time in Colombian history, government income no longer depended primarily on customs
revenues, and a potent source of political graft was thereby eliminated.

The moderate wing of the Liberals installed Eduardo Santos as President
1938–1942, and the reform movement began to slacken. Santos owned and
edited *El Tiempo,* one of the outstanding newspapers in the Americas, and
gave his strong support to the United States in World War II. When López
re-won the presidency 1942–1946, he carried on Santos' policy of support

for the allies. He was charged with a "no reform" attitude. It is true that his ministers were often millionaires and that the war years brought charges of corruption and even unsavory scandals touching the President's own family. After a series of unpleasant incidents, one of which was his own capture for several days by army elements in a provincial capital, López stepped down in August 1945, and Alberto Lleras Camargo was brought back from the Colombian Embassy in Washington with bipartisan support to serve out the last year of the presidential term.

The Conservatives regained power in 1946, when the veteran Conservative Laureano Gómez selected Mariano Ospina Pérez as his party's candidate, and won against a divided Liberal Party which had put up two candidates, one of whom, Jorge Eliécer Gaitán, stood for reforms for the benefit of the common people.

Colombia went steadily downhill under President Ospina. Inflation increased rapidly under the abnormal economic situation in the wake of the war, black marketeering became standard practice, and the cost of living for the masses rose sharply but not their income. The murder of Gaitán in 1948 sparked off an orgy of rioting that expressed an unstable political and social situation of long standing. When Laureano Gómez returned from Spain in 1948 to run for president, the gulf between the two parties became impassable. He won the election by a vote of 1,140,619 against 15, the Liberals abstaining from the polls. Some well-to-do Liberals welcomed his victory, for they were tired of instability and felt that a strong man like Gómez might be a salutary change.

● **Background for the Dictatorship of General Gustavo Rojas Pinilla.** Gómez as President surprised the country by appointing "technicians" to cabinets and other administrative levels; his regime was the beneficiary of higher coffee prices and freedom from wartime economic controls. Exports almost doubled during 1949–1953, labor organization was discouraged, and the index of living rose steeply. As he began to rule personally and autocratically, opposition began to form; even some members of his Conservative Party declared against his authoritarian rule. Gómez sent Colombian troops to Korea in cooperation with the United Nations, an action that was viewed as an attempted diversion from national troubles and as a way of transferring army control from the Liberals to the Conservatives. Liberals were considered "bandits" and hunted down mercilessly; two Liberal newspapers were burned and the rest controlled. Many of Gómez' followers were alienated by his proposed constitutional changes which would give the Catholic Church greater political and temporal power and set up a corporate fascist-like system of government. The army at last stepped in on June 15, 1953, Gómez fled, and General Rojas Pinilla's bloodless coup was hailed by a weary country close to exhaustion after years of uncertainty and violence. His popularity faded when he restored press censorship, incurred the enmity of the Church, and attempted to create a third party that would replace Conservative and Liberals.

His four-year rule did not pacify Colombia; he found he could accomplish little of the social reform he promised. Guerrilla warfare over political differences continued throughout the land along with plain banditry; in addition, the dictator and high Catholic officials charged that Protestants were Communists or Communist fronts. The countryside was kept in an uproar by the religious, political, and economic hostilities that divided the nation. With both parties united against him, Rojas Pinilla intensified the state of siege he had declared on coming to power. In desperation the Conservatives and Liberals joined hands to force him into exile on May 10, 1957. In 1959 he returned voluntarily to stand trial in Bogotá before the Senate; one of the charges was that he and his wife had illegally enriched themselves by millions of dollars; he was found guilty, by an overwhelming vote, of violating the constitution and of injuring the dignity of the presidency.

Rojas Pinilla's place in Colombian history will long be debated. He set in motion some economic projects recommended by the Currie Mission sent by the International Bank, inaugurated the Paz del Río steel mill, and pushed the Cauca Valley "TVA" project. Probably no government could have achieved much in a country so deeply disturbed; both parties were internally divided. One writer described the situation in these terms:

> the vast majority of the voters are either illiterate or totally un-educated, and the social system itself is unstable; the masses are subject to emotional, impractical, and self-interested propaganda, and now that they have learned their strength and tasted blood, it is going to be a hard task for any government to correct and control the political errors and exaggerations of the last thirty years.[6]

● **Bipartisan Government.** Two ex-presidents, the Conservative Laureano Gómez and the Liberal Alberto Lleras Camargo, meeting in the Spanish seaport Sitges, issued on July 20, 1957, a unique and notable agreement which aimed to bring political peace to their nation by proposing a bipartisan government for a period of twelve years. This historic moment brought together two of the most powerful and diverse figures in Colombian political annals.

Gómez, trained as an engineer, had early embarked on a political career in Congress where his invective and polemical power were given free rein. In 1938, for example, he denounced mild and scholarly President Santos as a "murderer . . . who sits in pools of Conservative blood." In the 1948–1953 era he tried to force on Colombia a dictatorship modeled after that of Franco in Spain, whom he admired. A demagogue with fascist tendencies, he believed that the Catholic Church must be, after government, the main force in society.

Lleras Camargo entered journalism as a youth and by his middle-twenties had achieved distinction as a writer; he was a Cabinet Minister at 29, Ambassador to Washington at 37, in 1945–1946 served as President when López left, and from 1948 to 1952 was the first Latin American to hold the office of Secretary General of the Organization of American States. He is not a Strong Man, but a wise one who since 1945 has believed that "National Union," a coalition of the two parties, is the only way to save Colombia. It was a traditional solution; for a century members of both parties had joined forces at times of special danger. The joint "Declaration of Benidorm" of these two men had in 1956 paved the way for a successful attack on Dictator Rojas Pinilla; the Pact of Sitges was a natural step in 1957.[7] The agreement made there to put the Congress, Cabinet, and Presidency under bipartisan auspices for twelve years was ratified in Colombia, later extended to a sixteen-year period, and led to the election of Lleras Camargo and his inauguration as President in August, 1958.

The National Front managed to survive throughout the full term of Liberal Lleras Camargo, and Conservative Guillermo León Valencia was peacefully elected to succeed him in 1962. The new president promised a vast program of social reforms to favor the lower-income workers, and insisted that the guerrilla warfare end. But political and economic conditions deteriorated steadily and by the summer of 1965 Valencia was a lonely man in the eighteenth-century palace in the heart of downtown Bogotá. Prices were up, he was in trouble with the Church, many of his decisions were judged erratic, la violencia had not been entirely conquered, and a new wave of kidnapping included the death of one of Colombia's best-known industrialists and former cabinet ministers, Harold Eder. Congress refused to pass Valencia's most cherished economic proposals, and the country generally was so bored with the bipartisan pact that only 2,200,000 voted in the Congressional elections of 1964 while twice that number abstained. The only success was General Rojas Pinilla, whose party made a considerable gain although he had been judicially deprived of his political rights after his overthrow in 1957. Will the truce endure? The National Front candidate, Carlos Lleras Restrepo, managed to win the presidential election in May, 1966, but opposition in Congress will probably continue to block badly needed economic and fiscal reforms. And even if Congress does take some action, will the country be peaceful enough for the government to carry out the fundamental economic and social reforms so urgently required?

● **"The Most Urgent Need of Colombia."** Lleras Camargo, a liberal, who twice risked the future of his party and his own political fortunes by joining with the controversial Conservative Gómez, appears to understand the gravity of the situation. He wrote in 1955:

The most urgent necessity of Colombia is that of preparing a numerous group of people with the capacity to manage and resolve the elemental problems of a collective type of life which is spreading over the planet with tremendous rapidity. This type of life is the consequence of the great industrial revolution which enlarged and made more dangerous the distance between the rich and the poor people . . . The new problems are . . . more general, because they concern human beings; masses, with a very definite consciousness of their rights.[8]

This "collective type of life" implies a change of outlook for the upper classes of Colombia and for the small middle class group which has usually sided with them. As the French Dominican Louis Lebret stated in a report made to the dictator Rojas Pinilla, but suppressed by him: "The primary Colombian problem is a social one, of irrational political quarrels in the face of realities obscured by poor statistics. There is a lack of directive courage capable of furnishing scientific leadership to the country. The leaders are not aware of Colombian social realities within the world scene, and consider any national progress in terms of an increase in their personal fortunes. The standard of living of the middle and working classes has declined, while financial inflation continues, and popular education is devoid of practical meaning and efficacy. The difference between the standard of living of the wealthy (5%) and that of the other economic classes in Colombia is greater than in more highly developed countries." [9] Lebret recommended various agricultural and other policies to avert the ruin that he predicted unless drastic reforms were made.

Light on Colombia's urgent needs has also been shed by Orlando Fals-Borda, one of the few Colombian sociologists who has analyzed social facts and problems by direct observation and measurement of social phenomena in the field, instead of relying on theoretical statements. His study of a small rural community near Bogotá combines statistical facts and generalizations of remarkable insight.[10] He concludes that the

rural people of Colombia are being swept into the whirl of social revolution that promises to be the distinguishing feature of our century. . . . As yet no clear-cut crisis has arisen in Colombian rural areas as a result of this historical transition, but there is unrest. This is not the same political unrest that attracted the attention of the world to Colombia during the last five years. It is, rather, an unprecedented feeling of dissatisfaction penetrating the masses of Colombia's farmers and laborers; it is an awakening due to an increasing class consciousness.[11]

This Colombian sociologist and government official knows the depth of poverty in the country, that the number of illiterates actually increased from 3.25 to 4 million during the period 1937 to 1947, and that the majority of the people live in houses of adobe or bamboo with earthen floors and straw-thatched roofs, and lack a water supply and sewage system. Do those who make the ultimate political decisions understand the implications of these facts? The Pact of Sitges was a political document without reference to economic or social affairs. If the peace sought by Gómez and Lleras Camargo at Sitges results merely in the union of what have been described as "the two conservative parties," the future of Colombia may be as stormy as her past fifteen years.

Some Colombians have been aware of the problems and the stakes for many years.[12] An enterprising publishing house, Ediciones Tercer Mundo, has started to publish stimulating social science studies including a sociological analysis of *la violencia*.[13] And some Colombians are proclaiming that their own efforts, rather than indefinite U.S. aid, should be the decisive factor.[14]

But the obstacles are formidable. The peasants in the many small communities are stirred by new thoughts, new desires. (*See Reading No. 51.*) The national party system, according to one observer, resembles:

> a voracious jungle in which concession is taken as a sign of weakness. . . . To the Liberal, the Conservative is a Renaissance-minded reactionary, bent upon retaining power and establishing an elitist rule in defiance of the people's needs, supported by the spiritual monopoly of Catholicism. His own party he considers alive, progressive, selfless, and bountifully endowed with wisdom. On the other hand, a Conservative views his opponent as anarchical, demagogic, atheistically anticlerical, and federalist to the point of state disintegration. Liberals are suspiciously close to communism, while Liberal policy would establish a slavery of conscience, destroying national principles and public morality through suppression of the clergy.[15]

Other observers are not so certain that the two parties differ on anything, except in attitudes toward the Church, and hold that the "National Front" has brought no grand new national visions but only apathy.[16] There are mysteries here, just as there are in efforts to explain *la violencia*. As one Colombian states: "it is difficult to understand the widespread and senseless violence . . . What element in Colombian national character and social structure fostered 'the violence'?" [17]

Evidence that new forces are at work in Colombian society may be seen in the activities of a few young priests who followed the doctrines of Pope John XXIII. Cardinal Luis Concha Córdoba and most of the hierarchy consider these ideas radical—the Cardinal condemned the bill introduced in Congress which would permit married women to hold property, and rebuked the woman deputy responsible—and have tried to silence the young priests. One of them, Camilo Torres, who came from an oligarchical family, was defrocked. Subsequently, he joined a guerrilla group and was killed in early 1966 by government troops while fighting in the mountains.

The rebellion among the young priests will probably run into strong opposition for some time, since the Church remains powerful in Colombia, but the fact that some priests there advocate divorce, birth control, and the wearing of trousers by the clergy instead of cassocks clearly shows that even the strongest institution in the country is beginning to feel the winds of change.

One of the most acute and intractable problems is the dramatically rising population. "Colombian culture puts a high premium on large families, a source of pride and a social asset, and only slow change in public attitudes can be hoped for at best." [18] Thus, "Colombia faces a future heavily charged with 'ifs.' The most important of these is if the National Front can hold together . . . The forces of a peaceful democratic order are weak . . . The question remains whether the bursting, shifting population of Colombia, now awakened after centuries of slumber, can continue on this slow and difficult road—or whether new violence lies in ambush around the next bend." [19]

[1] José Gutiérrez, *De la pseudo-aristocracia a la autenticidad: psicología social colombiana* (Mexico, 1961), p. 119.

[2] Arciniegas, *The State of Latin America* (New York: Knopf, 1952), pp. 386–392.

[3] Everett E. Hagen, *On the Theory of Social Change* (New York: Dorsey Press, 1962), p. 368.

[4] C. Langdon White and Donald J. Alderson, "Steel and Symbolism at Paz del Río," *Inter-American Economic Affairs*, IX (Spring, 1956), pp. 92–94.

[5] Juvenal Mejía Córdoba, as quoted by W. O. Galbraith, *Colombia. A General Survey* (London: Royal Institute of International Affairs, 1953), p. 23.

[6] Galbraith, *Colombia*, p. 135.

[7] Pat M. Holt, *Colombia Today—And Tomorrow* (New York: Praeger, 1964), pp. 55–56.

[8] As quoted by Vernon Lee Fluharty, *Dance of the Millions* (Pittsburgh: University of Pittsburgh Press, 1957), pp. 149–150.

[9] As given by *Hispanic American Report*, X (Stanford University, 1957), pp. 479–480.

[10] *Peasant Society in the Colombian Andes. A Sociological Study of Saucío* (Gainesville: University of Florida Press), p. 195.

[11] *Ibid.*, p. vii.

[12] Eduardo Caballero Calderón, *Cartas colombianas. Primera serie* (Bogatá: Kelly, 1950); Gonzalo Restrepo Jaramillo, "El absurdo político colombiano," *Universidad Pontificia Bolivariana*, XXV (1962), No. 90, pp. 195–212.

[13] Germán Guzmán Campos, Orlando Fals-Borda, and Eduardo Umaña Luna, *La violencia en Colombia*, 2 vols. (Bogotá: Ediciones Tercer Mundo, 1962–1964).

[14] Belisario Betancur, "Reflexiones sobre la sociedad colombiana," *Universidad Pontificia Bolivariana*, XXV (1962), No. 90, pp. 260, 275.

[15] John D. Martz, *Colombia. A Contemporary Political Survey* (Chapel Hill: University of North Carolina Press, 1962), p. 19.

[16] Personal communication to the author.

[17] *Caribbean Studies*, IV (1964), p. 64.

[18] Holt, *Colombia*, p. 194.

[19] *Ibid.*, pp. 195–197.

5
VENEZUELA

AREA: 347,029 sq. mi.

POPULATION IN MID-1966: 9,030,000

LARGEST CITIES:

Caracas (capital): 1,589,411
(metropolitan area, est. 1964)

Maracaibo: 502,693 (est. 1964)

PRINCIPAL EXPORTS (1961): petroleum,
iron ore, coffee

PRESIDENT: Raúl Leoni, civilian,
took office March 11, 1964,
for a 5-year term.

VENEZUELA

- **Bolívar, Dictators, and Oil.** When Rómulo Betancourt became President of Venezuela on February 12, 1959, he assumed the leadership of a country whose history has been linked to that of her neighbor Colombia by the Liberator Simón Bolívar, who freed both nations from Spain during the tumultuous revolutionary period 1810–1830. Otherwise the countries have little in common and relatively little to do with each other in spite of their physical proximity. Venezuela's nine million people are largely mestizos and thus much more homogeneous than Colombia's population, and Venezuela has no Church-State problem. After 1860 a strong anti-clerical movement reduced the privileges of the Church step by step; its financial independence was destroyed, its social leadership abolished, and in the end it became a relatively unimportant force in public and social life. Politically the Church has recently played a larger role, and participated in the overthrow of the Rómulo Gallegos government in 1948 and of the Pérez Jiménez regime in 1958.

Venezuela furnished many of the soldiers who followed Bolívar on his triumphant sweep through the lands now comprising Colombia, Ecuador, Peru, and even as far south as the mining center Potosí in Bolivia. On the summit of this mountain over 15,000 feet above sea level with the flags of the newly liberated nations fluttering in the breeze, the Liberator declaimed in 1825:

> We come victorious from the Atlantic coast. In fifteen years of continuous and terrific strife, we have destroyed the edifice that tyranny erected during three centuries of usurpation and uninterrupted violence . . . Standing here on this silver mountain of Potosí, whose rich veins were Spain's treasury for three hundred years, I must declare my belief that this material wealth is as nothing compared with the glory of bearing the ensign of freedom from the shores of the Orinoco to plant it on the summit of a mountain which is the admiration and envy of the world.[1]

This tradition of glory Bolívar bequeathed to his native land, Venezuela, which is still moved by the memory of the Liberator. A law still on the books, and still enforced, makes it a misdemeanor for any man to walk in front of the statue of Bolívar in the Plaza de Bolívar in Caracas if he is carrying a parcel or not wearing a coat.

One result of the revolution was heavy loss of life and property, for in Venezuela Spaniards and revolutionists fought the "Wars to the Death." One-quarter of the population, including a large proportion of the young men, is estimated to have died in battle, by disease, or in civil tumult. The economic confusion following independence and the political inexperience of her people help to explain the succeeding anarchy and despotism. Venezuela became notorious for her dictators in a continent where they flourished, and the purple prose used to flatter them became famous.

- **"Democratic Caesarism."** Venezuelan dictators were impressive in their variety. José Antonio Páez, the cowboy revolutionary leader who opposed Bolívar's grandiose schemes outside of Venezuela, served as a conservative dictator (1830–1846, 1861–1863); while in exile in New York City he wrote his memoirs. Antonio Guzmán Blanco, an educated gentleman familiar with European capitals, was a strong foe of the Church, and most famous for the centralized corruption during his eighteen-year rule (1870–1888). His vanity was colossal: he insisted upon being referred to as "Illustrious American" or "National Regenerator" and with even more bombastic titles. He loved music, built an imposing opera house in Caracas, and during his last years became a sybaritic waster in Paris. But his positive achievements, such as building the National Congress edifice in ninety days, are remembered today by a Venezuela which respects him as one of the few leaders who left something of value to the country.

Cipriano Castro (1899–1908), the most dissolute and one of the most corrupt, provoked a blockade by European naval units in 1902. Juan Vicente Gómez, Castro's trusted lieutenant who succeeded him in 1908, proved one of the most savage of all. A hard-working abstemious dictator, he stayed in Venezuela attending to his business, which made him the richest man in South America, since his hand dipped into almost every economic enterprise in Venezuela, particularly oil. He suffered from the disease that afflicts most dictators, the lust after decorations and titles; he even insisted that the Pope devise a new decoration for him.

Gómez maintained good relations with foreign powers, improved sanitation, and even built a few schools. His rule was called "Democratic Caesarism" by the intellectuals who largely accepted it as the only way to avoid chaos and anarchy. José Gil Fortoul, one of Venezuela's outstanding historians, saw no contradiction or betrayal of principles in serving the great dictator for many years as political advisor at home and as diplomat abroad.

In his eyes, only a "strong and good man" could give Venezuela what she needed most: peace, progress, and order. Gómez gave Venezuela peace, but the price was an army of spies and jails full of political prisoners, many of whom were severely tortured. When "The Well-Deserving" died in 1935, Venezuelans rioted in the streets and fired the homes of his numerous sons and henchmen. Mariano Picón Salas, the Venezuelan writer, once said that Venezuela did not enter the twentieth century until the death of this iron-fisted dictator. Yet, today there are some Venezuelans who feel that the public order and the beginnings of development he imposed have been underestimated.

● **Movement Toward Democracy, 1935–1959.** Venezuela's long experience of dictators did not prepare her for the problems of a less dictatorial government. General Eleazar López Contreras (1935–1940) headed a semi-dictatorial regime, but General Isaías Medina Angarita, who succeeded him in 1941, governed more moderately; he is hailed today because he clapped no political enemies into jail. He permitted opposition parties to exist, the largest of which was Acción Democrática (AD). The army seized control in October, 1945, with AD support. Led by Rómulo Betancourt, AD won the elections for a constituent assembly in 1946, and then elected the famous novelist Rómulo Gallegos as president in 1947. AD, made up of civilians, labor leaders, middle-class professionals and businessmen, incorporated the party's principles in a new constitution embodying social legislation which included the nation's right to expropriate oil properties and to elect the president by direct popular vote. Gallegos began his term of office in February, 1948, but served only nine months, for apparently the AD regime alarmed many important sectors of Venezuelan opinion by their advocacy of radical changes. When the army ousted Gallegos and Betancourt there was almost no reaction from the people, which some analysts have interpreted as an indication of AD's unpopularity at the time.

With the brief experiment in democracy ended, a military junta now exercised dictatorial power. AD went underground, the junta jailed opponents freely and used tear gas against demonstrating university students. The junta arranged for an election in November, 1952, but when unexpected opposition strength threatened, the dominant junta member, General Marcos Pérez Jiménez, simply announced that he had won by an overwhelming majority, and Venezuela was back again under a one-man dictatorship.

The Pérez Jiménez regime was a tough autocracy which insisted that the economic development of the nation was supreme, and that to bring traditional democracy would only precipitate chaos and interfere with the material progress of Venezuela. As the Interior Minister Dr. Laureano Vallenilla Lanz stated the case, in words reminiscent of "Democratic Caesarism": "It is absurd to attempt to build a democracy in a backward, uneducated nation." The AD leaders in exile accused the dictator of wasting the national wealth in spectacular but unproductive public works, and the Archbishop of Caracas, Msgr. Rafael Arias Blanco, on May 1, 1957, wrote in his pastoral letter that "nobody will dare affirm that wealth is distributed in a manner that reaches all the Venezuelans, since an immense mass of our people are living in conditions that cannot be designated as human."

An important fact of the social situation was, and continues to be, the instability of the Venezuelan home. "Marriage has never been a popular institution in Venezuela . . . In terms of cold statistics, 51.9 per cent of the children born in the country in 1949 were illegitimate; 7 per cent, though illegitimate, were recognized by their fathers, which presumably guaranteed some support; only 41.1 per cent, the products of legal marriages, would know the security of normal family relationship. What is more, some women —saddled with children they cannot feed—follow the example of the men. According to the Consejo del Niño, a branch of the Venezuelan Department of Justice, there are about 90,000 abandoned children in the country. That is roughly 2 per cent of Venezuela's total population." [2]

The Pérez Jiménez dictatorship remained in power through the support of the military establishment—whose clubs and other facilities made possible by oil revenues reached extraordinary heights of luxury—and through the control he exercised over the officers and others by the secret police. But all dictators fall at last. On January 23, 1958, dissident military units made possible the courageous and unanimous action by practically all elements of society in Venezuela. University students led the civil agitation, but labor unions, lawyers, people living in the miserable "ranchos" in the hills overlooking Caracas, and substantial businessmen also played active roles in the movement which overthrew Pérez Jiménez.

A great sense of freedom swept over the country, mixed with lively indignation against the United States which partially explains the rough treatment accorded Vice-President Nixon during his visit in 1958. Venezuelans had resented the friendly U.S. gestures made to Pérez Jiménez during the height of his oppressive rule, such as the medal bestowed on him, the gala reception in Washington for his dreaded police chief Pedro Estrada, the close personal relations between one U.S. ambassador and the dictator, and the fact that Pérez Jiménez was allowed to take up luxurious residence in Miami after the people had ejected him from Venezuela. After the Nixon incident, reports in U.S. newspapers and magazines that carried what Venezuelans considered greatly exaggerated estimates of communist influence in their country deepened Venezuelan displeasure and aroused a storm of anti-U.S. feeling. The charge was heard in Caracas—and was of course given currency by the communists themselves—that the United States was planning to inflate "the communist menace" in order to justify action in Venezuela as in the case of Guatemala.

The veteran AD leader Rómulo Betancourt won the presidential election in 1959, and on February 12 was inaugurated amid general rejoicing. He proved to be a resilient, determined, and democratic leader. Although the new government inherited a debt from the dictator of $1.5 billion, Venezuela's leading citizens shared President Betancourt's conviction, expressed in his declaration made in 1956 while in exile, that the Venezuelan people and the country are essentially sound. (*See Reading No. 52.*)

One of the most powerful reasons for Venezuelan optimism is the plenitude of oil, which deeply colors the country's economic and political life. No city in the Americas, with the possible exception of São Paulo in Brazil, has been so dramatically transformed during the last twenty-five years as Caracas. Once a delightful town with a certain colonial air, Caracas now has built a sort of Rockefeller Center downtown; four-lane super-highways are available for the many automobiles, which choke the older, narrow streets; luxurious hotels attract cosmopolitan guests, and life proceeds at a dizzy—and expensive—pace. Well-to-do Venezuelans find vacations in New York inexpensive, set up foundations for various purposes, and have supplanted Argentines as free-spenders abroad. All this has resulted from oil, whose power now rivals that of the earlier dictators.

● **The New Dictator: Oil.** Venezuelans have always been primarily farmers, and three-quarters of the population still live on the land. Most farmers wring a precarious living out of the steep slopes of the Andes on which in other countries farming would not be attempted. Until a generation ago, there was a mountainward movement due to political unrest on the plains and the prevalence there of malaria and the virulent fever known as *la económica* because it killed its victims so rapidly that there was no time to call a doctor. Cultivation methods are often primitive and wasteful, which helps to explain the yield of only two bushels of corn to the acre, as compared with 40 bushels in the United States. The average Venezuelan, therefore, is accustomed to austerity; his food intake has been estimated at about one quarter of that required by a European immigrant.

Some good agricultural lands are found in the Maracaibo lowlands, but the rest of Venezuela is disappointing to the farmer. The southernmost region, the Guayana Hinterland, is relatively inaccessible, little exploited, and in parts unexplored. The sandstone mountains, which inspired Sir Arthur Conan Doyle to write *The Lost World,* still await ornithologists, botanists, and other scientists to unravel their mysteries. Gold and diamonds are found in this vast region, but the greatest potential is in the rich iron deposits on its northern edge.

North of Guayana are the thinly settled plains (*llanos*) or grasslands which produced General Páez and his cowboy fighters who helped Bolívar win Venezuela's independence. The *llanos,* so well described by Rómulo Gallegos in *Doña Bárbara,* Venezuela's most famous novel, are subject to serious floods in the rainy season, and under the hot sun of the dry season their clay soils become hardpan. It was on or near these plains that T. S. Stribling located the story of that literary but credible dictator *Fombombo* (1923). Agriculture is being developed in Venezuela, but the solemn and limiting fact is that much of the land is difficult to cultivate or poor—hence, the spectacular importance of oil in Venezuela's economy—and no Venezuelan government has given agricultural development the attention it deserves because oil revenue is so much easier to obtain.

When the Spaniards arrived at Maracaibo in 1499 they found the Indians using oil for medicine and other purposes, but it was never commercially significant until the twentieth century. The nineteenth century, however, saw important laws passed on oil extraction. Subsoil deposits were made the property of the nation, not the surface owner, and the authority to grant oil leases was exclusively reserved for the President. As the world began to use oil, British, Dutch, and American companies moved into Venezuela, but the industry lagged until 1919. Dictator Gómez encouraged exploration by the 1922 basic oil law which has been called a "liberal, clear, simple, workable statute," though royalties of only 7.5 to 10 per cent were paid.[3] Gómez, however, had a bag of tricks which enabled him personally to secure additional profits. The years 1923–1929 were boom years when Venezuela rose from an insignificant producer to become second only to the United States among the world's petroleum producing nations. In Maracaibo, the hottest city in South America and the center of the nation's oil industry, living costs doubled and real-estate values tripled. By 1930 Gómez had completed paying off the entire foreign debt with oil revenues. When he died in 1935, "an economic dictator had already inherited Venezuela . . . the petroleum industry was the new ruler. The new tyrant was immortal, and political upheavals disturbed it little. It answered only to the demands of the market in the United States and in western Europe and waited for the signals to be called from abroad." [4]

● **Petroleum: Blessing or Curse?** At the death of Gómez, Venezuelans began to debate whether petroleum was a blessing or a curse to the country, and this argument continues. Those who take the affirmative side stress that the great oil development costs the government nothing, for the foreign companies built roads, mapped large areas, paid Venezuelans high wages, and improved their living conditions generally. They emphasize that taxes provide the chief source of revenue for the government.

The critics assert that the large profits made by the foreign companies have an unsettling effect on the nation's economy, that oil helped to keep corrupt dictators in power and hindered a real attack on such problems as education, health, and agriculture. Oil provides a slippery base for a nation's economy, they conclude, and insist that Venezuela is now dangerously dependent on a single foreign-owned industry which fluctuates violently due to the uncertain demands of a capricious world market.

One result of this debate was that, after Gómez, both military dictators and popularly elected presidents have energetically and persistently worked to increase Venezuela's share in oil profits. General Medina's basic 1943 law unified petroleum legislation and increased the government's share. The AD government upped this to 50 per cent of the profits—a revolutionary concept when it was written into this law. The Provisional Government of 1958 raised the percentage still higher, and since then the oil companies claim that about 70 per cent of the profit from oil goes to Venezuela.

What the post-Gómez governments have done with these profits is a much disputed story. Each successive government has proclaimed the policy of "sowing the petroleum," of ploughing the oil profits back into the soil of the nation in the form of roads, hospitals, and other public works. Roads have indeed been built, but ultramodern expressways pass through towns that have as yet no water, sewers, telephones, or medical facilities. A splendid new University of Caracas, an Officers' Club that offers the last word in comfort and elegance, a University hospital with more than 1,100 beds, and low-cost family housing are also products of this policy. More than half of the government funds for public works have been spent in or near the capital, Caracas. The most neglected area in the country probably is the State of Zulia, from which 75 per cent of the oil comes. One foreign observer has concluded that up to 1954 the policy had failed to benefit the country as a whole and that responsibility for this rested largely upon the army.

The debate on the proper place of oil in the nation's economy goes on, but Venezuela remains the world's third producer of oil and the largest exporter of crude and refined oil products, despite the fact that only 3 per cent of the labor force of Venezuela extracts the petroleum which accounts for over 90 per cent of Venezuela's foreign income and provides 63 per cent of her government revenues. The size of this "economic tyrant" may be seen from the fact that a single American company, Creole, has produced in Venezuela in recent years approximately half as much oil as the U.S.S.R., but this great industry may be challenged in the future when the huge iron deposits south of the Orinoco River are fully exploited. Bethlehem Steel started operations in 1951; United States Steel, which discovered a mountain, Cerro Bolívar, containing an estimated half billion tons of high-grade ore, invested $50 million in a railroad and other facilities, and began to mine ore in 1954. Meanwhile, oil still rules the economy of the nation: in 1963 taxes on iron ore produced about $20 million, while oil yielded $1,164,000,000.

- **Betancourt's Presidency, 1960–1964.** Betancourt succeeded in holding together a coalition government, started a much-needed land reform, won the backing of the World Bank for a long-term plan of economic and social improvements, and both held the military in line and maintained the majority of the people behind his government. He worked actively against both Trujillo and Castro, whose intervention in Venezuela through support for the guerrillas led to OAS sanctions against Cuba. To do all this, Betancourt needed all the courage, persistence, and political wisdom he had exhibited since he began his career as a student opponent of Dictator Gómez. He was imprisoned, then went into exile, and while in Costa Rica joined the communists for a short time in 1930, an experience he has described as a youthful infection that gave him permanent immunity. He was a founder of the AD party in 1941, which eventually led to the growth of other political parties with profound effect upon the course of Venezuelan history: "It is hard to envision the social, economic, and political transformation of the last five years outside the realm of a modern political party system." [5] This development has made possible the growth of legislative power, the weakening of the all-powerful executive, and the achievements of Betancourt.

Fidel Castro's seizure of power significantly affected Venezuela, as the leader of the Social Christian Party (Copei) has stated. Europe and the U.S. now began to consider Latin-American problems more seriously, and Latin Americans began to think more deeply about their future,[6] especially when the FALN (Armed Forces of National Liberation) was formed in late 1962 to coordinate terrorist activity against the government. Led by young and adventurous men and some women, inspired by Castro's Sierra Maestra insurrection and often Cuban-trained, it carried out various guerrilla activities: the murder of police and national guardsmen, the sabotage and bombing of U.S. companies, the U.S. Embassy, and Venezuelan government installations. (*See Reading No. 53.*) This urban terror was supplemented by a rural guerrilla movement of perhaps a thousand men. The FALN did not topple the government, but kept Betancourt so busy simply staying in power that it greatly hindered his own revolutionary program. The political tension also created a difficult atmosphere in which free speech existed somewhat precariously. (*See Reading No. 54.*)

One of the prime objectives of the FALN was to prevent the peaceful transference of presidential power, but it failed. Raúl Leoni, long time political associate of Betancourt, but not his choice for the presidency, won the free election of December 1, 1963, when a large majority of the people went to the polls. When Leoni was inaugurated without incident in March 1964, Betancourt was the first democratically elected president to have completed his term of office.[7]

● **Leoni's Government.** The new president was not as well-known as his predecessor; he was judged to be not as brilliant, and AD no longer enjoyed the cooperation of Copei, now the second largest party. But he has worked quietly to carry on the reforms sponsored by his party, has included two other political parties in his coalition (URD and FND), and has achieved a political consensus in the country which has surprised his critics and the doubters. This consensus was essential to Leoni's government because the AD party has steadily lost support; from 70 per cent of the electorate in 1948, it has fallen to some 30 per cent. Hence, the combination with other parties to form a somewhat shaky coalition. The Christian Democrats bide their time and have high hopes for a victory at the next election.

The Venezuelan economy continues to climb. Industrial production was up 8.7 per cent in 1963 and 15 per cent in 1964, and almost half the 1965 budget of $1.6 billion was allotted to schools, housing, industries, and major public works. The government owns airlines, luxury hotels, an oil company, a petro-chemical plant, a radio-television network, telephone and telegraph companies, a merchant marine fleet, and iron and steel plants. Venezuela's foreign reserves and the value of its international commerce are the highest of any Latin-American country. Her reserve of gold and foreign currency in 1964 was, in fact, higher than that of the U.S., and Venezuela took satisfaction in making an advance payment to the U.S. "to help the U.S. reduce its deficit in the international balance of payments."

But the guerrilla raids continue, students and intellectuals are dissatisfied with a government avowedly moderate and in some respects conservative. In February, 1965, left-wing students at the Central University prevented a memorial service for Mariano Picón Salas, one of Venezuela's most respected men of letters. Why? Because Arturo Uslar Pietri, another outstanding writer who had run unsuccessfully for the presidency and who had cooperated with the Betancourt government, was scheduled as one of the speakers.

The population increase is 3 to 4 per cent annually, with more than half of all Venezuelans under the age of 20.[8] Large families are common. In 1963 quintuplets were born to a couple in Maracaibo; the father had had 10 other children and the mother 7 by previous unions so that the couple then had a total of 22 children, not all of them at home; one of the mother's daughters (aged 17) already has borne a child.[9] Three decades of migration from farms to the cities have turned a 70 per cent rural population into a 70 per cent urban population. Only one quarter of the 2.37 million children between 10 and 19 are in school.

Although Venezuela's problems are numerous and urgent, her political ideals have not changed. Leoni explains that the "Venezuelan Revolution is a Revolution of free men." Her educational system aims to create "free citizens of a democratic country and not fanatics of a dogma that dehumanizes and destroys." [10] They remain alert against a *golpe* from the totalitarian left or right, and oppose both the intervention of Castro in Venezuela and intervention by the U.S. in the Dominican Republic. Leoni proudly declares: "We are thus building the foundations of a democracy which is conscious of its social mission. We place emphasis on the social content of our regime because without it all efforts to achieve dynamic change would be in vain.

And in spite of the threats posed and the aggression to which we are subjected, all Venezuelans—civilian or military, entrepreneur or worker, university student or technician—are, without loss of liberty, realizing the fruits of revolutionary change. Though we may have made a late entrance into the twentieth century, we now live in the serene conviction that we will arrive on time at the threshold of the twenty-first." [11]

[1] As quoted in the author's *Bartolomé Arzáns de Orsúa y Vela and His History of Potosí* (Providence: Brown University Press, 1965), p. 43.

[2] William D. and Amy L. Marsland, *Venezuela Through Its History* (New York: Thomas Y. Crowell Co., 1954) p. 262. For an even more somber picture of conditions, see Raúl Martínez Vera, "Explosión demográfica en Venezuela y algunas de sus consecuencias", *Revista Social C. F. A.* (Caracas, 1965?).

[3] Edwin Lieuwen, *Petroleum in Venezuela. A History* (Berkeley: University of California Press, 1954), p. 27.

[4] *Ibid.*, p. 71.

[5] Peter Snow, "The Political Party Spectrum in Venezuela," *Caribbean Studies,* IV (1965), No. 4, p. 47.

[6] Rafael Caldera, *El crecimiento de la democracia cristiana y su influencia sobre la realidad social de América Latina* (1965). Mimeographed.

[7] Timothy F. Harding and Saul Landau, "Terrorism, Guerrilla Warfare, and the Venezuelan Left," *Studies on the Left,* IV (1964), No. 4, pp. 118–128; "FALN. Our Errors," *Studies on the Left,* IV (1964), No. 4, pp. 129–130; Rómulo Betancourt, "The Venezuelan Miracle," *The Reporter* (August 13, 1964).

[8] Raúl Leoni, "View from Caracas," *Foreign Affairs,* XLIII, p. 644.

[9] *El Tiempo* (Bogotá, Sept. 10, 1963).

[10] Leoni, "View from Caracas," p. 640.

[11] *Ibid.*, p. 646.

GETULIO VARGAS—STRONGMAN AND PRESIDENT OF BRAZIL, 1930–1945, 1950–1954

SOUTH AMERICA

6
THE
INDIAN LANDS
OF THE ANDES

Ecuador

AREA: 104,506 sq. mi.

POPULATION IN MID-1966: 5,110,000

LARGEST CITIES:

Guayaquil: 506,037 (est. 1963)

Quito (capital): 368,217 (est. 1963)

PRINCIPAL EXPORTS (1960): bananas, coffee, cacao beans

PRESIDENT: Otto Arosemena Gómez, civilian, took office in November, 1966, to serve until constitutional order can be resumed.

Peru

AREA: 494,293 sq. mi.

POPULATION IN MID-1966: 12,012,000

LARGEST CITY:

Lima (capital): 1,436,231 (metropolitan area, 1961)

PRINCIPAL EXPORTS (1961): copper, cotton, fish products

PRESIDENT: Fernando Belaúnde Terry, civilian, took office July 29, 1963, for a 6-year term.

Bolivia

AREA: 424,163 sq. mi.

POPULATION IN MID-1966: 3,748,000

LARGEST CITY:

La Paz (de facto capital): 352,912 (est. 1962)

PRINCIPAL EXPORTS (1959): tin, lead, silver

PRESIDENT: René Barrientos Ortuño, military, took office August 6, 1966, for a 4-year term.

THE
INDIAN LANDS
OF THE ANDES

- **"The Huge Coiled Spring."** When the conquistadores arrived in the lands of the Andes more than 400 years ago, they found the Incas ruling over many subject peoples. The Spaniards established their seat of government in "The City of the Kings" (Lima) and from this capital their viceroys ruled over this vast area. Today three separate nations—Bolivia, Ecuador, and Peru—occupy the central portion of the Inca Empire in an area of more than one million square miles. Some 80 per cent of the 20 million inhabitants of these countries are pure Indians or of mixed Indian and Spanish blood; 10 to 15 per cent are considered white; and the rest are Negro, Mulatto, Chinese, and Japanese.

The commanding Andean mountain chain isolates the immense tropical jungles from the upland regions, and, in turn, from the low-lying areas of the Pacific coast. The topography creates serious problems, but the problem that towers like the Andes themselves above all others in these three countries is the presence of great Indian populations never fully assimilated into Spanish culture, although the Spaniards tried to impose it after their military conquest. Until recently, attempts to incorporate the Indians into national life accomplished relatively little; few spoke Spanish, few were familiar with any but the rudiments of Christianity, and some retreated as far as possible from a society they found alien.

At times the Indian "has climbed to altitudes so high and terrains so barren that white exploiters have found it unprofitable to follow. He has also retreated into himself, and his deep mind set toward the environment and white society has made him well-nigh impervious to outer influences." [1] In contrast, others, like the vigorous and attractive Otavalo Indians who dwell on the lower slopes of Mount Imbabura in Ecuador, have been able to absorb gradually the ways of the white world while remaining faithful to their ancient culture rooted in the land. The Otavaleños have developed a pros-

118

perous textile industry carried on in their homes to supplement their income from crops grown on small individual landholdings. They have discovered the power of education, when given access to schools, and have started to learn Spanish; they have demonstrated ability to compete with white craftsmen, and have become such independent and responsible citizens that anthropologists have described their achievements in an absorbing, beautifully illustrated, and lyric account entitled *The Awakening Valley*. Indians, assert these authors, "are the destiny of Ecuador, Peru, and Bolivia": the success achieved by the Otavalos "could be shared throughout the Andes, for their vitality is born of universal energies." [2]

The vitality of the Andean peoples depends to some extent on the policies adopted by governments. As Carlos Monge, the Director of the Institute of Andean Biology, has emphasized, "Andean life and society require their own special conditions of survival and welfare." Inca practice and Spanish legislation reveal a surprising knowledge of acclimatization in higher altitudes; although he was speaking of Peru, Monge might as well have been referring to the situation in all the Indian lands of the Andes until recently when he said that the government of modern Peru was still unaware of the problem of adapting Andean people to their physical environment.[3] Yet their greatest resource is their people, and it is a resource which has just begun to be developed.

The small number of whites in power have adopted various attitudes toward the Indians who, just as in the sixteenth century when contact was first made, are considered a drag on progress, or the hope of the future, or a complete enigma. None of the Andean countries have displayed the pride in their Indian culture that Mexico does. Ecuador and Peru have watched, with interest and some anxiety, Bolivia's recent revolution in which the needs of Indians have received more attention than ever before, for the small ruling classes know that the 6 to 7 million Indians of the Andean uplands "possess the latent energy and underdeveloped power of a huge coiled spring." [4]

Ecuador

● **"Ecuador Is a Very Difficult Country to Govern."** So said José María Velasco Ibarra, four times President between 1934 and 1961, and he should know. One of the poorest South American countries, Ecuador is also one of the smallest, with an area reduced to about 100,000 square miles since Peru won in 1942 a bitterly disputed boundary fight. Only Bolivia, Guyana, Paraguay, and Uruguay in South America have populations smaller than Ecuador's approximately 5 million people. Her economy has always been largely agricultural, although only a third of her potentially cultivable land is being used. High quality cacao production during the years 1910–1925 enabled a few families to become so wealthy that they could live luxuriously in Paris and, on returning to Ecuador for brief visits to their properties, some rather proudly spoke Spanish with a French accent. When disease attacked the cacao trees, rice culture increased; when rice exports dwindled, bananas saved the day, and today Ecuador has become one of the principal banana exporting nations of the world.

Primitive methods of cultivation are still the rule. The jet planes that land in Quito skim over fields being cultivated with wooden-bladed plows pulled by oxen or even by Indians. At the Guayaquil airport, however, fleets of modern crop dusting planes used by the banana industry illustrate the extreme contrasts to be found in Ecuador. But much remains to be done for agriculture if it is to meet the increasing competition from Central American bananas: more credit facilities, soil conservation, seed selection, and defense against insect pests.

Conservative monetary policies and salary scales have retarded Ecuador's economy. An American Embassy report in late 1965 stated: "The future of Ecuador's economy lies in the ability of the government, and its people, to develop the resources of agriculture by increasing productivity, diversifying its productive bases, employing modern techniques now available, training its manpower, and developing domestic as well as foreign markets." Moreover, mineral production has not developed as in Bolivia and Peru.

Ecuadoran geographers describe their country as one continuous tropical jungle running from the Pacific coastal region to the Amazon lowlands, fortuitously interrupted by a double line of formidable mountain peaks which range up to 20,000 feet in Mt. Chimborazo and Mt. Cotopaxi. Politically, Ecuador has been dominated by the conservative capital Quito, dramatically situated more than 9,000 feet high in a green Andean valley, and by the liberal coastal metropolis Guayaquil, through which Ecuador's products are shipped to the world. The two cities were connected by railway in 1908, a remarkable engineering feat accomplished by British capital and the energy of the Harmon brothers of Virginia.

After the port was freed of yellow fever in the 1920's, with help from the Rockfeller Foundation, ideas flowed into Ecuador from the outside world, carried by among others, anarchists, communists, fascists, and Nazi agents. Colonies of artists, intellectuals, and foreigners developed in Quito; there a new, well-to-do professional class existed side by side with traditional society. Guayaquil became noted for its vigorously polemical writers and socially conscious artists who generated some of the attacks upon the wealthy landlords and powerful clergy of Quito.

Tension between Quito and Guayaquil has long been a fundamental fact of Ecuadoran life. Today Guayaquil has well over 700,000 inhabitants, for its population has practically doubled during the last ten years, and Quito has about 500,000.

● **Too Many Presidents.** Few presidents have been able to serve out their constitutional terms since Ecuador set up an independent government in 1830. Cabinet ministers likewise have passed rapidly across the political stage; twelve successive foreign ministers attempted to administer foreign policy in a two month period in 1933. Although Ecuador has promulgated many constitutions, politics and political parties revolve around personalities; regionalism has a persistent influence, the coast always pitted against the capital. When the military took over in 1925 they installed a junta of 7 members, one of whom was to occupy the presidency, alternatively, for a week.[5] There followed a generation of uprisings, disorders, and recurrent instability.

President Carlos Arroyo del Río (1940–1944) brought a period of peace to Ecuador while the world was at war. He broke with the Axis and allowed the United States to build and occupy bases on the Galápagos Islands and on the mainland. Washington loans and technical assistance enabled Ecuador to revive the ailing cacao industry, improve the railways, and undertake other public works. For the election of 1944, Arroyo del Río handpicked his successor and declared ineligible José María Velasco Ibarra, who had served as president from 1934 to 1935, and was then conducting a determined campaign from exile in neighboring Colombia. Before the election could take place the army rose and installed Velasco Ibarra as President on June 1, 1944. His six-point program, widely hailed by the hemisphere's press, proposed to establish "true democracy," aid agriculture and industry, stimulate labor unions, improve sanitation, and cooperate with the other American republics and the United Nations.

Velasco Ibarra was an intellectual, called by his admirers "The National Personification." Feeling himself a man with a mission, he wrote prolifically and spoke with persuasive magnetism, opposing both communism and fascism, and considered himself a member of no political party. Some looked upon him as a demagogue, a sort of Andean Perón dedicated wholeheartedly to maintaining himself in power. He believed Ecuador unready for democracy: "the conflict between dreams and reality . . . has been the tragedy of Spanish America," he once wrote. "Unified by the Spanish soul, Americans have desired union, and have come up against infinite distances, gigantic mountains, varied climates, unhealthful valleys, and perpetually extended rivers and plains." [6]

A constructive achievement during his rule was the establishment in 1944 of the *Casa de Cultura Ecuatoriana,* a cultural institute the government financed with funds obtained from a tax on exports. Under the leadership of Benjamín Carrión, the Casa organized lectures, courses, recitals, concerts, art exhibitions, published books and periodicals and in many other ways works toward its objective, to "direct and guide national culture."

In spite of his undoubted gifts and lavish promises, Velasco Ibarra nevertheless lost the support of the army and the coalition of political forces which had brought him to power; in August, 1947, with his extensive program unfulfilled, he was overthrown. Confusion followed; in the next month three presidents succeeded one another rapidly in office.

Galo Plaza, regularly elected in 1948, will long stand out as a model president who brought stability to Ecuador. A wealthy and enlightened landowner trained in the United States, his administration made possible increased production of cacao, coffee, and bananas and hence a balanced budget. The press was free and democratic practices were honored. He completed in 1952 the full four year term, and was succeeded by, again, Velasco Ibarra who also served the full term, a peaceful period during which economic progress contined. A conservative president, Camilo Ponce Enríquez, followed, and completed his full term of office (1956–1960), despite some fear that he might try to restore the political power of the Church.

Ecuadorans have been sensitive over the religious issue ever since the nineteenth-century dictatorship of the famous Conservative Gabriel García Moreno, who was supported by the landowners, the army, and the Church. Though García Moreno was assassinated in 1875, conservative forces continued to dominate the country until Eloy Alfaro and the Liberals broke their power in 1895. State and Church were then separated, education secularized, huge Church estates confiscated, divorce laws—among the first in South America —introduced, and Protestant missionaries allowed to enter the country. In 1931 the inter-denomination World Radio Missionary Fellowship opened in Quito a powerful radio station, "The Voice of the Andes," whose five transmitters daily broadcast programs in nine languages that can be heard all over the world. Protestants have won few converts, but they encounter no governmental opposition and Ecuadorans seem determined to preserve the Church-State separation established at the turn of the century.

Velasco Ibarra won the presidency again in 1960, but was able to stay in power only 14 months of his fourth term. A fiery orator whose flamboyance appealed to the masses, he appointed only Velasquistas to office, whether Cabinet Ministers, humble doorkeepers, or policemen. He devalued the currency, which led to inflation and a flight of capital that dangerously reduced the nation's reserves. One of his unpredictable policy switches caused trouble with the Worker's Confederation and then the army, which abruptly brought him down in November, 1961. Vice-President Carlos Julio Arosemena succeeded him, but he too was forced out in July, 1963—reportedly because he was a compulsive drinker and erratic personality—by a junta headed by Rear Admiral Ramón Castro Jijón. The junta ruled with force, but so discreetly for a time that it was called a *dictablanda*. It kept demonstrations under control with tear gas and batons, rather than with pistols or machine guns. Under the prodding of the Alliance for Progress the junta had begun a number of much-needed reforms such as levying an income tax, improving the civil service, and effecting some agrarian changes. But increasing protests against military rule by university students and by Guayaquil merchants made the junta's rule more and more difficult. After bloody skirmishes with university students in Quito, the high command of the army forced out the junta in March, 1966, and installed a well-to-do Guayaquil businessman, Clemente Yerovi Indaburu as Provisional President.

Yerovi cancelled plans for presidential elections, which the junta had scheduled to be held in July, and called a constituent assembly. In November, 1966, a political unknown and member of the white oligarchy named Otto Arosemena Gómez managed to get himself elected interim President by the assembly, which led to further uncertainty. Presumably the veteran spellbinder José María Velasco Ibarra is still available to serve a fifth term as president, since he has always maintained that if someone would give him a balcony from which to speak he would be elected.

● **"Democracy in the Greek Sense."** Ever since the Spaniards arrived, the ruling minority has enjoyed what has been called "democracy in the Greek sense," in which effective citizenship was limited to the small number of men of education and culture, with all others rigidly barred from responsive participation. This comfortable doctrine for those in power is now under scrutiny; one student is convinced that fundamental political stability will be achieved in Ecuador only when the ruling class becomes willing to bring the submerged masses into the national life. (*See Reading No. 55.*)

The magnitude of the task may be gauged by what one writer describes as Ecuador's age-old problems, today almost as far from solution as ever:

> The general poverty that forbids the majority of the population to own more than the clothes they are wearing—and that means in the hot regions often little more than a torn shirt and a dirty pair of trousers; the tropical diseases to which must be added tuberculosis; the lack of population in vast undeveloped regions; the uneven distribution of land, producing a rural proletariat composed of nearly the entire Indian population and hundreds of thousands of mestizos, or Negroes and mulattoes along the coast; the absence of a balanced agricultural and industrial production; the lack of roads, of educational facilities for the dispersed population; the profound cleavage between Sierra and Coast.[7]

Some anthropologists believe that the future belongs to the Indians: "the Spanish must eventually be absorbed by the masses they have conquered. The growth of Ecuador must be the growth of the Indians; as long as they are held in subjugation, the cultural and economic progress of the land will be retarded. The destiny of the Andes is in the revival of Indian vitality that will open the doors to individual freedom and national unity." [8] If this revival is to come, the attitude of Indian women must be changed. The "guide and axis of the family" with much influence at the community level, they are also the traditional guardians of the "old ways." Any change, they fear, may imperil their families and thus they constitute a major obstacle to the programs for development in Ecuador.[9]

Other observers of Ecuador feel, however, that neither the present ruling minority nor the Indians will prevail; they believe that the best hope for the country lies in a greatly expanded role for the *cholo* (mestizo) class in Ecuadoran life. The cholos are a mixture of Spaniards and Indians who now participate in civic affairs to some extent—in commerce, agriculture, and the army. They are sensitive—as the Indians are not—to their exclusion from a fuller share in government and may in time induce or compel the ruling minority to accept fundamental changes in the economic, political, and social structure of Ecuador.

Will the elite accept changes without a revolution? Its opulent way of life reaches far back into history. In 1579 a friar indignantly reported from Quito to Philip II that most of the Spanish ladies there considered it beneath their dignity to suckle their own infants. The mestizo servants of the Spaniards had in turn their own Indian servants, and if "a Negro goes to market for his master, he takes along an Indian to carry home the meat." [10]

The temper and outlook of the elite may be judged by the results of the questionnaire directed a quarter of a century ago by an enterprising Quito citizen, Hipatia Cárdenas de Bustamante, to two hundred leading citizens. She asked only one question: "What should Ecuador do to free itself from dictatorships?" The replies she published from the 108 who answered provide valuable insights into the political ideas of this select group.

The first reply published, from one-time presidential candidate Neptali Bonifaz, struck a pessimistic note. Nothing can be done, he declared, unless the executive power, the army, and the legislative power are all abolished, for they all produce dictatorships. Still bitter from his experience in 1931 when he had been elected president with Conservative and Church support in Quito and had seen the election annulled by a Congress controlled by Guayaquil, he concluded: "It is surprising that we don't wear feathers instead of European clothes." [11]

Many agreed, in their replies to the questionnaire, that militarism was the big problem, and that the army should be shorn of political power; others called for more education. The leader of the Conservative Party believed the problem essentially a moral one: "we must restore . . . the spiritual factors —honor, patriotism, impartiality, and integrity." No one mentioned the concentration of land in the hands of a few; no one mentioned the *huasipungueros,* the half million Indians who exchange their services on haciendas for the right to till a bit of ground and live in semi-servitude. Only one person, an army colonel, referred to the Indians and mestizos at all; he urged that this large block, 80 per cent of the country's population, be immediately admitted into the civic life.[12]

A stark picture of Indian life appears in the Ecuadoran novelist Jorge Icaza's *Huasipungo,* a work that has been translated into Chinese, Russian, and other major languages, although the first English version was done in Moscow.[13] At long last Southern Illinois University Press brought out a translation in 1965.

Some of today's elite are undoubtedly more aware of Ecuador's basic needs than most of those who answered the questionnaire a generation ago. Ecuador has an able group of *Indianistas*—professors, lawyers, doctors, and writers— who have studied the Indian problem and produced valuable reports and recommendations. The first determined attempt to end the huasipunguero system, however, was made by the military junta after it assumed power in 1963. Indian life has changed: more huasipungueros now own their own land, are paid a wage, and are no longer serfs. In the last few years the Indian has become more mobile, thanks to Ecuadoran-made bicycles, and is likely to own a transistor radio.

How will these and other changes that Ecuador has experienced since the end of World War II affect the nation's future? Does obligatory voting for males over 18 mean that the structure of government has radically changed and that there will be from now on substantially greater citizen participation in the political process? Has the powerful influence of Spanish individualism in the upper classes sufficiently abated to permit the growth of a democratic consensus, including a realistic and respectful view of manual labor? If a peaceful transition to civilian control is finally achieved, Ecuador may enjoy another period of steady development because, for the first time in the country's history, "liberals, conservatives, and socialists are now capable of listening to each other." [14] If these hitherto mutually hostile components of Ecuadoran society do not find some agreement on national objectives, Ecuador is likely to remain "a very difficult country to govern."

Peru

● **Coast, Sierra, and Montaña.** Books on Peru ordinarily begin with this popular phrase, to indicate that this country of half a million square miles, five times the size of Ecuador, is divided geographically, economically and culturally into three distinct parts. In Hubert Herring's words:

> If any visitor would sense the drama of the three Perus, he can start out in the morning from Lima (choosing a car with trustworthy brakes), push across the hot sand of the coastal desert, climb the fine highway to the 15,680-foot divide, drop down to Oroya where copper smelters blanket the mountains with sulphur fumes, continue to Tarma, and find the road which leads to the Amazon Valley. That downward passage to the village of Merced gives the taste, the smell, the feeling of the montaña, with its heavy rain clouds, its dripping vegetation, its forests of mahogany and other hardwoods. Little streams are everywhere, growing in volume with every mile traversed, until at Merced they

have gathered into a roaring river, the Perene, one of the many which feed the Amazon. The traveler will have seen the three Perus between dawn and dusk.[15]

Transportation problems have preoccupied all Peruvian rulers, from the Incas, who built roads and bridges that are the wonder of the modern world, to President Fernando Belaúnde Terry today. The 1,200-mile coastline is paralleled by narrow deserts reputedly drier than the Sahara, and the Sierra region is so mountainous that the trip from Lima to Cajatambo, one of the provincial capitals of the Department of Lima, requires not only an eight-hour ride over rough roads by car, but a sixteen-hour horseback trip. Railroad construction provided a romantic chapter in nineteenth-century Peruvian history; both the line to Oroya, which is the highest standard gauge line in the world, and the road from Mollendo on the coast to Cuzco and eventually to La Paz, Bolivia, were planned and partially accomplished by Henry Meiggs, "the Yankee Pizarro." In recent years Peru has made significant attempts to open up its vast tropical hinterlands of the Andes. Its principal town, Iquitos on the upper Amazon, could formerly be reached from Lima only by an almost two-month sea voyage via Cape Horn or the Panama Canal and then a river passage 2,000 miles up the Amazon; now it is joined to the capital by four-hour airplane service. Roads in this remote region have been begun, and now towns are being established.

The Incas' seat of empire was Cuzco, high in the Andes; the Spaniards established their viceregal capital near the sea at Lima, the "City of the Kings," which today preserves an air of aristocratic distinction despite its 1,000 per cent increase in population since 1900 to a total of over 2 million inhabitants today. In this pleasant and impressive city live Peru's "forty families" and foreigners who are said to maintain economic control of the country, or a "strangle-hold" as some Peruvians call it. Here may be visited the great collections on Indian civilizations and of Spanish colonial art, all as yet privately owned; only modest activity has been displayed on behalf of public museums. In Lima also lives a large proportion of the white population, estimated at 10 per cent of the total of 11 million, which dominates Peru's political and social life. The approximately 4 million Indians live in the Sierra, and the 4 million mestizos are scattered through all parts of the republic. Some 90,000 Chinese coolies were imported in the nineteenth century, a third as many Japanese came after 1900. European immigration has been small, but some of the several thousand Italians and Germans have risen to important places in the business and industrial world.

Few Indians are seen in Lima, at least not in their native garb, and the city is saturated with Spanish influence; Catholic history and imperial traditions are still present and influential.

● **"Indians Are Peruvians."** In the first flush of revolutionary enthusiasm General José de San Martín, who shared with General Simón Bolívar the glory of liberating Peru from Spanish rule, declared in 1821: "Henceforth the aborigines shall not be called Indians; they are children and citizens of Peru, and they shall be known as Peruvians." [16] But the turbulent conditions of life in independent Peru were not propitious for the Indians. The Spanish crown provided them some protection, the Republic, even less; the great concentrations of land (*latifundia*) continued, and *gamonalismo* became the order of the day. This has been defined as "the condition of inequality of the Indian with respect to the other social classes . . . it is colonialism and clericalism projected through a century of independent life; it signifies spoiliation . . . the connivance of . . . authorities, clergy, and landholders in exploiting the Indians without conscience and without scruple." [17]

Guano, the excrement dropped by millions of birds on Peru's offshore islands, proved to be an excellent fertilizer and became a principal source of the country's wealth after 1840. Fortunes were made from the industry, and also from the extraction of nitrate in the southern desert region. Prosperity mushroomed, and large loans were floated in Europe; railroads were built, and easy money led to scandals and corruption. Chile defeated both Peru and Bolivia in the War of the Pacific (1879–1883), by which Peru lost the nitrate province of Tarapacá and eventually Arica. Chilean troops occupied Lima, used the buildings of sixteenth-century San Marcos University as barracks and stables, and took home much loot including books from the National Library and monkeys from the zoo.

The nation was shaken by these humiliating reverses, and a generation of writers sought to understand the reasons for the defeat and to reform Peruvian institutions to avoid similar disasters in the future. Four themes were developed which dominated the thought of some Peruvians as they confronted their reality: 1) concern for Indians and an exaltation of their ancient culture; 2) criticism of the wealthy, aristocratic class ruling the country from Lima; 3) attack on latifundia and gamonalismo; and 4) opposition to the Church for its great wealth in the midst of a poor people, for its indifference to the plight of the Indians, and its intimate alliance with the ruling class.

Outstanding in this "literature of disillusionment" were the writings of Manuel González Prada (1846–1918), a bitter anti-clerical who was deeply wounded by Peru's defeat in the "War of the Pacific," in which he had served. He felt that the leaders of the country were bankrupt: "Old Men to the Tomb, Young Men to Work" was the title of one of his many polemical writings. "Women, the Church's Slaves," was a phrase in another essay which pained his devout mother and sister. He refused to head a boy's school because the students were required to go to confession and receive communion, and in 1912 was appointed Director of the National Library. Wherever he looked he saw decay: "In Peru there is pus wherever you put your finger"; he was a skilled and pitiless prober of his country's problems, who ceaselessly attacked the Church for its economic power and its control of education. He denounced Peruvian revolutions as not true revolutions; he called them sham battles in which poor Indians killed each other for the benefit of their masters "who would afterwards gather around a festal board with fraternal embraces to divide the spoils."

González Prada lived out his last agitated years before Augusto B. Leguía established his dictatorship. Having served as President from 1908–1912, Leguía later went on to rule by force (1919–1930). During his long domination, Peru made significant material advances. Highways and railroads were extended, ports improved, irrigation developed, foreign mining companies encouraged, sanitary facilities installed in thirty towns; the dictator also built a marble palace for himself. He obtained $90 million in loans, mostly from the United States, at a time when U.S. bankers were unwisely vying with each other and, if necessary, bribing officials for the privilege of extending loans whether the security was adequate or not. They were called "champagne loans," because the proceeds often went into nonproductive ventures.

Leguía fancied himself a benevolent ruler; he organized schools, contracted for an educational mission from the United States, and for a time employed an American as Rector of the University of Cuzco. In 1920 he promulgated a new Constitution with many splendid democratic provisions, which he completely ignored. He jailed critics, closed down the University of San Marcos, and thereby provoked the first stirrings of political liberalism in Peru. He also affected to take up the cause of the neglected Indians, announcing with fanfare that their serfdom was over, and proclaimed them full citizens of Peru as San Martín had done a century before. No actual change in their lives occurred, however; they continued to suffer all the long-established abuses. There was such a slavish orientation to European society and so little recognition of the national problems in University circles that courses in sociology at the University of San Marcos in the 1920's included no reference to Peru or its problems. One of the rectors of San Marcos during the Leguía regime, the philosopher Alejandro O. Deustua, was convinced that the Indians could not be educated and looked upon them as an inert, deteriorating race: "The Indian is not, and cannot be, anything but a machine." [18] But the writings of González Prada and the discontent engendered by dictator Leguía led to the growth of the Aprista Party, one of the most interesting indigenous political parties in Latin America.

● **"Only Aprismo Can Save Peru."** José Carlos Mariátegui, the most serious political thinker ever to appear in Peru, was much influenced by González Prada and by his study in Europe, 1919–1923, made possible by Leguía. On his return to Peru he opposed the dictator, but as a thinker rather than as militant activist. He founded in 1926 the review *Amauta,* and when he decided in 1928 that he was an orthodox Marxist-Leninist moved to transform the review into more of an instrument of Communist propaganda. In 1929 he helped to found a party which while it was called Socialist was actually Peru's first Communist party and which in 1930, after Mariátegui's death, affiliated itself with the Communist International. His principal work, *Seven Interpretive Essays on Peruvian Reality* (1928), revealed him as a writer who, in an aseptic style, laid bare the great problems of his country—the depressed condition of the Indians, latifundia, regionalism, the political power of the Church, and an inadequate educational system.

Although many of his economic views seemed to be those of a party-line Communist, he advocated a return to a modified form of the old Incan system of communal use of land. Mariátegui opposed middle class reformers eyeing Europe and the United States and their idea that more European immigration would be the solution for Peru. He also opposed the dominant aristocratic concept of education; he wanted education provided for everyone, including Indians, and believed that students should have a large responsibility in running the university. This honest, lonely writer wanted Peru, above all, to work out its own type of socialism based on native American institutions; it ought not to copy a Marxism founded on modern European industrialism. He rejected the materialistic interpretation of history, was apparently something of a mystic who felt that communism was essentially a spiritual movement. During his life communism in Peru did not slavishly follow Soviet dogma, and had he lived longer he might "have produced a significant and lasting schism within the communist movement as it was developing in Latin America." [19] His early death in 1930 prevented him from accomplishing this; his role was in any case, he believed, to diffuse ideas, to prepare the way for the "great transformation."

Mariátegui had many followers in university circles, among them Víctor Raúl Haya de la Torre, who led student attacks on Leguía in 1923 when the dictator dedicated Peru formally to the Sacred Heart of Jesus. In the turbulence a student was killed, Haya delivered a stirring funeral oration, and his much disputed political career was under way. Exiled by Leguía, Haya announced from Mexico the formation of an international movement, APRA (Alianza Popular Revolucionaria Americana), which was henceforth to be an important element on the Peruvian political scene. Apristas were anti-imperialist and anti-United States in the early days, favored nationalization of land and industry, the internationalization of the Panama Canal, and the unity of Indo-America, as Haya proposed to rename Latin America. APRA ideas and aspirations gained great currency through the writings of such talented and articulate exiles as Luis Alberto Sánchez and Manuel Seoane. Haya was also a prolific writer and a wide-ranging thinker; but APRA has never become influential outside Peru, principally because the individual countries preferred their own nationalist developments even when adopting similar programs.

Political partisanship and myth still obscure the history of the APRA.[20] Haya early espoused the popular indigenista cause, but his fundamental appeal was to the insecure middle classes. He liked to be pictured as an admirer of Gandhi and nonviolence, but appeared to be convinced that violence would be needed to reform Peru. By 1930, when Leguía was at last overthrown, Peruvians were divided into two uncompromisingly hostile camps with apristas and their opponents preparing for a bitter struggle.

From the downfall of Leguía until today apristas have played an important role on the somewhat confused and ever-changing Peruvian political scene. Despite much popular support, APRA has never been able to exercise much positive power. It won the elections in 1936, but was prevented from assuming office by the "moderate dictator" General Oscar Benavides. When the middle-of-the-road aristocratic liberal José Luis Bustamante was elected President in 1945, thanks to APRA votes, and apristas sat in the cabinet and presided over the Senate, the Chamber of Deputies, and the University of San Marcos, no bold projects were put into effect to implement their long-proclaimed ideals.

Eventually, Bustamante was forced to dismiss the apristas, and their brief period of semi-power was over. Bustamante himself had to yield to a new dictator, General Manuel Odría, who simply took power in 1948 after the abortive revolution led by the left wing of APRA, and had himself elected for a regular six-year term in 1950. He bloodily persecuted apristas and largely restored control to the old government class in Lima. His emphasis was solely on material development; a steel mill was started, a hydroelectric plant built, oil wells were drilled, and mineral production—always an important part of Peru's economy—increased.

During Odría's rule and later, APRA seems to have lost its crusading fervor and to operate expediently, using the "fear and favors" technique of other political parties. The communists, who had won recruits among bank clerks, textile workers, teachers, and university students taunted: "Communism is a live party with a dead leader (Mariátegui), while APRA is a dead party with a live leader (Haya)." The long period when U.S. observers looked upon Aprismo as the great hope for Peru now came to a close. A recent analyst has written that most "apristas seemed totally unconcerned with the proletarian revolution and appeared to be thoroughly dedicated to the enjoyment of capitalism's benefits." [21]

The first free election in eight years was held in 1956, when a conservative, Manuel Prado, won over Fernando Belaúnde Terry, a 43-year-old architect trained at the University of Texas. Belaúnde ran on a platform of economic planning, social welfare, and a program of land reform which aimed at bringing into effective participation the 40 per cent of the population which did not vote—largely the sierra Indians. Belaúnde received 35 percent of the votes, many of them cast by intellectuals, young professional men, military officers, and several groups of large landholders, including owners of mechanized haciendas of the rich coastal strip who believed that the old system of obligatory unpaid work by Indians in return for the use of subsistence plots of land, and of haciendas leased simply to obtain the free labor of Indians attached to them, was economically inefficient and socially indefensible. They were convinced that Peru was on the verge of social change which would bring the Indian into greater participation in national life; but they wanted this change to come gradually and shuddered at what they consider the drastic, bloody, and inept way Bolivia's revolution had been carried on. Prado won, however; he was of a ruling family, son of a former president, and had also served in the office 1939–1945 during the war years when he aligned Peru against the Axis powers. In the 1956 election he had the support of APRA because he promised to legalize the party. Prado as president also allowed the Communist Party, technically illegal, a fairly free hand in political activity and labor organization. The result was a period of relative political stability despite an increasingly critical economic situation.

The election campaign of 1962 was to choose as president Haya de la Torre, backed by the Prado administration and described as "the kind of conservative we need in Peru," or Belaúnde, or Manuel Odría, trying to stage a comeback. None of the candidates received a majority and, amidst charges of voting frauds committed by the apristas, congress was called upon to exercise its constitutional function of choosing among the three highest candidates. Haya de la Torre and Odría joined forces against Belaúnde to produce one of the strangest combinations in Peru's political history. Odría was to become president, and APRA expected to rule the country through congressional control. The military under General Ricardo Pérez Godoy thwarted this plan by taking over power on July 18, 1962, and held free elections in June, 1963, as had been promised.

Belaúnde with his Popular Action party won the 1963 elections through the support of the middle classes, both urban and rural, and his victory was interpreted as an expression of the new economic and social forces. He immediately began to work for better roads, a decentralization of the national administrative apparatus, and for land reform.

The land question is complicated, one of the problems being the plan to move Indians down from the overpopulated high mountain valleys. Today the people of the Andes are trickling down to the warmer foothills or to the hot lowlands. Those who choose to remain in their mountain villages can change their way of life without moving, if the Cornell University Peru project is a true indication: "These Indigenous Communities are digging their own way out of their Andean isolation, punching through their own farm-market and access roads, bridging the gullies that cut them off from the national economy, providing school rooms for their children, quarters for their local officials, and starting on the task of providing basic modern public utilities. There can be no question as to the readiness of the majority of these Indigenous Communities to change their natural and social environments." [22] Communal habits are resistant to changes, the difficulty in getting Andean villagers to boil water being one example (*see Reading No. 56*), but the optimistic conclusions by Cornell anthropologists on the Vicos experiment are based on much experience, and may point the way to a promising new stage of Peru's development. (*See Reading No. 57.*)

One favorable circumstance is that Belaúnde is the first President of Peru who really believes in the capacity of the Indians. A member of an ancient family of conservative and traditional Arequipa, he hopes to mobilize the latent energies of the oppressed race. His declarations on "Peru as a doctrine" in his book *The Conquest of Peru by Peruvians* clearly show the quality of thought of this attractive and energetic leader. He manifests a genuine zeal for the development of a pluralistic country in which the coast with its westernized, capitalistic traditions and the sierra with its semisocialistic Inca customs can coexist. An APRA-Odría combination in congress still opposes many of his reform proposals, but Peru for the first time in the twentieth century is being guided by a strong and intelligent leader, with much popular support, who is moving with the times to strengthen the economic and social structure of the country as a whole.

● **A Final Reflection.** The tangled complexities of Peruvian politics in the twentieth century indicate the need for caution in attempting to characterize them. They cannot be interpreted simply as a struggle between the bad "oligarchs" and the good reformers. One writer has called this approach a "caricature that should be consciously discarded," and charges that such labels have been used as a substitute for analysis. He maintains that civilian violence and military intervention, both considered very "undemocratic" by orthodox political scientists, have led Peru to "the democratic norms of limited tenure of office and responsiveness of the office holders to citizen demands." [23]

Bolivia

● **Has the Revolution Ended?** When President Víctor Paz Estenssoro was overthrown by the Vice-President, General René Barrientos Ortuño, in November, 1964, Bolivia joined the lengthening list of Latin American countries under military rule. Barrientos proclaimed his coup as a *Revolución Restauradora* (Restoring Revolution), thus reminding the country that the new regime was a return to the early reform movement which led in 1941 to the foundation of the Nationalist Revolutionary Movement (MNR), in which other army officers had played an active role. But it was President Paz who gave that reform shape and substance in his two terms of office (1952–1956, 1960–1964), and the question arises whether a military junta can effectively bring about the working alliance between the miners, the nationalist middle class, and the campesinos who till the soil. Barrientos has the important assets of humble origin and of speaking fluent Quechua, so that he can talk directly with many of the country's four million people, about half of whom speak only this Indian language. Recent studies, too, have emphasized the fact that military rule is not necessarily blind and brutal,[24] and army spokesmen in the months before the coup—when the MNR was visibly degenerating from a revolutionary party into a patronage machine—were increasingly insistent on the importance, and selflessness, of the army's role in developing the nation's resources.[25] Whether Barrientos, who shared the power with General Alfredo Ovando Candia and in August, 1966, was elected president, can continue the reforms inaugurated in 1952 when the MNR first came to power is the important question. Though Bolivia received massive aid from the U.S.—at one time the largest per capita aid to any country in the world —a decisive factor in the Revolution's success was the support of the country generally for the MNR's objectives. Fundamental changes in the life of the country were achieved:

> Bolivia has accomplished a greater social revolution than Mexico in a fifth of the time. Yet it has done so under a nationalism that, unlike Cuba's, has preserved the forms of democracy. In a way its nationalism is pure—unaffected by anti-colonialism, anti-imperialism, anti-communism, etc. It is a nationalism concerned with the social, economic, and political integration of the people and with the national problems which this integration raises.[26]

Can the generals mobilize the country's reform forces to continue the attack on these national problems now that Paz is in exile in Lima, and other MNR leaders have gone to Asunción, Montevideo, and elsewhere? Whatever happens politically, the geographical problems remain.

● **Geographical Realities.** Though it has some of the most formidable mountain territory in the world, more than three-fifths of Bolivia's territory consists of tropical forests and plains a few hundred feet above sea level. As large as France, it is landlocked, having lost its access to the sea to Chile in the War of the Pacific (1879–1883), and no product or person can get in or out of Bolivia except by arduous travel.

The *Altiplano* or Andean plateau is cold, windswept, and arid, but for centuries has been the most densely populated part of the country. It "has the forsaken aspect of a landscape on some vaster and more ancient planet where life has long been obsolete. . . . It is a harsh, inhuman land, inhabited by a dour, unsmiling, toiling race. There are no trees. Except in the brief season of the rains there is no green. . . . There is a grandeur which humbles and turns one to admiration of those men who for centuries have made it their home." [27] Lake Titicaca in the northern Altiplano is the highest navigated lake in the world.

The Yungas, or semitropical valleys on the eastern slopes of the mountains, are a different world from the Altiplano. The vigor and variety of plant life there are incredible; yet vegetables, fruits, and other crops are largely unexploited because coca, from which cocaine is derived, yields such good returns that all else is neglected. The leaves of the coca plant have long been chewed by the Indians; the juice produces a feeling of euphoria which alleviates the harshness of daily life.

The lowland tropics (Oriente) in eastern Bolivia contain 70 per cent of its total territory. Underdeveloped, underpopulated, and isolated from the rest of the country by poor transportation, the Oriente with its dense tropical forests, vast pasture lands, and rolling savannas, may hold the key to the future of Bolivia. The tropical forests of northern Oriente, alone almost twice the size of Ecuador, were once the center for a wild-rubber empire. During the boom period 1906–1913, before Malaya rubber dominated the market, this was a no-man's land producing such provincial dictators as Don Nicanor Gonzalo Salvatierra, who lived like an Indian rajah, surrounded by a harem of native girls, occupying himself at times with correcting linguistic errors in the *Diccionario de la Real Academia de la Lengua Española.*

The open plains of Beni Province occupy the center of the Oriente, where herds of semiwild cattle range. The land is largely alluvial; for hundreds of miles one sees no hill, no stone, no gravel. From February to June, the Beni suffers annual floods; the countryside resembles a vast lake extending to the horizon.

The Chaco, a part of which was lost in the 1932–1935 war with Paraguay, is in southern Oriente. Here open woodlands and savannas, grazed by semi-wild herds of cattle and goats, suffer from drought during most of the year and also from floods and plagues of locusts. The many rivers, relatively use-less for transportation because they run eastward from the populated portions of the country toward the uninhabited interior, abound in succulent fish which, though in season they are so plentiful that they are scooped up in buckets, cannot be marketed for lack of transport.

The Altiplano and the Oriente are so separated that their peoples do not know each other well. Despite the campaign to unify the country after the Chaco War ended in 1935, the Altiplano is nearly a foreign country to those in the tropical lowlands, and neglect by the central government in La Paz has led to political disaffection in the Oriente.

Transportation is the "one problem upon which all else depends." [28] Air services are good and have done much in recent years to mitigate the psychological and physical isolation of the more remote populations. But the cost of air freight is high and the airports lack concrete runways; rain renders many of them unserviceable for days or weeks at a time. Argentine meat is cheaper in La Paz than that from the Beni, and some sugar is still imported from Peru and the United States.

Only 2,200 miles of railroads are operative in this huge country. Single track lines, constructed under conditions of great difficulty, connect La Paz with Cochabamba, second largest city, and with Argentina, Chile, and Peru. Lines from Santa Cruz, largest city in the Oriente, have recently reached Corumbá on the Brazilian border and Yacuiba in Argentina. For a time the government tried to run the railroads, but some of them are now operated again by British engineers though this arrangement may not be a permanent one.

"Bolivian roads are uniformly bad, usually incredibly bad, and most often dangerous." [29] Yet these roads bear the trucks which carry most of the internal traffic. Both the appalling geographical obstacles to roadbuilding and inadequate provision in the national budget have aggravated the situation for years. One urgent need, for an all-weather road between Cochabamba and Santa Cruz, was met in 1954 with the help of an Export-Import Bank Loan.

The Oriente may be on the verge of important economic advance, thanks to this road and agricultural changes under way in the Santa Cruz district. If more roads can be built, more peasants will leave the windswept Altiplano for the immense lowland regions. There some are already "changing habits of dress, of speech, of food, of hygiene. . . . The almost religiously traditional diet of potatoes is abandoned for yucca and rice. The ancient invocations to the Pachacama lose meaning as abundant crops, no longer threatened by drought and hail, yield more than the colonists can eat or sell." [30]

● **The Heritage of Potosí.** The revolutionary nature of the present attempts to redistribute people as well as land may be best appreciated by considering history and the many previous prescriptions for improvement. Bolivia has probably received more advice from foreigners for her ills than any other country in South America; enough surveys have been drawn up to fill a 5-foot shelf. One United Nations Mission, alone, in 1950 included experts in taxation, public finance, fiscal administration, mining production, transportation, electrical power production, labor legislation, social welfare, living standards, public education, soil analysis, cotton cultivation, and irrigation. A report on mining methods, by a New York consultant, fills three volumes. A rich and confusing literature has resulted from all these investigations.

But historically Bolivia's present plight goes back to the year 1545, when huge deposits of silver were found in Potosí, which quickly became one of the most famous mines in the history of the world despite its remoteness and altitude, several thousand feet higher than Lhasa in Tibet. *Vale un Potosí,* "as rich as Potosí," came to mean "indescribably wealthy." Today some historians hold Potosí responsible for fastening upon Bolivia a pernicious economic-social system which exalted quick profits from the mines and left agriculture so little regarded that its growth was dangerously neglected and a feudal-type society prolonged for centuries.

Until the 1952 revolution nationalized the three largest mine holdings, now producing tin, the owners' sole objective had been profit, and the mine workers lived short and miserable lives. Anthropologists, who have provided some fascinating studies on Bolivian workers both inside and outside the mines, emphasize the long-standing neglect of the Indians as at least a partial explanation for Bolivia's turbulent history and present difficulties.

● **"Sick People" (Pueblo Enfermo).** The Bolivian diplomat and writer, Alcides Arguedas, gave this title to one of his most widely discussed books. Arguedas looked at Bolivian society with a cold, analytical eye and found little to his liking. "Everything in Bolicia is immense; everything, except man," he wrote. The highland Indians were sad and doomed to extinction, the mestizos suffered from duplicity, drunkenness, and a lack of moral sense, while the dominant whites had their own special diseases: delusions of grandeur, excessive influence by the military, lack of education among the women. Only a sick people, argued Arguedas, would have produced so many revolutions, assassinations of presidents, and outlandish caudillos. He named the dictator Mariano Melgarejo (1864–1871), a powerful, dissolute, and illiterate soldier, as representative of the lot; Bolivians have told many fabulous stories, some of them true, of his exploits. He is said to have argued fiercely that Napoleon was a greater general than Bonaparte, and to have ordered the Bolivian army to march to Paris in 1870 to aid his friend the French Emperor, who had decorated him, but was persuaded that an intervening land mass—Brazil—and body of water—the Atlantic Ocean—made the project impracticable.

Whoever meditates seriously on Bolivia's problems, as many of her patriotic citizens have done, must consider the Indians who constitute the mass of the population. Though declared free by the Republic over a century ago at the time of independence from Spain, they remained outside the main currents of national life. The emergence of the Republic saw the abolition of laws which gave Indians preferential treatment.[31] During the 19th century, and later, mestizoes usually reenforced their economic dominance with political dominance, and maintained immense landholdings utilizing the unpaid labor of Indian serfs who no longer enjoyed even the appeal to protective legislation.

A slight improvement began some thirty years ago, partly due to the influence of the late Franz Tamayo, not yet well-known outside Bolivia, though "alone of Bolivian writers [he] ranks indisputably among the great creative poets of our time." [32] His basic work, on the kind of education Bolivia needs, is an exaltation of his countrymen, Indians and mestizoes alike. They need education and training suited to their special characteristics, but essentially they are sound, affirmed this son of a Spanish-speaking Bolivian father and an Indian mother.[33]

The Spanish conquerors of the 16th century debated furiously on the aptitude of Indians for Christian civilization; Bolivians are still deeply divided on the question of their innate character.

One school of thought represent (the Indian) as perfidious, cruel, egoistic, unsociable, venal, malicious, spiteful, suspicious, deceitful, without initiative or ambition, lazy, drunken, hypocritical, untrustworthy, cringing, and cowardly. Others, who know him well, assert that Indian morality is superior to that of the white and praise his high standards and strict performance of honesty, truthfulness, conjugal fidelity, respect for family ties, obedience to law, sobriety, patience, diligence, and tenacity.

Although they may seem so, these "two views are not irreconcilable, for the Indian in his own environment is a different being from an Indian who has joined a mining camp or the urban rabble." [34] (*See Readings Nos. 55–58.*)

Anthropologists note the addiction of Indians to native liquor (*chicha*) as a solemn fact of their social and economic existence. The working year is frequently broken by fiestas, which in Bolivia are competitive orgies so expensive that the host may go heavily into debt (at 5 per cent interest a month) in order to give a bigger and better fiesta than his neighbor. In some regions, almost 40 per cent of cash income goes for chicha, for drinking apart from fiestas is also phenomenal. One anthropological field study reported the almost unbelievable average of 979 bottles of chicha consumed in a certain province in 1953 for every adult man and woman. Many mestizos and whites are also heavy drinkers. The most important fact about the Indians today, however, is the emergence of a real class of farmers (*campesinos*), increasingly aware of themselves as Bolivian citizens with a stake in the nation's future.

● **Agrarian Reform.** The Chaco War (1932–1935) with Paraguay, a debilitating affair for both countries, was a turning point in the history of Bolivia. The loss of manpower and wealth was enormous; Indians saw other parts of the country for the first time, and the inadequacies of the nation's economic and social system became evident to many people.[35] Veterans of the war organized to redress grievances, and during World War II several new political parties were organized as a result of the ideological ferment. The MNR emerged as a loose coalition of groups with diverse political views, although its strongest support came from the organized miners and other labor unions including peasant syndicates. The platform of the MNR when it came to power in April, 1952, included one of the most comprehensive land reforms ever enacted. The word *indio* ("Indian, but with depreciatory connotations") was struck from the language and the more neutral *campesino* ("peasant or rural dweller") became the accepted term.[36] This revolution was no ordinary one accomplished by one of the traditional coups. The MNR in 1952 produced "a large-scale reorientation of the entire national culture. It almost completely destroyed the power of the former elite; and the immediate and profound modifications of political life and government policy have subsequently been codified in constitutional changes." [37]

The need for land reform was particularly great; a United Nations study reported that Bolivia had in 1950 the smallest proportion of agricultural crop land to total area in all Latin America—only 0.2 per cent of an acre per person because of the extremely high density of population in the agricultural regions. No reliable history of the Bolivian agrarian reform has yet been written, though important studies have been made. Whether the movement was imposed from above or the peasants achieved it from below is one of the disputed questions. Generalizations are dangerous, for the application of the reform "was as diverse as the geography that makes up Bolivia and the factions that make up the MNR." [38]

The beneficiaries of the reform had to be educated to profit from it and to accept the responsibilities it posed. Those who stood to lose were precisely those who had controlled the nation economically and politically. The administrative and technical personnel needed to operate the complex and revolutionary law was as scarce as in any underdeveloped country. Food production dropped at first. Yet one of the most qualified professional observers, familiar with land reform activities in Mexico and Venezuela, has concluded: "Considering the enormous physical and social obstacles to agrarian reform in the early 1950's it is amazing that so much has been accomplished." [39]

● **"A Beggar Sitting on a Chair of Gold."** Few countries have been endowed by nature with such an abundant diversity of essential raw materials, and Bolivians aware of their nation's poverty often apply to their country this picturesque phrase, which originated with the French explorer Alcides d'Orbigny over a century ago. From the discovery of the Potosí silver mine in 1545 until the nationalization of the tin mines in 1952, a few persons won great fortunes, though there were long periods of poor production. With the mines nationalized, some Bolivians felt that their problems were solved: the workers expected higher pay and shorter hours, now that the mines "belonged" to them; MNR officials calculated that profits hitherto pocketed by the "exploiting imperialists" would pay the increased costs of their socialized government. The harsh truth proved different; tin production dropped after nationalization, partly because of inefficient handling and the increasing depletion of the better deposits. Recent surveys disclose that many mines now being operated are uneconomic, due to the increasingly low grade of the ore, and should be closed. Surveys also reveal that other deposits are available for exploitation, but few new mines have been opened since 1952. The collapse of the international tin market in 1958 further deepened the mining crisis. Even the recent higher price for tin has not brought the industry out of its doldrums. The latest attempt to increase production by a combined U.S.-West Germany project has been abandoned.

President Hernán Siles Zuazo, who served as president (1956–1960) between the terms of President Paz, tackled the inflation problem when he entered office in 1956. The *boliviano* had so deteriorated that from 700 to the dollar in 1953 it had fallen to 16,000; with the help of the International Monetary Fund he halted runaway inflation in 1957 for a time, and stabilized the situation. Juan Lechín, who as leader of the left wing of the MNR and secretary general of the Bolivian Workers Union wielded considerable power, opposed stabilization because it involved closing the uneconomic mines, dismissing miners, and eliminating the main "social" cost of the mines and the subsidized commissary prices. The miners feel that their class has been exploited for centuries, and that they are justified in demanding benefits from any government.

Further development of the Oriente and the opening up of oil fields may in time improve the situation. Deposits of oil have been found in Santa Cruz, Chuquisaca, and Tarija, and elsewhere the rock formations are favorable; three refineries are in operation, a number of British, Canadian, and U.S. companies are at work, and in August, 1959, a Brazilian company received a concession. A considerable area is open to private firms but a government petroleum agency (YPFB) also exists.

Bolivia was the first Latin American state to nationalize a foreign petroleum industry, when it confiscated the holdings of the Standard Oil Company of Bolivia in 1937, a full year before Mexico acted.[40] When the MNR came to power in 1952 Bolivia again invited foreign oil companies to operate, but the terms have been modified from the old days. Friction has not been entirely eliminated and the situation remains explosive because of continued opposition from the extreme left and the nationalist right. Gulf Oil Company expected to begin to export oil by the end of 1965 when a pipeline to the Pacific cost port of Arica made possible a shipment of up to 50,000 barrels of crude oil a day.

● **The Future.** Bolivia has been struggling for years to turn the clock ahead, economically and socially, in a way that Peru has only recently begun to undertake and Ecuador has never seriously contemplated. Today, after more than a decade of incredible social confusion and economic uncertainty, Bolivia has reached another crossroad. The political party that somehow was able to hold together and to embark upon a notable revolution is no longer dominant. Will it be rejuvenated? Will the newly formed Social Christian Party displace it, or will it linger on to "become a cloak with which discredited Right-wing parties hide their nakedness?" [41] Meanwhile the army commands and at least provides a breathing spell before the decision to be made at the next election.

The campesinos seem at least somewhat better off economically than before. Though their lives may be just as hard as before the revolution, they have changed psychologically. They build schools, now more often possess arms, and are on the march.

The generals suppressed a number of unproductive fiesta days, and such mines as Potosí are producing more tin because of more efficient methods. The junta also broke the control of the miner's union over the administration of the mines. Wages were cut and bonuses abolished, which provoked in late 1965 a protest by the Archbishop of La Paz and other ecclesiastical leaders—the first time in many years that the Church spoke out on economic issues, and parish priests are taking definite stands on national problems. (*See Reading No. 24A.*) The mining still does not pay, but is maintained because it is the only source of foreign revenue. U.S. aid remains substantial but the practice of giving money for ordinary budget support, not done for other countries, is being phased out in favor of project support. Problems of mining and the miners harass every Bolivian government. Nationalization in 1952 affected the holdings of only three major companies—Hochschild, Aramayo, and Patiño—and more mines are still in private hands than under government control. Although miners "constitute a mere one per cent of the population, they are vocal and militant out of all proportion to their numbers, and they capitalize on the strategic importance of mining in the economy of the nation." [42]

Roads are being improved with Alliance for Progress funds. Some of the altiplano Indian tribes have proved their ability to thrive in the lowlands—thus disproving the anthropologist Alfred Métraux's charge that such a transfer would be genocide. Japanese colonists and investors have been useful economic stimulants. The *chola* (mestizo) women are as industrious and as independent as ever. They wear many elaborately designed skirts and wonderful stove-pipe hats, which they take off when entering a church or a movie theater. But their daughters wear western clothing, and some go to the university. The chola mothers sacrifice to put them through school, and even send some of their sons for training to Europe or the United States.

In the far reaches of this enormous country, far from the political trenches of La Paz, the Bolivian people continue to work to achieve the only thoroughgoing revolution now in progress in the lands of the Andes. Considering the violence in Bolivia's past, it has been a remarkably peaceful revolution up to now.

Everyone concerned for the future of this remarkable and difficult land will do well to remember the words of Jaime Mendoza:

Let us not underestimate the Indian. . . . He is the very basis of our nationality and has already demonstrated to us his value . . . He was the great producer who made possible the money spent by the conquistador. His contributions in industry, commerce, and communications have been enormous . . . He is still the most solid and productive element in our national economy. [43]

Behind all the political agitation and social change in Bolivia today stand the awakening Indians. They clearly can profit from new ideas, for illiterate farmers in the Santa Cruz area during 1951–1952 greatly increased their corn production by using Cuban yellow corn introduced by the Point Four Program.[44]

The energy and power of that "huge coiled spring," to which the Andean Indians have been likened, have begun to be released in Bolivia. No one knows for certain how this great force will spend itself.

[1] W. Stanley Rycroft, ed., *Indians of the High Andes* (New York: Committee on Cooperation with Latin America, 1946), p. 81.

[2] John Collier, Jr., and Aníbal Buitrón, *The Awakening Valley* (Chicago: University of Chicago Press, 1949), p. 2.

[3] Carlos Monge, *Acclimatization in the Andes* (Baltimore: The Johns Hopkins Press, 1948), pp. 114–115.

[4] Rycroft, *Indians of the High Andes*, p. 91.

[5] José Alfredo Llerena, *Frustración política en ventidos años* (Quito: Casa de la Cultura, 1959), p. 13.

[6] George L. Blanksten, *Ecuador: Constitutions and Caudillos* (Berkeley and Los Angeles: University of California Press, 1951), p. 48.

[7] Lilo Linke, *Andean Adventure. A Social and Political Study of Colombia, Ecuador and Bolivia* (London: Hutchinson, 1945), pp. 182–183.

[8] Collier and Buitrón, *The Awakening Valley*, p. 196.

[9] Beatriz Vázquez Fuller and Gladys Villavicencio, "La mujer indígena frente a los programas de desarrollo," *V. Congreso Indigenista* (Quito, 1965), IV, p. 11.

[10] Francisco María Compte, *Varones ilustres de la Orden Seráfica en el Ecuador, desde la fundación de Quito hasta nuestros días*, 2nd ed. (2 vols., Quito, 1885), I, p. 53.

[11] Hipatia Cárdenas de Bustamante, *Encuesta. ¿Qué debe hacer el Ecuador para librarse de las dictaduras?* (Quito: Imprenta Romero, 1939), p. 9. Another attempt to describe and analyze Ecuador's problems was made by the Unión Nacional de Periodistas del Ecuador, *Realidad y posibilidad del Ecuador* (Quito: Talleres gráficos nacionales, 1946).

[12] *Ibid.*, p. 63.

[13] Bernard Dulsey, "Jorge Icaza and his Ecuador," *Hispania* (March, 1961), p. 99. For a documented account of the life of the agricultural workers from ancient times, see Ezequiel Clavijo Martínez, "La condición social y jurídica de los trabajadores agrícolas ecuatorianos," *Anales de la Universidad de Cuenca*, V (1950), Nos. 3–4, pp. 107–200; Aníbal Buitrón and Barbara Salisbury Buitrón, *Condiciones de vida y trabajo del campesino de la provincia de Pichincha* (Quito: Instituto Nacional de Previsión, 1948).

[14] Llerena, *Frustración política*, p. 111.

[15] Hubert Herring, *A History of Latin America* (New York: Alfred A. Knopf, 1955), p. 511.

[16] Rycroft, *Indians of the High Andes*, p. 284.

[17] Thomas R. Ford, *Man and Land in Peru* (Gainesville: University of Florida Press, 1955), p. 111.

[18] As quoted by Luis Monguió, *La poesía postmodernista peruana* (Mexico: Fondo de Cultura Económica, 1954), p. 105. For an excellent bibliography on political ideas of this period, see Eugenio Chang Rodríguez, *La literatura política de González Prada, Mariátegui y Haya de la Torre* (Mexico: Ediciones de Andrea, 1957).

[19] Fredrick Pike, *A History of Modern Peru* (London: Weidenfeld and Nicholson, 1967), Chap. 8.

[20] This account of APRA is largely based on Pike's volume cited above, and on his article, "The Old and the New APRA in Peru," *Inter-American Economic Affairs*, XVIIII, No. 2 (1964), pp. 3–46, a challenging re-interpretation of APRA.

[21] *Ibid.*

[22] Raymond E. Crist, *Andean America: Some Aspects of Human Migration and Settlement* (Nashville: The Graduate Center for Latin American Studies, Vanderbilt University, 1964). For an analysis of the land reform proposals see Richard W. Patch, *The Peruvian Agrarian Reform Bill* (New York: American Universities Field Staff, 1964). The quotation comes from Henry F. Dobeyns, *The Social Matrix of Peruvian Indigeneous Communities* (Ithaca: Department of Anthropology, Cornell University, 1964), p. 96. See also Allan R. Holmberg. "The Changing Values and Institutions of Vicos in the Context of National Development," *The American Behavioral Scientist*, VIII, No. 7 (1965), pp. 1–8. For a comparative view see José R. Sabogal Wiesse, "La política en una aldea andina," *Revista Mexicana de Sociología*, XXIV (Jan.–April, 1962,) p. 25–34, which describes four villages whose conditions have changed little since colonial times.

[23] James L. Payne, *Labor and Politics in Peru* (New Haven: Yale University Press, 1965), p. 272.

[24] Lyle N. McAlister, "Changing Concepts of the Role of the Military in Latin America," *The Annals of the American Academy of Political and Social Science*, Vol. 360 (1965), pp. 85–98.

[25] Alistair Hennessey, "The Bolivian Coup d'état," *The World Today* (February, 1965), pp. 50–53.

[26] Richard W. Patch, "Peasantry and National Revolution: Bolivia," K. H. Silvert, ed., *Expectant Peoples. Nationalism and Development* (New York: Random House, 1963), p. 126.

[27] Harold Osborne, *Bolivia. A Land Divided*, 3rd ed. (London: Royal Institute of International Affairs, 1964), p. 9.

[28] *Ibid.*, p. 43.

[29] *Ibid.*, p. 43.

[30] Richard W. Patch, *Bolivia's Developing Interior* (New York: American Universities Field Staff, 1962), p. 13. See also Raymond E. Crist, "Bolivians Trek Eastward," *Américas*, XV (April, 1963), no. 4, p. 33–38.

[31] For a detailed view of the post-revolutionary period see Charles W. Arnade, *The Emergence of the Republic of Bolivia* (Gainesville: University of Florida Press, 1957).

[32] Osborne, *Bolivia. A Land Divided*, p. viii.

[33] Franz Tamayo, *Creación de la pedagogía nacional* (La Paz, 1910).

[34] Harold Osborne, *Indians of the Andes* (London: Routledge and Kegan Paul, 1952), p. 211.

[35] For details, see Murdo John MacLeod, "Bolivia and its Social Literature Before and After the Chaco War: A Historical Study of Social and Literary Revolution" (University of Florida dissertation, 1962–1963); David H. Zook, Jr., *The Conduct of the Chaco War* (New York: Bookman Associates, 1960).

[36] Dwight B. Heath, Charles J. Erasmus, and Hans C. Buechler, *Land Reform and Social Revolution in Bolivia*, 3 vols. (Madison: University of Wisconsin Land Tenure Center, 1965), I, p. 115. This splendid collection of material is in mimeographed form at present.

[37] *Ibid.*, I, pp. 115–116.

[38] *Ibid.*, I, p. 149.

[39] *Ibid.*, I, p. 157. See also Richard W. Patch, "Bolivia: diez años de revolución nacional," *Cuadernos*, No. 64 (Sept., 1962), pp. 18–35.

[40] Herbert S. Klein, "American Oil Companies in Latin America: The Bolivian Experience," *Inter-American Economic Affairs*, XVIII, No. 2 (1964), pp. 47–72.

[41] Hennessey, "The Bolivian coup d'état," p. 53.

[42] Dwight B. Heath, "Revolution and Stability in Bolivia," *Current History*, XLIX (Dec., 1965), pp. 328 ff. For a review of material on the revolution, see Charles W. Arnade's "Bolivia's Social Revolution, 1952–1959," *Journal of Inter-American Studies*, I (1959), pp. 341–352.

[43] Jaime Mendoza, *El factor geográfico en la nacionalidad boliviana* (Sucre, 1925), pp. 79–80.

[44] Charles J. Erasmus, *Man Takes Control. Cultural Development and American Aid* (Minneapolis: University of Minnesota Press, 1961), pp. 23–24.

7
SOUTHERN
SOUTH
AMERICA

Argentina

AREA: 1,072,068 sq. mi.

POPULATION IN MID-1966: 22,691,000

LARGEST CITIES:

Buenos Aires (capital): 7,000,000
(metropolitan area, est. 1960)

Rosario: 671,852 (est. 1960)

Córdoba: 589,153 (est. 1960)

PRINCIPAL EXPORTS (1961): meat,
cereals and linseed, wool, hides,
dairy products

PRESIDENT: Juan Carlos Onganía,
military, seized power June 28,
1966, and was inaugurated June 30,
1966, for an indefinite term.

Uruguay

AREA: 72,172 sq. mi.

POPULATION IN MID-1966: 2,749,000

LARGEST CITY:

Montevideo (capital): 1,202,890
(est. 1963)

PRINCIPAL EXPORTS (1962): wool,
meat, hides

PRESIDENT: Jorge Pacheco Areco
succeeded to the presidency
December, 1967, on the death
of Oscar Daniel Gestido.

Paraguay

AREA: 157,047 sq. mi.

POPULATION IN MID-1966: 2,094,000

LARGEST CITY:

Asunción (capital): 305,160 (1962)

PRINCIPAL EXPORTS (1960): meat
products, wood, quebracho extract

PRESIDENT: Alfredo Stroessner,
military, took office August, 1963,
for a 5-year term.

Chile

AREA: 286,400 sq. mi.

POPULATION IN MID-1966: 8,790,000

LARGEST CITY:

Santiago (capital): 2,270,738
(metropolitan area, est. 1963)

PRINCIPAL EXPORTS (1961): copper,
iron ore, saltpeter

PRESIDENT: Eduardo Frei Montalva,
civilian, took office November 3,
1964, for a 6-year term.

SOUTHERN SOUTH AMERICA

Paraguay

● **Arcadia?**   Travelers to this isolated region in the heart of South America have often described it as an Arcadia, ever since the Spaniards first established their capital there in 1537. After traversing the pampa for hundreds of miles, the Spaniards were delighted to find around Asunción an abundance of chickens, partridges, doves and ducks, mandioca, peanuts, maize, beans and pumpkin, deer, boars, river fish, and fruits in wondrous variety. The original inhabitants thought of Paradise in terms of their own land; it was called Yvaga in the Guaraní language, which means "a place of abundant fruit-trees."

Voltaire knew of Paraguay and arranged for his Candide to search there for happiness. A Scottish merchant, John Parish Robertson, visiting the country in 1811, was so impressed with the idyllic scene that his words may stand as typical of those who have found Arcadia in Paraguay:

> the pastures, protected by the trees, and irrigated by abundant streams, were in most places beautifully green; . . . hills, and more gently sloping eminences, contrasted beautifully with the valley and the lake. Wooded from the base to the top, those hills and slopes exhibited now the stately forest-tree, and anon the less-aspiring shrub, the lime, and the orange, each bearing, at the same time, both blossom and fruit. . . . Pendent from the boughs of many of the trees was to be seen, and yet more distinctly known by its fragrance, the air-plant. Squirrels leaped, and monkeys chattered among the branches; the parrot and the parroquet, the pheasant, the moigtu, the Toocan, the humming bird, the guacamayo or cockatoo, and innumerable others . . . inhabited, in all their gaudy variety of plumage, the woods through which I rode.[1]

This picture is still true today for that part of the country which lies east of the Paraguay River. But two-thirds of Paraguay, the Chaco, lying west of the river, is an entirely different world. These plains lack running water, are covered with dry grass and with trees that stand apart from each other and have few leaves, whose wood is as hard as steel. It is a harsh and lonely region, through which many expeditions in colonial days unsuccessfully tried to reach the silver mines in the Andes. One Paraguayan historian called the Chaco a dragon stretched out to protect the wealth of Peruvian mines.

Paraguay is not Arcadia; even with the fertile soil and healthy climate of the eastern portion the Paraguayans have not been able to live anything remotely resembling the proverbially "happy, simple, and natural life" ascribed to the shepherds and hunters in ancient Greek Arcadia. Economic and political conditions are so difficult that many Paraguayans choose to live outside their homeland, mostly in nearby Argentina, Brazil, and Uruguay. A dictator, General Alfredo Stroessner, sits in the presidential palace and maintains his rule by harsh methods. Paraguayan problems have been much the same for four centuries and merit some description as a background for present conditions.

● **The Iron Curtain Approach.** The conquest of Paraguay, under the direction of the first governor, Domingo Martínez de Irala, from the establishment of Asunción in 1537 until his death in 1556, was a humane undertaking. Irala "changed conquerors into colonizers, established friendly relations with many Guaraní tribes, and sought always to open the doors of the land, so that Paraguay might not be isolated, despite its location 1,000 miles inland." [2] He was truly the "Father of the Nation," for in his will he recognized as his own numerous children by six Indian women. Very soon Paraguay became essentially a mestizo colony; the close and permanent association of Indians and Spaniards in villages throughout the land led the Indians to assimilate Spanish culture traits, but the Guaraní language has survived as the principal Indian contribution to Paraguayan culture, and makes Paraguay the only truly bilingual country of the continent. Most Paraguayans speak Spanish, but the most authentic literature is in Guaraní. "The Paraguayans love, hate, and fight in Guaraní. In this tongue they shout on the football fields and whisper their declarations of love in the dark corners of the patios of their old colonial houses." [3]

After Irala Spanish interest shifted to Buenos Aires, Asunción grew slowly, and throughout the rest of the colonial period Paraguay was a defensive post to hold back the Indians and serve as a buffer province against the Portuguese in neighboring Brazil whose frontiersmen (*mamelucos*) were a constant threat. The Jesuits maintained their famous "Reductions" for almost 200 years until their expulsion in 1767. When their missions were at their most prosperous, as many as 100,000 Indians were under mission influence; yet the Jesuits exercised little or no permanent influence on the development of the country.

When Buenos Aires declared its independence from Spain in 1810, the Argentines—who felt then, as they do now, that they should exert special influence in Paraguay—called upon Asunción to follow them. When the Paraguayans refused, General Mariano Belgrano was despatched to force compliance, but he was decisively defeated. Asunción declared its own independence in 1811 and Paraguay was launched on its very uncertain future. An iron curtain was lowered around the country by José Gaspar Rodríguez de Francia. During his dictatorship, 1816–1840, well described for English readers in Edward Lucas White's novel *El Supremo,* Paraguay was almost completely isolated from the world. This policy was reversed by Carlos Antonio López (1842–1862), the best of her dictators, who encouraged immigration, built a cathedral, started schools, distributed land, constructed, in 1861, one of the first railroads in South America, and sent young Paraguayans to Europe for study. His son Francisco Solano López was sent to Paris to buy munitions; he returned with an ambitious and handsome Irish mistress, Madame Elisa Lynch. When young Solano López succeeded to power upon his father's death in 1862, he began to indulge in power politics; due to long standing and complex rivalries among Paraguay's powerful neighbors, he soon found himself confronted by a coalition of Argentina, Brazil, and Uruguay. The War of the Triple Alliance (1865–1870) was a disaster for Paraguay. Because her brave soldiers fought to the death, for this homogeneous people was defending its own soil, the population declined from 525,000 to 220,000, and only 28,000 men were left. During this dreadful holocaust, the dictator maintained his power; cholera raged and generals fought barefoot, but he was presented with a golden sword and jewels while people were starving in Asunción.

Paraguay's next fifty years were a desperate period, although some Mennonite, Australian, and Hutterite immigrants trickled in and, despite a series of revolutions and coups d'etat, the male population so reduced by the war gradually returned to normal. Now another tragedy befell the country—the Chaco War with Bolivia (1932–1935), which Paraguay "won" but only at great cost to her economy and manpower. Again her people displayed their formidable fighting power, this time against Bolivian Indians who felt no solidarity with their white officers. Paraguayans, whether officers or privates, were moved by a fierce national pride, and they used the common Guaraní language as a secret code which the Bolivians could not break. At the end of the struggle a group of war veterans under Colonel Rafael Franco, calling themselves *Febreristas,* attempted a totalitarian rule beginning in February, 1937, but they were forced out after they had announced a program calling for a "New Paraguay," some of whose elements have been used by later governments.

Colonel José Félix Estigarribia, the hero of the Chaco War, assumed power as a temporary dictator, and this able leader promulgated in 1940 a constitution tailored to Paraguay's needs, which provided for a "strong but not a despotic Executive." Unfortunately, he died in an airplane accident soon afterward, and a dictator of the traditional stripe followed, Higinio Morínigo, whose arbitrary but orderly rule began in 1940.

During Morínigo's regime, the United States provided some aid as a war measure to improve agriculture, public health, and transportation. The lack of minerals and industry makes Paraguay largely dependent upon a small export trade in her agricultural, forest, and pastoral products, and a modest internal market. Most of her people live in rural districts; the ratio of the population of the capital to the national population is 14 per cent, one of the lowest of any of the Latin-American nations. A scattered population, the cost of the marriage ceremony, and the fact that women exceed men in many places due to the toll of war and emigration, all help to account for the present social imbalance. In one town which was intensively studied, one household in three included no man and less than half of the births were legitimate, which resulted in the "economic and social disorganization of family life." [4]

After World War II Morínigo found it increasingly difficult to maintain control; he was overthrown in 1948. After the brief presidency of the noted writer Natalicio González and an uneasy period under Federico Chaves, General Alfredo Stroessner was "elected" president in July, 1954, in a typical Paraguayan election: only one candidate appeared on the ballot. The General is still in power, having been "reelected" at appropriate intervals.

● **"The Last Dictator in South America."** Although General Stroessner prefers to be known as President Stroessner, he is usually referred to as "the last dictator in South America" and pressure is strong to remove him. In Paraguay the Archbishop of Asunción considered the situation so grave that he has sent out a pastoral letter denouncing "excessive centralization of power" but also warning the opposition that it must cooperate "with a constructive spirit." As exiles in neighboring countries, thousands of Paraguayans impatiently await the fall of Stroessner.

He has proved to be a durable dictator. His first years were marked by ruthless oppression; jails swallowed up enemies of his regime. Then his continued army strength and his powerful Colorado party enabled him to feel secure enough to give the country a semblance of democracy. An opposition party voted in 1963 for the first time in 10 years, though the Liberals won few votes and some wits refer to it as "the omnibus party" because they claim all its members could ride in one bus. Twenty Liberals sit in the one-house congress but the government still controls every aspect of Paraguayan life.

Economic progress is evident. Paraguay's currency is stable. The population increase is moderate, there is no great rush of rural folk to the capital city, whose streets are now mostly paved. Few Asunceños appear barefoot on the streets, and Asunción has its first water-supply system. It has few trains, but they probably run on time. Every now and then Stroessner reports that his alert forces have snuffed out a Communist plot.

Dictators usually reach a point where they wish to be considered law abiding and even benevolent; Stroessner has now reached this point, for he boasts that Paraguayans never had so much freedom before and states: "I never had a man killed." Whether he remains in power or falls, Paraguay will continue to be an isolated nation living somewhat under the shadow of her neighbors, with basic problems impossible of quick alleviation. One of the prime obstacles to achieving political peace is the passion and intolerance Paraguayans display in their politics. Political opponents are always personal enemies.

"The tragedy of this natural Arcadia," George Pendle has written, "is that it can neither live in idyllic solitude nor compete on equal terms with the great nations that surround it." [5] Yet the inherent vitality of the people of Paraguay can be, as it has been in the past, one of her strongest assets for the future.

Uruguay

● **A Moderate Miracle.** The smallest country in South America, with less than 3 million people, Uruguay has had only one dictator in the twentieth century and is rightly considered one of the most stable democracies in the Americas. Its population is predominantly white, with no Indians, few Negroes, and perhaps 10 per cent mestizos. Nine out of ten inhabitants are first, second, or third generation Europeans, principally from Spain and Italy. The perceptive Lord Bryce described that country thus in 1910: "Uruguay has neither mountains, nor deserts, nor antiquities, nor aboriginal Indians. . . . It is a cheerful country, with scenery constructed, so to speak, on a small scale, as befits a small republic." [6]

Uruguay has participated in no war for many years, is plagued with no boundary controversy with its neighbors. Its people are relatively prosperous and well educated; its organized archives, National Library, vigorous newspapers, and University are all manifestations of a healthy nation proud of its past and determined to maintain its independent position in the world. Its army is small, its national social program impressive, and its system of national government through an Executive Council, without a president, was a symbol of its fear of domineering leaders.

No Church-State problem exists; the Church was disestablished in 1919, and the Uruguayans are not a conspicuously religious people. The official calendar makes no mention of Church festivals; December 25 is "Family Day," and Holy Week is a seven-day vacation period called "Tourist Week." In Uruguay women enjoy a much better economic, legal, and psychological status than in most other countries of Latin America. Divorce has been legalized for half a century, and may be obtained at the request of the wife, who need not state her reasons. The Uruguayan delegation to the United Nations Conference in San Francisco in 1945 was one of the few to include a woman.

Yet Uruguay was not always thus, and a brief view of her history shows what important changes can be achieved if a nation has outstanding leadership.

● **Uruguay Before Batlle.** During the colonial period Uruguay was merely a buffer state between the Portuguese in Brazil and the Spaniards in Argentina. Horses and cattle roamed at large, rival forces clashed, and the area was a no-man's land off the beaten path until the revolutionary period. Beginning in 1806 the British, Portuguese, Spaniards, and Buenos Aires forces all participated in the confused events of Uruguay's struggle for independence. The patriot leader José G. Artigas created a sense of nationality during the years of his influence up to 1820, and by 1828 Uruguay was proclaimed independent, largely through British influence.

The nineteenth century was a turbulent time for this little country: "Of the twenty-five governments that guided the Uruguayan ship of state from 1830 to 1903, nine were forced out of power, two were liquidated by assassination and one by grave injury, ten resisted successfully one or more revolutions, and three were free of serious disturbance during their period of office." [7] It was a thoroughly undramatic history; not even an outstanding dictator rose to power. Uruguay was so weak that her neighbors intervened, occasionally at the invitation of the Colorado Party when it wanted help against its opposition, the Blancos. By 1880 general chaos reigned; Colonel Latorre resigned the presidency declaring the Uruguayans ungovernable.

During these difficult years, Uruguay's remarkable transformation began. After the war against Paraguay ended in 1870, Argentina and Brazil ceased to intervene in Uruguayan politics and the two political parties began to develop programs. From 1886 on, all presidents were civilians, and in this same year young José Batlle y Ordóñez (1856–1929) founded the newspaper *El Día* and began in its columns his long battle for order and progress. By the mid-nineties he had made himself an outstanding political leader. Under his guidance modern Uruguay began to take shape; he served two terms as President (1903–1907, 1911–1915), and left a deep imprint on the country. "Neither Napoleon nor Hitler, Ataturk nor Gandhi influenced a single country as much or as variously as Batlle did his own beloved Uruguay."

● **What Batlle Accomplished.** In 1900 before Batlle's first term began, Uruguay was far behind Argentina in economic and social development. Its political instability frightened off capital and immigrants; land was in the hands of a few men, the armed forces consumed a large share of the budget, of which 40 per cent went to pay service on the national debt, which was per capita the highest in South America. Education lagged, despite the influence of José Pedro Varela (1845–1879), an outstanding educator. Some economic development had been achieved, thanks to the relative political peace after 1886—Uruguay had almost 2,000 kilometers of railroads at the turn of the century—but much remained to be done.

Beginning about 1905 President Batlle led Uruguay into the first real social and economic revolution in Latin America. He believed the State capable of operating public services and was certain that this step would both replace foreign influence and help to bridge "the enormous gap between the rich and the poor." Today the State operates many enterprises; it has a virtual monopoly of insurance, manufactures alcohol and refines petroleum, directs a meat-packing plant and owns fishing trawlers, and controls three powerful banks, the telephone system, and ports. Some of these enterprises make a profit; others consistently operate at a loss and have to be maintained by government subsidies. Batlle also fought for social legislation; today Uruguay has an impressive body of laws to protect and aid workers. Hours of work are limited to 8 per day and 48 per week, and other regulations provide holidays with pay, minimum wages, family allowances, workers' accident and unemployment compensation, and old age pensions.

To make social and economic reform politically possible, Batlle worked for honest elections and less presidential power. These he achieved in the Constitution of 1917, according to which executive power was divided between a President, in charge of foreign relations, national defense, and the police, and a National Council of Administration to control the other ministries. The Council of Nine was to have one-third of its members from the leading minority party. Abolished in 1933, the Council was briefly reinstated under President Alfredo Baldomir (1938–1942), and in 1951 the presidency was abolished altogether after wide popular discussion and vote. A "Collegiate Executive" was established called the National Council of Government, composed of nine members, six from the party having the largest vote, and three from the minority party with the largest vote. The President of the Council, chosen from the representatives of the majority party, served for one year under a plan of rotation.

During the early years of Batlle's great transformation, Uruguay produced one of the most influential writers of Spanish America, José Enrique Rodó (1872–1917). His *Ariel* portrayed the contrast between that materialistic "Caliban," the United States, and "Ariel," the embodiment of man's higher aspirations, represented by Spanish America. Although Rodó believed the United States might in time become less materialistic, the part of his message that appealed to his contemporaries was his attack on the United States. Now considered somewhat *passé* in Spanish America, for at least a generation his writing helped to mold the attitudes of Spanish Americans toward "the Titan of the North."

After 1950, it became evident that all was not well in Uruguay. Although it had become the first and most advanced welfare state in Latin America, certain vexing problems threatened to undermine its position as one of the most stable and democratic nations of the continent.

● **"Demographic Megalocephaly."** A political scientist has used this elaborate term to describe what he considers Uruguay's gravest problem—its failure to solve the perennial and growing imbalance between the capital and the interior. Montevideo, with over one million inhabitants, has at least one-third of the company's total population; it also has a practical monopoly on educational and cultural facilities, commercial opportunities, medical services, and the national intelligentsia.

The interior departments contain most of the national territory but only a small part of the population. Here live the ill-fed, ill-clothed, ill-housed agricultural workers on *rancheríos,* the infamous rural slums where "promiscuity, concubinage, prostitution, illegitimacy, and venereal disease are common." [8] The Blanco party leader Luis Alberto Herrera described the ranchería some years ago in the following terms, which are still largely applicable: "[it] constitutes a public calamity, a den of malignancy and thievery, the center of disease of all kinds, without hygiene, without schools."

Although this discouraging description applies principally to the northern departments, the interior as a whole has colonial status with respect to Montevideo, which irresistibly attracts the energetic, the progressive, the intelligent. The government has taken some steps to make country life more agreeable, but the industrialization fostered by the government has drawn many workers from the hinterland. Every day the imbalance increases between the underprivileged interior and the capital—the "suction pump" whose "castles have been built" and whose "streets have been paved with the beef, wool, and hides of the provinces." [9] Those who live in Montevideo are inclined to consider this description exaggerated, and to emphasize the advantages a metropolitan center affords for the country at large.

Uruguay's unique welfare services are almost entirely financed from exports—wool (50 per cent), meat (20 per cent), and hides (15 per cent)—produced in the interior. Fifty per cent of the population tend 23 million sheep and 8½ million head of cattle, and carry on the small amount of farming done. Thus Uruguay's economy rests squarely upon the ranching industry of the hinterland, whose rural population receives least benefit from the state welfare program. Until this inequity is diminished, Uruguay will suffer impoverishment, economic, spiritual, and psychological.

● **The Sick Welfare State.** The Welfare State is now a way of life in Uruguay, and no politician can hope to win votes by advocating austerity,

hard work, and the sacrifice of benefits enjoyed for many years. The widespread custom of taking off the summer afternoons of working days to enjoy the superb beaches that stretch from Montevideo beyond Punta del Este will not be easily broken.

One in every three adult citizens of Montevideo has a government job, and three-fourths or more of the national budget is normally allocated for the salaries of government employees who, with their families, constitute 20 per cent of the total population. Thoughtful Uruguayans and foreign observers wonder how long Uruguay can continue to support such bureaucracy and at the same time pay the generous social security provisions for which the country is famous. (*See Reading No. 61.*)

The crisis accelerated during the government of the conservative Blanco Party, which in 1958 returned to power for the first time since the Colorados won in 1856. That the transition occurred peacefully was an impressive demonstration of the maturity of Uruguay's political democracy, but Blanco political leadership has inspired little confidence, and the nine-man governing council is being "agonizingly reappraised" by both parties. Inflation proceeds at a dangerously rapid rate, unemployment is reaching 200,000 or 20 per cent of the country's active population, and a bank scandal closed virtually all the banks for several weeks in June, 1965. In August, 1965, Argentina and Brazil—which usually can find almost nothing to agree upon—were so disturbed by Uruguay's economic plight that they moved to take joint action to alleviate the crisis. A small but active Communist party, the pro-Fidelista Federation of Uruguayan Students, and the independent newspaper *Época* keep up a steady drum fire against both traditional political parties as representatives of the landowning oligarchy (one per cent of the population holds 33.5 per cent of the land). Most of the left's energy, however, is directed outside Uruguay: it supports the Peronist movement in Argentina, opposes the military government in Brazil, and denounces U.S. action almost everywhere. Voters turned out in large numbers in 1966 to change the executive branch of their government from the cumbersome Swiss-type to a Presidency. Uruguayans had been proud of their elaborate machinery for eliminating personal influence but it "involved the paradox that only a strong and determined man could make it work." [10] The machinery attracted the keen professional scrutiny of political scientists, but it did not serve to control inflation or to stop the 500 strikes staged by various groups of workers in 1966.

The first President elected under the new system was Óscar Daniel Gestido, which also was an indication of the voters' sophistication. He was a retired airforce general, and Uruguay cherishes its tradition of civilian rule, but he had won a reputation as a competent reorganizer of the country's railroads and national airline. He also won out in the stiff intraparty pre-election squabble over Jorge Batlle, the grand-nephew of the legendary political leader whose contributions to national unity still evoke patriotic memories. Moreover, he is a Colorado, so that once more the country witnessed a peaceful change of political parties.

General Gestido, who assumed office on March 1, 1967, campaigned on a platform of honesty and straight talk about Uruguayan problems. Uruguay's currency was devalued eleven times in 1966, and during the sixty days of 1967 preceding his inauguration there were 160 labor walkouts. Inflation hit an all-time high of almost 120 percent. After several months during which President Gestido attempted, unsuccessfully, to solve his country's pressing economic problems by persuasion, he embarked upon a get-tough policy which had long been advocated by the International Monetary Fund and numerous Uruguayan economists. He even indicated that he would introduce legislation calling upon Uruguayans to give up some of their cherished social security benefits. Then he died suddenly, in early December, 1967, and his whole economic belt-tightening austerity program was put in question, inasmuch as Vice President Jorge Pacheco Areco, who succeeded to the presidency, is expected to favor less stringent measures to solve Uruguay's economic problems.

One close student of Uruguay's history closes his book with a chapter "Trauma in Uruguay" and remarks that the country can no longer "afford the luxury" of failing to meet its well-known and long-standing problems: "The overtones today clearly are of approaching disintegration of a way of life." [11] A European traveler found Montevideo "full of charming, cultured, cynical intellectuals" who were pleased that their country had "no oil, no minerals, nothing" and one commented, with apparent complacent unconcern: "we are very advanced as consumers, but rather backward as producers." [12]

Yet Uruguay's democratic way of life and active parties, the Blancos and the Colorados, give hope for the future. These parties are among the oldest in the world and are probably better organized than any others in Latin America. Uruguay possesses one other great advantage in the present struggle: Her population growth is slow and thus adjustments should be possible without turmoil. But they will not be made easily.

Chile

- **The Lesson of Chile.** This relatively small country with some 7 million people has all the classic problems of most South American nations: large landholdings, inadequate transportation, poverty, and, since 1920, considerable political instability. Yet Chile occupies a special position, for it has been steadily working toward social and economic democracy by evolution rather than by a tremendous upheaval. Uruguay and Costa Rica have also followed this course, but they are smaller countries with smaller problems.

Culturally, Chile stands high; its universities, private and public, have long played an important national role; its musical and literary development is noteworthy; its pride in its own history and the competence of its historians has always been strong; and its excellent newspapers reflect the vigorous social and political thought of a lively and free people. It is fitting that the Chilean poet Gabriela Mistral was the first Latin American to win the Nobel Prize in the field of the humanities.

The army has remained "essentially obedient," as it was required to be by the conservative Constitution of 1833. The Catholic Church lost many of its political prerogatives during the nineteenth century and has maintained its religious influence since then by the quality of its prelates. Chile's secular, civilian atmosphere gives life there a flavor quite distinctive from that of her neighbors—Argentina, Bolivia, and Peru. But Chile has some serious problems. One of them, her geography, is of permanent importance.

● **"Chile Has a Crazy Geography."** A Chilean geographer made this statement, and many facts support it. With a coastline almost 3,000 miles long and an average land width of only 100 miles, Chileans are subject to an astonishing range of climates and geographical conditions. In the great northern desert are areas where rainfall has never been recorded; in the south it rains "13 months of the year" with some sections receiving 6 feet of rain annually. Lying between them is the central valley of Chile which has "the world's perfect climate" and the country's bread-basket. Chile has peaks almost as high as Aconcagua, the loftiest mountain in the New World, which rises on the Argentine side of the Andes, and near Chile's shoreline the bed of the Pacific Ocean sinks to one of its lowest depths. Chile has many peaks higher than any in continental United States; it has 30 rivers, but only two are navigable and these for only a short distance.

Although Chile's coast, including bays and fiords, extends for 6,000 miles, it provides few good natural harbors in the more populated zones. Valparaiso, however, the second largest Chilean city, is the largest harbor on the west coast of the Americas, except for San Francisco, California. "Only 8 per cent of Chile's surface supports agriculture. Another 9 per cent is suitable for pasture, and 22 per cent is forest, leaving 61 per cent not suitable for development. The initiative and industry of the Chilean people are demonstrated by the fact that these scanty agricultural and pasture areas now furnish 90 per cent of the population's food." [13]

Minerals in many parts of the world tend to appear in high or isolated spots; in Chile, this is spectacularly true. All the coal she needs comes from mines beneath the sea near Lota; two of her three principal copper mines, the nitrate industry, the sulphur resources, and many smaller mines are located in the dry north.

Chile is the world's foremost copper-exporting country; about 90 per cent of the more than 400,000 tons it sells abroad each year is produced by three United States enterprises; together they provide more than half of Chile's foreign exchange commerce. Chuquicamata has been one of the world's greatest copper centers since it began operations in 1915 and mines large quantities of ore and waste daily; its reserves are estimated to last for more than a century at the present consumption rate. Copper is so vital in her economy that when its price drops one cent on the world market, Chile stands to lose $6,000,000 of its foreign exchange per annum.

Chile's nitrate industry has been diminishing due to competition from European fertilizers but still holds second place in the national economy. Sulphur may soon surpass it, for Chile's sulphur reserves are of higher grade than any extensive deposits known elsewhere. Unfortunately they lie in rugged, uninhabited regions, atop the volcanoes that form an almost continuous range for some 600 miles in the north, at elevations of 17,000 to 20,000 feet. The Chilean miner is tough, and in no other industry is his fortitude tested more severely. Already 50,000 tons of sulphur are exported annually, despite the fact that large quantities are used in the national wine industry. Iron ore production has increased in recent years; it is expected to surpass nitrates in value, and may eventually be more important than copper in the national economy.

Chile was a pioneer in railroad construction in South America and now has some 6,000 miles of main and branch lines, but geographical obstacles are deterrents to both railroad and highway construction. Chileans and Chilean products therefore move principally on the sea or by air.

Chile looks to the south for future development. Its present area is 290,000 square miles, but the nation claims half a million square miles in Antarctica and has established there three permanent bases where scientific and mineral investigations are in progress. In Chile's portion of Tierra del Fuego, which Magellan passed on the first circumnavigation of the globe, wells are now producing petroleum and gas. Oil reserves are not considered large, but already Chile's dependence on foreign oil has decreased.

● **The Heart of Chile.** More than half of the country is uninhabited; it consists of high mountains, arid desert, and dense forest. One third of Chile's population is concentrated in the pleasant central valley, much like California, where the province of Santiago contains the capital city and many industries. This is the economic, educational, and political heart of the country. Here reside, for at least part of the year, the owners of the great estates, whose rural life has been so well described by George McBride in *Chile, Land and Society* (1936). Here rapid industrialization shows itself in a pall of smoke that sometimes obscures the snow-covered Andes and in the city slums where the workers crowd together. Here Chile's best musical performances are given, her famous ballet and theater flourish, the poetry, fiction, and history written that have given the country such a high literary reputation. Here lived José Toribio Medina (1852–1930), bibliographer and historian, whose 408 volumes remain a wonder to scholars. Here, to an advanced age, lived Francisco Encina, whose 20 volume *Historia de Chile* was in recent years a national best seller and is still keenly debated in classroom and cafe. Not surprisingly, in the light of Chile's long eminence in the field of history, here lives the new generation of historians, some of them now Marxist-oriented. Here live most of Chile's social scientists, who have long and searchingly studied the nation's problems. Here, at the universities, are the students who take an active part in national and international politics and Pablo Neruda, one of the great poets of the hemisphere, now a dedicated Communist. Here also are most of the members of the ecclesiastical hierarchy who increasingly speak out on Chile's need to improve the economic well-being of her people. Santiago, then, is where the drama of this relatively small country's struggle with its economic and political problems is being played today.

● **Arturo Alessandri's Revolution.** The conquistador Pedro de Valdivia founded Santiago in 1541. But Chile remained a frontier outpost subject to the viceroy in Lima for most of the colonial period. A few families dominated the land and, like their Peruvian counterparts, sought, bought, and relished titles of nobility. This landed elite, with its insignia, ribbons, and family coats of arms, was in control when the independence movement against Spain began in 1810. The revolutionary period was a confusing time, but Spanish power was broken in 1817 at the battle of Chacabuco. The Chilean leader, Bernardo O'Higgins, the illegitimate son of a Chilean mother and the Irish Ambrosio O'Higgins, former viceroy of Peru, now attempted a social revolution. He tried, unsuccessfully, to limit the power of the Church, break up the landed estates, revoke the privileges of the nobility, and reform the social habits of the people generally. He was forced out in 1823; by 1833 a conservative constitution was established under which Chile was governed until 1924.

The peace the conservative rule established made possible steady economic development and important educational advance. The University of Chile, founded in 1842, has been a vital intellectual center for more than a century. The Church's political privileges were gradually whittled down; freedom of the press was won in 1872, and public cemeteries and civil marriage were approved. Chile's victory in the War of the Pacific (1879–1883) stimulated her national spirit; the spoils of war in the form of nitrate territory in the north led to economic expansion. But the land system remained unchanged and the defeat of President José Manuel Balmaceda in the 1891 civil war led to the establishment of a "pseudo-parliamentary" regime. It was called the "Parliamentary Republic" by some; more realistic writers termed it the restoration of the oligarchy. "Members of the landed gentry who had called themselves conservatives and others who called themselves nationalists and liberals, had permitted representatives of a growing middle class, who called themselves radicals, to join forces with them to overthrow a too dictatorial president." [14]

Congress now became the devoted instrument of the aristocrats; ignoring the growing changes in the social and economic life of the nation and lacking a sense of responsibility to public opinion, they manipulated the national and local political machinery for their own benefit. Some lonely voices called for basic changes. Francisco Encina advocated a thorough overhauling of Chile's educational system. Always a caustic writer little given to sugar coating his pill of criticism, Encina issued his diagnosis, *Our Economic Inferiority: Its Causes and Its Consequences* (1912); it went largely largely unheeded. He feared political extremism, of the right or left, and believed that Chile urgently needed social legislation as well as a better educational system.

The outbreak of World War I and the resulting high prices for copper and nitrates created an artificial boom; in 1915 the conservatives forced the election of Juan Luis Sanfuentes, who believed that "social change was not only bad for business but an insult to Almighty God." [15]

Behind the façade of national prosperity, the common man of Chile lived in misery, with little share in the bounty which was enriching the aristocracy and creating new fortunes from mines and farms. *Inquilinos,* virtually bound to the land of their masters, still worked from sunup to sundown for a few cents a day. Miners sweated under the blinding sun of the Atacama Desert, or choked in the deep shafts of the coal mines, for as little as twenty cents a day, and had no insurance against industrial accident, disease, and death. Factory workers fared no better. Domestic servants and other menials served interminable hours at wages of a few cents a day. The luxuries of the golden age were reserved for two or three out of every hundred people; the reasonable comforts of modern society were shared by a few more; but more than nine-tenths of the people were packed into huts or tenements, wore rags, ate scant and poor food, and had no security against disaster. More than half the people could neither read nor write.[16]

The end of World War I brought falling prices and great misery to the people. The situation was ripe for change. President Arturo Alessandri, elected in 1920 by a minute margin, became the hero of the forces seeking that change. He promised separation of Church and State, votes for women, personal and corporate income taxes, social and welfare legislation, government control of the nitrate industry, more provincial autonomy, and more popular influence in political affairs. Alessandri could not fulfill all his promises; conservative senators blocked some of his reforms, and during the economic crisis of 1924 the army expelled him from the presidency and he went in exile to Mussolini's Italy. A period of confusion followed.

Socially minded army leaders brought Alessandri back in 1925; a new Constitution was drawn up in that year. A thoroughly Chilean document, influenced neither by the contemporary Mexican constitution nor the Weimar

Republic, the 1925 Constitution provided for separation of Church and State, restored presidential powers lost in the Civil War of 1891, in effect abolished parliamentary government, made the presidential term six years, and forbade consecutive re-election. No expropriation language was used but one article read, significantly: "The exercise of the right of ownership is subject to the limitation necessary for the maintenance of social order; and in that sense the law may impose obligation on services of public utility in behalf of the general interests of the State, the health of the people and the public well-being."

But constitutions do not bring peace and order unless the basic social and economic structure of the nation is in harmony with them, as Bernardo O'Higgins had declared a hundred years earlier. Chile now suffered many vicissitudes: Alessandri was ejected again and an army officer, Carlos Ibáñez, ruled as dictator from 1925 until 1931, when he was forced to resign. Alessandri returned as a sober, conservative president for a full term, 1932 to 1938. By the end of his term, the nation was tired of his conservatism and ready for a change. The "Lion of Tarapacá" ended his political career as he had begun it a generation earlier, as the object of criticism from all directions.[17]

In 1938 the Popular Front, a combination of political forces which included Communists, elected as President Pedro Aguirre Cerdá, a wealthy Radical whose program of economic nationalism and extensive social legislation made Chile a welfare state matched in the Americas only by Uruguay and not equaled by most European countries. An equal degree of state responsibility was "only realized by Britain since 1945." [18] Appropriately, one of the principal authorities in the Americas on social welfare legislation is Moisés Poblete Troncoso of Santiago.

The Chilean Development Corporation (Fomento) intensified state intervention into economic affairs by building a steel mill at Huachipato near Concepción which now exports steel to Argentina and the United States, by constructing hydroelectric power plants, and by energetically supporting Chile's industrialization program.

Although factories multiplied and social legislation protected their workers, the Radical Party neglected agriculture. The conservative landed families could not halt the technological and industrial changes transforming Chile, but kept almost intact their own economic and social order. The government granted loans and an irrigation program to the owners of the great wheat estates and the vineyards, but did little to relieve the miserable condition of their workers.

● **A New Era: The Electoral Victory of Frei.** The 1958 election of Jorge Alessandri, a son of the former president, brought to the presidency a Liberal who won very narrowly over the Socialist Party candidate, despite support

GABRIELA MISTRAL—CHILEAN NOBEL PRIZE WINNING POET
(Pan American Union)

from the Conservative Party and the middle class generally. His six-year term did little to change the basic economic and social situation; indeed, no one term could have done so. But the triumph of the Christian Democrat Eduardo Frei Montalva at the polls in 1964 was the most important political event of the year in Latin America. The Chilean Nobel Prize poet Gabriela Mistral once wrote: "Some day Eduardo Frei will be president of Chile, though I will be dead. On that day I will turn over in my tomb to applaud him." [19] Many people in and outside of Chile were delighted to see a strong and intelligent political figure, determined to achieve economic and social justice, assume the presidency. (*See Reading No. 59.*)

Frei has long pondered the problems of Chile and of the hemisphere, and has presented his views in several notable books. He has not hesitated to criticize those who demagogically cry out against "Yankee imperialism" while extending their hands for U.S. money to help them remain in power. He asked his fellow Latin Americans to consider what their situation would be if a nation of 150 million Frenchmen, Germans, Englishmen, Japanese, or Russians were their neighbor, instead of the United States: "We would find ourselves in many and greater difficulties than at present." [20]

Frei will not, however, follow U.S. leadership unless it coincides with his own platform. On his visit to Europe in July, 1965, he spoke freely and independently against U.S. unilateral military intervention in the Dominican Republic and has stated firmly that the Organization of American States must be radically improved if it is to survive. He urged at one time that Cuba should be brought back into the American family of nations, but since the tricontinental conference of revolutionary movements held in Havana in January, 1966, he has increasingly attacked the subversive plans formulated there for Chile: "guerrilla warfare . . . strikes, invasion of rural estates, collective demands, and revolutionary violence."

● **Promises and Reality.** On his return from his triumphal European tour, he found Chile's severe inflation continuing, that only the Copper Agreement of the many important pieces of legislation the previous Congress had blocked had been partially passed, and that even this remained controversial. Braden and Anaconda Copper had already been paying about 80 per cent of their profits to the Chilean government; the new arrangement gives the government a 50 per cent holding in the industry but, at least at first, may provide less rather than more revenue. Education has been strengthened at all levels, but the needed basic land reform has barely been started, in spite of widespread public support. The real problem may be "the institutionalized relationship between people." [21] A generation ago Chilean society was described as essentially patriarchal: "the landowner has commanded, a landless people has obeyed." [22] Such long-standing relationships can be changed neither easily nor quickly, in Chile any more than in the U.S., as the U.S. struggle for racial integration shows.

Ironically, the powerful influence of the advanced social security system is one of Chile's problems: some observers hold that Chile is becoming a "sick welfare state" like Uruguay. A quarter of a century ago the philosopher and educator Enrique Molina wrote: "Chileans are highly civilized in regard to consuming, but primitive when it comes to producing." [23]

The strength of the established elite in Chile must not be underrated. Some believe that Frei won the votes of the conservatives only because they feared even more drastic changes from his opponent, the Communist-supported Salvador Allende who lost the previous election by a narrow margin. The oligarchy are rather expecting Frei to forget at least some of his electoral promises. If Frei persists in trying to keep them, he will be strongly opposed on such key projects as agrarian reform.

The first two years of Frei's program for "Revolution with Freedom" included some victories and some defeats. In October, 1966, a Communist-led strike caused the rector to suspend the activities of the most important provincial university in Chile, which meant that 4,500 students lost a full school year. On the plus side, about the same time the Christian Democratic government won final approval for the plan to "Chileanize" the nation's copper industry. Not only does this make Chile the dominant partner in one of the world's largest copper mining operations, but if all goes well the new investment involved will double the industry's productive capacity to 102 million tons a year within five years.

The Chilean Senate, however, by a combination of left and right wing extremists refused Frei authorization to visit Washington. (*See Reading No. 60.*) At Christmas time 1966, Frei proudly announced that his government had decided to renounce the U.S. financial credit of about $80 million annually which had been used to buy essential imports and help meet public investment requirements. In early 1967 Christian Democratic candidates in municipal elections lost ground, which indicated at least a ground swell against the government. Back of all these political and economic maneuvers is one fundamental fact, stressed by the most recent analysis of Chile's present situation: Almost 90 per cent of persons receiving incomes cannot afford to maintain an average family at a minimum adequate standard of living. The situation at present may be even worse since Chile's per capita real income since 1942 has declined.[24]

The issue is now joined between those who want to maintain the status quo and those who insist on change. If the reform government stands firm and moves rapidly enough toward its primary objectives not only will communism be checked in Chile, but throughout the continent all those who believe in the possibility of social change without violent revolution will be encouraged, and it will be proven that communists have no monopoly on the idea and practice of economic improvement for the people.[25]

President Frei came to power with a clear mandate from the voters of Chile, and no more propitious country could be found for a test of the proposition that far-reaching changes can be achieved under the present form of government. Chile, with its energetic people, its tradition of free speech, and its devotion to education and democratic processes, has entered a crucial period of its national life.

Argentina

● **The Legacy of Perón.** How was it possible for Juan Domingo Perón and his Evita to dominate Argentine life so completely from 1945 until the dictator's fall in September, 1955? What had gone wrong in the old pre-Perón Argentina which for so many years had prided itself on being the richest, the best-educated, the least dictator-ridden country of Latin America? How can the immense physical and moral damage wrought during this decade of "national humiliation" be repaired? How can the nation build itself anew, avoiding the mistakes of the past, so that Argentina may take its rightful place again among the South American nations?

A flood of pamphlets, articles, and books has poured forth from Argentine presses since 1955 to answer such questions as these. A government-appointed National Investigation Commission produced in 1958 five thick volumes, which bring together carefully organized data on "the Peronista party, the legislators, publicity policies, political and social policies, economic policies and their disastrous results, . . . educational and cultural pursuits, corruption, vandalism, and disorder, the worst of the Peronista crimes, and the attempt to spread Peronismo to other lands." [26] A British writer emphasizes the strong and continuing influence of history in all the recent changes— "The past behind the present." (*See Reading No. 62.*)

No two persons offer the same prescription for recovery. Ezequiel Martínez Estrada declared on December 3, 1958, on the occasion of the twenty-fifth anniversary of the publication of his *Radiografía de la pampa*—considered by many the deepest expression of the nature of Argentina—that the present disorientation of Argentina is due,

> in part, to the fact that the great men of the past have died without heirs . . . The country has not changed. What we formerly saw under sumptuous garments we now see oppressed and spent, naked as if for clinical examination, in a surgical theater crowded with incompetent doctors and good medical students. No one paid any attention when I counselled that the photographic image should be ignored and the x-ray analyzed; for, according to my diagnosis, Argentina was suffering from no skin disease, but rather a glandular sickness. [27]

Another writer has rejected all explanations of the nature of the crisis thus far set forth; he asserts that the crisis existed before Perón, exists now, and will continue to exist until Argentina somehow acquires a sense of community it now lacks. (*See Reading No. 65.*)

This national inquiry is in one sense most un-Argentine and indicates the shock which the national ordeal dealt to Argentine sensibilities. In Brazil, Mexico, and other Latin-American countries, the literature of self-examination is extensive, but not in Argentina. Argentines have taken their national destiny for granted; until lately it has usually been foreigners who have analyzed Argentine character and found an essential sadness in the true Argentine tango, the dominance of the male in Argentine society, and the "defensive" nature of the people. Observers have often noted that the Argentines themselves—particularly those in Buenos Aires—tended to believe in their own superiority and were certain that their destiny was to become the leading nation of South America. (*See Reading No. 63.*)

● **The Background of Modern Argentina.** The four-hundredth anniversary of the establishment of Buenos Aires was celebrated in 1936 with great pomp, but it was the second founding of the city in 1580, not that of 1536, that marked the true beginning of Argentina. Buenos Aires was established on a strategic site which ensured its becoming one of the world's great ports; the herds of cattle which were to make the country famous were multiplying on the pampa; the people of the port (*porteños*) and those of the interior were living such separate and distinct lives that a gulf yawned between them; the porteños had already manifested the spirit of independence which has since characterized the development of the capital.

But the Argentine colonial period was on the whole a dull time; Spaniards seeking treasure disembarked in Buenos Aires only to hurry across the rich pampa lands toward the silver mines of Peru, and those who remained lived quietly, without the solace of Indians to do the hard labor.

A decisive event occurred in 1776, when Spain established the Viceroyalty of the Río de la Plata, a huge area that included approximately the territory of present-day Argentina, Bolivia, Paraguay, and Uruguay, with Buenos Aires as the capital; Argentines began to dream of imperial grandeur. The one printing press in the area was moved from inland Córdoba to the capital, and Buenos Aires became the cultural, economic, and political center of a vast region.

The confused revolutionary period began in 1806, but not until 1816 did the Argentines formally proclaim their independence from Spain. Civil strife continued until 1829 when Juan Manuel Rosas became dictator of the country, dominating it until 1852. He ruled with terror and a formidable apparatus of spies; everyone in Buenos Aires had to wear, as a sign of loyalty, a red ribbon inscribed "Death to the Savage Unitarians," as he termed his political opponents. "Even the ladies of the aristocracy did not dare to be seen in the street without their red ribbon or sash. Doña Encarnación, Rosas' wife and ardent assistant, wore evening dresses of scarlet satin." [28] Rosas made lavish gifts of land, thus laying the basis for some of the extensive landed estates, and consolidated national feeling by his defense against British and French invasions. At last a combination of his opponents managed to defeat him.

Following his downfall the Constitution of 1853 was drawn up in an atmosphere of great hope. Discussions were carried on at a high level, often by those who now returned after years of exile in Chile and Uruguay but had never ceased to ponder their country's problems, and aired various views on Church and State, presidential powers, personal liberties, navigation, banking and finance, and especially on the fundamental theme, regionalism and unification. The nonparticipation of powerful Buenos Aires in these deliberations accentuated the need to keep the port city and the interior provinces in some kind of workable harmony.

Juan Bautista Alberdi's ideas, expressed in his treatise *Bases and Starting Points for the Political Organization of the Argentine Republic,* were the principal focus for this discussion. He held that Argentina had declared her independence without being ready for freedom; he advocated hard work, immigration, railroad construction, and education. His proposals were couched in forceful language: "Foreign capital will be needed: attract it. The age of heroes has passed. We enter today in the age of common sense. The American type for grandeur is not Napoleon, but Washington, who represents not military virtues but prosperity, organization, and peace. South American liberators are the worst enemies of Liberty." He warned that the road was long: "We shall sow the seed for our grandchildren. Real freedom is a slow growth."

The 1853 Constitution encouraged immigration and adopted some other ideas of Alberdi. It provided a federal government, closely patterned on the United States Constitution but with significant differences. The national government was given the right to intervene in the provinces—even to the extent of displacing the elected governor and legislature and putting Federal Interventors in charge. Another difference lay in the powers assigned to the President: the Argentine President was made supreme over the legislature, a significant fact in Argentina's political history. He might declare a state of siege, a form of martial law which suspended the personal liberties guaranteed by the Bill of Rights and permitted him to rule the country by presidential decrees instead of legislation. The whole machinery of democracy might be ignored, except the civil courts which could not, however, pass judgment on any presidential action.

A period of uncertainty followed from 1853 to 1862, during which Buenos Aires remained outside the Confederation established by the Constitution; it somewhat resembled the difficult years the United States experienced under the Articles of Confederation. In 1862 Bartolomé Mitre brought the rich province of Buenos Aires into the Confederation and the capital was moved from inland Paraná to Buenos Aires. Mitre became

President and a consolidated Argentina was now ready to develop. Much of Mitre's presidency was taken up with the War of the Triple Alliance against Paraguay (1865–1870), but his prestige and competence did much for the nation. He was a many-sided patriot—soldier, orator, historian, skillful administrator, biographer of Argentina's revolutionary hero San Martín, translator of Horace and Dante—and a leader of profound honesty and morality. After completing his presidential term he founded in 1870 one of the outstanding newspapers of Latin America, *La Nación,* which became the voice of the conservative landed gentry.

Another remarkable Argentine followed him in the presidency, Domingo F. Sarmiento (1868–1874), under whom the Paraguayan War was ended and unprecedented economic expansion and change begun. Sarmiento was the schoolmaster of his country; his book *Facundo* (1845), ostensibly an attack on a provincial dictator, was also a plea for Argentina to throw off the tyranny of the *gaucho* (cowboy) mentality and adopt civilized European ways, though he was Argentine enough to admire gauchos, too. Clothes were a symbol of culture, he felt; he had fought against Rosas dressed to the nines: "My polished sword, buttoned coat, gloves, French overcoat and cap, everything was a protest against the gauchesque spirit." A teacher all his life, whether in exile in Chile, visiting Europe and the United States, serving as Argentine Minister in Washington or as President, Sarmiento virtually created the educational system of Argentina. He was a writer as well as man of action, as the 52-volume set of his publications testifies. A vigorous president, he intervened repeatedly in the provinces and stirred up animosity by his occasionally peremptory decisions. He was very serious; he never played a game in his life until ordered to do so as an old man by his physician. A powerful personality during a significant period of Argentina's growth, he will always be remembered in his country's annals as "a soldier in the never-ceasing war for the liberty of men's minds," [29] who considered the schoolroom the most important battlefield in America.

Sarmiento well understood the nature of the struggle, as he made clear in his speech to Congress on October 12, 1868, when he took the oath of office as President:

"The ills which afflict the Argentine Republic are not a matter of our day alone. The spectacle of provinces in the throes of 'risings' has been common for half a century . . . The same social phenomenon is to be seen everywhere in Spanish America. . . .

We cannot wait patiently . . . The time has come to show whether the government is what it ought to be under our republican institutions: an instrument for insuring the largest measure of happiness for the greatest possible number of individuals. . . .

We have inherited popular masses who are ignorant and destitute. We lack homogeneity and cohesion, the essential conditions for any society to survive. . . .

Nevertheless, our situation is not desperate or beyond remedy. If we lack people to fill our vast territory, the world asks only security and favorable laws to give us within a few years millions of its superfluous people. If distances are great, the steam engine will shorten them. But all resources must be allocated and made available by thoughtful and fair laws to see to it that while the elements of civilization appear on our coasts, the rest of the country is not handed over to barbarism. Otherwise, measures that should lead to progress will merely give rise to new disasters and anarchy."

In the years following Sarmiento's presidency, modern Argentina now began to take shape: "The immigrant and immigrant capital, the railway network, barbed wire, the refrigerator ship and the *frigorífico,* these were the instruments of a pastoral, an agrarian, and a commercial revolution which converted the country into the world's greatest exporter of meat and one of its largest producers of grain, raised land values to fabulous heights, and with unprecedented rapidity transformed a backward frontier area into a highly urbanized commercial civilization." [30] Between 1869 and 1914 the population rose from less than two million to almost eight million; despite several crises, these were years of vigorous expansion under a landed aristocracy in economic, social, and political control of the country. Two thousand families ruled Argentina, it is said, and they spent their wealth so freely in Paris that the "rich Argentine" became a well known literary figure.

During this period Buenos Aires definitely assumed leadership. The city grew by 84 per cent in the decade from 1880 to 1890, while the rest of the country increased by only 29 per cent.[31] It was in Buenos Aires in these years, too, that the remarkable men known as the Generation of Eighty flourished who brought Argentina onto the stage of world affairs: "provincial yet cosmopolitan; proud of their land and themselves yet quick to imitate the ways of other lands and other men; . . . liberal in economic matters but conservative in politics; sensitive to the nuances of European culture yet adolescent in its domestic application; proud of their history, but prouder of their future." [32] With the coming to power of the Generation of Eighty the days of the historic gaucho were numbered.

● **The Gaucho.** In colonial Argentina and well into the nineteenth century almost everyone rode a horse. Travelers told of beggars collecting their alms on horseback, and dentists filling teeth while both doctor and patient sat astride their mounts. The Indians, also, took to horses; one tribe, the Mbayas, abandoned agriculture completely and constituted themselves an aristocracy of horsemen and herders ruling over sedentary Indians. The gaucho, the Argentine counterpart of the American cowboy, was preeminently a horseman.

For more than two hundred years the gaucho of colonial days collected hides, and led an outlaw life away from the confines of society. During the first 75 years of the 19th century he took an active part in the frequent wars

of the period. As the rural life of the nation changed when the "desert" developed into enormous wheat and cattle producing areas, the free-wheeling gaucho almost became a man without a country. He was pressed, sometimes shanghaied, into army service to fight against the Indians, and the famous "Conquest of the Desert" by General Julio Roca was achieved (1878–1880) only by the ruthless expenditure of many gaucho lives. The gaucho became alienated from a society that despised him and considered him "uncivilized"; he rebelled against administrative controls by scattered revolts and other acts of violence. Then, just as the gaucho's traditional way of life was passing from the scene, he was rescued from oblivion by the magic of a poet's pen. *Martín Fierro* (1872), by José Hernández told the story of a gaucho so powerfully and so persuasively that it indelibly marked Argentine literature and provoked serious thought about the gaucho, his character, and his place in Argentine history. Some saw him as a violent rebel, resisting the onward march of progress; a bad citizen, an enemy of regular work and order who could or would not adapt to the civilized life the nation was straining to achieve, a lawless and ignorant horseman, so tough and rowdy that the drinking houses where he and his kind caroused had iron grilles to protect the barmen from their patrons. Others regarded the gaucho as basically noble, a heroic fighter for Argentina's independence, an inspired songster who embodied something authentically Argentine. The book *Martín Fierro* defended the gaucho, interpreting him to the nation in whose history he had played so dramatic a role. Thus Hernández, turning a spotlight on the poor marginal men of Argentine society, did something much like what the Brazilian Euclydes da Cunha accomplished later when his *Revolt in the Backlands* (1902) attacked his nation's indifference to the followers of the mystic Antonio Conselheiro in poverty-stricken northeast Brazil. Neither writer persuaded his contemporaries to action, but each produced a book of enduring significance in his own national literature and of great interest to students of modern Latin America.

The gaucho did not disappear. Instead he sank into the position of a faceless peon on a ranch, no longer a colorful element in Argentine life but an anonymous worker whose knowledge of horses and skill in their training contributed substantially to the nation's astonishing economic advance.

Like the Hollywood cowboy, the gaucho became and remains a symbol of certain national ideals—Argentine self-sufficiency, stoic courage, and authentic national character. Perhaps a popular native hero was needed to help nationalize the mass of immigrants flowing into Argentina. The politicians had to take account of him. In 1952, the Perón regime established a "Day of Tradition" in observance of the seventy-fifth anniversary of the poem's publication: the now idealized gaucho of the pampa officially became a central figure in Argentine life. The President of the National Commission of Culture announced a policy "to protect the world of the national spirit, guarding it from exotic influences. We will keep alive our native music and primitive dances, the vivid representatives of our past, reminding us of our native genius, our respect for the family, our cult for courage, the beauty of popular poetry, and our vernacular idiom."

● **The Pampa.** Although Argentina is six times the size of Spain and only smaller than Brazil among Latin-American nations, its effective territory until 1862 was limited to the province of Buenos Aires, the interior colonial city of Córdoba, and a few towns on the periphery of the country—Mendoza at the base of the Andes through which traffic flowed to Chile, and Salta in the north toward Bolivia. After the Indians of the south and west had been driven from their lands by the "Conquest of the Desert" ranches, railroads, and settlements rapidly expanded. Argentina now began its remarkable transformation into one of the world's most productive pastoral and agricultural areas. The pampa, of more than 30,000 square miles with deep, rich earth, generally dependable rainfall, mild winters and hot summers was "tamed, organized, and virtually harnessed to the economy of far-away Great Britain." [33] Alfalfa now fattened cattle instead of the wild, tough prairie grass of Rosas' day, and the stock itself was greatly improved with British pedigreed cattle. A small French refrigerator ship proved in 1876 that Argentine beef could be transported across the tropics to feed the growing industrial populations of Europe; within ten years 57 refrigerator ships were plying between Buenos Aires and British ports alone.

Over 6 million immigrants poured into Argentina between 1858 and 1930, most from Italy and Spain, but some from France, Germany, Russia, and Switzerland. Welsh immigrants sailed to Argentina, too, singing their rousing hymns as they entered upon a new life in the bleak southern regions of the country. It was these immigrants, plus refrigerator ships, wire fencing, and railroads, that transformed the pampa. Their industry was remarkable; the native Argentines despised farming, but the immigrants, particularly the Italians, working as tenant farmers, converted great tracts into farmland. By 1900 wheat and other agricultural products were even more important to the nation's economy than meat and other animal products, and the earlier pampa W. H. Hudson had described in his marvelous little book *Far Away and Long Ago* had disappeared forever.

The railroad connected the great port with the economic core of the country; after the Indians were pushed back vast tracts of land were bestowed upon officers of the Army of the Desert who had fought them. But the Province of Buenos Aires, the largest single section of the pampa, continued as the economic, political, and cultural center of the country.

The immigrants transformed more than the pampa. They created what José Luis Romero has termed "alluvial Argentina," by which he means the "social conglomeration" resulting from the incomplete nationalization of the immigrants. "No one can deny that this mixture continues to maintain its conglomerate character. . . . It would be difficult to state what we Argentines are . . . the Argentine soul is an enigma because the collective personality of the nation is still in the process of elaboration." [34] Another Argentine thinker, the late Ricardo Rojas, attributed a weakening of the moral fiber of the nation to the immigrant hordes. They went to Argentina to make money and in this they succeeded but, Rojas felt, their "get-rich-quick" attitude gave Argentine life an unhealthy materialist tone which prepared the way for Perón from the turn of the century.

● **The Background to Perón.** The development of the pampa led to widespread speculation, extravagance, and optimism. The aristocracy of landowners, the *estancieros,* made great fortunes and their president, Miguel Juárez Celman, boasted to Congress in 1889: "Everything goes up: the value of land, of livestock, of agriculture, of industry, commerce, credit, accumulation of capital, public and private incomes." [35] The bubble burst soon afterward; the Revolution of 1890, waged for wider political rights and in protest against the economic collapse, was put down by the oligarchy. Although the economy recovered somewhat after a year or so of uncertainty, the crash aroused dissatisfactions and anxieties which led to the formation of the Radical Party in 1892. Competent leaders such as Leandro Alem and, later, Hipólito Irigoyen with support from the middle classes, developed into the largest group opposed to the ruling conservatives. It was actually more liberal than radical; its platform included electoral reform, rights of petition and speech, constitutional liberties, and representative government. Economic reforms such as land division, collective bargaining, and social legislation were barely considered. Almost immediately doctrinal and other differences split its ranks. Juan B. Justo and others withdrew to found in 1894 a relatively weak Socialist Party which influenced the urban workers somewhat but divided the intellectuals. Lisandro de la Torre, an able and conscientious political leader alienated by Irigoyen's iron rule of the Radical Party, established his own Agrarian Party. Anarchist ideas were brought in by immigrants from Spain and Italy. But the nation's prosperity was such that no real urgency for reform was felt and the Conservatives quite easily maintained political control of the country. No detailed study of the Oligarchy has yet been published, and it may be that some of its members pushed for more reforms than is realized. But one member of this dominant society has declared that it consisted of "a powerful material prosperity, civic apathy, political disorganization, a malaise of the masses. . . . the wealthy plutocracy lived in a state of refined luxury, gave brilliant parties, owned magnificent country houses, and made frequent trips to Europe." [36]

By the end of the century, the Argentine economy had recovered. But the gap remained between Buenos Aires and the provinces, between urban and rural society, so that the nation remained unconsolidated, "a divided and uncertain people. . . ."

What was Argentina?

Was it the educated, progressive elite who administered the nation, as their patrimony, from the floor of congress or the stock exchange or over an after-dinner brandy at the Jockey Club, the Club del Progreso, or the Círculo de Armas? Or was it the burgeoning middle class so evident as grocers, clerks, office managers, and foremen in the coastal cities? Or was it the Indian working in the cane fields of Tucumán or the quebracho forests of the Chaco, the Italian sharecropper in his hovel on the pampas, the Irish sheepherder in Patagonia, or the native peon in the province of Buenos Aires? Or was it the rapidly expanding urban proletariat in the ports—the mestizo cook from Santiago del Estero, the Basque laborer in the slaughter house or packing plant, the porter from Galicia, or the Italian peddler? Little wonder was it that, after a century of Independence, Argentines were still searching for identity and that the nation presented simultaneously all shades of prosperity and poverty, progress and reaction, learning and illiteracy.[37]

Conservative rule during the early years of the 20th century, although selfish, was benign enough to produce enlightened presidents. President Carlos Pellegrini saw that the rising clamor for honest elections and democratic suffrage must be answered. Even while the Conservatives cynically and competently maintained themselves in power by rigged elections and the Radicals adopted a policy of abstention from the polls, Pellegrini warned his fellow oligarchs that "the floodgates must be opened" to the people: in his last speech in Congress in 1906, this enlightened conservative declared that "we will establish solidarity in the Argentine nation the day when all Argentines enjoy equal rights, the day when the Argentine is not faced with the sad alternative of either renouncing his citizenship or of appealing to force to recover the rights taken away from him." [38] Pellegrini did not go so far as to work for popular suffrage, and it remained for another Conservative president, Roque Saenz Peña (1910–1914) to take this decisive step.

Saenz Peña worked for the conservation of Argentina's natural resources —water rights, timber, and mineral resources. He presided over what was generally acknowledged to be the wealthiest and most civilized nation of Latin America, with a population of 8 million at the outbreak of World War I. It was a secure, self-centered society, with the Jockey Club on the then swank Avenida Florida in Buenos Aires symbolizing the life of the wealthy landed families who enjoyed principal control of the country. Saenz Peña did not share his fellow-Conservatives' disdain for the masses; in his presidential campaign he called for honest elections and pushed through an electoral law in 1912 which provided for universal and compulsory male suffrage, the secret ballot, and a strict system for the registration of voters. Thanks to this law, the Argentine people for the first time in their history freely elected a president in 1917. The experienced Radical leader Hipólito Irigoyen, who had fashioned a tightly controlled party through the years, won the election. His carriage was drawn through the streets of Buenos Aires by his jubilant middle class supporters.

Looking back at the period of Radical domination from 1916 to the crash of 1930, some Argentines believe that Radical "failure" helps to explain the appearance of Perón. Irigoyen took office with public support for some progressive changes, soon won great power as a war president, and probably could have effected some basic improvements. But with full control of the smoothly working political Radical machine, he chose to follow an essentially conservative policy. He suppressed the labor strike of 1919, and none of his policies took account of the crucial problems of the over-large rural estates and the depressed lot of the workers everywhere. It was an index of Argentine complacency and isolationism that Irigoyen and his party were influenced not at all by the revolutions in Mexico, Russia, or even nearby Uruguay.

Irigoyen maintained neutrality during World War I, which was good for Argentine business, and economic development remained rapid. In 1922 he set up a state oil company, putting into effect what the 1916 Mexican Constitution had provided in theory. Almost completely isolated in his personal as well as his political life, he conducted much of the business of state himself for, like the sixteenth-century super-bureaucrat Philip II, he trusted no one. He never married, though he had a succession of mistresses. He strongly defended the Catholic Church, opposed divorce laws, and gave clergymen important public posts. He intervened even more actively and frequently in the provinces than his Conservative predecessors.

Students constituted in 1918 the only vigorous reform element in Argentina. The "Manifesto from the Youth of Córdoba to the Free Men of South America" issued on June 21 was the beginning of continent-wide participation by university students in political as well as educational matters. The Manifesto condemned the universities as a "refuge of the mediocre, a source of income for the ignorant," which reflected "the sad spectacle of a senile immobility." It demanded a democratic government for universities in which students should have the right to rule themselves, to name professors, and to appoint administrators. Autocratic in many respects, Irigoyen apparently looked upon this movement as an attack upon the old guard that he detested and supported the students, who won many of their demands. Argentine universities improved; more fellowships were made available, ampler publication opportunities were provided, and "popular" universities for adult education were organized. Henceforth Argentine universities and university students were in politics, although some Argentines still consider this detrimental to academic standards.

Under the succeeding Radical president, Marcelo T. Alvear (1922–

1928), Argentina pursued "business as usual," much as the United States did during the Coolidge era. Buenos Aires dominated the national scene; immigration, which had been free and state-aided, was now on a quota system; the 1924 law specifically forbade immigrants from seeking homesteads or public lands from the state, restrictions also imposed on native Argentines. The Radicals during their years of power neither noticed the poverty of the interior provinces nor supported the social legislation proposed by the Socialists. It was a measure of the bankruptcy of his party, and of Argentine politics, that in 1928 Irigoyen was re-elected at the age of 75. "The President, who had never been clear-headed, was now senile; his rapacious subordinates, without his knowledge, robbed every department of the administration; and he himself was incapable of fulfilling the ordinary routine of his office; papers remained unsigned, salaries unpaid, and appointments with his ministers ignored." [39]

In September 1930, a palace revolution, which enjoyed much popular support, overthrew Irigoyen, who was completely unable to cope with the economic problems that followed the crash of 1929. An extreme Conservative, General José F. Uriburu, closely allied with the Catholic hierarchy, now seized power with the support of the army, which has remained a force in Argentine politics ever since. For thirteen years the Conservatives kept themselves in power by the old political stratagems of fraudulent elections and interventions in the provinces.

Argentina now entered a new economic phase; the State more and more intervened in economic affairs, and industry advanced rapidly. From 1935 to 1942 industrial production doubled, spurred on by economic nationalism and a shortage of goods during World War II. By 1942 it is estimated to have equaled agricultural and pastoral production combined.

The ostentation of the rich and unconcern for the masses that had largely marred Radical rule was now intensified. Eduardo Mallea, the novelist, asserted in 1937 that the nation had grown soft since 1900; there was nothing to challenge the immigrants, and youth had grown cynical. The ideals of Sarmiento the educator were no longer venerated, the primitive nationalism of the gaucho spirit revived; the country felt no sense of direction or destiny. Another Argentine, writing after Perón's fall in 1955, declared that the period from 1930 to 1943 damaged the country even more than Perón. Under Perón the opposition forces at least stayed alert, while under the Conservatives a period of moral and national relaxation weakened the nation profoundly: "A great lassitude and repugnance [had] existed because of the constant electoral fraud that the oligarchy organized, perfected, and practiced." [40]

At the death in 1933 of the old Radical ex-President Irigoyen, a drama was enacted which illustrates the rigidity of the Conservatives against the hopes of the people. The government refused to allow his body to lie in state in the Buenos Aires cathedral, but the workers persisted in honoring the man they thought had been their saintly leader.

The staircase up to his modest apartment was much too narrow to accommodate the thousands of mourners who wished to pay homage to the corpse on the cheap iron bedstead; so most of this vast multitude had to remain below, filling the street. They stood there for hour after hour, bareheaded, in silence. Trains from the provinces brought 100,000 country folk into town for the long vigil of three nights and days. . . . On the day of the funeral the government sent an escort of cavalry, but [it was] forced to withdraw. Men fought for the honor of carrying the coffin. There were a quarter of a million people in the funeral procession; and an equal number packed the flat roofs, the balconies, windows and trees along the route.[41]

The people needed to believe that they were important, even to the government from which they had received so little consideration. It was this widely felt frustration under all the surface prosperity that perhaps explains most clearly the rise to power of Juan Domingo Perón.

- **The Age of Perón, 1943–1955.** The literature on Perón and his epoch in Argentina is already copious and sharply controversial. The great debate on his place in history will continue for years. In some ways he was an Argentine *caudillo* much like the other dictatorial presidents who had governed the country under both Conservative and Radical regimes. The military coup of 1943 paved the way for his accession to power just as the army's ousting of Irigoyen did for the Conservatives. His foreign policy was traditional; he worked hard to establish Argentina's primacy over Brazil in South America, and his development of a "Third Position" somewhere between the Soviet Union and the United States may be seen as a natural continuation of the hostility to "The Colossus of the North" which had long been a principal plank of Argentine policy. He tried to liberate Argentina from the economic influence of Britain and the United States by putting into effect policies of economic nationalism long advocated by the Radical Party and strongly supported elsewhere. (*See Reading No. 64.*)

Yet Perón was different from his predecessors. The great grandson of an Italian immigrant, he had great personal charm and roused enthusiasm and sympathy among many different kinds of people. But, of his twin pillars of support, the army and the workers, it was labor upon which he particularly leaned. As Head of the Department of Labor and Social Security in the uncertain years 1943–1945, he had won the allegiance of the labor unions by undertaking many long overdue social reforms. "No matter how demagogic his methods, he had accomplished more for them in two years than the Socialist Party had achieved in decades of patient and constantly obstructed legislative effort." [42] It was the workers, or *descamisados* (shirtless ones), who made possible his election in February 1946, but they received some unwitting help from U.S. Ambassador Spruille Braden. His "pro-democratic" statements and his later involvement in the publication of the State Department's Bluebook, an exposé of Nazi activities in Argentina, were presented to the Argentine public as "intervention." The election was held under army supervision and, despite considerable help in the pre-election period from *peronista* goon squads, most observers believed that Perón was clearly the people's choice.[43]

Perón moved quickly to organize a social and economic revolution whose force is even now by no means spent. He aimed at economic independence; to this end he nationalized the Central Bank, made insurance a semi-state monopoly, purchased the United States-owned telephone system and British-owned railroads, and greatly expanded the state-owned merchant fleet. Through an Institute for the Promotion of Trade he was given the right to buy cheaply practically all of the country's wheat, meat, and other produce, and sell it wherever the best price could be obtained. During this early phase, when Miguel Miranda was riding high as Perón's economic advisor, industrialization was given a forward thrust to assure an improvement of the workers' living conditions. Great industrial progress was made, though at the expense of agricultural and pastoral products.

In 1949 a new Constitution was drawn up which increased the President's power, already great, removed the bar to immediate re-election, included a statement on the rights of labor and the aged, and permitted the rural worker to buy the land he worked. Armed with new powers, Perón now purged the Supreme Court, intervened in the universities, and in 1951 seized Argentina's great newspaper *La Prensa* thereby completing a process of press control that had begun in 1930.[44]

Beginning in 1951, Perón met increasing difficulties—economic, political and personal. He had probably never completely controlled the army; real tension developed when it forbade Eva Perón to run for the vice-presidency in 1951. The Church had at first supported the government brought in by the army putsch of 1943, and religious instruction in the schools was almost immediately restored. Cardinal Copello and the hierarchy helped Perón to power in the 1946 election but the situation changed radically after Eva Perón took control of public and private charity which the Church or Catholic organizations had previously organized. The campaign to exalt the Peróns deeply offended the Church; certainly the great landholding families that detested the Peróns personally, as well as politically, wielded powerful influence in the inner councils of the Church. Many Argentines were affronted by the signs set up all over the country: "Perón cumple; Evita dignifica." After his wife's death in 1952, Perón might have effected a reconciliation with the Church. Instead he provoked open conflict, perhaps fearing that the Church was undermining his influence with labor or to divert attention from the deteriorating economic situation. By November, 1954, he had publicly denounced certain members of the clergy as conspirators against his government, and when he proceeded to legalize divorce and brothels the break was decisive.

Perón's grandiose economic plans now began to crumble. Meat production dropped; to the horror of Argentine housewives, the government even decreed "beefless days." Later he was forced to import wheat from the United States, which brought home to the nation, as nothing else could, the depth of the crisis. In April, 1953, as if to warn his enemies and prove that the age of the oligarchs had ended, he permitted hoodlums to burn down the Jockey Club with its rare book collection and vintage wines. When he signed a contract with the California Oil Company to exploit Argentine oil resources, around which emotional nationalistic currents had always swirled, his plight was obviously desperate. This contract, plus the support the United States gave him toward the end of his rule—which was interpreted in Argentina as Yankee intervention—hastened the end of his era.

● **Argentina After Perón.** When the armed forces rose at last in 1955 against the dictator-President and he fled the country, many in the Argentine nation—particularly the middle and upper classes—felt both profound relief and profound shock. Disclosures of the unimaginable corruption and suffering which the regime had imposed were followed by national recognition that Argentina now faced the disastrous economic and moral consequences of his policies and his pillaging, while Perón himself enjoyed in exile abroad—and by 1965 in Spain with a new young wife—the immense personal fortune he had amassed and carried away. And yet, to many of the humble people of Argentina, Perón was their beloved champion. Ernesto Sábato, a well-known anti-Peronista, recorded a scene which disclosed this:

> That night in September of 1955 while we, the doctors, landowners, and writers were in the parlor noisily celebrating the fall of the tyrant, I noticed how two of the Indian women in a corner of the kitchen were working there with their eyes full of tears. And even though through all those years (the ten years of Perón) I had meditated on the tragic duality which cuts through the Argentine people, at that moment it appeared to me in its most poignant form. For what neater characterization could there have been of the drama of our country than that almost exemplary scene? . . . Great multitudes of humble compatriots were symbolized in those two Indian girls crying in a kitchen in Salta.[45]

Sábato called for national reconciliation, based on sympathetic understanding, of all classes of the population, which is now estimated at 21.5 million. He asked all Argentines to accept responsibility for Perón's rise to power, to surrender their old divisions and hostilities and to work together to build a unified new Argentina.

The smoke of the fires Perón lighted still hangs over Argentina, and Peronism is still the dominant issue in Argentine political life. The uncertainty left in his wake affected all groups: the labor unions, landowners, army, Church, industry, and political parties. Argentina returned to the 1853 Constitution in mid-1956, pending the drawing up of a new one. Caretaker governments under army sponsorship finally achieved enough stability to make presidential elections possible. The experienced Radical leader Arturo Frondizi was elected president in February, 1958. If, as A. P. Whitaker states, "one of the few constants in the shifting sands of Argentine opinion is a pronounced anti-imperialism which is tinged with Yankee-phobia," [46] President Frondizi showed courage in his attempt to achieve the economic recovery of Argentina. Ignoring his own previous pronouncements against imperialism and in favor of exclusively Argentine development of national oil resources, he entered into contracts with several big foreign oil companies. The dominant element remained the national petroleum agency (YPF), but Royal Dutch-Shell, Standard Oil of New Jersey, Pan American International Oil Company, and others were all at work on an ambitious program of exploration and development.

Equally courageous, and hazardous, was Frondizi's austerity message of December 29, 1958, when he warned Argentines that they "must face facts and adopt heroic measures." Pulling no punches, he reported in painful detail on the way in which Argentina had consumed more than it had produced during the previous fifteen years, and informed the nation of the sacrifices necessary to correct the dangerous state of its economy. Most extraordinary of all was Frondizi's trip to the United States in February, 1959, in the face of an unquiet situation at home and the strikingly different economic and national orientations of the two countries. No Argentine President had ever made a state visit to Washington before.

● **The Fall of Frondizi.** The new Argentina called for by many Argentines on the fall of Perón did not arise. Frondizi's program of rapid economic development based on the attraction of foreign capital for industrial development and reintegration of Peronists (but without Perón) failed. They were basically wise policies, but the times were out of joint, Frondizi was not a skillful enough politician to achieve a consensus for his policies, and the military, restless for power and determined to rule, removed him from office in March, 1962. A constitutional president. Arturo Illia, was elected in 1963. Relative calm returned to Argentina, but "the Argentine Problem" remained unsolved.

Even the analyses of Argentine character and of the nation's prolonged crisis remain much the same, although now it is social scientists rather than, as earlier, men of letters, who are subjecting Argentine society to the kind of attention a psychiatrist gives his patient. The sociologist, Gino Germani, emphasizes that Perón gave the worker a new sense of personal dignity, as well as material benefits;[47] another sociologist, José Luis de Imaz, analyzes the composition of selected leadership groups between 1936 and 1961 and concludes that the country has no "coherent elite." [48] This lack may result

JORGE LUIS BORGES—ARGENTINE AUTHOR AND POET
(Pan American Union)

from the "alluvial society" produced by massive immigration, which José Luis Romero so imaginatively described.[49] No matter which interpretation an Argentine follows, he is likely to feel a sense of failure and frustration, which comes from a kind of collective realization that the long-cherished Argentine dream of national glory and hemispheric power have simply not come true, and he has no confidence that the situation will improve for a long time.

Buenos Aires continues as an impressive concentration of urban power, and the pampas as a vast but sparsely settled fertile region. Argentines remain charming in private, and rude in public; they write copiously and read omnivorously. Bookstores have recently been opened in postoffices; publishers report much larger editions of translations of Italian novels than of the original books in Italy and of the 30,000 copies printed in Argentina of Jean Paul Sartre's latest volume, 10,000 were bought in Buenos Aires alone within 48 hours. The city also prides itself on being the most sophisticated music center in Latin America; world-famous artists appear at the Teatro Colón before large audiences and the handsome new San Martín theater probably has some of the most modern stage equipment in the world.

Argentina has not fought a war since 1870, but has a well-armed force of 150,000 which absorbs a large part of the national budget and controls the government. It apparently has determined to play a significant role in the nation's development, although views on what that role should be vary widely. (*See Reading No. 66.*) The military hierarchy abandoned its provisional stance of subordination to civilian authority in mid-1966. An astute editor-observer had written, "The first time President Illia telephones the Minister of War, 'I need your help', that [will be] the beginning of the end." [50]

Whether or not Illia made that appeal, the army overthrew him in June, 1966, and installed General Juan Carlos Onganía as head of a strong-fisted regime whose early repressive, even reportedly brutal, actions gave little hope for peaceful resolution to Argentina's problems. In July, 1966, the army abolished the traditional autonomy of Argentina's nine state universities, which aggravated the already serious "brain-drain" to other countries. The tripartite system of university self-government—by professors, students, and alumni—lost out. Now a regent plus a council determined by the government runs the universities, while a government-appointed team of educators drafts a code for administering the universities on a permanent basis. Another cause of widespread concern is the press law now being drafted "to guarantee freedom of the press" President Onganía announced on August 4, 1966, but which the highly respected *La Prensa* calls a sign of "the erroneous and dangerous tendency that seems to dominate the thinking of the Presidency."

This latest putsch and the army's announcement in April, 1967, that it expected to stay in power for ten years indicate anew that the end of the profound crisis that Argentina has been experiencing since 1930 is not yet in sight. The wounds the body politic suffered during the Perón regime have not yet healed, nor has an economic balance between agriculture and industry been fully achieved. The Peronistas remain on the political scene as a powerful force, but they are divided too. Like all political groups in the nation they are weakened by a lack of fundamental agreement on policies and practices.

Yet Argentina's great natural and human resources could still bring significant social and economic advances, provided that she achieves political stability and a sense of national purpose.

[1] J. P. and W. P. Robertson, *Four Years in Paraguay: Comprising an Account of the Republic, under the Government of Dictator Francia*, 2 vols. (Philadelphia: E. L. Carey & A. Hart, 1838). The quotation is in Vol. I, p. 174.

[2] Harris Gaylord Warren, *Paraguay. An Informal History* (Norman: University of Oklahoma Press, 1949), p. 79.

[3] As quoted from Walter Wey by George Pendle, *Paraguay. A Riverside Nation*, 2nd ed. (London: Royal Institute of International Affairs, 1956), p. 94.

[4] Emma Reh, *Paraguayan Rural Life: Survey of Food Problems* (Washington: Institute of Inter-American Affairs, 1946), pp. 21–22.

[5] Pendle, *Paraguay*, p. 94.

[6] As quoted by George Pendle, *Uruguay. South America's First Welfare State* (London, Royal Institute of Internation Affairs, 1952), p. 4.

[7] Simon G. Hanson, *Utopia in Uruguay. Chapters in the Economic History of Uruguay* (New York: Oxford University Press, 1938), p. 3. For a comprehensive survey of Uruguay's progressive labor laws, as embodied in more than 70 acts concerning hours, wages, industrial safety, and social insurance see Alberto Sanguinetti Freire, "Social Legislation in Uruguay," *International Labour Review*, Vol. 59, No. 3 (1946), pp. 271–296.

Two standard works now provide a detailed story up to 1933: Milton I. Vanger, *José Batlle y Ordóñez: Creator of his Times*, Vol. 1 (Harvard University Press, 1963); Göran G. Lindahl, *Uruguay's New Path. A Study in Politics during the First Colegiado, 1919–33* (Stockholm: Library and Institute of Ibero-American Studies, 1962).

[8] This and the following quotation come from Russell H. Fitzgibbon, *Uruguay. Portrait of a Democracy* (New Brunswick, New Jersey: Rutgers University Press, 1954), pp. 114–115.

[9] *Ibid.*, p. 117.

[10] As quoted by Pendle, *Uruguay. South America's First Welfare State*, 1st ed., p. 17.

[11] Philip B. Taylor, Jr., *Government and Politics of Uruguay* (New Orleans: Tulane University Studies in Political Science, 1960), p. 157. For a briefer study see Professor Taylor's "Interests and Institutional Dysfunction in Uruguay," *American Political Science Review*, LV (March, 1963), pp. 62–74.

[12] George Pendle, *Uruguay*, 3rd ed. (London: Oxford University Press, 1963), p. 122. The quotation comes from George Mikes, *Tango*.

[13] William E. Rudolph, "Chile," *Focus*, VII (American Geographical Society, May, 1957), No. 9, p. 1.

[14] I. J. Cox, "Chile," in A. Curtis Wilgus, ed., *Argentina, Brazil, and Chile Since Independence* (Washington, D.C.: The George Washington University Press, 1935), p. 360.

[15] Herring, *A History of Latin America*, p. 559.

[16] *Ibid.*, p. 558.

[17] For a detailed denunciation, with much information on the period, see Ricardo Donoso, *Alessandri. Agitador y demoledor*, 2 vols. (Mexico City: Fondo de Cultura Económica, 1952–1954).

[18] Gilbert J. Butland, *Chile. An Outline of Its Geography, Economics, and Politics*, rev. ed. (London: Royal Institute of International Affairs, 1953), p. 44.

[19] Quoted by Luis María Anson, *ABC* (Madrid, Sept. 6, 1964), p. 48.

[20] Eduardo Frei Montalva, *La verdad tiene su hora* (Santiago, 1955), pp. 129–165.

[21] Peter Dorner and Juan Carlos Collarte, "Land Reform in Chile: Proposal for an Institutional Innovation," *Inter-American Economic Affairs*, XIX (1965), No. 1, pp. 3–22.

[22] George M. McBride, *Chile, Land and Society* (New York: American Geographical Society, 1936), pp. 12–14.

[23] Fredrick Pike, *Chile and the United States* (Notre Dame: University of Notre Dame Press, 1963), p. 289.

[24] Federico G. Gil, *The Political System of Chile* (Boston: Houghton Mifflin, 1966), p. 17. For a description of variations from class to class see Óscar Álvarez Andrews, "El problema de la familia en Chile," *Revista Mexicana de Sociología*, vol. 20, No. 2 (May–August, 1958), pp. 413–428.

[25] Joseph H. Fichter, *Cambio social en Chile: Un estudio de actitudes* (Santiago: Editorial Universidad Católica, 1962), pp. 220–222.

[26] See Fritz I. Hoffmann, "Perón and After," *Hispanic American Historical Review*, XXXVI (1956), pp. 510–528; "Perón and After (Conclusion)," *ibid.*, XXXIX (1959), pp. 212–233, for a detailed and informative report on the flood of publications. The quotation comes from the second article, p. 214.

[27] "Discurso de Ezequiel Martínez Estrada en la Sociedad Argentina de Escritores," *La Gaceta, Publicación del Fondo de Cultura Económica, Año V* (Mexico City, 1959), No. 53, p. 1.

[28] George Pendle, *Argentina* (London: Royal Institute of International Affairs, 1955), p. 32.

[29] Harold Benjamin, "Sarmiento, the Educator," *Some Educational and Anthropological Aspects of Latin America* (Austin: University of Texas, Latin American Studies, V, 1948), p. 16.

[30] Robin A. Humphreys, *The Evolution of Modern Latin America* (London: Oxford University Press, 1946), p. 89.

[31] Thomas F. McGann, *Argentina, The United States, and the Inter-American System, 1880–1914* (Cambridge: Harvard University Press, 1957), p. 15.

[32] *Ibid.*, p. 65.

[33] Pendle, *Argentina*, p. 47.

[34] José Luis Romero, *Las ideas políticas en Argentina* (Mexico City: Fondo de Cultura Económica, 1946), pp. 227–230.

[35] As quoted by Ysabel F. Rennie, *The Argentine Republic* (New York: The Macmillan Co., 1945), p. 174.

[36] Carlos Ibarguren, *La historia que he vivido* (Buenos Aires: Ediciones Peuser, n.d.), pp. 239–240.

[37] James R. Scobie, *Argentina. A City and a Nation* (New York: Oxford University Press, 1964), p. 135. See also Scobie's *Revolution on the Pampas. A Social History of Argentine Wheat, 1860–1910* (Austin: University of Texas Press, 1964).

[38] Carlos Pellegrini, *La nación en marcha (Discursos y escritos políticos)*, prologue by Miguel Cané (Buenos Aires: W. M. Jackson, Inc., n.d.), p. 124.

[39] Pendle, *Argentina*, pp. 60–61.

[40] Luis Reissig, "El fin de un ciclo histórico en Argentina," *Cuadernos Americanos*, LXXXVIII (Mexico City, 1956).

[41] George Pendle, *Argentina* (New York: The Macmillan Co., 1957), p. 77. The Lands and Peoples Series.

[42] *Ibid.*, p. 83.

[43] For a challenging re-interpretation of this episode, see Thomas F. McGann, "The Ambassador and the Dictator: The Braden Mission to Argentina and its Significance for United States Relations with Latin America," *The Centennial Review*, VI, No. 3 (1962), pp. 343–357.

[44] Arthur P. Whitaker, *The United States and Argentina* (Cambridge: Harvard University Press, 1954), p. 158.

[45] Ernest Sábato, *El otro rostro del peronismo* (Buenos Aires: Imprenta López, 1956), p. 40.

[46] A. P. Whitaker, *Argentine Upheaval* (New York: Praeger, 1956), p. 144.

[47] Gino Germani, *Política y sociedad en una época de transición* (Buenos Aires: Editorial Paidos, 1962), pp. 243–244.

[48] José Luis Imaz, *Los que mandan* (Buenos Aires: Editorial Universitaria de Buenos Aires, 1964).

[49] José Luis Romero, *A History of Argentine Political Thought.* Introduction and translation by Thomas F. McGann (Stanford: Stanford University Press, 1963), pp. 167–182.

[50] James W. Rowe, *Argentina's Restless Military* (New York: American Universities Field Staff, Inc., 1964).

8
BRAZIL

AREA: 3,286,473 sq. mi.

POPULATION IN MID-1966: 84,679,000

LARGEST CITIES:

Rio de Janeiro: 3,223,408 (1960)

São Paulo: 3,164,804 (1960)

Recife: 788,569 (1960)

Belo Horizonte: 642,912 (1960)

Salvador: 630,878 (1960)

Pôrto Alegre: 617,629 (1960)

Brasília (capital): 130,968 (est. 1961)

PRINCIPAL EXPORTS (1961): coffee, cotton, sugar, iron ore

PRESIDENT: Arthur da Costa e Silva, military, assumed office March 15, 1967, for a 4-year term.

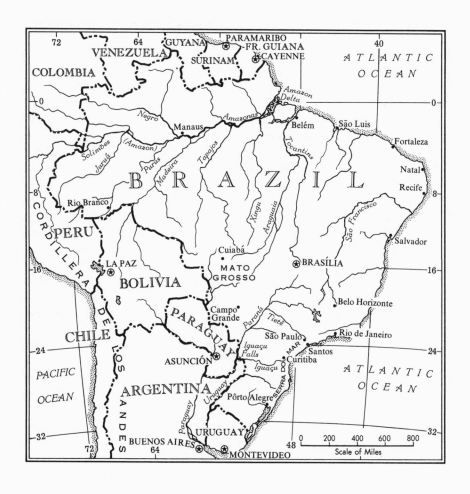

BRAZIL

● **Brazil Is a Giant.** Brazil has been called "the country in Latin America with the most of everything." It has the most people, the most persistent inflation, the most voters, the most workers, the most consumers, the most illiterates, and the greatest economic potential. Its population increases by over 2 million per year; five Latin American countries have populations smaller than its annual increase. (*See Reading No. 67.*) Another basic fact about this giant country—an uncertain and complex giant, but still a giant—is that it is very different from Spanish America. (*See Reading No. 68.*) Brazilians speak Portuguese, not Spanish; in a continent of sharply divisive racial strains, they alone have evolved a culture marked by the relatively peaceful fusion of European, Indian, and Negro stocks; and, situated among countries where political violence has often occurred, these more than 80 million people rarely use force to settle their disputes.[1]

The immense size and diversity of Brazil are the overriding facts of this largely tropical world. Its 3,294,000 square miles are large enough to hold continental United States with room for an extra Texas; it has the largest river in the world, the Amazon; two of its waterfalls, Iguassú and Paulo Afonso, are higher than Niagara; the island of Marajó at the mouth of the Amazon is as large as New England. Brazil produces much of the world's coffee, despite Africa's increasing competition, grows more bananas than any other country, possesses in Itabira an iron deposit estimated at more than a billion tons, and is so rich in plants that some 50,000—or one-fourth of all known species—are found within its borders.

Brazil has three distinct geographical regions, each one of great diversity. The Amazon dominates the immense region in the north as it sweeps from its sources in the Andes through dense undergrowth and thickly matted equatorial forests and, after flowing eastward for some 4,000 miles—more than 2,300 of them navigable by ocean-going vessels—pours itself into the Atlantic Ocean in such terrific volume that it turns the salt water fresh for about 200 miles. A 1963 joint Brazilian-U.S. scientific team determined that it discharges water into the ocean at the rate of 3,400,000,000 gallons per minute, or 12 times that of the Mississippi. Most of the Amazonian region is only a few hundred feet above sea level, with a climate uniformly hot and damp.

The Brazilian Northeast includes portions of the large state of Bahia as well as several smaller states, and consists largely of *caatinga,* or scrubland of semi-desert character. This region has long been subject to devastating droughts, but cotton, cacao, sugar cane, tobacco, and coffee are raised in the irrigated or humid sections. This wilderness of the northeast has acquired a mythical importance. A Brazilian from another region who goes there considers it the adventure of a lifetime, according to a U.S. political scientist, and "upon completing his travels Marco Polo could not have been accorded greater deference." [2] And Amazonia is almost as unknown to the average Brazilian in the south as is Africa.

The third region, the central and southern uplands, contains the most fertile lands, the great coffee *fazendas,* most of the minerals, railroads, manufacturing centers, and population. Most of Brazil falls within the tropical zone, but the large plateau regions of 600 to 3,000 feet in altitude in this third area enjoy a mild climate. The sheer size and diversity of the land make an indelible impression on the traveler, and would require a large book to describe adequately.

These three regions are so variegated in their historical developments and contemporary conditions, and so isolated from one another, that Brazil remains a difficult country to know and an almost impossible one to generalize about soundly.[3] The triangle bounded by the metropolitan areas of Rio de Janeiro, São Paulo, and Belo Horizonte contains the industrial heart of the nation, rich in manufacturing, mining, and agricultural production and relatively well endowed with transportation and power facilities. São Paulo alone produces almost one-third of the domestic income; Brazilians in less favored regions remark on the "imperialismo Paulista."

Great cultural variety exists, too, within each region. "A traveller leaving the international jet airport at São Paulo can find, within a few minutes, a little building dedicated to the cult of Xango, a St. Jerome assimilated by Africa, and there take part in a candomblé ceremony." [4]

● **The Spirit of Brazil.** Brazilians, more than any people in Latin America except the Mexicans, have analyzed their own national characteristics frankly and variously. One geographer has drawn up a list of "27 unfavorable realities of Brazil"; Paulo Prado began his interpretation, *Retrato do Brasil,* with the declaration: "In a radiant land lives a sad people." An historian, Sérgio Buarque de Holanda, considers the special contribution of Brazilians to civilization to be the "cordial man" who easily establishes a sense of intimacy with other people.[5] Still another famous Brazilian writer, Alceu Amoroso Lima, states:

> We are naturally pessimistic. We always see the dark side of affairs. We exaggerate our defeats. We do not believe in our victories. We only defend our own in front of foreigners. And then we throw ourselves into a facile pride which is merely another type of pessimism . . .
>
> At the same time our pessimism leaves us an inheritance of inconstancy. We are much more active as creators than as maintainers. We have more courage for beginnings than for endings, or, as José Bonifacio said, 'We undertake much and complete little.' We enjoy innovation, renovation, reformation, but not repetition, conservation, continuation. We build roads, but we do not maintain them. We raise buildings, but we willingly permit the facilities to get out of order.[6]

But a complex people cannot be truly characterized by a few quotations, and the exuberant human scene in Brazil is even more impressive than its geographical diversity.

One aspect of society which everyone notices and many writers generalize about is its racial democracy. Gilberto Freyre has presented a lyrical view of "the Brazilian melting pot"; the anthropologist Charles Wagley gives a more cautious appraisal. (*See Readings Nos. 68, 71–72.*) Race prejudice still exists; discrimination in such centers as São Paulo and Rio de Janeiro led the National Congress some years ago to pass a law making it a criminal offense, but there are no impassable racial barriers to social and economic advance. Brazilians are proud to have accommodated so many races and combinations of races in their country, but they do not want Brazil represented as non-white. A certain ambiguous feeling makes them pleased that the French film "Black Orpheus" won international prizes, but unhappy that it presents a black Brazil to the world in a carnival atmosphere. Alfredo Dias Gomes gives a more meaningful view of one aspect of Brazilian life in "Keeper of Vows," which won the Gold Palm for the best film at the 1962 Cannes Film Festival.[7]

Fortunately Brazilian social scientists are producing solid and sophisticated analyses of the composition of Brazilian society, especially of the results of the meeting of Indians, Negroes, and Portuguese. The belief that race mixture might produce a "new and marvelously organized nation" was expressed as early as 1845 by Karl Frederick Philipp von Martius in his famous essay on "How the History of Brazil Should Be Written," and Sylvio Romero went even further when he wrote in the late nineteenth century: "As we now understand it, the history of Brazil is not, as was formerly thought and repeated by the Lusophiles, exclusively the history of the Portuguese in America. Nor is it, as romanticism tried for a while to assert, the history of the Tupis nor, according to the day dreams of some of our Africanists, that of the Negro in the New World.

"Rather it is the history of the formation of a new type by the action of five factors, a semi-conscious formation in which miscegenation played a predominant role. Every Brazilian is a mestizo, if not biologically at least culturally. The agents which have brought about this basic situation are the Portuguese, the Negro, the Indian, the physical environment and imitation of foreign culture." [8] To maintain a proper balance in the study of the several cultural strains that have produced modern Brazil is a difficult task. Anthropologists have published so much interesting and valuable material on the Indian, Negro, and mestizo elements in Brazilian society, that the Portuguese element is in danger of being neglected.[9]

● **Brazilian Optimism.** An important fact about Brazilians today is their optimism, in the face of their country's urgent problems. Brazil throbs with plans and bounding predictions of future growth; this spirit is of long standing. An English traveler wrote in 1869: "I find in Brazil another symptom of strong and healthy national vitality. Men wage irreconcilable war with the present; they have no idea of the 'Rest and be thankful' state. They balance 'Whatever is, is good' by the equation 'whatever is, is bad'; yet they are neither optimists nor pessimists. They have as little idea of 'finality' as have New Yorkers. They will move and remove things quiet, and they will not leave well or ill alone." [10] Their confidence, as Preston James points out, "is just as real a factor of the Brazilian environment as are the hills and streams and forests." [11] Thus it is not surprising to find Brazil moving toward atomic power production. She activated her fourth atomic reactor in April, 1965, at the University of Brazil. It was put together by Brazilian nuclear engineers from components, 93 per cent of which were manufactured by Brazilian industry, and the nation confidently expects that atomic power plants will play an important role in her fast-growing industrial advance.

An example of this desire to improve matters, no matter what the cost and inconvenience, was President Juscelino Kubitschek's decision to build a new federal capital, Brasília, during his term of office, and thus fulfill an ambitious provision in the 1891 Constitution. No other nation in the Americas or elsewhere would have had the audacity, or energy, to move its long-established capital to a hitherto undeveloped area 500 miles in the interior. Brasília the "dream-city," rising near the geographical center of the country, though it strained the national resources and was vociferously opposed by many Brazilians, symbolizes for all elements of Brazilian society a dramatic national achievement.

Brazilians do not doubt their capacity to play a large role in the hemisphere. Kubitschek's advocacy of "Operation Pan America" before the birth of the Alliance for Progress reflected well the widespread Latin-American call for massive U.S. aid for economic development. Brazil thought in terms of billions of dollars over a period of years, and its objective was to lead the attack "against the festering sore of underdevelopment." No other Latin-American country had the authority or vision to propose such a program.[12]

The exultant, confident spirit that has moved many Brazilians throughout their history, and still exists despite the country's present economic and political distress, is well expressed in Ronald de Carvalho's poem, "Song of Brazil." (*See Reading No. 70.*) A popular Brazilian saying is that "God is a Brazilian."

● **The Unity of Brazilian History.** From the discovery of Brazil by Pedro Alvares Cabral in 1500 until the establishment of the Republic in 1889, Brazilian history followed a comparatively placid course. Brazil's colonial experiences of more than 300 years under Portugal was markedly different from that of the Spanish colonies. Portuguese colonizers moved much more slowly than the Spaniards, and remained for a long time near the coast. They made no great thrusts in the early years into the hinterland and the Indians they met were both relatively few in number and primitive in culture compared with the Aztecs, Incas, and Mayans in Spanish America. Negroes were therefore imported in considerable numbers from Africa to do the hard work on the sugar plantations in the northeast.

The patriarchal and aristocratic culture which slave owners on large plantations developed is brought vividly to life by Gilberto Freyre in his sociological study, *The Masters and the Slaves*. These families constituted a stable group whose economic and political interests soon became more Brazilian than Portuguese. Regional differences existed in domestic architecture, dress, and family life in general, but the important Brazilian families had in common a system, particularly with respect to the inheritance of property, in which the decisions of the family predominated over individual desires. Group interests were defended by the family council, an institution still powerful in Brazil.

In the seventeenth and eighteenth centuries, a hardy race of *bandeirantes* (frontiersmen) pushed out from poverty-stricken São Paulo in the south to explore and raid as far as the Andes, the Amazon, and the Río de la Plata area.[13] These mestizo pioneers established a still living tradition of far-flung adventuring and bold action in hitherto unexplored and unsettled areas. They went in search of gold, precious stones, and Indian slaves. The regions through which they passed became the strongholds of cowboys and outlaws, of Indians and halfbreeds, of bandits and bosses, of individualism and fanaticism. It was, and to some extent still is, Brazil's Wild West.

Mining developed late, but from 1710 to 1760 the General Mining District

GILBERTO FREYRE—BRAZILIAN SOCIAL HISTORIAN
(Pan American Union)

(*Minas Gerais*) produced about 500 metric tons of gold, an amount equivalent to half the entire world production in the preceding centuries. Gold flowed to London via Lisbon in sufficient volume to enable the British pound to become the first monetary unit to be placed on a gold standard, and to give European capitalism a powerful thrust forward.

In general, a quiet, almost vegetative society grew up in colonial Brazil. The Church was much weaker and poorer than in Spanish America, the Holy Office of the Inquisition was never formally established and Jews played a significant role in commercial life. No printing press was set up, and no universities were founded; wealthy families sent their sons to Coimbra, the ancient university in Portugal.

● **Royalty in the New World.** Brazil was a provincial society of about three million people when Napoleon invaded Portugal and sent the Royal Family scurrying across the Atlantic for safety. The women of Rio de Janeiro were so unacquainted with the ways of the world that when they saw the Portuguese court ladies debarking with shaved heads they hurried home and cut off their own hair in hasty emulation, not knowing that not Portuguese fashion but the need to cope with vermin on shipboard had decreed this drastic measure.

Dom João's arrival in 1808 conferred an invigorating new status on Brazil, now the heart of his empire. He brought a printing press, established a bank, public library, medical faculty, and powder factory, and opened Brazilian ports to the commerce of all friendly nations. The complications of the period 1808–1840 cannot be described here. Independence from Portugal was proclaimed in 1822 under Pedro I with no bloodshed or alteration of the patriarchal, slave-owning, landholding character of the Brazilian governing class. After a period of turbulence and a regency, Pedro's son was crowned Emperor Pedro II in 1841 and for almost half a century Brazil lived at peace and largely apart from the many Spanish-American nations struggling with the chaotic conditions that the violent wars of independence had left in their wake.

Pedro II maintained benevolent control; perhaps his greatest accomplishment was to hold Brazil together, huge and loosely organized as it was. He did not attempt to alter its essential character, "because he recognized it as the basis of his regime. In politics, though himself conservative and jealous of the imperial prerogatives, he encouraged the development of parliamentary forms and insisted on the orderly application of laws above men. But he was content to leave the country as a one-crop economy, dependent . . . on the fluctuations of world markets, while power shifted from the declining sugar growers of the northeast to the rising coffee planters of São Paulo. He permitted such industrialization as was useful to that shift, but in this, as in his eventual abolition of slavery, he insisted on only very gradual evolution." [14]

● **The End of Empire.** The immediate cause of the overthrow of the Empire was the abolition of Negro slavery in 1888 without appropriate compensation, but there were other reasons as well.

At the Emperor's forced abdication in 1889, Brazil had a population of 14 million, 6,000 miles of railroads, and immigration from Europe was beginning. But Brazil was unprepared for Republican life and when the Emperor's austere personal control of government was removed, new elements in society began to struggle for power. The army became a political force, a new working class came into being outside the old paternalistic structure, and the powerful states of Minas Gerais and São Paulo fell under the domination of regional bosses and oligarchies that assumed full political control and kept the people from active participation in politics. States, and combinations of states, controlled what national power existed. Within individual states, near anarchy often prevailed; politicians and powerful landowners employed private gangs in their struggle for power. The film "Cangaçeiro," whose locale was the dry northeast, and Jorge Amado's novel *Gabriela,* whose scenes are located in Bahia, convey the flavor of life in these regions. Many Brazilians carried guns (and in some northeast states, still do), a circumstance that tarnishes somewhat the article of Brazilian faith that their civilization is marked by peaceful and inter-cultural understanding.[15]

Rui Barbosa, one of Brazil's great statesmen, fought without success for civilian control of government but, significantly, helped to develop a civil conscience in the nation during these difficult days of the Republic. The Constitution of 1891 provided for a franchise limited to literate males, and included great presidential powers. Despite the centralized government, states were allowed some unusual privileges: they could tax exports, had other wide taxation powers, and maintained their own armed forces.

● **"Ordem e Progresso."** The motto on the Republican flag is "Ordem e Progresso," a phrase taken from the French Positivist Auguste Comte, but there was little order or progress in those days. A naval revolt was easily put down in 1893, but in 1896–1897 a religious fanatic named Antônio Conselheiro defied the government, which could only suppress the revolt he led by dispatching an overwhelming federal army to the rebel stronghold of Canudos in the dry and inhospitable northeast. The violence of this conflict shocked the nation into recognition that the neglected provinces (the "backlands") must be made an integral part of the nation. Conselheiro and almost all his illiterate, ragged followers died but the story of the epic struggle, which Euclydes da Cunha preserved in his *Rebellion in the Backlands,* has become a Brazilian classic.[16]

During the early years of the twentieth century Brazil made a determined effort to control disease, especially smallpox and yellow fever, which had long retarded the development of a healthy population. The success of this medical campaign, directed by the eminent scientist Oswaldo Cruz, is now recognized as one of the fundamental reasons for the growth of Brazil. (*See Reading No. 69.*)

In the years 1908–1910 a campaign to protect the Indians against threatened extermination by the advancing colonists and railroad men led to a national debate on the place of diverse races in Brazilian society. This resulted in the establishment in 1910 of the first Indian Service in Latin America, which was placed under the direction of the famous army officer Cândido Rondon, who believed in peaceful dealing with the Indians. Today this splendid initiative of Brazil has fallen on evil days. The Indian Service staff has dwindled, receives little government support, and cannot protect the Indians from exploitation by other Brazilians.[17] Historians recognize the early contributions Indian men and women made to the development of colonial Brazil and anthropologists emphasize the Indian origin of the hammock, the burning over of land before planting new crops, the roasting of fish over coals, the use of the coconut drinking cup, cashew nuts, manioca flour and Indian corn. But no monument in Brazil yet commemorates the Indian contribution as the Black Mother in São Paulo and the Black Father in Rio de Janeiro recall the contribution of the Negro to Brazil.

● **Brazil Looks North.** During the early years of the Republic Brazil began to orient its political policy toward closer friendship with the United States. French culture and British commerce continued to exert a powerful influence, but Brazil moved closer to the United States politically under the diplomatic leadership of the Baron Rio Branco and Joaquim Nabuco.[18]

Economic changes came, too. The fall of the monarchy had ushered in the reign of "King Coffee." Beginning in 1890, Brazil provided more than 50 per cent of world production; today it remains the major producer in the world. The dominance of coffee in Brazil's foreign trade may be seen from the fact that since 1900 it has averaged about 60 per cent of the total value of the nation's export trade. Since 1906 the coffee industry has been trying to perfect some system to defend itself in the world market. A Permanent Coffee Institute was set up in 1924 but no successful system has ever been devised to raise or to stabilize permanently world coffee prices, for coffee is now produced by many countries.

Rubber production boomed from 1900 to 1910, when the growing popularity of bicycles and automobiles in the United States created great demand for it. For a few years rubber prices soared to dizzy heights. The boom ended abruptly after the discovery that plantation rubber could be produced in Malaya far more cheaply than wild rubber could be gathered in Brazil. All that remains to testify to this gaudy period in Brazilian history is the imposing opera house in Manaus, 2,000 miles up the Amazon, to which rubber barons

RUBBER TAPPING

brought European opera companies in the heyday of the Brazilian rubber industry. This $10 million monument to jungle riches was built of white marble, topped by a dome tiled in green, blue, and gold, and decorated with European paintings commissioned at great expense. Operas with famous Italian singers were mounted on stage for the rubber barons, and world famous artists including the dancer Pavlova appeared there. Nothing seemed too costly for the rubber millionaires or their wives, who imported linens from London and Paris and are said to have sent them back to Europe to be laundered.[19]

● **Revolt of the "Tenentes".** High prices for Brazilian products during World War I brought some relief from economic uncertainties, but the postwar years were again difficult. The army failed to impose its presidential candidates and added considerably to the confusion and turmoil of the period. The discontent of the laboring and middle classes with the government and with general conditions gained a sympathetic response from some of the younger army officers (*tenentes*), most of whom were themselves of the middle class. In 1924 revolt broke out among these officers in São Paulo; they held the city for almost a month before government forces compelled them to flee westward. For three years, under the command of Luís Carlos Prestes, this fighting force, which at times dwindled to only a few hundred men, wandered back and forth across the vast interior of the country.

The Prestes Column never achieved its objective: to arouse the civilian population to force the government to comply with their demands for reform. But this indigenous nationalist and reform group, in setting forth their reasons for revolt and their ideals, drew up an indictment that suggests the conditions of the time:

> Reason: financial and economic disorder; exorbitant taxes; administrative dishonesty; lack of justice; perversion of the vote; subornation of the press; political persecution; disrespect for the autonomy of the states; lack of social legislation . . . Ideas: to assure a regime loyal to the republican Constitution; to establish free primary instruction and professional and technical training throughout the country; to assure liberty of thought; to unify justice, putting it under the aegis of the Supreme Court; to unify the treasury; to assure municipal liberty; to castigate the defrauders of the patrimony of the people; to abolish the anomaly whereby professional politicians become prosperous at the expense of the public purse; rigorous economy of public funds in keeping with efficient aid to the economic forces of the country.[20]

The Revolution of 1930 was the work of the *tenentes* (lieutenants), together with other discontented elements in several states. Although Prestes disassociated himself from it and soon afterward began his spectacular career with the Communist party, these young army officers contributed to the victory of Getúlio Vargas, who ushered in the modern age in Brazil.

● **The Age of Vargas, 1930–1954.** The history of the seething period in which Vargas dominated a sprawling but rapidly developing country remains to be written. A master politician who well understood his people, he shrewdly played off the army, big business, workingmen, and the various regional rivalries of Brazil against one another. His pronouncements always had a strongly nationalistic tone which appealed to the country even though his "March to the West" program was perhaps developed in part to distract attention from problems of the littoral.

Vargas handled such a crisis as the São Paulo revolt of 1932 in a statesmanlike manner. The coffee planters and industrialists in this powerful state demanded greater autonomy and more federal assistance. The ensuing civil war involved 50,000 or 60,000 men in arms on each side. The estimated 15,000 casualties, dead and wounded, horrified a nation accustomed to thinking of itself as a peaceful society. Alberto Santos-Dumont, the Brazilian air pioneer who anticipated the work of the Wright brothers by a couple of years, was so disturbed by the destructive uses to which airplanes were being put during the revolt that he committed suicide. The reaction to his death was very Brazilian: hostilities ceased for a day while both sides paid solemn tribute to a great national figure. When the Paulista rebels were defeated, Vargas acted again in the best national tradition by dealing generously with them, even to the extent of underwriting the expenses of the revolt by guaranteeing the bonds issued by the state government.

One result of the revolt was the Constitution of 1934 which provided for both a strong federal government and protection for workers. To correct the abuses that flourished during the individualistic regime of the Republic, Vargas had already created a Ministry of Labor, Industry and Commerce shortly after he came to power in 1930. The mass of workers had been "trampled under foot by both the feudal coffee planters and the rising industrialists," and in the new Constitution Vargas set out to redress the balance.

In the midst of the world-wide depression years in which he began his rule—coffee dropped from 29 cents a pound in 1929 to 7 cents in 1931— Vargas initiated university reform and increased the responsibility of the federal government toward education generally.

The almost four million immigrants who had entered Brazil between 1890 and 1937 represented an only partially assimilated population upon whom the winds of fascist, Nazi, and other doctrines blew. By 1937 one-fifth of the entire 40 million population consisted of immigrant stocks. Vargas met this crisis, or perhaps took political advantage of the confused economic and social situation, by increasing his own power through the establishment of a "New State" in 1937, which was in fact a dictatorship supported by the military. It lasted until 1945 when the army commanded him to resign. But it was a most Brazilian kind of dictatorship, with little of the harshness usually found in such regimes.

During these years Vargas—and his propaganda office—worked hard to gloss over the defects of his rule and, with the help of World War II, he held out for eight years. During the War Brazil played a greater international role than ever before; in contrast with its closest rival in South America—Argentina—which held aloof, Brazil not only declared war against Germany, Italy, and Japan but sent troops to Italy and, at home, made available sea and air bases of great strategic value to the United States.

Vargas pushed development of the Amazon, an ancient Brazilian dream—or mirage; he supported a TVA-type program for the São Francisco River basin, nationalized such resources as electricity and steamship lines, diversified both agriculture and industry, and in 1940 initiated a five-year industrialization plan which included a steel mill at Volta Redonda. This large installation began operation in 1946 and now produces over a million tons of steel a year, with more expansion in progress.

During a period of unprecedented social and economic ferment, which he encouraged, Vargas held Brazil together like a twentieth-century Emperor Pedro II. He was even so astute and so Brazilian as to surrender power peacefully; when the army told him to go in 1945 he retired. The next President, General Eurico Gaspar Dutra was, however, the dictator's choice and in general continued policies already in effect. Vargas neither sulked nor fled the country with millions of dollars in the tradition of Spanish American dictators: he ran for the Senate, and was elected.

As resounding proof of his political dexterity and his popularity among workers and industrialists alike, Vargas won the 1950 presidential election at the age of 67 despite the opposition of liberals, intellectuals, and the coffee lords. He committed suicide in August, 1954, apparently because of unsavory scandals in official circles that the army and air force were beginning to uncover. Students of the formative age of Vargas are beginning to believe that he was not only a master politician who succeeded in creating a federal, bureaucratic machine but also a follower of Castilhos, who had established in the southernmost state of Rio Grande do Sul a positivist and dictatorial regime: "the ideas and political habits which the gaúcho Vargas brought from his native state when he took power in 1930, and the 'New State' of 1937, was nothing more than 'The Republican Dictatorship' of Rio Grande do Sul dressed in more modern and more ornamental clothes." [21] This may prove to be too simple a diagnosis. When his regime receives the historical analysis it deserves, Vargas may be judged a uniquely flexible and skillful politician who well understood the needs and aspirations of his country.

● **The Army, Economics, and Oil.** Since 1945 the army has stood as the decisive force in Brazilian politics. Traditionally it is disposed to uphold established government and to guarantee constitutional and civilian rule. But it stands ready to act even against an existing government when it considers Brazilian institutions threatened from any direction. Army officers are usually of moderate or conservative political persuasion, and have feared the growing influence of labor. One observer is convinced that the army will continue to determine the course of political events in the foreseeable future.[22] Certainly the Kubitschek government made a distinct effort to keep the officers contented through high salaries and other emoluments.

The army, the communists, and Brazilians generally supported strongly the policies developed after World War II to free the country from foreign economic influence. Petrobrás (Brazilian Petroleum Co.) became a national symbol of economic independence, which few dared to criticize. A government-controlled stock company created in 1953, Petrobrás monopolized the extraction, refining and transportation of domestic petroleum, and also largely controlled the handling of imported petroleum. "O Petróleo é Nosso" (Petroleum belongs to Brazil) became the rallying cry for the nation, which effectively bottled up in the ground much of Brazil's known petroleum reserves, safely out of reach of what were labeled American capitalistic imperialists. The oil was also safely out of reach of the Brazilian economy, which desperately needed it.[23] Only native Brazilian citizens could become Petrobrás board members; foreign participation in Brazilian oil development has been limited to the granting of loans for exploration and for equipment. In 1963 a Soviet mission made a survey of prospects, as the negative findings of U.S. technicians had been challenged, but Petrobrás has made slow progress thus far in producing crude petroleum partly because Brazil lacks enough geologists or equipment. An output of 150,000 barrels a day had been achieved by December, 1966, and in 1967 Petrobrás announced it would begin to look for oil under Brazil's coastal waters.

Petrobrás has taken important strides in refining, and in producing natural gas. It now has some 35,000 employees in its various operations, which include a tanker fleet, and an annual business volume of about $2 billion.

Other examples of the economic nationalism which has exerted so powerful and pervasive an influence in Brazilian life was the 1962 law limiting annual profit remittances abroad to 10 per cent of registered capital and the plans to nationalize eventually all foreign public utility companies. Widespread public support existed at that time for measures to protect the national economy and tighten controls over foreign investment and profits.

● **Shifting Party Lines.** Political parties in Brazil reflect the state of its society, which is in rapid transition. Political power until very recently rested on a narrow base of landed elite, with the majority of the people excluded from political life. The Emperor, and later the President and heads of the state machines in such states as Minas Gerais, São Paulo, and Rio Grande do Sul, made the political decisions. At the local level, the bosses known as *coronéis* (colonels) delivered the vote which maintained the traditional regimes in power. The system of *coronelismo* has been declining, but in large parts of the north and northeast it remains largely untouched. Politics there remain the monopoly of large landholding families and the coronéis who maintain their dominant position through favors, purchase of votes and, when necessary, by violence.

Political parties are weak, have had brief histories, and have not yet received from political scientists the analytical attention needed to understand their role in national life. The present party system was hastily put together to meet the needs of the free election at the end of World War II. The Social Democratic Party (PSD) inherited most of the Vargas machine, while the National Democratic Union (UDN) attracted most of the opposition to Vargas, who organized The Brazilian Labor Party (PTB) to rally his immense popularity with orgranized labor. The Communist Party (PCB) dates from 1922 and has been led since 1935 by Luís Carlos Prestes. Immediately following World War II it was probably the best organized political party. Like everything else Brazilian, the PCB was large, at least during its most popular period 1945–1947.[24] Though illegal since 1948 it maintains its organization under Prestes' guidance, despite some division in it ranks. (*See Reading No. 74*). In true Brazilian emphasis on peaceful change, Prestes has maintained that "revolution is not a synonym of violence; it is fundamentally a change of classes in power and this is possible even in certain Latin American countries in present conditions, without civil war and without armed insurrection." [25]

Brazilian parties cut across class and racial lines, and personality plays a major role in all parties. The party system is unstable, with many minority groups, but this permits new elements to enter the political scene. It would be difficult, however, to understand Brazilian political thinking simply by study of her political parties, and the usual labels of "right," "left," and "center" have limited meaning. Roberto Campos, with much experience, puts it this way:

> It would be better to speak of the *conservatives,* who desire to preserve the status quo; the *reformists,* encompassing a broad political spectrum, ranging from the right of center to a large segment of the left, who may disagree on the type and intensity of reforms but agree on the basic postulate that they should be instituted through the democratic mechanism; and finally the *revolutionaries* who advocate violent change by totalitarian methods, encompassing the communists, the ultramontane nationalist left, and a small residuum of rightist revolutionaries.[26]

● **Brazil After Vargas.** With the suicide of Vargas in 1954, Brazil entered upon a period of almost continuous economic and political instability. Kubitschek's presidency (1955–1960) saw spiralling inflation, which many attributed to his building of Brasília and his lack of financial responsibility. His advocacy of economic development through industrialization, improvement of highways, and more electric power as well as the plan for an "Operation Pan America" made him popular, despite the frequent charges that he had acquired a personal fortune while president, and during his administration Brazilians became increasingly aware of the potential greatness of their country. Since Brazil was discovered in 1500 it had been influenced by Portugal or Great Britain and more recently by the U.S. Vargas particularly had given the Brazilian people a sense of national destiny, and Kubitschek gave vivid expression to this feeling in Brasília.

Ideas now began to influence Brazilian life more than ever before. The major turning points in her history—the establishment of a monarchy independent from Portugal in 1822, the shift to a republic in 1889, and the Vargas Revolution of 1930—all occurred without much planning or much mobilization of mass opinion. Gilberto Freyre and others regard Brazil's absence of sharp doctrinal conflicts and its national genius for compromise as among the nation's great assets. But during Kubitschek's years an almost hot-house growth of nationalist thinking developed; it gives a special tone to Brazilians' political thought. Writing in the publications of the Instituto Superior de Estudos Brasileiros (ISEB), the *Revista Brasiliense,* and the *Editôra Fulgor,* the nationalists call for "planned action toward a highly productive economy of self-sustained growth controlled by Brazilians, higher standards of living for all, an independent foreign policy, and an end to the alienation and discontent born of prolonged inferior status." [27]

The ISEB group included both "left" nationalists and "right" nationalists, who split in 1958 over the questions whether the Brazilian bourgeoisie can still take the lead in national development and whether a more conciliatory attitude should be taken toward foreign participation in the exploitation of Brazil's oil resources. This heterodox group has produced a remarkable body of students and of writing, and in a few years had "set an intellectual standard for nationalist writing of whatever political inspiration in Brazil." [28]

● **The Quadros Enigma.** Jânio Quadros was elected president in 1960, by the largest popular vote in history, of a Brazil whose economy was desperately strained by the building of Brasília and burdened by an enormous population growth. This enigmatic and unpredictable leader, after initiating many significant and important reforms, resigned suddenly in August, 1961, after only 7 months in office, and plunged Brazil into a political crisis from which it has not yet emerged. There was fortunately no bloodshed, though large armies had begun to mass for action. Quadros had promised to sweep out corruption, and had made a promising start; he had pushed through an agrarian reform bill against much opposition, and had embarked upon a foreign policy, very popular in many circles, that emphasized Brazil's independence of the United States. A political lone wolf, he was given to such dramatic acts as decorating Ernesto Ché Guevara, the Argentine communist, during the latter's visit to Brazil as the Cuban Minister of Economy, a move which scandalized the Brazilian conservatives as much as the earlier U.S. decorations of Latin-American dictators had distressed liberals throughout the Americas. Many reasons have been advanced for the dramatic resignation of Quadros; it is too soon to know whether his personal inadequacies, his political miscalculations, or "reactionary forces"—Quadros' own explanation—were responsible.[29] One analyst believes that he was a victim of a coup d'etat led by Carlos Lacerda, the vigorous and flamboyant Governor of Guanabara State; another element may have been the unresolved conflict between the "left" nationalists and the "right" nationalists. It seems clear that the enigmatic president was particularly shocked and frustrated by the opposition in Congress to his reform measures.

● **The Army Takes Over.** The armed forces considered Vice-President João Goulart too radical and only permitted him to be installed as president after presidential powers had been reduced by hurriedly instituting a parliamentary form of government. But by January, 1963, a plebiscite brought back the presidential form. Political uncertainty and economic distress continued, many began to fear that Goulart was moving toward an authoritarian regime, and on April 1, 1964 a military-civilian group removed him in what was called "the Democratic Revolution." At first it was widely reported, especially in the United States, that Brazil had been on the brink of the communist abyss, but few in Brazil today would support this view. Goulart was not an able administrator, his position on national problems was neither clear nor consistent, and he had not won the confidence of the country. His left-leaning regime was replaced by a military-dominated, middle-class-supported, government under Marshal Humberto Castelo Branco.[30]

Before Congress elected the General to the Presidency, the military leadership decreed an "Institutional Act." This amendment to the 1946 Constitution provided that the commanders-in-chief of the three armed services could oust any federal, state, or municipal official, including elected members of the legislatures, whom they considered to be an "extremist"; suspend for ten years the political rights, including the right to vote, or to be elected to any office, of any "extremist" citizen; and suspend the immunity of any judge, professor, or other officeholder for six months so that he too could be purged. The president was given the power to send any desired legislation to the national congress where it would have to be acted upon within thirty days;

if the congress did not act within that time the legislation would be considered approved. The remainder of the Constitution of 1946 was to remain in effect.[31]

● **Rule of the Marshals.** The new government was eager to clean out the "corruption" it had denounced; it cancelled for 10 years the political rights of many prominent Brazilians—former President Kubitschek, state governors, well-known educators, many legislators, and business men. Though generalizations about the confused political scene in Brazil are dangerous, it seems that since the feverish days of April, 1964, Castelo Branco's government had failed to win a strong following anywhere; the middle class no longer supports him as vocally as before, and a variety of opinions are expressed on this colorless, honest army officer. Inflation has slowed down, but the nation has no sense of forward movement, and the basic problems which have plagued Brazil for years still are waiting for the successor to Castelo Branco. During the uncertain years since the end of World War II, Brazil's tradition of peaceful change and conviction that brute force must be avoided have thus far been largely honored, but President Goulart's ouster severely strained the ties that bind Brazilians together. In November, 1965, Castelo Branco abolished, by decree, all existing political parties and substituted one "official" party and one "loyal opposition" and in February, 1966, ordered the indirect election of president, state governors, and municipal officers in state capitals, a further abrogation of the 1946 Constitution providing for direct, popular vote.

The election of Marshal Artur da Costa e Silva by Congress on October 3, 1966, introduced another uncertain element into Brazil's confused political situation. One hundred and seventy opposition Congressmen refused to vote in what they termed a rigged election, but the Marshal peacefully assumed the presidency in March, 1967. Whether he will "humanize" the revolution, as he promises, or will attempt, in a harsh military spirit, to solve the country's many problems remains to be seen. He was reported as telling a group of military men reluctant to support him: "My party is the army, and it is strong."

Since Marshal Costa e Silva's inauguration on March 15, 1967, he has limited himself to general statements, in which he promised to consider the needs of Brazil's most explosive groups—university students and the lower class workers. He did not repeal or liberalize the numerous decrees, mostly repressive of individual rights, which his predecessor put forth during his last days in power.

● **A Testing Time.** A testing time is now at hand, because the nations economic, educational and political problems are grave, and Brazilians are impatient for social and economic change that will truly benefit the people, particularly the rural masses in the northeast. Francisco Julião organized peasant leagues there in the early 1960's, violence broke out in the land, and the urban public discovered that many rural workers live no better today than the Indians the Portuguese found in 1500. Some churchmen became concerned, and the federal government called for land reform. Goulart and the Labor Party sponsored a bill, passed in 1962, which gave plantation workers the right to organize unions. Urban conservatives and landowners took fright, rumors flew of communist influence and foreign agitators, and Julião was eventually jailed. To confuse the picture further, an anthropologist has declared that Julião was not so much a wild-eyed radical or communist in his active period up to April, 1964 when the Castelo Branco government jailed him, as a well-educated, well-to-do lawyer who was organizing the peasants for his own political advantage rather than their welfare.

One prediction may be hazarded: Though the shock that Euclydes da Cunha administered to his countrymen at the turn of the century—when his *Revolt in the Backlands* described the poor, ignorant fanatics of the northeast led by Antônio Conselheiro—could be forgotten once the campaign was over, the poor and dispossessed in Brazil cannot be ignored today. As they crowd into the cities at an ever-increasing rate, they are highly visible. No longer dispersed in the vast reaches of the continent which is Brazil, or shipped off to the Amazon when drought drove them from their homes, now they go south—to Rio, São Paulo, and other already overcrowded cities where they are both seen and heard. A slum dweller wrote an account of her experiences in the favela and her view of life which became a best seller, read all over Brazil as well as abroad.[32]

Can Brazil muddle through? The "oligarchs" of Latin America receive less attention in some quarters than the leftists. Yet the influence of the conservatives in Brazil remains strong; if Brazil is to avoid a bloody showdown they will have to change their ways. Can they learn in time? There are differences among them; some have adapted themselves more easily to modern conditions than others.[33] But too often, in the past at least, as Stanley J. Stein has written, they have seemed oblivious to all else than their own immediate economic advantage. In the past they trod "the vicious circle of destroying virgin forests to plant coffee to pay debts to get credit for the purchase of slaves to destroy more forests and plant more coffee." [34] Newspaper reports that many wealthy Brazilians, some obtaining their dollars and other foreign currency illegally on the black market, are still putting their money in overseas banks are not reassuring.

Certain new forces have roused themselves in the last few years, however, to confront the nation with the economic and social crisis which the arrival of the submerged masses on the political scene poses: the Church and the universities. Professors and students, who often play significant political roles in other Latin-American countries, were rarely heard from in Brazil after the days of "tenentismo" in the 1920's except on the issue of nationalism.

Now the many rapidly growing universities are forums where Brazil's destiny is continuously discussed. Although from the middle class, this new political-minded group has become the "most radical element in Brazilian society in that they have been least willing to accept the stagnation and conservatism built into Brazilian government and politics."

● **Changes in the Church.** The Catholic Church, likewise, until fairly recently a fairly passive organization politically, is changing. Since the days of Portuguese colonization its influence has been ubiquitous in Brazilian life. With the largest Catholic population of any country in the world, for 90 per cent of its 80 million people are at least nominal Catholics, Brazil had in 1961 three cardinals, 32 archbishops, 128 bishops, and over 10,000 priests, representing a major concentration of the Church's manpower in Latin America. But the ratio of one priest to about every 6,000 Catholics is the lowest in Latin America; many Catholics in Brazil seldom see a priest or have access to the sacraments. Given the general absence of violence and extremes of passion in Brazilian political history, and the generally mild and non-political role the Church has played in society, the intransigent clericalism and bitter anti-clericalism found elsewhere in Latin America simply do not exist in Brazil. The Church itself has been shaped by Brazil; one student of colonial art remarked: "In Brazil, even Christ hangs comfortably on the cross."

Now the Church is inescapably caught up in the onrushing crisis of national development. (*See Reading No. 76.*) Though Church and State have been separated since 1890, Church leaders have been assuming ever stronger positions on economic and social problems; such prelates as Archbishop Câmara of Recife have become leaders in the demand for improvement in living conditions for the masses.[35] One of the first steps President Goulart took after his inauguration was to entertain the more prominent members of the Catholic hierarchy at the Presidential Palace in Brasília, where the exchange of deferences and reassurances between the assembled prelates and the President was intended as a clear sign to the nation that there was no immediate threat from Left or Right to the compromise solutions the administration had in mind.

Three years later the atmosphere had radically changed. Goulart attracted 150,000 persons for a "Reform Rally" on March 13, 1964, in Rio where he outlined for the wildly cheering crowd the measures he had just decreed or was sending to Congress: "Nationalization of the last privately-owned oil refineries; expropriation of vacant agricultural lands along federal roads, projects, and waterways; Constitutional amendments to permit a second straight term for the president, a vote to illiterates and soldiers, and authorization for noncommissioned officers to run for office." [36] But six days later a "spontaneous" demonstration of over 500,000 persons took place in São Paulo, the marchers carrying rosaries and national flags as well as anti-leftist, anti-

Goulart placards. This "March of the Family with God for Liberty" had been organized on short notice by various groups, including Sister Ana de Lourdes, Congressman Antônio Silva Cunha Bueno, and the São Paulo Civic Feminine Union to fill the streets of São Paulo for political purposes, on the Day of St. Joseph, patron saint of the family. Similar demonstrations occurred in many other places. The armed forces showed their sympathy in various ways, as when the Navy Minister ordered the arrest of a Marine Corporal (a university student in obligatory military service) whose agitation on behalf of Goulart's "reforms" technically violated naval regulations. Goulart's ejection from office was not long in coming, but the struggle within the Church continues between those who favor moderate reform and those who are convinced that drastic action must be taken.

The growth of Protestantism has also helped to develop greater political awareness in Brazil. Foreign Protestant missionaries have worked in Brazil for many years. Though the government stated when it established a Consulate General in Jerusalem that it was the "largest Catholic nation in the world," 4 to 5 million Brazilians live "under Protestant influence either directly or indirectly," according to Catholic Bishop Agnello Rossi.[37] Moreover, in true Brazilian fashion, their number is growing faster than in any other country in the world. Protestantism is now a distinctly national movement; there are as many native-born Protestant clergy as there are native-born Roman Catholic priests, despite the enormous disparity in the numbers of Protestants and Roman Catholics. Protestant Churches are proud that their members are literate and concerned with political movements. However, both Catholics and Protestants fear the growing power of the pentecostal groups on the fringe of Protestantism and of the movement known as "low spiritualism," a curious mixture of African paganism with Roman Catholic rites which is said to influence nearly 20 per cent of the population.[38] These movements of social concern, by both Catholics and Protestants, indicate clearly that the day is over when religious bodies can be passive or indifferent to national issues. Their leaders may not all agree on the political steps to be taken, but they are increasingly active in social and economic affairs.

Can one of those famous Brazilian compromises be reached, will the national genius for improvisation—called *jeito,* essentially an ingenuity in bending law, regulation, or principle to the moment's need—save the nation from economic collapse and general frustration?

● **Favela and University.**   Foreigners are often puzzled by the contradiction between the disquieting facts of Brazilian life and the optimism of many Brazilians. Is this a healthy belief in the possibilities of life on this troubled earth, or a refusal to face the facts of existence? Inflation has been rampant for years; prices rose steadily during Goulart's administration; the rate was about 100 per cent in his last months of office. Urban food riots and rural violence have led to widespread questioning of Brazil's essential peacefulness, and the dreadful slums known as favelas grow steadily, although some efforts are being made to substitute modest new low-cost housing outside of Rio.[39] Even the approach to favelas reveals the startling contrasts in Brazilian life:

Favela, a picturesque expression having a certain literary flavor, which has served as the motive for many prize-winning songs in the Carnival, means in real life filth, hunger, promiscuity, sickness, and prostitution.[40]

A recent U.S. educational analyst has declared that "the almost incredible" legalism and structure of Brazilian higher education retards its development: the University of Brazil, for example, gives elementary chemistry courses in six different faculties, with each part-time but independent professor struggling with inadequate equipment. Such a situation "assumes a fairytale quality. The fairy tale may well end on the pathetic note that this country continues to require massive foreign aid at frequent intervals to resolve its economic crises." (*See Reading No. 9.*) A Swedish writer feels that the ideas of racial tolerance propounded by Gilberto Freyre and others have led Brazilians to become so complacent about their situation as to ignore "the enthralling social and economic problems confronting the country and offered the reactionaries a convenient excuse for dismissing them as mere illusions." [41]

● **Cities Short of Food.** The food supply for Brazil's bursting cities epitomizes the nation's problems. Insufficient production is not the principal obstacle to achieving a satisfactory diet for Brazilians. But sources of food for most major cities are generally hundreds or even thousands of kilometers away. These great distances, coupled with inadequate transportation facilities, create a major obstacle to distribution. Cattle must often be walked to market or shipping points, with consequent loss of weight; trucks, the principal carriers of food, are hampered by poor roads that cause frequent mechanical breakdown; train service is slow, poorly organized, and subject to pilferage en route. A freight train moving from Rio de Janeiro to Belo Horizonte, a distance of about 300 miles, may take five to 30 days and averages about ten days. In addition, storage facilities are few, canning and refrigeration plants are rare, and marketing techniques are relatively primitive.

Attitudes toward food are important too. Many Brazilians scorn frozen and canned products, green vegetables are regarded as little more than "grass," milk is skimmed, and oranges are considered bad for the liver. What counts most is *peso no estomago*—the feeling of weight and fullness in the stomach. Thus a two- or three-helping meal of rice, beans, and dried beef is generally rated high in comparison with "weak" foods such as fish, poultry, fruit, and vegetables.

The instability of the nation's economy and the deeply ingrained "speculative" philosophy of the business community are additional explanations for the urban food-supply problem in Brazil. Inflation means that a crop at harvest time may be worth so little that the farmer may not even recover his costs. The difficulties most urban Brazilians experience in getting enough to eat are symptoms of Brazil's general economic distress.[42]

● **Brazil's Cultural Explosion.**   The cultural break with the past in Brazil came before the political revolution of 1930. Some writers believe that during World War I Brazil shed many of her older ideas and European influences began to wane; with the Modern Art Week in São Paulo in 1922 Brazil began a more independent artistic and literary life.[43] As one critic has described this significant event: "In São Paulo in 1922 Mário de Andrade struck a match and then lit the fuse to several sticks of dynamite; the explosions so far have been more than big noises. Earth has been moved, rock torn away, and mines opened up for the digging of vast literary wealth." [44] The Modern Art Week brought to national attention new forces and encouraged Brazilians to use 20th century themes and their own experience. Provincialism and dependence on French culture declined; Brazilians now developed their own styles in art, music, literature, and other creative forms. Aware of currents outside of Brazil, they began to paint, compose, write, and build in their own national idiom. Today Brazil's artistic and literary development is as noteworthy as her tremendous population increase or industrial development. Brazilian influence has spread abroad; those who have seen a ballet version of "Emperor Jones" danced to the music of the Brazilian composer, Heitor Villa-Lobos, or the murals in the Hispanic Foundation of the Library of Congress painted by Cândido Portinari, or have read a novel of the Sugar-Cane Cycle of José Lins do Rêgo know that Brazil has begun her independent creative life.

The freshness, vitality, and richness of Brazilian achievement is expressed in many ways. A delightful children's art museum has been opened in Copacabana, a suburb of Rio de Janeiro; the late Augusto Frederico Schmidt was a poet, a partner in a chain of supermarkets, a government economist; Aldemir Martins, an Indian, won the Grand Prize for design at the 1956 Venice International Art Show for his stark and powerful line drawings; conductor Eleazar de Carvalho is active at Berkshire Music Festivals; and Érico Veríssimo has reached such a large audience with his "Time and the Wind"—a sort of Brazilian "Forsyte Saga" depicting the development of southern Brazil through several generations—that for the first time a Brazilian creative writer can live by his pen. Much of the appeal of the Brazilian arts is that their roots lie in popular, folkloristic, native materials. Elsie Houston made Brazilian folk music famous wherever she sang those hauntingly beautiful songs. It is significant, too, that the poverty-stricken Northeast produced a quartette of first-rate novelists—Jorge Amado, José Lins do Rêgo, Rachel de Queiroz, Graciliano Ramos—who gave a heightened sense of nationhood to Brazil.

• **Brazil's Cultural Roots.** Brazil's present cultural position has deep roots: *Marvelous Journey. A Survey of Four Centuries of Brazilian Writing,* by Samuel Putnam, shows the country's literary past. The gold mines of colonial days made possible the construction of many remarkable churches. The inland towns of Ouro Prêto (Black Gold) and Congonhas are practically museums of colonial art, including the sculpture of the eighteenth-century Antônio Francisco Lisboa (Aleijadinho), whose monumental statues of prophets stand impressively in Congonhas.

Brazilian architects, whose buildings today are perhaps the country's most visible cultural achievement, have departed radically from their colonial past and the French Empire craze that produced the ornate Municipal Theatre and Fine Arts School in Rio de Janeiro. The technique of concrete reinforced with steel has enabled Brazilian architects to strike out on their own in a period of great building activity. Combining concrete with glass, stone, and painted wall tiles (a colonial art), and skillfully employing light, air, and tropical plants, they have molded new forms of imagination and grace. Lúcio Costa believes that Brazilian architecture "has succeeded in adding plastic lyricism and concern for human emotions to the structures in which we live and work." It will survive not because of its mere functionalism but "because it will still be able to touch the heart." [45] Oscar Niemeyer's slab-sided glass walled Ministry of Education building in Rio de Janeiro was a forerunner of the United Nations building in New York, in the design of which he collaborated. In houses and other intimate buildings Brazilian architects have demonstrated their skill and their "Brasilidade."

The attitude of the late composer Villa-Lobos may be taken as typical of many of Brazil's artists and writers. He, "the composer most likely to be remembered a century hence," knew European music and greatly admired Bach, but also spent much time with the people of interior Brazil. His "Bachianas Brasilieras" and other music employ violinophones, drums, wood blocks, and notched sticks from the exotic forests and rivers of Amazonia, whose folklore he knew so well.[46] (*See Reading No. 73.*)

The movement that came to world notice in São Paulo in 1922 has become a mighty force—nationalistic, confident, varied, and powerful, which recalls one of the first writers to reach Brazil, the official scribe of the Cabral expedition which touched Brazil in 1500. Pero Vaz de Caminha described for King Emanuel the richness of Brazil—the "groves everywhere" and the "waters many and endless"—and then he made a prediction concerning the future of Brazil: "This land, Sire, is exceeding fair and so fertile a one that,

if you care to cultivate it, it will yield everything." [47] A significant fact of twentieth-century Brazil, as important as the smoke billowing from Volta Redonda steel mill or the rolling waters of the mighty Amazon is that Brazil now cultivates its own cultural soil. The yield is rich and gives promise of much more to come.

• **A Study in Problems.** Everything about Brazil is large, including its problems. Geographers point out that the soil, from which the majority of her people in the "hoe-country" wring a meager living, is being steadily exhausted by the ancient slash and burn methods which destroy the organic matter and invite erosion. Becoming more frequent are "man-made calamities resulting from the destruction of the resource base by a people who did not know what they were doing to their own economy." [48]

The picture of human erosion in some of the backward agricultural regions of the interior is also dark. Here the illiteracy rates rise at times to 80 per cent. Here no real land reform has been undertaken; only 3 per cent of the land is put to use, and 8 per cent of the population own 73 per cent of the land. Politically these regions are underdeveloped; "coronéis" used to deliver the vote by giving the voters two pieces of paper: one the ballot of the favored candidate and the other a free lunch ticket. Now a change has set in, for the official ballot is to be used even in the rural regions. But political development remains slow.

Particularly in the industrial sections of the south, rapid economic change is accompanied by only a slow rate of social change. A principal problem is the lack of a large consumer base to support the industries springing up on all sides. As one economist explains it: "the domestic market does not expand since the cost of living rises and the rural population remains incapable of consuming; without a domestic market, industry fails to prosper, it fails to keep abreast of technological advances and must continually appeal for government protection." [49]

Detailed and objective study of these changes and the social structure generally, made by the universities and research centers, are hopeful signs. The Escola de Sociologia e Política in São Paulo, the Instituto de Joaquim Nabuco in Recife, the University of Brazil and the Getúlio Vargas Foundation in Rio de Janeiro, and other institutions have published many valuable monographs. The *Revista Brasileira de Estudos Políticos* of the University of Minas Gerais has been realistically analyzing political processes in Brazil, and the *Revista Brasileira dos Municípios* has published studies pointing out the tax inequities in the country's financial structures. University scholars are also making deep-probing analyses of the nature of her social structure.

Brazil continues to assimilate an impressive variety of ethnic strains: English, French, Germans, Irish, Italians, Japanese, Poles, Swiss, Syrians, Ukrainians and even descendants of former colonies of Confederate families

RIVER STEAMBOAT

unreconciled to the defeat of the South in the U.S., all of whom are integrated in various degrees into the Brazilian society whose basic strains represent Indian, Negro, or Portuguese backgrounds. The 19th century isolation of some of these groups is dissolving: a Kubitschek was President, a Trompowsky was Minister of Aeronautics, and one Yokishigue Tamura served as Federal Deputy from São Paulo. The telephone book of any Brazilian city demonstrates this tremendous ethnic variety.

● **The Need for a Formula.** Will Brazil find a formula to assimilate, as well as she has absorbed her immigrants, the foreign capital she needs so badly for her industrial programs? In the past, vociferous nationalists prevented effective oil exploration; Petrobrás, the government-controlled oil corporation was hedged about by ultra-nationalistic legislation.[50] Under Castelo Branco these laws have been either repealed or substantially modified. Roberto Campos, the competent economist who served as ambassador to the U.S. under Goulart, then chief architect of the Castelo Branco regime's economic program, promptly announced some of his objectives: to cut national deficits; keep wage increases down; generate new taxes and make certain that taxes are collected; end subsidies on utilities, bread, and fuel; open the door for new and private investment—both Brazilian and foreign. This program succeeded to some extent. Will the present government of Marshal Costa e Silva be able to continue it?

Does all the heightened concern for and by the people mean that Brazil will solve her problems? The Right appears to be as powerfully entrenched as before and as reluctant as ever to make meaningful concessions while the Left has thus far produced no dynamic national leader who can weld together the many dissident groups eager for change into an effective political force. The Sino-Soviet dispute split the Communist Party in late 1961, and the Cuban Revolution also divided the national groups such as the ISEB intellectuals who had done so much during Kubitschek's regime to define issues and develop a coherent ideology.

Brazilians have been conditioned since childhood to believe in the inexhaustible possibilities of their country—one of the first Portuguese to go there described it as "Brazil the infinite land." Doubting Thomases are considered unpatriotic, perhaps subversive. Yet obviously a country in which over half the population of 80 million is under 20 years of age has too few productive workers.[51] In the face of their grave economic problems, many Brazilians still expect some miracle to solve them. Even the slum dwellers without electricity, safe drinking water, elementary sanitation, or jobs believe that things will somehow get better. But uneasiness is widespread throughout the land; the intellectuals are increasingly dissatisfied with the repressive tendencies of the present government, as the dynamic young publisher Énio

Silveira made clear in his open letter to President Castelo Branco.[52] Debate flourishes, too, on the exact nature of the independent foreign policy that Brazilians overwhelmingly desire. Is it to be primarily anti-U.S. or neutralist or something else? Is Brazil ideally equipped, as some proclaim, to become a world power through her relative absence of color prejudice which will attract the many new African nations to follow her leadership? [53] (See Reading No. 77.)

● **The Future of Brazil.** Foreigners who have studied and lived in Brazil long enough to develop a lasting affection for its people, usually speculate on its future. One has written a pentrating essay entitled "If I were a Brazilian," [54] and another has answered affirmatively the question of whether indeed Brazil *is* the land of the future, but with these reservations: "providing Brazilians learn and apply even more of the medical and sanitary techniques which alone can make life healthful in the tropics; providing they make the fullest use of modern technology and cease their fierce destruction of natural resources; providing they borrow or devise a more equitable system for distributing the results of the productive process among capital, management, and labor; and providing they apply much more of what mankind has learned about urban life, so as to reduce the precariousness of life for the millions who now are flocking into her cities and towns." [55]

This huge Brazil is clearly a giant society capable of great advances. But it confronts today terribly pressing problems, with increasingly powerful sectors of society determined to improve the condition of its masses. If it is to avoid violent revolution during the next decade, it will need to call upon all its humor, its social tolerance, and its tradition of peaceful change.

[1] For an up-to-date view of Brazil as a whole by an experienced anthropologist, see Charles Wagley, *An Introduction to Brazil* (New York: Columbia University Press, 1963). Other valuable works are Thales de Azevedo, *Social Change in Brazil* (Gainesville: University of Florida Press, 1963); Frank Bonilla, "Rural Reform in Brazil. Diminishing Prospects for a Democratic Solution," American University Field Staff Reports Service, VIII, No. 4 (New York, 1961); Florestan Fernandes, "Reflexões sobre a mudança social no Brasil," *Revista Brasileira de Estudos Políticos* (Belo Horizonte: Universidade de Minas Gerais, 1963), pp. 31–71; José Honório Rodrigues, *Aspirações Nacionais. Interpretação históricopolítica* (Rio de Janeiro: Editora Fulgor, 1963); Hilgard O'Reilly Sternberg, "Brazil, Complex Giant," *Foreign Affairs* (January, 1965).

[2] George J. Blanksten, "The Politics of Latin America," Gabriel A. Almond and James S. Coleman, eds., *The Politics of Developing Areas* (Princeton: Princeton University Press, 1960), p. 466.

[3] A Russian geographer has produced an outstanding contribution on regionalism, V. V. Pokshishevsky, "The Major Economic Regions of Brazil," *Soviet Geography, I* (January–February, 1960), pp. 48–68.

[4] Georges Friedmann, "A Frenchman Looks at Brazil," *Americas* (January, 1962), p. 39.

[5] For these and other opinions see Fernando de Azevedo, *Brazilian Culture* (New York: Macmillan, 1950) pp. 115–136. See also E. L. Berlinck, *Fatores adversos na*

formação brasileira (São Paulo: Imprensa IPSIS, 1949); Rodrigues, *Aspirações nacionais.*

[6] Alceu Amoroso Lima, *A realidade americana. Ensaio de interpretação dos Estados Unidos,* 2nd ed. (Rio de Janeiro: Livraria Agir Editora, 1955), pp. 229–230.

[7] James C. Brewer, *A First Look at Race Relations* (New York: Institute of Current World Affairs, 1964). See also Kalervo Oberg, "Race Relations in Brazil," *Sociologia,* XX (March, 1958), pp. 340–351; Francis A. Dutra, "The Theater of Dias Gomes: Brazil's Social Conscience," *Cithara. Essays in the Judaeo-Christian Tradition,* IV (St. Bonaventure University, May, 1965), pp. 3–13.

[8] Sylvio Romero, *Historia da litteratura brasileira,* 2nd ed., 2 vols. (Rio de Janeiro: H. Garnier, 1902), I, p. 4.

[9] Stuart B. Schwartz, "The Uncourted *Menina:* Brazil's Portuguese Heritage," *Luso-Brazilian Review,* II (1965), No. 1, pp. 67–80.

[10] Richard F. Burton, *Explorations of the Highlands of the Brazil With a Full Account of the Gold and Diamond Mines,* 2 vols. (London: Tinsley, 1869), I, pp. 373–374.

[11] Preston James, "The Cultural Regions of Brazil," T. Flynn Smith and Alexander Marchant, eds., *Brazil. Portrait of Half a Continent* (New York: The Dryden Press, 1951), p. 99.

[12] For documentation and Brazilian opinion on OPA, see *Revista Brasileira de Política International,* ano II (Rio de Janeiro, March, 1959), No. 5, pp. 44–77, 90–114, 137–158; and Operação Pan-Americana, 3 vols. (Rio de Janeiro: Presidencia da Republica, 1958).

[13] Richard M. Morse, *The Bandeirantes. The Historical Role of the Brazilian Pathfinders* (New York: Knopf, 1965). For collections of material on Brazilian history as a whole, see the volumes edited by E. Bradford Burns, *Documentary History of Brazil* (New York: Knopf, 1966); *Perspectives on Brazilian History* (New York: Columbia University Press, 1967).

[14] Alexander Marchant, "The Unity of Brazilian History," Smith and Marchant, eds., *Brazil. Portrait of Half a Continent,* p. 40.

[15] James L. Busey, "Brazil's Reputation for Political Stability," *The Western Political Quarterly, XVIII* (Dec. 1965), pp. 866–880.

[16] Translated by Samuel Putnam (Chicago: University of Chicago Press, 1944).

[17] James C. Brewer, *Brazil's Indian Service* (New York: Institute of Current World Affairs, 1965).

[18] E. Bradford Burns, *The Unwritten Alliance. Rio-Branco and Brazilian-American Relations* (New York: Columbia University Press, 1966).

[19] For a recent description see E. Bradford Burns, "Manaus, 1910: Portrait of a Boom Town," *Journal of Inter-American Studies,* VII, No. 3 (July, 1965), pp. 400–421.

[20] Robert J. Alexander, "Brazilian Tenentismo," *Hispanic American Historical Review,* XXXVI (1965), p. 234. See also John Wirth, "Tenentismo in the Brazilian Revolution of 1930," *ibid.,* XLIV (1964), pp. 161–180.

[21] Tocary Assis Bastos, *O positivismo e a realidade brasileira* (Belo Horizonte: Edicões da Revista Brasileira de Estudos Políticos, 1965), p. 128.

[22] John J. Johnson, *Political Change in Latin America. The Emergence of the Middle Sectors* (Stanford: Stanford University Press, 1958), p. 179. Detailed studies on the Vargas period and later are just beginning to appear. See Thomas E. Skidmore, *Politics in Brazil, 1930–1964. An Experiment in Democracy* (New York: Oxford University Press, 1967); John Foster Dulles, *The Age of Vargas* (Austin: University of Texas Press, 1967).

[23] Theodore Wyckoff, "Brazilian Political Parties," *The South Atlantic Quarterly,* LVI (1957), p. 289.

[24] Rollie Poppino, "Communism in Postwar Brazil," *Hispanic American Historical Review,* XLIII (1963), pp. 313–345.

[25] Luis Aguilar, *Marxism in Latin America* (New York: Knopf, 1967), Introduction.

[26] Campos, in Irving Horowitz, *Revolution in Brazil* (New York: Random House, 1964), p. 353.

[27] Frank Bonilla, "A National Ideology for Development: Brazil," K. H. Silvert, ed., *Expectant Peoples. Nationalism and Development* (New York: Random House, 1963), pp. 223–234.

[28] *Ibid.*, pp. 238–239.

[29] Hélio Jaguaribe, "La renuncia del Presidente Quadros y la crisis política brasileira," *Política*, No. 18 (Caracas, 1961), pp. 32–60.

[30] James W. Rowe, *Revolution or Counter Revolution in Brazil? An interim assessment of the "April Movement"* (New York: American Universities Field Staff, 1964). The discussions and the bibliography on the 1964 movement have already reached impressive proportions. See Amaury de Souza, "Março ou Abril? Una bibliografia comentada sobre o movimento político de 1964 no Brasil," *Dados* (Rio de Janeiro, 1966) 2° semestre, pp. 160–175. For another example of the searching nature of Brazilian political analyses, see the issue of the outstanding review, *Cadernos Brasileiros* directed by Afrânio Coutinho devoted to "Os Militares" (Nov.–Dec., 1966).

[31] Phyllis Peterson, "Brazil: Institutionalized Confusion," in Martin C. Needler, ed., *Political Systems of Latin America* (Princeton: Van Nostrand, 1964), pp. 476–477.

[32] Carolina Maria de Jesus, *Child of the Dark* (New York: Dutton, 1962).

[33] Maria Isaura Pereira de Queiroz, "A estratificação e a mobilidade social nas comunidades agrarias do vale do Paraiba," *Revista de História*, I (1950), pp. 195–218.

[34] Stein, *Vassouras* (Cambridge: Harvard University Press, 1957), p. 30. See also his *Brazilian Cotton Manufacture* (Cambridge: Harvard University Press, 1957), pp. 186–187.

[35] See Dom Helder Câmara's address at his inauguration as Archbishop of Olinda, April 12, 1964, as translated by the Commission for International Development of New York City. Another example is the letter by Bishop Jorge Marcos de Oliveira published in *Ultima Hora* (Rio de Janeiro, May 20, 1965).

[36] Rowe, *Revolution or Counter Revolution in Brazil?*

[37] *Christian Century* (March 20, 1957), p. 366.

[38] M. Richard Shaull, "Church and Culture in Latin America," *Theology Today,* XII (Princeton, 1950), p. 50.

[39] For a view of the favelas in Rio, see José Arthur Rios, "Aspectos humanos da favela carioca," *O Estado de São Paulo* (suplemento, No. 13, April, 1960).

[40] Maria Luiza Moniz de Aragão, "¿Favela-vivem ou vegetam as 1,111 familias da Barreira do Vasco?"; *Serviço Social*, ano 9, No. 54 (São Paulo, 1949), pp. 65–74.

[41] Cited by Magnus Mörner, "Race and Class in Twentieth Century Latin America," *Cahiers d'Histoire Mondiale*, VIII (1964), No. 2, p. 304.

[42] Based on studies by Kempton Webb, *Geography of Food Supply in Central Minas Gerais* (Washington: National Research Council, 1959); "Origins and Development of a Food Economy in Central Minas Gerais," *Annals of the Association of American Geographers*, XLIX (1959), pp. 409–419.

[43] Richard M. Morse, *From Community to Metropolis. A Biography of São Paulo, Brazil* (Gainesville: University of Florida Press, 1958), p. 259.

[44] John Nist, ed. and trans., *Modern Brazilian Poetry* (Bloomington: Indiana University Press, 1962), Introduction.

[45] Lúcio Costa, "Testimony of a *Carioca* Architect. Concrete, Sun, and Vegetation," *Perspective of Brazil* (*Atlantic Monthly*, February, 1956), p. 43.

[46] Vasco Mariz, *Heitor Villa-Lobos, Brazilian Composer* (Gainesville: University of Florida Press, 1963).

[47] As quoted by Samuel Putnam, *Marvelous Journey* (New York: Knopf, 1948), p. 3.

[48] Preston E. James, "Patterns of Land Use in Northeast Brazil," *Annals of the Association of American Geographers*, XLIII (1953), p. 26.

[49] As quoted by Stein, *Brazilian Cotton Manufacture*, p. 188.

[50] Werner Baer and Mario Henrique Simonson, "American Capital and Brazilian Nationalism," *The Yale Review*, LIII (1964), pp. 192–198.

[51] Birth control methods are widely used, at least in urban Brazil, Sugiyama Iutaka, *Inter-Generational Mobility and Family Planning in Brazil* (Austin, Texas, 1965). Mimeographed report.

[52] "Primeira Epistola ao Marechal: Sôbre o Delito de Opinião," *Revista Civilização Brasileira*, ano 1 (July, 1965), No. 3, pp. 3–11.

[53] For a favorable view of the importance of Brazil's relation to Africa, see José Honório Rodrigues, "The Influence of Africa on Brazil and of Brazil on Africa,"

Journal of African History, III, No. 1 (1962), pp. 49–67. A more cautious interpretation is given by Maria Y. Leite Linhares, "Brazilian Foreign Policy and Africa," *The World Today,* XVIII (1962), pp. 532–540.

[54] Charles Wagley, *An Introduction to Brazil,* pp. 267–297.

[55] T. Lynn Smith, *Brazil, People and Institutions,* rev. ed. (Baton Rouge: Louisiana State University Press, 1963), p. 619.

CONCLUDING REFLECTIONS

• **Persistent Clichés.** The contemporary Latin American scene is too complicated and too variegated for any book, especially one of this kind, to offer resounding conclusions. (*Readings Nos. 1–5, 12–32.*) One may, however, emphasize how urgently both citizens of the United States and of the Latin-American countries need to develop reciprocal relations based upon realistic appraisals of Latin America's present problems and those of the United States. For the governments and people of both Americas must find ways to relax the present dangerous tensions. Unfortunately, past and present clichés still becloud the real problems, which are grim enough, and continue to be believed throughout the Americas, and thus to determine attitudes and affect the course of events. Two of the oldest clichés, which although they were never sound are still tossed back and forth, are that most Latin-American needs will be met by the application of more U.S. aid and that Latin America is profoundly spiritual while the U.S. is primarily materialistic.

Those who are inclined to denounce Spain or Portugal for all the ills of today, especially the large landholdings which so dominate Latin-American agrarian life, should realize that land was "grabbed" during the period from 1810 to 1880 at a rate far exceeding that of the entire colonial period.[1] The social welfare laws and economic planning that have developed in the Latin American nations since the early 1930's came partly from twentieth century Europe, but may derive as well from the ancient traditions of Mediterranean culture transplanted in colonial Latin America by Spain and Portugal. State intervention in the life of the people and the systems of restricted economy now being practiced in Latin America constitute a policy revolution—but a revolution of return to the past.[2]

It is true, as the geographer James Parsons has observed, that "everywhere in Latin America the hand of the past lies heavily on the land," [3] but a colonial-type mentality persists which has discovered new villains to blame for the troubles of the present—Yanqui imperialism or communism of what-

219

ever variety. With the growth of a powerful spirit of nationalism in every country, the situation becomes extraordinarily confused. In the felicitous phrase of the historian R. A. Humphreys, "there is both the tradition of revolt in Latin America and a revolt against tradition." [4]

The discovery in Mexico a few years ago of the alleged bones of Cuauthémoc, the last Aztec emperor, whom Cortez killed, led to a sharp political controversy over the nature of Spanish rule in America.[5] This controversy was particularly sharp because the economic, social, and racial problems the conquest created still exist. The struggle for justice on behalf of the Indians, which began in the sixteenth century and continued throughout the colonial period, has today been broadened to include social and economic justice for the mass of people in Latin America who have never been adequately fed, housed, or educated. The increasing number of persons concerned with these problems are facing the fact, as one agricultural specialist wrote, describing the desperate plight of workers on the land: "In Brazil, Haiti, and the eighteen Spanish American countries as a whole at least one half of the agriculturists are dependent upon methods of extracting a living from the soil that are more primitive, less efficient, and more wasteful of human energy than those the Egyptians were using at the dawn of history." [6]

Latin Americans are now debating how to modernize their countries: "What is under debate is the whole heritage of the archaic society—the economic, political, and intellectual heritage, as well as the archaic society itself —its structure, its values, its prospects." [7]

No one knows what will happen next month, much less during the coming years, in this immense territory with its remarkable fusions and divisions of races and cultures. But no one can study or visit Latin America without noting certain important trends. The following pages represent a tentative assessment of some developments which are general to this area of the world.

● **The Role of Women.** The abundant literature on contemporary Latin America contains few references to the fundamental changes now affecting the lives of over half its population—women. The more than 3,000 doctoral dissertations prepared on Latin American topics in the United States since 1900 shed only a faint light on the distinctive role of women in the past and on their possible future. Not even such a deeply-rooted institution as the mistress has much interested sociologists though some brief descriptions are available. (*See Reading No. 42.*) The intense and widespread discussions of the need for a "revolution" of the structure of Latin-American life pay almost no attention to the part women can be expected to play in it.[8]

One anthropologist has observed: "The cult of the Holy Virgin was a major symbolization of the virtues of womanhood. The double sex standard was deeply rooted, as was the notion that 'ladies' were incapable either of work or of logical thinking, whereas lower-class women were created mainly for work and men's sexual pleasure but, of course, were not equipped with brains." Yet the facts were otherwise. "The 'respectable woman,' whether of the aristocracy or of the working classes, has for many generations been the anchor of the home and the family."

Man's sphere was outside the household; he had much "freedom" and was encouraged in various sorts of "masculine adventures." [9] The result was a certain masculine irresponsibility and exaggerated sense of virility, the *machismo* so evident in Latin-American life and literature. Girls were kept under strict surveillance, often educated by nuns who usually developed in them a sense of responsibility to maintain the integrity of the family and at the same time inculcated an acquiescent attitude toward male "prerogatives." Women were expected to stay at home, and attend to family affairs. When a public-spirited Brazilian woman wanted to speak on behalf of a protective policy for the Indians in the early years of the 20th century she found it impossible to persuade the men leading the campaign to allow her to do so or even to attend the meetings. But in 1923 the Fifth Pan-American Conference passed a resolution recommending the abolition of sex discriminations and, though legal discriminations still exist, since that time steady pressure for a larger role for women has been exerted. Some of the results of this campaign are visible to the public: "Things have come to such a pass that a couple of years ago the lady mayor of San Juan, Puerto Rico, made a highly-publicized visit to the lady mayor of Santiago de Chile." [10]

The position of the Latin-American woman is definitely changing, though at somewhat different rates from country to country and from class to class. The great majority of the "women of the people" have probably always worked hard, as responsible members of their relatively simple though changing society. In some countries these tradition-bound women oppose change as potentially harmful to their families, and constitute an important obstacle to plans for development. Middle- and upper-class women are beginning to participate in the changes affecting their societies, and in some countries now work outside the home even when there is no economic necessity to do so. Women hold paying jobs in business offices, libraries, government agencies, airplanes, legislatures, and even in some diplomatic services. Women almost everywhere have the vote; Eduardo Frei is now President of Chile partly because the women's vote, which both candidates solicited, went heavily to him. In a number of countries Catholic women are using contraceptive devices forbidden by their Church. Even in such a conservative nation as Colombia, women are beginning to participate in dialogues between lay people and the hierarchy on economic aid and social questions. Divorce is discussed more insistently and more publicly than ever before, with women actively engaged in this highly controversial and delicate subject.

The extent of these changes should not be exaggerated. The woman who has written one of the few books available on the Mexican family reports that the Mexican Revolution, despite the many drastic changes it brought, "has not yet succeeded in sweeping from the feminine mind the preconceptions about her incapacity, her dependence on man, and her absolute need for resignation that traditionally have weighed her down for centuries." [11]

● **A Change in Social Fashion.** Yet, changes are taking place throughout Latin America, including Mexico. Experienced analysts of the social scene there report that during the last ten years it has become unfashionable for prominent men to have mistresses; it is no longer "in" behavior. And in 1965 Mexico elected her first woman member of its Chamber of Deputies.

What will be the social, economic, and political consequences of women's growing emancipation? Will their femininity be endangered when they compete in the market place with men? Will they tend to indulge in sexual adventures as the men do? Will advances in their education prepare them to become better companions for their husbands, to give more intelligent guidance to their children, and thus to offer a new kind of partnership within marriage? How will upper-class women, now dependent on servants, adapt to the gradual diminution of the servant class as more and more young girls prefer to enter other fields of work, and the devoted family servant disappears as an institution? These and other questions deserve attention. But a brief survey must concentrate on the larger role women in Latin America are beginning to play.

One observer believes that the change now under way, "paradoxical as it sounds, provides an element of stability that has been so long lacking in the public life of many Latin-American countries." He holds that if the long tradition of responsible womanhood "is translated to the level of public affairs, it may well be that a new factor of stability will be introduced into the Latin-American situation." [12]

The fact that women have begun to feel the urge to develop themselves in new ways and to exercise more direct influence on affairs outside the home, is undoubtedly of high importance for the future of Latin America. The attitudes men adopt toward this new, actually world-wide, development will, however, markedly affect this movement, for it must be stressed that male domination in the life of most countries there seems even stronger and more resistant to fundamental change than the entrenched power of the oligarchs.

But the entrance of many young women into the universities and professions, and the emergence of a number of women novelists, have potential significance. Expectations of women and indeed their determination to work for positive gains, especially in those fields most related to women's traditional roles—translated into active concern for education, care of the sick, the amelioration of intolerable poverty—indicate that the women of Latin America are beginning to respond strongly to the challenges of the time.

● **Religion and the Church.** The answers to some of the questions relating to the growing recognition of women's rights, and the emergence of women as an important, sometimes powerful, factor in public life are intimately connected with the future of the Roman Catholic Church in Latin America. For since women make up the majority of observing Catholics—except in a few countries, notably Colombia—they may be supposed to follow more submissively than men the social doctrine of the Church.

But what is this doctrine, particularly as it applies to such emotion-laden topics as birth control, agrarian reform, capitalism, foreign investment, workers' wages and nationalization of industry? The Center of Intercultural Documentation in Cuernavaca, Mexico, publishes a selection of the remarkable variety of fact and opinion, drawn mostly from Latin-American sources, on the present widespread agonizing reappraisal of these problems by both clergy and laity.[13]

During the centuries since Spain and Portugal first began to colonize the New World, the Catholic Church usually sided with the conservatives and yet largely failed to impress upon the wealthy their fundamental duties to the laboring classes. The double threat today of communism's appeal and the population explosion has led churchmen to involve themselves as never before in an attempt to improve the miserable conditions in which so many Latin Americans live. (*See Readings Nos. 21–24A.*)

The liberating example of Pope John XXIII and the deliberations of Vatican Councils I and II, in which Latin-American ecclesiastics played an important role, have exerted profound influence. The Church increasingly tends to acknowledge that its historic mission to evangelize the world is jeopardized in societies where men and women see it as unresponsive to their urgent human needs. A half century ago the Jesuit Fernando Vives Solar was exiled from Chile when he helped to organize workers and did not insist, as the hierarchy did, that they vote solidly for the Conservative party.[14] Today many ecclesiastics, from cardinals to parish priests and members of the various orders, are in the front lines working with those struggling for social justice. They differ greatly among themselves on what this justice is and on how to achieve it, just as the sixteenth-century missionaries disagreed on the Christian way to treat the Indians. But the Church can no longer be regarded as a monolithic institution closely allied to the Conservative view in politics and some churchmen in every country would probably concur with the following analysis of the present situation: "An immense and ever growing majority of the masses is discovering its power, realizing its misery and becoming conscious of the injustice of that political, juridical, social and economic order which obliges it to accept things the way they are. The majority is not likely to wait any longer. Rapid, deep, and complete change of structures is demanded. If violence is necessary, they are ready to use it." [15]

● **Protestant Growth.** In addition to the papal influence, the growth of Protestantism has had a noticeable effect. The Jesuit Prudencio Damboriona has publicly stated that the Catholic Church "has lost more people to Protestantism in twentieth-century Latin America than it did in Europe during the Reformation." [16] Moreover, the Belgian Jesuit with many years of experience in Latin America, Roger E. Vekemans, has written that "unless the Catholic Church can undergo a cultural mutation that will cause it to begin to stress the capitalistic virtues commonly associated with the Protestant Ethic, then there may be no possibility of a non-Marxist solution for the problems of Latin America." [17] Clearly the Church no longer dominates the non-spiritual realms, and must compete henceforth with the variety of private and state-controlled institutions in its growing concern for the material well-being of man. The Christian Democrats stress the non-confessional nature of their movement, their lack of official connection with the Church, and their conviction of the need for religious pluralism.

Thus to be effective in helping to improve man's material conditions on earth, the Church must cooperate with many other groups. This has led to considerable economic, political, and social activity by some Church leaders. Cardinal Luis Concha Córdoba of Colombia, noted both for his ultra-conservative views which oppose Church participation in "politics" and for the sporty automobile he drives, severely lectured such radical priests as Camilo Torres Restrepo for engaging in these matters.[18] This priest eventually left the priesthood, and was killed in early 1966 while fighting with guerrillas in the mountains against Colombian government forces. One must wonder whether Camilo Torres might have remained within the Church as a leader in social reform if he had not been subject to a particularly conservative archbishop's discipline.

● **Reform from Below.** In the early decades of the twentieth century the Church tried, unsuccessfully, to influence the directing classes toward paternalistic measures to mitigate the poverty of the masses. Perhaps because some voluble and influential Church leaders believed that fascism was the way to reform society, the Church after 1945—when fascism ceased to be a tenable philosophy—lost intellectual leadership, and some leaders decided to instigate reform from below. Fredrick Pike compared this shift with the early history of America, and has sounded a warning:

> In turning to the masses and seeking reform from below, churchmen of the post-1945 era in Latin America present a remarkable similarity to some of the missionaries of sixteenth-century New Spain. Disillusioned by alleged Spanish depravity, these missionaries turned for a time to the Indians as a group endowed with superior virtue. Disillusioned in the mid-twentieth century by their failures to lead a reform from above, some churchmen incline to dismiss the upper

classes as hopelessly benighted, and to suggest that only the lower classes are endowed with virtue. . . .

If churchmen concentrate exclusively on bringing about reform from below, by appealing to the lower mass for direct action and ignoring the possibility of renewed cooperation with upper social sectors, then along with communists and other extremists they seem destined to be a divisive force in society that can impede or disrupt the constructive endeavors of the state.

Pike illustrates this thesis by describing the attitude of Ricardo Talavera Campos whose essay on "Catholic Thought on Property" won the first prize in a contest sponsored by the Catholic University in Lima in 1963:

In addition to demanding immediate social justice and material comfort for all peasants and urban laboring masses, Talavera makes a lengthy analysis of capitalism. Convinced that in no part of the world has there been a genuine development away from classically liberal capitalism, Talavera asserts that the unscrupulous, avaricious captains of industry are gaining control over every aspect of the Capitalist system. He maintains that capitalism inevitably corrupts democracy by leading to the purchase of political parties and preventing the honest dissemination of news. Capitalism, he avers, echoing incidentally much of the message that has been propounded by Christian Democrats in Chile and elsewhere, can be based only on human selfishness and lust for profit, and thus can never be reconciled with Catholic morality. He argues further that capitalism cannot survive because it does not have a soul to save and is absolutely devoid of ideals and ideas. Catholics must, therefore, abandon all support of the discredited system. If they do not leap from the sinking Capitalist ship, it will be only non-Catholics who reconstruct the economic and social order once capitalism is totally submerged. Quoting the Jesuit priest Angel Arin Ormazabel to confirm his views, Talavera states that the rich should give their goods to the poor. If they do not wish to, then the poor, by capturing control of the means of government, should force them to.[19]

If the Church must compete in promises with the Communists in order to attract and hold the allegiance of the masses, the question arises whether it or at least some of its spokesmen have not promised too much. Some experts believe that the population explosion will further depress even the desperate living conditions in some underdeveloped countries. If the Church demands "that resignation be stamped out overnight and replaced with militant insistence upon immediate attainment of the comfortable material life" and at the same time preaches "that the sole and end purpose of matrimony is procreation," [20] will not widespread frustration, perhaps rebellion, result?

● **The Reform of Reform.** The much disputed role of the Church is obviously a complex subject, and the above considerations present only selected aspects of the rapidly changing situation. Enlightened and inspiring leaders are coming forward and Church action programs developed which rest upon a realistic assessment of the problems involved. Father Vekemans, for example, calls for a "reform of reforms" and states: "We must ask first not *what* reforms are needed, but rather *how* to reform any area of society. Man's answer to the modern world cannot be simply the satisfaction of wants but must include the reform of society, of men's relationship to each other." [21]

Other priests and some Catholic laymen fear that the Church's preoccupation with material matters has turned it away from its essential spiritual tasks. A Canadian priest with long experience in Latin America is convinced that the Church is using unreligious weapons to fight the wrong battle. He does not fear communism as much as he fears the Church engaged in politics, for "His Kingdom is not of this world." The "only alternative" to communism, he writes, "is not Christian Democracy, it is the Word of God." [22] Professor Pike, in a somewhat similar vein, calls for less action by priests ill-informed in economic matters and more attention to inculcating "the natural virtues." He even believes that "the clergy in Peru and elsewhere in Latin America has historically been fatally attracted toward intervening in spheres somewhat removed from its primary area of concern." [23] He is also convinced that the challenge of rolling back the tide of materialistic atheism cannot be met unless Catholicism and its increasingly important potential partners Protestantism and Judaism become more and more actual partners.

The mutual growing respect and cooperation in Latin America between Catholics and Protestants is a healthy sign of Christian ecumenicism in action, and the spirit of the 1956 joint pastoral letter of Central American bishops "which in effect lumped together Protestantism, gambling, alcoholism, and prostitution as the major menaces of the region is less and less in evidence." [24] Gone are the days when the National Catholic Welfare Conference in Washington could issue, as it did on November 14, 1942, a manifesto entitled "Victory and Peace" against Protestant missionaries in Latin America.[25] Many Protestants, too, have lost their bellicosity toward Catholics. Christian leaders in Latin America are apparently learning that, in order to meet the needs of Latin America today, they must simultaneously concern themselves with the human living conditions of their people, and work in harmony with all of the Christian tradition who are similarly concerned and active.

● **The Population Explosion.** Economists, who constitute a new kind of priesthood on the international scene, do not ordinarily write much about the danger of population growth in Latin America. With some notable exceptions, their discussions are more likely to revolve around such issues as the "structuralist" school versus the "monetarist" school on inflation, land reform, regional trading groups, and the like. Many writers, however, including some economists, have remarked upon the spectacular growth of population in

Latin America, especially in the urban areas where the population has increased from about 65 million to about 95 million in the last decade and is estimated to reach 138 million by 1970, or double that of 1950.[26] Though the rural population grows more slowly, Latin America has the world's highest rate of population increase, and present forecasts are that the annual rate will rise to above 3 per cent. If so, the more than 200 million inhabitants of 1960 will grow to 360 million by 1980, which means that Latin America will somehow have to feed, clothe, house, and provide work for 150 million more people.[27] For the world as a whole, especially Asia, Africa, and Latin America, it should be obvious that "there must be declines in birth rates if economic development is to become a continuing process," and a recent conference formally agreed that "the vast majority of the people of the world, including a large proportion of the people of the United States, do not yet recognize the full implications of the present population trends." [28]

If the Latin-American nations decide to undertake a birth control campaign, it is likely that the women and the Catholic Church will be important factors, although the ignorance of the people concerning contraceptive methods and their inability to buy them will also be important in many countries. Enough statistics have already been gathered to indicate that in some cities over 50 per cent of women who regularly attend mass now use birth control devices. Church leaders are cautiously exploring the implication of this delicate subject, while they await the establishment of official church doctrine by the papal commission charged with this responsibility. Meanwhile, discussions are held in Church centers and ecclesiastical publications. One of the papers presented to the first public conference on birth control, held at Cali, Colombia, in August 1965, under the auspices of the American Assembly of Columbia University and the Population Council, was written by the highly respected young Colombian priest Father Gustavo Pérez Ramírez of the Center of Social Research in Bogotá. (*See Reading No. 3.*)

● **The Debate over Birth Control.** Change is coming and expectancy is in the air. But will Latin Americans accept the thesis Frank Notestein advanced at this First Pan-American Assembly on Population that "the nation that chooses to be both prosperous and large in the long run can speed the day by reducing its birth rate drastically and at once?" It seems clear that many Latin-American women want relief from the excessive burden of child bearing and too large families; startling figures were given at the conference on the rate of illegal abortions in Latin America, among married as well as unmarried women.

But doctrinal change and practice will both come slowly, for deeply-imbedded habits and centuries-old convictions will have to be drastically altered. The words of the Cuban poet and patriot, José Martí, evoke a sympathetic response from many Latin Americans: "There is no contra-

diction in nature; the earth will know how to feed all the men it creates."
Both the *machismo* complex of male virility and cold-war politics will influence the future. The Communist daily in Santiago, Chile, had a long article
against "Yanqui Malthusianism" which denounced efforts "to regulate fertility
in Latin America" as a nefarious imperialist plot concocted in Wall Street.[29]
Some economists would probably agree with Víctor L. Urquidi: "Fundamentally, population control is a cultural problem. I am an economist. I don't
believe it is a problem for an economist." [30] But other writers argue that
most Latin American nations are thinly populated in relation to their immense territories, and that this inhibits mass production and attendant economic growth which could improve social conditions, a viewpoint that has
been described as "the sophisticated Marxist position." [31] The vigorous anticommunist leader, N. Viera Altamirano of El Salvador, strongly denounces
birth control as a trick of the leftists to pave the way for the socialization and
regimentation of Latin America—"a secret racial campaign." [32]

Some political leaders in Latin America seem to be even more opposed
than the Church to any effort to curb the "dynamism" of their people and apparently have the same blind faith as Martí, taking the position that education
and economic development will eventually slow down the rate of growth "as
has inevitably occurred in Western European countries." [33]

The study of the cultural, political, and religious aspects of birth control
in Latin America has just begun. Pioneer studies, such as those by Corwin
and Stycos, have collected much useful information which needs to be carefully evaluated. One basic conclusion that emerges from this inquiry is that
birth control always has political implications. Professor Corwin explains the
failure of Mexican leaders to face squarely the problem of demographic
planning because they fear this would smack of defeatism, an acknowledgement that the Mexican Revolution is not a success. "It would be an admission
that land distribution and other social welfare remedies are no longer an adequate solution to the problem of social injustice." [34] Some political leaders,
however, are beginning to recognize publicly the existence of the problem.
President Frei cautiously welcomed the eighth conference of the International
Planned Parenthood Federation to Santiago, Chile, in April, 1967, with these
words: "The problem of the world population explosion can't be avoided." [35]

If political leaders in Latin America eventually decide to embark on birth
control programs, can they achieve them without a formal change in the
Church's doctrine and practice? Some Catholic leaders have been willing to
issue strong statements on social and economic changes needed and to exhort
governments to change their ways. But ecclesiastics seem as reluctant as the
politicians to admit that birth control might result in material and spiritual
improvement of their people. Though government influence may eventually
be the decisive force in favor of birth control methods unless the Church also
definitely takes a position of leadership, it may be a long time before these
methods are widely used, particularly in the rural regions.

- **The Means of Control.** The means of control are at hand, however. The Church now is putting itself in a position to reach the rural masses through its radio-schools, along the lines established in Colombia a few years ago. Television as a group teaching device is being experimented with in Chile,[36] and President Frei is responsible for the statement that the "transistor radio is a much more revolutionary influence than Karl Marx," and illustrated this with a story of finding an illiterate shepherd at the end of Chile in far off Patagonia listening to Beethoven's Seventh Symphony by means of a transistor.[37] But in Latin America, as elsewhere, radio programs are not limited to classical music, and the real question facing Latin America and indeed the world is the content of the messages sent. The American Maryknoll priests have established a powerful radio station at Puno, Peru, which within a few years may reach the million inhabitants, mostly Indians, of the Department. When a recent Catholic visitor remarked that they were wasting their time unless these splendid facilities were used to spread knowledge of contraceptives and to encourage birth control, two of the priests agreed and two did not.

The future number of Latin Americans has a vital bearing on the amount of aid countries may ask for or demand, and also on the movement of Latin Americans to the U.S. The Johnson administration exerted intense pressure to strike from the 1965 immigration reform bill a provision which would have placed a limit on migration into the U.S. from other American countries. The flood of Puerto Ricans which poured into New York at one time and the rush of West Indians to Britain during the last fifteen years, which Britain has already begun to limit, are only tokens of the vast numbers that might some day wish to leave their homelands. If Latin Americans fail to damp their population explosion and if their economic problems remain acute, mass emigration to the U.S. might result, which could bring new and unparalleled tensions in relations between the U.S. and Latin America.

- **Continental Provincialism.** César Graña introduces his penetrating analysis of cultural nationalism in Spanish America with a story from the Father of History: "Herodotus, after visiting the Egyptians, concluded that they were a puzzling people. Women went to market while the men remained at home to weave. And, most strange, they wrote from right to left. He noted, however, the surprise of the Egyptians at his observation. It was not they, the Egyptians said, who wrote from right to left, but the Greeks who wrote from left to right." [38] Ethnocentrism has existed for a long time and one should not be surprised to find it powerful from Maine to Patagonia. "American history," to the hundreds of thousands of students in the U.S. who are now taking courses in the field, means the history of the United States; in Spanish-speaking America the same words mean the history of Spanish America with an occasional reference to the United States, Canada, and Brazil. In Brazil, "American history" may contain some reference to that of Spanish America but often treats it as the experience of a variety of rather quarrelsome folk frequently subject to military dictators, in marked contrast to the peaceful annals of Brazil where the relative racial harmony serves, in turn, to highlight the present struggle against discrimination in the United States.[39]

Students and visitors from the U.S. are often surprised to find that, despite a warm welcome from colleagues and even casual acquaintances, the Latin-American press carries much material hostile to their country's policies and culture. An examination of the columns of twenty leading dailies in Latin-American capitals revealed a fairly broad representation of images but considerable emphasis upon the affluent American at play; the American aware only of Europe; the sinister, imperialistic, arrogant American, the friend of dictators.[40]

Latin Americans believe that their countries are similarly misrepresented in our press, and that, knowing little about them and their culture, we think all the individual countries are alike. Assurances that over a thousand courses are offered in U.S. universities on Latin American subjects do not impress them, nor does the absence in Latin America of courses on U.S. history or culture much concern their educators; where such courses exist they have been promoted by U.S. embassies or foundations. Cold war tensions added to cultural nationalism have produced a situation in which each sector of the Americas tends to feel that its own method of "writing," to return to Herodotus, is the right way.

● **The Image of the United States.** Certainly some of Washington's policies and pronouncements over the years have tarnished the Latin-American image of the United States, which during much of the nineteenth century was highly respected by some of Latin America's educators and statesmen. A distinct change came when Secretary of State Richard Olney fatuously declared in 1895 that "the U.S. is practically sovereign on this continent, and its fiat is law upon the subjects to which it confines its interposition." Then followed the Spanish American War, the "taking" of Panama in 1903 by Theodore Roosevelt, and other U.S. interventions in the Caribbean. The nadir was reached, in the opinion of many Latin Americans, when the U.S. House of Representatives in 1965 announced, after intervention in the Dominican Republic, support for possible future unilateral U.S. military interventions in any Latin-American country where in its judgment communism threatened. In an area where many thoughtful persons have long feared the influence of the military in holding back democratic development, the U.S. Army-initiated project "Camelot," set up with millions of dollars through an American university and designed to investigate "subversion and possible revolution" in Chile, was intolerable. "Camelot" was begun without the knowledge of the U.S. Ambassador in Chile, whose vigorous protests caused President Johnson to cancel it but not before many Latin Americans saw confirmed the communist allegation that the Pentagon now calls the tune in Washington. Henceforth, U.S. researchers must expect that their efforts to learn about Latin America by study in the field will be met with this question: for exactly what purpose are you undertaking this research, and with whose funds?[41]

One's vision of the world, no matter in what country, depends a good deal upon the kind of education one is exposed to, and it should be remembered that a noticeable emphasis on Europe has prevailed thus far at all levels of the U.S. school system. Changes in this orientation are under way, but as one G.I. explained in West Berlin in 1961: "The point is, it's really Europe that matters to Americans, not Asia or Africa or Latin America. I studied history in college. Europe is what we stand for too." [42] The need for greater effort to include Latin America in our school programs from the primary grades to the university—as Vice-President Hubert Humphrey has advocated—is clearly apparent.

No matter how much information and interpretation of U.S. history and culture Latin Americans receive through educational channels, they will, of course, judge the U.S. by the way it behaves towards them, and will interpret this behavior in terms of both reality and of clichés. The powerful presence of the U.S. in Latin America cannot escape notice. Nor should the U.S. be surprised that Latin Americans find it difficult to reconcile the various faces the U.S. has turned to them over the years. The Venezuelan writer and senator Arturo Uslar-Pietri has described this difficulty clearly:

There is the United States with its liberal doctrines, admired and emulated by our democratic leaders of the nineteenth century. There is the United States of political expansion and military might that has left unhappy memories in many lands. There is the United States that, in many areas, has only the hard, aggressive face of great private-business enterprise. There is the United States of a hardhearted, insensitive, and thundering foreign policy that rides roughshod over the interests and feelings of many countries in Latin America. And then there is the United States whose thought and culture have always won the respectful applause of Latin Americans. In most countries, Jefferson, Lincoln, and Whitman are held in the highest regard, while Teddy Roosevelt's 'big stick' and the brazenly cynical attitude of Foster Dulles towards dictatorships are disdained and detested. [He concludes:] No one knows with any certainty which of the faces that speak is the real face of the U.S., and this persisting uncertainty is one of the main causes of misunderstanding between the Americas.[43]

Of all misunderstandings one stands out above all: Intervention. Hemispheric efforts to devise a workable inter-American political system have been gravely hampered by a fundamental clash between Latin America and the U.S. on when intervention is justified and how it should be carried out. Doubts have even been expressed that the Organization of American States can survive another crisis like the Dominican situation.

• **Does the OAS Have a Future?** The weakness of the Organization of American States is apparent to everyone. (*See Readings Nos. 78–86.*) Some look upon it as an ineffective debating society which the U.S. Government maintains for ceremonial purposes; certainly Washington has never been represented there by a delegation comparable to the diplomatic and political personages who have spoken for the United States at the United Nations. The Peruvian writer Francisco García Calderón once sarcastically described Latin America's role in the organization as that "of a Grand Eunuch; distinguished, but of slight influence." Today Latin American nations enjoy in the United Nations, especially in its Economic Commission for Latin America and in the cultural organization UNESCO, an authority and sense of freedom from domination by the U.S. that they have never had in the OAS.[44]

President Frei of Chile has declared: "The Organization of American States no longer has any real vitality. The moment is approaching for a decision whether to bring it up-to-date with a rapidly changing world and in line with the goals of the Alliance for Progress, or to let it become a sarcophagus of outmoded ideas." The OAS is now clearly of relatively little importance to the peace and welfare of the hemisphere. Some of the gravest crises in all its history confront the Americas today, yet the meeting of the OAS, the inter-American conference, is continually postponed. Scheduled for 1960 in Quito, the Eleventh Conference has not yet met. Originally the hostile attitude of Ecuador toward Peru over territorial questions prevented its convening. Since then one or more nations have judged it "inconvenient" to attend a full-fledged meeting where responsible political leaders might debate. While the United Nations holds regular sessions, no matter how many member nations disagree violently with each other's policies, it is difficult to assemble even a majority of the foreign ministers of the hemisphere to consult together on their many serious problems. One Argentine Foreign Minister warned that the OAS is giving the world the idea that it is suffering an acute case of "postponitis" at a time "when it should be asserting its prestige through decisive and imaginative actions." [45] A U.S. diplomat with long experience in inter-American affairs asks: "Is the OAS capable of coping with contemporary problems that beset the hemisphere? Or is it essentially a tangle of juridical inhibitions that render positive and effective action impossible? . . . Is a major reformation of the hemisphere system called for? Or must we consider the awful alternative of abandoning the effort of half a century of inter-American cooperation and returning to the unilateral exercise of power as the only reliable means of achieving necessary ends?" [46]

• **Ignoring the OAS Charter.** The U.S. is now facing this "awful alternative," whether it fully realizes the fact or not, since both President Johnson and the House of Representatives are apparently ready to ignore fundamental provisions of the 1948 OAS charter whenever they consider such action necessary. Article 15 states: "No state or group of states has the right to intervene, directly or indirectly, in the internal or external affairs of any other state. The foregoing principle prohibits not only armed forces but also any other form of interference or attempted threat against its political, economic, and cultural elements." Article 17 is equally emphatic: "The territory of a state is inviolate; it may not be the object, even temporarily, of military occupation or of other measures of force taken by another state, directly or indirectly, on any ground whatsoever."

Article 19, however, demonstrates the flexibility of the legal mind and the ingenuity some lawyers display in devising statements which lead to conflicting conclusions: "Measures adopted for the maintenance of peace and security in accordance with existing treaties do not constitute a violation of the principles set forth in Articles 15 and 17." [47]

In analyzing the present impasse between the U.S., fearful of communist influence in the hemisphere, and Latin America, equally fearful of U.S. interventions—each side considering the other hysterical—one must remember that the paternalistic attitude of the U.S. toward Latin America that existed for a long time included elements of both dominance and responsibility, sometimes in accord but sometimes in conflict.

The following colloquy, which took place in London between British Foreign Secretary Lord Grey and U.S. Ambassador to Britain Walter Hines Page, represents an unpleasant mixture of both attitudes expressed in the moralizing tone of a high official of Woodrow Wilson's administration:

Grey: Suppose you have to intervene, what then?
Page: Make 'em vote and live by their decisions.
Grey: But suppose they will not so live?
Page: We'll go in again and make 'em vote again.
Grey: And keep this up for 200 years?
Page: Yes. The United States will be here for 200 years and it can continue to shoot men for that little space till they learn to vote and rule themselves. [48]

The policy of supporting "free elections" has not been particularly effective. Stability of a sort has been created at best on only a temporary basis. Moreover, the policy had the "unintended, ironical, and self-contradictory result of paving the way for strong dictatorships as in Nicaragua, Cuba, and the Dominican Republic." [49]

Herodotus would probably see this policy as another example of ethnocentrism, but a U.S. observer in 1950 used harsher words:

Almost invariably, national self-righteousness is dominant in the breasts of the interventionists or quasi-interventionists who advocate forcing Latin Americans to live up to our concept of political democracy. It is outspoken among those who would have us turn our backs on the other American republics because they are unworthy of us.[50]

Belligerent voices were raised in the U.S. during the 1962 missile crisis, for the Olney "fiat" spirit of 1895 is not yet dead.[51]

● **Myths About Latin America.** Myths still influence the feelings and the actions of many people inside and outside of Latin America. (*See Reading No. 86.*) Convictions on economic problems generate much ill-feeling: witness the bitter complaints by José Figueres and many others in Latin America that the U.S. has not done enough to raise and stabilize the prices of their primary products. Yet the matter is not so simple as it may appear. Ex-Senator Paul H. Douglas, a liberal economist, for example, questioned the value of price increases for coffee in discussing the International Coffee Agreement which went into effect in 1963 after strong support from the United States:

> It is urged in support of this agreement that it is necessary both to raise the standard of living of the poverty-stricken peasant who raises the coffee and give greater stability to hard pressed governments such as that of Brazil. Those are both desirable purposes and it is probably that the previous price of 34 cents a pound was altogether too low. But it is questionable whether the peasants who do the physical labor would get much of any increase in price. They did not in the previous periods of high prices. The profits were instead largely intercepted by the relatively small group of wealthy planters and traders. In El Salvador, for example, the well known fourteen families largely control the land and with their associates reaped the major share of the benefits from the high prices of the early 1950's. It was much the same way in Brazil and Colombia. It must be granted, however, that an increased price does increase the revenues which producing countries can raise through export taxes and that, to this extent, it amounts to an indirect subsidy to the governments and wealthy planters with some crumbs falling from the table into the mouths of the hungry peasants at the bottom of the Latin American social structure.[52]

Chronic overproduction and the rising competition of African coffee still threaten the economic stability of Latin America, despite the efforts of Brazil and other countries to diversify their crops and create new industries. For coffee production has been running roughly 20 percent ahead of world demand and world consumption is growing at annually only 2.5 to 3 per cent. And there was a surplus in Brazil of 87.5 million bags of 132 pounds each in January, 1967.

Industrialization has been considered another path away from "colonialism" by many Latin Americans. The U.S. is now pushing common market plans to assist the process of economic integration. But Raúl Prebisch, the Argentine economist, has sounded a warning: "Recent events in the motor vehicle industry are highly instructive. Not only are there a number of countries all trying to do the same thing, but there is an incredible proliferation of anti-economic plants within a single country." [53]

For better or for worse, U.S. policies and pressures have long made a strong impact on many Latin American problems and will continue to do so. How to develop and implement policies wisely and whether to exert pressure must continually be debated. Dean Acheson had these sober reflections:

> We must be careful not to act as the schoolmistress of the Western Hemisphere. We have a proper stake in how their governments behave toward us and affect our interests. We can properly object to infringements of them, or to conduct or to relations with our enemies or potential enemies likely to weaken the security of all of us. We can properly act to help them to participate in the life and to reap the benefits of a free world economic system. When we begin to take action as a government, to oppose suspensions of representative government and *habeas corpus,* and to berate those responsible, we are moving out of the area of proper conduct. Here I am preaching what I have learned the hard way. To express collective indignation may bring the glow of moral principles vindicated without effort; but it is usually futile, and, more often than not, harmful . . . There is reason to believe that in the hemisphere acceptance of the principles of the Bill of Rights may be best advanced by economic development and diffusing its benefits.[54]

President Kennedy, who was to face the most serious threat of foreign intervention in the Americas in this century, had this to say:

> Cuba is not an isolated case. We can still show our concern for liberty and our opposition to the *status quo* in our relations with the other Latin American dictators who now, or in the future, try to suppress their people's aspirations. And we can take the long-delayed positive measures that are required to enable the revolutionary wave sweeping Latin America to move through relatively peaceful channels and to be harnessed to the great constructive tasks at hand.[55]

● **U.S. Intervention and the Cold War.** A powerful, relatively new element now complicates the workings of U.S. policy—the cold war struggle with the communist world. This fact and the traditional mistrust of the U.S. endemic in many parts of Latin America help to explain the present deadlock in the OAS over "unilateral intervention" and a "collective intervention" carried out by the proposed inter-American armed force. U.S. policy no longer follows the Walter Hines Page prescription of unlimited intervention for the "good" of Latin Americans, but the problem still exists of determining when a danger exists to the hemisphere and what, if anything, to do about it. When the U.S. sends Marines to the Dominican Republic to prevent "another Communist Cuba" it does so to protect itself and also to save Latin America from what it considers a grave peril; when a Latin-American nation opposes intervention, it does so on behalf of what it believes to be its own national integrity, and the integrity of all Latin America, which it sees as threatened by the power of the Colossus of the North. (*See Readings Nos. 78–94.*)

Though "intervention" is often defined in the very specific sense of the landing of troops on foreign soil, it has other faces. One diplomat maintains that non-intervention simply doesn't exist, "because what the American Government refrains from doing may, because of our preponderant power in the hemisphere, constitute an exercise of influence almost as weighty as intervention itself." [56] Dr. Ferrara of Cuba pointed out in 1928 that the principle of non-intervention, which was intended to guarantee freedom and the right of self-determination, might well become the very means by which tyranny could be perpetuated. This was the same position Fidel Castro and his Minister of Foreign Relations took a quarter of a century later when they insisted that the principle of non-intervention must not be allowed to serve as a shield behind which dictators such as Trujillo could hide.[57] While the Latin American governments generally still regard non-intervention as fundamental to the inter-American system, the U.S. State Department seems to be beginning to campaign to substitute something less absolute and less binding than Articles 15 and 17 of the OAS Charter.[58] Whatever theoretical views the nations of the hemisphere hold, the fact of intervention has not been abolished in the Americas: "In the past two decades Central America and the Caribbean have probably seen more cases of intervention than any area of the world outside the Soviet sphere. Furthermore, few if any States in the area can honestly plead innocence." [59]

The next few years may well see the U.S. abandon certain so-called "American principles." President Kennedy warned during the Cuban missile crisis that "if the nations of this hemisphere should fail to meet their commitments against outside communist penetration . . . the Government will not hesitate in meeting its primary obligations." [60] His declaration, although it differed very little from the House of Representatives resolution of 1965 so bitterly criticized in Latin America, seems not to have provoked the same indignant response. Perhaps this was because the world at that moment was holding its breath as the nuclear giants stood face to face; moreover, President Kennedy's enlightened policy vis-à-vis Latin America was evident and both his personality and his later assassination set him apart in the minds of Latin Americans.

● **The Prospects for Unity.** Perhaps the animosities and rivalries in the hemisphere, when combined with the different economic and political interests of the individual countries, will make any important Latin American unity impossible, except on such a negative issue as opposition to U.S. intervention. Daniel Cosío Villegas, the Mexican writer noted for his penetrating comments, has charged that no single Latin American country today has a clearly defined foreign policy resting upon an adequate political philosophy, and he fears that such a task would require "more talent and, above all, more rectitude than the present public figures of Latin America apparently possess." [61]

Alberto Lleras Camargo, the first Latin American to serve as Secretary General of the OAS, who probably knows as much as anyone about the strengths and weaknesses of the inter-American system as well as about Latin American politics, concluded in 1954: "The Organization is neither good nor bad; it can be nothing else than what the Governments which are members of the Organization want it to be." [62] So the real question confronting both Latin America and the U.S. is: Can cynicism and distrust of the U.S. be abated enough to permit a new and healthier relationship to be worked out? The question is a formidable one and many, but far from all, of the answers will have to come from Washington, in both word and deed. (*See Readings Nos. 87–94.*)

Many of the answers will have to come from Latin America, as the summit conference of presidents at Punta del Este in April, 1967, emphasized. The recognition there by such leaders as Fernando Belaúnde Terry, Gustavo Díaz Ordaz, and Eduardo Frei Montalva of the responsibility of Latin America to confront its own problems rather than to depend forever on foreign aid is one of the most hopeful signs in recent years.

[1] Leslie N. Gay Jr., "Problems of Land Ownership in Latin America," *Journal of Farm Economy,* XXXII (1950), pp. 258–270.

[2] Eastin Nelson, "A Revolution in Economic Policy: An Hypothesis of Social Dynamics in Latin America," *Southwestern Social Science Quarterly* (December, 1953), pp. 3–16.

[3] *Social Science Research on Latin America,* edited by Charles Wagley (New York: Columbia University Press, 1964), p. 61.

[4] R. A. Humphreys, *Tradition and Revolt in Latin America* (London: The Athlone Press, 1965), p. 20.

[5] See the author's "The Bones of Cuauhtémoc," *Encounter* (September, 1965), pp. 79–85.

[6] T. Lynn Smith, *Agrarian Reform in Latin America* (New York: Knopf, 1965), p. 40.

[7] Costa Pinto, as quoted in Wagley, *Social Science Research in Latin America,* p. 244.

[8] Exceptions are Felícitas Klimpel Alvarado, *La mujer chilena. El aporte femenino al progreso de Chile, 1910–1960,* Santiago: Editorial Andrés Bello, 1962; Fryda Schultz de Mantovani, *La mujer en la vida nacional,* Buenos Aires: Ediciones Galatea-Nueva Visión, 1960. As an example of the way women are beginning to speak up and assess their position in the world, see the forum "La mujer en la política. Por que no ha llegado a desempeñar los más altos cargos," *El Nacional* (Caracas, January 17, 1966). For a sober, factual account of working women, see the *Informe presentado por la Comisión Interamericana de Mujeres sobre la condición económica de la mujer trabajadora en las Repúblicas Americanas,* Washington, D.C.: Secretaría General de la Organización de los Estados Americanos, 1959. For the background on women in Spain, see the sections on "Don Juanismo" and "machismo" in Condesa de Campos Alange, *La mujer España. Cien años de su historia* (Madrid: Aguilar, 1964).

[9] The quotations in this paragraph come from John Gillin, "Changing Depths in Latin America," *Journal of Inter-American Studies,* I (1959), pp. 379–389.

[10] *Ibid.*

[11] Arthur F. Corwin, *Contemporary Mexican Attitudes Toward Population, Poverty, and Public Opinion* (Gainesville: University of Florida Press, 1963), p. 46, quoting María Elvira Bermúdez, *La vida familiar del Mexicano* (Mexico: Robredo, 1955).

[12] Gillin, "Changing Depths in Latin America," p. 388.

[13] This Center maintains an extensive file of material on contemporary religious change in Latin America, and issues twice a month reports on a wide variety of developments. The Center published in 1962–1963 a collection of *Recent Church Documents from Latin America* which included the "Pastoral Plan of the Bishops of Chile," "Emergency Plan of the Bishops of Brazil," "Pastoral Letter on Social Problems (1962) Chile," "Pastoral Letter on Social Reform (1963) Brazil," "Pastoral Letter on Social Reform (1963) Peru," and "Rules and Standards of the Latin American Confederation of Religions."

[14] "El Padre Vives, un luchador social," *Mensaje*, No. 143 (Santiago: Centro Bellarmino, 1965), pp. 545–550.

[15] Roger E. Vekemans, "Psycho-Social Analysis of Latin America's Pre-Revolutionary Situation," *CIF Reports*, I (Cuernavaca, Mexico: Center of Intercultural Documentation, 1963), No. 9, p. 409. This issue is a digest of a substantial number of *Mensaje* (Santiago) entitled: "Revolution in Latin America: A Christian Vision."

[16] Father Damboriena, a Spanish Jesuit, taught in the Universidad Javeriana, Bogotá. His statement appeared in a bulletin of the National Catholic Welfare Conference of Washington, D.C. The quotation comes from *The Christian Century*, LXXXII (June 2, 1965), p. 699. See also Padre Damboriena's *El Protestantismo en América Latina* (Bogotá: Oficina Internacional de Investigaciones Feres, 1962); Pierre Chaunu, "Pour une sociologie du protestantisme latinoamericain. Problèmes de méthode," *Cahiers de Sociologie Économique*, No. 12 (Le Havre: Centre de Recherches et D'Etudes de Psychologie des Peuples et de Sociologie Économique, 1965), pp. 5–18; Magdalaine Villeroy, "Enquête sur les églises protestantes dans le Brésil en crise des années 1962–1965," (*ibid.*), pp. 19–80.

[17] Vekemans, "Economic Development, Social Change, and Cultural Mutation in Latin America," in William V. D'Antonino and Fredrick B. Pike's, *Religion, Revolution, and Reform: New Forces for Change in Latin America* (New York: Praeger, 1964), pp. 129–142.

[18] "Carta del señor Cardenal al Padre Camilo Torres," June 9, 1965, in *El "caso" del Padre Camilo Torres* (Bogotá: Ediciones Tercer Mundo, 1965), pp. 33–34.

[19] Fredrick B. Pike, "Church and State in Mid-Twentieth Century Latin America: A Catholic's View," an address delivered in May, 1965, published subsequently by the National Council of the Churches of Christ in the U.S.A. (New York). For a significant exchange of opinions on the doctrine of the Church on property, see "Diálogo en torno a la propiedad," *Mensaje*, XIV (Santiago, 1965), No. 143, pp. 567–573.

[20] Pike, "Church and State in Mid-Twentieth Century America."

[21] "Revolutionary Reforms in Latin America: A Christian Vision," *CIF Reports*, II (Cuernavaca, Mexico: Center of Intercultural Documentation, 1963), No. 6, pp. 245–272. This issue is largely a résumé of the October, 1963, *Mensaje* published by the Centro Bellarmino in Santiago, Chile. See also João Gonçalves de Souza, "A situação da América Latina em face dos idéas da cristianidade," *Síntese Política Económica Social*, IV (Rio de Janeiro, January–March, 1962), pp. 26–42.

[22] Ivan Labelle, "Las armas con que combatimos no han de ser carnales!"; *Finis Terrae*, año XII, No. 50 (Santiago, 1965), pp. 23–28.

[23] Pike, "The Modernized Church in Peru: Two Aspects," *The Review of Politics*, XXVI (Notre Dame, 1964), pp. 314–315.

[24] *Primera Carta Pastoral del Episcopado de Centro America y Panama*, May 27, 1956 (Managua, Nicaragua, 1956), as quoted by Pike in note 20 above.

[25] Wade Crawford Barclay, *Greater Good Neighbor Policy* (1945), pp. 40–41. Barclay and the Jesuit historian Peter Dunne were the pioneers in the present-day rapprochement of Catholics and Protestant missionaries in Latin America.

[26] John P. Powelson and Anatole A. Solow, "Urban and Rural Development in Latin America," in Latin America Tomorrow, *The Annals of the American Academy of Political and Social Science*, Vol. 360 (1965), p. 49.

[27] Jacques Chonchol, "Land Tenure and Development in Latin America," in Claudio Véliz, ed., *Obstacles to Change in Latin America* (London: Royal Institute of International Affairs, 1965), p. 75.

[28] Philip M. Hauser, ed., *The Population Dilemma* (Englewood Cliffs, New Jersey: Prentice-Hall, 1963), pp. 32, 183.

[29] Orlando Millas, "Malthusianismo yanqui," *El Siglo* (Santiago, October 20, 1965).

[30] As quoted by Corwin, *Contemporary Mexican Attitudes*, p. 6.

[31] *The New York Times*, August 14, 1965.

[32] "¿Contra el hambre o contra el hombre?" in *Día a día en El Diario de Hoy* (San Salvador: El Diario de Hoy), pp. 9–11.

[33] J. Mayone Stycos, "Population Growth and the Alliance for Progress," *Population Bulletin*, XVIII (1962), No. 6, pp. 112–134.

[34] Corwin, *Contemporary Mexican Attitudes*, p. 49. For a comprehensive and well-organized summary, see J. Mayone Stycos, "Opinions of Latin American Intellectuals on Population Problems and Birth Control," Latin America Tomorrow, *The Annals of the American Academy of Political and Social Science*, Vol. 360 (1965), pp. 11–26.

[35] *The New York Times*, April 10, 1967.

[36] Teresa Donoso Loero, "El campesino chileno y la televisión," *Finis Terrae*, Año XII (Santiago, 1965), No. 50, pp. 54–56.

[37] "El Diario 'Il Giorno' de Milán, entrevista al Presidente Eduardo Frei," *Política y Espíritu*, Año XIX (Santiago, 1965), No. 291, p. 35.

[38] Graña, "Cultural Nationalism: The Idea of Historical Destiny in Spanish America," *Social Research*, XXIX–XXX (1962–1963), pp. 395–418, 37–52. The quotation appears in XXIX, p. 396.

[39] See the author's *Do the Americas Have a Common History? A Critique of the Bolton Theory* (New York: Knopf, 1964).

[40] Wayne Wolfe, "Images of the United States in the Latin American Press," *Journalism Quarterly*, XLV (1964), pp. 79–86.

[41] For thoughtful critiques of Camelot and its implications for research in Latin America, see Kalman H. Silvert, *American Academic Ethics and Social Research Abroad* (New York: American Universities Field Staff, 1965); F.J.C., "Camelot: Proyecto con dos caras," *Mensaje*, XIV (Santiago, October, 1965), pp. 577–580; Irving Horowitz.

[42] "What Berlin Means to the Berliners," *The New York Times* (August 27, 1961), p. 71.

[43] Uslar-Pietri, "No Panacea for Latin America," in Joseph Maier and Richard W. Weatherhead, eds., *Politics of Change in Latin America* (New York: Praeger, 1964), p. 79.

[44] Bryce Wood and Minerva Morales M., "Latin America and the United Nations," *International Organization*, XIX (1965), No. 3, pp. 714–727.

[45] *The New York Times*, July 22, 1965.

[46] John C. Dreier, *The Organization of American States and the Hemisphere Crisis* (New York: Harper and Row, 1962), p. 9.

[47] *Ibid.*, pp. 22–33.

[48] As quoted by William Franklin Sands, *Our Jungle Diplomacy* (Chapel Hill: University of North Carolina Press, 1944), p. 121.

[49] Theodore P. Wright, "Free Elections in U.S. Latin American Policy," *Political Science Quarterly*, LXXIV (1959), p. 112.

[50] Y, "On a Certain Impatience with Latin America," *Foreign Affairs* (July, 1950), p. 577.

[51] See the collection of strong statements assembled by Samuel Shapiro, *Invisible Latin America* (Boston: Beacon Press, 1963), p. 139.

[52] Paul H. Douglas, *America in the Market Place* (New York: Holt, Rinehart, and Winston, 1966), p. 189.

[53] "Surmounting Obstacles to a Latin American Common Market," in *Latin American Economic Integration*, Miguel S. Wionczek, ed. (New York: Praeger, 1966), p. 145. See also Sidney Dell, *A Latin American Common Market?* (London: Oxford University Press, 1966).

[54] Dean Acheson, *Power and Diplomacy* (New York, 1958), pp. 80–82, *passim*.

[55] John F. Kennedy, *The Strategy of Peace* (New York, 1960).

[56] Ellis Briggs, *Farewell to Foggy Bottom* (New York: David McKay, 1964), p. 180.

[57] C. Neale Ronning, *Intervention, International Law, and the Inter-American System* (New York: Wiley, 1963), pp. 67–68.

[58] See the *Address by the Honorable Leonard C. Meeker, Legal Advisor, Department of State, Before the Foreign Law Association, June 9, 1965*. Dept. of State Press Release No. 147.

[59] Ronning, *Intervention, International Law, and the Inter-American System*, p. 81.

[60] *Ibid.*, pp. 160–162.

[61] Cosío Villegas, "Crisis de la diplomacia latino-americana," *Cuadernos*, No. 100 (Paris, September, 1965), p. 22.

[62] O. Carlos Stoetzer, *The Organization of American States. An Introduction* (New York: Praeger, 1965), p. 42. Originally published in German in 1964, this volume is a guide to the present problems and prospects of the OAS.

SIGNING OF THE SOVIET-CUBAN DECLARATION OF FRIENDSHIP IN THE
KREMLIN, MAY 23, 1963.

READINGS

SECTION I

General

<hr>

Political instability is one of the facts of life in Latin America. Since 1930 there have been 106 illegal political changes there, including chiefs of state who were assassinated, committed suicide, or forced from office. Only Mexico has achieved stability.[1] Merle Kling, a political scientist at Washington University, analyzes what is meant by "instability" and emphasizes the limited nature of the power exercised by Latin American rulers. (Reading No. 1.)

Even dictators cannot be supreme, as R. A. Humphreys, the leading British Latin Americanist, makes clear in his historical view of the caudillo tradition. (Reading No. 2.) Prediction on the course of political events is perilous, for one author rashly observed in a book published in 1929: "the Argentine is today one of the most stable and well-ordered states in the world; it is one in which revolution is as improbable as in England."[2] The population explosion constitutes the most dramatic and dangerous development today (Reading No. 3), but nationalism is a strong competitor. John J. Johnson of Stanford University provides a succinct and informed analysis of the "new nationalism" which contains many old elements. (Reading No. 4.)

Sharp differences concerning the nature of Latin American society and its future directions have been responsible for a publication explosion. One experienced observer has written that "in the last eight or ten years in the United States there have been published more good, analytical books on Latin America than in the previous 100 years."[3] This abundant literature has not produced a consensus, however, as Rodolfo Stavenhagen shows in his "Seven Mistaken Theses on Latin America." (Reading No. 5.)

[1] Willard F. Barber and C. Neale Ronning, *Internal Security and Military Power. Counterinsurgency and Civic Action in Latin America*, Columbus: Ohio State University Press, 1966, p. 4. A detailed list of these political changes is given in Appendix A (pp. 249–265).

[2] As quoted by R. A. Humphreys, p. 154.

[3] Robert G. Mead, Jr., "Literature and Politics: Our Image and Our Policy in Latin America," *Hispania*, XLIX (1966), No. 2, p. 302.

242

1 KLING, A Theory of Power and Political Instability in Latin America

Political instability in Latin America is distinguished by three characteristics: (1) it is chronic; (2) it frequently is accompanied by limited violence; (3) it produces no basic shifts in economic, social or political policies.

Political instability in a Latin American country cannot be evaluated as a temporary deviation in a pattern of peaceful rotation in office. In many Latin American republics, despite prescriptions of written constitutions, an abrupt change of governmental personnel through violence is a regular and recurrent phenomenon. In Honduras, "from 1824 to 1950, a period of 126 years, the executive office changed hands 116 times." "During the nine-year interval ending in 1940, Ecuador had no less than fourteen presidents, [and had] four of them during the single month which ended on September 17, 1947. Instability is likewise dramatized on the cabinet level: twenty-seven different ministers occupying eight cabinet posts between May 29, 1944, and August 23, 1947. Twelve foreign ministers attempted to administer Ecuadoran foreign policy in the two-month period between August and October 1933." And the observations of a member of a United Nations mission to Bolivia in 1951 would not be inapplicable in substance to many Latin American states: "In the past ten years, Bolivia has had nine major revolutions. None of its Presidents has served out his constitutional term of office during the last twenty-five years. There have been eighteen Ministers of Labor in four years; eight Ministers of Finance in eighteen months." . . .

Occupancy of key governmental positions, consequently, has been secured at least 31 times in disregard of formal procedures since the Second World War. Nor does the above list take into account the numerous "unsuccessful" plots, suppressed uprisings, arrests, deportations, declarations of state of siege, boycotts, riots and fraudulent "elections" which have punctuated Latin American politics in the last decade. . . .

Revolts, uprisings and coups d'état, moreover, constitute incomplete evidence of the range of political instability in Latin America. For obscured by data of these kinds is the presence of "concealed" instability. The protracted tenure of a Vargas in Brazil (1930–1945), of an Ubico in Guatemala (1930–1944), the single candidate (candidato único) "elections" of Paraguay, Honduras, the Dominican Republic, Nicaragua and Colombia, the abortive "elections" of 1952 in Venezuela are not to be construed, of course, as symptomatic of political stability. For these also constitute instances in which governmental authority has been retained by the exercise of force in disregard of formal requirements. *Continuismo,* prolonged office-holding by a strong *caudillo,* in its essence represents the reverse side of the

Merle Kling, "Towards a Theory of Power and Political Instability in Latin America," *The Western Political Quarterly,* IX, No. 1 (March, 1956), 21–35, *passim.* Reprinted by permission.

shield of political instability. *Continuismo* signifies not the absence of political instability, but the effective suppression of potential and incipient rebellions by competing *caudillos. Continuismo,* in fact, may be regarded as perpetuation in office by means of a series of successful *anticipatory* revolts. . . .

Although violence provides a continuing strand in the fabric of Latin American politics, revolution, in the sense of a fundamental transformation of society, "is rare in Latin America, and even mass participation in violence is only occasionally found." A leader may be assassinated or exiled, a new junta may assume the posts of political authority, but control of the economic bases of power is not shifted and the hierarchy of social classes is not affected; in short, there is no restructuring of society. The label "palace revolution," as defined by Lasswell and Kaplan, can be appropriately applied to the pattern of political change in Latin America; for political instability in Latin America, like a palace revolution, involves "a change in governors contrary to the political formula but retaining it." Again violence in Latin America, in conformity with the characteristics of a palace revolution, produces a "change in government without corresponding changes in government policy." General Gustavo Rojas Pinilla may be a party to a successful revolt in Colombia, and General Zenón Noriega may be a party to an unsuccessful revolt in Peru; but the basic economic, social and political policies of Colombia and Peru are not altered by either the successful or the unsuccessful general. Violence is virtually always present; fundamental change is virtually always absent. . . .

Chronic political instability is a function of the contradiction between the realities of a colonial economy and the political requirements of legal sovereignty among the Latin American states.

Significant implications for both public policy and research appear inherent in the interpretation of Latin American politics here formulated. In the field of public policy, this interpretation implies that it is not possible for the United States to have powerful allies in Latin America so long as present economic patterns persist. . . .

While the achievement of political stability would augment the power of the Latin American states, the elimination of a status of economic colonialism may diminish the diplomatic reliability of their governments! And the dilemma thus brought to the surface by the interpretation of Latin American politics offered in this study has never been publicly acknowledged by the United States Department of State. . . .

For research, the implications of this interpretation of Latin American politics are rather obvious. If political studies of the Latin American area are to rest on more than superficial foundations, they can rest neither on formal analyses of constitutions nor on the diplomatic exchanges between the United States and various Latin American countries. Nor, in the light of this interpretation, can a study nourish the illusion that it has penetrated to the realities of Latin American politics when it has applied the label "dictator" to a particular holder of governmental office in Latin America. The Latin American *caudillo,* according to the implications of the interpretation presented here, operates within a narrowly-circumscribed range of power, since he may not tamper with the traditional economic bases of power. Serious attempts to analyze the nature of politics in Latin America, therefore, must seek to identify the ambits of political maneuverability within which power may be exercised by those who occupy posts of governmental authority in sovereign states with colonial economies. The successful conclusion of such attempts should result in a new awareness of the limitations on the nature of the power actually exercised by presidents and junta members in the politically unstable environment of Latin America.

2 *HUMPHREYS, The Caudillo Tradition*

. . . Like the fifteenth-century Italian despot, the nineteenth-century caudillo was an expression of the needs and conditions of his time. But caudillismo was older than the "age of the caudillos." Its roots lay deep in the colonial past and in the structure, the character and the traditions of Spanish American society. Spain's empire in the New World had been an absolutism, a paternal absolutism, it is true, but an absolutism none the less. Its principle was the principle of authority. Loyalty to the Crown was the cement which held the vast, heterogeneous structure together, and, after three hundred years of Spanish imperial rule, it still needed the shock of the Napoleonic invasions of the Iberian peninsula and the consequent crisis of the Spanish monarchy to precipitate the revolutions which led to independence. But the Spaniards are a highly individualistic people. Anarchy, says Salvador de Madariaga, is their "natural state." And in the Indies Spaniards and Spanish Americans were distant indeed from Spain. They were used to authority. But they were used also to ignoring authority. "Obedezco, pero no cumplo," "I obey, but I do not execute." Who but a Spaniard could have devised so ingenious a formula for nullifying the royal will, as nullified it so frequently was? It was not merely in civic tumults or even in occasional rebellions that what Pedro Henríquez-Ureña calls "the latent anarchy of the colonial régime" was revealed. The comment of Antonio de Ulloa, visiting Perú in the seventeen-forties, comes forcibly to mind. "Here . . . ," he reported, "everyone considers himself a sovereign."

The principle of authority destroyed, loyalty to the Crown dissolved, it was the anarchical element that prevailed. The collapse of the empire was the collapse of the State, whose ally, the Church, was itself gravely compromised. It was in vain that the architects of a new order attempted to establish a rational pattern of freedom in constitutions which, too often, borrowed eclectically from abroad, and conformed too rarely to political and social realities at home. Once the old basis of political obligation had been undermined, there was no firm foundation, as

R. A. Humphreys, "Latin America," in Michael Howard, ed., *Soldiers and Governments. Nine Studies in Civil-Military Relations.* (London: Eyre and Spottiswoode, 1957), pp. 155–163. Reprinted by permission.

General O'Leary noted in his famous memoirs, on which political institutions could be built. There were exceptions. In Chile the landed gentry early drew together to give the country stability and to open the way for the slow unfolding of its economic life. And Brazil, an empire amidst republics, was always a case apart. But in most of the new republics of Spanish America there was little cohesive force, little sense of *communitas,* to weld into a whole the diverse elements of which society was composed; and while the masses were sunk in poverty and ignorance the dominant social class had yet to learn to govern itself before it could govern others. Politically at least these states were not the adult heirs of imperial Spain; they were her orphan children, their homelands ravaged, their prosperity destroyed, their economic life disrupted during the enormous catastrophe of civil war. "Many tyrants will arise upon my tomb," wrote Bolívar in 1826, and the prophecy was fulfilled. The constitutionalists, as Professor Morse remarks, those who "avowed the existence in fact of a state-community," were "swept away before the winds of personalism." Authority revived not in the impersonal state but in the person of the caudillo. Dictatorship became the norm of government, revolution the method of changing it. "We convulsed a continent for our independence," says Martin Decoud in Conrad's *Nostromo,* "only to become the passive prey of a democratic parody."

A military class enjoying special privileges, the so-called *fuero militar,* had made its appearance in Spanish America before the wars of independence began. But it was the wars that fastened militarism on so many of the new republics. A relatively large standing army, such as was retained in Mexico, too often proved a menace rather than a protection to the state whose security it was designed to serve. Military interests became distinct from civil interests, military loyalties from civic loyalties. Generals who had commanded armies, moreover, aspired to govern countries. "The presence of a fortunate soldier," San Martín had said in his famous farewell proclamation to the people of Perú, ". . . is dangerous to newly constituted states." But it was the soldiers, who, in their own view, were the indispensable men. Most of the early presidents-dictators, and of the lesser local and provincial caudillos as well, were military leaders, veterans of the revolutionary armies, ambitious local commanders, and, in Argentina, gaucho chieftains of the plains. A civilian autocrat, such as the formidable Dr José Gaspar Rodríguez de Francia, whose ruthless reign in Paraguay attracted, inevitably, the half-admiring attention of Carlyle, was the exception rather than the rule.

The caudillos ruled by force. And, mostly, they fell by force. Some, like the infamous Carlos Solano López of Paraguay, were destroyed in war. Some, like the theocratic Gabriel García Moreno of Ecuador, one of the most remarkable of the later civilian caudillos, were assassinated. Some, like Rosas, the greatest and the worst of the Argentine tyrants, ended their days in exile. But few died peacefully in power. Dr Francia in Paraguay and Rafael Carrera in Guatemala were notable exceptions. And few, once they had tasted power, voluntarily relinquished it. Most of them had some basis of general support in one or another segment of the population, and most, also, were capable of inspiring a passionate loyalty among their immediate followers. In Argentina Darwin was told that a man who had murdered another, "when arrested and questioned concerning his motive, answered, 'He spoke disrespectfully of General Rosas, so I killed him.'" "At the end of a week," adds Darwin, "the murderer was at liberty." Nor were the caudillos all of one sort. There were autocrats who waded through blood to presidential thrones, ignorant adventurers, like Mariano Melgarejo of Bolivia, who perpetrated unspeakable crimes. And there were astute and cynical despots who had nothing to learn from the pages of Machiavelli. But not all the caudillos were tyrants. Among them were sincere and high-minded men, not without honour or undeserving of honour in the countries which they ruled; and even among the worst there were some who, by breaking and moulding lesser despots to their will, helped to substitute a larger conception of the state as a nation for the agglomeration of personal and local loyalties which had hindered its action and restrained its growth.

When the "age of the caudillos" ended, if ended it has, is a matter of debate. In some of the Spanish American states the struggle for stability, the problem of how to reconcile freedom with order, had not been resolved even when the nineteenth century closed. In some it has not been resolved to-day. But the turbulent years of the first half-century were certainly the worst. Slowly, however, the temper of politics began to change. The cruder forms of military despotism began to vanish. Civilian oligarchies took control and a new type of presidential autocrat arose. In Argentina the unity of the nation and its constitutional organization were at last attained by the eighteen-sixties. And thereafter the face of the great pampa, where the gauchos had fought and the Indians roamed, was transformed. The great currents of European capital and immigration, the coming of the railway net-work, the invention of wire-fencing and of the refrigerator and the refrigerator ship, all spelt the advent of a new age. In Brazil the monarchy which had served the country so long and so well, which had preserved its unity and had given to it a political education, was displaced by a federal republic. But though a military conspiracy destroyed the empire, its fall was bloodless and its legacy to Brazil was a tradition of constitutionalism. Mexico, after the great reform movement of the mid-nineteenth century and the tragic episodes of foreign intervention and the empire of Maximilian, finally found peace and stability under the long dictatorship of Porfirio Díaz; and Díaz was indeed the new type of caudillo. The régime rested, no doubt, on military force. But it was grounded also on economic interests, business interests as well as landed interests. Díaz could refer to his legislators as "my herd of tame horses." Like Aristotle's tyrants he preferred foreigners to citizens. But the Pax Porfiriana offered substantial rewards—the approval of foreign powers, the economic prosperity of the supporting groups, and the modernization of Mexico.

What were the results of this great transformation? Bryce summed them up in what is perhaps the best of all travel books on South America, published in 1912. There were, he found, three classes of states in Latin America. First, there were "true republics in the European sense," countries, that is, in which authority had been obtained under constitutional forms, not by armed force, and where the machinery of constitutional government functioned with regularity and reasonable fairness. Secondly, there were the "petty despotisms," more or less oppressive and corrupt, and created and maintained by military force. And, thirdly, there was a fairly large intermediary class, a group in which the machinery of constitutional government indeed existed but worked more or less irregularly and imperfectly. In the first class Bryce placed two countries only—the "aristocratic republic" of Chile, whose history had always been distinctive, and Argentina. Mexico, he believed, belonged to the intermediary class and Haiti was by far the worst of the despotic. At this point Bryce ceased to particularize.

Such, then, was the situation at the opening of the present century. But again a great transformation scene occurred. Uruguay embarked on the great experiment of state socialism. The state entered into commerce and industry; it assumed new social responsibilities; its political machinery was overhauled. And what had formerly been one of the most backward and turbulent of the Latin American republics was transformed, within a few years, into one of the most vigorous and most progressive. Colombia, a land where dictators had never flourished long, but whose political life had been fevered in the extreme, substituted ballots for bullets, developed a two-party system, and won for itself by the nineteen-thirties a reputation for maturity and stability which was seemingly well-deserved. The little state of Costa Rica in Central America, with the advantages of a comparatively homogeneous population, a high degree of literacy and a fairly wide distribution of property, grew into a "true republic," in Bryce's sense of the word, an oasis of democracy amidst a desert of Central American dictators. And in Mexico the Pax Porfiriana was broken. Díaz was driven from office. The pent-up passions of the people, the suppressed desires for social and economic liberation, burst into conflagration, and Mexico became the scene of the first genuine social revolution in the New World.

The observations upon which Lord Bryce's book had been founded were made in 1910. What changes had been wrought in the political pattern of the Latin American republics twenty-five years later, and what variations have subsequently occurred? In the first place, it seemed fairly obvious, in the decade of the nineteen-thirties, that Costa Rica and Colombia ought now properly to be included in the category of what Bryce called "bona fide" republics, republics, that is, in which the constitutional machinery was "a reality and not a sham." The high-handed proceedings of President Gabriel Terra raised doubts about Uruguay. But whereas in Uruguay and Costa Rica the structure of democratic government was strengthened rather than weakened in succeeding years, though at the cost of a brief civil war in the latter country in 1948, in Colombia it crumbled, and there, in 1953, a military government was installed.

Secondly, of the two states which Bryce had labelled "constitutional" republics in 1910, namely Argentina and Chile, Argentina's claim to that title was already far more equivocal than Chile's. It is true that Chile's evolutionary constitutional development had been rudely interrupted in 1924–5, when the army entered politics, and not till 1932, after an embarrassing sequence of *coups d'état,* were normal political procedures fully restored. But restored they were, and though the stresses and strains of political life are acute, Chile has held fast to the democratic ideal. In Argentina, on the other hand, where the army also entered politics in 1930, the revolution of that year entrenched a conservative oligarchy in power, and by force and fraud it remained in power until a series of barrack-room revolutions in 1943 and 1944 prepared the way for the Peronista dictatorship.

Finally, as an example of his "intermediary" class of states, neither true constitutional republics on the one hand nor mere autocracies or military despotisms on the other, Bryce, in 1910, selected Mexico. Brazil, perhaps, would have been a better choice. But Brazil, in 1930, abandoned constitutionalism altogether. Only in the years after the Second World War was it slowly and haltingly restored. As for Mexico, whose social revolution seemed to have run its course by the early nineteen-thirties but was now, on the contrary, to enter upon its most active phase, it could not be denied that the government was in fact a dictatorship clothed in legal forms and that the army was its chief source of power. And whatever the political as well as the social gains that the Revolution has made, Mexico must still be classed among the "intermediary" states.

Despite, then, the bright democratic faith that burns in the majority of the constitutions of the Latin American states, democracy in Latin America is a plant of slow growth, whose shoots easily wither and decay. Nor could it be otherwise. Democracy, says the famous Mexican Constitution of 1917, should be considered

> not solely as a juridical structure and a political system, but as a system of life based on the continuous economic, social and cultural improvement of the people.

There is the rub. There can be no political democracy without a measure of social democracy. And the social structure of the majority of the Latin American states is still profoundly undemocratic. The illiteracy and poverty so evident in most of the republics, the great cultural cleavages in the societies of the Indian and mestizo states, the glaring social inequalities, the land system which has concentrated political as well as social power in the hands of small minorities, these are not the foundations on which the structure of democratic government is easily built. And they have been combined with a tradition of authoritarianism in Church and State on the one hand, and, on the other, with a highly personalist interpretation of politics.

It is true that the social landscape has been changing, rapidly changing in Argentina and Mexico and Brazil, but much more slowly in Perú or Bolivia or Ecuador. The great technological revolution of modern times, the rapid expansion of the cities, the rise of a middle class and of the urban industrial and labouring classes, all are threats to the traditional social order. And while the functions of the state have themselves been enormously expanded to meet new responsibilities, new elements have entered into political calculations. President Alessandri recognized them in Chile in the nineteen-twenties. Dr Vargas appealed to them in Brazil in the nineteen-thirties. And Colonel Perón exploited them in

PERCY LAU

Argentina in the nineteen-forties. But social change is one thing, social solidarity is quite another. And the integration which Uruguay has achieved on one side of the Río de la Plata, Argentina has failed to achieve on the other.

The rule of an oligarchy or the rule of a dictator, these have been the traditional forms of Latin American government. They are still the prevailing forms to-day. There have been enlightened oligarchies, and unenlightened oligarchies, dictatorships serving limited interests, sometimes, indeed, little more than personal interests, and dictatorships which have looked to a general interest. But whatever the ends proposed or the interests served, régimes of force have been as common in the twentieth century as they were in the nineteenth century. The terms upon which political power may for long be held have, in most countries, changed, or are in process of change. The sphere of government has been greatly enlarged. New doctrines—doctrines which undergo a sea-change as they cross the Atlantic—have been imported from abroad. The twin forces of nationalism and socialism have newly been released. But the caudillo tradition survives. The dictator of the present age, whether he belongs, like the late President Somoza, to a type that is vanishing, or whether, like Colonel Perón, he adopts all the trappings of modernity, is the heir of the nineteenth-century caudillo, and his lineage, perhaps, is older still. Was it not Gonzalo Pizarro whom the citizens of Lima saluted, in 1546, as "Liberator, and Protector of the people?"

A study of the social origins—usually comparatively humble—and of the early careers of the twentieth-century caudillos, if caudillos they may be called, would make fascinating reading. It would range from the ex-private of marines in the Dominican Republic, now Generalissimo Trujillo, to the ex-professor of law in the University of Guayaquil, Dr José María Velasco Ibarra, lately President of Ecuador. Dr Vargas would occupy a distinguished place, and so would Colonel Perón. But soldiers would be more prominently represented than civilians. For the army, if not the only road to power, is still the major road to power, and the roll of colonels and generals who have exchanged military for political command is long.

Nor is it surprising. For in the last analysis it is upon the army that oligarchies and dictatorships alike depend. The army is a permanent national institution, parallel to the civil and ecclesiastical institutions of the state. Its rank and file count for little. They are there to obey. But its officers form a class apart, a professional class, with professional loyalties. And they are possessed of force. No revolution can now take place without the aid or connivance of at least a part of the armed forces, and most revolutions are in fact *coups d'état* which the armed forces carry out. It is a wise government that cherishes its own army.

The army has been disbanded in Costa Rica. Its influence in Uruguay is negligible. It has generally kept aloof from politics in Chile. And it has only recently assumed the responsibility of intervening in civil affairs in Colombia. But in most Latin American countries the army is at once an instrument of power and a political force in its own right.

WOMEN AT THE WELL

If a Latin American country's military establishment, writes Professor Fitzgibbon, is kept within due bounds and, more importantly, is recognized, by itself and the general public, as subordinate to the civilian authority of the state, the country has taken a long step in democratic development.

And so long as these things are not true soldiers will continue to play a predominant part in politics.

3 First Pan-American Assembly on Population: Final Report

At the close of their discussions the participants in the First Pan-American Assembly on Population reviewed as a group the following statement. The statement represents general agreement; however no one was asked to sign it, and it should not be assumed that every participant necessarily subscribes to every recommendation.

The extraordinary rates of population growth in many of the American countries in recent decades have aggravated and will continue to aggravate problems in almost every sphere of life, from the diet of the peasant to the investment necessary to accelerate economic and social development. There is considerable variation among the American nations in their demographic situation—size, density, population distribution and velocity of growth. While not faced with severe demographic problems at this time, Northern America is undergoing rates of population growth which may cause serious problems in the future. Most Latin American nations, on the other hand, have rates of population growth which are high, both in terms of their growth of national product, and in comparison with the demographic growth of nations in other areas or eras. As a result of rapid and continuing declines in death rates, along with continued high natality, the population of the region will double in about 25 years, but the number and severity of the problems will increase by an even higher factor.

● **Distribution.** Although over-all population density in Latin America is low, the distribution of population is uneven. Since urban areas are growing much more rapidly than rural, the problem of mal-distribution is steadily growing more severe. The "bands of misery" around many Latin American cities grow thicker as rural inhabitants leave the farms, as a result of rural population growth and other social and economic changes.

● **Economic Development.** Among the factors which impair economic development, excessively high rates of population growth may be cited, because they

This report was issued by The American Assembly, Columbia University. Reprinted by permission. For the papers presented at this conference, held in August, 1965, in Cali, Colombia, see *Population Dilemma in Latin America,* edited by J. Mayone Stycos and Jorge Arias (Washington, D.C.: Potomac Books, 1966).

require higher proportions of national income to be saved and invested merely to maintain current levels of per-capita income. Further, because of the large proportion of young people in high fertility nations, capital is diverted from production to consumption. There is increasing difficulty in making per-capita improvements in community services when new population tends to absorb the new homes, classrooms and hospitals.

● **Family Welfare.** High population growth rates also affect the family. The family with many children can save and invest very little and must spend a higher proportion of its income on consumption than the family with few children. Problems of the degree and kind of education are also aggravated. Equally important are aspects of health and morality. Scientific surveys indicate that the average Latin American woman (at least in cities) wants fewer children than she has, but as a result of reductions in infant mortality, family size in Latin America has been increasing. Latin American women have not been unresponsive to this discrepancy, and high rates of induced abortion prevail in the countries studied thus far, creating a broad range of legal, moral and medical problems.

The above reasoning does not imply that Latin America is currently "overpopulated," only that the present rates of growth are impeding social and economic development. Nor does it imply that Latin American nations should stop growing, or have some fixed population, but that a slower rate of population growth has many advantages. Most important of all, it does not imply that attention should be shifted from the great and imperative needs for basic social and economic reforms.

For the kind of problems we have been discussing, there are demographic and other than demographic solutions. The latter refer to the usual ingredients of economic and social development—investment, industrial and agricultural development, higher educational levels, a more balanced distribution of income, social security measures, etc. We have seen that these are difficult to achieve in the face of high rates of population growth but even low rates, without growth in the factors cited above, would result in intolerably slow social and economic improvements. While the present recommendations concentrate on population, it should be understood that a judicious combination of demographic and other solutions is essential.

In all instances, whether or not the approach be demographic, the ultimate ends of improvement in the cultural, economic, and physical well-being of the individual human being must be kept in view. Our recommendations are intended as means to these ends, as ways of further liberating man in his pursuit of higher goals.

RECOMMENDATIONS

1) Every nation, according to its special cultural, economic, religious and demographic circumstances, should develop a population policy embodying broad national objectives with respect to population distribution, velocity of population growth, and levels of mortality, fertility and migration, as an integral part of its

policy of economic development. The creation of such a policy should be preceded by adequate public discussion and thorough analysis of demographic, economic and social data.

2) American governments should assign high priority to the improvement of collection, processing and analysis of demographic and related data. Further, the appropriate ministries and planning boards dealing with such problems as health, education, housing, and manpower, should include demographers as part of their personnel.

3) Governments should aim toward the enlightenment of the community with respect to family and sexual problems, with the end of encouraging responsible paternity. This means efforts to reduce illegitimacy and to encourage couples to have the number of children consistent with their own ideals and compatible with the possibilities available to them for the education and care to which they are entitled.

4) Private national organizations have important roles to play in dealing with population problems. Until governments adopt policies, such agencies should serve to awaken public opinion, encourage government participation and serve as a continuing stimulus for programs in research, communication and service. By means of pilot programs they can demonstrate demand, feasibility and range of alternative population and sex education programs. Even after governments adopt a program, the private agency should remain a continuing stimulus for new ideas, pioneering new avenues of approach to family planning and sex education, and adopting experimental programs.

It is highly important that such organizations be composed of representatives from a broad spectrum of the professional community—such as physicians, sociologists, economists, business men, educators and clerics—as well as representatives of labor and farm organizations.

5) In realization of the educational aims of the governments enunciated previously, and in recognition of the high incidence of criminal abortion, and in recognition of the manifest desire of many couples to properly space their children's births, the governments, through their appropriate ministries, should make family planning services accessible to the people who desire them and educate the people to their availability. These services should provide a sufficient variety of medically approved methods so that they can be chosen in accordance with the dictates of the individual conscience.

6) Considering the fact that most nations have excessively high rates of urban growth, special attention is needed to problems associated with internal migration and population density. With respect to external migration, governments should encourage personnel essential to economic and social development to remain in the region.

7) Recognition of the dangers of population growth and formulation of the policies which may be applied to population problems should not divert attention from the necessity for basic social and economic reforms.

8) Intergovernmental institutions should provide financial and technical assistance for the establishment of national population programs, providing information and consultative services with respect to administrative and technical alternatives in population programming.

9) Bilaterial arrangements with foreign organizations of public and private character should be considered by governments and private institutions for technical and financial assistance in the study, execution and evaluation of population programs.

10) Universities and other institutions of higher learning should seek ways of introducing the scientific study of population to all relevant university curricula in such fields as law, theology, education, economics, sociology, medicine, public health, biology and planning. In cooperation with government and private agencies, and with each other, universities and other institutions of higher learning should take the lead in pure and applied research on population problems, in the preparation and training of personnel and in the determination of the appropriate methods of education in sexual and family matters. The university and other institutions of higher learning should be focal points for high level public discussion and diffusion of ideas on the population question. They should also participate actively in programs related to population problems and coordinate by means of centers or work groups the interdisciplinary study, research and discussion indispensable to integrated planning for the solution of demographic problems.

11) Religious leaders should be continually provided with the best available scientific information on biological, social and economic aspects of population problems. This information should be made available to all levels of the church hierarchy. In turn, religious leaders of all faiths should intensify communication with scientists in order that the public may fully comprehend the continual development of church thought.

4 JOHNSON, The New Latin American Nationalism

The most important single phenomenon in Latin America today is the rapid growth of nationalism. The nationalist ferment there, as in other developing areas, reflects the passionate efforts of millions of people to create something for themselves and to attain greater status in the world. Neither all the people nor all the twenty republics in Latin America are approaching those goals at the same pace, but nearly everywhere—from huge Brazil to tiny Panama—the movement is underway, and the tempo of the advance is quickening. . . .

By 1930 nationalism in Latin America had begun to acquire the populist quality which has since remained its trademark. In Mexico this development was a by-product of the social revolution of 1910. Elsewhere, it was a logical derivative

John J. Johnson, "The New Latin American Nationalism," *Yale Review* (Winter, 1965) pp. 187–204, *passim*. Reprinted by permission from *The Yale Review,* copyright Yale University.

of secularizing and modernizing processes which dated from the late nineteenth century, and which by the 1920's had already shifted the more advanced republics (Chile, Uruguay, Argentina, and to a lesser extent Cuba) well away from feudal agrarianism toward urban industrial life. One major consequence of this transformation was a political revolution that greatly strengthened the new urban middle sectors—entrepreneurs, managers, professional men, and bureaucrats—at the expense of the traditional landholding elites. . . .

The new nationalism contrasted sharply with the aristocratic nationalism which it was replacing. Since the worker's entrance into the political arena had made him an *homo economicus,* popular nationalism played upon social and economic urges rather than upon cultural ambitions. It stressed the needs and aspirations of society, and in so doing it struck a hard blow against the liberal tradition and the "inactive" state inherited from the nineteenth century and still defended after the First World War by the intellectuals. Implicit in this stand was a conviction that the central government should possess not only the administrative, technical, and financial capabilities to regulate national development but also the power to impose its will on all persons and corporations within the nation, including foreigners and foreign companies. . . .

By enhancing the status of the worker, who was ordinarily from the *gente de color* (people of color), the proponents of popular nationalism placed themselves under two major obligations: to establish that the laborer was worthy of his new role, and to demonstrate concern for his welfare. . . .

Since the population of Mexico and more than a dozen other nations was predominantly European-American or European-African, a natural extension of the new favorable judgment of the working man was to upgrade persons of mixed blood. The racist theories of LeBon and Gobineau and certain schools of positivism, especially those in Argentina and Peru, which had lingered on from the nineteenth century, were finally laid to rest. They were replaced by the theory that the crossing of native American blood with that from Europe produced a better human specimen than the offspring of either strain alone.

The mestizo thus came to hold the key to spiritual and cultural attainment. In Mexico, José Vasconcelos prophesied that mestizo nations would fulfill the great dream of human synthesis, a harmonious fusion of two opposite worlds. In Brazil, the sociologist Gilberto Freyre played upon the same theme but in a lower key. . . .

Legislation against foreigners proliferated. The Brazilian constitution of 1934, for example, proposed to protect the worker by placing restrictive quotas on the admission of European and Asiatic immigrant groups who might supplant Brazilians nationals in their jobs. Elsewhere foreign operatives of banana and sugar plantations, mines, transportation companies, public utilities, and manufacturing and commercial enterprises were instructed to hire more nationals and to guarantee them equal pay for equal work. Colombia's so-called "ten-twenty-thirty law" of 1936 stipulated that in large enterprises, whether foreign or domestic, aliens could not constitute more than 10 per cent of the wage workers or 20 per cent of the salaried employees, and that no more than 30 per cent of total salaries could be paid to non-Colombians. . . .

Since the Second World War popular nationalism has taken on important new dimensions. . . . No longer worried, even remotely, about United States territorial designs upon the Hemisphere, nationalists in countries like Chile, Peru, and Ecuador have themselves become aggressive. They now press for national control over adjacent waters and submerged lands, often far beyond the limits recognized by international law. They insist that Latin America can never be completely sovereign as long as a European colony remains in the Hemisphere; they oppose colonialism in any form and in all quarters, and they make a point of demonstrating their own "non-imperialism."

The new nationalism less often seeks respectability in the world arena, and more often stresses domestic problems. One consequence of this attitude is that most of the republics express an intense desire to participate in international decision-making but also insist that internal problems require all their resources and become reluctant to share the cost of implementing the decisions they help to reach. In the United Nations, the Latin-American states constantly request more committee posts and greater representation in the General Assembly while continually calling for lowered UN assessments and regularly voting against increases.

Since 1945 new leaders have transformed Brazil, Argentina, and perhaps Panama into strong, self-willed republics. Theirs is essentially an economic nationalism. Whereas their predecessors stressed the conservation of unreplenishable resources, the production of consumer goods and semi-durables, and the defense of workers from foreign exploitation, they have pointed to the "collective humiliations" accompanying economic dependence, which they associate with production of raw materials. In this regard ex-President Juscelino Kubitschek of Brazil once said, "We want to be on the side of the West, but we do not want to be its proletariat." As a corollary the new economic nationalists demand the industrial capacity to produce capital goods; they have chosen to make the integrated iron and steel plant and the petrochemical factory the marks of their countries' developmental aspirations and the showcases of their national achievements. Belching smokestacks may lack economic justification, but one can hardly question their startling psychological impact. The Paraíba Valley in Brazil is now proudly called the "Valley of the Chimneys."

Economic nationalism fathered xenophobia, whose most legitimate heir to date has been neutralism. For Mexico, neutralism has already become an all-embracing passion, manifested on several occasions in its refusal to be coerced into radically altering its original stand on Castro's Cuba. (In Brazil during the administrations of Jânio Quadros and João Goulart, who was overthrown on April 1, 1964, the current of neutralism became stronger almost by the day.) The other republics, besides being encouraged by these "declarations of independence" by Mexico and Brazil, know that the United Nations—where each state has one vote, and all member states proclaim the right of self-determination—is on their side;

and they, too, are on their way to making neutralism the cardinal principle of their foreign policies. . . .

Neutralism can, of course, provide techniques for needling the United States, or the USSR, or both. It can even be a means of engaging in international blackmail, as Egypt, India, Yugoslavia, and Indonesia have occasionally been accused of doing. It is undoubtedly true, as Albert Hirschman has said, that the realization that they can maneuver between the Eastern and Western blocs must be exhilarating to neutralists.

But to assume that blackmail is the essence of Latin-American neutralism, or that it is only a political gimmick, is to miss a most important point. Neutralism, above all, is Latin America's way of saying that it is entering a new era in its basic relationships with the United States and the rest of the world. . . .

Many hypotheses have been offered to explain the changed direction of popular nationalism since the Second World War. The one most generally advanced in the United States is the growth of communism in the area— a development that was given a great boost by the launching of the first Russian satellite in 1957, and which has been strengthened, in some circles, by the Kremlin's defense of the Castro regime in Cuba when it has been under extreme pressure from the United States.

There is no denying that Latin American Communists have embraced nationalism, and with good reason. Drawing support from all sectors of society as it does, nationalism provides the Communists with a cloak of repectability; and in its anti-foreign manifestations nationalism is directed most often against the United States. . . .

But popular nationalism of a decidedly radical nature probably would have asserted itself without the stimuli of communism and Castroism. . . .

Students have . . . proved to be major allies of the ultranationalists. In each of the more advanced countries, the students are one of the few groups organized on a nationwide basis; Brazil's 80,000 to 100,000 university students, for example, are welded together in a single major national organization. As nationalist propagandists students have still another advantage: the high station accorded them in their culture permits them to engage in agitational politics with greater immunity from police intervention than any other group from which the extreme nationalists draw their mass support.

Mass communications media are employed constantly by the Communists and ultranationalists to feed the rising spirit of nationalism and assure that nationalist issues are kept current. They use the press and television, but most of all radio: Brazil has more than 700 radio stations and 7,000,000 receivers, many of which are public (in bars, plazas, etc.). . . .

There is no doubt that nationalism will continue to flourish in Latin America. As in the rest of the developing world, radical nationalism in Latin America is essentially an urban phenomenon, and the major cities of the Hemisphere are growing at an annual rate of 5 per cent or more per year, compared to approximately 3 per cent for the population as a whole. . . .

It is no longer a question of whether or not there will be nationalism in Latin America; it is here and here to stay. It is only a question of who will give it direction. If this fact could be accepted within and without Latin America, then the banners of popular nationalism might be wrested from the spokesmen of the irresponsible Left. Should such a recovery prove possible, there might be time to use nationalism as a constructive force in essentially democratic approaches to national reform and development.

5 *STAVENHAGEN, Seven Mistaken Theses on Latin America*

In the abundant literature produced during the last few years on social and economic development, a number of erroneous or ambiguous theses and affirmations have appeared. Many of these ideas are currently considered valid by our intellectuals, politicians, students and professors. Indeed, they have come to form an integral part of any thought concerning Latin America. But the facts often contradict these ideas. In recent years several investigations and studies have disproved them totally, or at least have caused their veracity to be seriously questioned. Yet they continue to acquire respectability, and in some cases they almost become dogma, due to constant repetition in countless books and articles (generally written abroad) on the problems of development and underdevelopment in Latin America.

● **First Thesis: The Latin American Nations Are Dual Societies.** In essence, this thesis holds that the Latin American nations are composed of two distinct societies which, although partially independent of one another, have a necessary connection. One is described as archaic, traditional, agrarian, stagnant and retrograde, while the other is pictured as a modern, urban, industrialized, dynamic, progressive society undergoing rapid development. The "archaic" society is supposedly characterized essentially by family and personal relationships, traditional institutions, and a rigid social stratification. Its norms and values exalt the status quo and traditional modes of life which pose obstacles to "rational" economic thought.

The "modern" society supposedly consists of social relationships (which sociologists would term "secondary") determined by interpersonal actions and directed toward rational, utilitarian ends. It is characterized by functional institutions and social mobility. Status is obtained through personal effort and is determined by income, education, or occupation. In this "modern" society, a person's norms and values tend to be oriented toward change, progress, innovation and economic rationality.

According to this thesis, each of these two societies has its own system of

CIF reports, IV, No. 16 (Cuernavaca, Mexico: Center of Intercultural Formation, Aug. 16, 1965), pp. 119–123. Reprinted by permission. The article, by Rodolfo Stavenhagen, appeared originally in Spanish in *El Día* (Mexico City, June 25–26, 1965).

dynamics. The "archaic" society has its roots in the pre-colonial eras and has preserved very ancient social and cultural elements. It either excludes change entirely, or only allows it to occur gradually. Changes are not generated from within this society, but are imposed upon it by "modern" society. It is this "modern" society which is truly oriented toward change, which generates its own modifications and is the source of economic development, while "archaic" society constitutes an obstacle to all development.

On a more sophisticated level (and perhaps a false one), the thesis of the dual society is expressed as the theoretical opposition of feudalism and capitalism in our nations. It claims that a feudal social and economic structure exists in Latin America, supported by reactionary, conservative social and economic groups, (the landed aristocracy, the oligarchy, local political bosses, etc.). On the other hand, theoretically, nuclei of a capitalistic economy exist within the ambitious, progressive urbanized middle classes. Implicit in this thesis is the idea that feudalism constitutes an obstacle to the development of our nations and should be eliminated in favor of progressive capitalism. The latter system would then be developed by the enterprising capitalists for the over-all benefit of the nation.

We do not deny the existence of extreme contrasts in social and economic life in the Latin American nations. There are enormous gulfs separating the rural and urban areas, the indigenous and non-indigenous populations, the mass of the peasants and the urban and rural elite, backward and developed regions. Who can deny that in certain isolated and backward areas there are huge plantations on which the relationship between peasant and owner amounts to serfdom, if not slavery?

Nevertheless, these differences do not justify the dual-society concept for two reasons: first, these two opposing societies are the result of a *single historical process;* and second, because the mutual relationship which exists between the "archaic" or "feudal" groups and the "modern" or "capitalistic" groups represent the manner in which an *over-all, single society* functions. Both extremes are integral parts of this society.

Concerning the historical process: from the very beginning the conquest of America had commercial characteristics. Essentially, the conquest was accomplished by mercantile companies who represented large investments of private capital, together with certain aid and intervention by the State. In some regions vast plantations were created by using the "encomienda" system (the endowment of Indians to the conquerors by the Crown, with the understanding that the former would see to their welfare, both spiritual and physical. The Indian would repay this service by working the land of the plantation owner). The conquered Indian populations were submitted to brutal oppression and exploitation by the Spanish. Yet "feudalism" in the indigenous zones of America was not based on a closed, self-sufficient economy as in classic European feudalism. American feudalism first, developed a mining industry for the exportation of mineral wealth and second, produced foodstuffs which supplied both the mining centers and European markets.

(. . .) The existence of two "societies" is, in itself, unimportant. What is important are the relationships between these two "worlds" in the measure that local development in certain areas of Latin America is based on cheap labor (and is this not why foreign capital is attracted to our nations?), the backward regions which produce this cheap labor have a specific function in national society. They are *not* merely underdeveloped areas. Moreover, these "archaic" areas usually export cheap raw materials to urban centers and foreign nations. Therefore, underdeveloped areas tend to become even *more* underdeveloped. Gunnar Myrdal refers to this process as "cumulative circular causation." In other words, in these "archaic" or "traditional" areas of our nations the same process occurs as in today's colonial nations with respect to the metropolis (e.g., Africa). Our underdeveloped regions serve as *internal colonies*. Instead of explaining the situation of Latin American nations in terms of a "dual society," it would be preferable to speak in terms of "internal colonialism."

● **Second Thesis: Progress in Latin America Could Be Realized by Diffusion Factors Producing Industrialization into Backward, Archaic and Traditionalist Areas.** This "diffusionist" theory is found on many levels. Some speak of an urban or Western culture which is gradually extending itself throughout the world and absorbing backward and primitive peoples. Others speak of the spread of modernism like a pool of oil which, from a central source, gradually moves outward over an ever-larger area. Still other experts claim that all stimulus for change in rural areas must necessarily come from urban zones. Supporters of this thesis argue that even in the remotest corners of the world bicycles, transistor radios, tooth paste and Coca-Cola are familiar items. The thesis also implies other elements which are not always so explicit: 1) that the development of the modern, essentially expansionist sector of society will inevitably cause the development of the traditional or archaic sector; 2) that the transition to modernism is a real, permanent and inevitable process which all the world's traditional societies will eventually experience; 3) that the present centers of development are simply the result of the diffusion of "modernist" elements—technology, know-how, the business spirit and, of course, capital from the developed nations.

This second thesis is mistaken for the following reasons: 1) Although it is true that an infinite number of consumer articles have reached the underdeveloped areas within the last few years, their presence does not mean that these zones will automatically begin to develop (if development is understood as an increase in general social well-being). In many cases the result is simply the spreading of the "culture of poverty" to already backward areas. 2) The introduction of industrially manufactured articles into backward areas often displaces flourishing local industries or hand crafts and destroys the productive base of a large population. "Rural proletarization," rural exodus and economic stagnation are then provoked.

(. . .) The correct thesis would be: progress takes place in the modern, urban and industrialized areas of Latin America at the expense of backward, archaic and traditionalist areas. In other words, drawing capital, raw materials, foodstuffs and labor forces from the "backward" areas permits rapid development in the developing zones, while condemning the backward areas to perpetual stagnation and underdevelopment. The relation of the modern urban centers to backward rural areas parallels the situation of the developed nations in relation to underdeveloped nations.

● **Third Thesis: The Existence of Backward, Traditionalist Rural Areas Is an Obstacle to the Formation of an Internal Market and the Development of National Progressive Capitalism.** This thesis claims that national, progressive capitalism, located in modern and industrialized urban centers, wants agrarian reform, the development of indigenous communities, a raise in minimum wages for farm labor, and other similar programs. This is a mistaken idea because:

1) Except in rare cases, there is no progressive, national capitalism in Latin America; neither do international conditions favor its development.

2) To date, and within the foreseeable future, there is and will be a sufficient internal urban market. This market is growing constantly and has great potential which has not been sufficiently exploited. At the same time, urban industrial capacity has been only half-utilized (e.g. the textile industry). Such industry has nothing to do with the internal market, but is simply a problem of luxuries—supplying the urban demands. Areas like Lima-Callao, São Paulo, Santiago and Mexico City, then, can grow economically for years without necessarily bringing about profound structural change in backward, rural areas (the "internal colonies"). On the contrary, the growth of modern zones is very probably the result of the current social and economic structures existing in the backward areas of our nations.

● **Fourth Thesis: The National Bourgeoisie Wishes to Destroy the Power and Domination of the Landed Oligarchy.** It is often said that the interests of the new elite (made up of modern industrialists and impresarios) and those of the traditional upper classes (consisting generally of the landed gentry) conflict. Although it is true that in some Latin American nations the land-owning aristocracy has been eliminated by revolution (always by the people, never by the bourgeoisie), it is also fact that in others such a conflict of interests does not take place. On the contrary, agricultural, financial and industrial interests are often found within the same economic groups, companies and even families.

(. . .) The disappearance of the landed gentry in Latin America has been the exclusive work of mass movements and has never involved the bourgeoisie. The bourgeoisie find in the landholding oligarchy an ally in their struggle to maintain the internal colonialism which is beneficial to both groups.

● **Fifth Thesis: Development in Latin America Is the Creation and Task of a Progressive, Enterprising, Dynamic and Nationalistic Class. The Objective of the Social and Economic Policies of Our Governments Should Stimulate "Social Mobility" and the Development of That Class.** This is perhaps the most popular theory on Latin America. It is supported by scientific investigators and researchers, journalists, politicians and statesmen, who give countless seminars and conferences, and write books on the subject. It forms one of the basic tenets of the Alliance for Progress. Indeed, it has become dogma. But this thesis is mistaken for many reasons.

1) The concept of the "middle class" is both ambiguous and erroneous. If this group is thought of as the level of society which earns an average income and is located between two extremes on the economic scale, then it merely consists of a statistical aggregation and is not a social class. But generally, the concept is applied to those people who have a certain type of occupation, particularly in the third sector of the economy—business and services—and principally in urban areas. This group includes administrative employees, bureaucrats, businessmen and a certain type of professional man. (. . .)

2) Often the term "middle class" is a euphemism for the "dominating class." When the role of the impresarios, financers, and industrialists is discussed in our nations, reference is made to a social class which is already in power. This group has reached an economic, social and political apex. Together its members make the decisions which affect our nations. In such a case, the social class being discussed is certainly not a "middle class," but is termed so by writers who do not wish to call it by its real name for obvious ideological reasons.

3) In this thesis, "middle class" means the group which will eventually include the majority of the population. Supposedly it will be recruited from the lower levels of society, and sooner or later will occupy the entire social spectrum. The very high level of society will lose its economic importance, while the very low classes will virtually disappear. Nothing could be more utopian or false. Neither does the growth of the third sector of the economy guarantee development, nor does an increase in the average-income sectors of society (a statistical fiction) result in the disappearance of economic and social inequalities. No matter how fast this middle group grows in Latin America, the low-income sectors will increase at an even greater pace. Despite the existence of the so-called "middle classes," economic inequality in Latin America is growing every day.

It is possible to distinguish intermediate economic groups on the levels of both income and consumption. At one extreme are those who consume luxury items out of reach of the majority, and at the other, are those who cannot even afford to purchase furniture or beer. Yet a social class is not defined by the articles which it consumes, and aspirations do not indicate the structure of social institutions and the quality of human relations between groups. The diffusion of industrially manufactured goods results from both the overall level of technology and effective demand. The majority of the population (particularly the urban population) can enjoy this kind of consumption to a degree without basic change in class structure, inequalities in income, social position, political power and working conditions.

(. . .) At the same time, economic studies have shown that in Latin America the average national salary decreases as the luxuries and benefits of a minority group increase. This tendency has been verified in recent years by an inflationary process which has occurred in Argentina, Brazil, Chile, Bolivia, and Colombia. It certainly does not reinforce the idea of a harmonious, gradual increase in the "middle class."

The strengthening of the "middle class"—as a socio-political fact instead of a sociological one—does not have the economic development of a nation as its goal. It only means the creation of a political force capable of supporting the dominating classes and delaying a class struggle which could endanger the stability of the present socio-economic structure. "Middle class" ideologists often lament the fact that in Cuba there was no class strong enough to oppose the socialist revolution. On the other hand, they credit the "middle class" with the fact that the Mexican and Bolivian revolutions have become "established" and "institutionalized." (. . .)

● **Sixth Thesis: National Integration in America Is the Result of a Racial Mixture.** This idea is frequently supported in those nations which have ethnic problems—those which have a high percentage of Indians, and Brazil, with its Negro population. Its supporters claim that the Iberian colonization of America brought two racial groups and two civilizations face to face, and that national integration represents a simultaneous biological and cultural mixture. They further claim that in the nations of indigenous America this mixture is a universal process in which the principle differences between "white" or "occidental" dominant minority and the indigenous masses have disappeared. Theoretically, from this traditional, bipolar social structure a new, intermediate biological and cultural element has risen —the "mestizo," "ladino," "cholo" or "mulatto." This mixed group supposedly represents the "essence of the nationality," and its members possess all the qualities necessary for the progress of their nations.

The fallacy of this thesis is obvious. A biological and cultural mixture does not in itself constitute a change in the existing social structure. (. . .)

The "mixture" theory also includes racial prejudice, although it is often unconscious. In the nations where the majority of the population has some Indian features, racial mixture has meant a "whitening" process. Thus the "mestizo" or "mulatto" virtues conceal an anti-Indian prejudice. The so-called "cultural mixture" really means the disappearance of the indigenous cultures. But today nobody believes in racial arguments, so prejudice is manifested in a cultural sense. To make this mixture the necessary condition for national integration is to condemn the Indians of America, still many millions, to slow, cultural torment.

● **Seventh Thesis: Progress in Latin America Can Only Result from an Alliance of the Workers and the Peasants. Such an Alliance Would Stress the Common Interests of the Two Groups.** We cannot end this critique without mentioning this idea, which is so common among the orthodox leftists. Basing their ideas on the theories developed by Lenin and Mao Tse-Tung, they claim that the success of the democratic revolution in Latin America depends on the formation of a common front of the peasant and working classes against the reactionary bourgeoisie and imperialism. In answer to this idea, I present the following facts:

1) A necessary step in any democratic revolution is agrarian reform. But if peasants are given land through a non-collectivist reform program, they become

landholders whose interests are similar to those of landowners in all places in all times.

2) Concerning land reform, the objective interests of the workers and the peasants are not the same. An agrarian reform generally causes an initial rise in the cost of foodstuffs in cities, which would directly affect the workers. It also implies the channeling of public investment into the rural sector of society. In turn, this would harm the urban sector which (due to internal colonialism) is really the only group in society benefitting from economic development.

3) As long as internal colonialism persists in Latin America, there will be few possibilities for an authentic political alliance between the workers and the peasants. Brazil and Bolivia offer recent examples of this problem.

These seven theses do not include all the mistaken theories and concepts on the social structure of Latin America. But the others are related to or derived from these seven ideas, and the reader will recognize them when he encounters them.

Education

Education is both a hope and a challenge in Latin America, as in the world generally. If approached statistically, and by comparison with Europe or the U.S., Latin America is far behind in the race to train her human resources. A Chilean educator, Oscar Vera, considers the present situation in education a difficult one, but encouraging in some respects. (Reading No. 6.)

Latin American universities usually break into the news when their students go on strike or denounce the U.S. for its policies and actions in Latin America or Vietnam. During Vice-President Richard Nixon's famous visit to South America in 1958 he was not only harassed in Venezuela by a mob but the Federation of University Students of San Marcos in Lima, Peru, formally declared him unwelcome in a political manifesto detailing their doubts and dissatisfactions with the U.S. (Reading No. 7.) Kalman Silvert of New York University, who gained an intimate knowledge of Latin American university life as a representative of the American Universities Field Staff, draws a balanced picture of the role of university students there. (Reading No. 8.) Other specialists have warned against picturing all university students as flaming radicals,[1] but it is probably true that many of them have serious doubts about the U.S., as President Eisenhower found out in an exchange of correspondence he had with Chilean students in 1960 and as anyone visiting a Latin American university today can discover for himself.

But there is much more to the story of higher education in Latin America than the political manifestations of university students; universities everywhere are expanding their services to meet the needs of the tremendous number of young people. Everywhere, universities face grave problems and unless they solve some of them at least the future is bleak indeed. Harold Benjamin, a veteran U.S. educator, puts the crisis in perspective by analyzing developments in all the American Republics. (Reading No. 9.) Orlando Albornoz, a Latin American

---

[1] Daniel Goldrich, "Panamanian Students' Orientation Toward Government and Democracy," *Journal of Inter-American Studies,* V (1963), pp. 397–404.

educator, explains the special importance of universities in underdeveloped countries and offers a negative view of the "university reform" movement in Latin America. (Reading No. 10.)

The lack of trained agriculturists is great, though not treated in these readings. More than half of all Latin Americans are engaged in agriculture, whereas only ten per cent of the U.S. population are farmers. Yet we graduate more than six times as many students in this fundamental field: "less than 1100 professional agriculture graduates in all of Latin America per year! This is indeed a shocking fact, but it becomes more so when their level of preparation is taken into account. . . . Most of their agricultural schools are weak and their graduates poorly trained." [2] Even in such an advanced country as Chile, the English educator, Joseph A. Lauwerys, has stated that the university structure there is at least a century behind the times.[3] The Chilean director of the Inter-American Development Bank, Felipe Herrera, stresses the responsibility of Latin American nations to confront and solve their own university problems. (Reading No. 11.) Some leaders understand the desperate need for Latin America to train her human resources. President Frei of Chile, in an address to the 1965 Conference on the Application of Science and Technology to the Development of Latin America, declared: "In the last century, the wagon constructed by the Chilean pioneers to make their way south differed little from the covered wagon of the North American settlers who advanced westwards. But nowadays, the North Americans are constructing space ships. . . . It is evident that the gap between the highly developed and the developing peoples, instead of diminishing, is increasing considerably." [4]

[2] Lewis Roberts, "New Directions in Agricultural Education in Latin America," *Agriculture and the University* (New York: Institute of International Education, 1965), p. 33.

[3] "El Dr. Lauwerys enjuicia nuestra educación superior," *Boletín de la Universidad de Chile*, No. 34 (Oct. 1962), pp. 13–17.

[4] "Science, Technology and the Development of Latin America," *UNESCO Chronicle*, XI, No. 11 (Nov., 1965), p. 417.

The literature on universities is growing, though still is not satisfactory. For some representative discussions see John P. Harrison, "The Confrontation with the Political University," in Robert Burr, ed., Latin America's Nationalistic Revolutions, special issue of The Annals of the American Academy of Political and Social Science (March, 1961), pp. 74–83; Rudolph P. Atcorn, "La universidad latino-americana," Eco, VII (Bogotá, 1963), Nos. 1–3, pp. 1–169; Jaime Jaramillo Uribe, "Observaciones al informe Acton, ibid., pp. 170–186; Eugenio Gonzáles, "Palabras en la inauguración del año académico 1964," Boletín de la Universidad de Chile (May, 1964), No. 47, pp. 4–11; Luis Maira, "Discurso del Presidente de la Federación de Estudiantes de Chile," ibid., pp. 12–16; L. Ronald Scheman, "The Brazilian Law Student: Background, Habits, Attitudes," Journal of Inter-American Studies, V (1963), pp. 333–356.

6 VERA, The Educational Situation and Requirements in Latin America

The educational situation in Latin America, as outlined in this study, may, if compared with the situation in North America and Europe, present a rather depressing picture; but if the comparison is made with other regions of the world such as Asia, Africa or the Near East, or, as it should be, with the educational situation as it was in Latin America thirty or forty years ago, the picture is frankly encouraging.

From the brief survey of the quantitative and qualitative aspects of education in Latin America just presented, the following main conclusions emerge:

The average level of education in the region was, in 1950, 2.2 school years for the whole of the population of 15 years of age and over, with a maximum of 4.2 years in Chile and a minimum of 0.5 years in Haiti, and of 4.4 school years for the mass of the population which had had the opportunity of attending school, with variations ranging from 5.3 years in Chile to 3.2 years in the Dominican Republic. The results of the censuses of population being carried out in 1960 and 1961 will no doubt reveal an appreciable increase in the level of schooling among adults in all the countries, corresponding to the expansion of educational services that has taken place during the last fifty years. . . .

In all the countries the sectors of the population with a high social and economic status enjoy educational opportunities comparable very often with those existing in more developed countries in other regions of the world; for the great majority of the population, however, such opportunities are very limited, particularly in rural areas. . . .

The degree of premature school-leaving is very high. A few years ago, even in the most developed countries in the region, it was roughly 75 per cent in the case of primary education and 68 per cent in the case of secondary education; but only 5 per cent of the pupils who began primary education went on to complete secondary education. . . .

Available data make it difficult to judge the results of literacy campaigns and adult education in Latin America; there is no doubt, however, that the development of such programmes, technically well devised and executed, is the only short-term method of raising the educational level of the population, in view of the fact that it is only at the end of a few decades that the expansion of normal school services begins to have an appreciable effect upon the adult level of education.

The structure, contents and tendencies of education at all levels are derived in the main from the conception of educational needs implicitly maintained by

Oscar Vera, "The Educational Situation and Requirements in Latin Ameria," in *Social Aspects of Economic Development in Latin America,* Vol. I, Papers submitted to the Expert Working Group on Social Aspects of Economic Development in Latin America, Mexico City, 12 to 21 December 1960, edited by Egbert de Vries and José Medina Echavarría (UNESCO, 1963), pp. 302–305, *passim.* Reprinted by permission.

small sectors of the population, rather than from a careful and well-balanced analysis of the universal demands of culture and present-day life, and the characteristics and requirements peculiar to the country and its different areas, as seen from the point of economic, social and political development. . . .

Standards in teacher training, salary levels and other conditions under which teachers and executive and administrative personnel in education have to work are, in general, unsatisfactory in the majority of the countries. About 45 per cent of those engaged in teaching in primary schools are unqualified; this percentage is very much higher in secondary schools. . . .

Sums of money for financing education are clearly insufficient to ensure satisfactory standards in educational services and to allow for the expansion of these services. It is estimated that the average annual cost per primary school pupil in the region is equivalent to U.S. $20.

The control and administration of educational systems present, in general, very serious deficiencies. These derive principally from the lack of planning and continuity in educational policy and the little relation this bears with other basic features of national development policy; from the influence of considerations often incompatible with technical requirements in administrative structure, in the selection of personnel and in the running of educational services; from the lack of specialists in research, inspection and administration and of technical advisers. However, in an increasing number of countries, great attention is being paid to the application of the principles of systematic planning in education, and some have already embarked upon careful studies of their educational needs in order to ensure more efficient and rational use of resources and the co-ordination of educational development plans with over-all plans for national development.

From these conclusions can be deduced the most important educational needs in Latin America, as well as some of the measures required to meet these needs within a reasonable period of time. Naturally, a suitable and efficient plan of action demands a careful and detailed study of the situation in each country not only so as to be able to state basic aims to be followed in determining educational policy, but also to be able to define the specific goals that can be attained within a certain number of years.

7 The Federation of University Students of San Marcos in Lima, Peru, Declares Vice-President Nixon Unwelcome

The Federation of University Students of San Marcos, in its motion passed May 5 declared Vice-President Nixon unwelcome. The complete motion follows.

"Considering:

"1. That there has been announced the visit to Peru of Mr. Richard Nixon, Vice President of the United States of North America;

From *Nixon in Peru*, by Richard W. Patch, an AUFS Report, Copyright 1958 by American Universities Field Staff, Inc. Reprinted by permission.

"2. That confronting this situation, the reform students as a consequence of our essentially anti-imperialist position wish to remember some acts and attitudes which are definitely American and which fully reveal their imperialistic character before the world;

"3. That in a continental view the 'Good Neighbor' and 'defense of democracy' policies of the Government of North America are false and insincere because of that country's easy understanding with military dictators: Odría, Pérez Jiménez, Trujillo, Somoza, Rojas Pinilla, Stroessner, Batista, etc., which have harassed popular democratic movements;

"4. That the United States, and specifically the Department of State, obeying the interests of the great capitalists of Wall Street, recognized and applauded the coup of Odría, and encouraged the criminal devaluation of our currency with the euphemism 'free exchange' which perpetuated the anti-Peruvian tyranny;

"5. That the President of the United States of North America, General Eisenhower, decorated Odría, in spite of his being a genocide and a vulgar ruler-by-force who placed outside the law the popular parties of Peru, and who persecuted, imprisoned, and assassinated leaders who fought for the liberty of our people;

"6. That the North American imperialism forced Peruvian legislative reforms, such as the Mineral Code, which permitted them, in ominous conditions, to take power over the iron of Marcona and Toquepala and the national petroleum wealth. And that even today we are threatened with new tariffs upon our exports: copper, lead, zinc—as they have already done with tuna; and with dumping, or unfair competition, of our raw materials such as cotton;

"7. That the United States and Odría agreed to a military pact which meant the gift of arms to a tyrant, as they are today helping Batista, and the submission of our people, and which, in addition to being a sacrifice of our national economy, places our youth in the danger of becoming flesh for the cannons of imperialism. Because by means of these pacts they have imposed upon our countries the unfriendly and discriminatory tactic of giving or denying arms to this or the other government, inflaming rivalries and risking internal conflicts; and insinuating its intentions to establish atomic bases in our America in its measureless warlike eagerness which the Indo-American people have already rejected;

"8. That still present in the minds of all is the insolent aggression perpetuated by the imperialists of the United States on our sister republic of Guatemala, where the United Fruit Company was adversely affected by the agrarian reform, and by the gallant and patriotic stance of the democratic government such as those of Dr. Juan José Arévalo and Jacobo Arbenz, and by the strict economic control placed over the North American monopolies. These interests mobilized their influence and pressed the government of Washington to intervene and provoke a fratricidal war which crushed the popular revolution of Guatemala, demonstrating before continental opinion that the much vaunted democracy which the United States pretends to defend was neither nationally nor continentally defended, but was rather trampled upon and bloodied with the arms of military pacts and the dollar loans of the American treasury;

"9. That economically, while the United States scatters thousands of millions of dollars to finance its European colonial allies, it systematically denies tenths of this amount to develop technical help for Indo-America in its eagerness to arrest the development of our continent and maintain us in an underdeveloped position as simple producers of raw materials and for the satisfaction of its mercantilist appetite. For these reasons, defending despotic regimes, the great imperialist capitalists make themselves the proprietors of our natural riches, fixing a price which strangles and impoverishes our people, and impeding trade with other countries of the world, as was done in the epoch of colonial Spain;

"10. That the aid given by the government of the United States to the great colonial powers such as England, France, and Holland, against the peoples who fight for their independence, violates the profound nationalist sentiment and conviction of our brother countries, and they are seen as even further wounded by the example of Puerto Rico, which is today a North American colony with its nationalist leaders such as the patriot, Dr. Pedro Albizú Campos, suffering persecution, prison, and exile, for the crime of fighting for the emancipation of their fatherland;

"11. That the United States has apportioned economic and military assistance to the Dictator Batista in Cuba, who at this very moment continues with impunity to bloody the glorious land of José Martí, in full view and with the approbation of our international organizations such as the Organization of American States and the United Nations;

"12. That this maneuver of deception and the protestation of good faith, inevitable and inherent characteristic of the development of imperialism, has extended itself among all the peoples of Indo-America who are wearied by the hard lessons learned in the past two World Wars and their respective consequences. On both occasions the handsome promises formulated before and during the conflicts vanished, and there reappeared the bitter reality of a large country, powerful and armed, which blocks our political and economic progress, which stimulates intrigues threatening the unity of Indo-America, which attacks with acerbity the popular regimes which do not prostrate themselves, which imposes a monopoly of commerce assuring the low price of its imports and the high price of its exports;

"13. That all of these irrefutable facts, apart from others beyond this list, make up the typical aspects of the imperialism of the government of the United States of North America, of whose aggressive activities in our America there remains evident the deeply graven tracks in Haiti, Nicaragua, Santo Domingo, Cuba, Panama, Puerto Rico, Honduras, and our never-forgotten sister republic of Guatemala;

"We agree:

"1. To ratify the anti-imperialist position of the students of San Marcos in particular and the students of Peru in general, and to express our fraternal salute to North American students and to the North American people, whose democratic virtues we recognize, and who have been so often sacrificed in imperialist wars;

"2. To declare *non grata* the presence in Peru of the Vice-President of the

United States of North America, Mr. Richard Nixon, because he embodies the plutocratic and imperialist interest of the North American government;

"3. That the visit of Mr. Richard Nixon to our University is without the approval of any student organization.

"Lima, May 5, 1958."

8 *SILVERT, Social Change and the University Student*

A complex mythology of the Latin-American student has grown up in the United States, in large measure a result of the excited findings of observers scurrying to make up for irrevocably lost time. We hear that the Latin-American student is a radical, uninterested in study, the pawn of professional agitators, the persecutor of his professors, and the bane of responsible university administrators. Some students are all these things. Others are serious and questioning young people working well and serenely in rapidly improving faculties and departments. Still others are apathetic playboys, or yearners after the glories of National Socialism, or social climbers thirsting to become oligarchs, or desiccated youths who aspire to no more than the routine life of the bookkeeper. Probably the majority of students in the state universities are more secularist than not, more nationalist than not, more middle-class than not, more center and left-of-center than not, and more worried about individual fortune than the fate of the state. They form the reservoir of modern men and women upon whom the nation can draw for its development, susceptible to national leadership and willing to take the risks demanded when societies break from one world of thought and action into another.

The Latin-American university student is the child of his parents. To assume that the student is but a hot-eyed revolutionary is to presume that somehow registering in a university is sufficient to cut family ties, break class and other group identifications, and produce a special kind of creature divorced from his society. The intellectual community can be "ahead" of society as a whole, but it must have identifications with some sectors of the community, and can pull along only those people susceptible to its particular suggestions or prodding. To single out the Latin-American student for special disdain is to forget that it is truly debatable whether he is more irresponsible, rapacious, corrupt, and foolish than his elders on the farm, in the government, in the bank, or in the trade union. Indeed, there is some reason for advancing the thesis that the student is at least temporarily a better citizen than his elders.

The simple fact of youth also crucially distinguishes the Latin-American student from his parents. He still remains free to believe in and to attempt to apply the long-held ideals of the old liberal aristocracy—those desires for freedom, dignity, growth and progress so often honored in the breach since Independence. With whatever ideological superficiality, misplaced enthusiasm, and youthful conviction of ultimate right, the reformists have preserved and modernized these ideals, and often have displayed a courage and selflessness in their defense that merit admiration rather than contempt or condescension.

Over and above nationalistic feeling and the commitments to party, there exists a set of canons governing and inspiring student action. In Chile these are not often articulated but they are recognized as going back to the very beginnings of the student federation. . . . They include the courage to hold and defend a point of view on fundamental issues, a readiness for self-sacrifice, loyalty in friendship, love of country, hatred and distrust of the military, a sentimental identification with the working classes, and solidarity with the youth of other Latin-American countries. Students have been a force of progress within the university.

9 BENJAMIN, The Future of Higher Education in Latin America

The most pressing problem of professional preparation confronting all these countries in the next three decades will be that of educating professors for higher educational institutions. This problem will be acute in the United States, Brazil, and Haiti, but it will assume catastrophic proportions in the eighteen Spanish-speaking republics. At present the most advanced of the latter countries barely indicate any recognition of such a problem. Without greatly increased and improved graduate programs in key universities of Mexico, Central America, and Spanish South America, even the present level of instruction and research in the higher education of these countries will deteriorate.

Spanish America, however, runs a peculiar risk of permitting national frontiers and the compartmentalization of traditional faculties to impede proper education for the thousands of new university professors who will be needed in 1970, 1975, 1980, and later. Ten important graduate schools preparing an average annual cadre each of 100 holders of the doctorate in various fields would produce only 1,000 new professors per year, even if all those who earned the doctor's degree went into university teaching in Spanish America. In the next twenty years at least twice this number will be needed annually.

Although it is academically fashionable in most Spanish-American countries to draw up various plans for educating large numbers of their graduate students in the United States or in Europe, the barriers of linguistic differences and of transportation and subsistence costs in foreign countries will continue to keep the numbers of such students relatively small. Even if funds were available and the linguistic barriers did not exist, it would still be educationally undesirable to have more than a relatively few Spanish-American professors get their graduate training outside of Spanish America. It is true that at first many of the new graduate schools of Spanish America will have to be manned largely by people who have been trained in European and United States graduate schools, but the shift to people oriented in their research and instruction toward Spanish-American problems will need to be made promptly. It will have to be made sooner than most European or United States graduate school authorities would recommend. To do otherwise is to encourage the continued establishment of pathetic imitations of foreign research and other advanced-study institutions—imitations that are often nurtured by foreign aid until they die on the vine. Even then their remains are likely to be cherished and to impede the development of new Spanish-American graduate schools to serve Spanish-American ends.

Every university in the eighteen Spanish-speaking countries of the Americas with an enrollment exceeding 5,000 students faces a special challenge in this regard. Some of them will never recognize the challenge. Others will try to meet it but will fail for lack of financial, instructional, or administrative resources. Those which meet the challenge successfully in the next twenty-five years will be among the world's most distinguished universities.

General education in Brazil stops at the secondary school, a seven-year institution divided into two cycles of four and three years based on a four- or five-year elementary school. The secondary school program is so encyclopedic that it becomes a complex memorizing machine where instruction in Portuguese, foreign languages, mathematics, physics, biology, history, geography, philosophy, and drawing is given under pressure to a group of students who are highly selected, but mostly for economic and social reasons.

The ordinary entrant to a Brazilian university has had no modern general education of consequence; he has merely undergone a general memorization activity. The university has to give him general education and does so in various disguised ways. The popularity of law and, in more recent years, of economics arises to a considerable degree from the general-education phases of those studies.

When the University of São Paulo set up a Faculty of Philosophy, Sciences, and Letters, it had the idea of making it the central agency for basic scientific and humanistic education for all students in the University. The Faculties of Medicine, Engineering, and Law blocked this first Brazilian plan for a central, unifying university institution by refusing to allow their students to take basic courses in the new school. This first Faculty of Philosophy and also the second, set up in 1939 in the University of Brazil, appealed to foreign cultural centers for help in a determined attempt to create in Brazil better conditions for developing the various fields of knowledge. The philosophical faculties were multiplied by legal grants until by 1962 there were more than sixty of them, all created by improvising facilities and professors.

The concept of the lifelong proprietorship of the cátedra [chair] . . . , is one of the principal difficulties in developing the programs of Brazilian higher educational institutions. For example, one cátedra in a certain faculty of medicine, having sixty microscopes and corresponding sets of slides, claims it cannot admit more than sixty students, even though a group of sixty uses this equipment only a few hours a week, because having another shift would upset the routine of the cátedra, and that would be impossible. This explains why the traditional schools of medicine which twenty years ago graduated 200 to 400 physicians today admit only 100 students on the plea that they have had to raise their standards.

The competitive examination for degrees and professorships is another colonial inheritance which impedes higher educational progress in Brazil.

In administration and control of higher education, marked changes will occur during the remaining decades of the present century. In Brazil, for example, the excessive legalism and formalism of the higher educational system, so pronounced as to be almost incredible, will tend to break down under its own weight. The situation in 1961 at the University of Brazil, an institution of relatively modest size, with 533 "autonomous," separate chairs (cátedras) including eighteen in mathematics, twenty-three in economics, twenty-eight in physics, and thirty-nine in chemistry, will be changed whenever minimum notions of administrative efficiency seep through the University's ivy-clad walls. A university with a total enrollment of only 9,000 which gives elementary instruction in chemistry independently in the Faculties of Engineering, Philosophy, Industrial Chemistry, Pharmacy, Dentistry, and Medicine, with each cátedra having its own equipment, laboratories, libraries, and autonomous team of professors and assistants, assumes a fairy-tale quality. The fairy tale may well end on the pathetic note that this country continues to require massive foreign aid at frequent intervals to resolve its economic crises.

10 *ALBORNOZ, Academic Freedom*

The issue of academic freedom has received substantial attention in the United States in recent years. There seems to be a fairly general agreement among scholars, with substantial public concurrence, that academic freedom is a necessary part of higher education. Academic freedom also has as important a role in the developing nations although it has been a good deal less secure in these nations than in many of the industrially advanced countries.

It can be argued that the quality of university life is even more important in the developing areas than in the advanced nations because of its crucial role in modernization and in technical training. Because academic freedom is a key element in determining the tone of academic life and is generally agreed to be an important component of scholarly research, it is a vital issue in any consideration of higher education and the progress of democracy in the developing nations. . . .

Despite the undoubted relationship between academic freedom and the broader political situation in a nation, it is nevertheless also true that the universities in Latin America, as in other countries, have often retained a considerable degree of freedom even in the face of authoritarian regimes. The fact that the universities are

Orlando Albornoz, "Academic Freedom and Higher Education in Latin America," *Comparative Education Review,* X, No. 2 (June, 1966), 250–256, *passim.* Reprinted by permission.

sometimes the last stronghold of political discussion under dictatorial regimes increases their importance. Thus, while the university must in the last analysis keep in step with trends in the broader society, it has shown a good deal of independence. . . .

To see in detail the current problems of academic freedom in Latin America I propose to discuss the different ingredients of the situation—the universities, the students, the professors, and the intellectuals.

The universities are, generally speaking, primary instruments in the process of social change, since they train the future elites of the country in scientific, humanistic and professional areas. To accomplish this task, universities are obliged to seek to further the universalistic objective of finding truth, as S. M. Lipset has pointed out in his much-quoted article on "University Students and Politics in Underdeveloped Countries."

The need for academic freedom requires that the university give institutional backing to professors against the particularistic tendencies which in every country seek to prevent innovation and change. The struggle for academic freedom in Latin America may be seen as an aspect of the struggle between those who are concerned with universalistic values, with the need for modernization and social change, and those who try to prevent such changes, who want to preserve the traditional establishment.

Such issues take on varying aspects in public and Catholic universities. There are many variations between the two. The main difference concerning academic freedom is that the latter tend to have internal consensus about basic values and ways of finding truth, which the former lack. In the Catholic universities, truth is generally established by principle, without any possibility of discussion. Truth in this case has a dogmatic basis. In the state universities, the situation is quite different. Hence, the political issue of academic freedom in Latin America, almost by definition, is a problem of the state universities. . . .

Catholic and state universities may also be distinguished by the fact that the former tend to support traditional values, while the state universities often foster criticism of the established order. In this sense, the latter are instruments of change. The scholarly weaknesses of the state universities, which have been partly a consequence of political instability and intra-university political conflict, have created support for the private secular universities and research institutes. Those interested in a fruitful intellectual life increasingly find it advantageous to participate in the private institutions as a way of escaping the political tensions involved in working in a state university. These give the scholar and teacher more academic freedom, precisely because they are less involved in politics and religion. Many concerned with freeing Latin American scholars from non-academic pressures, whether those of the politicians, the church, or the student groups, have furthered the growth of secular private universities, and of independent non-profit academic research institutions. These may eventually provide the needed "demonstration effect" in the area of academic freedom for both state and Catholic universities.

Limitations on academic freedom in the public universities are to a considerable degree related to the role of students in politics. The politically active students in the universities in much of Latin America can and often do intimidate their professors. The political parties look on the *campus* as a major arena for political activities. The continued strength of political activities within the universities is, in turn, related to two elements: co-government (students' participation in the administration of the university), and the inviolability of the campus inherent in the concept of autonomy. . . .

If autonomy contributes to the politicization of the campus, the institution of co-government increases the chances that student political activity will endanger academic freedom. *Cogobierno* means that the students share directly in the government of the university, that they have a voice in the different bodies that have power inside the university, especially at the level of the *Consejos de Facultad* (Faculty Council), where university decisions are made. It has given them substantial power on matters of academic policy and personnel. This student power has often been used for political purposes; their involvement in academic decision-making has often resulted in considerable corruption and a high degree of factionalism. Corruption means misuse. In the case of students, corruption derives directly from the power that university students have to participate in the government of the university. There are many examples of such corruption, enough to suggest the existence of a pattern in the universities of the continent. In one case (I am not in a position to name the university in question) the student members of a special body which awarded scholarships did so only to those students who agreed to "kick back" part of the scholarship stipend to the student political leaders, whether for personal or political use, one will never know. In another case, a researcher appointed five assistants, but in fact hired only two. The salaries for the other three went to students who served on the university committee which had given funds to this researcher.

Even more important are the occurrences in which professors have been nominated for *catedras* after they agreed to give back part of their salaries to student leaders. As *The Economist* has pointed out in a recent discussion of Peruvian universities, the "power granted to students has led to a system of bribery, both with money and with high marks, by faculty members. 'I am now correcting exam papers,' said one Cuzco professor, 'and at least half of these poor bastards deserve to fail. They don't know anything and they don't come to class. But if I failed them they would fire me. Believe me, I take a great risk in flunking 10 per cent of my students, which few other professors would dare to do.' " These provide vivid examples of the perils to development of competent scholarship and academic freedom which, involving students directly in the process of choosing faculty, have created for various Latin American universities.

Many Latin American professors will privately acknowledge having to say and publish things that they do not believe, including favorable citations to leftist authorities, in order to win or retain the support of the student activists. To publicly approve of North American scholarship opens one to the charges of being a lackey of Yankee power, an agent of cultural imperialism. And to be viewed in this light may affect one's chances to attain or keep a position, or more commonly to retain the good-will of the academic community, particularly of the students.

Of course, if we consider the lack of scholarly competence and particularly of objectivity of many Latin American professors, it may be argued that the faculty inhibit efforts to sustain academic freedom by their inadequacy as scholars and teachers. In much of Latin America competent faculty simply do not exist yet. Being a professor is often an honorific post which men seek not for the sake of the small honorarium, but to enhance their general social prestige and opportunities in the professions or politics. Most faculty do not devote themselves to full-time activity at the university. The part-time professor who earns most of his income in a totally nonacademic occupation is still the standard. Some would like to become full time academics, but too many, particularly in the social sciences, prefer to keep the professoriate as an honorific position, which enable them to advance themselves in professional or political life.

It should also be noted that the distinction between teaching and indoctrination which, as Max Weber noted, must always be in the consciousness of university professors, does not exist in much of Latin America. Teaching *is* indoctrination in many cases. Most professors, particularly in social sciences, feel obliged to take a strong stand on many unverifiable aspects of knowledge. Thus the continued presence of incompetent scholars and highly subjective teachers constitutes one of the principal impediments for the emergence of academic freedom in Latin America. . . .

In conclusion I would reiterate that discussion of the relationship of academic freedom, higher education and the process of modernization in Latin American society lacks any substantial empirical underpinning. Research on the effects of co-government, autonomy, and other factors on academic freedom is just beginning to be done. It is, however, evident that though the university in Latin America must undergo substantial reforms, the principles of Reform which emerged in Cordoba almost fifty years ago are no longer as progressive as they seemed then. The concept of university autonomy has become an illusion, a medieval concept applied to a modern or, more accurately, modernizing society. The same thing is true for the idea of university co-government.

These ideas, of course, have a remarkably democratic sound, the notion that students hand-in-hand with their professors should try to make the best possible use of the university without external interference can hardly be disputed. In practice, however, they have not led to the improvement of the academy. It cannot be repeated too often that the politically active students are not interested in improving education through establishing academic freedom, but rather in finding political allies.

11   HERRERA, The Function of the University in the Development of Latin America

We must recognize the fact that many of the problems and difficulties faced by Latin America do not result from unjust trade agreements with the outside world or from the structural deficiencies and limitations of a socio-economic nature which condition our insufficient development. Numerous problems also arise from the fundamental backwardness of certain basic aspects of the individual organization of each nation, and from a poor distribution of the resources and potentials in Latin America as a whole. A typical example of this situation is the precarious condition of the Latin American university. I would like to ask the following question: who, if not we Latin Americans, is responsible for allocating in each one of our respective countries the necessary public funds to allow the universities to fulfill their important missions? Whose obligation is it, if it is not ours, to create the necessary conditions for our systems of higher education to absorb and spread the scientific knowledge and techniques of other, more advanced nations? Who, if not we Chileans and Panamanians, Nicaraguans and Argentines, Paraguayans and Venezuelans, are responsible for awakening in our university students a love of science and culture, a vocation for study and investigation, not only for the sake of knowledge, but also so that they might transmit this acquired knowledge to new generations through dedication to the university and teaching?

We cannot escape this responsibility, nor can we transfer it to an area outside our own countries. It belongs to our own collectivities, to our governments, our intellectuals, our scientists, and our universities. To avoid this responsibility means to renounce the vital elements which shape our communities' characteristics.

The great European universities were not created with foreign funds. They were constructed on a foundation of study, of passionate dedication to culture, by the nations which they serve. In the United States private aid contributes to the progress of the university, which is a product of the very social organizations to which it belongs.

It is obvious that in young nations like ours, which have so many urgent problems to be solved, first priority must be given to the formation of new groups of leaders who have a real sense of responsibility, together with the capacity and preparation which such responsibility necessitates. And I do not mean leaders in only political and business life, but in all fields of science and culture. Today's complex socio-economic processes call for more leaders than those in government and congress. Leaders are also needed in laboratories and technical areas, in the administration of public and private enterprise, in the school and in the factory, in finance and planning, in hydro-electric projects and in colonization. They should

Felipe Herrera, "The Function of the University in the Development of Latin America," *CIF reports*, V (Cuernavaca, Mexico: Center of Intercultural Formation, Oct. 1, 1966), pp. 145–149, *passim*. Reprinted by permission. The article originally appeared in *Eco* (Bogotá, January, 1966).

all participate in the common patrimony which identifies people with their own community and gives them a clear sense of the values and potentials of that community, and of the common goals which can be reached by exalting and developing both.

Unfortunately, in the plans for national development in our countries too little importance has been given to investment in university education. It seems that the vast and multiple influences which the university can have on the over-all development of our nations has been underestimated.

The Inter-American Bank, as it realizes its activities in financial cooperation, vigorously insists on the need for orienting a good part of the collective effort in this direction. It also points out the responsibility which, in this case, governments have—to understand the importance of the university, and to allot increasing funds to them and to other institutions of higher education which cannot wait with their arms folded for national subsidies or international aid.

The possibility of public financing in Latin America is limited by serious problems. The very deficiencies in our development make it difficult for us to supply the universities with the quantity of funds which they need. We are very familiar with the budget difficulties of the great majority of the Latin American governments. Nevertheless, upon examining those budgets, it can often be seen that the universities are not assigned even the share of funds which they should receive, despite the inadequacy of public finances. Nothing is so troublesome as attending to the formation of capable and qualified leaders who are so urgently needed for the great task of our regional and national development.

Consequently, each nation should provide sufficient resources for the adequate financing and increasing perfection of its university system: yet Latin America is now passing through a decisive era which demands prodigious resources to enable her to consolidate the foundations of her future development. Once this era has passed, the Latin American universities should not base their future development on exterior aid. . . .

There is a more or less generalized fear—especially in more conservative circles, or in those which have had little contact with our historical reality— regarding what is designated the "uneasiness" or "instability" of the Latin American university.

In effect, some see in the active participation of the student in the politics of his respective country, and in the pronouncements of student organizations on socio-political or international questions, the existence of a profound crisis which not only undermines the real university spirit, but also compromises the very future of the university itself.

Regarding this fear, we should not even pretend that the universities do not reflect the tremendous problems and critical circumstances which characterize our reality as a region undergoing development. There are certain realities which will certainly be reflected in the universities: difficulties and tensions arising from a general situation in which there is insufficient economic development and a simultaneous increase in demographic pressure; an unjust distribution of wealth at a time when the great masses are anxiously awaiting their betterment; the exodus of the rural population to the cities at a time when an incipient industry is incapable of absorbing a displaced labor force; the growth, despite all adversities, of a new middle class which is demanding new opportunities and responsibilities; the influence of the world-wide ideological debate, etc. It is inevitable that the anxieties of our political and intellectual leaders also appear in the universities and in the attitude of their students in the measure that it is proclaimed that our continent must progress, and that this progress occurs in the form of leaps, radically reforming or transforming old and feeble structures. It would be strange, unusual, and alarming if this did *not* happen. A passive, quiet university in nations undergoing such an intense process of transformation would be absurd, perhaps even a hindrance.

I do not mean to defend permanent imbalance, disorder or lack of discipline as fatal conditions in our universities. I am only trying to point out the difference between the inevitable restlessness arising from the historical moment in which we live (and which we are not going to calm simply with exhortations for discipline or with force) and protests and disorders which create critical tensions and climate, and are instigated by people who attempt to use them for other ends. . . .

Perhaps the most transcendent responsibility of the Latin American universities is the preservation of our continent's inherited spiritual patrimony. Our history, our deeply rooted institutions, our traditions, our language, our literature do not have to be enslaved or perverted under the pretext of the necessity for adaptation to scientific advances. We can already witness the sterile, cultural hybrids created by some countries undergoing development which have put up with cultural penetration as contraband from investments and collaboration for scientific and technical progress. This is a danger which becomes more immediate every day, and its prevention specifically calls for the intervention of the universities as a major task.

(. . .) Also, for the formation of the intellectual leaders which our development will continue to require in the fields of Philosophy, Law, the Political Sciences, Sociology, Economy and Anthropology, our universities must get in stride with the new concepts and theories, techniques and methods of investigation which are part of the amazing advances we are seeing today in the social sciences of the developed nations. This progress is so significant that it can no longer be assumed with yesterday's assurance that progress in the physical sciences is much greater than in the social sciences. The social investigation which is taking place in the United States, the Soviet Union and Germany is revolutionary. But we are absorbing few of these advances in Latin America . . .

At this particular moment Latin America needs more than ever before the study of political philosophy which she seems to have abandoned. We lack thinkers to renew on our soil the creative tradition of the great sowers of autochthonous ideas. Thinkers who penetrate the deepest reaches of our reality with American eyes, who analyze its problems with the exact perception of historical causality and who discover possible solutions with the most elevated of ideological flights.

Thinkers who can lift the process of our regional integration from the pragmatic level on which it is now developing to great guiding principles which must determine its institutionalization. We can rightly qualify as tragic the negligence in the formation of the top echelon leaders who have been called upon to preside over integration.

We can only prepare them in the measure that our universities are capacitated to nurture them with a solid background in philosophy and an adequate ideological preparation, both resulting from a thorough knowledge of our historical development, our geography, and our sociology, together with a knowledge of the social and political experiences of other areas, and its application to the process of Latin America's integration. Are our universities complying with this labor with sufficient funds, and in the measure required?

Rural Life and the Rush to the Cities

So much attention has been given in recent years to the industrialization of Latin America that the importance of tropical agriculture sometimes has been overlooked. Raymond Crist, an experienced geographer at the University of Florida, redresses the balance and in so doing helps to explain the massive movement of farmers to urban centers. (Reading No. 12.) A veteran sociologist, T. Lynn Smith, also of the University of Florida, points out the results of the combination of a great upsurge of population and the rural exodus. (Reading No. 13.) Yet some return to the land and serve as "cultural brokers," to employ the felicitous phrase of Charles Wagley of Columbia University. (Reading No. 14.)

12 CRIST, Tropical Agriculture Remains a Way of Life for Millions

It is estimated that some 200 millions of people in the tropical areas of Latin America, Africa, and Asia—even in areas usually thought of as densely populated, such as the Indian subcontinent—make their living by practicing some form of "shifting agriculture," "slash-and-burn farming," "forest fallow," "nomadic agriculture," or whatever the local name for it. . . . This remarkable system of agriculture, developed on a trial-and-error basis millennia before the principles of modern science were dreamed of, consists of clearing land of tropical forest or bush, except for huge trees which are left standing but killed by girdling; burning the trash when dry; and planting to crops for from 1 to 5 years. As yields decline owing to the leaching out of soluble salts and plant nutrients, as weeds take possession, and as rodent, bird, and insect populations build up, this land is abandoned

Raymond E. Crist, "Tropical Subsistence Agriculture in Latin America: Some Neglected Aspects and Implications," *Smithsonian Report for 1963* (Washington: Smithsonian Institution, 1964), pp. 503–519, *passim*. Reprinted by permission. See also Hilgard O'Reilly Sternberg, "Land and Man in the Tropics," *Academy of Political Science Proceedings*, XXVII (May, 1964), No. 4, pp. 11–21.

for another nearby plot. The jungle takes over for anywhere from 3 to 20 or 30 years, and the cycle is repeated. . . .

Over millennia this primitive farmer has evolved a sure-fire crop complex: Corn, yuca, beans, and pumpkins or squash. To this list has been added, since the Spanish Conquest, the cooking banana. The techniques of this kind of primitive farming [are fairly simple]. The great toe of the farmer's bare foot is used—or a dibble stick if one is fancy—to make a hole in the soft earth of the burnt-over plot, preferably after the first rain; two or three grains of corn and a few beans and squash or pumpkin seeds are put in, and the hole is covered up by a swipe of the foot and the earth is tamped down by being stepped on. The corn comes up rapidly and shoots up fast, its green stalk forming a living pole for the beans to climb up on; it will be harvested in about 90 days, the beans a month or so later. . . .

The subsistence farmer is in a closed, almost hermetically sealed, economic unit or cocoon that he spins around himself; he may try to work his way out of this cell by taking to market a bag of raw cotton, or perhaps an extra bunch of cooking bananas, or even a few kilos of yuca, but these small surpluses usually are not produced by design. The load of firewood or charcoal, however, carried by mule or canoe or even on one's back, is expressly cut or made for sale and is often the only and seemingly very tenuous economic thread that gives the slash-and-burn cultivator contact with his fellows on the regional scene. . . .

But the forest is his home, as it has usually been for all of his ancestors. It has no terrors for him because he and his ancestors have wrested their living from it; he is really terrified, and with good reason, of the landlord, or local cacique, or boss, with his bespectacled lawyer whose briefcase is full of lengthy documents that are backed up by the police. He knows all too well that he will lose in any fight with them, for he and his kind have always lost when confronted with those representing urban power—*así es la vida.*

Millions of human beings, poorly qualified and equipped to cope with modern agricultural problems, are relegated by cultural controls precisely to those areas where the problems of soil management are most difficult. . . .

As the outsider looks at Latin America he is aware of the fact that there is a lack of continuity in many spheres. Political groups shoot their way into and are shot out of office with sickening regularity. A man may be a newspaper editor one day, a college professor another, only to be a salesman for a large importing firm the next day, or his country's representative abroad, traveling for his health. And so on. But the institution of the subsistence farmer is one that is centuries old, and shows very little chance of losing continuity; it may bend, to be sure, but the possibility of a complete break with the past seems remote. . . .

The average small-scale subsistence farmer is not surplus or market-minded, and, even if he should be, the road or river tends to be a one-way street—i.e., the products that move over them tend to lose most of their value en route, as they must pay high transportation costs, or high taxes, or suffer outright confiscation at the hands of one who claims to own the land on which the produce was grown.

Further, native peoples, ignorant of the official language, who occasionally try to enter the market economy are frequently, and sometimes even openly and flagrantly, robbed by small village shopkeepers, who consider themselves civilized. As long as these things go on, it will be difficult to make the subsistence farmer market-oriented. . . .

The diet of such hand-to-mouth farmers is extremely monotonous for months at a time; protective foods such as meat, eggs, and milk products are in short supply; the protein intake of these families is often inadequate and many of the members show signs of undernourishment or malnutrition—a bad skin condition, depigmentation of the hair, the so-called "Dutch hair" in Brazil, and so on. One of the consequences of inadequacy in protein intake (kwashiorkor) is cirrhosis of the liver, which is extremely common even among children in many tropical countries; such people are extremely susceptible to infections and infestation to which better-fed people would either be immune or highly resistant. . . .

The millions of subsistence farmers have for the most part lived out their obscure lives beyond the impact of almost all those factors that we associate with modern life. Education has not penetrated their world, which means that, among other things, the fundamentals of modern hygiene and asepsis are not known—even the boiling of water to kill noxious, waterborne bacteria is not knowingly practiced. Fortunately for the visitor to the little thatch-roofed hut in the forest, water has first to be boiled to make the coffee or the sweetened water that is so hospitably proffered by one's host. These primitive farmers are not only illiterate, they know next to nothing about balanced diets, soil science, seed selection, technology, mechanics. . . .

At present the self-sufficient farmer operates in a kind of social, economic, and political no-man's land that officially belongs to a nation or political entity, yet the area under cultivation, or forest fallow, is not an "effective" part of the nation. The Jesuits early saw the necessity of having the seminomadic Indians of many parts of the Americas assembled in villages, or *misiones,* if they were to have effective control over their charges. Modern governments may perhaps have to act in a similar manner, for it would seem that their leaders can hardly afford to allow their unskilled farmers to swell the slum sectors of cities where their labor cannot be utilized. It would seem more rational to keep them on the land by having them engaged in tasks they *can* perform, such as the building of roads and dams, drainage ditches and canals, and even crude schools, houses, and community centers, and so on, rather than to be allowed to agglomerate into an amorphous mass in shanty towns, without streets, lights, water, or doctors, thus creating a kind of cancerous growth, a subproletariat, a class of pariahs or untouchables. Once they have enjoyed just a few of the amenities associated with the bright city lights, the modern Lorelei, once they have lived in modern times, even if just barely on the margin of modernity, getting literally fringe or crumb benefits, they will never willingly return to isolation and a way of life that has not changed in thousands of years—their eyes will continue to be on the stars, rather than on the pitfalls of slumdwellers. Even illiterates can enjoy electric lights, moviehouses, radios, television, music, asphalt streets, running water, and sanitation, and they can dream of the time when they might enter the Promised Land of decent houses, schools, libraries, and supermarkets; one of the ways then to build up uninhabited or sparsely settled rural areas is to make some of these amenities available in the country as well as in town.

13 SMITH, The Upsurge of Population and the Rush to the Cities

The small minority of the elite who long have been accustomed to command and direct seem to have become convinced that industrialization is the only solution for the host of chronic and acute problems with which their societies must deal; and millions of simple country folk are fleeing the huge estates of their landlords and flocking into the cities or squatting in the huge circular belts of shanty towns that are mushrooming on the outskirts of all the urban centers. In a few locations, such as the area in and about the cities of São Paulo and Rio de Janeiro, Brazil, Mexico City and Monterrey, Mexico, Buenos Aires, Argentina, and Bogotá, Cali, and Medellín, Colombia, great industrial complexes are arising; but most Latin-American cities still have no substantial industrial bases. Industry is almost non-existent in many large and rapidly growing centers. Moreover, few of the uprooted peons and peasants have more than the most rudimentary ideas about their chances for remunerative work and improved levels of living in and about the urban centers to which they are migrating. . . . For decades the populations of the various Latin American countries have been increasing at a pace greatly exceeding that of other rapidly growing parts of the world. This fact has provided a basis for the mushrooming of cities and towns throughout the immense area which lies between the Rio Grande and Cape Horn.

When in 1900 the living members of the human race had come to number about 1.6 billions, the inhabitants of the twenty Latin-American countries accounted for approximately 43 million, or 2.7 per cent of the total. During the first half of the twentieth century, however, the rate of population increase was so much more rapid throughout Latin America than it was in other parts of the world, that by 1950 when the population of the earth had risen to 2.5 billions, that of the Latin-American segment had mounted to some 145 million, or about 6.2 per cent of all. Nearly all the Latin-American countries had rising rates of growth, although by 1950 they already had the highest rates in the world. As a result between 1950 and 1960 while the world total was increasing to almost 3 billion, in the upsurge that so popularly and so inappropriately has been known as an "explosion," the number of people in Latin America shot up to 200 million or to 6.7 per cent of all living persons. . . . The forces and factors that have pro-

T. Lynn Smith, "Why the Cities?; Observations on Urbanization in Latin America." *Latin America Problems,* edited by Philip L. Astuto and Ralph A. Leal (Jamaica, New York: St. John's University Press, 1964), pp. 17–33, *passim.* Reprinted by permission.

duced the recent rapid multiplication of human beings in Latin America have neither expended their energy nor lessened their intensity. For at least several decades to come, the increase of population throughout Latin America is likely to be fully as rapid as it has been since 1950. In all probability it will be even faster. . . . In Brazil, which alone contains one-third of all Latin Americans, the increase of population between 1940 and 1950 amounted to the high figure of 26.0 per cent; whereas that between 1950 and 1960, to the surprise of all including those in charge of Brazilian statistical offices and the present writer, was an amazing 36.5 per cent. Similarly, in Mexico, second most populous of the Latin-American countries, a tremendous increase of 31.2 per cent between 1940 and 1950 was followed by another of 35.4 per cent during the decade ending in 1960. . . .

It is possible to show directly and easily that in 1950 almost one-half of the persons living in the Federal Districts of Brazil, Mexico, and Venezuela had been born in other parts of those countries. In each case the Federal District was somewhat coterminous with the national capital, which indicated that millions of migrants from other parts of Brazil, Mexico, and Venezuela had contributed to the growth of Rio de Janeiro, Mexico City, and Caracas, respectively. . . . By 1952 most Latin-American leaders were convinced that the "rural exodus" was one of the major problems confronting their societies. . . . The rate of natural increase of the rural population is far higher than that of the urban population. Nevertheless in the period between censuses ending in 1950 or thereabouts the growth of towns and cities far outstripped that of the rural sections. Thus, for example, in Brazil during the decade 1940–1950, the urban population increased by 46 per cent, the rural population by only 17 per cent; in Mexico during the same decade, the urban population mounted by 59 per cent and the rural only 16 per cent; in Argentina, over the period 1914 to 1947, an increase of 139 per cent in the urban population was accompanied by one of only 60 per cent in the rural population; and in Venezuela between 1941 and 1950 an upsurge of 79 per cent in the urban population took place while the rural population was decreasing by 1 per cent. The materials for the period since 1950 are more fragmentary, but those that are available indicate rather conclusively that the tendency for Latin Americans to concentrate in urban centers was even greater during the opening years of the second half of the twentieth century than it was in the closing decades of the first half. Fortunately, the materials for the Brazilian third of Latin America are available from the census of 1960 as well as from the 1940 and 1950 enumerations. These show that while the total number of Brazilians was rising from 41 million in 1940 to 52 million in 1950 and 71 million in 1960, the proportion of those classified as urban rose from 31.2 per cent in 1940 to 36.2 per cent at midcentury and to 45.1 per cent in 1960. Such changes were possible only because the bulk of Brazil's large increase during the first and second decades was accounted for by the growth of its urban centers.

The best known feature of the phenomenal growth of cities in Brazil is of course, the population build up in the cities of Rio de Janeiro and São Paulo. As late as 1920 there were only about 1,250,000 persons residing in Rio de Janeiro and its suburbs. Today, some 40 years later, there are at least five million inhabitants. When the nineteenth century opened there were only 240,000 people in São Paulo and the rest of the *município*, or county, of which it formed a part. Thereafter, a remarkable growth of the city brought this total to 579,000 by 1920. In 1960, however, as capital of a state having more than thirteen million inhabitants, with more than two-thirds classified as urban, São Paulo was the greatest industrial center in Latin America and one of the more important manufacturing cities of the world. By then its built-up areas had expanded far beyond the limits of the *município*. Its center alone contained 3,288,000 residents; and it was the central city in a metropolitan complex of well over five million inhabitants. The tendency of Brazilians to crowd into towns and cities, however, is not limited to these two great metropolises in the South. This phenomenon is evident throughout the nation. . . .

Mexico, second most populous of the Latin-American nations, is another country for which considerable information from a census taken in 1960 also is available. If one considers Mexico's 35 million people along with Brazil's 71 million, one can take into account fully one-half of all Latin Americans. As a basis for the inference that Mexico, too, is experiencing a mass movement of population from the rural districts to the urban areas, one need note that Mexico's enumerated population rose swiftly from 16,552,722 in 1930 to 34,923,129 in 1960, and that during the same thirty-year period her urban population shot up from 5,540,631 to 17,705,118. As a result the number of Mexicans residing in places of 2,500 or more inhabitants, which constituted only one-third of the population in 1930, actually made up a majority of all Mexicans by 1960. Most striking of all, of course, was the growth of Mexico City and its environs, which now constitute a metropolitan community of more than five million persons, or one of about the same size of Rio de Janeiro or São Paulo. . . .

Many pages might be filled by an enumeration and discussion of the broad social and economic changes which Latin America has experienced since 1900. In the analysis, these are the factors or forces responsible for the tremendous flow of population from country to city, and which, therefore, are highly pertinent to any discussion of "why the cities?" The development and extension of modern means of communication and transportation not only helps to link one country with another but also to unite the various sections of a given country. During the nineteenth century in most parts of Latin America the application of steam for ships and trains did not revolutionize the system of transportation to the degree that it helped to speed up and cheapen the cost of transporting things and persons in Europe, the United States, and Canada. Even today adequate rail facilities are few and far between in Latin America. Similarly, prior to 1920 the telephone and the telegraph did relatively little to modernize communication facilities in most of the countries under consideration. But since 1930, and especially since 1950, the automobile and the motor truck, airplanes, and radio and television have, with startling suddenness, brought rapid and relatively inexpensive means of transportation and communication to practically all occupied parts of Mexico, Central America, the Island Republics, and South America. For example, roads and trails in the interior of Brazil, Colombia, and Mexico, on which less than 20 years ago the present writer spent days and weeks in which he encountered very few vehicles, today are jammed with trucks, busses, and automobiles moving thousands of persons and many tons of produce and merchandise from place to place. All of this expansion has done much to set the stage and provide the means for the rural exodus. . . .

Great social ferment among the rural masses during the second half of the twentieth century is another great force in promoting the movement of people from the open country into the thickly populated urban districts. Once docile and tractable under the paternalistic direction of their land-owning masters, these humble people by the millions are growing increasingly discontented with their lot in life and the prospects for their children's future. . . .

The enactment in all of the Latin-American countries of large bodies of social legislation since the end of the First World War must also be included in even a short list of broad changes which are contributing heavily to the flight of people from the land. Ever since the organization of the old League of Nations, Brazil and the Spanish-American countries have been among the first to enact into law the numerous models of social legislation that were designed by the various international agencies. Measures dealing with hours of work, minimum wages, security of tenure, severance pay, paid vacations, sick leave, and the like are on the list. Granted that many of these measures have been largely ineffectual, the fact remains that they have been much more effective in urban rather than in rural areas. This has helped to broaden the already wide differentials of working conditions in the two areas. Indeed, in many cities these social enactments have done much to better the lot of the workers, and word of this has spread quickly to the rural districts. This factor, too, has played an important role in causing rural folk to flock into the urban centers. . . .

Throughout all the Spanish-American countries an image favorable to city life has prevailed for over four hundred years, and in Brazil its existence goes back at least to the national crisis which accompanied the abolition of slavery (1888) and the establishment of the Republic (1889). The fundamental change is that in recent years the rural masses gradually have been liberated from economic, social, cultural, and legal bonds which have tied them to the soil in the rural sections of their respective countries. Of course in their desire to become urban residents, which seems to be the most widespread current societal driving force in Latin America, the rural folks are merely imitating the upper classes of the societies of which they make up the numerically dominant part.

14 WAGLEY, The New Cultural Brokers

The new cultural broker works generally for change. Some new cultural brokers are native sons of the community in which they live, and thus are fully aware of the traditional values and of the local social system. But even these native sons have lived in and learned something of the larger society, and they have accepted the values of the outside world. Throughout highland Latin America, there are a growing number of bilingual Indians who have spent considerable time on plantations and in large cities, and who have returned to live in their native communities. Many of them reject what they saw and learned while away from home, and attempt to reintegrate themselves into the local community. Others become innovators and cultural brokers. They have learned of the power of labor unions, political parties, and the judicial process. The young Indian political leaders who appeared in so many Guatemalan communities after the revolution of 1944 are a good example.

Among mestizo peasants, cultural brokers originating in the community are, of course, more numerous, since there is a greater awareness of the outside world and no linguistic barrier. Yet it would seem probable that few potential cultural brokers with experience outside their local communities actually return to perform that role in mestizo communities. The mestizo peasant community lacks the distinctive set of values and integration that encourage so many Indians to return. Mestizo peasants, already consciously a part of the larger society, are more likely than Indians never to return home, especially if they are successful in the larger society. As in the United States, every village and small town in Latin America has its native sons who were successful in the city and never returned. Still, there are a few who do return, and they are important in interpreting the outside society to their compatriots.

Finally, one must consider the new cultural brokers who come from outside the local community. As national institutions penetrate peasant communities, they bring cultural brokers from the outside—teachers, agronomists, public health officers, Peace Corps personnel, Protestant and Catholic missionaries, and politicians. Most of these people cannot fulfill the role of a cultural broker, for they do not understand the local society in which they are assigned to work. But, increasingly, they are being taught to be cultural brokers—by UNESCO in its school at Patzcuaro, by the Peace Corps, and by Latin American governments, which realize the great gulf that exists between technically trained personnel from the cities and the mass of people with whom they must work. Important among the new brokers from outside the community are, of course, politicians, labor leaders, and others who are deliberately attempting to awaken political consciousness among

Reprinted from *Continuity and Change in Latin America*, edited by John J. Johnson, with the permission of the publishers, Stanford University Press. © Copyright 1964 by the Board of Trustees of the Leland Stanford Junior University.

peasant groups. More and more, politicians find the peasants ready to listen and to participate. Often the peasants do not fully understand the leaders from the outside, and, in many countries where literacy is a requirement for voting, they have no recourse to the polls. The time may not be too far off, however, when nationally organized peasant groups will wield decisive political power in many nations of Latin America. Already in several Latin American nations, such as Venezuela, Colombia, Bolivia, and Mexico, the peasant is considered an important locus of political power. Crucial to the form and direction that such political movements will take are the people we have called the new cultural brokers.

Problems of Economic and Social Development

A copious and controversial literature has grown up on almost every aspect of the economic and social changes now occurring in Latin America. No one has done more to increase the analysis and informed discussion of developmental problems there than Raúl Prebisch, the Argentine economist. As Director of the United Nations' Economic Commission for Latin America, he proved to be an articulate, independent and competent spokesman whose pronouncements were carefully studied in Europe and the Americas. (Reading No. 15.)

Yankees with their "can-do" attitude are often puzzled by what they consider the snail's pace of desirable changes under way, and some are even inclined to apply to Latin Americans Professor Higgins' indignant and complacent question about women in "My Fair Lady": "Why can't they be more like us?" William S. Stokes wrote that Latin Americans—or at least the important segment of their leaders called pensadores—*don't really want technological change because they prefer not to be like the U.S.[1] T. Lynn Smith, University of Florida sociologist, believes that certain Latin American ideas and institutions constitute obstacles to change. (Reading No. 16.)*

Claudio Véliz, a Chilean economic historian who was for some years a research associate for the Royal Institute of International Affairs, London, would place much of the blame for the present situation on the rising middle classes in Latin America. It is possible that this provocative interpretation is too broad to apply to all of Latin America, and may rest upon a mistaken notion of the role of the middle classes in Europe but it is a stimulating thesis. (Reading No. 17.) For more information on this subject, see the volume of papers by a number of Latin American scholars edited by Dr. Véliz, Obstacles to Change in Latin America *(London: Royal Institute of International Affairs, 1965).*

Simon G. Hanson, editor of the quarterly review Inter-American Economic

---

[1] William S. Stokes, "The Drag of the Pensadores," in James W. Wiggins and Helmut Schoeck, eds., *Foreign Aid Reexamined* (Washington, D.C.: Public Affairs Press, 1958), pp. 62–79.

Affairs, *is a free-lance economist resident in Washington, D.C., with access to the voluminous current reports on Latin America available to the public through such government agencies as the Department of Commerce and the Library of Congress. In this statement he challenges the prescriptions offered by the economists, whom he calls "the new sophisticates." (Reading No. 18.)*

More private initiative is a favorite prescription given by many in the U.S. and Frank Brandenburg, with long experience in Mexico, outlines this viewpoint. (Reading No. 19.) One of the most active agencies in promoting sound, long-range action in Latin America is the newly-established Inter-American Development Bank, whose annual reports have become one of the principal sources today for accurate and up-to-date information. (Reading No. 20.)

15 PREBISCH, A Dynamic Policy is Needed

The ills besetting the Latin-American economy are not determined by circumstantial or transient factors. They are an expression of the critical state of affairs in our time and of the incapacity of the economic system—owing to structural defects that it has been beyond our ability or our power to remedy—to achieve and maintain a rate of development consonant with the growth of the population and with its demands for a speedy improvement in its levels of living.

The increase in the population is certainly phenomenal. At the beginning of the century, there were 63 million inhabitants in Latin America, and the annual rate of demographic growth was 1.8 per cent. Now we number 220 million, and we are multiplying at an annual rate of 2.9 per cent which shows signs of rising even higher.

On the basis of conjectural data, it may be estimated that about half of the existing population has a tiny average personal income of 120 dollars a year. And this vast social aggregate accounts for only about one-fifth of total personal consumption in Latin America, showing the highest coefficients of undernourishment, poor clothing and worse housing, as well as of disease and illiteracy; and, at the same time, the highest rates of reproduction.

The social contrast is striking indeed. While 50 per cent of the population accounts for approximately two-tenths of total personal consumption, at the other end of the scale of distribution 5 per cent of the inhabitants of the region enjoy nearly three-tenths of that total, according to the conjectural estimates referred to above. A policy of austerity mainly affecting this latter social group, and supplemented by the contribution of international resources, would permit an increase in net capital formation and the attainment of the above-mentioned growth target for per capita income, while at the same time redistribution policy would see to it that the income increment thus obtained was passed on to the lower strata of the social aggregate.

Raúl Prebisch, *Towards a Dynamic Development Policy for Latin America* (New York: United Nations, 1963), pp. 3–20 *passim*. Reprinted by permission.

Herein lies the essence of redistribution policy. It is not a matter of taking income away from the upper minority and simply distributing it among the broad masses of the population, for with per capita personal income in Latin America as a whole barely amounting to 370 dollars, the benefits of such a redistribution would not stretch very far. But if, on the other hand, restrictions on the consumption of the privileged groups were reflected in a steady increase in net capital formation, the standard of living of the bulk of the population would rise progressively faster. . . .

There is no doubt that the most persistent bottleneck in the whole of Latin America's development process is generally to be found in agricultural production. Several factors are jointly responsible for this: the system of land tenure, which makes it difficult for modern techniques to be assimilated; inadequate State aid in the work of adapting and diffusing these techniques; and the unsatisfactory investment situation. However thoroughly these three problems are coped with, unless farmers are given proper incentives, efforts to accelerate development are likely to find their most formidable stumbling-block in the agricultural sector, as has been the case in a number of countries with differing economic systems.

The incentives may be of various kinds, but the most important is that agriculture should reap the benefits of the technical progress it makes, as regards both external aspects and the interplay of internal economic forces. This is the only way in which the wide gap between average income figures in rural and in urban areas can be gradually narrowed. The fact is that the impoverished half of the population is largely to be found in rural areas. . . .

One dominant idea runs through the whole of this paper: Latin America must quicken its rate of economic development and redistribute income in favour of the broad masses of the population. The attainment of this objective cannot be indefinitely postponed, nor are there grounds for expecting that economic development will take place first and be followed in the natural course of events by social development. Both must be achieved gradually and side by side. This will entail rational and deliberate action to influence the forces of development; the spontaneous interplay of these forces will not suffice here, as it did in the capitalistic evolution of the advanced countries. . . .

These internal structural changes, and international cooperation in development, are the subject-matter of the present document. It is designed as much for those who resist such changes within their own countries as for those who propose to carry them out. It is also directed at those outside the region who fail to grasp the nature and gravity of events in Latin America.

To the first of these groups, we should like to demonstrate the ineluctable necessity of introducing the changes in question into the social structure so that the pattern of production and the structure of the economy can respond to development requirements. If they are anxious to keep their position in the distribution scale inviolate, we would emphasize for their benefit that a point in history has been reached when it is no longer feasible to maintain consumption patterns that imply the dissipation of a substantial capital formation potential, in a fashion totally incompatible with the region's vast capital formation requirements. And if they are concerned for the future of democracy, it will not be amiss to suggest that nothing will do more to strengthen it in Latin America than social mobility, the emergence and rise of the dynamic elements of society, by virtue of the reforms in question; and that stubborn opposition to such measures might compel other men, whose ultimate motive was the same, to ride roughshod over democratic procedure in order to achieve this aim, perhaps in the illusory belief that the opportunities for sound democratic development which would thus be lost in social strife could be recovered in the course of time.

Those who are resolved to carry out the reforms are faced with a tremendous responsibility. Considerable emotional force is building up in Latin America, the emotional force of great mass movements. It must be channelled towards clear and constructive ends. Nothing can be accomplished without thought and rational planning. But neither can bold decisions be taken—such decisions as our countries need—without the driving-power of this force. The acid test of ultimate efficacy will lie in the ability of the leaders to fuse these elements into a development policy. . . .

Development policy must be based on a correct interpretation of the real state of affairs in Latin America. The theories that we have taken up, and are still taking up, from the countries at the centre of the world economy often make a fallacious claim to be generally applicable. It is essentially incumbent on us who are on the periphery to play our part in correcting these theories and introducing the dynamic elements needed to bring them into line with our own situation. . . .

The rapid assimilation of technology entails new patterns of living and new attitudes of mind. Nevertheless, there is nothing in this vast process of change that requires the relegation of human values to second place. On the contrary, present-day technology opens up infinite possibilities for a variety of ways of life and a freedom of individual choice that until recently, in terms of history, were confined to a small fraction of mankind.

But the production technique of today also makes possible an enormous concentration of economic power in a few hands, and this is perhaps even more true of information techniques and mass communication of ideas. Everything depends on the use we make of such techniques for the purpose of exercising conscious and deliberate control over the forces of economic and social development—on whether we use them to place some men under the dominion of others, or to enhance the dignity of the human personality. . . .

It would be a tragedy if in order to free man from want we had to sacrifice other values and subject him to the demands of an arbitrary power. The very idea is fundamentally incompatible with the genius of the Latin-American peoples, with their latent urge to shake off the trammels of poverty in order to liberate the human personality and give full rein, by means of economic development, to democracy and human rights, especially as regards the underprivileged half of the population of Latin America; in order to ensure that both there and in all strata of society, social mobility will allow the best elements to move upwards, for the good of economic development and of democracy. The goal must be a social order free from privilege, and not only economic privilege, but also that baneful sort whereby some men usurp dominion over the ideas of the rest, over the creative forces of the spirit and over the deepest feeling of the heart.

16 SMITH, Why Economic Development Lags

From the very first, the Spaniards and the Portuguese who sought their fortunes in the New World were thoroughly imbued with the idea of securing others to work for them, on their lands and in their mines. . . . Latin American society early became differentiated into a small, wealthy, highly-educated, white elite for whom nothing in the world was considered too good, and a mass of humble, poverty-stricken, disease-ridden, illiterate, colored or mixed-blood agricultural laborers. Although hundreds of thousands of the most demoralized segments of the lower class recently have flocked into the rapidly growing towns and cities, this has not radically changed the class system. It has merely transformed a part of the lower classes into a degraded urban proletariat.

Naturally such a system of social stratification generated and perpetuated many basic values with respect to human behavior and social relationships. Most important of all those which became and have remained almost universally accepted with respect to human labor and toil. Throughout Latin America, work with the hands, manual labor of almost any type, any activity that has been the work of slaves or peons, is looked upon as the stigma of servile or semi-servile social status. Anyone not resigned to life as a member of the lower classes must avoid it as he would the plague . . . the fundamental problem that such ideas about manual labor pose in relation to our technical cooperation with Latin Americans is, of course, how the ordinary tasks on the farm can be made socially acceptable to others than those definitely known and admitted to be of lower-class status.

Closely related . . . is the idea which views labor as being of so little value or consequence that it may be expended with the utmost abandon in the productive process. . . . Labor is one thing in the production process that is expended lavishly. Except in pastoral activities, land certainly is not used extensively. . . . Capital is used so sparingly that even the most rudimentary tools or implements, not to mention work stock or other sources of power, are largely lacking. Men and women work for the most part almost with their bare hands; and the amount of human toil that goes into the production of a ton of sugar, a bag of coffee, a sack of beans, a bushel of wheat or corn, or a unit of any other product, in most parts of Latin America, is almost beyond belief. Probably more than half of all the people in Latin America today are gaining their livelihood through a system of agricultural techniques or a system of farming that is more primitive than that the Egyptians were using at the dawn of history. . . .

T. Lynn Smith, "Values Held by People in Latin America which Affect Technical Cooperation," *Rural Sociology*, XXI (1956), pp. 68–75, *passim*. Reprinted by permission.

Closely related to the nature of the class structure . . . is what may be styled a mind-set of resignation, a deep-seated pessimistic outlook on life . . . a deep-rooted belief, almost fatalistically entrenched, in the futility of any undertaking of a long-range nature, in the certainty that accomplishments must be achieved quickly or all is in vain. . . . From the very first the concentration of land ownership and control, the system of large estates, the separation of society into the small class of elite and the mass at the bottom of the scale, absenteeism (with the large landowners residing in state and national capitals), and political control by the favored few, have placed local and departmental government in a strait jacket. Through constitutional provisions which prohibit the residents of the *municipios* or counties from levying any tax on the land, the members of the upper classes have deprived the rural masses of the population from using the tried and tested method of pooling local efforts in order to provide the services they need. Land is an asylum for the capital of the absentee landlords, and the people in the rural communities must suffer from want of schools, protection for life and property, health and sanitary services, roads and bridges, etc. As a result, local leadership and responsibility are practically nil. Everything must come from the national capital and the federal government. Hence, inevitably, the Latin Americans with whom we deal are those currently basking in the favor of the regime in power. If there is a revolution of the Latin-American variety, or any other change in government, they quickly will be numbered among the "outs," and their places will be taken by the kinfolk and other political leaders who have gained control.

17 VÉLIZ, Obstacles to Reform in Latin America

The well-intentioned attempt to identify a liberal, industrious, frugal and reformist middle class in the present Latin American social structure is destined to early facile success and eventual catastrophic failure. There are groups which have the superficial characteristics of the middle class; they even talk, write, and think of themselves as being middle class, but objectively they are not, and it is very hard to see how they can ever bridge the distance which separates their intrinsic conservatism, their respect for hierarchical values, their admiration for their natural aristocracies, their overwhelming desire to rise and be accepted by those they regard as their betters, from the dynamic reformism which is usually associated with middle-class idiosyncrasy.

This unexpectedly conservative attitude on the part of the Latin American urban middle sectors is relatively new. Until the Second World War their political leadership had maintained a reformist position and had even become associated

This material originally appeared in an article "Obstacles to Reform in Latin America" by Dr. Claudio Véliz in the January 1963 issue of *The World Today*, the monthly journal published by The Royal Institute of International Affairs, London. Reprinted by permission. See also Charles Wagley, "The Dilemma of the Latin American Middle Classes," *Proceedings of the Academy of Political Science*, XXVII (1964), No. 4, pp. 2–10.

COASTAL FISHERMEN

with a number of national Communist and Socialist parties. In fact, during the years between the wars, several reformist political movements, broadly based on urban middle-class support, managed to get near the sources of political power in their respective countries. . . . The urban middle sectors of Latin America, however, reached the sources of political power with the support of the popular vote, while they were still economically unimportant. They did not represent growing industrial pressure groups nor were they associated with the traditionally foreign-dominated extractive industries. The land was still held by the old aristocracy and commercial activity was controlled either by foreign business houses or by well-established minor local firms. There was no area of the economy from which the rising urban groups could derive substantial financial support. . . .

The outbreak of the Second World War created a new situation which opened unprecedented opportunities for rapid industrial growth. European and U.S. exports ceased to reach Latin American markets and, in the vacuum thus created, a fantastic mushrooming of industry took place. The consequences of this were obvious. In less than a decade, the leadership of the urban middle sectors became extremely wealthy. Using their access to the sources of power and their influence with the bureaucracy, they allocated tenders, granted licenses, exercised the traditional rights of patronage, and, even without outright corruption, accumulated considerable fortunes. These economic changes were too swift, unexpected, and accidental to result in significant social changes. No apparent contradictions developed between the aristocratic landowner and the wealthy radical leader: on the contrary, they became fast friends and political colleagues once the rising bureaucrat had bought land and racehorses, joined the local country club, and taken his first golf lessons. Thus in a relatively brief period of time, the violently outspoken reformist leaders of 1938 became the sedate, technically minded, and moderate statesmen of the 1950's. Once their foot was in the door, there was no more talk of demolition: now the problem was how to get inside the mansion of privilege. The leadership of the urban middle sectors had gained access to the very sources of political power which they now shared with the traditional landed aristocracy. They had also acquired considerable wealth and, as new and well-protected industrialists and bureaucrats, also stood as equals with the wealthy landowners. The one thing they lacked, and which they could only obtain from their enemies of a generation ago, was social prestige. . . .

In Latin America there survives what is perhaps one of the largest and oldest aristocratic establishments in the Western world. Through countless revolutions, civil wars, and other catastrophes, it has managed to hold on to most of its land, a considerable part of its power, and all of its social prestige. Generals, 'caudillos,' and colonels come and go, but the aristocracy remains. There are a large number of families, in countries like Chile, Colombia, Argentina, and Peru that have contributed presidents, senators, prelates, scholars, judges, high ranking military officers, and even Spanish colonial officials in practically every generation for the last two centuries. . . .

The fact of the survival of these aristocratic groups, in spite of revolutions, palace revolts, and the like, immediately qualifies all the popular notions about political or institutional stability in Latin America. It can even be said that the continent's record of stability is almost without parallel in the Western world. There are very few countries—perhaps with the exception of Spain and Portugal— that can boast of having had practically the same social structure for over two centuries. These aristocratic groups represent the social peaks which the urban middle sectors want to climb. Now, throughout the continent, the middle sectors are willing and ready to outdo the conservatives in their devotion to established institutions. If they have acquired land for purposes of prestige during the last two or three decades, they are certainly not going to give it away just because the Alliance for Progress is suggesting such a thing. In fact, it is not altogether difficult to suppose that the traditional landed aristocracy, precisely because of their talent for adaptation, are more prepared to give their land away, if they feel this to be necessary for survival, than are the newcomers who have just achieved the landed proprietors clubs. Social climbing has thus become a political institution. . . .

This fundamental isolation, both emotional and intellectual, of the urban middle sectors from their social and cultural environment can be dramatically illustrated in their basic cultural sterility. The middle classes of Europe did not look to the aristocracy or to any foreign influence for guidance in their cultural creativity. Their dress, manner of living, gastronomic and architectural tastes, and their inclinations in painting and music were their own and, if anything, their creators were smug and stubborn in their loyalty to their own tastes and values. Not so with the urban middle sectors of Latin America. At the highest levels, they follow the sartorial, domestic and artistic guidance of the aristocracy they so much admire and hope to join. . . .

Most of the continent's intellectuals are in opposition and have adopted a quiet but forcefully critical attitude. There are extremely few writers, poets, musicians, economists, architects, or historians of the last generation who are willing to identify themselves with the political and social arrangements made by the leadership of the urban middle sectors. This does not mean that they are all members of the Socialist or Communist parties. In fact, most intellectuals are not members of any parties at all. It simply means that they do not think—like Dickens, Balzac, Dumas, or, for that matter, Walt Whitman, Mark Twain, or Ralph Waldo Emerson—that they are living in a dynamic society where occasional injustices and mistakes can be put right with goodwill and bourgeois decency. On the contrary, they are extremely sceptical, critical, and pessimistic. Hopelessness seems to dominate their view of contemporary affairs and indifference is only overcome when something like the Bolivian or the Cuban revolution, the victory of Betancourt in Venezuela or Frondizi in Argentina, promises to achieve the reforms which could initiate the period of vigorous growth which everybody is hoping for.

Meanwhile the urban middle sectors, essentially conservative and conformist, fundamentally inclined to defend the *status quo,* emotionally ready to cast in their lot with that of the old order, are precisely the sectors which are now being asked to reform, to change, to lead their nations into a new era of development. It does not take very much political acumen to realize that they cannot do this, no matter what incentives are provided from abroad, for the simple reason that for them the opportunity for social advancement at home—the chance of entering the glittering mansion—is the best of all possible rewards. . . .

In the absence of reformist leadership from the urban middle sectors, the forgotten elements in Latin American society, the workers and the peasants, may very well join the dissident intelligentsia and take into their own hands the responsibilities of implementing the fundamental structural changes which are urgently needed.

18   HANSON, The Administrators Are at Fault

In Latin America, the Roman Catholic Church is often depicted as the reactionary, fat, torpid, unconcerned guardian of the *status quo*—a caricature easily drawn and purposefully propagated. And there are the familiar case interpretations of the Mexican Revolution, say, where the "achievements" (cited presumably in ignorance of the increased inequality in distribution of national income and the infliction of rarely paralleled social injustice) were said to have been "a result of the severing of the relations with the Church and the firing of the priests out of the schools". . . .

Also at fault in Latin America, the textbooks said, was the ineffective organization of economic and human resources that kept personal incomes well below $400 per capita, and left very sizable blocs of people with incomes below $100 per capita. . . .

The textbooks go on to identify the wide difference between rich and poor in Latin America as another source of the country's problems. This gulf between rich and poor forms a "carapace over the rich," making them incurious, unconcerned, content to avoid taxes and social responsibility, to hold the land idle, to reject labor organization, to exploit and exploit and exploit while engaging in a riot of conspicuous consumption and in a skilled movement of their assets to Switzerland. . . .

Sophisticated theoreticians also claimed as a cause of Latin America's dilemma the "frustrated" process of economic development in which production and exports of foodstuffs and raw materials tended to grow less rapidly than those of manufactured goods—a process in which the now-disproved terms-of-trade analysis once generated by Raúl Prebisch figured largely. Latin America had been "able" to reduce its share of world exports from 11.1 per cent in 1950 to 6.7 per cent in 1960, but there was a disinclination to remember that this reduction had stemmed in large part from the area's own policies soberly entered upon rather

Religion, Revolution, and Reform. New Forces for Change in Latin America, edited by Fredrick B. Pike and William V. D'Antonio (New York: Praeger, 1964), pp. 186–196. Reprinted by permission.

than from the mystical "dynamics of development." World exports of manufactured goods, these theoreticians mourned, had risen 103 per cent from 1928 to
1955–57 while Latin-American exports of basic commodities excluding petroleum
had risen only 14 per cent. . . .

It is the fashion of the Latin-American politician to issue pronouncements
that the conditions are not going to continue, that they must not continue, that they
cannot continue. Thus, he feeds the "revolution of rising expectations" with daily
reminders. "The Dominican people," the new president declaims typically, "demand a better life!" . . .

The Archbishop of Rio de Janeiro, Don Helder Pessoa Camara, shows even
less restraint: He reminds Brazil's Catholics that "freedom is but an empty word
for two-thirds of mankind who lack shelter, clothes, food and a minimum education or authentic employment." He concedes graciously that "the yearly aid of
$2 billion from the United States is undoubtedly a token of good will," but in his
desire to create a new image for the Church, he refers to this aid as "inexpressive
in terms of real economic development." He proclaims that the Alliance for
Progress is dead. . . .

The economist's role is first and foremost to emphasize that Latin America's
problems arise from the fact that the Latin American does not live in what
Huxley calls "symbiotic harmony with [his] environment." Nowhere in Latin
America is there any inclination to face up to the ecological problem that there
is virtually no chance for members of a society whose population is doubling in
twenty-five years or less, and whose nonproducers relative to its producers will
thus grow disadvantageously, to meet the deficiencies in food and shelter and
clothing and the amenities that make life tolerable. Irene Taeuber at Princeton
has estimated that there are now 850 to 900 youth and aged for each 1,000 adults
aged fifteen to sixty-four, and that in 1975 there will be 890 to 940 such de-
pendents for each 1,000 adults. . . .

The economist must not be blinded by his "do-gooding" instincts to the realities of public policy. What are those realities?

First it is not alone, or even primarily, the landowner, the priest or his bishop,
or the tax-evading industrialist who should be blamed for the resistance to and
the ultimate failure of the revolution of rising expectations. It is the new managerial class in Latin America that is to be blamed—the bureaucrat, the economic
planner, the international-agency bureaucrat—the new makers of public policy,
those who so glibly excite expectations (despite the fact that they are well aware
that the race with the rising population is an almost impossible one), but who are
not prepared to direct their countries' energies and resources toward the realization
of these expectations.

It must be doubted seriously that the Latin Americans who are conducting
the debate on reform and development have really grasped the great issues and
are capable of articulating them. And in the briefcase brigade that is proceeding
from Washington to Latin America, that incredible, hastily mobilized parade of
mediocrity, there is even less capacity to grasp and articulate the great issues. . . .

At one time Latin America's leaders believed that it was possible to import—and the leaders of Europe and North America believed that it was possible to export—the "basic political skills and the arts of freedom" to the hundreds of millions who acclaimed the name of freedom and democracy without any significant understanding of the matter. For many years, the traffic in constitutions, in forms, and in political institutions flourished. But it failed! And the Latins were left desperately remote from political democracy, subject to unending constitutional crisis, a victim at home of chaos illuminated from time to time by *coups d'état,* and a victim abroad of derision as the dictators enthusiastically subscribed to democracy and to "respect for the fundamental freedoms of man" at successive inter-American conferences, even as they trampled on those freedoms and made a mockery of democracy.

And now, more than a hundred years later, effective government still absent, literacy unachieved, and administrative capacity unavailable, the new sophisticates believe, erroneously, that there is a new, instant formula for the social and economic problems, just as their forebears believed that there was an instant formula for the political problems. To this end, we have the endless traffic of missions from North to South and from South to North happily learning what is already known. And we have the statisticians offering up their sophisticated capital-output ratios, when there are not even adequate basic statistics to deal with. And we have the planners expressing contempt for those who insist on studies of relative cost patterns, capacity to compete, and the like, and insisting that only additions to productive capacity are important. And we have the agricultural economists concerned with creating less food for more people in the hectic distribution of land. And we have the political economists willing to discourage the inflow of productive capital and the advance of technology. . . .

Is it not possible that our fundamental error is that we are allowing ourselves to be seduced by the rhetoric of the new managerial class, by their promises of affluence, by their alleged discovery of an instant formula? All the time that we are focusing our dissatisfaction on the landowner and the priest and the allegedly tax-evading industrialist, is it not possible that we are in fact accepting a managerial element that is destined to provide the greatest disappointment of all?

19 BRANDENBURG, Does Private Enterprise have a Future in Latin America?

The century-old debate on the merits of private versus public ownership assumes a very special importance in Latin America today. Latin American private enterprise, which can make a crucial contribution to economic growth and democratic evolution in a region long troubled by violent, authoritarian, and extremist politics, has entered upon a critical period. Choices have already been made and

Frank Brandenburg, *The Development of Latin American Private Enterprise* (Washington: National Planning Association, 1964), *passim.* Reprinted by permission.

are now being made which decisively affect the concentration of economic power, and thus of political power as well. The advocates of statism are articulate and politically effective. The advocates of private enterprise appear to be less so.

If private enterprise is valuable for the economic growth and democratic evolution of Latin American countries, effective policies and programs should be devised for its support because its position is more vulnerable there than in the relatively more advanced countries.

The classical arguments about the relative merits of public and private enterprise were worked out during the 19th century, primarily in the context of the economically more advanced countries. Although the nationalization of large productive enterprises has often appeared to the relatively low income countries to be the easiest solution to problems of political strength and economic justice, the trend toward socialization may threaten future wealth, creativity, and freedom unless it is checked in some countries and reversed in others. The situation in Latin America today also differs in that public ownership in Latin America is more dominant than in the classical European and North American economies of the 19th century. . . .

In recent years the trend toward government ownership of the largest enterprises has been increasing to the point where the threat of monopoly control in Latin America today comes much more from public than from private enterprises. . . .

An analysis of the distribution of ownership of the 30 leading enterprises in six Latin American countries shows the extent of nationalization of industry, the largest single problem in governmental relations with private enterprise in Latin America.

In simplified form, the distribution of ownership between government, local private capital, and foreign private capital is as follows:

	Government	Domestic Private	Foreign Private
Argentina	61.3%	20.5%	18.2%
Brazil	59.1	20.0	20.9
Chile*	63.3	18.0	18.7
Colombia	54.1	39.1	6.1
Mexico	82.2	13.9	3.9
Venezuela	74.0	22.9	3.1
Average for six countries	65.8%	22.4%	11.8%

* Excluding copper and nitrate exporters

. . . In developing economies like those of Latin America, the relationships between the government and private enterprise and the relative emphasis placed on the public and private sectors need to be flexible and responsive to changing needs and capabilities. The essential requirements are that a developing country recognize the vital role which modern private enterprise can play in national development and that it be prepared to adopt and implement the government policies and programs conducive to the growth of private enterprise.

The success of policies and programs of the U.S. government, other governments, and international aid agencies that would give promise of materially strengthening the growth of Latin American private enterprise within the framework of the Alliance for Progress depends on three major considerations: the capacity of foreign governments and international agencies to assist domestic private enterprise, the attitudes of Latin American governments toward such assistance, and the absorption capacity of Latin American recipients.

The future of free enterprise in Latin America depends on many factors. If entrepreneurs are lazy or concerned only with their own and their families' welfare and not at all with that of their employees, their survival is impossible. If national governments harass business with unpredictable taxes and tariff duties, with rampant inflation and expanding expropriation, they can stifle free enterprise. If foreign industrialists maintain rigid barriers against domestic employees and concern themselves exclusively with taking profits out of the country, they can dim the prospects for economic independence. And if international agencies confine their contacts to government circles, they will be giving less help than they could, and may at times actually hinder the evolution of democracy.

Whatever actions may be taken by governmental, international, and foreign organizations will be of no help to Latin American private entrepreneurs unless they help themselves. In Latin America today, native businessmen dominate small and medium industry and still hold a small proportion of large industry. Their current prevalence gives them a large part of the responsibility for future developments. Whether or not they make a real contribution toward realizing the social and economic aspirations of their communities is likely to determine not only their own future but also that of freedom itself in Latin America.

20 Background, Purposes and Administration of the Social Progress Trust Fund

The immediate origin of the Social Progress Trust Fund can be traced directly to the proposal of the United States to establish a Special Inter-American Fund for Social Development to be administered principally by the Inter-American Development Bank. This proposal was accepted by the governments of Latin America in the Act of Bogotá in September 1960. In June 1961, immediately after funds were authorized by the Congress of the United States, the President of the United States, John F. Kennedy, and the President of the Bank, Felipe Herrera, signed the Social Progress Trust Fund Agreement. Under this Agreement, the Government of the United States entrusted to the IDB the management of the resources of the

Social Progress Trust Fund, Fifth Annual Report, 1965, Washington: Inter-American Development Bank, 1966, pp. 1–4, *passim.* Reprinted by permission.

Fund, US$ 394 million. In February 1964, in accordance with an additional protocol to the Agreement, the Government of the United States increased the resources of the Fund by US$ 131 million, thus raising total resources available to US$ 525 million. . . .

In accordance with the principles and directives of the Social Progress Trust Fund Agreement, the Fund is administered by the Inter-American Development Bank. The fundamental purpose of the Fund is to provide financial resources and technical assistance, on flexible terms and conditions, to support the efforts made by the Latin American countries that are prepared to undertake effective and extensive institutional improvements, and to adopt measures for the efficient employment of their own resources toward achieving greater social progress and more balanced economic growth.

The resources of the Trust Fund may be utilized to provide loans and technical assistance designed to encourage progress in the member countries in the following fields:

1. Land settlement and improved land use, including access and feeder roads, assistance to agricultural credit institutions, assistance to supervised credit and agricultural extension, and development of storage and marketing facilities, provided that the resources of the Fund shall not be used for the purchase of agricultural land;

2. Housing for low-income groups, through assistance to self-help housing and to institutions providing long-term housing finance and engaged in mobilizing domestic resources for this purpose;

3. Community water supply and sanitation facilities;

4. Such supplementary financing of facilities for advanced education and training related to economic and social development as may be agreed upon from time to time between the United States and the IDB.

In addition, the IDB may utilize the Fund resources to finance the cost of technical assistance related to projects and programs in the foregoing fields or in conjunction with the mobilization of domestic financial resources and the establishment of financial institutions. This technical assistance can be reimbursable or non-reimbursable.

Under the Trust Fund Agreement, the IDB must be guided by certain general criteria in considering applications for loans and technical assistance which are submitted to it.

1. Financial and technical assistance shall be made available for projects and programs which are related to effective self-help measures in member countries of the Bank, where institutional improvements are being initiated or broadened and where a country's own resources are being utilized effectively in order to achieve greater social progress and more balanced economic growth.

2. Proposals which form part of national development programs will receive special consideration. Therefore, the review and analysis of economic and social progress and problems in each country, carried out at the annual meetings of the Inter-American Economic and Social Council, shall be taken into account.

3. Before acting favorably on a loan request, the IDB shall be satisfied that the measures necessary for the success of the particular project or program have been or will be undertaken.

4. Loans shall be granted only for projects or programs in which the applicant bears an appropriate share of the total costs. However, loans may be granted to cover the total cost of a specific project, provided that such a project forms an integral part of an expanding program in the same field financed to an appropriate extent by the applicant. Moreover, the borrower or another appropriate entity must be prepared to assume the costs of the continued support of the project or program, including the costs of maintenance and operation of any structure, installation and equipment connected therewith.

5. Before committing resources of the Trust Fund, the IDB shall take into account whether the financial or technical assistance required can be obtained from national or international agencies or from private sources on terms which in the opinion of the IDB are reasonable for the recipient, considering all pertinent factors.

6. Loans may be made to national governments, government institutions and agencies, local and municipal governments, and private borrowers within a country eligible within the terms of the Trust Fund Agreement, including cooperatives and organizations affiliated with or sponsored by labor unions.

7. The resources of the Trust Fund shall be provided under such flexible terms and conditions of repayment as are most appropriate to carry out the purposes of the Fund in each country.

8. No financial or technical assistance shall be extended to any country which was not a member of the IDB as of September 12, 1960, or which is being subjected to economic or diplomatic sanctions by the Organization of American States.

9. Loans may be made repayable, in whole or in part, in the currency of the borrower. . . .

10. Dollar funds made available shall be used for the purchase of goods and services from the United States or for the acquisition of goods or services of local origin in the country where the assistance is received. However, the IDB may authorize the use of such funds for the acquisition of goods or services produced in other countries which are members of the Bank if such a transaction would be advantageous to the borrower. . . .

SECTION V

The Churches and Change

A new spirit is stirring in the Roman Catholic Church in Latin America, as elsewhere in the world. Richard Shaull of Princeton Theological Seminary analyzes this change in relation to communism. (Reading No. 21.) One powerful obstacle to religious development in Latin America is the shortage of priests, which has caused grave concern. Extraordinary efforts have been made in Europe and the U.S. as well as in Latin America to help meet this need, so much so that at least one voice has been raised to suggest that the outside money and men constitute a kind of cultural imperialism.[1] For a reasoned and reasonable interpretation of this controversy, see the explanation of Joseph P. Fitzpatrick, S.J., of Fordham University. (Reading No. 24B.) Antonine Tibesar, historian and member of the Academy of American Franciscan History of Washington, D.C., brings to bear a historical perspective on this problem in his deeply-probing evaluation of a learned German work on the shortage of priests. (Reading No. 22.)

One of the most careful analyses of the present state of Latin America and what the Catholic Church should do comes from the pen of Manuel Larraín, Bishop of Talca in Chile. (Reading No. 23.) Pronouncements on these matters usually are made by the hierarchy[2]; an unusual declaration was made by parish priests in Sucre, Bolivia, which indicates that the ferment of change is at work at all levels. (Reading No. 24A.)

21 SHAULL, *The Catholic Church and Social Questions*

The last two papal encyclicals of John XXIII marked a decisive evolution in the Roman Catholic position on social questions. Parallel to this, and partly occa-

M. Richard Shaull, "The Church in the World," *Theology Today* (October, 1963), pp. 401–11, *passim*. Reprinted by permission from *Theology Today*.

[1] Ivan D. Illich, S.J., "The Seamy Side of Charity," *America*, V. 116, No. 3 (New York: Jan. 21, 1967).

[2] *Recent Church Documents from Latin America* (Cuernavaca, Mexico: Center of Intercultural Formation, 1962–1963).

sioned by it, is the intensification of Catholic participation in movements which are working for the radical change of social structures. This is especially evident in Latin America, where such a large proportion of the world's Catholics live, and where the church has been traditionally identified with the forces of reaction in a society of extreme privilege and social injustice.

The beginnings of this were seen some years ago when, in one country after another, the hierarchy began to cut itself loose from any close identification with unpopular rightist dictators. Today the leadership of the church in some areas is making a concerted effort to change the image of the church in the minds of the people. It is attempting to demonstrate clearly that it is not identified with the forces of the *status quo,* but rather decidedly on the side of social change, and that it has abandoned its traditional attitude of paternalism. The most striking example of this is the Pastoral of the Chilean bishops, published in September of last year, which studies openly how widespread is the poverty and social injustice which exist in the country and stresses the need for basic changes in the structures of that society. It is likely that this emphasis represents only a relatively small minority in the Latin American hierarchy. The church still is one of the institutions which sustains the *status quo* in many places and a more progressive attitude is considered pro-Communist. But a new spirit is stirring. . . .

In various countries, Catholic Action groups—of students, workers, and in some cases peasants—are fully involved in the present social struggle, and Christian Democratic parties are having a new lease on life in those instances where they have appeared with a revolutionary program that might offer an alternative to Communism. . . .

The crucial question which here arises is that of the Christian position in relation to Marxism. When any group in Latin America becomes convinced of the urgent need to change structures of a society which has been firmly established for 400 years, it is soon almost overwhelmed by the size and difficulty of the task. The forces of the *status quo* are so powerful that there is as yet no clear sign that change can be brought about. Moreover, when Christians become involved in movements which are working for such change, they immediately discover that the Marxists were there before them and are more prepared than anyone else for this work. For the Catholic to concentrate his energies on fighting the Marxist for control of the revolutionary movement, or in order to eliminate the Marxist influence in it, seems quite absurd. If social change is to come about fast enough to avoid a complete breakdown in Latin American society, in some cases at least it will have to come as the result of a joint effort of Catholics and Marxists. . . .

One thing at least is certain. We must not attempt any longer to define our attitude to the Latin American revolution in terms of the categories which we developed in our struggle with Communism in the United States in the 1930's. If we hope to meet the present problem creatively as Christians, we must recognize the complexity and ambiguity of the new situation, and be open to new ways of thought and new definitions of our responsibility. Otherwise, in our struggle against

Communism, we will be contributing ultimately to Communist domination in other parts of the continent.

22 *TIBESAR, The Shortage of Priests in Latin America*

This book is a major study of one of the most serious problems of the Church in Latin America today, the shortage of priests, by the Secretary General of the Latin-American College of Louvain University. Ten years have been devoted to research, and this effort is reflected in the extensive bibliography, numerous statistical tables, and the wide range of facts contained in the text. In a word, this study is a notable effort to understand and explain the lack of priests in an area which is traditionally looked upon as Catholic.

The volume opens with a country-by-country survey of the state of the question today. This survey reveals that in 1963 each priest in Latin America had to care for an average of 4,891 persons: 41,583 priests for 203,415,000 people. Of the continental Americas, Honduras has the poorest ratio of priest to people, with 11,044 persons per priest, and Chile the best, with 2,692 persons per priest. To make matters worse, of the priests in Latin America more than 40%—17,045— are foreigners, with Spain leading in supplying workers, with 8,000 priests, while the United States contributes only 1,850. Only Mexico has relatively few foreign clergymen.

After this survey of present conditions, the author in several chapters turns to the colonial period. He seems surprised by the fact that no shortage of priests existed in either Spanish or Portuguese America, with the possible exception of Honduras. Mexico, after the first few decades, maintained during the colonial period a ratio of priests to people which fluctuated between one priest to 600 to 800 people. Brazil in 1759 had 2,700 priests for about 3,000,000 inhabitants, while today it has only 11,144 priests for 69,335,000 people. The scarcity of priests, both diocesan and regular, in Latin America is very definitely a post-independence problem. This is studied in depth in the second section of the volume.

In the second section, the author lists and then studies what he considers the causes of the problem: first the historical, then the psychological, sociological, economic, etc. The reviewer is limited by his competence to the historical factors mentioned by the author and he can neither deny nor affirm the validity of the others. Essentially the historical causes are five: the church-state system of colonial Latin America, the method of instruction of the Indians, the lack of an Indian priesthood, the expulsion of the Jesuits, and the anti-clericalism of the newly independent states in the nineteenth century. It is the usual list, sustained for the most part by the pertinent literature, mostly of European origin and some of it quite out of date. . . .

Antonine Tibesar, O.F.M., "The Shortage of Priests in Latin America: A Historical Evaluation of Werner Promper's *Priesternot in Lateinamerika*," *The Americas*, XXII (1960), pp. 413–420, *passim*. Reprinted by permission.

Lastly, there is the matter of the anti-church and anti-clerical policies of the newly independent states in the nineteenth century. In most instances, the statement is true. However, it should be proven and not merely presumed that there is a true causal relation between that attitude and today's lack of priests. Certainly the most effective means of reducing the number of clergy, short of bloodshed, is to do away with the ordaining bishops. Yet the hesitancy of Rome to acknowledge the independence of most Latin American countries occasioned just that measure and in some instances for many years. In Lima, where the hiatus between bishops lasted only ten years, we find that up to about 1865 the archbishop was ordaining an average of about 15 priests a year, with a slow decline after that date to an average of about seven by about 1900. Today, the annual average is closer to one or two. On the other hand there is Mexico with the most hostile government of all towards the church. Yet, Mexico today has the least foreign priests and the largest annual number of ordinations. Clearly, there seem to be other factors operative here and a great deal of study is still required before we can put our finger on the exact causes of the lack of sufficient clergy in Latin America.

With this, we come to an end of the historical causes offered by the author for the present shortage of clergy south of our border. None of them seem to this reviewer to be very cogent. Instead, may he suggest that the search be directed down other paths. It is a well established fact that the clergy, diocesan and regular, exercised a wide influence in the newly founded Latin American republics. Numerous priests were elected to the first national congresses; in some cases, as in Peru, a priest was even the presiding official. As such, priests had an important voice in drawing up the basic laws and policies of the new nations: policies which are frequently classified as anticlerical or less frequently anti-church. Yet as we look at these first aspirations we are surprised as far as religion is concerned. For, what did they seek? The Mass in the vernacular, less pomp in church services, an increase in the power and prestige of the bishop with a correlative decrease in the disciplinary power of the pope, a return to the primitive church, a reform or abolition of the Roman curia, the suppression of the Inquisition and of the index, freedom of conscience, relaxation of celibacy for at least some of the clergy, a "poor" church, and some manner of limitation of the number of religious. Somehow this sounds almost as though we were discussing the agenda of Vatican II, except for the matter of celibacy which never got to the floor for discussion. The "poor" church indeed got to the floor of Vatican II but never got off it.

In their time, the priests who sponsored these proposals thought that they were loyal Catholics and that their suggestions would aid the Church in its mission among their peoples. But, their proposals were sternly rejected by Europe and, if the priests continued to espouse them, they were condemned. Now, in the light of Vatican II, could it just be that Latin America was 150 years ahead of Europe and that Rome, so solidly fascinated by European maneuverings, repeated the mistake of an Alexander VI, who esteemed a European bishopric for one of his sons more valuable than both Americas? At any rate, those nineteenth century American priests were condemned or silenced with the accompaniment of much head-wagging. Today, when their program has been so substantially adopted, they are forgotten and we are called upon instead, to admire the work of the "liberal" Belgian or French, or Dutch elements in awakening the Church, while other Europeans write books about the laggard Latin Americans, who were 150 years ahead of them and perhaps grew a little tired of waiting for Europe and Rome to enter their nineteenth century.

Perhaps an inquiry along these lines might provide greater insight into the problem of the scarcity of clergy in the Latin America of 1965.

23 *LARRAÍN, Latin America Looks to Catholic Action for a Program of Social Reform*

In general terms we may describe the social physiognomy of Latin America as follows:

An aristocratic class which goes back to colonial times and which maintains up to the present the psychology of a ruling class. A plutocracy—which does not always coincide with the aristocracy—generally descended from European or Middle Eastern tradesmen who immigrated after the beginning of the republican era (second half of the nineteenth century to the present). The total absence through the nineteenth century and the beginning of the twentieth of a strong middle class comparable to the European *bourgeoisie*. The populace, the product of the intermingling of races, in a debased intellectual and economic situation. Great development of large land holdings and as a consequence a peasant class which has not come of age socially speaking. Add to this another social factor of decisive importance, common to all of Latin America: the weakness of the family as an institution. Without any attempt at statistical exactness, we can cite the high proportion of illegitimately born as a social fact common to all the Latin American nations. Various causes, also common, have brought about this situation: historically, the conquerors did not marry with the Indian women, so that the first fusion of the European with the indigenous races came about under the stigma of illegitimacy; ethnically, the tradition of polygamy among the greater part of the Indian tribes of America; socially, the fact that the European immigrant of the nineteenth century came generally without his family, and hence did not bring with him a strong family tradition (unlike the immigrants of the eighteenth century, who came with their families, whence a solid family tradition which still maintains itself); materially, an irregular way of life due to the lack of an economic basis sufficient to support settled family existence.

Manuel Larraín, "Lo que espera de la Acción Católica la América Latina de hoy," *Revista Javeriana*, XLVII (Bogotá, June, 1957) No. 235, pp. 251–264, *passim*. Reprinted by permission.

Finally, we must not forget the Indian problem of most Latin American nations, in many of which the Indian is only externally assimilated to western civilization. This, then, in broad outline, is the social situation of these countries. . . .

The Latin American republics came into being during a period which was especially difficult for the Church in Europe. It was the time of the triumphs of the liberal ideas of the encyclopaedists in the French Revolution. These ideas fired the men of the independence movement. Then came the most thriving period of Masonry in Europe with its anticlerical and naturalistic concepts. Next, after the mid-nineteenth century, came the rise of socialism.

All these ideas were allowed to operate powerfully on Latin America. All the American nations can tell the story of struggles, diverse in detail but identical in their basis.

What resistance did these ideas encounter from Catholic opinion? The twenty years following the achievement of independence, when the Church was almost without hierarchy, produced a great deal of confusion in the internal life of the Church in Latin America. The crisis of the seminaries brought about a decrease of the number of priests, which during the nineteenth century came to an extremely low ebb. Hence the advance of these ideas did not meet with sufficient resistance. Three areas reflect this situation: the fields of intellectual, social and political activity. I will speak only of the first two. . . .

Latin America is a continent on the verge of profound social reforms. The terrible social inequality already described, the great proletarian and subproletarian masses which live under inhuman conditions, the continued toleration of large land holdings united to a feudal regime in rural areas, the lack of any sense of social responsibility among many of the Catholics who enjoy a comfortable economic condition, these are factors which bring home to us the urgency of taking a definite stand in this question of social reform. As His Excellency the Archbishop of Manaos said at Manizales: "Social reform will come about, whether through our efforts or in spite of them. But in the latter case, it will be anti-Catholic. . . ."

This view of the matter implies a problem: in the new world which is rapidly coming into being, does Latin America have a decisive role to play? What will that role be? Will it be an atheistic, anticlerical, materialistic role? Or will it be a Christian role, constructive and charged with hopes? . . .

The social problem has assumed an extreme seriousness in Latin America for three reasons: (a) because of the enormous social differences, greater than those which exist on any other continent, (b) because of the subhuman situation of large groups within Latin American society (the peasants, Indians, and subproletarian masses), (c) because of the rapid technological evolution of the continent, which is progressing not by easy stages, but by dizzying leaps and bounds.

This situation is aggravated by the lack of strong traditions of family life, social cohesion, and respect for labor. The Church does not have sufficient influence in the field of organized labor. The great syndical movements do not reflect a decisive Catholic influence.

Social disquiet is becoming more and more acute.

The power of syndicalism is becoming almost omnipotent.

Neither in national nor international affairs is there the least sign of a plan for concerted action. Latin America, due to the inequitable distribution of its arable lands, due to the abuses which have arisen from this cause, and due to the material and social condition in which the peasant exists, is ripe for agricultural reform at a very near date, although this may vary from nation to nation (for example, Mexico and Bolivia). The nature and inspiration of this reform depends upon Catholic international action. . . .

24 A and B Contrasting Attitudes Toward Aid by Foreigners to the Catholic Church in Latin America

24A. VIEWS OF PARISH PRIESTS IN BOLIVIA

● **1. The Social Context within which the Bolivian Church Operates.** Latin America has been called a continent in revolution which desperately needs a reformation of its socio-economic structures. Bolivia, perhaps more than any other Latin American nation, has lived for many years under the tension of a latent revolution. We are seeking new roads to the future, but all our attempts at renovation have been smothered by basic problems that our people seem to carry in their blood—slavery, domination, indifference and a strange sort of historical fatalism.

Nevertheless, some ancient structures are collapsing. The peasant masses are awakening, while a strong conviction is growing among the middle and working classes that Bolivia must break with a past which has led to ignorance, illiteracy and injustice—in other words, underdeveloped humanity.

The Marxists have found abundant material to promote their cause in the misery, hunger, malnutrition, promiscuity and illiteracy of our people. The Church has identified herself with the wealthy classes, who have interpreted Marxist prophecy only as resentment and the desire for revolution among a few intellectuals. The wealthy have blindfolded themselves to the magnitude of our problems.

And now Marxism is inspiring hundreds of teachers—to universities, primary and secondary schools, and in private educational institutions. It also dominates the thinking of many labor leaders and politicians. Marxism is presented to the oppressed classes as the only solution for our country's terrible social and political problems.

● **2. Solutions Offered to Socio-Political Problems**

a. Solutions offered by the United States:

The U.S. position is completely political. Its ultimate goal is to control the nation. Bolivia must be faithful to the political line of the United States. Politicians

"Uneasiness Among Clergy in Sucre," *CIF Reports* (Cuernavaca: Center of Cultural Formation, 1965), pp. 101–102, *passim.* Reprinted by permission.

from all parties have accepted the terms laid down by North American policy. If they don't, they soon lose their positions. Government officials depend on the U.S. aid for the budget, the sale of tin and even for the solution of such domestic problems as water, electricity and construction projects. They are forced to play the pitiful role of "good children" so that Uncle Sam will not lose his temper.

By its attitude, the United States has shown that it has no interest in Bolivia's economic development, nor does it realize the urgent need for promotion among the peasants, workers and the middle class.

b. The solution offered from within:

Bolivian leaders have obviously been influenced by Marxism. They have tried to solve the nation's problems by taking inflexible defensive or offensive positions, but have only succeeded in dividing the masses, particularly the peasants, workers and students. No constructive measures have been taken to educate new technicians, labor leaders or politicians. The result is a continual coming and going of governments, each more unscrupulous and superficial than the one which preceded it.

c. The activity of the Church:

The Church has been busy readjusting her internal structures. Her biggest problems are: 1) the scarcity of priests; 2) the poor physical and vocational quality of seminaries; 3) aid for disorganized parishes; 4) money to sustain a Catholic newspaper; 5) the lack of Catholic teachers for private and public schools. She has been attempting to solve these problems without either long or short range planning. Furthermore, her own problems have become so important to her that she has partially forgotten the drama being lived by the masses.

d. Marxism's answer:

It is widely known that even the smallest communist party has at its disposal at least $500,000 a year for propaganda purposes. With this money it exercises direct influence over our citizens, especially students and professional people. Bolivian Communists have never built a rural school nor constructed even a small medical dispensary. But, they teach in state, private and Catholic schools. They work in the universities and in labor unions. All of their activity is directed toward the masses, and naturally, their influence is heavy. . . .

We have arrived at the following conclusions:

a. Bolivia is faced with drastic socio-economic transformation. Any such transformation can take place either peacefully or through violent revolution. The Church *could* contribute to a revolution based on liberty for all. Fortunately, she is finally realizing the extent of Bolivia's social problems through her own sad experiences. The working classes are beginning to put their faith in the Church instead of Marxist leaders. Now is the time, therefore, to take positive and effective action. But the Church is faced with a serious problem: she has ignored the people too long, and has neglected to form leaders. Leaders are her greatest and most urgent need.

b. The failure of North American aid is a significant fact. Good intentions are not enough. Any aid which is not aimed at the education and promotion of the peasants and workers is wasted. The Church should concentrate her effort on creating the Church of Christ instead of dedicating herself exclusively to the construction of new buildings. The latter might someday be abandoned, used for Marxist purposes, or destroyed in a full-scale revolution. We must begin to plan for the future by carefully examining our nation's needs.

c. The awakening of pastoral activity in Bolivia is inspiring. Laymen have taught us how efficiently they can evangelize. "The poor are evangelized"—that is the ultimate goal of any pastoral program. All the effort and money poured into evangelization will never be wasted.

24B. FITZPATRICK: AMERICAN CATHOLICS AND LATIN AMERICA

The article by Monsignor Illich, "The Seamy Side of Charity," (*America*, 1/21/67) is a hard statement. The resentment it has provoked is understandable. The article does not present a new idea. It represents the culmination of a long and bitter controversy about the theory, policy and program which should guide American Catholic efforts in Latin America. It is important that it be placed in some historical perspective. The article raises very serious issues which must be given careful consideration. Americans are a spontaneous, open and very generous people. But our generosity is often unreflective. When we are challenged to examine or explain what we are doing, we easily become defensive and angry. Reflection that leads to self-awareness, however, is a blessing. And a self-awareness about our activities in Latin America can lead to a maturity and confidence that will issue in great benefits both for the Latins and for ourselves.

When Illich left Puerto Rico in 1960, due to difficulties which arose over his opposition to the so-called "Catholic" party in the 1960 elections, he immediately took steps to set up a center for training, dialogue and research which would help to link Latin America with the foreign nations which were seeking to send support in terms of financial aid or presonnel. No sooner had this center been started (The Center of Intercultural Formation in Cuernavaca, Morelos, Mexico) than the same controversy which had focused around him in Puerto Rico, began to appear on a much wider and more complicated scale. It was not a question of Puerto Rico, but the whole of Latin America at a time when the Papal request for ten per cent of the religious from the United States to be in Latin America by 1970, was generating an extraordinary enthusiasm for that area of the world. Together with religious personnel, the Latin America Bureau of the then N.C.W.C. began to promote a lay apostolic program in Latin America, whereby Catholic lay people supported from home (dioceses, organizations, schools, etc.) would dedicate themselves to three years of service to the Church. This program was given the name of the Papal Volunteers for Latin America (PAVLA).

Joseph P. Fitzpatrick, S.J., "American Catholics and Latin America," *CIF Reports*, VI, No. 7 (Cuernavaca, Mexico: Center of Intercultural Formation, April 1, 1967), pp. 51–56, *passim*. Reprinted by permission.

Illich immediately clashed with the Papal Volunteers. About twenty of them were sent to Cuernavaca for training in the summer of 1961. Half way through the course, Monsignor Illich dismissed half of them as unfit for Latin American work. This was hardly the way to win friends in the Latin America Bureau.

In relation to the Papal Volunteers and to the religious who were going to Latin America, Illich insisted on three things:

1. —They must be culturally sensitive to the values of Latin American life and seek to be of assistance to Latin American developments rather than appear to be coming to bring the answers themselves.

2. —Lay people, particularly, should not go to Latin America unless they could bring a skill or a competence which was very much needed but was not available. It was not wise to send people who had simply good will, sincerity and a desire to help, but who had nothing to contribute which the Latins did not already have. Why send an American Papal Volunteer to teach catechism when the cost of a single volunteer could maintain three full-time paid native catechists in Latin America.

3. —Care should be taken to make sure that people going to Latin America were not escaping from a problem at home. Mature, well-balanced people were needed!

In theory, most people (including PAVLA) came to agree with these guides. But, in practice, they were the focus of repeated difficulty and controversy. In the first place, the process of sending aid from the United States has often been haphazard. Everyone has talked about the need for coordination and planning, but no one has even been able to execute it. Many religious communities and some of the lay-sending organizations continued to send people to Latin America with no preliminary training, no introduction to the culture, and often with little understanding of what they were to do. I remember meeting the first three Jesuits from New England who went to Brazil. They were following an improvised language course in a Jesuit Novitiate near Campinas; and none of them had a clear idea what they were supposed to do when their training was finished. They have since settled into what appears to be a fruitful apostolate. But they did it the hard way. They were not by any means alone in their un-certainties. "Americanos" are not the only ones who play it by ear. Europeans and Canadians have often done likewise.

The German Bishops operate through a research and advisory corporation in Latin America called DESAL (Desarrollo Económico y Social Latinoamericano— Latin American Social and Economic Development). This is directed by Father Roger Vekemans in Santiago, Chile. When someone seeks aid from the German Bishops, he submits a formal proposal which is reviewed by DESAL. If DESAL recommends it, the proposal will probably be funded. If not, DESAL will seek to assist the petitioner to prepare a project and a proposal that will be funded. DESAL does not affect the sending of German personnel by religious communities or others. It supervises the allocation of funds for projects. But it represents a type of coordination which has been missing from the American effort.

For five years, we have been trying to arrange for some kind of coordinated effort between Jesuit universities in Latin America and the United States. There is still no progress. . . .

The problem of the political posture of American religious personnel suggested in the Illich article, namely: safe, reliable protectors of those interests which support the United States, is not simply a problem for American religious personnel. It is a problem for all personnel, native or foreign, in Latin America. It is not simply a religious problem. It touches every aspect of Latin life because it touches the issues related to the basic changes needed in social, economic, political and religious structures. The problem has two dimensions: 1) what social, economic or political changes should be supported in Latin America? This is a very difficult thing to determine; 2) even if determined, what part should the priest, religious or layman take in the promotion of change?

I have not met an American in Latin America, whether he or she be a religious, a businessman or government official, who does not insist every hour of the day that profound social and economic changes are absolutely necessary if Latin America is to survive. But every intelligent and thoughtful Latin says the same thing. The important point is what they mean by "change." There are two basic themes in the approach to progressive change in Latin America. There are many variations on these themes. But they may be described roughly as follows. The first theme stresses the need for profound change through rapid but orderly industrial and economic development. It promotes the development of business, largely in the private sector, which will provide jobs, open up opportunities, expand education and training, and enable the people of a nation to advance to higher social and economic levels. It stresses stability in government and the security of business investment, together with the responsibility to apply personal and corporate wealth to national development. It strives for cooperative processes between employers and employees, between business and government, between nations. The main proponents of this first theme are the new business classes, the emerging middle class that is slowly "making it," and enlightened foreign business interests who want very much to eliminate poverty by creating an economic and social structure which resembles, with modifications, the American model.

The second theme stresses the need for profound change in a rapid and radical change of structures. It ranges from an extreme Marxist, but anti-communist, position to a rather moderate position demanding extensive government involvement in economic activities, public control over private wealth and enterprise, and extensive participation of the poor in political and economic processes. It generally insists that the deep conflict of interests inherent in the present structures be made explicit; that the poor be brought to a consciousness of themselves, the injustices they suffer, the resources they can muster, and become organized to bargain from a position of strength about the political and economic structures on which their welfare depends. The proponents of the second theme are many of the intellectuals and university students who call themselves Marxist; but in its more moderate sector, it involves many of the vigorous Catholic Action groups and Social Democratic movements.

This is a deep ideological difference and within it could be ranged on one side men like Father Dan McClellan who seek to give the poor a fulcrum in the economic system through the organization of cooperatives, or Father Vicente Andrade of Bogotá who seeks to promote a strong center movement through moderate trade unions, and on the other side men like Father Alejandro Del Corro who organized TECHO, the great cooperative of Santiago, or the ill-fated Camilo Torres. In it could be ranged on one side a man like Bishop Mark McGrath of Panama, and on the other, Bishop Helder Camara of Recife, Brazil.

These are all dedicated and progressive men, but they perceive the nature and pace of change in very different perspectives. Christian Democrats generally strive to maintain a powerful center between these two strong forces, and, like Eduardo Frei Montalva in Chile, they move into power when they elicit enough confidence from both forces to get themselves elected. But it is a delicate and dangerous balance. The progressive business forces, in their fear of communism, can become overpowered by the extreme right (Brazil); the Marxist forces in their effort toward radical change can become overpowered by the communists (Cuba).

Within this maze of conflicting ideologies, it is difficult to pick one's way securely. Actually in his article, I do not think that Monsignor Illich was suggesting that American Catholics or any other Catholics identify themselves with the second theme described above. If I understand him correctly, he is criticizing them for permitting themslves to be identified with the first theme. He would insist that the men of the Gospel should be prepared to work within the framework of any political or economic system to the extent to which this is possible, but never to run the risk of giving the impression that Christ depends for His saving work on one economic or political structure rather than another.

In general, American business interests are associated with the first theme. They want extensive change, but within the orderly creation of a stable economic and political system which will enable them to promote vigorous development with a reasonable profit to themselves (what is reasonable is a bitterly debated point). The American government is seen as supporting the same interests as American business. In this situation, American priests and religious tend to take a position which is "safe" from the viewpoint of American business and government. American Catholics are notoriously absent from progressive movements even at home. They are generally very careful not to involve themselves with the Marxist forces in Latin America. They are not alone in this. Many Latin Catholics take the same position. Catholic universities in general are considered "safe" in contrast to the Marxist ferment in most of the National universities. It is interesting to note that a constant complaint of Catholic groups in Latin America is their charge that the United States Government and private American foundations provide abundant models for the support of Marxist groups, and neglect the Catholic groups and institutions which presumably are "on the American side." As a result, the people representing the second theme described above, the Marxist forces, and an increasing number of the Catholic population who are willing to cooperate with the Marxist groups, look upon American Catholics as having a character similar to that of American business and government. It is an easy leap to an identification of all three.

If this were only an association of American interests with the progressive business forces of Latin America, it would not be so bad. But the image of the United States, both that of business and government, has been badly soiled by many embarrassing involvements in Latin America. The Latins, even those of the emerging middle classes, are deeply afraid of the economic power of massive American business, and of the political and military power of the American government. The road back to confidence will be a slow, painful and often humiliating one. . . .

How is it possible for Americans to avoid this image and this identification? The effort need not always take the form it took in Panama in January, 1965, when the Chicago priests openly supported the Panamanian people who demonstrated violently against the United States. If the priests and religious are genuinely with their people, they will hardly be misjudged. But it is difficult to understand how they could be genuinely with an oppressed and struggling people without understanding, even if they do not participate in, their resort to conflict in a struggle for justice. In the struggle in Santo Domingo in the spring of 1965, even after the American troops intervened, American Peace Corps personnel were among the only ones trusted by all sides. Among other things, they took over for safe keeping the school of a group of Canadian Sisters who fled when hostilities began. Why the Sisters did not enjoy the same confidence as the Peace Corps workers is a question which should seriously be asked. The fact that they were foreign was not the critical point. It appears from reports that very few of the priests or religious even among the natives would have been trusted by the Rebels.

It is important that American business and government interests understand that, if the religious personnel are going to establish the confidence they need to work intimately with the people, particularly the poor and oppressed, they cannot be expected to support positions which appear to favor American interests. However completely convinced American business and government people may be that the American model offers the brightest hope to Latin America, this is not by any means a universally accepted position. If the impression is given that the advancement of the work of Christ depends on the establishment of the American model, the Church is in grave danger!

SECTION VI

Ideas and Attitudes

To official Washington and probably to the U.S. public as well, one of the most baffling aspects of Latin America has been the sympathy which is displayed there toward communism. Rollie E. Poppino of the University of California, Davis, presents a convincing explanation based on much study and experience. (Reading No. 25.)

Controversy over the Alliance for Progress centers on attitudes toward agrarian reform, business investment, the prices of primary products, inflation, economic integration, foreign aid, national planning. John P. Powelson, a U.S. economist, had an excellent opportunity to appreciate the divergent convictions on these topics through prolonged discussions with university students and professors in Bolivia, Mexico, and elsewhere. He sets forth succinctly his findings, which should be studied closely before engaging in discussion of Latin America's economic problems. (Reading No. 26.)

Poets and philosophers have long enjoyed a powerful influence in Latin America in both intellectual and political circles. The attitude expressed by Nicaraguan Rubén Darío in his ode to Theodore Roosevelt is still found far and wide below the Rio Grande. (Reading No. 27.) *Leopoldo Zea of the University of Mexico expresses another view strongly held by Latin Americans: there is an urgent need for inter-American understanding, but Latin America is more aware of this than is the U.S.* (Reading No. 28.)

25 POPPINO, *The Appeal of Communism in Latin America*

The apparent universality of Communist doctrine holds, and will probably continue to hold, a fascinating attraction for those educated in the humanistic

Rollie E. Poppino, *International Communism in Latin America* (Glencoe: The Free Press of Glencoe, 1964), pp. 214–15. Reprinted by permission.

tradition of Latin American universities. In this period of profound change, when traditional values and systems are being questioned, many individuals from the Latin American intelligentsia are finding that communism provides a rational explanation for the social ferment and confusion that surrounds them. Thus, even though so very many of them have not and probably will not become Communists in the literal sense, they, as internationalists and humanitarians, encounter almost no difficulty in accepting Marxist-Leninist interpretations of history and predictions about the destiny of man. They view Latin America as part of one great world that is moving rapidly toward socialism. They interpret the collapse of old colonial empires and the advances of communism elsewhere as verification of Marxist predictions. They tend to accept uncritically Communist claims that in the continuing clash between Marxists and "reactionaries" the oppression of imperialism and the vestiges of feudalism are gradually being eliminated, and they are persuaded to hope that when these evils are finally destroyed at home and abroad the millennium will be realized. There is little reason to anticipate any dramatic change in the outlook of this group.

The Communist appeal is by no means confined to the tiny minority of university graduates in Latin American society. To a broad segment of the Latin American public, many Communist views and proposals for social, economic, and political change seem neither unreasonable nor radical. The people of Latin America may be expected to continue to approve of those Communist views which they believe to coincide with their own, and to be increasingly reluctant to object to the source of proposals since they do not object to the proposals themselves. In fact, as noted above, the programs and ultimate objectives of some noncommunist parties are already virtually indistinguishable from the avowed programs and immediate objectives of the Latin American Communists. Indeed, although the overriding concern of most Latin Americans for rapid and spectacular economic growth was not caused by Communist propaganda, the Communists have been able, nevertheless, to identify themselves with this almost universal sentiment. Moreover, the Communists have no monopoly on Marxism or on the tendency to turn to the Soviet bloc to reduce Latin American dependence on the United States. Some of the noncommunist leftist parties even equal the Communists in their opposition to capitalism and to "capitalistic imperialism." The ultranationalism of many Latin Americans and the tendency to regard the United States as an "imperialist" enemy of the Latin American people exist independently of the Communists, although their propaganda hammers incessantly on both themes. Communist denunciations of present governments for their failure to satisfy the insistent demands of an exploding populace for higher living standards are no more bitter nor vehement than attacks by noncommunist opposition parties. Far more Latin Americans than can be found in the Communist movement have lost or are losing faith in the ability of the democratic process—as it is understood in Latin America—to meet the staggering socio-economic needs of the area. Many in addition to the Communists protest that Latin America has neither social justice, true political freedom, full national sovereignty, nor an adequate rate of economic progress. It seems clear that even without the Communists, much of the revolutionary program they advocate will be pursued in Latin America. By the same token, a large portion of the politically active population finds it only logical and proper that the Communists should participate in the common effort to achieve these objectives.

Preparatory techniques usually include use of the old Roman principle of *Columnare audactor, semper aliquid haered,* that is, "Always slander, something sticks." Stories attacking the government in power are invented and given wide circulation. Time-tried themes are the corruption of the officials, privileges accorded favored business interests, and treaties entered into by the government which run contrary to the sovereignty, economic welfare, or democratic traditions of the country. Small details are exaggerated and distorted until they appear as major crimes. The *Junta* strikes before the slanders can be neutralized by counter-propaganda. . . .

But what conclusions do they lead to? How can the United Nations or friends outside Latin America aid in establishing political stability and guarantees of constitutional democratic procedures in the countries to the south?

There are no easy answers. Latin-American political factors are derivative of other internal factors, including problems of economy, communication, education, population groups, and terrain. External diplomatic or economic pressures can in no way alter the internal structure of these countries.

26 POWELSON, *The Meaning of the Alliance for Progress: Conflicts of Opinion*

[It would be impossible here to enumerate all shades of sentiment that make their way into conversations, the classroom, and articles in the learned journals. But a general impression of the area of controversy can be gained by examining opposite pairs of extreme positions.]

Two sample opinions are cited below on each issue. The first set (opinions numbered 1) are held mainly in the United States, but they are also seconded by some Latin Americans, including civil servants, businessmen, and students. The second (opinions numbered 2) are heard primarily in Latin America, although a few North Americans would endorse them. They represent the group that distrusts the United States in varying degrees or believes it is mistaken in official policies. Holders of these views in their most anti-United States version, such as some students and professors in the economics and law faculties of the universities, believe most strongly that North American participation in the Alliance for Progress constitutes a revision of strategy, not a change of heart.

From *Latin America. Today's Economic and Social Revolution,* by John P. Powelson. Copyright 1964 by McGraw-Hill Book Co. Used by permission, from pp. 187–193.

ON AGRARIAN REFORM

Opinion 1. Apathetic for many years, the United States has at last awakened to the urgency of agrarian reform. Its interest stems in part from genuine concern for the welfare of the masses. But, mainly, it is aware that social justice is a requisite for avoiding repetition in other countries of the Communist inroads into Cuba. Only if peasants own their land will they have a personal stake in maintenance of political and economic institutions.

Opinion 2. The United States has never favored agrarian reform and never will. North Americans are prominent among the powerful owners whose pocketbooks will be compromised if land is confiscated. But Washington is aware that the revolutionary winds are becoming more intense, and it is no longer possible to suppress them by the traditional means. The most rational strategy is to pretend to be in favor of agrarian reform, to infiltrate the movement, and to gain control. Then it can be diverted into "painless" programs of resettlement on public lands, minor tax revisions, and a few confiscations of generally unproductive land, where the impact on the landlords will be minimal.

ON THE MARKET MECHANISM

Opinion 1. With rare exceptions, market prices are the most rational way of selecting goods and services to be produced and the people who will buy them. They respond to the desires of the people and predict the exhaustion of scarce resources. They distinguish successful ventures from failures. Any subsidies for the latter become aboveboard, and they are measured. Price ceilings and artificial or multiple exchange rates, on the other hand, not only pervert the rational use of resources but inevitably fail in their objectives. Over the long run, even the most pervasive controls can be avoided in a democratic society.

Opinion 2. Complete freedom of pricing favors the wealthy and injures the poor. Since income is a factor in determining demand, the unhampered operation of the laws of supply and demand will satisfy the whims of the wealthy while subsistence needs of the poor go unattended. Prices of basic goods and services such as transportation, electricity, fuel, food, and water must be kept low, for these are the consumption of the poor. Any foreign enterprises interfering with this *sine qua non* must be nationalized. Exchange controls are necessary for increased imports of capital goods to promote the nation's development.

ON FOREIGN INVESTMENT

Opinion 1. Investment by United States and European companies contributes to the economic development of Latin America. Foreign companies bring foreign exchange, which provides essential imports. Through their taxes, they often supply a significant percentage of the government's revenue. They share technical knowledge, train workers, and frequently pay higher wages than are earned elsewhere in the economy. They also require supplies from local companies, thus increasing demand and creating employment. Some companies have promoted Latin Americans into top management positions and have appointed them to boards of directors. Many have built schools, hospitals, and housing for their workers that are far superior to what they would otherwise have had.

Opinion 2. Foreign enterprise in Latin America has been largely of the extractive type. For whatever values it has contributed, it has taken more away. Foreign companies have acquired vast concessions in oil fields and other mineral deposits by bribing local dictators not elected by the people. They have followed repressive labor policies, often calling on the dictator to use troops against strikers, spilling their blood. Many companies do not promote Latin Americans into top positions, and when a Latin American and North American hold similar jobs, the latter often earns a higher salary than the former. Sometimes the foreign companies are more powerful than the government. They have exerted tremendous pressure to influence legislation, oppose agrarian reform, and keep their taxes low, and have even overthrown governments.

ON THE PRICES OF PRIMARY PRODUCTS

Opinion 1. It has never been proved that long-run changes in the terms of trade are adverse to Latin America. World demand for manufactured goods is increasing in proportion to that for primary products, but the absolute demand for both is rising. Commodity agreements to hold prices of primary products high are dangerous to the supplier, because buyers will seek synthetic substitutes or other ways of economizing. Furthermore, artificial prices will promote inefficient production, since mining companies and farmers will not be forced by competition to use less costly techniques.

Opinion 2. The prices of the goods that Latin America sells and the prices of the goods she buys are both set in the United States by large monopolies. Over the years the terms of trade have been turning against Latin America, so that a given quantity of raw-material exports buys much less in manufactured goods than it did in the nineteenth century. Fluctuations in the prices of primary products make it difficult for Latin American countries to plan their economic development or even balance their national budget. The United States should pay a fair price for the raw materials it buys, and this should be established by intergovernmental agreement.

ON INFLATION

Opinion 1. Inflation is caused by irresponsible monetary and fiscal management by governments. It discourages saving and impairs the quality of investment, by channeling funds into speculative rather than productive capital. It causes irrational choices of economic activity. It leads to price and exchange controls that suppress agriculture and encourage the domestic production of luxury goods whose import has been forbidden. It causes a drain on the balance of payments and leads the country into hopeless foreign debt.

Opinion 2. While runaway inflation is disastrous, nevertheless a conscious policy of mild inflation will encourage economic growth. It is, in fact, the inevitable consequence of growth, since some sectors of the economy will expand more rapidly than others, and prices will necessarily rise in the latter. But the growth of the former would be suppressed if overall price stability is required. Some say the United States discourages inflation because it wants to impede Latin American growth; the International Monetary Fund is a "lackey of the imperialists," whose objective is to strangle the forward movement of the economy.

ON ECONOMIC INTEGRATION

Opinion 1. Attempts to integrate the economies of Latin America and to establish common tariffs are bound to arrest economic growth. Less than 10 per cent of Latin American imports and exports are with other countries in the area. The bulk of trade is with the United States and Europe. Costs will be higher if Latin American countries are forced to buy from each other rather than traditional suppliers. Thus real incomes will be lower, and ability to save for capital formation correspondingly impaired. Similarly, the formation of a payments union does not justify the effort and expense. With world currencies increasingly convertible, Latin America will be just as well off settling intra-area accounts in dollars or other currencies traditionally used for this purpose.

Opinion 2. The small size of markets is a principal reason for underdevelopment in Latin America. If each of the twenty republics fosters growth of the same industries, none will become large enough to enjoy cost reductions on account of scale. Granted that the countries do not now trade with each other very much, nevertheless this need not be so in the future. Through international conferences, Latin American countries will determine which will specialize in which industry. Despite the liberalization of currencies, Latin America still suffers from a dollar shortage, and a payments union—similar to the one that was so successful in Europe—is desirable.

The United States has long opposed integration in Latin America because she did not wish to lose her export markets. Her present, mildly favorable attitude does not stem from conviction but from a resigned acceptance that integration is inevitable.

ON FOREIGN AID

Opinion 1. The United States extends foreign aid to Latin America partly from a genuine desire to help a neighbor. But more importantly, it is widely believed that foreign aid will help combat communism. This is so not only because poor people are susceptible to demagoguery but because the proper kind of aid, extended under the right conditions, can encourage growth along democratic channels. If the latter is to occur, however, certain reforms must be undertaken by the Latin Americans themselves, and aid should be made contingent upon them.

Another basis for foreign aid relates more to the self-interest of the United States. Economists have observed that high-income nations are the best customers for each other. North Americans want to promote Latin-American economic growth, because they know the Latins will then buy more United States exports, thus promoting mutual prosperity.

Opinion 2. To comprehend the reasons for foreign aid, one must first understand that the United States is opposed to economic growth in Latin America. Wages would rise, and the consequent increased prices of raw materials would be detrimental to North American industry. Furthermore, the development of consumer goods industries in Latin America would deprive the United States of markets.

Foreign aid is a means of disposing of capitalist surpluses, which arise as part of the final stage of capitalism, before its inevitable demise. In particular the agricultural surpluses shipped by the United States are intended to compete with Latin-American farmers and to retard the increase in their productivity. In other programs, the United States *gives* industrial commodities (primarily consumer goods) to politicians, who *sell* them to the people and pocket the proceeds. Thus aid strengthens the compact between the imperialists and the oligarchy and rarely filters down to the people who need it most.

Finally, foreign aid is part of the overall strategy of the United States to maintain its economic domination over Latin America. Instead of (or in addition to) United States businessmen's bribing corrupt politicians, the United States government is now doing so.

ON NATIONAL ECONOMIC PLANNING

Opinion 1. National planning is essential to economic growth in Latin America. Unfortunately, the country plans currently formulated are too heavily weighted toward a macro-, or overall, approach. They make elaborate projections of gross national product, investment by sectors, saving, taxes, and other data interesting to the intellectually curious. Such an overall plan may create a false sense of security, making development strategists feel comfortable even though they have not undertaken the less precise, more difficult, but vital tasks of seeking out and analyzing sufficient projects. Furthermore, planning may distort the government's statistical machinery. Scarce talent will be used to collect macro-type data, relating to total output, consumption, and saving. But there is a limited usefulness in analyzing the overall national economy, as opposed to studying the technical, economic, and marketing feasibility of specific projects. Statisticians would serve better by ferreting out more fundamental information, such as industrial statistics, on the basis of which entrepreneurial decisions are made.

Opinion 2. Overall national planning is vital to rapid development. Latin

America has neither the time nor the resources to make the mistakes undergone by the United States in its haphazard growth. These are evidenced by the number of business failures, with consequent loss in resources. The individual entrepreneur, unguided by national policy, will consider only the effect of his decisions upon himself, and not how they fit into a total picture of economic growth. If development is slow, as it was in the United States in the nineteenth century, the errors of such individualism are minimized, for the external conditions on which the entrepreneur bases his decision are not much changed for many years. If growth is fast, as is contemplated for Latin America, an entrepreneur who bases his calculations on what he sees about him at the moment is apt to be fooled some years hence. He will not realize what potential competitors, suppliers, or customers are simultaneously doing. But if his enterprise fits into the framework of a national plan, those entrusted with the overall direction of the economy will already have taken these factors into account.

27 *RUBÉN DARÍO (1867–1916), To Roosevelt*

The United States are rich, they're powerful and great
(They join the cult of Mammon to that of Hercules),
And when they stir and roar, the very Andes shake . . .
But our America, which since the ancient time . . .
Has had its native poets; which lives on fire and light,
On perfumes and on love; our vast America
The land of Montezuma, the Inca's mighty realm,
Of Christopher Columbus the fair America,
America the Spanish, the Roman Catholic, . . .
O men of Saxon eyes and fierce, barbaric soul,
This land still lives and dreams, and loves and stirs!
  Take care!
The daughter of the Sun, the Spanish land, doth live!
And from the Spanish lion a thousand whelps have sprung!
'Tis need, O Roosevelt, that you be God himself,
The fear-inspiring Rifler and Champion of the chase,
If you would hold us in your grasping, iron claws.
With all that you possess, one thing is lacking:
  God!

Thomas Walsh, ed., *Hispanic Anthology* (New York: Hispanic Society of America, 1920), pp. 597–598. Adapted from the translation by Elijah Clarence Hills. Reprinted by permission.

28 ZEA, Ibero-American and North American Cultures

In our times, there is much talk of international understanding. Well then, I believe we ought to begin with what is most urgent: inter-American understanding. This conference, of which the outstanding feature is the presence of those who have studied diligently the philosophies of both Americas, is already an effective step taken in the approach to a goal so much desired. It is to be wished that conferences such as this will be multiplied, in order to come to know one another better, and concomitant with this, to understand one another.

Now then, what steps must we take to arrive at an authentic knowledge of one another's ways of being—to achieve a full cultural interpenetration between the two Americas? First, I believe we should put into equilibrium the idea or ideas which each has of the other. Such an equilibration would permit us to stimulate accurate knowledge, or correct that which is not. We Ibero-Americans would be very much interested in an equilibration of the ideas which the North Americans hold concerning us. And the reverse: I believe they would be very much interested in an equilibration of the ideas which we have concerning them. Then why not bring it about? With this realized, false ideas or faulty interpretations would give way to the one thing which should occupy those who, like us, aspire to an authentic inter-American understanding—the truth.

In the countries beyond the sea, in Ibero-America, this country, North America, has always been present through the course of history, sometimes in positive form, at other times in negative. Sometimes North America has been thought of as the expression of the spirit of all the liberties; at other times, as the expression of the most crude materialism. Sometimes she has been admired, and at other times rejected. Before the consciousness of the Ibero-Americas there has passed in review the North America of Washington proclaiming the rights of man, the North America of Lincoln abolishing slavery, of Roosevelt proclaiming universal democracy. But alongside this North America there has marched one with territorial ambitions, the North America of "manifest destiny," of racial discrimination, and of imperialism. Against the first view, the defects of our own race and our peoples are plainly evident, making Ibero-America feel herself inferior; against the second, qualities become evident which before had passed unnoticed.

The history of ideas in Ibero-America demonstrates that two visions of North America have been held. On the one hand, there was the vision of our liberators Hidalgo, Bolívar, and San Martín, who found in the United States the model for what our people were to be. This same was the vision of Sarmiento, Lastarria, Bilbao, Rodríguez, Luz y Caballero, and Mora and others who found

Leopoldo Zea, The Interpenetration of the Ibero-American and North American Cultures," *Philosophy and Phenomenological Research*, IX (1948–1949), pp. 538–544, *passim*. Reprinted by permission.

themselves opposed by the so-called colonial spirit, the inheritance of the Spanish metropolis, when they tried to make of our America something similar to the admired North America. But also alongside this, one finds the vision of Justo Sierra, who admires, but at the same time fears the "Colossus of the North," which well might snatch from Mexico the last bit of her land; there is the vision of José Enrique Rodó, the Uruguayan teacher, confronted with the materialistic spirit which the North American glories in; that of the Chilean, Francisco Bilbao—over against the racial discrimination in the South of this country. That of José Vasconcelos against a race which does not wish to be contaminated.

Two North Americas have been thus present in the consciousness of the Ibero-Americans. There is the one which made Sarmiento say "Let us recognize the tree by its fruit: they are bad, bitter at times, and always scarce. . . . South America is falling behind, and she will lose her providential mission as a branch of modern civilization. Let us not hinder the United States in her march. . . . Let us be America, as the waters are the ocean. Let us be United States. . . . Let us call ourselves the United States of South America and the sentiment of human dignity and a noble emulation will conspire not to make an insult of a name with which grand ideas are associated." There is the other vision, that of Rodó, which impels him to say: "North American life describes effectively the vicious circle which Pascal presents in the eager pursuit of a sense of well-being which has no end outside itself. Its prosperity is as great as its impossibility of satisfying a moderate conception of human destiny. . . . The orphan of its own profound and orienting traditions, this people has been unable to substitute for the inspiring idealism of the past, a high and disinterested conception of the future. It lives for the immediate reality of the present, and because of this, subordinates all its activity to the egotism of personal and collective wellbeing."

At times the same mind has presented, in apparent contradiction, two opposite ideas about North America, such as those given by the Chilean Francisco Bilbao. "Those Puritans, or their sons," he said, "have presented to the world the most beautiful of constitutions, directing the destinies of the greatest, the richest, the wisest, and the most free of all peoples. That nation is in history today, what Greece was in the past—the luminary of the world, the word of the times, the most positive revelation of divinity—in philosophy, in art, and in politics. That nation has given this word, 'self-government,' as the Greeks did 'autonomy,' and what is better, they practice what they preach, attaining that which they think and believe necessary to the moral and material perfectability of the human species. . . . It is the nation which makes more discoveries, invents machines, which transforms nature more rapidly into an instrument for her service. . . . It is the nation possessed of the 'demos,' the demon of perfectability in every branch. It is a creative nation because it is the sovereign nation, because its sovereignty is omnipresent in the individual, in the association, and in the people. . . . Her free life, individual and political, and all her marvels, depend, then, upon individual sovereignty and the reason for this sovereignty—the free-

dom of thought. . . . What a contrast with South America, with what was Spanish America." But this same thinker who, faced with the good qualities of North
America feels his America to be inferior, must, on considering the defects of
the United States, feel that Hispano-America has on her side great positive
values. "Free thought, self-government, moral franchise, and land open to the
immigrant have been the causes of her aggrandizement and her glory," he said,
referring to the United States. "This was the heroic moment in her annals. Every
thing grew: richness, population, power, and liberty." "But," he adds, "despising
traditions and systems, and creating a spirit which devours time and space, they
have formed a nation a particular genius, and turning and contemplating themselves so great, they have fallen into the temptation of Titans, believing themselves
the arbiters of the earth, and even the holders of Olympus." The United States,
a nation so great and powerful, "did not abolish slavery in her states and did not
conserve her heroic races of Indians, nor have they constituted themselves the
champions of universal individualism, but of the Saxon branch of individualism."
The North, continues this Chilean thinker, has positive values. It has liberty; it
was born with it. On the other hand, the South has the slavery which she inherited
from theocratic Spain. Nevertheless and in spite of this inheritance, in South
America "there was the word, there was light in the bosom of grief, and we broke
the sepulchral stone and buried those centuries of darkness in the grave of the
centuries destined for us." After this, "we have had to organize everything. We
have had to consecrate the sovereignty of the people in the very heart of theocratic
education." But in spite of all, surpassing all those difficulties, "we have forced
the disappearance of slavery in all the republics of the south, we, the poor, while
you the happy and the rich have not done it; we have incorporated and are in-
corporating the primitive races which in Peru form almost the totality of the
nation, because we believe them our blood and our flesh, and you submit them to
a hypocritical extermination." We "do not see in the earth or in the pleasures of
the earth the definitive end of man; the Negro, the Indian, the disinherited, the
unhappy, the weak, all find in us the respect due the title and the dignity of the
human being. I have here," Bilbao concludes, "what the republicans of South
America dare to place in the balance, alongside the pride, the riches, and the
power of North America."

To sum up—the foregoing examples, to which one might add numerous others,
show how South America has taken cognizance of North America—how one
America has known another. It is partial knowledge, motivated by special historical circumstances. The inveterate despotisms of Ibero-America have made
us admire North America, the paladin of the liberties and rights of man. But the
support which certain forces of the same North America have given to those
despotisms of ours, in defense of private interests, has caused the Ibero-Americans to reject the North America symbolized by mere material comfort. Thus is
explained the apparent contradiction between the different visions of North America—the positive vision of a Sarmiento and the negative vision of a Rodó, as

well as the double vision of Francisco Bilbao. Before the eyes of a divided Ibero-America, in open struggle against her negative forces, there has been clearly shown a double countenance of North America.

Now, then, the important thing is to show, elaborating upon what was said a little earlier, one fact—the persistent presence of North America in the Ibero-American consciousness. We do not perhaps find many examples of such persistence of one country in the consciousness of another. Sometimes the presence has been positive, at other times negative, but the fact remains that there has been this presence of North America in almost the totality of Ibero-American history. Shall we be able to say the same of Ibero-America in regard to North America? I dare to declare with certainty—No!

With perhaps very few exceptions, North America has not been able to feel for South America any interest beyond a purely material one—the interest of a manufacturer in markets which furnish an easy outlet for certain products, or the interest of an industrialist in the raw materials which enable him to manufacture such products, or that of a financier who wants to broaden his field of speculation. It is of this North America which Rodó spoke, the North America which could have no interest in another Ibero-America than that of the depotisms and armed convulsions which serve her interests best. From this situation are derived the false or partial visions which in the past years each of the Americans have had of the others—visions purely negative. Little or nothing did each know of the spirit of the other. Ibero-America, feeling herself impotent in the field of the material, sublimated her impotence by considering herself the maximum expression of spirit in America, while assigning to North America a purely material role. For her part, North America saw in Ibero-America nothing but a group of half-savage tumultuous peoples, worthy only of despotic government. Mutually, the two Americas denied one another's spiritual capacity, and absolute misunderstanding came to rule their necessary relations.

Here we ought to return to our point of departure, the motive of the foregoing disquisitions, the interpenetration of the Ibero-American and North American cultures. The conference being realized here indicates that at last we are on the road leading to an authentic cultural interpenetration. This conference shows, on the part of North America, another interest which no longer has anything to do with markets, raw materials, and finances. Spirit is interested in spirit. The North America interested only in dealing with the Ibero-America of the despotisms gives way to the North America of the liberties, upon gathering here several of the men who, desiring the same liberty in their lands, suffer persecution and exile from such despotisms. And in her turn, South America, the positive Ibero-America, prepares to renew the old admiration which throughout her history she has felt towards North America, which has known how to offer the world models for institutions of liberty and democracy. This conference shows that no longer does either of the Americas begrudge the other cultural or spiritual capacity. The only thing asked is a knowledge, each time more extensive, which would permit continually better understanding.

Cultural Matters

<hr>

Anthropologists have long studied the archaeological remains of ancient civilization in America and of living Indians. Recently they have turned their attention to the contemporary culture in Latin America. John Gillin, of the University of Pittsburgh, has briefly presented his views on the emerging cultures in Latin America. (Reading No. 29.) He has elsewhere analyzed in more detail the following traditional values and changes in Latin American society: demography, position of women, emerging middle class, paternalism and personalism, labor movements, education and science, social stratification, political orientation, traditional values, family ties, idealism or transcendentalism, the place of emotions, and fatalism.[1]

Latin Americans have long studied their own aspirations and own position in the world. One of their concerns, almost as widespread as their questioning of U.S. values, has been their desire for cultural independence from Europe and their determination to make an original contribution based on New World conditions and needs. The Mexican painter José Clemente Orozco thought deeply on these matters. (Reading No. 30.)

Many foreign students of Latin America concentrate on its political instability and economic underdevelopment. The Uruguayan literary critic Emir Rodríguez Monegal, now editor of Nuevo Mundo *in Paris, urges us to look at the prose fiction if we would see the new face of Latin America. (Reading No. 31.) The writers whose works he analyzes to demonstrate this thesis are Juan Carlos Onetti, Carlos Fuentes, Julio Cortázar, Mario Vargas Llosa, Alejo Carpentier, João Guimarães Rosa, and Juan Rulfo.*

Music has long been cultivated in both Latin America and the U.S., but until after World War I there was little mutual recognition of this fact, as the U.S. composer Aaron Copland points out in a perceptive estimate of the distinctive nature of Latin American music. (Reading No. 32.)

[1] "Changing Depths in Latin America," *Journal of Inter-American Studies,* II (1960), No. 2, pp. 379–389.

Artistic development has accompanied political and economic development: "with the rush of national and social self-consciousness has come a pell-mell rush to evolve a new style, a new voice. And the voice is inseparable from the noisy political choruses around it." [2] A new responsibility has been expressed, too, for creation in Latin America rather than in New York or Paris.[3]

29 GILLIN, *Modern Latin American Culture*

Our tendency and that of most Europeans has been to identify the modern way of life in Latin America, either with some indigenous configuration or with European civilization in one or other of its European national traditions. We have persisted in viewing the Latin Americans either as degenerate Indians struggling with the ruins of a conquest-wrecked native culture or as tainted Iberians fumbling with the traditions of Spain and Portugal. . . .

The general culture of our southern neighbors seems to be neither basically Indian (except in tribally organized communities) nor is it basically Spanish, Portuguese, or "modern European"—except within the walls of luxury hotels and on the boulevards of capital cities.

Latin American seems a better term to apply to the new culture than the word "mestizo," which, although it has often been used with reference to culture, basically implies racial mixture. Although genetic hybridization has everywhere paralleled the development of the Latin American culture, it is not a necessary cause of the latter, and the use of the term mestizo tends to confuse biological and cultural processes. . . .

All are nominally Roman Catholic, and many of the details of content and organization are those of Iberian Catholicism as distinguished from the North European type: e.g., cult of the saints, public fiestas and parades, greater development of sodalities (cofradías, hermandades, etc.), more emphasis upon monastic orders. . . . The Spanish language itself with sundry modifications has become a part of Latin American culture. Ideologically this culture is humanistic, rather than puritanical, if such a contrast is permissible. Intellectually, it is characterized by logic and dialectics, rather than by empiricism and pragmatics; the word is valued more highly than the thing; the manipulation of symbols (as in argument) is more cultivated than the manipulation of natural forces and objects (as in mechanics). Patterns of medieval and sixteenth century mysticism are strong in the culture, and these patterns show no inconsistency with those of argumentation,

[2] David Drew Zingg, "The Winds of Change. A lively New Generation of Artists Is Coming of Age in South America," *Show*, No. 11 (November, 1962), p. 60.

[3] Luis Felipe Noe, "La responsabilidad del artista que se va de América Latina y la del que se queda," *Mirador*, Vol. I, No. 7 (New York, 1966), pp. 3–4.

John Gillin, "Modern Latin American Culture," in Olen E. Leonard and Charles P. Loomis, eds., *Readings in Latin Social Organization and Institutions* (East Lansing, Michigan: Michigan State College Press, 1953), pp. 10–13. Reprinted by permission.

for, as with medieval scholastics, the worth of the logic lies in the manipulation of concepts, not in the empirical investigation of premises.

. . . If we were to analyze the Latin American culture as a whole we would find a vast variety of ideas, derived from numerous sources—ideas from the Enlightenment; from the French and American Revolutions; and, more recently, from Marxism, etc. The content of the ideas themselves is in many cases not Spanish, but the patterns of argumentation probably represent heritages from Spain.

On the more mundane level of life, we see other Spanish or Spanish Colonial patterns fixed in the Latin American culture. For example, in town planning the "plaza plan" rather than the "main street" plan; in family organization, official male dominance, double standard of sex morality, functioning patterns of ceremonial kinship (godparenthood and the like); in the preeminence of the ox and the ass as traction and transport animals; in certain features of domestic architecture, e.g., the patio or courtyard in some form, the barred window, the house front flush with the street or sidewalk; in the broad-brimmed hat either of felt or straw; in the use of cloth head covering by women such as mantilla, head shawl or decorative towel, either universally or on certain ceremonial occasions (as in church); in the preference for the single-handled plow in agriculture; in specific concepts of "personal honor" and emphasis upon form in interpersonal relations; in the patterns of Roman law and certain political statuses still persisting from the colonial system. . . .

The Latin American culture in general (ignoring for the moment its regional and local subtypes and its various "phases") is still in process of consolidation. The society which it serves is a class society and the culture manifests itself in various forms which are related to the various categories of the society, as well as in geographical and social peculiarities. Thus many of the members of the "sophisticated," "cosmopolitan" set . . . might perhaps at first deny any Latin American (Creole) content in their culture, for much of their prestige depends upon their having assimilated the manners and mode of life of such "cultural centers" as New York or Paris. Yet it is probable that a careful study would reveal the presence in the higher social strata of certain cultural common denominators of the Creole culture . . . (the term most employed in that country to refer to the Latin American culture). Identification with the Latin American culture will become a matter of pride in such circles, even as it already has in many others. . . .

Latin American culture is not a servile copying of either foreign or indigenous models, but a new and vigorous expression of modern life.

30 *OROZCO, New World, New Races, and New Art*

The art of the New World cannot take root in the old traditions of the Old World nor in the aboriginal traditions represented by the remains of our ancient Indian peoples. Although the art of all races and of all times has a common value—human, universal—each new cycle must work for itself, must create, must yield its own production, its individual share to the common good.

To go solicitously to Europe, bent on poking about its ruins in order to import them and servilely to copy them, is no greater error than is the looting of the indigenous remains of the New World with the object of copying with equal servility its ruins or its present folk-lore. However picturesque and interesting these may be, however productive and useful ethnology may find them, they cannot furnish a point of departure for the new creation. To lean upon the art of the aborigines, whether it be of antiquity or of the present day, is a sure indication of impotence and of cowardice, in fact, of fraud.

If *new* races have appeared upon the lands of the *New World,* such races have the unavoidable duty to produce a *New Art* in a new spiritual and physical medium. Any other road is plain cowardice. . . .

The highest, the most logical, the purest and strongest form of painting is the mural. In this form alone, is it one with the other arts—with all the others. It is, too, the most disinterested form, for it cannot be made a matter of private gain; it cannot be hidden away for the benefit of a certain privileged few.

It is for the people. It is for ALL.

31 *RODRÍGUEZ MONEGAL, The New Novelists*

If one is looking for the new face of Latin America—not the Latin America of coups and revolutions, hunger and underdevelopment, but a new continent, groping for solutions, learning to find its way in the world—one will find this face mirrored in its prose fiction. All over Latin America—in Mexico and Argentina, in Brazil and Ecuador—new novelists are coming forward to investigate and map, with remarkable energy and invention, its complex, rapidly-changing features. But their aim is not only to record. They are trying to grasp the hidden meanings of this change, this revolution; and they are concentrating on the new man that

Textos de Orozco, edited by Justino Fernández (Mexico City: Instituto de Investigaciones Estéticas, Universidad Nacional Autónoma de México, 1955), pp. 42–43. Reprinted by permission. For a succinct analysis and description of Orozco's work, see Alfred Neumeyer, "Orozco's Mission," *College Art Journal,* X (1951), No. 2, pp. 121–130.

Emir Rodríguez Monegal, "The New Novelists," *Encounter,* XXV (September, 1965), No. 3, pp. 97–109, *passim.* Reprinted by permission.

the vast subcontinent is helping to produce. They are projecting into the future their vision of the people and the land. Like all artists, what they are seeing and describing to-day will mould the vision of later generations. Their novels are mirrors and, at the same time, anticipations. It is this latter quality that makes the new Latin American novel so exciting and original.

In the work of the established novelists of an older generation—writers such as the Mexican Mariano Azuela, the Argentine Ricardo Güiraldes, the Venezuelan Rómulo Gallegos, the Brazilian José Lins do Rêgo—American nature and American landscape so dominated man, so crushed and moulded him, that the human individual disappeared. The rendering of human conflicts was generalised; man's passions became anonymous. Abstract economic and social forces—in particular, the political power and aspirations of the ruling class—were pitted, say, against the disinherited and oppressed of the Andes, the Amazonian forest, the Argentine *pampa*. The human individual was reduced to a cypher in an inhospitable universe. Geography was everything, man nothing.

For the new novelists Latin America is now producing, the centre of gravity has shifted radically—from a landscape created by God to a landscape created by men and inhabited by men. The *pampa* and the *cordillera* have yielded to the great city. Whereas, for the older novelists, the city was no more than a remote presence, arbitrary and mysterious, for these new writers the city is the axis, the place to which the protagonist is drawn, ineluctably. The somewhat de-personalised vision of the novelists of the beginning of the century has re-acquired flesh and blood. Suddenly, powerful, complex fictional beings are emerging from the anonymous masses of the great cities. This dramatic change—it corre-sponds sociologically to the growth of the conurbations, but it also reflects the spreading influence of psycho-analysis—has not spared the novelists who stick by and large to rural themes. Even if superficially they still record the traditional struggle of man against nature, the characters they are now presenting are no longer abstractions, cyphers to justify some political or sociological approach. They are complex and ambiguous human beings. . . .

These new novelists are a good deal more than imitators of European and American models. Though linked to their originals by a continuous, living tradition, by study of their technique and vision, the new novelists combine an acute social and political awareness with a remarkable subtlety, personal engage-ment with sensitivity to other, transcendental dimensions. It is in these men that Latin America shows its face to the world and communicates its hopes and despairs. A new man is emerging from the chaos and revolutions, and the Latin American novelists are the prophets of this new man. . . .

The Latin American novel is beginning to take wing beyond its present linguistic limits. It is being translated, discovered, and discussed, as one hears, in Europe and the United States; the prizes and the editions are beginning to multiply. Some impact is being made in *milieux* rather sceptical until quite re-cently about Latin American writing. Perhaps not since the introduction of the

Russian novelists to 19th-century France, or of the modern Americans into postwar Europe, have similar potentialities existed, both for Latin American writers and for their potential readers overseas.

In the present situation of the Western novel, dominated by the arid writers of the *roman objectif* or by the secluded, private fiction of the best American, British, or Italian novelists, the all-embracing and over-confident attitude of the new Latin American novelists is worth considering. An enterprise of such vastness and courage—the summing up of a whole new society and the representation of a contradictory, not yet classified, type of man—is seldom attempted with such vigour in our days. I believe that the Latin American novelists have a vision to communicate and to share: it is the common vision of a continent, torn by revolution and inflation, but also emboldened by anger and mounting expectations, by its awareness that it is the spokesman of an emerging world. In these books the Western nations are being shown the face of a new Latin America. It is a face that is often deeply marked by crisis and bitter conflict. But it is a face that bears equally, I think, the marks of hope.

32 COPLAND, *Latin American Music*

The first thing I think you ought to know about Latin American music is that it is an art in the process of becoming. You can not be interested in it unless you are interested in growing things. Latin America is not filled with Beethovens and Bachs, and if you only like the greatest masterworks and nothing less than the very finest music will suit you, you can just forget about Latin America because they haven't arrived that far as yet. They are at the beginning of a whole creative musical development, which I think is going to be fascinating to watch, which is already fascinating to watch. But it is one aspect of their life which is definitely in a process of growth, and in thinking about it one should always keep that in mind.

The other thing that you must always remember when thinking about Latin America is the fact that there is no one music which represents all of Latin America. Latin America is a variety of countries with a variety of musics; with different solutions for different problems, sometimes for the same problems; and it is very difficult to consider the Southern Hemisphere as a single entity. When you think about South America and Central America and even Mexico you are thinking about civilizations which grew up through a variety of circumstances, some the same and some very different.

The subject of Latin American music in recent years has become a very lively one. Music festivals have been held in various centers. Most recently Washington began its series of biennial Pan-American Music Festivals, under

Aaron Copland, "Latin American Music," *Symposium on Latin America; presented by the Barnette Miller Foundation of Wellesley College, February 12 and 13, 1963* (Wellesley, Mass.: Wellesley College, 1963, pp. 181–194). Reprinted by permission.

the wing of the Pan-American Union, making use of our National Symphony Orchestra and all the best musicians in Washington.

Previously, in the late fifties, there were two festivals that I attended in Caracas, Venezuela, and there have been festivals of contemporary Latin American music in Mexico and Montevideo. It is therefore, of growing concern, and an increasing interest is being shown in the whole subject.

One of the curiosities of our cultural relations with the countries to the south of us is the fact that, to an extraordinary degree, we paid no attention to each other until after the First World War. It was as if we were mesmerized, both of us, by Europe; all culture seemed to emanate from Europe so that much of our time was spent merely in getting to know the European masterpieces. I felt a certain kinship when I met muscians of my own generation from neighboring southern countries. I felt that we came out of a similar musico-cultural background which gave us a sense of belonging together because we faced some of the same problems,—principally how you manage to establish a music of your own in a country of your own. Formerly they had been influenced principally by France. French culture has had an enormous influence in countries like Argentina and Brazil; and perhaps secondarily they have been influenced by Italy, and of course by Spain. But France especially. The whole panorama of Gallic civilization is registered on their minds very strongly, and many of the works of art that they have created were influenced, certainly up to the First World War, by various forms of French art.

Then after the First World War, instead of looking always to Europe, we began to look at each other. This sense that we had some of the same problems helped, and of course the growing musical development of the United States helped also. Suddenly they became aware of the fact that we had some thirty major symphonic organizations of high quality, that we could play their compositions here, that we could encourage publication of their works, that we could help occasionally with fellowships, and even that we were writing a music different from that of Europe and yet, naturally, partly in the European tradition.

That was all very helpful. It made for a human-plus-musical relationship which is so important if you are really going to make friends with a people and are not just acting *pro forma*.

Generally, in considering countries of colonial origin both here and to the south of us, you can identify three main periods in their musical history. The first step takes place when the Europeans come and settle in the new colonial world, bringing with them the music they loved at home. In Hispano-America the Catholic missionaries performed a major role in spreading knowledge of Western music among the peoples that they found in those countries. The situation was quite different from that in our own country, where our earliest musicians came mostly from England. Later on, during the nineteenth century, we had a great wave of German musicians, around 1848 and just after that, and then an influx of musicians from Italy and many other countries. In Latin America we witness a similar happening: at various periods the arrival of musicians from abroad who, as I say, helped to establish the whole idea of Western musical culture.

The next step is the finding of gifted musical people who are born in their native country, but decide that in order really to learn their job they have to go abroad. We had that period here, too, especially around 1890 to 1910. Even when I was a younger man than I am now, it was thought that you had to go abroad to be "finished." You could not be finished here. That is no longer true except in the sense that everybody likes to go abroad and culturally to broaden his horizons.

The young Latin American musicians all went abroad; and many of them went to France; some of them went to Germany; some went to Italy, according to their interests. And then they came back, and spread the word, from the standpoint of a native musician, of the glories of Mendelssohn and Schumann and Wagner and Brahms and later Debussy and Ravel, and even later than that, of Stravinsky and Schoenburg.

But finally we arrive at the generation, this present one, of native musicians who accept the idea that abroad is wonderful and European masterpieces are exactly that, but nevertheless realize that if they are ever to have a music of their own, if they are ever to add to the great stream of music, they have to do it in their own way, in their own country.

Now that presents various problems. How *do* you, after all, write a music that seems to express the spirit of Brazil, or even of Brooklyn? It *is* a problem, and you do not solve it just by thinking about it. Something has to be alive in the atmosphere about you that makes it possible for you to find a music which reflects the life of your own country. In that respect the individual folklores of the Latin American countries were of enormous importance. But folklorism, or the use of folklore materials, which is in a sense an easy solution, can also be a pitfall for a serious classical-minded music. It is almost too easy to sound Brazilian if you simply make use of Brazilian folk materials. The Latin American composers who first found that solution, which seemed so revolutionary in each country, would not now be accepted in quite the same way; the feeling would be that that phase had been gone through, and the problem had become a little deeper. The problem really is: How do you give music which does not quote any folklore, a sense of country? Can it be done through the unconscious use of local materials? That is a more complicated problem which is still in the process of being handled, of being thought about and worked through.

We mustn't forget that there have also been composers who have been violently anti-folklore, who feel that you limit music too much in that way, and who insist on the fact that music at certain periods in musical history has been international in style. The Bach-Händel period is an example—sometimes it is a little difficult to tell them apart and, during the eighteenth century, you might have had some trouble deciding who was an Italian composer and who was English. We are living in such a period today. Nationalism, as such, has become unpopular in sophisticated musical circles. Nobody wants to discuss it seriously any more. The last of the great nationalist composers, I suppose, was Bela Bartok. Somehow he was able to use folk materials in such a way that he transformed them. Nevertheless, the history of Latin American music is unthinkable without the important ingredient of their folk materials.

If we consider the separate countries you will see that they are quite varied. Brazil, for example, has the richest strain of folk materials. They have Indian, Negro, Spanish and Portuguese musical backgrounds to draw upon. The Negro, of course, is enormously important in Brazil, undoubtedly the most important influence. (Villa Lobos has made extraordinary use of Negro folk materials.) In Cuba they have the strong combination of Spanish and Negro materials. In Mexico, on the other hand, there is very little Negro influence because there is very little Negro population. There the mixture is Spanish with pure Indian, and the latter, which is so very primary in the makeup of Mexico is stronger than most of us know.

In countries like Peru and Colombia there is also a strong Indian basis— though different, of course, from Mexican Indians—and, I am almost certain that that is going to help younger Peruvian and Colombian composers find themselves. A country like Argentina is in strong contrast to the others because it enjoys the most sophisticated musical life. We would probably feel most at home musically in Buenos Aires. It has the atmosphere of a *big* town, with a big opera house, and a number of excellent symphony orchestras. The musical public has heard the finest artists, the best performances, a wider repertoire; obviously they are more cultivated musically. But they do not have so pronounced a basic folklore element, as is true of the other countries I have mentioned, and that fact has strongly influenced the nature of the music composed there. Chile has an active musical life, not unlike that of Argentina on a smaller scale.

When we get to the smaller countries, Uruguay, Venezuela, Ecuador, we find a picture which is influenced by their size and economic situation, and by the amount of musical activity that goes on there. In still smaller countries like the Central American ones, Costa Rica, Guatemala, Panama, you find a lack of the very basic materials out of which to make a serious musical culture. People do not appreciate the numbers of things that have to happen before you can hope to create a musical culture. An elaborate superstructure underpins our musical life, from piano tuners to xylophone manufacturers. Organized musical groups must be formed and these groups—and this does not happen automatically— have to be put at the service of the local composers. These groups, when first organized, are intent on playing standard repertoire, but gradually a moment comes when they realize that there are some local composers around who would like to hear their works. Until that moment comes, it is hopeless to expect to develop a native school of composers of any significance.

Musical superstructure would also have bearing on the training of Latin American musicians. They lack, in many areas, really up-to-date and well or- ganized music schools. That applies, not so much to the bigger towns, but it does certainly to the lesser towns. I have gone to some of the smaller towns; I have gone into their conservatories, and I had the feeling I was stepping right into the nineteenth century. Everything looked slightly musty; the teaching methods seemed not to have changed for seventy-five years; they were unaware of the latest developments in music; and one had the feeling that a good wind would have to blow in order to get things off to a fresher start before important, well-trained musicians could possibly be hoped for.

On the other hand, in a city like Buenos Aires, they are about to establish a very important school of higher education for composers. They have set it up for a mere handful of twelve composers, all of whom will be scholarship students, the course to last two years. They are going to bring teachers from abroad, as well as use local teachers, and for the first time, a fully adequate at- tempt will be made to train their own composers right there in South America. The head of the new school will be Alberto Ginastera, one of the leading com- posers of South America, now about forty-five years of age.

What is it that gives Latin American music its profile for us? As I indicated before, the first thing that comes to mind is the rhythmic element. But beyond the rhythmic element there is often a general picturesqueness about it, as in the music of Villa Lobos, for example. One senses the jungle, with its bird life; one senses thick textures and exciting "underneath" rhythm, thud-like sounds. It has a local color attraction which is dangerous ground for a composer. I say that because one can exaggerate the importance of local color, forgetting that its very picturesqueness and colorfulness tends to pall with repeated bearings.

The origins of the rhythmic life of Latin American music have not been sufficiently investigated, it seems to me. They do not seem to be purely Negro, but they are certainly, let us say 75% Negro in origin. I had the experience of being taken to what is called in Rio a *favela,* that is, a poor quarter of town. I was taken there by Villa Lobos some years ago to hear some of the typical drumming of the Negro population in that area. He was showing it to me as something very typically Brazilian, but the moment I heard it I said, "I've heard drumming of an exactly similar kind before." He said, "Where?" I said, "In Cuba." He said, "That is not possible." I said, "Yes, I am absolutely certain." And I later found that a portion of the Negro population in Cuba and Brazil had come from the same part of Africa. They were the Nyanigo Negro tribes who had brought their exciting rhythms to these different sections of Latin America. What we recognize now as Latin American in rhythm, may be, as I say, about 75% Negro in origin. But somehow the Spaniards, either through the Arabs having lived so long in Spain, or because of contact with the Negro world of Africa, or just because of something innate in themselves, produced a rhythmic texture which is a combination of this partly Negro, partly Arab, partly Spanish world. It is by nature polyrhythmic by which I mean we hear not just one rhythm, but numbers of rhythms going on at the same time. We tend to think of rhythms in a nice comfortable way, with a strong down beat; you almost always know where the strong beat is: *one* two three, *one* two three, *one* two three—no problem at all. Such rhythms can get dull unless a Chopin works with them; but that is not the Negro idea of rhythm. In the nineteenth century, composers seemed to be primarily concerned with the harmonic development of music. Beethoven greatly advanced our harmonic language, and by the time we get to Wagner at the end of the century, harmonies had become very complex. But this was done at the cost of neglecting rhythm in the sense that the Negroes were thinking about it. It would be a mistake to consider the Negroes as playing a primitive rhythmic role; on the contrary, their rhythm is very sophisticated and very complicated by comparison with our nineteenth-century rhythms.

Latin Americans enjoy polyrhythms. By putting three or four different rhythms together with, possibly, three or four different down beats, they produce an original rhythmic texture. In Cuba when they want to set up exciting rhythms they get six drummers, five of whom each gets hold of one steady rhythm of his own. Sometimes it is meshed in with the others, sometimes it is very independent. Then the sixth player is added, as a kind of "prima donna." He invents any rhythm is likes; he is completely free; he does not "know" where the down beat is. When you combine all that you get a complex, rich, developed rhythmic life such as we are not accustomed to, and I think that that is also the basis of the rhythmic excitement of Latin American music, and also the basis of our excitement with it in its most popular forms.

It is a curious thing that these polyrhythmic aspects of Latin American music happened, or rather, were brought to our attention, just at the moment that Western serious music had developed renewed interest in rhythm. One can trace its origins to Russia, with its exciting peasant rhythms not in equal metrical units such as ours but introducing rhythms of 7/8 and 5/4 at the end of the nineteenth century. Gradually that interest, by way of Russia (and Stravinsky) in serious music and this other interest by way of Latin America met, so that our music of today, in the sixties, is rhythmically a much richer manifestation than anything that had happened to Western music in a long time.

In order to make all this a little less general, perhaps I should discuss the work of some of the better known Latin American composers of today. I have already mentioned the name of Villa Lobos. Heitor Villa Lobos is probably *the* most famous Latin American composer. He died a few years ago. During his lifetime he made a great point of being an independent soul. The story goes that when he first went to Paris he made it perfectly clear to everybody that he was not coming there to learn anything. He was coming there to *show* them what he had done. That was a new note. Everyone was quite astonished, and this famous remark was repeated everywhere. Enormously prolific, and rather uncritical, he wrote more pieces than I have ever seen a list of. I rather doubt whether he himself *had* a complete list of everything that he had written. That is characteristic of the Brazilian scene, a wonderful richness, a natural human overflowing richness which makes the country so exciting. Because of the great amount that Villa Lobos wrote, his music is naturally not all of equal value; in fact, even within the same piece you will often find music of unequal value. Most musicians would agree that he was not as self-critical as he should have been.

But the good parts are very good indeed. They are vivid, they are fully alive, they are original. He had a special way with instruments, especially percussion instruments. He once showed me his personal collection of native percussion instruments—I had never seen such things before, I did not know they existed. The Brazilians seem to be especially gifted in inventing new kinds of noise makers, unearthly sounds, very peculiar, bird-like sounds. When he performed some of his orchestral works Villa Lobos had to bring with him the percussion instruments he called for in order to perform them adequately. So he is a kind of monument in Brazilian music; but, even more generally in Latin America, wherever music is known they know the music of Villa Lobos.

A younger man, now perhaps in his fifties, is Camargo Guarnieri. He lives in Sao Paulo. Sao Paulo bears about the same relation to Rio that Chicago does to New York. It is a big industrial town, lots of skyscrapers, everybody making lots of money. Sao Paulo boasts its own symphony orchestra. Guarnieri is a very accomplished musician, more careful, better trained, perhaps, than Villa Lobos, though not quite so stimulating. Guarnieri, to speak frankly, typifies a problem that I have found quite often in Latin American countries, namely, the ability to develop as a creative artist. There is something about the Latin American "ambiente" which does not help a man to develop. Perhaps there is just not enough competition. You accomplish a certain thing, everybody says it is awfully good, and then they all wait for you to do something even better; but somehow you get stuck with what was awfully good, and you keep doing that same thing over and over again. Every creative artist is faced with the problem of renewing his gift with each new work, but in Latin America it seems harder for their painters, writers and composers to surpass themselves. The stimulus within their own country that makes them want to go on to different and better things appears to be lacking. Thus, the things that Guarnieri was composing twenty years ago when I first met him and heard his work, are not so very different from what he is doing now, and that naturally brings a certain sense of disappointment; but he is a fine composer, nevertheless, and certainly at the head of the present day group of Brazilian composers.

Mexico I know probably best of all because I have been there more often than in any of the other countries. (I even once wrote a piece using Mexican themes.) Mexico is very different from Brazil, since it is a country of Indian-Spanish origins. There is something very stolid about a Mexican; you can not budge him, he is an obstinate fellow. Once he gets an idea in his head you can tell him ten reasons why it will not work; he will do it anyhow; there is a certain fatefulness in his attitude. Mexico too has by now developed its own music and, incidentally, its own symphony orchestra. The whole job of bringing Mexico up-to-date in terms of contemporary music was accomplished by one man, Carlos Chavez. Chavez has been in the United States many times, he has conducted practically all our important symphony orchestras, and is Mexico's best known composer. As a young man, he visited Berlin and Paris, with the intention of staying a while, but instead, he ended up, of all places, in New York. That is where I met him. He lived in New York more or less the way we live in Paris: that is to say, New York was his Paris, and the years he spent in New York towards the end of the twenties had a great influence on him.

He went back to Mexico and became extremely active, not only as composer but also as conductor, educator and leader of their musical life. He became the head of the conservatory; he established *the* Symphony Orchestra in Mexico City, and remained its musical director for about twenty-five years. Later he was Minister of Fine Arts under several governments. Now he is retired from that post, devoting all his time to composing or conducting. He is a man in his early sixties, full of energy and full of interest in the whole field of contemporary music, not only that of Mexico. His music is of two kinds: a piece like the *Sinfonia India* which I recommend to you (it is on records if you have not heard it) based on Indian tunes, played in a manner that is somehow suggestive of primitive music, though it is a highly sophisticated version of primitive music. It is primitive in the way that the *Rite of Spring* is primitive, and here again you may see in the relationship of Chavez' rhythms and Stravinsky's rhythms the meeting of tendencies that I was talking about in relation to Russia and Latin America.

But Chavez also has another side, a more international side, to his music. That developed later; it is a style in which the Mexican influences are less consciously present. They are there, certainly; something in the rhythmic life of the piece is not European. But the melodic materials and the harmonies are closer to those of Europe; there is no attempt to Mexicanize them as such. Basically his music gets its Mexican character from its overall quality: that persistent sticking to a point and hammering it home which I connect with the Indian psyche. Chavez himself is part Indian and part Spanish and in that sense typically Mexican.

The person who is generally named along with Chavez as being next in importance in Mexican music is Silvestre Revueltas. Revueltas had some of his composing training here in the United States. (He was also an accomplished violinist.) Unfortunately he died in 1940 in his forty-first year so that his talent never fully matured. His was a more colorful music than that of Chavez, more obviously folk-Mexican in sound. He was fascinated with the curious sonority that a Mexican band makes when it plays in a little provincial square on a Sunday morning. They have a way of playing out of tune which is absolutely unique. How Revueltas managed to recreate that out-of-tuneness, so to speak, I really do not know, but it is in his music. He loved writing for instruments that Mexicans have made peculiarly their own: clarinets and trumpets, to name a few, and had a special fondness for the tuba. He may write a piece for seven instruments, but you can be pretty sure that one of them will be the tuba.

Revueltas was not a composer of symphonies; instead he wrote a dozen shorter orchestral pieces, lively and colorful works, strikingly orchestrated and often strikingly named. One such is called *Sensemaya*. Here again you will probably hear rhythms that you may connect with Stravinsky, which he may have gotten by way of Stravinsky, but they have a Mexican insistence, a rhythmic hammering home of the point which I believe to be truly indigenous. And the overall color of it, the tunes that he uses are flavorsome Mexican tunes. It is easy to confuse Mexican tunes with Spanish tunes. If you play them a Mexican piece people will say, "oh, that is Spanish, isn't it?" And sometimes it is Spanish by origin. Revueltas' music helps to dispel the confusion, because in his music you will get some idea of what Mexico really sounds like.

Cuba, some years ago, had developed two composers, Amadeo Roldan and Alejandro Garciá Caturla who seemed to be getting the country off to a music of its own. Unfortunately both died at an early age. In more recent years they have had a composer brought to Cuba from Spain at the age of eleven, Julian Orbón, by name, who I think is one of the most gifted of the young Latin American composers. He feels very Cuban now, although he is living in Mexico at the moment. He does not write music based on Cuban themes. His early pieces were influenced by Manuel deFalla's music. It has the elegance of deFalla and some of his coloring, but also considerable originality and expertise. Incidentally, those Latin American composers who are neo-classically minded have been very influenced by deFalla, just as Americans were very influenced by Stravinsky. De Falla took Stravinsky's role in South America. If you happen to know deFalla's *Harpsichord Concerto* you will know one of the key pieces which was a germinal source for Latin Americans.

Argentina has, as I indicated, a special problem in that they work mostly without folklore materials. They will tell you that they do use their own Argentinian folklore, but to us it sounds quite Spanish, more Spanish than that of any of the other countries I have mentioned. Their leading musical family is named Castro. Of three Castro brothers, one is Juan José, a very accomplished conductor and a fine composer, his older brother José Maria, and the youngest brother Washington Castro.

The Castro brothers are the Bach family of Argentina; they have been important in the development of recent music in their country. I myself have been most interested in the music of José Maria Castro. I do not believe he has ever been outside of Argentina. Some years ago, he wrote a music that was neo-classic in character, with lots of invention, cleanly written, and that sounded well. Almost none of his music has been heard in the United States.

Luis Gianneo is another composer who also interested me when I was in Argentina. He is a man of sixty-five, very accomplished, who also writes a colorful music, not particularly nationalistic in style. Then there is the figure of Juan Carlos Paz. Paz was one of the first of the Latin American composers to become interested in twelve-tone music. He was a one man propaganda machine for the Viennese School of Arnold Schoenberg. He established his own series of concerts, taught pupils, wrote music himself, somewhat in the Schoenberg manner, and a little too dry for my taste. He became an important figure in the life of Argentina, and still is. I suppose one can say he has triumphed, in the sense that many of the younger composers in Argentina have become interested in the intricacies of the twelve-tone method.

In Chile we find Domingo Santa Cruz, who is dean of the Chilean school of composers, and head of the Faculty of Fine Arts at the University of Chile. Chilean musical life is well developed, as is manifest from the numbers of gifted men now composing there.

And now let us consider some of the composers of the younger generation. In Argentina the outstanding figure is that of Alberto Ginastera. He is a composer of thorough training, a leader by nature; a man who knows how to orchestrate wonderfully well and whose compositions are always interesting and effective. At the present time he is Latin America's best known living composer of his generation, and deservedly so.

In Mexico, among the students of Chavez the outstanding composer is Blas Galindo. He writes music a little bit too closely allied to the manner of his elders for my taste, but nonetheless, he is an interesting composer. A full-blooded Indian, no Spanish at all in his makeup, he possesses that same stolid and rather determined character of his racial forbears.

In Uruguay they have a brilliantly gifted younger man, Hector Tosar. We have not heard as much of his music here as we should. He has written choral works, symphonies, string symphonies, and chamber music. He happens to be living in Puerto Rico now, teaching at the conservatory there. We certainly should hear more from him in the future.

In Chile there is Juan Orrego Salas. Salas writes a rather delicate and elegant and rather Spanish-inspired music, not particularly Latin American unless you know Latin America very well and can distinguish between the original thing that was Spain and the thing that became Latin America from Spanish sources. Juan Orrego Salas is now in our country. He has a grant from the Ford Foundation, in order to set up a school of Latin American studies at the University of Indiana. He is very intelligent and a very cultivated musician.

In Panama there is a gifted composer whose name is Roque Cordero. Think what it must mean to be a gifted composer in Panama! I hope I am not hurting the feelings of any Panamanians here; in fact, I am sure they would agree with me The truth is that Panama is a small country and has only very limited musical resources. Cordero is the head of the conservatory there, and conductor of the local symphony. He has written me about the difficulties of obtaining and retaining players who will stay in Panama permanently. It is hard to develop as a musician under such circumstances. Cordero has done brilliantly under those circumstances. He has recently written a violin concerto under commission from the Koussevitzky Foundation here, which illustrates once again the help that we have given to Latin American musicians in recent years by publishing and commissioning works, and seeing to it that they are performed. But Cordero will probably some day wish to be part of a more cosmopolitan milieu, and, eventually, Panama will be very proud of him. Those are the crude realities—his is a name that you should remember.

In Venezuela they have Antonio Esteves. He writes a very attractive music, very lively. I heard a work of his for chorus and orchestra at the Caracas Music Festival in 1957. He is a favorite son there; there was an audience of six thousand people in an open amphitheatere who shouted for him the way I once heard an audience shout for George Gershwin. It was very exciting to be there that evening. The music is not entirely original, but there is something very spontaneous about it. It makes one want to hear it again, and to excuse whatever seems inadequate from a technical, formal standpoint. It is a little bit like Gershwin, you know. When Gershwin was alive, we tended to be rather severe with him. Those in the know pointed out that the form was not terribly good: you could tell where the seams were. He did not seem to know quite how to get smoothly from one theme to the next theme, or from one key to the next key. We were perfectly right you know, the seams are not very good. But we could not have been more wrong in the sense that it was music that the whole world loves. So one has to be very careful in judging the music of a composer who comes out of a musical background that does not necessarily supply the beautiful, finished, professional character that we think of as an ideal. Sometimes, as in the case of Gershwin, you may become a composer who is loved universally, despite technical shortcomings. When one thinks how little there is of serious music by Gershwin it is positively fantastic that people can hear these same few pieces over and over again, all over the world, and not get tired of them. Such is the power of personality.

Something of the same thing might happen to a Latin American composer, and I think of Esteves as that sort of figure.

It is of interest that the younger composers in Latin America are writing in the larger forms. Their elders concentrated too much on smaller forms. They wrote so many songs, so many short piano pieces, that they tended to shy away from facing the larger problem of writing an extended work. If there had been more symphonies of theirs that were playable, more operas, larger works, I think that their music would have imposed itself more.

It is interesting, I think, that almost all these men have been in the United States at some time or other, either just to take part in our musical life or even study here. I, myself, have had contact with at least a dozen gifted younger composers at Tanglewood, where they come to see what American musical life is like, sometimes as students, sometimes as onlookers. The Latin American field is filled with potentialities, and if you are interested in music, and if after this conference you are interested in Latin America (and I hope you are) I feel sure that there is a field there for you to explore.

SECTION VIII

Mexico

The one-party system in Mexico has been the subject of much speculation, and Professor Needler of the University of New Mexico weighs its advantages and disadvantages. (Reading No. 33.) Another important question is the role of the Leftists, here given sophisticated treatment by Daniel Cosío Villegas. (Reading No. 34.) Licenciado Cosío Villegas has shown notable catholicity of intellectual interests and capacities. Trained as a lawyer, he carried on advanced studies in economics in Europe and the United States, served as professor in various institutions of his country, Mexico, and represented it at numerous international conferences. Founder of the review El Trimestre Económico, he also established and directed from 1934 to 1948 the Fondo de Cultura Económica, one of the most imaginative publishing houses in the hemisphere. In recent years, with the help of the Rockefeller Foundation, he has embarked upon a new career as historian, by organizing a group of younger scholars who have been producing with him an ambitious Historia Moderna de México (6 vols., 1955–1964).

Many Mexicans consider anthropology an essential, perhaps the essential, part of history. Among the most widely read books on Latin America today are Five Families and The Children of Sánchez by the University of Illinois anthropologist Oscar Lewis. They are works of art as well as of research, and should be read entire to appreciate his full portrayal of poverty, but here is a useful résumé of some of his principal points. (Reading No. 35.)

The colorful and powerful murals which were painted during the Mexican Revolution were political documents as well as artistic creations. Diego Rivera symbolized the artist-politician type of those years: José Clemente Orozco viewed such a mixture with suspicion and irony. (Reading No. 36.) A young but already distinguished painter, José Luis Cuevas, illustrates the present vigor of Mexican art in his insistence on freedom of expression. (Reading No. 37.) Mexican culture cannot be easily described, but the poet Octavio Paz gives an impressionistic interpretation (Reading No. 38) in his series of brilliant essays, The Labyrinth of Solitude.

Mexico's impressive economic development has been achieved without massive aid from the U.S., and today Mexico insists on independence in reaching its own economic and political decisions. Simon Hanson, the economic specialist on Latin American affairs whose weekly letter is widely read in government and business circles, criticizes U.S. business men for not recognizing this obvious and important fact. (Reading No. 39.)

33 NEEDLER, *The Lesson of Mexico*

Mexico's political experience over the last fifty years—since the Revolution of 1910—is highly significant, not only for the rest of Latin America, but for much of the rest of the world. For Mexico has accomplished the exceedingly difficult feat of breaking out of the vicious circle of dictatorship, misery, and revolution, and finding a way to a regime that is at once increasingly democratic, stable, and progressive. Despite a relative lack of many of the social, economic, and cultural characteristics which are often treated as prerequisites of stable democracy, Mexico seems to have solved the problem of assuring peaceful succession to leadership positions, while at the same time permitting wide participation in policy formation and allowing full civil freedom.

This type of end-result is almost always the conscious goal of political leaders throughout Latin America, Africa, and Asia. While the Mexican road is hardly likely to be followed exactly elsewhere, other countries, to reach the same goal, will have to find equivalents for the solutions that Mexico has devised, for the obstacles in their paths are much the same. A study of the difficulties which Mexico has faced and how they were overcome may therefore have a generic interest, as being suggestive of some broader hypotheses about political development.

Much has been written about the seeming paradox that Mexico is clearly a democracy and yet has a one-party system; and parallels with putative one-party democracies in Africa and Asia are often drawn. I will not deal here with the question, compounded of definition and fact, whether the full complement of characteristics usually attributed to democracies can ever exist in a one-party system. It is enough for present purposes that Mexico, with her special brand of political institutions, has been more democratic and more stable, either than she was before, or than most Latin American countries have been, under more common arrangements, during the same period. Her system deserves to be judged in this relative light, rather than by absolute standards. . . .

In sum, the style of Mexican politics over the last half-century has been undergoing steady modification. The emergence of a preponderance of force on the side of the Revolutionary *status quo* and the subsequent atrophy of violence were

Martin C. Needler, "The Political Development of Mexico," *The American Political Science Review,* LV (June, 1961), pp. 308–312 *passim.* Reprinted by permission.

of crucial importance; graft and bribery had a role to perform; and the political effects of the land reform and of economic growth were significant.

The role of the official party has been, throughout the period of transition so far traversed, to contain dispute, to minimize the friction of change. The one-party system has striking achievements to its credit, which North Americans, trying to impose normative patterns familiar to themselves, generally overlook. Put briefly, the one-party system in Mexico has assured peaceful succession to power, while allowing for civil freedoms. In itself, this is a dual achievement worthy of note in Latin America. In addition, the system has permitted—indeed, has fostered—economic and political development.

Yet one must be wary of going to the other extreme, and of seeing the virtues of the system without acknowledging its faults. Mexico under the PRI is full of bossism, opportunism, favoritism, and careerism. Candidates are all too often imposed on the local party organization against its will. Too often major political figures are mere sycophants of the President.

With all its advantages—by comparison with what went before in Mexico, with what would probably have occurred in Mexico without it, with what has taken place elsewhere in Latin America—the one-party system, admirably suited though it has been to the politics of this transitional period in Mexican life, is most likely itself a transitional form. The old arguments for a system of effective party competition where a society can support it are still good ones. And the models which ascribe properties of equilibrium to the systems of two- or multi-party competition, but not of one-party dominance, are still accurate. It is unlikely, to put it another way, that in a democratic and "developed" society a one-party system can persist. By its success in contributing to Mexico's development, the one-party system may have made itself obsolete there. But it can hardly be denied that it performed its historical role well.

34 COSIO VILLEGAS, The Mexican Left

The position of the Left is difficult in Mexico because the society in which it operates is both new and receptive to the pressures of change. The Left cannot resort to the hackneyed method of destroying society with a stick of dynamite, as it might do in the petrified class systems of many Latin American countries. Unless he is a Communist, the Mexican leftist must necessarily offer remedies or progressive cures, and is forced to renounce the use of demagogic techniques, perhaps effective elsewhere, or he is obliged, if he intends to present a plan for progressive change, to show just how to implement it.

There is still another circumstance—as "special" as the foregoing one—that

Daniel Cosío Villegas, "The Mexican Left." Reprinted from The Politics of Change in Latin America, pp. 126–139, passim, edited by Joseph Maier and Richard W. Weatherhead, Frederick A. Praeger, Inc., Publishers, New York, 1964.

undercuts his position. The Mexican Revolution, in spite of all that it destroyed and in spite of how much it has created, is an unfinished work: Like Schubert's Unfinished Symphony, it has only two movements and needs at least one more to be completed. If the word "revolution" means, as already indicated, a rapid and profound transformation, it is scarcely a matter of debate that Mexico has not lived at a revolutionary tempo from 1940, let us say, until today. This does not mean, however, that in 1940 everything "the Revolution" proposed to do was accomplished; nor does it mean that the revolutionary word and gesture have completely disappeared from the political scene. On the contrary, many of the things that were to be done were left half finished when the initial, really revolutionary energy was exhausted and replaced by a cautious evolutionary approach to change. The governing group refuses to admit that this is the state of affairs and maintains that the third movement of the Unfinished Symphony still has to be written.

The Left is an amorphous group, the largest segment of which is made up of people who have never tried to define their ideas and feelings about the principal problems of the country and its leading public men. They simply feel or guess that things are going badly or that things ought to be better, that their government officials are inept or dishonest or that they lack the necessary training or the indispensable scruples of true public servants. In short, it must be remembered that governmental leaders in Mexico, the men whose public functions should put them in the limelight (deputies, senators, cabinet members, governors of states), have regulated their political behavior by two rules or principles: The first can be expressed in the popular saying "Silence is golden," and the second is that the role of the oracle is the exclusive right and property of the president. . . .

Do these disparate factions of the Mexican Left share any common ideological ground? There are, in fact, some areas of agreement. Viewed from the negative side of things, they are anti-clerical, anti-imperialist, and above all anti-Yankee; on the positive side, they are fervently nationalistic and outspoken advocates of statism, particularly in the control of economic affairs. They have other common traits, although not specifically ideological. They do not believe that there has been any real progress or general advancement of the country. For example, although they do not deny the clear statistic that Mexico today has thousands of kilometers of highway she never had before, they complain that the time, money, and effort needed for their construction ought to have been expended on something else. They are skeptical about the ability of today's or tomorrow's leaders to guide Mexico along the path they would like it to follow. The curious but actual meaning of this is that their general attitude, the little they do, say, or write, is based not on the way things happen in Mexico, but on the way they happen in foreign countries they rarely know and do not even attempt to study. The answers given by the Mexican Leftists are so plainly remote, unreal, and crude that they do not really impress anyone. . . .

The Mexican Left has exerted a good influence, although unwittingly so. . . . In Mexico, the undeniable progress, and the merciless publicity given to it by the government, creates an easy atmosphere of unjustified and unjustifiable complacency that the Left healthily denies or dispels. It is both consoling and reassuring to see the dissenter's boldness, even if, as we have seen, it is modest and risk-free, and to see a government that is tolerant and even generous. In sum, today's imperfect version of the Left may be the forerunner or seed of a more effective Left in the future. . . .

Now we can consider what elements would go into making a better Mexican Left. The first condition, I think, is intelligence, which certainly until now has been lacking—not so much because there is no keen mind in the ranks of the Left but because the few intelligent men it has have not used their wits to formulate their ideas and organize a party. One of its weaknesses—indeed, the one that has emasculated today's Mexican Left—is its irrational, capricious, and superficial reaction to national problems. The second prerequisite is of a moral order. It would be foolish to ask every member of a political faction or party to be a martyr, ready to sacrifice his life and his family's for his political convictions. Still, it is high time to admit that it is contradictory and repugnant to call for the salvation of the oppressed and the destitute when the "crusader" owns a sumptuous mansion and two automobiles and makes a mistress out of every secretary.

The third condition is intellectual and can be expressed in a brief motto: Avoid appearing the seer in the streets and the blind man at home; study and think first, and then, and only then, speak and get to work. The Mexican Left will never be regenerated as long as it preaches that Castro, Mao, or Nikita will solve Mexico's problems. Mexico might sink with all of them, but surely none of them will save Mexico.

The fourth stipulation would be for the Left to limit for the moment its role, to concentrate its attention and activity upon a single but far-reaching problem, for example, economic and social development. If it could devise a first, though necessarily rough, outline, subject to later revisions, in which both immediate and future goals are stated as clearly as possible, the new Left would almost overnight take on an authority it does not have, and will not have in any other way. In such a tentative outline, the Left ought to clarify the great question of the role of private enterprise in Mexico's march toward greater progress.

35 LEWIS, The Culture of Poverty

Poverty in modern nations is not only a state of economic deprivation, of disorganization, or the absence of something; it is also something positive . . . a way of life, remarkably stable and persistent. . . . Certainly in Mexico it has been

Oscar Lewis, "The Culture of Poverty," *Explosive Forces in Latin America,* edited by John J. TePaske and Sydney Nettleton Fisher (Columbus: Ohio State University Press, 1964), pp. 149–173, *passim.* Reprinted by permission of Ohio State University Press. Quoted material from *The Children of Sánchez* used by permission of Random House, Inc. For a detailed analysis of Lewis' work, see John Paddock, "Oscar Lewis' Mexico," *American Anthropologist,* XXXIV (1961), No. 3, pp. 129–149.

a more or less permanent phenomenon since the Spanish conquest of 1519 when the process of detribalization and the movement of peasants to the cities began. Only the size, location, and composition of the slums has been in flux. . . .

In Mexico, the culture of poverty includes at least the lower third of the rural and urban population. This population is characterized by a relatively higher death rate, a lower life expectancy, a higher proportion of individuals in the younger age groups, and, because of child labor and working women, a higher proportion of gainfully employed. Some of these indices are higher in the poor *colonias* or sections of Mexico City than in rural Mexico as a whole.

The culture of poverty in Mexico is a provincial and locally oriented culture. Its members are only partially integrated into national institutions and are marginal people even when they live in the heart of a great city. In Mexico City, for example, most of the poor have a low level of education and literacy, do not belong to labor unions, are not members of a political party, do not participate in the medical care, maternity, and old-age benefits of the national welfare agency known as *Seguro Social,* and make very little use of the city's banks, hospitals, department stores, museums, art galleries, and airports.

The economic traits which are most characteristic of the culture of poverty include the constant struggle for survival, unemployment and under-employment, low wages, a miscellany of unskilled occupations, child labor, the absence of savings, a chronic shortage of cash, the absence of food reserves in the home, the pattern of frequent buying of small quantities of food many times a day as the need arises, the pawning of personal goods, borrowing from local money lenders at usurious rates of interest, spontaneous informal credit devices (*tandas*), and the use of second-hand clothing and furniture.

Some of the social and psychological characteristics include living in crowded quarters, a lack of privacy, gregariousness, a high incidence of alcoholism, frequent resort to violence in the settlement of quarrels, frequent use of physical violence in the training of children, wife beating, early initiation into sex, free unions of consensual marriages, a relatively high incidence of the abandonment of mothers and children, a trend toward mother-centered families and a much greater knowledge of maternal relatives, the predominance of the nuclear family, a strong predisposition to authoritarianism, and a great emphasis upon family solidarity—an ideal only rarely achieved. Other traits include a strong present-time orientation with relatively little ability to defer gratification and plan for the future, a sense of resignation and fatalism based upon the realities of their difficult life situation, a belief in male superiority which reaches its crystalization in *machismo* or the cult of masculinity, a corresponding martyr complex among women, and finally, a high tolerance for psychological pathology of all sorts.

Many of the traits of the culture of poverty can be viewed as attempts at local solutions for problems not met by existing institutions and agencies because the people are not eligible for them, cannot afford them, or are suspicious of them. For example, unable to obtain credit from banks, they are thrown upon their own resources and organize informal credit devices without interest. Unable to afford doctors, who are used only in dire emergencies, and suspicious of hospitals "where one goes only to die," they rely upon herbs or other home remedies and upon local curers and midwives. Critical of priests "who are human and therefore sinners like all of us," they rarely go to confession or mass and rely upon prayer to the images of saints in their own homes and upon pilgrimages to popular shrines.

A critical attitude toward some of the values and institutions of the dominant classes, hatred of the police, mistrust of government and those in high position, and a cynicism which extends even to the church gives the culture of poverty a counter quality and a potential for being used in political movements aimed against the existing social order. Finally, the culture of poverty also has a residual quality in the sense that its members are attempting to utilize and integrate into a workable way of life the remnants of beliefs and customs of diverse origins.

The people in the culture of poverty have a strong feeling of marginality, of helplessness, of dependency, of not belonging. They are like aliens in their own country, convinced that the existing institutions do not serve their interests and needs. Along with this feeling of powerlessness is a widespread feeling of inferiority, of personal unworthiness. This is even true of the slum dwellers of Mexico City, who do not constitute a distinct ethnic or racial group and do not suffer from racial discrimination. . . .

As someone has said, "It is easier to praise poverty than to live in it"; yet some of the positive aspects which may flow from these traits must not be overlooked. Living in the present may develop a capacity for spontaneity, for the enjoyment of the sensual, the indulgence of impulse, which is often blunted in the middle-class, future-oriented man. . . . One might take exception to the trend in some sociological studies to identify the lower class almost exclusively with vice, crime, and juvenile delinquency, as if most poor people were thieves, beggars, ruffians, murderers, or prostitutes. Certainly in my own experience in Mexico, I found most of the poor to be decent, upright, courageous, and lovable human beings.

36   *OROZCO, Art and Politics in Mexico*

One of the themes which has most preoccupied Mexican muralists has been the history of Mexico. Some have enlisted themselves among one of the factions of historians and others have been independent thinkers, but all have become experts and commentators of great force and penetration. It is really wonderful. The discrepancy evident in the paintings is the reflection of the anarchy and confusion of historical studies, the cause or effect of the fact that our personality is not yet well defined in our consciousness, although it is of course perfectly defined in the field of action. We do not yet know who we are, like a nation suffering from amnesia. We are continuously classifying ourselves as Indians, creoles, or *mestizos*, thinking only of the mixture of bloods, as though we were dealing

José Clemente Orozco, *Autobiografía* (Mexico: Ediciones Occidente, 1945), pp. 99–106, *passim*. Reprinted by permission.

with race horses, and from this system of classification parties have arisen saturated with hatred, which are engaged in a life struggle, the indigenists and the Hispanists. . . .

The whole history of Mexico seems to be written exclusively from the point of view of race. Apparently the problem is to proclaim or force the opponent to accept the superiority of one of the two races, and the worst of it is that this is no domestic quarrel, for foreign pens have taken part and are taking part in the writing of our history, often for questionable purposes. The work of our historians seems like a boxing match between Indianists and Hispanists, with a foreigner for referee.

The theory that Mexico is necessarily Indian, Spanish, or mestizo is a false basis for the definition of our personality. The Spanish race is not one, but many and diverse. Spain was formed by Iberians, Celts, Romans, Greeks, Phoenicians, Jews, Arabs, Goths, Berbers, and Gypsies and each one of these groups was itself mixed. What is the race of the Spaniards and the Portuguese who have come to the Americas in the last four centuries?

In modern times other races have entered into the populations of Spain, Portugal and Hispanic America, one might say all the races of the world, and in considerable number. Nor does it appear that the American indigenes were of a single race, to judge by the diversity of type, custom, language, and degree of culture to which they had attained before contact with Europe.

The consequences of this emphasis upon the racial theory to the exclusion of all others are very grave. The antagonism between the races is stimulated. The conquest of Mexico by Hernando Cortés and his hosts seems to have taken place only yesterday. It is more alive today than the outrages of Pancho Villa. It seems that the assault on the great Teocalli and the Noche Triste and the destruction of Tenochtitlán could not have taken place four centuries ago, but rather last year, or even yesterday. . . . This antagonism is fatal because all the races are extremely proud. Not one will admit defeat or final submission. . . .

To achieve unity, peace and progress it might suffice to do away forever with the question of race; never again to talk of Indians, Spaniards and mestizos; to relegate the whole business of the conquest to purely speculative studies and to leave it where it belongs, in the sixteenth century; to treat the Indian, not as an "Indian," but as a man, equal to any other man, as we would treat a Basque or a Spaniard from Andalucia. If we must have a Department of Indian Affairs, why not a Department of Mestizo or Creole Affairs, too? These Indian Affairs remind one of a Department of Poor Devils, Department of Unfortunates Not Yet of Age who will never be able to do anything for themselves and require people of other races to think for them and provide them graciously with whatever they need. . . . A Department of the Licentious or of the Sick would be less humiliating. The indigenous race should be nothing other than one of many who have gone to make up the Hispanic race, of the same category and with the same rights as all the others. . . .

But this lovely ideal would be ruined by the indigenists. In their opinion the conquest was not as it ought to have been. Instead of sending cruel, ambitious captains, Spain should have sent a numerous delegation of ethnologists, anthropologists, archeologists, civil engineers, dental surgeons, veterinarians, doctors, rural school teachers, agronomists, Red Cross nurses, philosophers, philologists, biologists, art critics, muralists, and learnéd historians. Upon arriving in Veracruz allegorical carts decorated with flowers would debark from the caravels, and in one of them Cortés and his captains, each carrying a little basket of Easter lilies, a great quantity of flowers, confetti and streamers for use along the road to Tlaxcala and the great Tenochtitlán; and then to pay homage to the powerful Moctezuma, to establish bacteriological, urological, x-ray and ultra-violet ray laboratories, a Department of Public Assistance, universities, kindergartens, libraries and savings and loan associations. The Spaniards, instead of accepting the frequent gifts of Aztec and Toltec maidens, should have brought handsome girls from Andalucia and Galicia to be offered to Moctezuma and Cuauhtemoc. Alvarado, Ordaz, Sandoval and the other heroes of the conquest should have been assigned the task of guarding the cities in ruins so that nothing would be lost of the tremendous pre-Columbian art. The Spaniards should have learned the seven hundred eighty-two different languages then in use here; respected the indigenous religion and left Huitzilopochtli in his place; given free hand-outs of seeds, agricultural machinery and livestock; constructed houses and given them to the peasants; organized the *ejidos* and cooperatives; built highways and bridges; taught new industries and sports, all in a nice way, gently and with affection; encouraged human sacrifice and founded a great packing house for human meat with a fattening division and modern machinery for refrigeration and canning; suggested most respectfully to Moctezuma the possibility of establishing democracy, but without taking any of their privileges away from the aristocracy, in order to please everybody.

37 CUEVAS, The Cactus Curtain—Conformity in Mexican Art

I do not pretend to be a leader of the young, and I am not trying to recruit an army of rebels to storm the Palace of Fine Arts. I will limit myself to stating what I firmly believe to be the convictions of other members of my generation both in the fine arts and in other intellectual fields. . . .

Juan is a fictional character, but he is based on the actual people who swarm around our national culture. They stifle and terrify it, while those who ought to fight back are too apathetic or too frightened to speak up. . . .

Juan was fifteen years old. His father was a plumber, or a cobbler, or perhaps a minor official, one of those who, for a ten peso bribe, will settle within the legal period what would otherwise take months.

José Luis Cuevas, "The Cactus Curtain. An Open Letter on Conformity in Mexican Art," *Evergreen Review*, No. 7 (New York, 1959), pp. 111–120, *passim*. Reprinted by permission. The footnotes reproduced appear in the article. For more on the painter's life and opinions, see his autobiography *Cuevas* (Mexico: Editorial Era, 1965).

Juan was born with a talent that occurs very often among the population of the Republic of Mexico. This talent, this rich and ancient legacy, was not that of taking bribes, an infection poisoning the blood of the whole country, but of creating another, unknown world, the world of art.

Juan stood out in grade-school because of his excellent drawings. A school inspector saw them and told his teacher to encourage him. This continued until one day, Juan was given a prize and entered art school. . . .

They had taught Juan at La Esmeralda to draw simplified figures—smooth, undulant, curvilinear, with large hands and feet—and to use special effects such as foreshortening, so that certain intellectuals would say that he produced "strong" works of profound popular origin. They were not two-dimensional works. They tried to achieve three-dimensionality by an almost automatic method of drawing, a strict, uniform intensity of line. With such a formula, all is solved: it works equally well for portraying a man with a bandanna, an Indian woman selling flowers in the market, a worker in the oil fields, or one of those proletarian mother-and-child scenes which have been turned out for over thirty years without there having intervened, for the good of Mexican art, a single Malthusian or neo-Malthusian to hinder such an empty repetition of maternity.

Juan had not had access to books on the art of other countries either in school or in the public library, much less in the Palace of Fine Arts. Nor were there any museums in which he could see foreign art of the present or the past. When there was an exhibit of some artist who was not Mexican or who refused to follow the style he had been taught to believe was the only one, Juan's friends told him it was not worth seeing, because it pertained to an exhausted, degenerate culture, to inferior races that have nothing like the grandeur and purity of the Mexican race, which is the only one in the world that has complete command of the truth. . . .

But one day in a bookstore on the Alameda Juan saw an art magazine containing things very different from his own work. Some of them were unintelligible to him, and others struck him as absurd, but all of them fascinated him. "So there are artists in other countries too," he said to himself, "not just here in Mexico."

. . . He joined a national association, where both his errors and good judgment would be protected as long as he followed the line traced previously by who knows what comrade. There were conquests to be realized both in the salon and the association, and new demands to be made: "Give us more walls to decorate for the people!" Juan's two friends told him that this was the newest and clearest demand of the courageous young men who paint in Mexico, but he had read in a history of Mexican painting that it had been the hue and cry for almost forty years. However, it was convenient for him to follow the majority. Perhaps he would receive a fat commission. When the others shook their clenched fists, he did too. . . .

I have not wanted to become a Juan; on the contrary, I have fought against the Juans all my life. Against vulgarity and mediocrity. Against superficiality and

PERCY LAU

conformity. Against the standardized opinions that are parroted over and over again, without interruption, from the opening of an exhibit to the discussion afterwards at the café. I protest against this crude, limited, provincial, nationalistic Mexico of the Juans, but thus far I have been answered only with personal attacks, even though my own attacks have always been aimed at works of art and the theories behind them, never at personalities. . . .

I should also admit that the Mexico I have attacked is not the only one. There is another Mexico, one that I deeply respect and admire: the Mexico of Orozco, Alfonso Reyes, Silvestre Revueltas, Antonio Caso, Carlos Chávez, Goitia, Tamayo, Octavio Paz, Octavio Barreda, Carlos Pellicer, Manuel Bravo, Nacho López.* I am proud there is a publishing project in Mexico like the Fondo de Cultura Económica, and a rostrum like *México en la Cultura*† the expression of nonconformist opinions. I am delighted when I hear praise for *Los Olvidados* and *Raíces*§ in other countries, although both films were box-office failures at home. It is this other Mexico that encourages me to protest, because it is the true, universal Mexico, open to the whole world without losing its own essential characteristics.

There is a younger generation in Mexico with ideals similar to those I have been discussing. I wish to associate myself with it. I am not setting myself up as an arbiter, and I am not seeking disciples. I approve of many different tendencies and directions, of many roads in art . . . but only when they are free and meaningful extensions of life itself. What I want in my country's art are broad highways leading out to the rest of the world, rather than narrow trails connecting one adobe village with another.

38 PAZ, The Mexican Fiesta

The solitary Mexican loves fiestas and public gatherings. Any occasion for getting together will serve, any pretext to stop the flow of time and commemorate men and events with festivals and ceremonies. We are a ritual people, and this characteristic enriches both our imaginations and our sensibilities, which are equally sharp and alert. The art of the fiestas has been debased almost everywhere else, but not in Mexico. There are few places in the world where it is possible to take part in a spectacle like our great religious fiestas with their violent primary colors, their bizarre costumes and dances, their fireworks and ceremonies, and their inexhaustible welter of surprises: the fruit, candy, toys and other objects sold on these days in the plazas and open-air markets.

* The late Orozco was a famous painter, as are Goitia and Tamayo. Alfonso Reyes, Antonio Caso, Octavio Paz, Octavio Barreda and Carlos Pellicer are writers. The late Silvestre Revueltas was a composer, as is Carlos Chávez. Manuel Alvarez Bravo and Nacho López are photographers.

† *México en la Cultura* is the weekly cultural supplement of the daily *Novedades*.

§ *Los Olvidados* was shown as *The Young and the Damned*, and *Raíces* as *The Roots*.

Octavio Paz, "Todos Santos, Día de Muertos," *Evergreen Review*, No. 7 (New York, 1959), pp. 22–27, *passim*. Reprinted by permission.

Our calendar is crowded with fiestas. There are certain days when the whole country, from the most remote villages to the largest cities, prays, shouts, feasts, gets drunk and kills, in honor of the Virgin of Guadalupe or Benito Juárez. . . .

But the fiestas which the Church and State provide for the country as a whole are not enough. The life of every city and village is ruled by a patron saint whose blessing is celebrated with devout regularity. Neighborhoods and trades also have their annual fiestas, their ceremonies and fairs. And each one of us—atheist, Catholic, or merely indifferent—has his own saint's day, which he observes every year. . . .

. . . How could a poor Mexican live without the two or three annual fiestas that make up for his poverty and misery? Fiestas are our only luxury. They replace, and are perhaps better than, the theater and vacations, Anglo-Saxon weekends and cocktail parties, the bourgeois reception, the Mediterranean café.

In all of these ceremonies—national or local, trade or family—the Mexican opens out. They all give him a chance to reveal himself and to converse with God, country, friends or relations. During these days the silent Mexican whistles, shouts, sings, shoots off fireworks, discharges his pistol into the air. He discharges his soul. And his shout, like the rockets we love so much, ascends to the heavens, explodes into green, red, blue and white lights, and falls dizzily to earth with a trail of golden sparks. This is the night when friends who have not exchanged more than the prescribed courtesies for months get drunk together, trade confidences, weep over the same troubles, discover that they are brothers, and sometimes, to prove it, kill each other. The night is full of songs and loud cries. . . . Now and then, it is true, the happiness ends badly, in quarrels, insults, pistol shots, stabbings. But these too are part of the fiesta, for the Mexican does not seek amusement: he seeks to escape from himself, to leap over the wall of solitude that confines him during the rest of the year. All are possessed by violence and frenzy. Their souls explode like the colors and voices and emotions. Do they forget themselves and show their true faces? Nobody knows. The important thing is to go out, open a way, get drunk on noise, people, colors. Mexico is celebrating a fiesta. And this fiesta, shot through with lightning and delirium, is the brilliant reverse to our silence and apathy, our reticence and gloom. . . .

Thanks to the fiesta the Mexican opens out, participates, communes with his fellows and with the values that give meaning to his religious or political existence. And it is significant that a country as sorrowful as ours should have so many and such joyous fiestas. Their frequency, their brilliance and excitement, the enthusiasm with which we take part, all suggest that without them we would explode. They free us, if only momentarily, from the thwarted impulses, the inflammable desires that we carry within us. . . .

Our fiestas are explosions. Life and death, joy and sorrow, music and mere noise are united, not to recreate or recognize themselves, but to swallow each other up. There is nothing so joyous as a Mexican fiesta, but there is also nothing so sorrowful. Fiesta night is also a night of mourning.

39 HANSON, Mexico is an Independent Nation

"The atmosphere for foreign private investment in Mexico is beginning to sour."
. . . *New York Times.*

"I suggest that no responsible government can look at the present degree of non-resident control (in *Canada*) with any great feeling of confidence, far less complacency." . . . Finance Minister Sharp (Canada).

"Putting the squeeze on foreign companies to sell out to local interests or take them in as partner is an old *Mexican* custom . . . a recurring bugaboo for U.S. investors . . . currently the drive is on." . . . *Business Week.*

"*Canadians* should employ every possible means to buy back Canadian businesses now controlled by foreigners. At the same time the sale to foreigners of businesses now controlled in Canada should be discouraged."
. . . Former Finance Minister Gordon (Canada).

Mexico is getting a bad press in the United States. Two points are pertinent: (1) It will continue to get a bad press because foreign reporting in the United States proceeds largely by osmosis, and reporters looking for something to write about, especially on initial safari in Mexico, look at what the last piece written by someone said and then start filing, feeling that at least one piece is in the bag. And when the papers have printed the story enough times, the news magazines (Time and Newsweek) take it over. (2) This is not a public-relations problem, and it is not subject to solution by engaging public-relations men, or even "management consultants." The issue is central to Mexico's existence as an independent country. It stems in the case of Mexico as in the case of Canada and many western European countries not from simple political nationalism, but from considered judgments by fully trained and respected economists and public-policy analysts.

The situation dictates certain limits which should be respected by U.S. firms in their lobbying in Washington, lest this lobbying backfire badly on the companies. And the situation dictates maximum analysis of the national interest by the Mexicans themselves, lest the policy backfire on Mexico through poor execution. Let us examine some of the data.

The U.S. Department of Commerce finds that 10% or more of the gross national product of Mexico is now produced by U.S. controlled companies. No figure has as yet been set by Mexican economists as the limit at which point the independence of Mexico is threatened from the sheer weight of non-resident control of production. In the case of Canada, the Finance Minister has said that "no other country (other than Canada) has such a large proportion of its produc-

Hanson's Latin American Letter no. 1134. (Washington, D.C.: Dec. 10, 1966). Reprinted by permission.

tion in the hands of corporations that take direction from parent firms in other countries." There is no specific comparison to be offered between the degree of outside control that can be safely tolerated in Canada as against the degree in Mexico. Nor is there any mathematical formula which can define the danger point. But we do know that the danger point will be the farther the better the American companies can act so as to eliminate concern with the inevitable pressures from such non-resident control.

Former Finance Minister Gordon has said in the case of Canada that "I do not suggest that there is anything unnatural or unsavory about these pressures," referring to his own experience with "the influence that financial and business interests in the United States had in Canadian policy (which) was continually brought home to me." Similarly there is no evidence of unnatural or unsavory pressures by American interests in Mexico.

On the other hand, when American companies like Ford lobbied in Washington as some seventeen of them did to force Mexico to sign an investment guarantee treaty at a time when the Mexicans made it clear that they had no intention to surrender sovereignty or the supremacy of Mexican courts to the American Embassy or anybody else, they were being doubly foolish: (1) because the issue of independence and the threat of non-resident control is so embedded in Mexican foreign economic policy that any pressure of this kind has an adverse multiplier effect, and (2) because Mexico had at no time, despite its strong support of the concept of the Alliance for Progress, indicated that it was prepared to trade its independence and sovereignty for donations from Washington.

Indeed, it should have been clear to Ford and the others that at no time, despite Mexico's relatively lower standard of living and despite its capacity to use funds for social progress effectively as against the waste in other countries, had the U.S. ever shown any intention to give Mexico proportionate assistance. (See the table below.) And of course Mexico has now been cut off from donations and concealed donations, although funds are still going forth to countries like Venezuela which has an average GNP double that of Mexico, and to Chile whose Ambassador in Washington, justifying the recent purchase of modern fighter planes, boasted it has one of the highest per capita incomes in Latin America (actually higher than that of Mexico incidentally).

Disbursements:
Donations and Concealed Donations
First Five Years of the Alliance for Progress
Per Capita

Chile	$60.00
Venezuela	14.00
Mexico	2.30

Under the circumstances, to have demanded pressure on Mexico was pure stupidity and calculated in Mexican eyes to be a vindication of their suspicion that, as former Finance Minister Gordon said in the case of Canada, "we should not take our independence for granted."

This is the type of approach which demands the continuing alertness of U.S. firms. Most companies have been too intelligent to make such errors. But it is their small minority whose failure to grasp the central issues in dealing with an independent nation like Mexico as against the client states elsewhere in the Alliance that could shatter the climate of investment for everybody.

The other side of the coin was equally well identified by Finance Minister Sharp in Canada when, expressing his concern with the large proportion of production under non-resident control, he noted that Canadians must be appreciative of "the great contribution that such firms have made and continue to make to our standard of living." This clearly is the guideline governing the extent to which the formula for Mexican independence can be implemented safely.

In the case of Mexico, in 1965, the latest year for which data are available, American manufacturing and mining affiliates produced roughly $1.8 billion in goods. They remitted profits of $50 million as the reward for investors for this activity. And they produced exports from Mexico exceeding $175 million. In other words, Mexico had an extremely favorable balance of payments relationship as a result of the activity of U.S. companies. In addition to which it had the benefit to the standard of living of some $1.6 billion of U.S. enterprise-produced goods placed on the Mexican market.

Obviously, the contribution to Mexican well-being is great and any discouragement of capital inflow would require full attention from the skilled Mexican economists who have to weigh the potential discomfort of non-resident control of production against the immediate advantages in terms of standard of living.

In the table below, there is a comparison of manufacturing activity by U.S. firms in several countries. The Product-mix in each country differs but the data are of some interest:

1965 sales of U.S. Manufacturing Affiliates
(millions of dollars)

	Sales	*Earnings*	*Remittances*	*On Investment of:*
Mexico	$1,560	$62	$42	$606
Argentina	1,450	84	21	500
Brazil	1,098	64	13	668

In Canada, former Finance Minister Gordon has argued that while this is a capital-deficient area which must have more and more outside capital, "the capital still needed should arrive increasingly in the form of debt and decreasingly in the form of direct investment." Latin Americanists will recognize this as an old theme in the economic literature of Latin America, and especially in the thinking of Mexican economists. It is of course the point of impact between the philosophy of a potential threat from non-resident control beyond a certain point which prompts the "Mexicanization" effort, and the demands for unrestricted opportunity for foreign capital.

The sniping in fact at Mexico has already arisen in such journals as *Barron's* which protests the manner in which Mexican indebtedness abroad is mounting, and in the conclusion that "most Mexican borrowings abroad serve in effect to revolve existing liabilities." And *Barron's* goes on to point ominously to its ` suspicion that Mexican net exchange reserves are equal roughly to only three months imports.

Some further analysis would have been much to the point. Without serious assistance from the United States in a non-commercial manner, Mexico in the first five years of the Alliance for Progress accounted for *one-third* of the total rise in the gross national product of Latin America despite the fact that it has only one-sixth of the population of the area. It has been getting the per-capita gains in gross national product in the face of one of the most difficult population-increase rates in the area. And it has been increasingly probing for and finding the means to make the per-capita growth rate meaningful for the larger mass of the people, however tedious that job may be.

Again, when *Barron's* protests that Mexico has only 13 weeks net reserve coverage for imports, and implies the corresponding worry over the peso, it ignores the fact that this contrasts *very impressively* with the situation in our client states, Colombia, Chile, Brazil, where the reserves are much smaller and where they consist only of transfers by donations and concealed donations from the U.S. Treasury.

We would not expect either Mexico or *Barron's* to agree with us, but in terms of the overall objectives of U.S. policy and in terms of the practical balance of payments considerations, it may well be that the Mexican performance warrants a complementing of its self-help effort with renewal of concessionary financing. It has been amply demonstrated that a dollar of U.S. soft financing brings greater improvement in human welfare in Mexico than it does in any of the client states to which the bulk of the Alliance funds are being transferred en route to safe havens in Europe. In strictly practical terms, it remains true that a dollar of investment in Mexico brings better returns to U.S. investors, without the use of U.S. donations to finance profit remittances, than it does in any of the client states. And it remains true that a market on a commercial basis for $1.2 billion of U.S. exports has no chance of duplication in this area.

At year-end 1966, some conclusions emerge: (1) No U.S. firm should enter Mexico with the thought that it can eliminate the underlying premise of Mexican economic policy that a responsible government must continue to observe carefully the degree of non-resident control as a matter of protecting its independence. (2) No U.S. firm should enter Mexico with the thought that Washington can ever pressure Mexico into abandoning that thesis. (3) Even more importantly, even if it is so large a company as Ford Motors, no company should ever ask Washington to force Mexico to alter the fundamental concepts of its foreign policy—political or economic, for it must immediately backfire on the company to engage in such attempted interference. (4) It is wasteful to engage either public relations firms or management consultant firms to spew forth propaganda on the weaknesses of such policy. It is more likely that we shall see an expansion of this thesis rather than a contradiction of it under pressure or propaganda.

Mexico this year has been one of the half-dozen best world markets for U.S. exports. It is the only Latin American country where serious volumes of capital have gone from the United States by attraction to profit-making potential rather than through the willingness of the U.S. Government to assume the risk of investment. And it has become the only Latin American country *not* on the dole. It can continue to be the major market, it can continue to offer great opportunity for further investment, it has shown that it does not expropriate without just prompt and effective compensation, and it has provided profit remittances in suitable degree. But the display of concern with independence which is seen as fully in Canada as in Mexico should not be toyed with as a "souring" of the climate of investment, or as a vehicle for sniping. We are not used to the existence of an independent nation in this area but we have one now and it is the function of the business executive to recognize it and to accommodate himself to the situation.

SECTION IX

Central America

Land problems dominate the economic development of most countries in Latin America, but nowhere is the essential and inescapable poverty caused by soil exhaustion more dramatic than in El Salvador. (Reading No. 40.) Political questions cannot be treated in general terms in Central America, for the countries vary greatly from one to another. Honduras, for example, has had a rocky political history but the late William S. Stokes of Claremont Graduate School stated: "Paradoxical as it may seem, the average Honduran is to a large extent a free agent." (Reading No. 41.)

Panamanians and U.S. citizens alike tend to consider the Canal as the great fact of their relationship. Yet a deeper conflict exists, according to sociologists— a difference in culture patterns. To appreciate fully these differences, a historical perspective is necessary. The prevalence of the mistress in Panamanian society of all levels, for example—a situation to be found to some extent throughout most of Latin America—cannot be understood without taking into account the facts of the Spanish and Portuguese conquests of America in which few European women participated and the conquerors took their mates from the subject races.

This is a subject on which much remains to be said. When Latin Americans look at divorce statistics in the United States, they conclude that we have little family life and that we are a promiscuous people. The selection on Panama comes from a book by a man and wife team of U.S. sociologists. (Reading No. 42.)

The Panama Canal has long been a source of friction between Panama and the U.S., as well as an economic benefit to the world. Now, the need for a new canal brings a new question: Where shall it be constructed, and should nuclear power be used? Brigadier General Stratton, a retired Corps of Engineers officer, served as Director of the 1926–1948 studies of canal sites and construction costs, and gives his views on what should be done now. (Reading No. 43.)

369

40 PACHECO and MARTÍNEZ, Land Use in El Salvador

Cuscatlán (Indian name for "El Salvador") meaning "land of abundance" is becoming less deserving of the name. . . . Only on a small part of the land— the 5 per cent under coffee cultivation—are adequate or semiadequate conservation practices being employed. On the balance of the land the methods of cultivation used are exhausting the soil in one way or another, in the great majority of cases . . . there is only one hectare of land for each Salvadorian, of which 8 per cent is arable land, 3 per cent is flooded land, 46 per cent is fairly fertile, but not level, land, and the balance produces very little.

From this one hectare of land, the Salvadorian is able to produce approximately some 100 colons ($40 U.S. currency) per year. . . . It should surprise no one that 80 per cent of the population of El Salvador are suffering from malnutrition. . . . In El Salvador natural resources are diminishing and the population increasing. . . . Each new increase in population means a greater demand on resources, with an acceleration in losses, and the problem of education becomes increasingly difficult to solve.

41 STOKES, Political Power in Honduras

Frequently violence has led to political power in Honduras, and unrestrained executive authority sanctioned by force has been more the rule than the exception. However the subject of government is examined, by the microscope or the telescope, the result is the same. Government in action is government by *caudillo, él que manda* (the one who commands), the military man on horseback, the *doctor en filosofía* from the lecture hall. The average Honduran knows that wherever government is able to operate the final authority is the executive.

In the administrative branch, in the legislature, in the administration of justice, and in departmental and local politics—everywhere, the hand of the executive can be seen. The structure is hierarchical; the working principle, authoritarian. It would be presumptuous to assign the origin of this system to any one source. One would have to consider a large number of geographical and cultural factors; but in large measure the system is the product of Spanish schooling in social, economic, and political authoritarianism for over 300 years. The institutions of the family, church, and army were largely authoritarian, and the political institution of monarchy fostered a feudal economic system.

(40) Mario Pacheco and Alfredo Martínez, "Population of El Salvador and Its Natural Resources," *Proceedings of the Inter-American Conference on Conservation of Renewable Natural Resources, Denver, Colorado, September 7–20, 1948* (Washington, D.C. [1949]), pp. 129–132, *passim.* Reprinted by permission.

(41) William S. Stokes, *Honduras, An Area Study in Government* (Madison: University of Wisconsin Press, 1950), pp. 294–300, *passim.* Reprinted by permission.

Nevertheless, however paradoxical it may seem, the average Honduran is to a large extent a free agent, possessing the liberty to organize his household, operate his business, dispose of his property, and pursue his pleasures without great governmental regulation or control. It is therefore only within the sphere of a relatively small number of functions which the government performs that the executive's influence is absolute, or nearly so. These functions are mainly police, education, health, sanitation, and adjudication. . . .

If it can be demonstrated that the citizen enjoys considerable freedom in economic and social fields why should not one decide that the Honduran political system is highly desirable, and that it should be protected and perpetuated? The reasons are (1) that authority without responsibility has encouraged repudiation of government through revolution, a primitive expression of dissatisfaction which is socially undesirable; (2) that there is no incentive for the development of service functions through government; and (3) that the precedent of authoritarianism within a narrowly outlined sphere of activity is a dangerous stepping stone to totalitarianism.

Hondurans have repeatedly expressed dissatisfaction with their political system through revolutions, yet they have frequently said: "Our revolutions are not against principles but men." It is true that there has been general acceptance of the basic principles of the liberal democratic state since the 1880's—that is, government by the majority, protection of minority rights through equality before the law, and the welfare concept of utilitarianism. Yet Hondurans have failed to develop governmental institutions through which power can be popularly mobilized, held responsible, and changed periodically by honest and peaceful elections. For practical purposes, therefore, the "principles" represent at best long-term objectives, at worst, window-dressing for dictatorship. . . .

One cannot leave the field of research in Honduran government and politics with completely negative results. Indeed there is much to praise in both the theory and the actual working of government, which offers encouragement for even more favorable developments in the future. Racially homogeneous, nationalistic, with an economic system based on widespread ownership of land, Hondurans have a deep, almost profound appreciation of the dignity of man. Liberal democratic principles incorporated in all the modern constitutions have at least a symbolic value. The absence of a self-perpetuating social aristocracy, the fluidity and flexibility in the social classes, the large measure of equality of opportunity, all these point to considerable social and economic democracy. It is not inconceivable that the principles of political democracy, already widely accepted, will gradually be implemented. One must not forget that there has been a reasonably satisfactory beginning of a two-party system, in which the political parties are based more on principle and program than on *personalismo;* that the national elections of 1923, 1928, and 1932 were fair; that there is at least the birth of that spirit of sportsmanship in accepting defeat which is indispensable to the democratic process.

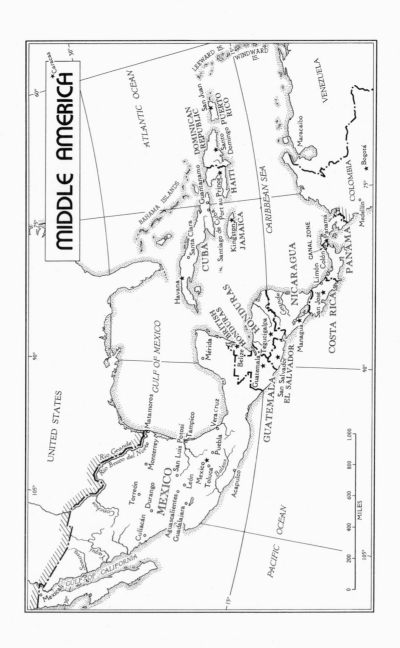

MIDDLE AMERICA

42 *BIESANZ, Panama: The "Gringo" and the "Spig"*

With caste differences placing the American in a superior position over the native Panamanians lumped with other non-Americans below, with Americans acting as if the Zone were their particular private preserve and Panamanians smarting under wounds to their sovereignty, one could hardly expect close and harmonious relations between persons of the two nations. Add to this the language barrier, differences in customs, the economic self-interest of each group, the contrasts in political systems, economic organization, levels of living, and racial composition of the two groups, and we can see that resentments, frictions, and conflicts are inevitable.

The Canal-digger of construction days worked under conditions which made home seem like "God's country," a feeling which he expressed in no uncertain terms. He had little but contempt for the "natives" who lived in such filth and disease, who did not speak his language, who were not of his race, whose moral code was different, who took life as easily as possible. They were different; therefore they were inferior. . . .

By the time the Canal was finished, the Zone had become quite a comfortable and attractive place to live, and the Americans wanted to stay and keep the best jobs for themselves. The old-timers took great pride in their accomplishment; it was *their* Canal and *their* Zone. Through the years they and their children, with a trickle of new recruits who came in slowly enough to be incorporated into Zone ways with little trouble, built up a self-sufficient community which depended on Panama for little except menial labor. Few Zonians met any Panamanians except maids, lottery vendors, perhaps a few silver workers. After decades there, many of them did not even know how to ask for a bottle of beer at the beer garden in adequate Spanish. The majority were utterly indifferent to and ignorant of the language, the customs, and the beliefs of their neighbors. Many accepted the stereotyped notion that a "spig" was an ignorant, lazy "nigger" who was none too clean, ungrateful for all that the United States had done for him, a gambler, a person of loose morals, a chiseler who thought the world, and most especially Uncle Sam, owed him a living. The Zonian thought he had assumed a fair share of "the white man's burden," for where would Panama be without the Americans? Still savage, backward, unsanitated. . . .

Except for the few Zonians they met when they ventured across the street to ask for a job, most Panamanians saw Americans only as the roistering soldiers and sailors who occasionally figured in lurid episodes, or as wealthy tourists or businessmen who kept to their own crowd. Given these limited contacts and humiliating experiences, they could hardly form a rosy picture of their "good neighbor." Stereotypes typically take form when one contrasts the ideal behavior of one's own kind with the worst behavior of the other group. The gringo was

John and Mavis Biesanz, *The People of Panama* (New York: Columbia University Press, 1955), pp. 178–181, 298–300, *passim*. Reprinted by permission.

conceived of as an immature, cocky, swaggering blond who considered himself superior to anyone else, especially to those with any Negro blood, and who enjoyed himself in foolish, rowdy ways. He was "money mad" and had no "culture." His women were loose. His nation was the Colossus of the North, run by imperialist bankers in Wall Street.

From the twenties on, the tide of nationalism rose steadily. Panamanians tried to stem the tide of Americanization. "Speak Spanish and count in balboas," reiterated Arnulfo Arias's *Acción Comunal*. They fostered pride in folk culture. They hotly defended "national sovereignty and territorial integrity" against "Yankee imperialism." They worked up a fever of resentment that simmered down only temporarily during the early years of the "good neighbor" policy, and then burned hotter than ever after the war, finally exploding in the rejection of the bases treaty in 1947.

La querida—the mistress—is found on all social levels, from the policeman or Zone laborer who tries to support two or three women and their children to the aristocrat who proves his masculinity by eloping with every lower-class Queen of the Carnival who proves willing.

The traditional seclusion of upper-class girls until marriage, the unbridled liberty of their brothers, and the existence of a large underprivileged group have made the *casa chica* (little house) a widespread institution in Latin America. In Colonial Panama, men . . . went . . . in search of premarital and extramarital adventure. Many of them recognized their illegitimate children and this gave rise to the large number of lower-class families who bear the same surnames as the aristocracy. Marriage was traditionally arranged to suit the parents' convenience; romance was found elsewhere if it did not happen to coincide with marriage. In theory concubinage has always been condemned by the Catholic Church; in practice the local clergy has done little to enforce this disapproval and in fact counsels patience and resignation on the part of wives. . . .

The *querida* is a prestige item, like a Cadillac. Men flaunt their mistresses, take other men to call on them, provide them with luxuries usually far more expensive than those they give their wives. Panamanians boast, "We do not hide our mistresses like the Costa Ricans." *Queridas* are the subject of gossip at the market and in the park; everyone seems to know all about such relationships and to tolerate them. It is generally agreed that a man has a right to as many mistresses as he can afford.

43 STRATTON, *Sea-Level Canal—How and Where*

President Johnson's announcement on December 18, 1964, that the United States is prepared to renegotiate the 1903 Panama Canal Treaty apparently has

James H. Stratton, "Sea-Level Canal: How and Where," *Foreign Affairs*, XLIII (April, 1965), pp. 513–518, *passim*. Reprinted by special permission from *Foreign Affairs*. Copyright by the Council on Foreign Relations, Inc., New York.

given encouragement to the efforts of the new Panama Government to find a basis for reconciling the differences between the two countries and has stiffened its determination to control the dissidents who have been planning further demonstrations of the kind that led to the flag-raising incident and riots of January 1964. . . .

The President's expressed interest in sea-level canal routes in Colombia and in Costa Rica-Nicaragua, as well as in two possible routes in Panama, conveys the impression that they are fully competitive. Actually, Panama enjoys a double advantage in the fact that the two best routes are both within her borders. Preliminary studies have favored a sea-level canal excavated by the use of nuclear explosives in eastern Panama close to the Colombian border. If nuclear explosives cannot be used in the construction, then the conversion of the existing lock canal to sea level is for many reasons the best solution. Indeed, it is preferable in any case.

Since the first indication some months ago that the United States was interested in several possible routes in the general area extending from Mexico to Colombia, a suspicion has developed that we would not be above playing the several countries against one another. This assumes that treaty concessions relating to the construction and operation of a sea-level canal would be the prime factor in the negotiations. Yet there is no evidence that any of the isthmian countries would yield such "rights, power and authority" as we now possess in the 1903 Panama Canal Treaty; moreover, the President's statement neither demands nor appears to expect a similar treaty arrangement for a new sea-level canal. Thus, the bargaining, if it should come to that, would seem to revolve around the factors of construction cost, the sharing of toll receipts and the managerial and administrative arrangements for the control of the canal and its operations. . . .

One of the basic decisions to be made is whether the new canal is to be dug by nuclear or conventional methods. Advocates of nuclear explosives claim that the great savings can be made in the total cost. The estimates for a canal on the site in eastern Panama range from $500 million to $700 million, of which about two-thirds would be for the excavation and the balance for the infra-structure and other features necessary for the canal's operation. The $2.3 billion estimate for the conversion of the existing lock canal to sea level by conventional methods provides approximately $1.1 billion for the control of tidal currents, the control of flood flows from streams emptying into the canal, new highways, a vehicular tunnel crossing under the canal, power and other utilities, sanitation, relocations, housing for construction workers over the ten-year construction period, and other miscellaneous items. Many, if not most, of these elements would also be required in the construction of any sea-level canal in a remote area—and remote it must be if nuclear explosives are to be used. . . .

The extensive studies conducted in 1946–48 under Congressional authorization remain relevant. Thirty sea-level routes, from Tehuantepec in Mexico to the Atrato River in Colombia, were evaluated. The recommended route was the site of the present lock canal. The estimated cost of conversion was $2.3 billion, and since then improved technology has offset rising prices so that the figure is still valid. A sea-level canal constructed by conventional methods in any other country would cost twice as much as converting the present Panama Canal.

The merits of the Panama route, which led originally to its selection by the French, far overshadow all others for either a lock-type or a sea-level canal. . . .

Far more important than the engineering factors entering into the choice of route and the dubious savings that might be made by using nuclear explosives are the political considerations involved in deciding whether to build the new canal on the present site, elsewhere in Panama or in another country. The President's statement set forth the concept of a changing relationship between the United States and Panama, in which the first step would be a new treaty to replace the treaty of 1903. Under the arrangement proposed, the United States would retain the rights necessary for the effective operation of the canal and the administration of the areas required for these purposes. The new treaty would recognize the sovereignty of Panama, provide for the effective discharge of common responsibilities for hemispheric defense and provide for its own termination when a sea-level canal comes into operation. The statement gave no inkling of the terms to be asked by the United States in entering into an arrangement for a sea-level canal and presumably these are left for eventual negotiation. Possibilities are joint participation in the operation, management by a Users' Association, or even hemispheric participation in the financing, construction and operation. . . .

The need for a canal invulnerable to attack and of sufficient capacity to meet the growing needs of commerce is becoming increasingly acute. A single sea-level canal could handle all traffic in the foreseeable future, and it would be needlessly expensive to keep the existing canal in service if a sea-level canal is constructed elsewhere. But to abandon the existing canal would seriously disrupt the large sector of the Panamanian economy which depends on the present Canal Zone. The Canal is Panama's largest industry and its largest employer. As has often been noted, the withdrawal of the United States would be a catastrophe for the Panamanians. This would be true whether it was preliminary to opening a new canal in another Latin American country or building a new canal elsewhere in Panama. . . .

Since the cost of construction does not weigh heavily, if at all, in making the choice of route, and since the United States is unlikely to obtain from any other country more favorable treaty arrangements than it can from Panama, the question must be asked: What purpose will be accomplished by the extensive route studies now proposed? Is there not the possibility that we will be accused of playing one country against the other and that we will thereby alienate many of our Latin American friends? We can well afford to be generous with Panama, as the President has indicated we are prepared to be. It will then be up to Panama to accept the President's offer in the spirit in which it was tendered. The conversion of the existing canal is the best possible solution, and there can be no excuse for failure to achieve it.

The Cuban Revolution

The French Revolution still engages historians in lively disputation, and the Cuban Revolution will certainly have a similar effect. Today, therefore, while the Revolution goes on and while documentation is only partially available, the assessments must be tentative. The Declaration of Havana (Reading No. 44) gives a comprehensive view of the objectives of the Revolution. Castro has spoken millions of words, but his speech before the United Nations on Sept. 26, 1960 (Reading No. 45) is probably a fair sample of his explanation for a world audience of how the Revolution came. The English writer Hugh Thomas, who has already proved his competence in dealing with complicated questions upon which men differ passionately in The Spanish Civil War, *gives (Reading No. 46) a careful analysis with historical depth. What to do with Cuba is a puzzle to many people, and Senator Fulbright has a provocative answer. (Reading No. 47.) As chairman of the Senate Foreign Relations Committee, he has long aimed "to stimulate public thought and discussion free of the rigid and outdated stereotypes which stultify many of our foreign policy makers," by trying out what he terms "unthinkable thoughts" such as his remarks on Cuba.*

44   *Declaration of Havana*

The people of Cuba, free territory of America, acting with the inalienable powers that flow from an effective exercise of their sovereignty through direct,

Declaration of Havana (Peking: Foreign Languages Press, 1962), pp. 1–8, *passim.* Other material published in Peking in English includes Fidel Castro's remarks on various occasions: *Closing Speech to the Congress of Women of the Americas* (1964); *Some Problems on the Methods and Forms of Work of the ORI* (1963); *Speech at the Mass Rally in Celebration of the Fourth Anniversary of the Cuban Revolution* (1964); *Television Speech Delivered on November 1, 1962* (1963). All of these items were also issued in French and Spanish, and some were published in Arabic and Japanese. Ernesto (Ché) Guevara's *Guerrilla Warfare: A Method* (1964) had previously been translated into Chinese for *Renmin Ribas* (*People's Daily*).

public and universal suffrage, have formed themselves in National General Assembly close to the monument and memory of José Martí.

The National General Assembly of the People of Cuba, as its own act and as an expression of the sense of the people of Our America:

1) Condemns in its entirety the so-called "Declaration of San José, Costa Rica," a document that offends, under dictation from the imperialism of North America, the sovereignty and dignity of the other peoples of the Continent and the right of each nation to self-determination.

2) The National General Assembly of the People of Cuba strongly condemns the imperialism of North America for its gross and criminal domination, lasting for more than a century, of all the peoples of Latin America, who more than once have seen the soil of Mexico, Nicaragua, Haiti, Santo Domingo and Cuba invaded; who have lost to a greedy imperialism such wide and rich lands as Texas, such vital strategic zones as the Panama Canal, and even, as in the case of Puerto Rico, entire countries converted into territories of occupation; who have suffered the insults of the Marines toward our wives and daughters and toward the most cherished memorials of the history of our lands, among them the figure of José Martí.

That domination, built upon superior military power, upon unfair treaties and upon the shameful collaboration of traitorous governments, has for more than a hundred years made of Our America—the America that Bolívar, Hidalgo, Juárez, San Martín, O'Higgins, Sucre and Martí wished to see free—a zone of exploitation, a backyard in the financial and political empire of the United States, a reserve supply of votes in international organizations where we of the Latin American countries have always been regarded as beasts of burden to a "rough and brutal North that despises us." . . .

3) The National General Assembly of the People of Cuba rejects as well the attempt to perpetuate the Monroe Doctrine, until now utilized "to extend the dominion in America" of greedy imperialist, as José Martí foresaw, and to inject more easily "the poison of loans, of canals and railroads," also denounced by José Martí long ago. Therefore, in defiance of that false Pan-Americanism which is merely prostration of spineless governments before Washington and rule over the interests of our peoples by the monopolies of the United States, the Assembly of the People of Cuba proclaims the liberating Latin-Americanism of Martí and Benito Juárez. Further, while extending the hand of friendship to the people of the United States of America—a people that includes persecuted intellectuals, Negroes theatened with lynchings, and workers subjected to the control of gangsters—the Assembly reaffirms its will to march "with the whole world and not just a part of it."

4) The National General Assembly of the People of Cuba declares that the spontaneous offer of the Soviet Union to help Cuba if our country is attacked by imperialist military forces cannot be considered an act of intervention, but rather an open act of solidarity. . . .

5) The National General Assembly of the People of Cuba denies absolutely that there has existed on the part of the Soviet Union and the People's Republic of

China any aim "to make use of the economic, political and social situation in Cuba . . . in order to break continental unity and to endanger hemispheric unity." . . .

6) The National General Assembly of the People of Cuba—confident that it is expressing the general opinion of the peoples of Latin America—affirms that democracy is not compatible with financial oligarchy; with discrimination against the Negro; with disturbances by a Ku Klux Klan; nor with the persecution that drove scientists like Oppenheimer from their posts, deprived the world for years of the marvelous voice of Paul Robeson, held prisoner in his own country, and sent the Rosenbergs to their death against the protests of a shocked world including the appeals of many governments and of Pope Pius XII.

The National General Assembly of the People of Cuba expresses the Cuban conviction that democracy does not consist solely in elections that are nearly always managed by rich landowners and professional politicians to produce fictitious results, but rather in the right of citizens to determine, as this Assembly of the People is now doing, their own destiny. Furthermore, democracy will come to exist in Latin America only when people are really free to make choices, when the poor are not reduced—by hunger, social discrimination, illiteracy and the judicial system—to sinister desperation. . . .

We certify that this Declaration of Havana was read and approved by the National General Assembly of the People of Cuba, held in the Martí Plaza, Havana, Cuba, Free Territory of America, on 2 September 1960.

OSVALDO DORTICÓS TORRADO,   FIDEL CASTRO RUZ,
President   Prime Minister

45 CASTRO, The Purpose of the Revolution in Cuba

The problem of Cuba? Some representatives are perhaps well-informed; some of them not so well—it depends on your sources of information—but there is no doubt that for the world as a whole the Cuban problem is one that has arisen in the last two years; it is a new problem. Formerly the world had little reason to know that Cuba existed. To many people it was rather like an appendix to the United States. Even for many citizens of this country, Cuba was a colony of the United States. It was not so on the map. On the map we were shown in a different colour from the United States; in reality, we were a colony. . . .

The Government of Fulgencio Batista was a typical government of force, a government which suited the United States monopolies in Cuba. But it was not, of course, the type of government which suited the Cuban people. With great loss of life and much sacrifice the Cuban people overthrew that Government.

What did the revolution find after it succeeded in Cuba? What wonders did it

United Nations. *Official Records of the General Assembly.* Fifteenth Session, Part I, Vol. I (1960), pp. 117–136.

find? If found, first of all, that 600,000 Cubans fit for work were permanently un-employed—a figure which is, in proportion, equal to the number of unemployed in the United States at the time of the great depression which shook this country and almost led to disaster. Three million people, out of a total population of a little over 6 million, had no electric light and enjoyed none of the benefits and comforts of electricity. Three and a half million people, out of a total population of a little over 6 million, were living in hovels and huts unfit for human habitation. In the towns rents accounted for as much as one third of family incomes. Electricity rates and rents were among the highest in the world.

Thirty-seven and a half per cent of our population were illiterate, unable to read or write. Seventy per cent of the children in the rural areas were without teachers. Two per cent of our population were suffering from tuberculosis, that is to say, 100,000 people out of a total of a little over 6 million. Ninety-five per cent of the children in rural areas were suffering from diseases caused by parasites. Infant mortality was consequently very high. The average life span was very short. In addition, 85 per cent of small farmers were paying rent for their lands amount-ing to as much as 30 per cent of their gross incomes, while 1½ per cent of all the landowners controlled 46 per cent of the total area of the country. The proportion of hospital beds to the number of inhabitants of the country was ludicrous when compared with countries with average medical services. Public utilities, electricity and telephone companies were owned by United States monopolies. A large part of the banking and import business, the oil refineries, the greater part of the sugar production, the best land, and the chief industries of all types in Cuba belonged to United States companies. In the last ten years, the balance of payments between Cuba and the United States has been in the latter's favour to the extent of $1,000 million, and that does not take into account the millions and hundreds of millions of dollars removed from the public treasury by the corrupt and tyrannical rulers and deposited in United States or European banks. One thousand million dollars in ten years! The poor and underdeveloped country of the Caribbean, with 600,000 unemployed, contributing to the economic development of the most highly indus-trialized country in the world!

That was the situation which confronted us; a situation which is not unknown to many of the countries represented in this Assembly because, in the final analysis, what we have said about Cuba is merely a general X-ray photograph, so to speak, which is valid for the majority of countries represented here. . . .

In short, we are for all the noble aspirations of all the peoples. That is our position. We are and always shall be for everything just; against colonialism, exploi-tation, monopolies, militarism, the arms race, and warmongering. We shall always be against those things. That will be our position.

To conclude, in performing what we regard as our duty, I quote to this Assem-bly the essential part of the Havana Declaration. The Havana Declaration was the Cuban people's answer to the Declaration of San José, Costa Rica.* Not ten, nor

* August 28, 1961, a conference of the Organization of American States approved this Declaration rejecting U.S.S.R. and Chinese communist influence in the hemisphere without mentioning Cuba. [Ed.]

100, nor 100,000, but more than 1 million Cubans gathered together. Whoever doubts it may go and count them at the next mass meeting or general assembly that we hold in Cuba, assured that they are going to see the spectacle of a fervent and informed people, which they rarely had the opportunity of seeing, and which is seen only when a people is ardently defending its most sacred interests.

At that assembly, which was convened in response to the Declaration of Costa Rica, these principles were proclaimed, in consultation with the people and by the acclamation of the people, as the principles of the Cuban revolution.

The national general assembly of the Cuban people condemns large-scale landowning as a source of poverty for the peasant and a backward and inhuman system of agricultural production; it condemns starvation wages and the iniquitous exploitation of human labour by illegitimate and privileged interests; it condemns illiteracy, the lack of teachers, schools, doctors and hospitals; the lack of assistance to the aged in the American countries; it condemns discrimination against the Negro and the Indian; it condemns the inequality and the exploitation of women; it condemns political and military oligarchies which keep our people in poverty, impede their democratic development and the full exercise of their sovereignty; it condemns concessions of our countries' natural resources to foreign monopolies as a policy sacrificing and betraying the peoples' interests; it condemns Governments which turn a deaf ear to the demands of their people so that they may obey orders from abroad; it condemns the systematic deception of the peoples by mass communication media which serve the interests of the oligarchies and the policy of imperialist oppression; it condemns the news monopoly held by monopolist agencies, which are instruments of monopolist trusts and agents of such interests; it condemns repressive laws which prevent the workers, the peasants, the students and the intellectuals, the great majorities in each country, from forming associations and fighting for their social and patriotic demands; it condemns the imperialist monopolies and enterprises which continually plunder our wealth, exploit our workers and peasants, bleed our economies and keep them backward, and subordinate Latin American politics to their designs and interests. In short, the National General Assembly of the Cuban people condemns the exploitation of man by man and the exploitation of underdeveloped countries by imperialist capital.

Consequently, the National General Assembly of the Cuban people proclaims before America, and proclaims here before the world, the right of the peasants to the land; the right of the workers to the fruits of their labour; the right of children to education; the right of the sick to medical care and hospitalization; the right of young people to work; the right of students to free vocational training and scientific education; the right of Negroes and Indians to full human dignity; the right of women to civil, social and political equality; the right of the elderly to security in their old age; the right of intellectuals, artists and scientists to fight through their works for a better world; the right of States to nationalize imperialist monopolies, thus rescuing the national wealth and resources; the right of countries to trade freely with all the countries of the world; the right of nations to their complete sovereignty; the right of peoples to convert their military fortresses into schools and to arm their workers (because in this we have to be arms-conscious and to arm our people to defence against imperialist attacks), their peasants, their students, their intellectuals, Negroes, Indians, women, young people, old people, all the oppressed and exploited, so that they may themselves defend their rights and their destinies.

Some people wanted to know what the line of the Revolutionary Government of Cuba was. Well then, there you have our line.

46 THOMAS, The Origin of the Cuban Revolution

The present Cuban explanation of events is that Cuba, previously a semi-colonialist society, was so severely exploited by U.S. and Cuban capitalists that the condition of the working class eventually became intolerable, the tension being especially sharpened under the tyrant Batista (1952–8); Castro's 26th of July Movement and the Communist Party therefore formed the *elite* which led the masses towards a coherent realization of their misery and the country towards the 'objective conditions' for revolution. Yet this explanation is also inadequate. Cuba, although a poor country in many respects, was certainly among the richer countries of Latin America. *Per capita* income reached a figure of $341 at its highest level in 1947. The average daily salary about the same time for the best-paid sugar worker was $3.25, which probably would have given him an annual wage (with a six-day week for the five-month sugar harvest) of nearly $500. This is a small wage, but in many countries in Latin America it would be considered high. Wages apart, however, the general availability of consumer goods, the social services per head, the labour laws, the communications system, literacy rates, all normal criteria indicate that Cuba was among the leading nations of Latin America—to be ranked in terms of development below only Argentina and Uruguay, and perhaps on a level with Chile. Certainly, Cuba had had for two generations before the revolution the highest standard of living of any tropical area in the world. It does not therefore seem to be poverty, any more than North American foolishness, that caused the revolution to take the turn it did.

The difficulty of explaining what happened in Cuba in Marxist terms has led some people to another extreme: they have seen the whole series of events as dictated by the whims of one man. The trouble with this argument is that it really credits Castro with greater powers than any man can singly possess. Instead of describing a monster, this argument creates a god.

The origins of the revolution seem more likely to be found in the fact that Cuban society was not so much underdeveloped as stagnant: semi-developed perhaps, with some of the characteristics of advanced countries when they enter decline. Cuba was not a country in the depths of poverty, but one extraordinarily frustrated, where opportunities existed for economic and social progress but where

This material originally appeared in an article "The Origins of the Cuban Revolution" by Hugh Thomas in the October 1963 issue of *The World Today*, the monthly journal published by The Royal Institute of International Affairs, London. Reprinted by permission.

these were wasted—and the fact of the waste was evident. The undoubted advances whetted the imagination of the working class, but did not satisfy it. The case of the well-paid sugar worker symbolizes the situation; getting $3.25 a day for the five months of the harvest, afterwards he could expect to earn nothing. Unused to saving, and perhaps incapable of doing so since he had to pay off debts incurred during the previous dead season, his life collapsed. For half the year he was comparatively well off, able to choose between a quite wide selection of consumer goods; for the rest of the year he lived in resentment, possibly more extreme than if it had been unemployed all the time, as a large fraction (around one-fifth) of his colleagues in the trade were. About 500,000 persons were in this frustrating position, nearly one-third of the total labour force of about 1.7 million. Nearly all of them were in debt throughout their lives—being disposed for that reason alone to hope for a violent upturn in society, which might declare a moratorium on, or even an annulment of, debts. The key to Cuban society before the revolution is, in fact, the sugar industry. . . .

In addition to being the world's largest producer of sugar, Cuba was, for about a century, the major single source of sugar for the United States, and for a time after the Civil War her sole source of sugar. For most of this century up to 1960, Cuba supplied between 40 and 60 per cent of U.S. sugar, with a drop towards 30 per cent and for a time 25 per cent during the 1930s depression. After this unstable period, Cuba secured a part of the U.S. market by a specific quota, allocated annually according to the U.S. Secretary for Agriculture's estimate of U.S. sugar needs. . . . The quota was a great advantage but also a great bondage, and therefore there is a certain logic in the Cuban Revolutionary Government's criticism of its existence in early 1960 and denunciation of its disappearance in August of the same year. The tragedy of the Cuban sugar industry in the years before the revolution is that it was hard to see how, even with the most effective methods of production, it could expand its share of the world market, or its own production. Both U.S. and world markets were quota-controlled and tariff-protected to the point where expansion was almost forbidden.

One should note, however, that a large percentage of Cuban sugar mills were in fact U.S.-owned. . . . Of course, it was natural for Cubans to denounce the high percentage of foreign ownership, throughout this long period, of the staple product of the country, especially when other sections of the commanding heights of industry were also U.S.-owned; these included almost all public utilities in Havana, railways, and banks, which had been largely U.S.- and Canadian-owned since the bank crash in the 1920's. However, there were some advantages in this: foreign ownership could help to keep the door open to new ideas in technology and research; some of the best schools in Cuba seem to have been run by Americans, some being financed as a public obligation, others privately; American firms were also probably less given to tax evasion than Cuban. The overall effect of U.S. ownership of such prosperity as there was in Cuba was that Americans could not avoid being blamed when things went wrong with the economy; and the economy had been in crisis for as long as anyone could remember.

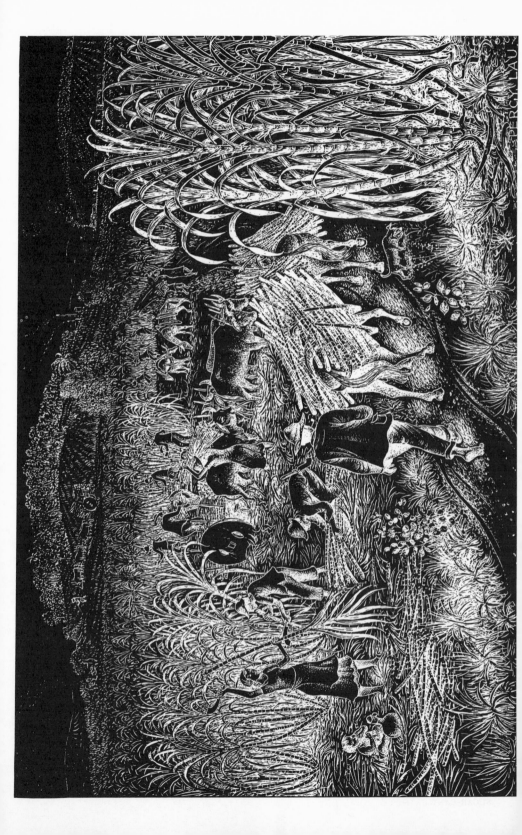

In fact, Cuban sugar before the revolution was going through the classic experience of a great industry in decline. Cuban sugar-growers never sought to make the best use of their ground, the yield per acre, for instance, being far below that of Puerto Rico or Hawaii. Irrigation was not only rare but not apparently even planned, though it was obvious that it gave a higher yield. There was very little research as to the type of cane best suited for Cuban conditions: the agricultural research center at Sagua la Grande was hardly able to carry on, since even the meagre ear-marked funds often 'disappeared' before they got there. Further, the industry was hamstrung by bureaucratic control. . . .

The country was also at the mercy of world sugar demand. Changes of a percentage of a cent in the world market price of sugar not only meant the creation or ruin of fortunes in Cuba, but also indicated whether ordinary life was intolerable or acceptable. . . . For example, in 1950 under the impact of post-Korean rearmament, the whole of Cuba's molasses from the 1951 harvest was sold at 20 cents a gallon, instead of 5 cents a gallon a year earlier. . . .

Credit was almost impossible to obtain unless the proposed project was in some way connected with sugar, yet investment in new industries (perhaps making use of sugar byproducts) and diversification of agriculture were the only way forward. This blockage could be observed throughout the economy. Education, health, social services of all kinds, public services, commerce, departments of agriculture other than sugar, trade unions, all gave the impression of being not only incapable of development, but also afraid of it. The Cuban educational system had deteriorated between 1925 and 1959. A smaller proportion of school-age children were enrolled in Cuban schools in 1950 than in 1925. . . .

Other Latin American economies were, and are, as unstable and as unbalanced as that of Cuba: and the central cause of the trouble, the monocrop, appears elsewhere. At the same time, none of the countries whose economies are to a lesser or greater extent monocultures actually depend on sugar, whose price has always been highly volatile. . . .

The institutions of Cuba in 1958–9 were amazingly weak. The large middle and upper class had failed to create any effective defence against the demands on what may be taken to be the majority when those demands came at last to be clearly expressed, as they did in January 1959, by a group self-confessedly middle class in origin. Perhaps the first and strongest factor working in favour of the revolution was the absence of any regionally based obstacles. . . .

To the absence of a regional restraining force was added the weakness of two other traditional conservative forces—the Church and the regular army. The Cuban Church has never really found an identity. Churches are few in Cuba. The Church played no part in the development of the Cuban spirit of independence, which instead was nurtured by freemasonry and rationalism. Few priests before 1898 were Cuban born, and even after 1900 the majority continued to come from Spain. Church and State had been separated in the Constitution of 1901, State subsidies also disappearing. Later on, the Church made something of a comeback, a large number of Catholic schools being founded in the 1930's; in

1946 a Catholic university was also founded. In the 1950's this educational emphasis led to the appearance of almost radical Catholic groups which opposed Batista. In Oriente, there was, in the early stages, some degree of relationship between the 26th of July Movement and the Church—chiefly since it was widely known that the intervention of the Archbishop of Santiago had helped save Castro's life after the Moncada attack in 1953. The leading Catholic and conservative newspaper, the *Diario de la Marina* was, on the other hand, among the first to suggest that the 26th of July Movement was communist.

After Castro got to power, the Church made no serious move to gather middle-class opposition, and it was only in 1960, when it was too late, that a series of sporadic pastoral letters appeared denouncing communism. All church schools and convents were closed by the end of 1961, and most foreign priests and secular clergy (i.e. the majority) were expelled. Since then there has been a surprising calm in the relations between Church and State, presumably by mutual consent; the Church in Cuba has, in short, never been a serious factor in the situation.

The regular army, the second traditional opponent of revolutionary regimes, was even less of an obstacle. By early 1959 it had in fact ceased to exist—not simply due to its demoralization in 1957 and 1958, when fighting Castro in the Sierra, but also to the repeated divisions which had weakened its *esprit de corps* during preceding years. . . .

The trade unions also could offer no serious opposition to the revolution; yet the revolution destroyed them, or anyway converted them into departments of the Ministry of Labour. Cuban labour began to be effectively organized under the shadow of the depression and the Machado dictatorship. Batista enabled the communists to form and dominate a congress of unions in the late 1930's—in return for communist electoral support for himself. Between 1938 and 1947 the unions were, if not structurally, at least in effect a section of the Ministry of Labour. The rather cynical alliance of Batista and the communists (till 1944) was responsible for some enlightened labour legislation: a minimum wage; minimum vacation of one month; forty-four-hour week and forty-eight-hour-week pay; nine days of annual sick leave; security of tenure except on proof of one of fourteen specific causes of dismissal, and so on—all admirable measures in themselves, enshrined in the 1940 Constitution, and all in effect till 1959. These measures were in fact so favourable to labour in the 1940's and early 1950's as undeniably to hinder the economic development of Cuba; labour opposition to mechanization, for example, seems to have been a serious handicap. The general impression to be gained from the labour scene just before Batista's second *coup* was less that of solid benefits won by a progressive working class than of a number of isolated redoubts, held with great difficulty and with continuous casualties, in a predominantly hostile territory. . . .

It was equally hopeless to expect the civil service to be a restraining factor in the revolution, although, with nearly 200,000 employees, it was the second largest source of employment, ranking after the sugar workers. Despite the passage of numerous laws, starting in 1908 under the Magoon administration, no Government was able to depend on a reliable civil service. With the exception of the National Bank, during the short period from its inception in 1949 to the Batista *coup,* all departments of state were regarded as the legitimate spoils of political victors. Of course, in this Cuba was no different from other countries. But in few countries of a comparable degree of wealth was the absence of an administrative career in government so conspicuous. In some Ministries, employees never seem to have appeared except to collect pay; the absence of responsibility was possibly most marked in the Ministry of Education. Also, since the salary scale was low, there was every incentive for employees of all grades to dip their hands in the government till, as their political masters did. Since governmental and non-governmental pension funds, which were lodged in the Treasury, had been used by the Grau Government to help pay other lavish but unspecified government expenses, it was very difficult after 1947 to allow any employee to retire. Many people thought that in fact 30,000–40,000 government employees were really pensioners. Thus government employment was a kind of social assistance.

The scandal of the old bureaucracy is certainly a reason why, after the victory of the 26th of July Movement in 1959, the idea of a total break with the past seemed so attractive. The word government had been debased for so long; not only the old bureaucracy but the old political parties were widely and with justice regarded as organizations for the private distribution of public funds. Who in 1959, even after seven years of Batista, had really forgotten the scandal of Grau's schoolteachers; or of Grau's Minister of Education, Alemán, who had arrived suddenly one day in Miami with was it $10 million or was it $20 million in cash in a suitcase? In what way was Batista's cheating in the State lottery worse than Prío's? It was all very well to return to the Constitution of 1940: but how far had it worked between 1940 and 1952? It had in many instances merely laid down general principles; the subsequent legislation had never been carried out to implement it. . . .

Some of the best-intentioned sections of the Constitution were in fact a little absurd, such as the provision in Article 52 that the annual salary of a primary school-teacher should never be less than a millionth part of the national budget. At the same time, not many people, even sincere democrats, could summon up enthusiasm for the 1940 Constitution, since it had been established with the backing of Batista and the communists. And at a deeper level, there was a genuine doubt among many in Cuba in 1958–9 about the structure of previous Cuban Constitutions ever since independence. Batista's police were certainly bloody, but the old days of gangsterism under the democratic rule of Grau were hardly much better. There was a time, for instance, in 1947, when three separate political gangster groups were fighting each other in the streets of Havana, each being separately backed by different divisions of the police, whose chiefs had been specifically appointed by the President to balance them off.

Although Castro did not come to power with a real party organization, or even a real political plan, he nevertheless did have behind him a real revolutionary tradition, a tradition which was firmly rooted in the previous sixty years of Cuban politics, almost the whole of which had been passed in perpetual crisis. . . . All the time between 1902 and 1959, Cubans were trying to prove themselves worthy of the heroic figures of the War of Independence—Martí, Gómez, or Maceo. Efforts were made, understandably, necessarily perhaps, by Castro to make himself, Camilo Cienfuegos, and others the equals of the past. The men of 1959 were undoubtedly in many cases the real sons of the men who made the revolution in 1933. Castro was to do the things that many people had been talking about before. Many moderately middle-class Cubans suspected, without much economic knowledge, that the only way out of the chronic sugar crisis, the only way to diversify agriculture, was to embark on very radical measures; to nationalize American property and to force a break in commercial relations with the United States.

Amateur Marxism was a strong force on the left wing of the *Ortodoxo* Party in the early 1950's, though it is now proving an illusion to suppose that even Marxist-Leninism can bring a swift diversification of agriculture. One can see how the illusion nevertheless became widespread, how anyone who seemed likely to realize it was certain of backing, regardless of whether he trampled on formal democracy. There can be only one reason why the moderates in the Cuban Cabinet of 1959—the admirable professional and liberal persons who now perhaps back Manuel Ray and argue that Castro has betrayed the revolution—failed to unite and resist Castro, backed by the considerable strength of the Cuban middle class: the reason is surely that they half felt all the time that, given the betrayal of so many previous revolutions, Castro was right. Many moderates after all did stay in Cuba, and many are still there.

What of the communists? They have never dictated events, but merely profited from opportunities offered to to them. . . . The communists got 117,000 votes in the presidential elections of 1944, but they were by that time in a curious position, being less a party of revolution than one which had a great deal to lose, almost conservative in their reactions in fact. Thereafter their influence waned, throughout the intermediate period between then and the Castro civil war, until mid-1958 when, after some difficulty, they established a working alliance with Castro, whom they had previously dismissed as a *putschista*. Since then, they have, of course, come into their own in many respects, if not quite absolutely; but their role in the origins of the Cuban revolution seems to have been small.

To sum up: the origins of the Cuban revolution must be sought in the state of the Cuban sugar industry. Similar conditions may exist in other countries of Latin America, in respect to other crops; these have hitherto been less pronounced. Even although other revolutions in the area may in fact be equally due, they have been hindered by the strength of institutions or regional habits, which in Cuba, for historical reasons, were especially weak. Finally, the Cuban revolution of 1959, far from being an isolated event, was the culmination of a long series of thwarted revolutions.

47 FULBRIGHT, Old Myths and New Realities of Cuba

One of the inhibitions to a realistic approach to the problem of Cuba is the myth that we are still in the era when, as Secretary of State Richard Olney put it in 1895, "the United States is practically sovereign on this continent, and its fiat is law upon those subjects to which it confines its interposition." This might have been so in 1895 (though even that can be argued), but it is clearly not so in 1964. The trouble is that a great many people apparently wish it were so, and persist in demanding that the United States Government act as if it were. The near-hysteria that has afflicted many Americans over Cuba comes more from wounded pride than from anything else. We are told that the Castro regime is "intolerable," despite the plain fact that, rightly or wrongly, we have tolerated it for more than five years. . . .

Neither the overthrow of the Castro regime nor its complete isolation would solve the problems of the United States in Latin America. These problems are aggravated by Castro, but they are not caused by him. They are the result of a process of rapid and profound change in societies which are stubbornly resistant to change. If Cuba were to sink below the Caribbean tomorrow, and if Moscow were suddenly and miraculously to recall all of its agents in the Western Hemisphere, much of Latin America would still be agitated by unrest, radicalism, and revolution. . . .

I believe that the United States under present conditions should maintain its *own* political and economic boycott of the Castro regime. Communist Cuba is hostile to the United States and poses a continuing threat of subversion in Latin America. As long as this remains true, it is clearly not in our interests to do anything that would help the Castro regime to sustain itself.

The boycott policy—or, more precisely, the policy of seeking to bring about the fall of the Castro regime through a concerted free-world boycott—has not failed because of any "weakness" or "timidity" on the part of our government. This charge, so frequently heard, is one of the most pernicious myths to have been inflicted on the American people. The boycott policy has failed because the United States is not omnipotent and cannot be. The basic reality to be faced is that it is simply not within our power to compel our allies to cut off their trade with Cuba, unless we are prepared to take drastic sanctions against them, such as closing our own markets to any foreign company that does business in Cuba. . . . It seems to me that we are left, then, with the acceptance of the continued existence of the Castro regime as a distasteful nuisance but not an intolerable danger so long as the nations of the Hemisphere are prepared to meet their obligations of collective defense under the Rio Treaty.

In recent years we have become transfixed with Cuba, making it far more important in both our foreign relations and in our domestic life than its size and influence warrant. We have flattered a noisy but minor demagogue by treating him as if he were a Napoleonic menace. Communist Cuba has been a disruptive and subversive influence in Venezuela and other countries of the Hemisphere, and there is no doubt that both we and our Latin American partners would be better off if the Castro regime did not exist. But it is important to bear in mind that, despite their best efforts, the Cuban Communists have not succeeded in subverting the Hemisphere, and that in Venezuela, for example, where communism has made a major effort to gain power through terrorism, it has been repudiated in a free election by a people who have committed themselves to the course of liberal democracy. It is necessary to weigh the desirability of an objective against the feasibility of its attainment, and when we do this with respect to Cuba, I think we are bound to conclude that Castro is a nuisance but not a grave threat to the United States and that he cannot be gotten rid of except by means that are wholly disproportionate to the objective. Cuban communism does pose a grave threat to other Latin American countries, but this threat can be dealt with by prompt and vigorous use of the established procedures of the inter-American system against any act of aggression. . . . But the defense of Latin America is ultimately a Latin American responsibility; however much we may wish to do so, we cannot protect people who are not interested in protecting themselves. . . .

In summary, I think that we must abandon the myth that Cuban communism is a transitory menace and face up to two basic realities about Cuba: first, that the Castro regime is not on the verge of collapse and is not likely to be overthrown by any policies which we are now pursuing or can reasonably undertake; and second, that the continued existence of the Castro regime, though inimical to our interests and policies, is not an insuperable obstacle to the attainment of our objectives, unless we make it so by permitting it to poison our politics at home and to divert us from more important tasks in the Hemisphere . . .

SECTION XI

The Position of Puerto Rico

One of the frequent charges made in Latin America and elsewhere is that Puerto Rico is a "North American colony" that has betrayed its Hispanic past. A lively debate goes on in Puerto Rico, and elsewhere, on this subject. Reading No. 48 *sets forth the views of Jaime Benítez, the eloquent and thoughtful Rector of the University of Puerto Rico, as stated before the United States-Puerto Rico Commission on the Status of Puerto Rico.* Reading No. 49 *gives the interpretations of Gordon Lewis, a Welsh Socialist who has written one of the fundamental volumes on Puerto Rico.*

48 BENÍTEZ, *The Meaning of the Commonwealth*

In the Americas, North, Central and South, the greatest threat to tolerance of diversity comes not from communism. It comes from nationalism. This is so, not because communism is better but because nationalism is closer to our deepest emotions and easier to spread. There is a much greater danger of nationalism than of communism in the United States. The same is true in Puerto Rico, in the Dominican Republic, in Panama, in Mexico, in Peru, in Argentina, everywhere throughout this hemisphere, except of course in Cuba. In Cuba communism would not have been possible except for its exploitation of deep nationalistic feelings imbedded in Cuban education. If communism spreads elsewhere in Latin America, it will be not upon the merits of its performance in Cuba but upon the strength of the hostilities created by nationalistic propaganda.

I find that my best hopes for our common future are incompatible with nationalism in Puerto Rico as well as incompatible with nationalism in the United States. I am a loyal, non-nationalistic Puerto Rican and a loyal non-nationalistic

Unfinished Notes on Commonwealth. Statement read by Dr. Benítez before the Commission on the Status of Puerto Rico in San Juan, July 31, 1965, pp. 2–14, *passim.* Reprinted by permission.

citizen of the United States. These two loyalties are and must continue to be compatible with one another as well as mutually supporting. . . .

One outstanding sensitive area is the language question. Spanish has been the language of this community for over four centuries. We do not wish to change that. We want Spanish to continue to be the normal vehicle of communication in Puerto Rico for ourselves, for our children and for our children's children, regardless of political status.

And yet, I have chosen to address you in English. It will be said I do it because I am colonially minded. This, I reply, is the strangest kind of colonialism for at this juncture the shoe of inferiority pinches the continental foot, not mine. Being able to converse in more than one language is no detriment to anyone. Europeans long ago discovered its indispensability. Americans will have to become increasingly bilingual and even trilingual as interdependency grows.

Concerning my choice of languages today, I may point out that politeness to visitors and a determination to make them feel at home is part of the Spanish heritage I wish to retain. . . .

Our identification with the Spanish language and with the universal Spanish values are part and parcel of the basic heritage of our community. I consider such identification compatible with American citizenship and values as well as with any form of association with the United States. I can think of many reasons why even in the eventuality of Statehood it would be compatible with national interest for Puerto Rico to preserve and enhance the Spanish heritage. This is a changing world. The United States itself is changing very rapidly and appreciation of pluralism is part of that change. . . .

Many, perhaps most, of the tensions, misunderstandings and hostilities which have clouded our relationships have centered on the language question. Official Commonwealth policy and practice today is that Spanish is our regular language of communication, expression and instruction; that English is an essential, desirable and required second language. This in my judgment, is as it should be, under Commonwealth, under Statehood or under Independence.

There was a time when official policy in Puerto Rico was oriented towards using the language of instruction as leverage for Americanization; when it was held that teachers who did not know English should teach in English students who did not know English either. At that time it was implied that education and democracy were things that happened in English or not at all. I lived through those days in the 1930's. As a young man trained and educated in the best tradition associated with Spanish and American liberal thought and experiences, my reaction was at first one of amazement, then of irritation, protest and at times despair. Under this climate of intransigence I became what my good friend in your Commission, Mr. Concepción de Gracia, is still now, an Independentist with a liberal background; a person for whom the only possible avenue of self fulfillment for Puerto Rico required complete dissociation from the political ties with the United States. That policy and others germane to it drew many of us into what I have come to regard as a blind alley. I make no apologies for having favored Independence when I did and while I did. I favored it fully and openly and at a time when there was much less tolerance of minority views than today. I make no apologies now for having moved away from Independence. I have reached the conclusion that the best hope for the future of Puerto Rico lies in continued association with the United States.

HISTORICAL ISSUES AND THE COMMONWEALTH FORMULA

What is the nature of this association now? What should its future nature be?

Present association is the result of an evolutionary process which began in 1898, which has not ended yet, and which is known in Spanish as "Estado Libre Asociado" and in English as Commonwealth Government.

As a social and political arrangement, Commonwealth is unique in the Western Hemisphere, perhaps in the world. What makes it unique?

POLITICAL ADVANTAGES AND PSYCHOLOGICAL ENTANGLEMENT

First, Puerto Rico is the only part of the old Spanish Empire which is neither an independent nation nor an integral part of the United States. As a result of the fortunes of war, in 1898 Puerto Rico came under the jurisdiction of the United States Congress. The question of what has happened to Congressional jurisdiction over the years has been a matter of considerable debate in the Courts, in Puerto Rico, in Congress, in the United Nations, throughout Latin America. As Puerto Rico has become more and more important and as the United States has become more and more significant, the nature of the present status has tended to become more controversial. There is a discrepancy between the political *de facto* reality and the documents presumably expressing that reality. We feel and Congress apparently also feels this relationship between Puerto Rico and the United States ought to be given a long hard look with an eye at possible clarifications and improvements. This Commission has been created as an instrument leading to these purposes. The Commission is expected to assess the present ordination and to recommend:

a) Improvement of Commonwealth, or

b) Departure from Commonwealth.

Possible departures are Statehood or Independence. . . .

Secondly, the 1898 involvement created frontiers, horizons, relationships, problems which neither the United States nor Puerto Rico had anticipated. The ultimate political objectives of the United States were left indefinite and have remained indefinite to this day. Perhaps this is as it had to be, given the confusion of the times, and certainly it is the way it must be now. . . .

The present arrangement, with its many advantages, lacks glaringly that basic formulation of theory which many minds find essential to intellectual tranquility. The expression *in the nature of a compact* in Law 600 was meant to provide a term of reference. But many of the ideological architects of Commonwealth find that it does not provide sufficient coverage now. In consequence, we are searching for a more satisfactory and concise formulation.

THE GREAT ACHIEVEMENTS

From 1898 to 1965 enormous, almost unbelievable, mostly beneficial changes have taken place in Puerto Rico. In education, health, longevity, human equality, personal freedom, opportunity, productivity, science, technology and modernity, general welfare, integrity in public administration, change through law and law through the democratic process, Puerto Rico and Puerto Ricans stand in the forefront of the hemisphere. Judged by any and all objective standards presently available to test social progress and human welfare, we approach the category of the well to do nations.

This experience of threescore and seven years of living together has left a decisive imprint upon all of us. We cannot act as if our life values had not undergone significant transformations during this period. We cannot pretend that we are writing upon a tabula rasa dated 1898. Over 95% of the people of Puerto Rico living today were born under the American flag. As to your inquiry where we go from here, I reply we must go ahead and we must go together.

Three significant events stand out as political landmarks during this period of sixty-seven years: First, in 1917 the United States citizenship was extended to Puerto Rico. This was a far reaching decision. Until then we had been held to be by the Supreme Court of the United States citizens of Puerto Rico and nationals of the United States. After that legislation we continue to be citizens of Puerto Rico entitled at the same time to the privileges, immunities and responsibilities of citizens of the United States. Even if these rights and privileges did not come to full fruition, Congressional action of 1917 represented a departure from a colonial relationship and a basic obligation to redress democratic shortcomings. Under the best American tradition citizenship is incompatible with discrimination. . . .

A second significant political development in Puerto Rico was the incorporation into our social, human and political outlook of the basic values and objectives of the open society, of the New Deal, of the Welfare State, of the dedication of government to the task of rectifying social injustices through law and providing real opportunities for all. Thus, our political responsibilities became something beyond and aside from political status objectives.

In the third place, the present Commonwealth status and relationships were formally worked out from 1950 to 1952. I have said *formally* to underscore one basic fact. Commonwealth is not a brilliant formula conceived and brought about by a flash of genius. No one wishes to detract from the extraordinary leadership which Mr. Muñoz Marín has symbolized and has so outstandingly exerted in the orientation of this particular political ordination. But we must remember that his leadership was effective also because it represented a deep perception of basic realities, aspirations and trends, both in Puerto Rico and in the United States. . . .

THE ROAD AHEAD

We come now to the present search for future goals. I think it can be said in summary, that the great majority of the people of Puerto Rico are proud of the progress and achievements our political ordination has facilitated while at the same time some are troubled by the fact that our Commonwealth Government does not fit easily into any of the conceptual categories resulting from the political science schemes of the Nineteenth Century. Thus, most of us are happy we are not Cuba, or the Dominican Republic, or Haiti. . . .

Can we amend Commonwealth status so as to eliminate all its imperfections and retain all of its advantages? The answer is no. Reality is not that simple. We cannot have the good things in life only. Except in Utopia, and Utopia means nowhere. We may learn from these deliberations that there is no perfect or final political solution in an imperfect and changing political world. Perhaps we may discover that the best political ordination permits the widest range of differences within a viable structure of legality, common values, social solidarity and human freedom. Measured against these criteria I would say of Commonwealth what Winston Churchill used to say of Democracy: "It is the worst form of government, after all others."

I speak of Commonwealth as the living experience in which all of us are engaged; the political ordination of freedom, justice and opportunity this community enjoys and which, in my judgment, it wishes to retain and to enhance. . . .

Commonwealth was and is a break through of intelligence over intelligentsia, of rationality over rationalism, of reality over utopia, of political pragmatism over political ideology. Under it a Caribbean community of Spanish origin and American citizenship, clustered in a small island, devoid of natural resources, beset by social, political, economic, cultural, educational maladjustments, has managed to live, struggle and progress in peace, with full regard for human rights, with ample opportunity and protection for challengers of the political ordination itself. . . .

I believe that one of the advantages, I repeat, one of the advantages of Commonwealth is that it neither calls nor makes any Puerto Rican a traitor. Quite the contrary. It is much more respectful of differences and more tolerant of them than all other alternatives. Not because it is weaker, but because it is stronger.

I regard Commonwealth as an evolving, flexible, elastic form of political relationship. I favor therefore changes in Commonwealth, provided they do not jeopardize the basic meaning of Commonwealth.

49 LEWIS, *The Puerto Rican Independence Movement*

Certainly ever since the abortive Tydings Bill of 1936 independence for Puerto Rico, meaning a complete separation from the United States, has seemed a feasible

Gordon K. Lewis, *Puerto Rico: Freedom and Power in the Caribbean* (New York: Monthly Review Press, 1963), pp. 396–402, *passim*. Reprinted by permission.

goal to one continuing section of local political thought and opinion. The local custodian of the ideal, since 1948, has been the *Partido Independentista Puerto-rriqueño*. Electorally, it has recently been on the decline, having been replaced in 1956 by the Republican Statehood Party as the leading opposition group. Its vote in that year indeed dropped catastrophically from some 126,000 to nearly a half of that figure, 86,101, and in only six towns did it manage to poll as much as 25 per cent of the total votes cast; and that it fared no better in 1960 was in large measure due to the fact that all liberal opinion appears in that year to have gone in sympathetic support to the Governor in his stand against clericalist politics. What are the reasons for this? Before that question is answered it ought to be noted that the ideal of an independent republic has been an honorable one in the island for a century or more. It animated the liberal spirits under Spain—Ruiz Belvis, Acosta, Betances, de Hostos. It was the main reason why many Puerto Ricans supported the American intervention in 1898. It was accepted for years after that event by the early Unionist Party as a legitimate alternative to state-hood and self-governing autonomy within the American system. It is true that Governor Muñoz, in his now celebrated Cidra Declaration of 1959, ruled out independence as a candidate for plebiscitary acceptance or rejection, and thereby dealt the party a brutal and illiberal blow calculated to place in jeopardy its very survival as a party legitimately seeking the support of the Puerto Rican voter. . . .

The fear of the economic consequences of independence is undoubtedly a major factor in the party's recent decline. People fear the effect of political separatism upon American capital investment and the whole future of the new prosperity under the industrialization program. The fear is certainly cleverly ex-ploited as a means of dampening enthusiasm for independence. Yet it is probable that it is ill founded. . . . At the same time, even while this is so, it is true to say that the party leadership has done little itself to mollify the fear. It ought to address itself, at the least, to a study of the economic consequences of in-dependence; it ought to draw up plans covering the successive stages within which the necessary economic adjustments could be made with least damage to the economy; above all, it ought to demand, as a leading item in its economic program, the arrangement of a long-term economic treaty with the United States whereby the American power would be required to undertake a sort of Marshall Plan aid to the economy during the transitional period from dependence to independence as a token of its moral obligations to the Caribbean ward. But little enough along these lines has been attempted. Nor indeed are people reassured when the party attempts to belittle the very real achievements of Operation Bootstrap. For to argue that the island's inclusion within the continental free-trade system has benefited only two or three lines of local business is to ignore the fact that the inclusion benefits the Commonwealth regime as a whole to something like $150 million or $175 million each year and, beyond that, the fact that the rate of general social return to government cost in the industrialization program has paid off with handsome dividends for living standards as a whole (from 1950 to 1956, for example, a total cost of some $30 million brought in a total benefit of some $106 million).

The party's appeal is further handicapped because in its social and economic program it accepts the mixed-economy and welfare-state policies of the government party and only recommends additions of degree rather than changes of kind: a more careful concern for agriculture, a more "nativist" industrializing program, a more effective control of absentee capital and the extension of public holdings for the benefit of the small farmer. . . .

The leading weakness of the *independentista* forces, until recently, has been their disability to construct a united front, as well as the fact that, lacking a striking leader, they fail to meet one of the basic requirements of a personalist politics. . . .

It would . . . be a profound error of judgment to believe that, whatever happens to its party expressions, the *independentista* ideal in the island will gradually disappear. The party expressions will no doubt continue to oscillate between a kaleidoscopic variety of groups. But its basic sentiment, that of a proud people yearning for a national identity, clear and distinct, seeking to become a coherent entity rather than a rootless multitude, is far too deeply entrenched, even perhaps in many members of the ruling party, to be lightly dismissed.

SECTION XII

Colombia and Venezuela

Few books or special studies exist on the oligarchies, those small groups of privileged persons who have ruled for years in most Latin American countries. The late Vernon Lee Fluharty, a U.S. scholar, sketches in a general way the contours of the oligarchy in Colombia. (Reading No. 50.) Bogotá is the capital of the country, but no one can understand the changes under way in highly diversified Colombia without taking into account events occurring in the remote villages. Gerardo and Alicia Reichel-Dolmatoff are able to interpret village life as a result of their many years spent studying social change. (Reading No. 51.)

Venezuela passed through a severe testing period during Rómulo Betancourt's presidency. An experienced political strategist and long-time leader of the Acción Democrática party, he had faith in democratic processes and faith in the Venezuelan people. (Reading No. 52.) Despite an almost continuous reign of terror by guerrilla extremist elements (Reading No. 53), he was able to complete his term of office. Arturo Uslar Pietri, an outstanding writer and statesman, dramatically describes the need for true free speech and true responsibility if democracy is to survive in Venezuela. (Reading No. 54.)

50 *FLUHARTY, The Colombian Upper Class— White, Privileged, Competent*

The gaps between the classes in Colombia are so great and so rigid that in a time of social ferment violence is always potentially present. Even when social and economic resentments merely simmer below the surface, the stream of national life may give a deceptive appearance of placidity that belies the facts and misleads the observer.

Vernon Lee Fluharty, *Dance of the Millions* (Pittsburgh: University of Pittsburgh Press, 1957), pp. 182–187, *passim*, Reprinted by permission.

To a very great extent, this is due to the frames of reference created by the upper classes themselves. Colombian upperclass people take their place in society by right of birth. The Great Families are still names to conjure with, and connections with them by marriage, bloodlines, or financial and social ties are both desirable and a kind of *Paz y Salvo* (safe-conduct card) to most areas of preference and privilege.

Due to the centuries-old tradition of caste, those born into the upper classes inherit the unshakable assumption that the lower classes are by nature inferior— they are those who cook, serve, clean, run errands, bow and scrape, and perform the hard and the menial tasks of the society. . . .

There is, then, considerable justification for the maintenance of control monopoly by the upper crust of Colombia's social layer cake. But that is not to justify, nor to indicate that the monopoly should be continued indefinitely. The real question, however, arises from the long tradition of the monopoly: how to break it without doing harm to the whole society; how to admit the masses to fuller participation as they impatiently demand a voice in directions.

This dilemma must be resolved in terms of the willingness of the upper class to share power, a willingness so far not demonstrated. Status in society in Colombia has always been determined by birth and by ownership of land. . . .

But to say that the upper classes of Colombia are an élite percentage of the population is not to say enough. Basically, the white Colombian is a Spaniard, with a complex racial heritage and he is therefore, a complex personality. Charming and witty, he is skeptical often to the point of cynicism, capable of extreme violence and frequent cruelty. . . .

Theories and disputations over abstractions charm him unutterably. But he is also extremely clear-headed and practical in everyday affairs. This upper-class Colombian has made his mistakes, but he has also done a first-class job of building the national economy and the national culture into a respectable edifice worthy of admiration. In brief, he is quite a fellow. His one blind spot is that he has always felt that the economy was for *him;* that culture (not necessarily esthetics) was for his sole consumption. . . .

As a young man, this upper-class Colombian was probably educated in a Colombian prep school or university, and later went to the United States or Europe for further study. Very likely he plays polo, or did before easy living made the game too strenuous for both him and the horse. Still, he keeps up an interest in sports, gambles with moderation, holds large quantities of whiskey (Scotch preferred) well, and loves a good story, either from himself or others.

Quite often he is highly literate, having gone through a youthful period of writing doggerel, although now he prefers the stock reports to Valencia or Mistral. Rather earlier than North Americans, he learned about women, and he will maintain an active, practicing interest in them long after he has married the daughter of his father's best friend who, like himself, is of the élite. His interest in politics may take him to Congress or to a cabinet post, or to service on the directorate of his party, even while he heads his own company or runs his coffee business or hovers over his investments. Book and ideas will be a part of his life, running always a little ahead of practical matters. . . .

All summaries are oversimplification, and this one does not tell all of the upper classes in Colombia. Perhaps it rather understates the case for the oligarchy: the culture, the industry, the tenaciousness, the vision in certain regards, the true gentility, the many-sided comprehension which marks these upperclass people. But it can never, on the other hand, overstate the case of the mental rigidity of the upper-class social outlook, a rigidity which prevents the development of a truly national outlook for all Colombians.

For this same high-caste Colombian has tended, and still tends, to worship at the shrine of social immobility through the vertical stratum; to perpetuate a set of values which excludes the great mass of people from participation in the national life; and in this regard, he is both arbitrary and short-sighted.

51 REICHEL-DOLMATOFF, The People of Aritama

In the late thirties and early forties of the present century, a new period of change made itself felt in the village. This time changes were brought about mainly by improved communications and the necessity for making use of them, under the pressure of new needs. In these years practically all of the lowland towns were connected by highways, and transportation by truck or bus became the rule. With it came the newspapers, the cinema, the loudspeakers, the travelers. And with them came party politics, commercial foods and textiles, fashions and furnitures, aluminum vessels and iron tools, barbed wire, dyes and paints, leatherwares, cosmetics, cheap rum, flashlights, Coca Cola, medicines, phonograph records of Mexican and Cuban music. This was 'progress.' Because of the monopoly exercised by the store-owners of the village, as well as because of the increasing scarcity of nearby agricultural lands for daily food production, the population increase, the credit system, and the new labor problems, people were being forced to think not only in terms of the lowland markets but in terms of lowland Creole culture. A lowland-style Sunday suit, a handbag containing cosmetics, an umbrella, a colored kerchief, a patent-leather belt, aluminum kitchenware, kerosene lamps—they all became status symbols, everchanging, ever increasing in number and variety, ever to be bought anew. . . .

The . . . stores are, of course, major foci of Creole influence. Their owners are among the few, or rather are the only ones, who live on a Creole level. These stores dictate the prices of cash crops and all locally manufactured goods, as well as tastes and fashions in fabrics, cosmetics, combs, kerchiefs. It is the store-owner and his wife who advise the customer in the choice of color, style,

Reprinted from *The People of Aritama* by Gerardo and Alicia Reichel-Dolmatoff, by permission of the University of Chicago Press. © Gerardo and Alicia Reichel-Dolmatoff, 1961.

and quality of dress, and it is he who prescribes commercial medicines or even gives injections. They are the first to criticize and ridicule people for being ill-dressed, in order to make them buy new clothes at their stores. The store-owner is a banker, pharmacist, family counselor, accountant, public scribe, and a news service. His wife is the one who introduces the new hairdo, the new soap or perfume, and the new style in dress. The store-owners can write to a government agency and ask for new seeds; they can ask for loans in a lowland town; they know lawyers and judges and can carry on suits; they can travel to buy and sell their wares—all this because their educational level enables them. Disliked and distrusted as they are because of imposing ever-new necessities and status requirements, they fulfil an important role in the change toward Creole revalues, and even if their main motivation is more often than not material gain, they frequently show a sincere concern for the 'progress' of the community, often more than do the official authorities or other leading families. However, the local stores have not yet become gathering places where people may come to discuss daily events of local or national importance as is the custom in the lowlands. In this sense the stores are still isolated and their function is limited, but nonetheless their owners, clients, and wares are closely watched by all, and the appearance of a new item or a casual remark overheard while passing by may have, perhaps, a stronger influence than long conversations with a group of people. . . .

There is a bitter irony in this situation. In reality, those despised as 'unprogressive Indians' stand ideologically closer to Western civilization than the local 'Spaniards' or the lowland Creoles. The conservative Indian peasant lives by a value system and demonstrates a personality type which are far more Western than the emerging Creole outlook on life. Among the former, their eighteenth-century Catholicism and their respect for due process of law, for family life, and village authority are in obvious opposition to the materialism of the average Creole, his hedonism, his disregard for law and authority, and his disrupted family life.

But neither can there be any doubt as to the final outcome. Not only Aritama but the whole of the Creole world, it seems, are steadily becoming less Western.

52 BETANCOURT, Venezuela Can Achieve A Stable, Civilized Government

One might suppose that the possibility of reestablishing and stabilizing a civilized system of government in Venezuela is remote indeed. The uninterrupted flow of petroleum, with the financial returns which come from this export, and the international complicities which have been an effective support for dictatorial regimes in our country, seem to guarantee a rosy future for dictatorship in

Rómulo Betancourt, *Venezuela: Política y petroleo* (Mexico City: Fondo de Cultura Económica, 1956), pp. 768–770, 774, *passim*. Reprinted by permission.

Venezuela. This conclusion is the result of a hasty analysis. In Venezuela the collective will to recover lost liberties, encouraged and channeled by the political forces organized by the parties, has not died out. And history proves that in any country where there are numerous groups within the population—the best armed intellectually and morally, in the long run—which persevere in their resistance to institutionalized arbitrariness, these groups always succeed eventually in imposing democratic norms of government and administration.

This is what Andrés Eloy Blanco said, in the well chosen words of a great poet and intuitive politician, in the lecture which was his last will and testament, given a few hours before he died, before the members of *Acción Democrática* in exile in Mexico: "It is necessary to acknowledge the importance of the economic realities, but we must also remember the reality of our people. They are as a people backward economically and resplendent in their epic struggle; underdeveloped by any economic criterion and millionaires in human wealth; small in number but great in their heroism. Among the people emotional values and above all the human factor are vital. Our prime material and our greatest wealth is our human wealth."

But other tendencies, which also go toward putting an optimistic face on the political future of Venezuela, should be noted. Some of these are related to the national reality itself; others result from recent historical events, universal in scale, which have occurred within the American scene.

Regarding Venezuela, it is coming to be realized that the regime imposed upon the nation without its consent is a historical anachronism, which goes against the degree of development already achieved by the country. . . . Its daring disdain of all norms of good government are as contrary to the needs of a highly evolved society as its police methods of dealing with the citizenry are repugnant to the entire population. The fact is that Venezuela is no longer what she was in the days of Castro and of Gómez, when she had scarcely two million inhabitants and was a backward, bucolic nation, without industries, isolated from the world in an era of difficult communications, and with a population scourged by yellow fever and lack of culture. Today we form part of a modern nation, a nation which has passed through the industrial revolution of the twentieth century, with a national territory largely made safe from tropical diseases, and with a population which exceeds five million, of whom half a million are workers living in industrial and extractive centers. Large segments of this population are cultured and there is a numerous, well informed middle class. The nation is no longer a walled island but, on the contrary, due to its geographic location and its economic potential, it is a plexis of aereal and maritime inter-communications. The radio has nullified the attempts of the governors to isolate us from the world as Paraguay was isolated in the nineteenth century under Francia. Thus one can understand why the determining majority of Venezuelans . . . is against a regime which makes every effort to continue to apply the tribal methods of Cipriano Castro and Juan Vicente Gómez to an adult nation in the process of accelerated growth. . . .

And if the Venezuelan nation is different today from what it was in the times of Gómez, today's army is also distinct from the mountaineers of that era, a primitive horde commanded by ignorant cut-throats. The requirements of national growth itself and the technological complexity of modern arms have forced the rise of groups of officials possessing appreciable personal culture in some branches of the armed forces, especially the Navy and the Air Force. It was groups from among these cultivated sectors of the armed forces who have contributed to the changes overcoming anti-democratic situations in some Latin American countries. . . .

Our reasoned and profound conviction is that it will be possible to create a stable form of government in our country which will respect popular liberties, and among them the fundamental right of suffrage; a government concerned to resolve by modern and rational means the problems of the collectivity; a government honorable in its handling of public monies and disposed to convince foreign investors that their capital may enter the nation for the purpose of legal business, and not to despoil our natural resources and trample upon the rights of the Venezuelan worker. In short, a government capable of orienting and conducting the national democratic revolution that is at the present moment a historical necessity for Venezuela, and which can no longer be postponed.

53 *Terrorism in Venezuela, September 13–October 1, 1962*

September 13—Policeman and a police patrol in Caracas are attacked with submachine gun fire.

September 14—Police patrol in Barquisimeto is attacked with gunfire.

September 14—Judge investigating terrorist assassination is threatened with death.

September 16—Peasant warning to police frustrates terrorist attack on Socony Oil pipeline in plains region east of Barquisimeto.

September 17—Estimated 200 Communist youths demonstrate and riot in Caracas; one is killed.

September 17—Eight armed men seize radio station in Valencia.

September 18—Terrorists attack office of the Military Directorate of Justice for third time, kill guard, wound three military policemen.

September 18—Bomb is found in Caracas radio station.

September 18—Terrorists armed with submachine guns attack bank truck in Caracas; three persons are killed.

September 18—Terrorists provoke street violence and gunfire in a Caracas neighborhood; one person is killed, three wounded.

Castro-Communist Insurgency in Venezuela. A Study of Insurgency and Counter-Insurgency Operations and Techniques in Venezuela, 1960–1964 (Georgetown Research Project, Alexandria, Va. 1965), pp. 65–66. Reprinted by permission. For an interpretation of the institutionalized use of violence in Latin American politics, see William S. Stokes, "Violence. The South American Way," *United Nations World*, V (1951), No. 12, pp. 51–54.

September 19—Policeman is seriously wounded by bomb explosion in Barcelona.

September 20—Terrorists fire submachine gun blasts at offices of Colgate-Palmolive factory and a cement factory in Valencia.

September 20—Bomb is found in political party office in Caracas.

September 20—Terrorists submachine gun home of Prefect in Valencia for the second straight day.

September 21—Bombs are thrown into political party meeting in La Guaira.

September 21—Two bombs are discovered in gas works at Puerto Cabello.

September 21—Two bombs explode in Caracas bus station.

September 22—Terrorists attack home of policeman in Valencia.

September 22—Terrorists inflict serious injuries on man who refuses to place bomb in Caracas supermarket.

September 23—Bomb explodes in municipal government office at Caracas.

September 24—Terrorists set fire to oil pipeline near Maracaibo.

September 25—Three terrorists break into home of retired miltary officer in town near Caracas and steal arms.

September 25—Terrorists attack and try to burn three buses in Caracas; small bombs are found in large office building.

September 26—Terrorists attack Coca-Cola plant in Caracas, burn three trucks, wound guard.

September 26—Bomb explodes in automobile at Barcelona.

September 27—Police capture 5 terrorists in Caracas after gunfight in streets.

September 27—Bomb explodes in trade union office at Caracas; another in a secondary school.

September 27—Terrorist group is captured trying to assassinate policeman in Caracas; members of group are accused of complicity in murders of 14 policemen.

September 28—Terrorists try to intercept and burn oil tank truck near Maracaibo.

September 28—Guard is wounded in terrorist attack on political party office in Caracas.

September 29—Bomb explodes in Caracas neighborhood.

October 1—A force of 35 to 40 armed terrorists, moving by automobiles and trucks from Caracas, briefly seizes the village of El Hatillo in Miranda State. They surprise and disarm the local police, cut communications lines, burn a local political party office, and paint signs advertising the operation as the work of the Castro-Communist "revolutionary army."

54 USLAR PIETRI, *Freedom of the Press Is Not in Jeopardy in Venezuela*

What is in peril in Venezuela, gentlemen, is not liberty of expression. Lies! Nobody is threatening that. It is sufficient to read the newspapers every morning in

Shorthand text of Senator Dr. Arturo Uslar Pietri's speech at the Senate session of March 18, 1965, Venezuela: Oficina Central de Información. Reprinted by permission.

which everything that can be said and can not be said is printed with the greatest liberty. . . .

In no civilized country would they tolerate a twentieth of what is said in the Venezuelan newspapers every morning. Here they commit moral assassinations daily more serious than physical assassinations, because if a man goes to the corner with a revolver in his hand and shoots the first passer-by, he goes to jail because he has hurt someone; but if a man fortified by his money, and the impunity that certain conventions guarantee him, dedicates himself to poisoning a country, closing avenues, deceiving, casting suspicion on the most reliable persons, this man is attacking the life and well-being of millions of people and his guilt is immense.

But, nevertheless, this man presumes impunity, this man pretends that there is no right to apply any law against him.

Here, gentlemen, freedom of the press is not in jeopardy. . . .

In Venezuela there has always been a mixture which is most dangerous to democracy, namely that of ignorance and bad faith. There are many people who believe that in our country, where the majority of our population is ignorant, and being ignorant, they can be deceived, they can be made to believe things, and thus bad faith is used openly, to deceive and divert the people on the basis of their ignorance.

Thus this people has been led to act many times against its best and most obvious interests. . . .

So, what is involved here, gentlemen, is no threat to the freedom of the press; what is involved is the defense of Venezuelan democracy. Every day a certain press publishes the most scandalous news, whose purpose are these clear objectives—to tell the country that the men ruling it are unworthy, inept, and of ill faith, or are marked by dreadful faults, and who, therefore, do not deserve to rule. That the government pact that has united three parties is a pact of infamy, indefensible, made in the union of three unconfessable appetites. This pursues the end that the country may lose its faith in those governing it and in the government system. . . .

It is obvious that it is a conspiracy to discredit democracy, the democratic institutions and the democratic government. And we must face that conspiracy with serenity, avoiding provocations. We are in Venezuela, gentlemen, in a very peculiar situation that comes many times to our encounter; and that situation is none other than this; this is a country that has lived for a long time, too long, under dictatorial regimes, and therefore suffers of huge legal gaps. We do not have a set of laws covering all aspects of the needs of social life and the conflicts that emanate from it. We do not have even a tradition of legal life; Dictatorships do not have many problems of this kind, because it is enough with the will of one man, or a handful of men, for things to go as they want, and shut down newspapers, jail or exile people, or do whatever they want, to defend that sacrosanct public order that favors them. But when we in Venezuela pretend to live in good faith in a democratic regime, we face the huge gaps in our legislation, and the terrible lack of a tradition. . . .

So in this moment we find ourselves in Venezuela with a group that, on behalf of an alleged right to freedom of speech, what they pretend is a right to irresponsibility, the right to be irresponsible, the right to assassinate morally, the right to calumniate, the right to lie, the right to deceive, the right to counterfeit facts with no responsibility. And if somebody is bold enough to raise his voice and say: "That is a crime, that is incompatible with a juridical regime." he is told immediately: "You are an enemy of the freedom of speech."

This stupendous comedy would be a laughing stock, gentlemen, if a tragic fact were not living at its bottom—the destiny of the Venezuelan democracy and the liberty of that people.

SECTION XIII

Andean Countries

Can these largely Indian states achieve a political stability based upon the needs and aspirations of their people? It will be difficult in Ecuador, according to the analysis by George I. Blanksten, a political scientist at Northwestern University. (Reading No. 55.)

Sometimes it is forgotten that improvements in the health of Latin Americans must be effected in a multitude of small communities whose customs and practices are determined largely by ancient traditions. Experienced applied anthropologists point out how resistant all cultures are to change, and how disappointingly limited and partial have been the successes in even the most intelligently planned and executed programs for conscious improvement. The following report (Reading No. 56) helps to explain why only 11 out of a total of 200 families in a Peruvian village were persuaded to boil their dangerously contaminated drinking water regularly after a two-year conscientious campaign by a resident hygiene worker.

No problem is more ancient or more debated today in the Andean countries than the true capacity of the Indian and his proper role in the life of Bolivia, Ecuador, and Peru. Here are three Bolivian opinions (Reading No. 57) on this vital subject by (1) Gabriel René-Moreno, foremost nineteenth-century bibliographer and historian; (2) Franz Tamayo, twentieth-century poet and philosopher; (3) Fernando Díez de Medina, recent Minister of Education. The last comment (Reading No. 58) comes from an American observer who describes the revolution in attitudes toward the Indian following the Agrarian Reform of August, 1953.

55 BLANKSTEN, The Political System in Ecuador

The "national life" of Ecuador has continued to be dominated by a small ruling class. These "whites" constitute approximately 20 per cent of the population

George I. Blanksten, *Ecuador: Constitutions and Caudillos* (Berkeley: University of California Press, 1951), pp. 169–170, 174–175. Reprinted by permission.

407

of the republic. The Ecuadoran political process rests on a brand of anarchy or chaos within the ruling class. This condition is occasionally referred to by Ecuadorans as "democracy in the Greek sense": a considerable degree of liberty and equality has developed within the "white" group so far as intra-class behavior is concerned. The nation's rigid class system imposes an impressively strong barrier between the "white" and the overwhelming mass of the people of the country.

Ecuador's "democracy in the Greek sense" has meant a chaotic intra-class struggle conducted by the "whites," an anarchical contest in which the lower classes do not participate and in which they normally exhibit little or no interest. The battle of the "whites" among themselves frequently crystallizes along personal and regional lines, ideological differences usually being a distinctly minor factor. Victory in the contest is typically brief, and the victors preside over unstable and uncertain governments.

This political system, like the dominant position of the "whites," rests upon those instruments of power which exclude the lower classes from active participation in what Ecuadorans call the "national life." These instruments are: (1) the pattern of landownership; (2) the Roman Catholic Church; (3) armed force; (4) the class distribution of literacy; (5) the status system, which confers marked prestige upon the "whites"; (6) the division of labor which bestows upon the "whites" a monopoly on laws of the republic. The last of these instruments of power is generally less effective than the other six. . . .

Fundamental reform would involve a far-reaching change in the pattern of landownership, the reduction of the large haciendas, the destruction of the present landowning class, and the introduction of a new group of small individual holders of land. It would mean the reduction of the Church as an instrument of power, its disestablishment, and its removal from national politics. It would demand a radical alteration in the present class distribution of literacy, a termination of the ruling class's virtual monopoly on formal education. It would call for an attitude which would permit "gentlemen" to work with their hands without losing caste, it would demand an alteration in the hierarchy of social classes. And the army would be required to defend the frontiers instead of the class structure of the republic. It the "whites" desire political and constitutional stability, they must themselves undertake a sweeping program which would run essentially counter to their own short-range vital interests. Faced with a choice, most of the "whites" would undoubtedly prefer to retain their present class position—and with it political instability.

Fundamental reform, moreover, cannot be achieved overnight, as many a disillusioned Ecuadoran revolutionist knows. Institutions must take root and grow in the peculiar environment in which they are to live. As the republic's present political system is rooted deep in the character of the nation, so must another be if the system is to change.

56 WELLIN, Water Boiling in a Peruvian Town

A major concern of the Ica Departmental Health Service, a regional health department in Peru, is the attempt to introduce hygienic measures at family levels. A specific problem in the rural reaches of its jurisdiction is to induce people to boil their contaminated drinking water. After two years' effort in Los Molinos, a town of 200 families, a resident hygiene worker visiting individual homes has persuaded 11 housewives to boil water. In this she was aided by a physician, who gave occasional public talks. In addition, there were 15 housewives who were already in the habit of boiling their water prior to the hygiene worker's arrival in town.

A family-by-family investigation disclosed that housewives who decided to boil water did so for different and even opposing reasons. The diversity of motives also applied to the majority of residents who decided to continue consuming unboiled drinking water. Several boiled water because they were sickly, in conformity with pervasive theories about illness and its relation to the local dichotomy between "hot" and "cold" foods. Others boiled water because they rejected local cleanliness values and other standards. Of those who yielded to health department persuasions, some boiled their drinking water because the hygiene workers recommended it; others wanted to heed the hygiene worker but did not boil drinking water until the physician publicly "authorized" their departure from prevailing norms of water usage.

Among those who did not boil drinking water, as among those who did, motives differed. Some did not boil water because they did not have available an after-breakfast interval which, by virtue of local circumstances and belief, was the only possible and appropriate time to boil water. Included among those who decided not to do so were many whose allegiance to cultural values precluded acceptance of new and competing health values.

The hygiene worker was apparently able to secure more positive results with housewives whose economic level and cultural background were similar to her own. Her own background was middle class by Los Molinos standards, and she belonged to the majority cholo group. She was apparently unable to secure equally positive results when dealing with Negroes or with families of markedly different socioeconomic level from her own.

The Los Molinos experience supports the notion that action programs in regions like Ica can effectively supplement professional personnel with local people trained as auxiliary health workers. The study suggests that detailed knowledge of social and cultural factors of the community is vital to the efficiency of the water-boiling program. It also suggests that useful wisdom comes not simply from knowing the scattered items of cultural belief and practice but from

Edward Wellin, "Water Boiling in a Peruvian Town," in Benjamin D. Paul, ed., *Health, Culture, and Community* (New York: Russell Sage Foundation. 1955), pp. 101–102. Reprinted by permission.

the appreciation that they constitute a system in which the individual parts are linked to form a meaningful structure.

57 The Place of the Indian in Bolivia

(1) The red man gave up the struggle centuries ago. The power and civilization of the Empire of Peru could not withstand the first contact with the power and civilization of a group of white adventurers. No new factor whatsoever was contributed by that race to culture or to the conduct of modern life. The Inca Indian is useless. But by some monstrous deformity the Indian is indeed a living force in Bolivia, a passive, inert mass, a stone blocking the viscera of the social program.

---

(2) We must bring about a great, new movement among the upper classes, to whom circumstances have given control over the destiny of the Indian. We must begin the tasks which we irresponsibly failed to undertake three hundred years ago. The situation requires collective action, wise, analytical, and reasoned, as well as justified. A crooked and unsavory way of thinking about the Indian and his meaning within the Bolivian nation must be rectified. We are plagued by anti-scientific prejudices which are basically highly immoral and foreign to the very spirit of nationality. To consider the Indian less than human, ignoring the qualities of his race that are superior to those of the dominant classes, is true inhumanity. . . . This absurd way of thinking about the Indian was the principal cause of the downfall of Spain in America. . . . But who will undertake this movement which we do not hesitate to call national regeneration? Not the Indian directly, but rather we, the thinkers, the directors, the governors, who are beginning to understand more clearly the whole of our life and the true history of our nature. We must begin by realizing the degree to which we have outraged the human dignity of the Indian, the degree of our ignorance of his true strengths and capacities, the abasement we have created, and the ruin worked upon the original masters of this land we now possess. Then we must understand that all this injustice will, in the end, be turned against us, and that, though the apparent victim is the Indian, we are the final and transcendent losers, and that we are in reality destroying the only sources of life and energy which nature offers to us. We will realize that above all we must concede to the Indian respect, justice, dignity and love, acknowledging that his misery is in many respects our work, and that his resurrection will be our salvation.

(1) Gabriel René-Moreno, *Bolivia y Argentina. Notas biográficas y bibliográficas* (Santiago de Chile, 1901), pp. 142–143; (2) Franz Tamayo, *La creación de la pedagogía nacional* (2nd ed., La Paz, 1945), pp. 157–158; (3) Robert J. Alexander, *The Bolivian National Revolution* (New Brunswick, New Jersey: Rutgers University Press, 1958), p. 17. Reprinted by permission.

(3) The Indian is a sphinx. He inhabits a hermetic world, inaccessible to the white and the mestizo. We don't understand his forms of life, nor his mental mechanism. The sociologist and the narrator don't succeed in molding the living material. . . . We speak of the Indian as a mass factor in the nation; in truth we are ignorant of his individual psyche and his collective drama. The Indian lives. The Indian acts and produces. The Indian does not allow himself to be understood, he doesn't desire communication. Retiring, silent, immutable, he inhabits a closed world. The Indian is an enigma.

58 *Agrarian Reform and the Peasant*

The agrarian reform has had a profound effect upon the peasant. This began to be felt even before the task of dividing the haciendas of the landlords among the peasants had begun. Antezana notes this change, then he says:

"A profound psychological transformation was produced in the peasants when the announcement of the reform was made; they began to walk on their own land and to feel free, as if they were standing on the top of a mountain. They learned to speak in a loud voice, with pride and without fear."

One interesting aspect of this psychological change was an alteration of the popular vocabulary. Antezana explains this in the following words:

"From that moment the word 'Indian' disappeared and was wiped from the language to become a relic in the dictionary. Now there existed the 'peasant.' The worker of the countryside had been dignified by being given land and liberty in all of its aspects. 'Indians,' a feudal concept, was the serf of an epoch which had disappeared. Today the peasant is the equal of anyone. . . . The peasant is a human being capable of receiving instruction, of reaching the University, of being owner of the land he works and of making it produce, since the land belongs to him who works it.

"This change in the psychology of the Indian was noted by the officials of the Ministry of Peasant Affairs, which was more closely in touch with him than any other branch of the government. Although the peasants who came to present their problems and their requests to the Ministry continued to show respect for the authorities, they tended to become increasingly insistent in demanding a solution for their difficulties, whatever they might be. They no longer were coming hat in hand to ask favors, but were coming to demand what they now had come to consider their rights."

Robert J. Alexander, *The Bolivian National Revolution* (New Brunswick, New Jersey: Rutgers University Press, 1958), pp. 75–76. Reprinted by permission.

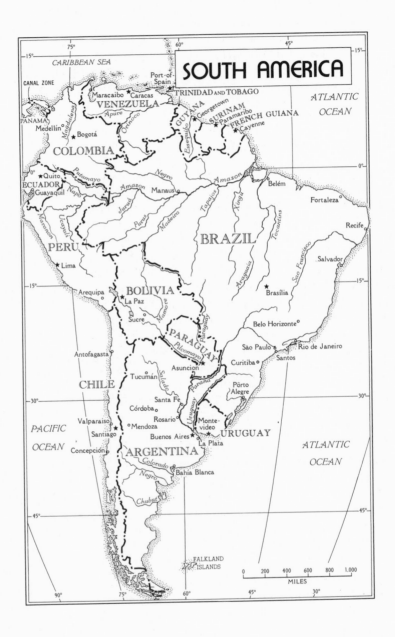

SOUTH AMERICA

CARIBBEAN SEA

CANAL ZONE

ATLANTIC
OCEAN

Port-of-Spain

PANAMA
Medellín
Maracaibo ★Caracas   TRINIDAD AND TOBAGO
VENEZUELA
Apure   Georgetown
Magdalena   Orinoco   GUYANA SURINAM FRENCH GUIANA
★Bogotá   Paramaribo
COLOMBIA   Esequibo   Cayenne

0°   ★Quito   Putamayo
ECUADOR   Napo   Negro   Amazon   Belém
Guayaquil   Manaus   0°

Amazon   Fortaleza
Juruá   Tapajos
Marañon   Ucayali   Purus   Madeira   Xingu   Recife

PERU   Tocantins
★Lima   São Francisco   Salvador

15°   Arequipa   BOLIVIA   15°
★La Paz   Mamoré   Araguaia   ★Brasília
Sucre

PARAGUAY   Belo Horizonte
Antofagasta   Pilcomayo   Paraguay   São Paulo   Rio de Janeiro
                    Asuncion   Curitiba   Santos
CHILE   Tucumán   Salado   Paraná
                                        Pôrto Alegre
30°   Santa Fe   30°
Valparaiso   Córdoba   Rosario   Uruguay   Monte-
Santiago   Mendoza   video   URUGUAY
PACIFIC   Concepción   Buenos Aires ★ La Plata   ATLANTIC
OCEAN   ARGENTINA   OCEAN
                    Colorado
                    Negro   Bahía Blanca

                    Chubut

45°   45°

FALKLAND
ISLANDS   0   200   400   600   800   1,000
                        MILES

90°   75°   60°   45°   30°

Chile

A new phase of Chilean history began with the election in 1964 of Eduardo Frei Montalva as president of Chile. This experienced and vigorous leader of the Christian Democratic party knew what he wanted to accomplish and explained his program in clear and persuasive language. (Reading No. 59.) Chile is a democratic country, but this does not mean that it supports U.S. policies. Fredrick Pike of the University of Notre Dame has analyzed the reasons for opposition by both the Right and the anti-communist Left in Chile. (Reading No. 60.)

59 President Frei Explains His Program

On the occasion of my inauguration as President of the Republic of Chile I directed my remarks not only to my own people, but extended my sentiments and greetings to peoples in every part of the world:

. . . to the brother peoples of Latin America, with whom we no longer wish to live on the bases of the old and worn-out juridical and diplomatic formulas of the past, for they do not satisfy the urgent needs of integration, cooperation and unity. The attainment of these objectives is not only the mandate of geography, tradition, language and history, but is the indispensable condition for reaching the advanced frontiers of creative thought, scientific effort, and technical efficiency which alone will enable us to expand our economy, achieve justice, and acquire a respectful and vigorous voice in the world community. . . . to our friends, the people of the United States, likewise a part of our Great America, with whom we wish a real association based on genuine equality; an association which does not rest on an imbalance of power and wealth but in a real Alliance that permits us to advance in freedom, as pointed out by a man who has died, but whose message is still alive and ever present.

William Manger, ed., The Two Americas. Dialogue on Progress and Problems (New York: Kenedy, 1965), pp. x–xiii, passim. Reprinted by permission.

. . . to the peoples of old Europe, whose presence, image, and ideas have nourished our spirit and have educated us in their long and glorious history, and who now have taught us the miracle of their prodigious recovery and of their growing integration by overcoming age-old antagonisms. Today they are beginning to discover Latin America, and to realize what a grave error it would be for them and for the world not to have a feeling of solidarity with peoples so closely linked with the very essence of their civilization.

. . . to the peoples of the Afro-Asian world, who are undergoing a great revolution for the conquest of political and economic independence and who are struggling for just international relations, without which peace and freedom would only have a precarious existence.

. . . to the people of the so-called socialist world, whose dramatic human adventure we cannot disregard. It would be blindness on our part to do so, despite the deep ideological differences that separate us, since the fact of their existence in the world community cannot be erased and peace cannot be attained without coexistence with them.

In the Presidential elections of 1964 the people of Chile faced a historic crossroads. After a long process of free discussion and conscious reflection, they chose a path which calls for profound changes and for swift advances in the social and economic fields under a government which respects the freedom and dignity of man. The people of Chile did not vote for a man alone. They gave broad, vigorous, and unquestionable support for a course and a program, for a philosophy which inspires the Christian Democratic movement, for a national and popular position which received the generous backing of other political forces and of large independent sectors.

The election heralded a new era in national life. It is the product of a new generation with a new orientation, which seeks to bring education to all Chilean children and give them every opportunity, in the certainty that a nation that conquers ignorance will inevitably conquer misery and servitude.

My administration intends that in an ever increasing manner the peasants will be owners of the land and that property will not be concentrated in the hands of the few; that those who work in the fields will have a just wage and income, and that the laws of the nation will be strictly obeyed. Its aim is that all Chilean families will live in their own homes in a decent community where their children can live in dignity and happiness. It intends to promote economic development and free initiative so that we may increase the production of foodstuffs, expand our industries, and develop our mineral resources for the benefit of Chile.

It proposes to stop inflation, to protect the value of the currency, to provide steady employment and give youth an opportunity; to break the rigidity of a social order which no longer responds to the demands of the times, and thereby afford access to culture and to a real participation in the wealth and the advantages which mark contemporary affluent societies. . . .

On the difficult problem of Cuba that confronts our inter-American regional system, I hope that it may be possible to initiate an action, which I trust will be joint and not individual, with other American states to seek a peaceful solution, a solution that will signify respect for the principle of self-determination of peoples and of nonintervention in their internal problems.

Following my election as President of the Republic, I made the statement that "the Organization of American States no longer has any real vitality. The moment is approaching for a decision whether to bring it up to date with a rapidly changing world and in line with the goals of the Alliance for Progress, or to let it become a sarcophagus of outmoded ideas."

60 PIKE, *The Chilean Right and the Anti-Communist Left*

The social structure and aims of the United States are unappealing to many Chileans. Particularly offensive is the acceptance of social mobility and of the degree of class competition that is inevitable in a pluralistic society. Chile's directing classes, even if they concede the need for social reform, remain generally committed to the stratified, non-open, hierarchical society. Within this structure they are willing to encourage "fraternity," but certainly not equality, nor necessarily even liberty, at least so far as the lower classes and minorities are concerned. "Fraternity" is to be achieved through the paternalism and charity practiced by the aristocracy. And "fraternity" is to be guaranteed by seeing that the lower classes are not allowed to become powerful enough to challenge their leaders and demand their rights. They must remain content, in short, to accept gratefully what is bestowed upon them from above, without ever claiming anything from their superiors.

This spirit was well summarized in a letter that Ambassador to the Holy See Ramón Subercaseaux directed in 1928 to the Chilean Ministry of Foreign Relations. Subercaseaux lamented that social action movements in Chile and elsewhere in the world had not produced hoped-for results because many of their leaders, including even a few priests, had forgotten that the true end was the achievement of social solidarity based on paternalism. As a consequence, the immoral class conflict had vitiated most reform movements. The valid goal of social reformers, asserted Subercaseaux, was not to change the circumstances of men, but to encourage greater love of them as they are, no matter how mean the conditions in which they live.

This attitude is expressed by a multitude of Chilean politicians and intellectuals who are often self-proclaimed champions of social justice. Over one hundred of them have published twentieth-century works that although advocating some reform are as hostile to basic United States social, economic and political patterns as to Russian communism. A striking feature of this body of literature is the accord which the authors, even those of the most recent years, have maintained with the 1928 views of Subercaseaux. . . .

Fredrick Pike, *Chile and the United States, 1880–1962* (Notre Dame: University of Notre Dame Press, 1963), pp. 253–256, *passim*. Reprinted by permission.

Today, many of the reformers of the noncommunist left have come to embrace the ideology of social mobility, direct democracy, pluralism, and some degree of class competition. They oppose the United States because its alliance with Chile's right has placed it in apparent opposition to the very principles to which they aspire. . . .

If the United States is to proceed consistently along these lines, it must first face up to the fact that the traditionalist groups in Chile for whom friendship has been reserved are, in spite of their charm, sophistication, broad culture, gracious way of life, and unquestioned anticommunist fervor, the guardians of a social system that growing thousands are finding intolerable. Yet, not until 1961 did the United States begin to waver in its uncritical support of these groups. It thereby contributed to a situation in which inhered the increasing likelihood that its influence, along with that of the groups it backed, would be swept away before the advancing tide of the very principles which it has long championed within its own boundaries.

Uruguay and Argentina

Uruguay has long been considered a model of democratic and effective gov-
ernment. Economic difficulties have increased during the last few years, to such
an extent that Russell H. Fitzgibbon, a veteran political scientist now on the
faculty of the University of California, Santa Barbara, has asked some probing
questions on the future of Uruguay. (Reading No. 61.)

Argentina has suffered many ups and downs, but the present situation has a
vital relationship to the past as George Pendle, the British Latin Americanist,
shows. (Reading No. 62.)

It is difficult and dangerous to try to capture in a few words the true spirit
of any people, particularly the Argentines. Reading No. 63 *gives five samples of*
opinions: (1) by the Argentine Domingo F. Sarmiento who served as President
(1868–1874); from his classic work on Argentine society Facundo *(1845); (2)*
by the Spanish philosopher José Ortega y Gasset; (3) by Rosita Forbes, who looks
at Argentine men through the eyes of an Englishwoman; (4) by Marcelo T. Al-
vear, President of Argentina, 1922–1928; and (5) James Bruce, United States
Ambassador to Argentina, 1947–1949. Probably no one of these opinions is
wholly correct, for Argentine character is complicated, far from clear-cut phenom-
enon. Other studies have appeared: A. J. Pérez Amuchástegui, Mentalidades argen-
tinas (1860–1930), *Buenos Aires: UDEBA, 1965; Thomas F. McGann,* Argentina: The Divided Land, *Princeton, New Jersey: Van Nostrand, 1966; Jaime Rest,*
Cuatro hipótesis de la Argentina, *Bahía Blanca, Argentina: Universidad Nacional*
del Sur, 1961; Samuel Schapiro, *"Yankees and Argentines,"* The Centennial
Review, *V (1961), pp. 339–349; Tomás Roberto Fillol,* Social Factors in Economic Development. The Argentine Case, *Cambridge, Mass.: The M.I.T. Press,*
1961.

Perón, like most modern dictators, explained his doctrine in many publications.
(Reading No. 64.) *After Perón was overthrown in 1955 a great soul-searching*
began in Argentina to discover why he had come into power, what the long-range
effects of his rule were, and how Argentina was to recover. An Argentine writer,

H. A. Murena, examined all these problems in a long essay in Sur, *the blue-ribbon literary review directed by Victoria Ocampo.* (Reading No. 65.)

The armed forces have been receiving in recent years more attention and a more sophisticated analysis by students of Latin American affairs. James W. Rowe, as a representative of the American Field Service in Argentina, enjoyed an excellent opportunity to assess the complicated influences at work among the generals and gives below an idea of the complexities involved in trying to assess these influences. (Reading No. 66.)

61 *FITZGIBBON, Uruguay: A Model for Freedom and Reform in Latin America?*

Has Uruguay provided by now a sad demonstration of the inability of a democratic state—traditionally regarded as Latin America's most democratic—to preserve hard-won and admirable advantages to the individual in the face of intricate and perhaps selfish political and economic pressures in a complex world? Is Uruguay facing bankruptcy, political anarchy or impotence, or psychological civil war? . . .

In the colonial period Uruguay had little distinct personality of its own. It was simply an appendage of the vast area across the Plata, economically, culturally, and psychologically tributary to Buenos Aires, and at times a bone of political and territorial contention between Spain and Portugal or their more direct agents, the Viceroyalty of La Plata and Brazil. . . .

Most of the nineteenth century saw the record of Uruguay written in about as undistinguished fashion as that of any Latin American country. There was not even the distinction of outstanding dictatorships, bad or good: Uruguay produced no Rosas, no García Moreno, no Díaz, no Gúzman Blanco.

Then, in a relatively short time, say a generation, Uruguay made a remarkable transformation. It is easy to oversimplify the explanation and assign all the credit to one man. As I have written elsewhere, "Probably in no other country in the world in the past two centuries has any one man so deeply left his imprint upon the life and character of a country as had José Batlle y Ordóñez upon Uruguay." That evaluation can still stand. Neither Napoleon nor Hitler, Ataturk nor Gandhi influenced a single country as much or as variously as Batlle did his own beloved Uruguay.

In some degree, though perhaps less certainly, speedily, and pointedly, the spectacular changes which Uruguay experienced over the turn of the century would have come anyway. The country was ripe for an awakening by late in the nineteenth century; it lacked the obstacle of a large unassimilated and perhaps partly unassimilable alien ethnic group; it had favorable climatic, topographic, and other features. But Batlle was initially a catalyst and later a captain of the ferment and change which came to Uruguay. The ten or a dozen years following

Fredrick Pike, ed., *Freedom and Reform in Latin America* (South Bend, Indiana: University of Notre Dame, 1959), Chap. XI, *passim.* Reprinted by permission.

approximately 1905 saw Uruguay experiencing a social and economic revolution of a very real sort. It was the first such reorganization of life and activity that any Latin American state had undergone, antedating by several years the far more highly publicized Mexican revolution. Some of the Uruguayan changes were good, others were perhaps questionable or at least premature, but the net result was to make the government more democratically responsive and a significant fraction of the people more politically conscious and articulate than in any other country of Latin America.

Uruguay's recent planning unfortunately appears jerry-built and in some instances the product of emergency and erratic response to exigencies as they developed one by one. What is probably needed in this wise is another Batlle, not necessarily a son or nephew of Uruguay's outstanding figure, but a figurative Batlle, a man of great moral stature, influence, and wisdom who could lead the country out of the political and economic difficulties into which it has fallen.

The new Batlle would have to be a consummate politician to be able to sell a democratic country a program and policy which would of necessity be initially unpopular in greater or lesser degree. But more than that, he would have to be a statesman of outstanding character, integrity, and vision who would provide constructive rather than simply machinative leadership. There seems little doubt that the economic policies and actions of Uruguay have in various instances been unwise. The remedy for this may have to be an unwonted austerity.

Where is Uruguay headed? In facing a question of this sort we see only as through a glass, darkly. It seems obvious that the country cannot go on indefinitely in the direction and at the pace it recently has. Overpadded personnel rolls are an item: three-fourths or more of the budget is normally allocated for payment of personnel and twenty per cent or more of the whole Uruguayan population (including family members) depend for their livelihood on wages, salaries, or other income from the government. The proportion of Uruguayans in government employ is significantly higher than is the case in the United States despite the fact that this country has a federal and hence more elaborate form of governmental organization.

Another item is the nature of the retirement system. Uruguay is justly famous for the conscientious care it gives to the superannuated and for the advanced social security legislation it has adopted with regard to them. There is grave question, however, as to whether the pattern is actuarially sound. A byline correspondent in the *New York Times* points out that some employees can retire at age fifty if they have by that time worked for thirty years, and adds: "One of the attractive features of retirement is that the pensions are higher than the take-home pay received before retirement. This increase, which may amount to 15 per cent, results from the ending of deductions for social security." Even if such a situation could be actuarially defended it would still be subject to question on psychological grounds.

Uruguay has experienced an accretion of successive gains which temporary injury to the economy and polity of the country cannot efface. Many other Latin

American states are still far behind Uruguay when criteria of any practical or useful variety are applied. . . .

Fortunately, very fortunately, Uruguay fails to be possessed of at least two characteristics which would make its financial plight still worse: (a) it has no psychosis of "keeping up with the Joneses" which would lead it into extravagant expenditures simply to maintain governmental fashions or appearances, and (b) it has no pathological urge to develop a large military establishment, that voracious devourer of pesos, dollars, pounds, or whatnot with which so many contemporary countries are saddled. And yet, Uruguay's fiscal management has not, especially in recent years, been sound. No government can operate on a basis of deficit financing as frequently as has Uruguay's and not find itself in increasing fiscal difficulties. . . .

On the other hand, there has been no diminution—not could there well be— in the political consciousness and articulateness of the average, humble Uruguayan citizen. . . .

62 PENDLE, The Past Behind the Present in Argentina

The absence of a 'stabilized and integral collective life' in Argentina is partly the consequence of the country's extraordinary geographical diversity—sub-tropical luxuriance in the north; Andean deserts, and oases, in the west; temperate, fertile plains in the centre; the windswept south—and the great distances that separate the chief groups of population.

Argentina has been divided by history no less than by geography. In colonial times the Spaniards, whose main base in South America was on the Pacific coast at Lima, generally approached the area now named Argentina from that side of the Andes; and they established their principal settlements in the Andean foothills and marginal mountain ranges, where they founded Salta, Tucumán, Santiago del Estero, Mendoza, Córdoba. To the east, across the vast pampa, on the muddy estuary of the Río de la Plata, Buenos Aires was no more than a sad little outpost of the Empire. Thus geographical separation was confirmed by the pattern of settlement.

When, in the second half of the eighteenth century, Buenos Aires became the seat of administration of a new Spanish vice-royalty that stretched from the Andes to the Atlantic, the people in the east and west of the country were not united. This development merely reversed the relative importance of Buenos Aires and the Andean towns. Buenos Aires grew in prosperity, while the western towns declined. Liberation from Spanish rule in the early years of the nineteenth century, and the opening of Buenos Aires to the shipping of all nations, carried the separation further. The merchants in Buenos Aires now found it cheaper to obtain woollen *ponchos* from Yorkshire by sea than overland by ox-cart from Santiago del Estero,

George Pendle, "Argentina: The Past Behind the Present," *International Affairs*, XXXVIII, No. 4 (October, 1962), 494–500. Reprinted by permission.

HOUSEBOAT

cheaper to get wine from France than from Mendoza, sugar from Brazil than from Tucumán. As Domingo Faustino Sarmiento wrote in his classic work on the period, *Facundo,* Argentina contained two incompatible types of society: on the one hand there was, in Buenos Aires, an urban civilization on the Spanish and European model; on the other hand, in the countryside, the wild life of the uneducated and lawless *gaucho.* Moreover Buenos Aires, being the nation's only port, received and appropriated to itself all the Customs duties, leaving the other provinces almost without public income.

For many years after the attainment of independence from Spain there was no national government, though Buenos Aires constantly fought to extend its authority westwards across the pampa. The dictator Rosas during his long rule (1835–52) ruthlessly crushed rebellious provincial *caudillos,* but he could not entirely subdue them. In 1853 the provinces set up a Confederation, which Buenos Aires refused to join, and Argentina was in fact two states until, at the battle of Pavón in 1861, the Buenos Aires army defeated the Confederate forces. Thereafter, Argentina was in organization one nation. But successive presidents of the republic, by using their constitutional powers to 'intervene' in the provinces, kept alive the old resentment. Time after time, when they disapproved of the results of provincial elections, they would depose provincial governors, members of the provincial legislatures, municipal officials, and judges and install their own representative— an *interventor*—to manage provincial affairs and to 'supervise' the next elections. This procedure continues today.

*   *   *

After the 1850s the economy of the pampa was transformed by the building of railways, the development of cattle-raising to satisfy European (chiefly British) demand, and the coming of a flood of agricultural labourers from Italy and Spain. But this extraordinary economic growth did not greatly contribute to the unification of Argentine society. The railways were not designed to draw the population together: their purpose was to carry the pastoral and agricultural produce of the interior by the shortest route to the shores of the Río de la Plata for shipment abroad. The European immigrants, arriving in such numbers, naturally did not help to form a 'stabilized and integral collective life'. (In 1895 the population of Argentina was about 4 million, of whom one million were foreigners.) Nor was the preponderance of Buenos Aires reduced. The landowners, enormously enriched, built extravagant mansions for themselves in the capital, while the standard of living of the rural workers was no better than before.

*   *   *

In 1890–1 a brief interruption occurred in the rising national prosperity. Excessive optimism and public extravagance had produced a high degree of inflation. The crisis revealed another conflict of interests, though this proved to be less fundamental than it seemed at that time.

During the period of inflation the conservative landowners—who were now in permanent control of the central government—welcomed the fall in the value of the Argentine currency because they sold their meat and grain for British pounds or French francs, and in consequence of the depreciation they received a higher peso income for their exports. On the other hand, the inflation threatened to ruin the Buenos Aires merchants, who had to pay at soaring peso rates for the British manufactures, the French wines, and the olive oil which they imported. A large proportion of the merchant and shopkeeping class were of European birth, or the sons of immigrant parents, and their outlook had little in common with that of the landowners.

This urban middle class were the main strength of a Radical Party which arose out of the crisis of 1890–1. Their principal demand was for free suffrage and honest elections—in other words, that their own class should be given an opportunity to share in the management of the country. In the second decade of the twentieth century the Radicals made their first experiment in government; but of course by then they were just as Argentine as the Conservatives, and when their leader, Hipólito Irigoyen, was elected president of the republic in 1916 he ruled just as autocratically as his predecessors. Indeed, Irigoyen outdid all previous rulers in the use—or abuse—of his powers of intervention in the provinces.

Again and again liberal-minded men sincerely tried to set up representative government of the British or North American kind, but when a more or less democratic régime was established it almost invariably evolved into a dictatorship or was overthrown by a coup d'état. It would not be an exaggeration to say that the conflict between imported democratic ideas and the local tradition of personal leadership—*caudillismo*—has been the central theme of political development in Argentina, as in other South American republics. Parkinson has even suggested that 'it is to South America that we must look, in the first instance, for dictatorship introduced and perpetuated as an admitted necessity; defended by thinkers of integrity and seen by historians as a positive good. . . . All modern dictatorship owes its inspiration to Simón Bolívar.'

* * *

Under Irigoyen the Radicals wasted their opportunity, and they were replaced in 1930–1 by a military-Conservative alliance. In fact the Radicals—the name was a misnomer—had discovered that they did not really desire any drastic alteration in the economic system. Consequently they, almost as much as the Conservatives, failed to gain the support of the urban working class, who were rapidly growing in strength and could not indefinitely be denied participation in public affairs. Nor were the workers greatly attracted to Socialism, which they were inclined to regard as a foreign creed. When the stream of immigration was cut off after the economic crisis of 1930 the workers became more and more Argentine in outlook and ready to follow a *caudillo* who would appeal to their nationalist sentiments and who would offer to improve their standard of living—an improvement which they were unable to achieve by parliamentary means.

The army, too, were increasingly dissatisfied with the Conservatives, into whose hands the government had passed again. A group of younger officers, in particular, were determined that Argentina should be transformed into a modern industrialized state, and they realized that the conservative oligarchy were obstructing that transformation. So the military coup d'état which occurred in 1943 not only removed the Conservatives but prepared the way for a new era.

In the next two years, however, the senior officers grew alarmed by the activities of one of their colleagues, Colonel Juan Perón, who, as Secretary of Labour and Social Welfare, was gaining extraordinary popularity among the working class by promoting their interests with great zeal and publicity. In 1945, in an attempt to halt this process, Perón's military critics compelled him to resign from the government. Perón defiantly appealed to the workers for support. He was then placed under arrest. Working-class riots followed, and the trade union leaders—feverishly assisted by the young radio performer Eva Duarte who, like Perón himself, was of humble social origin—organized large-scale demonstrations. To appease the crowds, Perón was released.

*   *   *

As President of Argentina Perón raised the standard of living of the workers. He encouraged the expansion of urban industry—not only in Buenos Aires, but also in provincial towns such as Córdoba. He would have developed the southern oil-fields if he had remained longer in power.

In making these and other contributions to social and economic progress, however, and in his manoeuvres to maintain himself in power, Perón aggravated the fragmentation which for so many years had been characteristic of Argentine society. By playing one sector of the community against another—politicians, land-owners, businessmen, workers—he weakened the opposition but increased internal disunity.

Perón's military successors likewise, by repressing and ostracizing the *Peronistas,* made it impossible for an 'integral collective life' to come into being. The Aramburu government dedicated itself to the purging of the country of every trace of *Peronismo.* Those who had been connected with that régime were dismissed from the federal and provincial administrations, and from universities, law-courts, and embassies abroad. Military *interventores* were placed in charge of the trade unions, and the *Peronista* Party was outlawed. The workers retaliated with strikes and sabotage. Employers (as the Buenos Aires Correspondent of *The Times* wrote) now treated the workers with deliberate lack of consideration, their attitude being: 'Well, you fellows: you have had your day. Now it is our turn.'

As the *Peronistas*—comprising about one third of the electorate—were not permitted to nominate their own candidates for the general elections in 1958, they voted for the faction of the Radical Party that was headed by Dr Arturo Frondizi, who had indicated that he would give them a fair deal if he were elected. With the *Peronistas'* assistance Frondizi won an overwhelming victory, and in spite of the protests of some members of the military hierarchy General Aramburu allowed him to be inaugurated in the presidency.

Frondizi had declared that he would govern, not for any one party, but for the whole nation, and it was evident that he intended to bring the *Peronistas* back into the community. Soon after assuming office he ordered a general increase in wages, granted an amnesty to those who were in prison or exile for political offences, and enabled *Peronistas* to re-enter the public service. The military leaders objected to these concessions, and during the next three years they repeatedly compelled the president to dismiss from official posts those whom they suspected of having Peronista sympathies. Nevertheless, at the congressional and provincial elections in March 1962 Frondizi rather rashly allowed the *Peronistas* to vote for their own candidates. This was doubtless another attempt to close the rift in the community; at the same time Frondizi probably judged that the *Peronistas,* having been proscribed for six years, would no longer vote as a bloc. In the event, the *Peronistas* won more than half of the available seats in the Chamber of Deputies and the majority of the available provincial governorships. Thereupon the leaders of the armed forces, fearing that Frondizi would permit the revival of *Peronismo* to continue, deposed him, imprisoned him, and ordered the annulment of the elections. The generals and admirals now had no clear policy for the nation. Their one aim was to keep the *Peronista* workers out of politics, to drive them back to where they properly belonged—to the meat-packing plants, the textile factories, etc., whence Perón had so irresponsibly brought them forth.

*   *   *

In deposing Frondizi, as when overthrowing Perón, the military were serving the interests of the upper class (now consisting not only of the landowners, but also of industrialists, bankers, and merchants). It is true that the majority of the military officers today are of *petit bourgeois* origin, but they (and their wives) saw a career in the armed forces as means to social advancement. During the 1930s and 1940s they were pampered by military governments, and in the social upsurge of the Perón era they gained prestige and quite comfortable prosperity. After the revolution which overthrew Perón in September 1955, officers with *Peronista* left-wing tendencies were placed in retirement, and the disputes which subsequently occurred within the armed forces arose mainly from disagreement on the measures to be adopted for preserving order and the traditional social structure.

In Argentina, as in other Latin American countries, the desire of the present military hierarchy, as of the civilian oligarchy, is that the capitalist system shall be perpetuated, and that whatever modifications may have to be made to adjust it to modern conditions shall cause the least possible inconvenience to the privileged members of the community.

*   *   *

Conditions are constantly changing, but to a considerable extent we can find in the past the explanation of why the Argentines behave as they do today. During the nineteenth century, as we have observed, they acquired the habit of *not* co-operating with one another. *Caudillo* was against *caudillo,* the capital city against the provinces. Landowners who amassed vast wealth soon became (with some notable exceptions) absentee owners, inhabiting quite another world from that of their *peones*. When foreign settlers arrived, they were allowed to live their own lives in their own way; and while their children were taught at school to sing the Argentine national anthem and to honour the national heroes, they learned also to be Argentine individualists, each one of them a *'Señor Yo'*, a 'Mister I'. Military officers—feather-bedded heirs of the soldiers who marched across the Andes with San Martín—today still pay lip service to parliamentary democracy but take it for granted that government by decree is the only practical method of preserving order.

Of course, many of the characteristics and conditons described in the present article are by no means peculiar to Argentina. A combination of *all* of them does not exist, however, in any other country. Critics—foreigners, and Argentines too— contend that the Argentine way of conducting affairs is deplorable. Nevertheless, it is in this way that Argentina became, and still manages to remain, the most highly developed nation in Latin America.

Most foreigners—and, indeed, most Argentines whom one meets abroad— know little of Argentina outside Buenos Aires and the nearby holiday resorts. But Buenos Aires is a deceptive city. In appearance, and in its way of life, it is the most European of all Latin America's major cities, so one is apt to forget that it only exists by reason of the very *un*-European hinterland, which it dominates but which, since the pastures and grainfields provide the city's wealth, does, in a sense, domi- nate the city in return.

Buenos Aires is swept by a wind that comes from the desolate south; a wind that has passed over the dreary adobe villages of the remote regions, and over the rich *pampa;* a wind which, meeting the warm air currents from the north, creates violent storms upon the capital. Likewise, Buenos Aires, in spite of its European aspect, is affected by powerful social and political pressures that are provincial, disturbing and, above all, South American. This is nothing new. It has always been so.

63   *"The Originality and Peculiarities of Argentines"*

1. GOD HELP PEOPLE WHO DO NOT HAVE FAITH IN THEMSELVES!

Argentines of whatever class, civilized or ignorant, have a high opinion of their own worth as a people. The other American peoples throw this vanity in their faces and act offended at their presumption and arrogance. I believe that the charge is

A Sarmiento Anthology, edited by Allison W. Bunkley, trans. by Stuart Edgar Grummon (Princeton: Princeton University Press, 1948), p. 116. Reprinted by per- mission. (2) José Ortega y Gasset, *Obras* (3rd ed., 2 vols., Madrid: Espasa-Calpe, 1943), I, 659–679, *passim.* Reprinted by permission. (3) Rosita Forbes, *Eight Republics in Search of a Future* (London: Cassell, 1933), p. 109, *passim.* Reprinted by permission. (4) As quoted by James Bruce, *Those Perplexing Argentines* (New York: Longmans, Green & Co., 1953), p. 7. (5) *Ibid.,* pp. 24–34, *passim.*

not unwarranted, but I am not concerned about it. God help the people who do not have faith in themselves! Great things have not been wrought for them!

2. ARGENTINA'S FABULOUS TREASURE

The Argentine people are not content to be one nation among many; they require an exalted destiny, they demand of themselves a proud future, they have no taste for a history without triumph and are determined to command. They may or may not succeed, but it is extremely interesting to witness the historical trajectory of a people called to empire. . . .

Argentine society has been formed and more and more lives under waves of immigration. Thousands and thousands of new men arrive on the Atlantic coast of Argentina with no other spiritual possession than a fierce individual hunger; men abnormally lacking in all interior discipline, men uprooted from their native societies, where they have lived, without realizing it, morally disciplined by a sort of stabilized and integral collective life. But the immigrant is not an Italian, nor a Spaniard, nor a Syrian. He is an abstract being whose personality has been reduced to the exclusive aim of seeking a fortune. . . .

The immoderate appetite for fortune, boldness, incompetence, and the lack of adherence to and love for any trade or job are recognized characteristics endemic in any trading post. And it is precisely this set of characteristics which distinguishes the abstract and alluvial society of a trading post from a native, organic society. . . .

The Argentine is a marvellously gifted man who does not abandon himself to anything, who has never surrendered his existence irrevocably in the service of anything exterior to himself. . . .

In Buenos Aires I have heard many Argentines complain of the frequent egoism of their compatriots. But, in my opinion, this stricture is erroneous. A nation of the calibre of modern Argentina is not made by egoists in a century. In addition, this supposed congenital egoism does not explain any of the other peculiarities of the Argentine.

The Argentine is pleased with the image he has made of himself. In this image, imprecise in its totality, of vague qualities and attributes, there are, nevertheless, some clear traits. For example, one of its ingredients is *argentinidad* itself. To be from the Argentine nation, to be of this people, this is a reason for elemental, irrefutable, and axiomatic pride for any true Argentine. . . . It is born within the individual along with a blind faith in the glorious destiny of his nation; he considers all the future grandeurs already accomplished, and feeling himself a part of them, he appropriates to his own person the glory of this collective future as if it were a present reality. . . .

This dynamic is Argentina's fabulous treasure. I repeat, I know of no other modern nation which possesses a basic and decisive resource with greater potentialities.

3. BUENOS AIRES BELONGS TO MEN

Buenos Aires belongs to men. They crowd the narrow pavements and congregate in groups at street corners. They loiter on steps of clubs and public buildings. They fill the cafés which are unusually silent, and impede the traffic with their haphazard wandering, for there is no hurry in the streets of Buenos Aires. . . . For most of the day, the streets are masculine and inordinately sober. There are no smiles. The faces leaning across the café tables, while their owners throw dice to see who shall pay for drinks, are as serious as those monotonously progressing some five feet above the pavements. The Argentine takes his pleasures as solemnly as his business. . . . There are no smiles in Buenos Aires till the shopgirls come out for lunch, or till that convivial hour when traffic is swept from Calle Florida and women, in twos and threes, never alone, rarely in company of a man, take possession of the scene. . . .

The private life of Buenos Aires is Spanish. To a certain extent it is even Eastern, for there are restaurants where men and women eat in different sections. Except on a golf course it is unusual to see a man and a woman walking together. Male and female are sharply divided. The men have their offices and their clubs. The women occupy themselves with their enormous families, their clothes, bridge and formal hospitality. . . . It is the women who represent contemporary culture for they read the best literature in several languages. They follow the latest movements in art and music. They are admirable housekeepers, and the rooms they live in, the meals they offer their guests, are as perfected in detail as the clothes they wear. . . .

At present there is no necessity for the average Argentine woman to compete with man. She has not lost the pride of being wholly and only a woman. She is willing to be leisured and detached, cherished, elusive and pursued. She is fully occupied with the large families on which the future of her country depends. . . .

The country women, living in mud huts thatched with reeds, working from sunrise to sunset, cooking, cleaning and looking after their children, between long spells of harvesting cane or maize; the wives of construction engineers, of architects, builders and camp-men, living in temporary galvanized-iron sheds without any comforts at all on the edge of a growing railway, a bridge that is building, land that is being developed—these also are Argentines. They represent the courage and the enterprise of a new country intent on growth. Their days are measured by hard work, or by a still harder endurance.

4. THOSE PERPLEXING ARGENTINES

Argentines refuse to accept any truth which makes them inferior to anyone else. Theirs is the greatest city in the world, their frontier mountains the highest and their *pampas* the widest; theirs the most beautiful lakes, the best cattle, the richest vineyards, and the loveliest women. They accept no qualifications nor the fact that there might be some other country which surpasses them in anything . . . perhaps it is this overwhelming pride of the Argentines that leads them to believe they can live aloof from any interdependence of nations; that they are self-sufficient without possessing even elementary industries; and that they need have no fear of whatever changes may come.

5. THE ARGENTINE CONCEPT OF DIGNIDAD

The Argentine concept of *dignidad* takes many forms. All Latin Americans share this concept, but the Argentine form is most acute. To an Argentine, *dignidad* means no man can be criticized in front of his friend. Employees have been known to resign for lesser cause. Even office boys and porters, streetcar conductors and the sanitation men are treated with the same sort of *dignidad,* lest they become enemies. Argentine students must be strictly obedient to teachers, just as the private obeys his officer. Anything less would be *contra la dignidad.* . . .

There is something essentially sad about the Argentine character that is quickly apparent, especially to the newcomer. It shows in Argentine music, dress, and conversation, and, despite his optimism, in the average Argentine's outlook. Many of the stories popular in Buenos Aires are not locally created, but imports dressed up in local verbiage. Many of the comic strips are translations from abroad. Most locally produced humorous films are with few exceptions not really funny. Rather, they are drawing-room farces filled with talk. . . .

Argentines love the sport and drama of argument. They like to punctuate what they say with verbal thrusts and stinging barbs. Points are often made to win the approval of listeners rather than overwhelm opponents with logic. A stranger, first seeing a pair of Argentines in conversation, often feels that an explosion is imminent. To Argentines, a good rousing argument is a vital part of living. They like talk for talk's sake. Contradicting one's friends or enemies is routine. . . .

The habit of contradiction, and the refusal of the average Argentine to take orders may, however, some day be their country's salvation, for, no matter who is in control, the Argentines, although moving slowly, have always somehow managed to contradict. . . .

For those he knows, the Argentine can be the world's most courteous and charming individual. Unknowns get short shrift. Relatively few Argentines have any sense of public politeness. They frequently bump into people while scurrying round town, refusing all written or unwritten rules about keeping to the right or left, or giving the right of way to man, beast, or vehicle. . . .

Argentines want most to live peacefully. They seek a tranquil existence, hence are willing to talk but go along rather than fight back. Some feel this characteristic has stemmed from the vast flat *pampa* where the temperature is mild all year round and the cattle are placid, bland, and phlegmatic. True, the trait of tranquility is more notable in the interior than in Buenos Aires. Yet even among those Argentines who are excitable and passionate in other ways, the desire to keep out of trouble, to remain uninvolved, to refuse to upset oneself unduly, is traditional.

64 *Perón Expounds His Doctrine*

1. THE RULING CLASS

An attempt has been made to lead the public to believe that the oligarchy, that untoward lodge of demagogues, represented the ruling class in the country, its elite, and as such was made up of wise, rich and good people. We must observe that "the wise are seldom rich, and the rich seldom good." Nor must we forget that neither the wise nor the good found a place among Argentine politicians. (October 15th, 1944)

2. OBJECTIVES

From today onwards we shall industrialize the country so that our work may be done by Argentine workers and so that they may earn what foreign workers earned before. This is what industrialization means to us. To accomplish this cycle we shall complete and intensify the economic cycle of production and consumption, we shall produce more, and value that production in view of our own industrialization and commerce, avoiding exploitation and increasing the consumption. When this cycle is closed, we shall be able to provide our country with 80 or 90 per cent of our production and we shall only export 10 or 20 per cent, because it is necessary to convince ourselves that the money of a man from Catamarca or Santiago del Estero is worth as much as that of the English, Americans or Japanese. All this problem is in itself simple if one tries to solve it, but it gets complicated when one cannot or does not want to solve it. We have our orientation clearly defined and a plan of action that will take us directly to the achievement of the objectives we are looking for. (July 30th, 1947)

3. EVERYTHING SHOULD BE ARGENTINE

Foundations have already been laid for the national tin-plate factory—an article of trade which is taking too long in getting to our country—in which the containers we need to export our production in will be manufactured. Due to the lack of a factory of tin-plate containers, the Republic has lost many thousands of millions of pesos; and we have not had any tin-plate factory before because certain foreigners that negotiated with our food production, objected to it. But in the future we shall have the containers that our production requires, the ships necessary to transport it, and those who in previous times commanded here as if they were in their own land, will have to submit and receive our products canned

Items 1–3 are from Juan Domingo Perón, *Perón Expounds His Doctrine* (Buenos Aires, 1948), pp. 53, 146–147, 149; items 4–5 are from Juan Domingo Perón, *The Voice of Perón* (Buenos Aires: Subsecretaría de Informaciones de la Presidencia de la Nación Argentina, 1950), pp. 131–132.

by Argentine hands, transported by Argentine railways and taken to Europe by Argentine ships. (March 2nd, 1947)

4. ANOTHER SOCIAL SERVICE

It would never occur to anyone that the air, the sun, the light, and the water in the rivers were the exclusive heritage of a chosen few. The very idea seems absurd to us. The time will come when it will also seem absurd to us that culture and advantages of industrial civilization, petroleum, and sources of energy should be exploited by a privileged few.

In the same way, I understand that, with the passing of the years, the distribution of food supplies will become another social service, because proper nourishment is one of the most powerful sources of energy, and one which is most directly responsible for the development and perfecting of a community of human beings. (April 29th, 1949)

5. ARGENTINE RAILWAYS

We have reached our "coming of age" which enables us, to the same extent as anybody else, to estimate our true value and to govern our country by ourselves. For this reason it is of vital importance that basic industries should be national, sometimes controlled by the State and at others privately owned, but always in the hands of Argentines. In achieving this purpose and effecting this policy of recovery, it is of vital importance that the railways should be nationalized, to say nothing of reasons of sovereignty which are easy to understand. (September 17th, 1946)

65 MURENA, The Nature of the Argentine Crisis

For how long has Argentina been in a state of crisis? From its foundation? If so, there was, nevertheless, during the nineteenth century an "animal" instinct, if I may use that expression, which carried the country onward in spite of itself. And there was also, at the end of the last century and at the beginning of the present, the illusion that a community had taken form. . . . Now, for the last few decades, for the last thirty years, we are witnessing the crisis of the crisis. What has become of that "animal" instinct, which was doubtless the source of the famous optimism of the cattle men? In some way it grew tired, it disappeared, although it is still breathing its last, unconvincing moos.

The only force which could have taken its place, the community spirit, was never formed. The proof: that the country is sunk in paralysis. The sick one has fallen on his bed, at last. Wherever I look, at the statistics, the way of life, or international prestige, I see the same. Of course, the world situation has changed. There is also the universal crisis: many tell me that the Argentine crisis is but

H. A. Murena, "Notas sobre la crisis argentina," *Sur,* No. 248 (Buenos Aires, 1957), pp. 1–16, *passim.* Reprinted by permission.

part of the universal. But I cannot help thinking of Brazil: this country has faced general problems, but also others which are not universal but which are almost identical to the problems of Argentina. Nevertheless, it is not paralyzed. What is more, it has managed to pass to the head of the Latin American nations.

Argentina often hits the front page of foreign newspapers. Thanks to our military *coups d'état* . . . we have revealed ourselves to be just what we used to boast that we were not: South Americans. Since 1930 military *coups*—triumphant, defeated, or abortive—exceed three dozen in number. . . .

. . . Under the name of various political parties the forces of the oligarchy had the power in their hands for a long time. They did what they did: much of it good, much bad . . . the oligarchy was one of the forces which molded *Peronismo*. It refused to listen to half the country, it mocked half the nation by ignoring it. Not out of avarice, as some suppose, but out of a pride which wore the mask of a beneficent "patriarchalism." . . .

The crisis is not an economic problem. How could that be the case in a country which enjoys one of the highest standards of living in the world? There are economic problems, but the problem is not economic . . . the crisis is not a social problem. It is not the problem of any particular class, which has been inflicted upon the whole nation. It is a problem of all the classes, because all of them have failed to meet it, and all of them have contributed to it. It is, as a result, a common problem. A problem of the community, I am tempted to say. But I know I ought not to, for I know also that the problem is precisely the lack of *community*. . . .

There is no community in Argentina. We do not form a body, though we may form a conglomeration. We behave as if each one were unique and as if he were alone, with the unfortunate consequences which result when that is the situation. The hand knoweth not what the head thinketh, the mouth ignoreth the stomach, *et cetera*. . . . When a situation cannot be resolved within the framework of the community, then there must be a revolution, in order to modify that framework. Party struggles and revolution are the resources which assure the community of life. Instead of life, Argentina has rancorous, factious chaos, periodically illuminated by *coups d'état*. It is not an organism of which all feel themselves a part. Each organ believes itself the whole, and functions as if it were more important than the whole. Is there any more succinct definition of sickness? Who is to blame? No one. Everyone.

66 ROWE, The Role of the Military

Despite the occasional rhetoric of romantics—in the Peronist trade-union sector at one extreme or the pockets of literary nationalism at the other—it is safe to say that very few Argentines can tolerate the notion of outright dictatorship headed by a military *caudillo*. Similarly, except for a few of the more romantic

From *Argentina's Restless Military*, by James W. Rowe, an AUFS Report, Copyright 1964 by American Universities Field Staff, Inc. Reprinted by permission.

Radical orators, no one talks of the shriveling of the military role to a status similar to that which is found, say, in Costa Rica, or even Uruguay. Within these outer limits, however, at least four views regarding the role of the military in Argentine society have some currency.

The first view, which was actual practice during the Provisional Government and came near to being reestablished in 1962, holds that a period of tutelage is necessary while the country is being cleansed of totalitarian threats and corruption in preparation for full democracy. The military govern as trustee, but permit widespread civilian participation in the decision-making machinery, encourage impersonalism, and observe institutional forms if possible. This was the view of the more extreme elements of the Colorado movement inside the military, and during the anarchic months of 1962 it was embraced by a variety of civilian leaders more influential than numerous. The prestige of this school has been considerably diminished by the successive Azul victories of 1962 and 1963.

A second view is the "Doctrine of Vigilance" practiced during the Frondizi administration. It was enunciated bluntly by its chief practitioner, General Carlos Severo Toranzo Montero in March 1960:

. . . The national government, with its initial "integrationist" political line, stimulated Peronist appetites. This line was abandoned because of pressure of the Armed Forces. . . . Pressure action by the Armed Forces, acting within the constitutional order, contributed to the change. . . . In case of national catastrophe, of a succession crisis, or of the drift of government toward tyranny, the Armed Forces, disciplined in republican principles, are the best guarantee . . . The Armed Forces, politically impartial and directed by men true to their word, can and do act from time to time as a legitimate force of gravitation in the institutional order, and contribute to the hastening of national recovery.

"Vigilance," then, permits the normal play of civilian politics and administration within certain boundaries. As conceived by Toranzo Montero, it implies circumscription by means of suasion, and within an order of institutions and legality —not mere fiat. It is questionable whether such a theory corresponded to the reality of 1959–1962, since the "vigilantes" usually needed the support of allies more interested in terminating the administration than controlling it. "Vigilance" also implies a degree of institutional coherence and unity which simply did not exist either in the Army or the services as a body. As a policy, it had to be abandoned in favor of a *golpe* to contain Frondizi, and slipped toward "tutelage" before the Azules struck in 1962.

A third view sees the military's role as that of "the great mute"—highly professional corps dedicated exclusively to its "specific task." Professionalization and modernization of the Army took place around the turn of the present century under the direction of General Pablo Richieri. Despite the tergiversations of the past three decades, a persistent strand of thinking in the Armed Forces has insisted on the incompatibility of military and political activity. In 1962 this view received new impetus when the Azul sector triumphed and General Juan Carlos Onganía became Army Commander in Chief. Both Onganía and the Azul documents stressed repeatedly that the Armed Forces, after setting Argentina back onto the path of law and constitutionality, should return to their specific professional duties.

A fourth view holds that the energies of the Armed Forces must be harnessed to the task of economic development. Argentina has a strong tradition of military involvement in industrial and developmental enterprise, dating from the activities of General Mosconi with the state oil monopoly (Yacimientos Petrolíferos Fiscales) in the 1920's and those of General Manuel N. Savio with heavy industry in the 1940's. The latter was largely responsible for laws establishing an infant iron and steel industry at San Nicolás and a complex of military industries known as the Dirección General de Fabricaciones Militares. The Air Force and Navy also established industrial activities extending well beyond mere arsenals. During the Perón era, individual officers and the services themselves entered a wide variety of paramilitary activities, and despite retrenchment during both the Aramburu and Frondizi periods, the influence of the military in state industrial enterprises is still heavy. In social development activities which other countries now call military "civic action," antecedents can be traced to Roca's Army of the Desert in the 1870's. Even such a beleaguered target of military intromission as Arturo Frondizi has indicated disagreement with the notion of Armed Forces limitation to the "specific task," and urges that they be enlisted in the struggle for economic development. Although the semiofficial creed of the present military hierarchy is "professionalization and abstention," a number of younger officers appear to favor more vigorous paramilitary activity. Sometimes loosely termed "Nasserists" by the Argentine and foreign press, they include such officers as General Carlos J. Rosas and Colonel Carlos María Zavalla. In March 1964 this viewpoint was espoused by General Juan E. Gugliamelli, Director of the Superior War School, who suggested that a "third way"—between political intromission and professional abstention—could be found in the notion of "the Army at the service of economic development."

SECTION XVI

Brazil

Two basic convictions of many Brazilians may be summed up in these phrases: "Brazil has more of everything," and "Brazil is different from Spanish America." John J. Johnson of Stanford University and Charles Wagley of Columbia University—both long-time Brazil watchers—examine these conditions. (Readings No. 67–68.)

Disease has had a tremendous influence on the course of Brazilian history, a fact which has not always been recognized as a vital part of her developmental problem. Donald B. Cooper of Tulane University, one of the few U.S. writers concerned with the medical history of Latin America, has explained the contribution of Brazil's greatest medical scientist, Oswaldo Cruz, in conquering yellow fever. (Reading No. 69.)

Brazil is also poetry, and Ronald de Carvalho has captured, in a Whitmanesque spirit, in his "Song of Brazil" some of the essential qualities of his country—its exuberance, optimism, variety, and vigor. (Reading No. 70.)

Gilberto Freyre, born in 1900 in Pernambuco, was trained as a social anthropologist under Franz Boas at Columbia University. Prolific author, delegate to the General Assembly of the United Nations, member of the Brazilian Parliament from 1945 to 1950, professor at various universities in the United States and Europe as well as in his own country, Freyre has become one of the foremost spokesmen for Brazil. His studies, The Masters and the Slaves, and Brazil: An Interpretation, and other contributions have become widely known in English as well as in many other languages. He gives a well-known and much-discussed interpretation of Brazil's racial history. (Reading No. 71.)

Anthropologists have made significant contributions during the last twenty years to the study of Brazil. Here, Charles Wagley and several associates present their findings (Reading No. 72), which confirm to some extent the lyrical attitude of such writers as Gilberto Freyre but also set forth present and future problems.

Carleton Sprague Smith, of New York University, considers Heitor Villa-

Lobos the twentieth-century Latin American composer most likely to be remembered a century hence. *"His is an undisciplined genius—but it is genius. And the kind that will outlast the twentieth century."* (Reading No. 73.)

Communists in Brazil, as elsewhere, have come to doctrinal blows over whether to follow Moscow or Peking. (Reading No. 74.) *The Left in Brazil is fragmented, but there are many influences at work, as indicated by two U.S. students, Timothy F. Harding and Barbara Hall. Mr. Harding made his observations while a Stanford University graduate student. Miss Hall's work as a staff member of the YWCA enabled her to work closely with Brazilian students and to see national problems through their eyes.* (Readings No. 75–76.)

One widely held political view is that Brazil must decide upon and maintain its own independent foreign policy, a position vigorously set forth by the historian José Honório Rodrigues. (Reading No. 77.) *His statement was written in 1962 during the presidency of João Goulart, and appeared in the first number of the new publication edited by Enio Silveira, whose title*—Brasil Independente—*indicates its orientation.*

67 *JOHNSON, Brazil Has More of Everything*

Brazil has been called "the country in Latin America with the most of everything." The claim is figuratively, if not literally, true. Brazil has the most area, a half of South America. It has the most people, and its population is increasing at a phenomenal 2,250,000 per year (five Latin American countries have populations smaller than the annual increase in Brazil). Brazil has the most foreign debt ($2.7 billion at the end of 1962); amortization and interest charges, were they to be met, would require over 40 per cent of the Republic's foreign exchange earnings. Brazil has the most inflation. It has the most illiterates. It has the most people living under substandard conditions. It has an urban housing shortage of between two and three million units. Rio de Janeiro alone has 650,000 persons massed in its deplorable *favelas*. Everywhere one sees grim poverty and glaring deficiencies in education, housing, and public health. Only 14 million out of a total of 77 million are served by water works and sewer systems. Brazil has the most voters, the most workers, the most consumers, and the greatest economic potential. Also, to date Brazil has received the most assistance from the United States. . . .

In writing about Brazil today four essential problems must be considered—inflation, the economic slow-down, educational backwardness, and the position of the bureaucrats.

INFLATION

During the past months inflation has captured most of the headlines from Brazil. Living costs, after rising by 40 per cent in 1961 and 50 per cent in 1962,

John J. Johnson, "Potential in Brazil," *Current History* (January, 1964), 1–7, *passim.* Reprinted by permission of the author and of *Current History, Inc.*

continued to soar in 1963. As the year drew to a close it was anticipated that 1963 would show an increase of at least 70 per cent in living costs. Other figures, using 1958 as a base, indicate that consumer price levels in the city of São Paulo had almost quadrupled by 1962. . . .

It is probable that the inflation will get worse before it improves. This is because there are still individuals in positions of influence who believe in inflation or, at least, do not find the alternatives acceptable. . . .

The evidence, however, appears to support those who contend that inflation in Brazil no longer promotes development, or benefits any social-economic group. This "anti-inflationist" element claims that the inflation has resulted from large government deficits, financed by increasing the money in circulation, and from irresponsible expansion of credit, much of which has been wasted in non-productive channels. They also contend that Brazil's rate of economic growth can be explained in terms of its favorable international trade position until the early 1950's and, since then, by the large loans made by the United States largely to repay Brazilian creditors. The anti-inflationists feel that if inflation is to be stopped before it generates explosive tensions, Brazil must promptly institute sweeping monetary and fiscal reforms supported by still more massive loans.

ECONOMIC SLOW-DOWN

Brazil's economy has drifted since 1960 and the GNP rate of growth currently stands at approximately one half or less of the 1950–1960 average. The slow-down has served to point up several dangerous flaws in the nation's economic structure. Management personnel is incompetent; too often the criteria for selection of key officers in private industry are family relationships rather than managerial skills. The State refuses to pay salaries that will attract top quality men and then tolerates corruption by the generally mediocre individuals it relies upon to run public-controlled enterprises. Skilled laborers who might be trained as competent shop foremen are extremely scarce and shift from job to job haphazardly. The collection of statistical data is in an elementary state of development. Neither private producers nor the Government know what the population needs or wants. Power and transportation (except perhaps air transportation) are inadequate to satisfy the requirements of an expanding industrial economy. . . .

The seriousness of the present industrial slow-down and the lag in the agricultural sector become apparent when it is realized that Brazil, because of its very rapid rate of population growth, must create approximately the number of new jobs each year as does the United States, which has a population two and one half times Brazil's.

EDUCATIONAL BACKWARDNESS

Educational opportunity is the key to social mobility and constructive social change. Brazil has a miserable record on offering its people a chance for self-improvement through academic training. No major country in Latin America has been so irresponsible in this regard. Half of Brazil's school-age population is illiterate, as opposed to approximately 12 per cent in Argentina. No more than 25 per cent of the population has attained the third grade level. Less than one per cent of those who enter school graduate from a university. In 1962, only one in three of those who were prepared to enter a university could be accommodated. . . .

THE BUREAUCRATS

Needless to say, there are many capable, dedicated civil servants in Brazil, but the Brazilian bureaucrats in general leave much to be desired, in terms of both skill and dedication. At least 40 per cent of government expenditures are allocated to civil servants' wages, compared to 14 per cent in the United States. Still, any comparison of the services rendered in the two countries would not be valid: bureaucrats are ridiculously underpaid in Brazil. . . .

THE POLITICAL CLIMATE

The Brazilians are among the most politically sophisticated people of Latin America. In January of 1963, when a plebiscite by a five-to-one vote returned the country to the presidential system after a brief and stormy foray into parliamentarianism, the nation once again reaffirmed its capacity for peaceful resolution of its political controversies. Earlier, in October of 1962, Brazilian voters, of whom there are now 17.5 million, continued their movement to the left, while also showing their preference for political moderation. With few exceptions they rejected extremists of both the right and left, which may be taken to mean that the articulate minority was not yet ready to seek desperate solutions to its problems. . . .

THE STUDENTS

Brazilian university students give important ideological support to the Communists and *fidelistas*. The students, who number about 80,000, are organized on a nation-wide basis. Many of them have an exaggerated sense of national pride. This causes them: 1) to fear and resent foreign economic and political influence, 2) to search for quick social and economic solutions of the kind that the extreme left promises, and 3) to advocate "positive neutrality." Of course, not all students belong to the Communist left. On the contrary, this group constitutes a relatively small section of the national student body. A larger group, representing the militant non-Communist left, probably provides a useful antidote to politically more conservative elders. . . .

BRAZILIAN–UNITED STATES RELATIONS

At least since World War II, Brazil has aspired to become a world power, but it has gone largely unheeded in world councils. For some time, Brazilian leaders have contended that their nation's failure to receive international recognition results from the world's image of Brazil as a "satellite" of the United States. Especially since the abbreviated term of President Quadros, Brazil's statesmen have been at pains to change that image. They have actively sought to strengthen Brazilian ties with Western Europe and the Communist bloc and to win acceptance as one of the leaders of the "neutral" countries. They believe that success in these areas would permit Brazil to pursue a truly "independent" foreign policy. . . .

More important perhaps to an understanding of the relations between the two countries is the fact that although Brazil pretends to be "free," it in truth is not and cannot be. The United States is Brazil's principle market and major supplier, as well as its primary source of loans and investment capital. This is why, to some in the United States, it has seemed illogical that Brazil should withdraw its traditional support of United States' foreign policy while expecting the United States to resolve Brazil's financial chaos and to guarantee an important part of its developmental program.

68 *WAGLEY, Brazil Is Different from Spanish America*

. . . The national culture of Brazil is clearly distinguishable from that of other Latin American countries such as the Spanish-Indian culture of Bolivia, Peru, and Ecuador, and as the European-Spanish culture of Argentina, Uruguay, and Chile. It differs from these not only in specific formal customs and culture patterns but especially in the singularly Brazilian interpretation and orientation which common features are given. The result is a different way of life and a different way of looking at the world. . . . Attempts to describe Latin America as a unit have all used the expression "except for Brazil" with remarkable frequency.

. . . Although Brazilians are not without a certain race prejudice, . . . in general, one finds here less emphasis on color as a symbol of superiority or inferiority than elsewhere . . . in Brazil it might almost be said that there is a cult of the family . . . it is still a large and decidedly an intimate group. Social life of many Brazilians is carried on predominantly with relatives. . . . Foods and food habits also differ from those of the surrounding Latin American cultures. . . . The carnival period before Lent . . . is the most important festival of the year to Brazilians, overshadowing both patriotic and religious holidays. The zeal with which the Brazilian people lose themselves in dancing and music for four days and the manner of celebrating carnival is not found elsewhere.

. . . Brazilians are said to be more overt and more voluble than the comparatively taciturn Argentinians; they are less proud and less worried about losing face than the Spanish-American. To the Argentinians, Brazilians are not dignified, so they call them "monkeys." Even Brazilians agree that there is something pro-

Charles Wagley, "Brazil," in *Most of the World*, edited by Ralph Linton (New York: Columbia University Press, 1949), pp. 258–270, *passim*. Reprinted by permission.

foundly Brazilian about the personality of José Carioca, the sly, friendly, and talkative parrot created by Walter Disney. Yet, many writers, both native and foreign, mention a certain sadness, a softness, and a melancholy about the Brazilian. "In a radiant land lives a sad people" is the opening line of Paulo Prado's famous interpretative work on Brazil. This is another side of the Brazilian personality. This same author describes the excess of sensuality and the great love for luxury of the Brazilians. . . . With these traits goes a desire "to get rich quick" and a love of gambling. The economic history of the country is made up of a series of speculative booms, and almost all Brazilians gamble in some form— either in the *jogo do bicho* (a sort of numbers racket), in the federal or state lotteries, or until recently in the luxurious casinos.

Brazilians give a uniquely Brazilian twist to institutions and concepts which they share with the Western world. The Brazilian monarchial system, Brazilian democracy, and Brazilian dictatorship were unlike similar forms of government as they existed in Europe. Even the recent dictatorship, despite its aping of European patterns, never became a harsh system with strict control over the people. Jokes about the dictator, complaints and discussions of the lack of freedom of expression, and rumors of growing opposition were discussed openly in cafés and salons. When the dictator was finally overthrown, it was a typical bloodless Brazilian revolution. As one student of colonial art remarked: "In Brazil, even Christ hangs comfortably on the cross."

. . . Potentially, Brazil has most of the necessary equipment to make it one of the great nations of the world. For the time being, however, "Brazil is rich and Brazilians are poor," as the people sigh with their rather fatalistic sense of humor. Brazil must learn to make use of its natural wealth by developing its human potentialities unless it is to remain forever a land of false promises.

69 COOPER, Oswaldo Cruz and the Impact of Yellow Fever on Brazilian History

The medical history of Latin America remains a field largely unworked by historians. There is as yet no satisfactory general medical history of the region, and relatively few solid monographs on which to base such a work. Reliable information on the medical history of Brazil—a nation with an area larger than the continental United States and a much older history—is especially scarce. Perhaps the major gap in this field is the lack of any comprehensive study of the historical impact of yellow fever. All the general histories of Brazil agree that this disease has produced major socioeconomic and political consequences, particularly in the second half of the nineteenth century.

The long history of yellow fever in Brazil began, however, many years before

Donald B. Cooper, "Oswaldo Cruz and the Impact of Yellow Fever on Brazilian History," *The Bulletin of the Tulane University Medical Faculty,* XXVI, No. 1 (February, 1967), 49–52. Reprinted by permission.

that time. It seems likely that it originated in Africa, and that it was introduced to the New World as a consequence of the slave trade. It was reported in Northeastern Brazil between 1686 and 1694. João Ferreira da Rosa mentions in his famous book, *Tratado unico da constituição pestilencial de Pernambuco*, that this prolonged epidemic killed thousands of persons. Rosa's book is the first work published anywhere on yellow fever, and today it is one of the rarest volumes in the world. After 1694 yellow fever epidemics were not reported again in Brazil during the colonial period, although they were widespread in the Caribbean area, Mexico and Central America.

In 1849 yellow fever was again reported in Brazil in the city of Salvador, capital of the State of Bahia. Contemporary Brazilian accounts assumed that this was a re-introduction of the disease, and most of them blamed the ensuing epidemic on the arrival of an American ship that had touched recently at both New Orleans and Havana. In any event the epidemic spread southward through the coastal cities and reached Rio de Janeiro early in 1850. Before this first epidemic had run its course more the 90,000 persons had contracted the disease, and 4,160 died in Rio alone. The disease was endemic there for the remainder of the nineteenth century. The highland areas that lay just back of the narrow coastal plain remained relatively free of the disease, and constituted through the years the usual refuge for those persons able to flee the cities during the yellow fever season.

The recurrent epidemics of yellow fever posed a serious drain on the economy of the country. Large amounts of both public and private funds had to be diverted from more productive channels to pay for prevention and treatment of this disease. Much of this money was wasted since the true manner of spreading the disease was not confirmed until the work of Walter Reed and his associates in Cuba in 1900. Foreign residents of the port of Santos, for example, commuted daily by train from the highlands because of speculation that "night airs" might cause yellow fever. During the yellow fever season there was a mass exodus from the seaports—led by the Emperor himself who went to Petrópolis—and the recurrent interruptions, losses, and delays in the area of trade and commerce caused much permanent loss of income.

The presence of yellow fever was a serious deterrent to European immigration, since the unacclimated foreigner was the usual victim of the disease. The great Brazilian author, lawyer, and political figure, Ruy Barbosa, wrote in 1899 that the fear of yellow fever diverted thousands of potential immigrants away from Brazil, and on to Uruguay or Argentina where the disease was rarely encountered. The need for immigrants was keenly felt after the abolition of slavery in 1888—Brazil was the last nation in the New World to take this humanitarian step—and the country's reputation as a hothouse of tropical disease complicated recruiting efforts. In 1896 the Italian government cautioned Italians about immigration to Brazil as a result of the famous *Lombardia* incident. An Italian cruiser of that name entered the harbor of Rio de Janeiro in October, 1895, carrying a crew of 340 officers and men. Of this number only 7 persons failed to contract yellow fever, and 234 perished. The English seemed particularly vulnerable, and a walk through an English graveyard revealed the names of hundreds of victims of Yellow Jack. North Americans who succumbed to yellow fever include the first Presbyterian missionary from the United States to Brazil, Ashbel Green Simonton, and Edward Lane, a Presbyterian missionary of the late nineteenth century. Few travelers who wrote accounts failed to warn their readers of the dangers of yellow fever. Henry Walter Bates, author of the classic study, *The Naturalist on the River Amazons,* first published in 1863, was among those who contracted the disease. In 1903 an editorial in the newspaper *A Gazeta* said: "We all know what yellow fever is: It is the ruin, shame, infamy and curse of our land."

In that very year, however, a comprehensive program was launched by the Brazilian government which succeeded in eradicating yellow fever (and also smallpox) in most parts of the country within five years' time. President Francisco de Paula Rodrigues Alves (1902–06) is credited with various progressive innovations, including tax and fiscal reforms, extensive railroad construction, and modernization of cities and seaports, but it was the aggressive public health measures which he endorsed and supported that constituted his most lasting achievement. His progressive health policies did much to move Brazil toward implementation of the national motto of "order and progress" that had been optimistically adopted when the monarchy was overthrown in Brazil in 1889.

Major credit for the successful fight against yellow fever (and smallpox) must always go to the young physician whom Rodrigues Alves named Director-General of Public Health in March, 1903. Oswaldo Gonçalves Cruz (1872–1917) proved such a resourceful and tenacious fighter against disease that he soon won international acclaim. His name is now the most honored one in the field of public health and sanitation anywhere in Latin America. Scientifically Cruz was not a major innovator. His conquest of yellow fever rested squarely on the techniques developed and employed earlier by Walter Reed and his associates in Cuba. But they had not been employed previously on a national scale in Brazil, and Cruz carefully adapted them to the Brazilian setting.

Oswaldo Cruz was born in 1872 in the city of São Luis do Paraitinga in the state of São Paulo. By 1892—at only 20 years of age!—he obtained his M.D. degree from the Faculty of Medicine of Rio de Janeiro. From 1896 to 1898 he studied microbiology and experimental pathology at the Pasteur Institute of Paris—the first of his countrymen to do so. In 1899, having just returned from France, he won his first victory over epidemic disease by cutting short an epidemic of the dreaded bubonic plague in Santos, the seaport of São Paulo. When Rodrigues Alves sought leadership at the national level for his public health program, Oswaldo Cruz, despite his relative youth, had the winning combination of expert training and practical experience.

Under the forceful leadership of Cruz the federal government of Brazil launched a war of eradication against the *Aedes aegypti* mosquito which Reed had proved was the vector of yellow fever. Teams of inspectors combed the urban areas along the coast, and nearby rural environs, particularly in the vicinity of Rio de Janeiro, taking note of all swamps, pools, puddles, or even rooftop gutters where the mosquitoes might breed. A massive public education program was launched at the same time which sought to persuade the citizenry to lend their utmost cooperation in eradicating yellow fever. Tough new federal legislation, which was contained in a comprehensive "Sanitary Code," insured the ultimate if occasionally reluctant cooperation of the public. Many persons considered the legal right of the "mosquito inspectors" to enter private property, indeed the home itself, in search of potential breeding places of mosquitoes as an unjustifiable invasion of privacy. But Cruz and the president never backed down in the face of vehement and occasionally violent opposition.

In November, 1904, opposition to the unpopular Sanitary Code culminated in outright armed rebellion against the government. Units of the army joined the rebellion and several lives were lost. The opposition charged with considerable justice that the Sanitary Code authorized the massive use of federal "police power" in areas traditionally reserved to state and local governments. The most controversial provision of the Code was one which required *compulsory* vaccination against smallpox. The influential Positivists, for example, who clearly understood the dangers of yellow fever and smallpox, feared governmental compulsion of any sort, including compulsory education, no matter what the reason. They saw the campaign against yellow fever and smallpox as a kind of Trojan horse which under the pretext of preserving the public health would establish strong and dangerous precedents for future federal encroachments. Other opponents included respected physicians who doubted or resented the "new school" of scientific and experimental medicine as epitomized by the young Doctor Cruz, and political agitators who saw an "exploitable" issue that might prove to be the means of bringing down the government. Prompt military action ended the brief rebellion, and insured the continuation of the Rodrigues Alves government as well as the fight against epidemics. The efforts of Cruz and his associates had the intended effect since by 1908 both yellow fever and smallpox had been virtually eliminated. Of the two diseases yellow fever had been far more destructive in that it had claimed about 60,000 victims since the epidemic of 1850.

There were many significant consequences of the sanitary campaign of Cruz. After 1908 the eradication of yellow fever contributed in no small way to the rise of land values, increased settlement, and rapid industrialization of former fever-ridden areas, particularly at Rio de Janeiro, Santos, the Paraíba valley, and adjacent coastal lands. Elimination of yellow fever is one of several factors which help explain the spurt in European immigration to Brazil between 1908 and 1914. Perhaps most important of all, after the victories of Cruz it was evident that many of the alleged deficiencies of residents of tropical lands, such as lack of energy, vitality, and "ambition," ought to be attributed more to the effects of disease rather than to inherent racial or climatic factors. The work of Cruz and his associates demonstrated that the use of modern scientific and medical techniques, executed if not necessarily originated by Brazilians, could impede and in some cases stop the customary ravages of epidemics. Nationalists now talked more of the blessings of living in tropical lands and less about the dangers of such lands. According to the historian José Maria Bello: "All of Brazil seemed to take on new life, with greater confidence and pride in herself." It is obvious that the conquest of yellow fever by Oswaldo Cruz marks a major turning point in the history of Brazil. Moreover, when it becomes possible in later years to write a general medical history of Latin America, the impact of yellow fever on this region, particularly in Brazil, will comprise a lengthy chapter.

70 CARVALHO, Song of Brazil

I hear the vast song of Brazil!
I hear the thundering steeds of Iguassú pounding the naked rocks, prancing in
  the wet air, trampling with watery feet the morning of spume and green trills;
I hear thy solemn melody, thy barbaric and solemn melody, Amazon, the melody
  of thy lazy flood, heavy as oil, that swells greater and ever greater, licking the
  mud of banks, gnawing roots, dragging along islands, goring the listless ocean
  like a bull infuriated with rods, darts, branches and leaves;
I hear the earth crackling in the hot northeast wind, earth that heaves beneath
  the bare bronze foot of the outlaw, earth that turns to dust and whirls in silent
  clouds through the streets of Joazeiro and falls to powder on the dry plains of
  Crato;
I hear the chirping of jungles—trills, pipings, peepings, quavers, whistles, whirrings,
  tapping of beaks, deep tones that hum like taut wires, clearly vibrating drums,
  throats that creak, wings that click and flicker, cries like the cricket's whispers,
  dreamy calls, long languid calls—jungles beneath the sky! . . .
I hear the millstones grinding sugar cane, the gurgle of sweet juice flowing into
  vats, the clank of pails among rubber trees;
  and axes opening paths,
  and saws cutting timber, . . .
  and mangroves leafing in the sun,
  and peccaries snapping their jaws at alligators asleep in the tepid mud of
    bayous . . .
I hear all Brazil singing, humming, calling,
  shouting! . . .
  factories grinding, pounding, panting, screaming, howling and snoring,
  cylinders exploding,
  cranes revolving,
  wheels turning,
  rails trembling,

Dudley Fitts, ed., *Anthology of Contemporary Latin-American Poetry* (Norfolk, Conn.: New Directions, 1942), pp. 131–135. Translation by Charles Poore. Reprinted by permission.

noises of foothills and plateaux, cattlebells, neighings, cowboy songs, and
lowings,
chiming of bells, bursting of rockets, Ouro-Preto, Baía, Congonhas, Sabará,
clamor of stock-exchanges shrieking numbers like parrots,
tumult of streets that seethe beneath skyscrapers,
voices of all the races that the wind of the seaports tosses into the jungle! . . .
But what I hear, above all, in this hour of pure sunlight . . . is the song of thy
cradles, Brazil, of all thy cradles in which there sleeps, mouth dripping with
milk, dusky, trusting,
the man of tomorrow!

71 FREYRE, Brazilian Melting Pot

Brazil is an American extension of Portugal. . . . The Portuguese colonists
found in tropical America an ideal place for the expansion and development of
their ethnically democratic but culturally aristocratic civilization. . . . In 450
years, the Portuguese have assimilated not only the vast population of Amerindians
. . . but also large numbers of Africans who were imported to work as slaves on
the plantations. . . . The settlers—Portuguese, Spanish, Italian, German, and
Polish—through union with colored women, made up for the extremely small
number of whites available for the task of colonization. . . . The colonizers
propagated a vigorous and ductile mestiço population that was still more adaptable
to the tropical climate. . . .

And today Brazil is a genuinely unified country, although some of the newest
groups of immigrants are still in the first stages of assimilation . . . the tendency
toward fusion-ethnic and cultural—has been the decisive factor in Brazilian history. . . . Brazil does not have race conflicts, but she has powerful class antagonisms, and these have grown out of her acute interregional maladjustments.

In Brazil, both before and after the break with the Empire [in 1889], ethnic
problems have been easily solved. The abolition of slavery in 1888 was achieved
peacefully and with little political disturbance. The "Indian problem," which
has been so prominent in Peru, Mexico, Bolivia, and other Latin-American republics, has scarcely existed. The average Brazilian is unaware of the possibility of
political, cultural, or social conflict among the races. . . .

Perhaps the most important point to emphasize is that there really are second-
generation Brazilians who are politicians. . . . In the early years of the republican
regime, Lauro Müller, who had been born in Santa Catarina in a family of German colonists, became one of the most astute and influential politicians in Brazil.
. . . For years Müller was a presidential possibility, as was David Campista, the
Brazilian son of a German Jew . . . who became the Minister of Finance. Both
men came close to being the President of the Brazilian Republic, and in neither

"Perspective of Brazil," *Atlantic Monthly*, February, 1956, pp. 8–12, *passim*. The
supplement was also issued separately. Reprinted by permission.

case did their failure have anything to do with the fact that they were sons of non-Portuguese colonists. . . .

Sons and grandsons of modest immigrants are rapidly rising in Brazil to positions of leadership in business, industry, politics, religion, and the press. In medicine there are men like Mario Pinotti; in science, Cesar Lattes; in art, Candido Portinari; in architecture, Henrique Mindlin; in music, Francisco Mignone. Even in literature, where the vested cultural interests of the aristocracy are likely to be most firmly entrenched, the newcomers are surpassing the descendants of the old Portuguese families. In the last century, Machado de Assis, who was Brazil's greatest writer of fiction, was of Portuguese ancestry, although his novels sometimes derived from African and plebeian sources. But today many non-Portuguese Brazilians are contributing to contemporary literature—for example, Augusto Meyer, the scholarly and enthusiastic analyst of Portuguese classics; Viana Moog, the novelist and essayist; Menotti del Picchia, the nationalist poet; Augusto Frederico Schmidt, another poet whose works are very popular; Sergio Milliet, the literary critic; Marcos Konder, a young poet; Gastao Cruls, a novelist who has specialized in the dramatic conflicts between the elemental values of the Amazonian region and the bourgeois values of Rio society; Raúl Bopp, a poet who has written excellent lyrics based on Amazonian themes; and many others.

When the processes of assimilation go far enough to include literature of the most lyrical and introspective kinds, it means that in Brazil people of European non-Portuguese origin are really becoming a new force in the life and culture of the nation. . . . They symbolize the whole Brazilian melting pot, the dynamic and creative tropical culture which nevertheless derives across the centuries directly from the European Renaissance.

72 Race and Class in Brazil

Brazil is renowned in the world for its racial democracy. . . . It may be said that Brazil has no 'race problem' in the same sense that it exists in many other parts of the world; people of three racial stocks, and mixtures of all varieties of these stocks, live in what are essentially peaceful relations. All of them are Brazilians proud of their immense nation and sharing in its numerous problems and potentialities.

This does not mean, however, that all Brazilians have equal rights and advantages. Brazil is indeed a country of striking contrasts. There is a great difference between social conditions in modern industrial São Paulo or cosmopolitan Rio de Janeiro, and those in the backward frontier regions of the west and north of Brazil. There is a wide social and economic gap between the wealthy who live in fine homes and modern apartments in Rio, and the miserably poor who inhabit the *favelas* (slums) only a few blocks away. Brazil has many social prob-

Charles Wagley, ed., *Race and Class in Rural Brazil* (Paris: UNESCO, 1952), pp. 7–8, 140, 144, 154–155, *passim*. Reprinted by permission.

RIVER FISHERMEN

lems to overcome if it is to become a great nation with full social democracy. The standard of living of the majority of its people is well below that of most industrialized western nations. More than 50 per cent of all Brazilians are still illiterate. Transportation, industry, and agriculture are insufficiently developed to provide a sound economic basis for the country.

Nor will Brazilians who are aware of the social realities in their country deny . . . that a mild form of racial discrimination exists and is growing in certain areas. There are well-known stereotypes and attitudes, traditional in Brazil, which indicate dispraisal of the Negro and of the mulatto. There are also well-known barriers to the social ascension of 'people of colour' who are the descendants of slaves. Increasing discrimination in such centers as São Paulo and Rio de Janeiro caused the National Congress to pass a law making racial discrimination a criminal offence. . . .

. . . Social conditions have not been favorable to the ascension in the socio-economic hierarchy of the descendants of former slaves and of indentured 'semi-slaves.' Thus people of Indian and Negro physical type continue to hold an inferior social position. The physical characteristics of the Indian and the Negro, therefore, continue to be a symbol of low social rank, of descent from slaves or peons. . . .

Class lines are still rigidly drawn in Brazil. The descendants of the old white aristocracy with the new upper class which results from new fortunes and from relatively recent political success, form a small upper class which maintains many of the ideals of the old slave-owning aristocratic caste. These people follow a comfortable, even luxurious, way of life with all the educational advantages, the forms of recreation, and the technological equipment available to the economically well-off in any modern Western country. There is, however, a rapidly expanding middle class which is comprised of government employees, professional groups, commercial and industrial employees, owners of small business enterprises, and so on. The members of this Brazilian middle class generally identify themselves with the upper class, sharing to great extent in their 'aristocratic' values and ideals, and follow an upper-class pattern of life so far as their smaller incomes allow. They differ thus from the middle class of other Western countries which forms the numerical backbone of the nation and is proud of its values and way of life. Finally, in modern Brazil there is a large 'lower class,' mostly illiterate, whose miserable standard of living offers a striking contrast to that of the contemporary upper class, even to that of the growing middle class. It is composed of the many subsistence farmers throughout the country, the workers on plantations, the industrial workers, the domestic servants, and the innumerable groups of people who perform manual labour of all sorts. . . .

. . . The system of inter-racial relations which has taken form in Brazil, with all its faults and its advantages, provides a comparatively favourable and fertile basis for the future growth of Brazilian society. Brazil has taken the form of a multi-racial society unlike that found in most colonial areas of the world where a rigid 'colour line' is usual. In most colonial areas, the intense and emotionally charged feelings of the native population (generally of Mongoloid or Negroid racial stock) toward the dominant European 'caste,' and the clash of economic interests between the racial castes, create numerous barriers to the improvement of social and economic conditions. Brazil has avoided developing a caste society such as that of the United States, where the strict line between the Negro and the white has been a costly drain upon the nation and the individual. With the rapid economic development of Brazil, which is now under way, there should be more numerous opportunities for individuals to improve their economic status throughout the country, and Brazil should be able to make educational facilities available to its people on a much broader basis than at present. As the standard of living and the educational level of the lower strata of Brazilian society improve, the people of darker skin colour now occupying the lower ranks should take their place in the middle ranks of society. There are no serious racial barriers to social and economic advance and, as opportunities increase, larger numbers of people will rise in the social system. The great contrasts in social and economic conditions between the darker lower strata and the predominantly white upper class should disappear.

There are dangers, however, along the road to this ideal. There are indications both in the present studies and in reports from the great metropolitan centres of the country that discrimination, tensions, and prejudices based on race are appearing. As has been pointed out, when the number of individuals of Negro or mixed ancestry improve their educational and economic position, they challenge the dominant position of the white upper class. This might well result in emphasis upon 'race' as a criterion for social position, in greater prejudice, in tension between racial groups, and even in discrimination. Furthermore, as Brazil becomes more closely tied to the Western industrial and commercial world, and develops its technological equipment, it will be exposed to the ideology of the more industrialized and technologically developed nations. . . . Both Brazilians and foreign observers have the impression that Western attitudes and concepts of racism are entering Brazil along with industrial and technological improvements. But there is no inherent relationship between Western industrialism and technology and Western racism, no necessary connexion between the widespread improvement of social conditions and the development, through competition, of tensions and discrimination between racial or minority groups. Aware of the dangers and pitfalls and taking care to avoid them, Brazil may enjoy the benefits of technological change, and of greater rewards for its underdeveloped potentialities, without losing its rich heritage of racial democracy.

73 *MARX, Heitor Villa-lobos, The Brazilian Composer*

Villa-lobos is, in my opinion, the first nationalist composer of the Americas; one must not only be native to a country, but must also possess genius to evoke the

Burle Marx, "Brazilian Portrait—Villa-Lobos," *Modern Music*, XVII (October–November, 1939), 10–17, *passim*. Reprinted by permission.

sound and feeling of a whole people and its culture. He is as unmistakably Brazilian as Moussorgsky is Russian.

At his father's death Villa-lobos, who was then eleven, put an abrupt end to his schooling by getting expelled for general rebellion. . . . Then began a long struggle to win livelihood for himself and his family. At first he played the various instruments for which he has such an amazing aptitude in theatre and cafe orchestras. . . . Until 1910, when he was twenty-nine, no exact details of his life are known except that he studied by himself, examining the scores of old masters and European contemporaries and also that he composed incessantly. . . .

Undeniably the year 1912, when he joined a scientific expedition into the interior of Brazil to study the customs and music of Indian tribes, marked the great turning point of his life. For a temperament like that of Villa-lobos, inclined to the strange, fantastic, and exotic, such direct contact with a primitive culture would lead naturally to a new path and a new goal. . . . Villa-lobos not only recorded, learned and absorbed, but he merged what he found with that which he recognized as his own. . . . After these researches into primitive Indian melodies, he proceeded further to make an all-embracing study of the folk, popular and indigenous music of Brazil. . . .

The creative fruits of that work appeared in 1914; the *Suite Popular Brasileira,* for guitar; *Cirandinha,* a cycle of twelve pieces for piano; *Danças Caracteristicas Africanas,* a set of three pieces for piano; and the first *Sonata Fantasia,* for violin and piano. *The Danças* are based on tunes of the Caripunas African-Indians in Matto Grosso, and are scored for African and other exotic instruments. . . . In 1915, Rio heard its first all Villa-lobos concert. . . .

When Villa-lobos came to Europe for the first time in 1922, on a scholarship granted by the Brazilian government, he was already a man of forty-one years. He was not entirely ignorant of the musical movements then agitating Paris and other centers. . . . Indeed, one may say even now, that the part of Villa-lobos which is not Brazilian . . . is impressionist and post-impressionist French. But this French influence . . . is in the final summing up of Villa-lobos a surface effect. He was a composer already formed when he came to Paris; his musical compulsion was more powerful and rich than that of most Europeans. He arrived with curiosity but supreme confidence; his attitude was, "I didn't come to study with you, I came to show you what I've done."

. . . His inordinate love of the saxophone seems to dominate his entire musical existence. He has been known to use it for a Beethoven symphony when the bassoon was lacking. And at one time he even worked his way out of a jail in the interior of Matto Grosso by playing his beloved instrument for the chief of police. . . .

Another important facet in Villa-lobos' range of interests is his preoccupation with Bach. He has long studied that master's works and claims familiarity with over four hundred. Since 1932 he has written five suites, called *Bachianas Brasileiras,* which are not so much evocations of Bach in a contemporary manner, as an attempt to transmit the Bach spirit, which to Villa-lobos is the universal spirit, a source and end into itself, into the soul of Brazil. . . .

Less known in the United States but famous all over Latin America is Villa-lobos' achievement as a director of musical education in the schools of Rio de Janeiro. The composer had long cherished a desire to contribute directly to the cultural development of the Brazilian people. In 1931, when the government sought a man to fill the new post of Supervisor and Director of Musical Education, . . . I suggested him as logical for the task. . . .

The first task was to form a choir of school teachers, who were required by decree (this was a revolutionary period) to work with him two or three times a week. They became the nucleus for all his experiments, the vehicle for spreading his work to the schools. He then devised an altogether new system of musical notation, which was designed to teach children in less than the usual time, and also to lessen boredom and interference with the pleasure of singing. . . . As a contribution to this work, he has also compiled an enormous collection of folk and popular music to be used in the schools. . . .

Since the revolution of 1930 he has been an important national figure, a center of interest not only for Brazilians but for artists and intellectuals all over South America.

74 The Central Committee of the Communist Party of Brazil Denounces Khrushchev, July 27, 1963

The struggles which are going on in Latin America have also proved the correctness of the Chinese Communist Party's thesis concerning the national-liberation movement of oppressed nations and the role of these struggles in the world situation as a whole. The peoples of Latin America cannot afford to wait for their liberation by "peaceful competition." They are brutally oppressed by U.S. imperialism which interferes ever more flagrantly in their internal affairs, propping up this or overthrowing that government, tramples on their national sentiments and, under the cover of the false philanthropic "Alliance for Progress," intensifies the ruthless exploitation of the various countries on this continent. Latin America is a battlefield of silent warfare between U.S. imperialism and the masses of people. Therefore, only the most vigorous struggles, especially armed struggles, can pave the way for the liberation of the oppressed nations of this hemisphere. This is proved by the Cuban revolution, the uprisings in Venezuela and the guerrillas expanding in other countries.

The revisionist policy spreads illusions about U.S. imperialism, bows to its dictates and tries to damp down the struggle against it and the internal reactionaries. This policy seriously harms the revolutionary movement in Latin America. All

Reply to Khrushchev. Resolution of the Central Committee of the Communist Party of Brazil (Peking: Foreign Languages Press, 1964), pp. 11–14, *passim.*

those who are not prepared to expose resolutely the U.S. imperialists and drive them out of their own country are doomed to complete failure. Genuine revolutionaries cannot agree to Khrushchev's statements prettifying U.S. imperialism and are opposed to his frequent eulogizing of Kennedy. How can one agree to the assertion that the top chieftain of imperialism is interested in peace, that he can act sensibly in face of the contradictions between the people and imperialism? How can one believe that Kennedy, who planned the invasion of Cuba, wages "special warfare" in south Viet Nam, organizes military coups in Latin America and is engaging in an unprecedented arms drive, is a representative of the less aggressive, less reactionary group of U.S. monopolists? To Latin Americans, Kennedy is the most ferocious enemy of peace and independence of the peoples. Thus, the broad masses of our continent see that what Khrushchev has said are lies.

Especially serious is the fact that while creating illusions about U.S. imperialism, Khrushchev crudely attacks the Chinese Communists who have led a most important revolution of our time and who have opened a new state in the struggle for liberation of the oppressed nations. He said that China wanted thermo-nuclear war, that it wanted to bring about victory of socialism throughout the world on the ruins of an atomic explosion. Such utterances are an insult to the conscience of the people of the world. . . . The allegation made by Khrushchev and certain leaders of some Parties that the Chinese leaders want to drag mankind into a thermo-nuclear war is unworthy of Communists. All the attempts to show that the Chinese Communists are out of step, and falsely presenting them as advocates of atomic war, will be condemned by revolutionaries and all honest people.

75 HARDING, *The Failure of the Left in Brazil*

To understand the failure of the left to stave off a rightist coup and the prospects for revolution in the future we must examine leftist leadership in Brazil.

The Communist Party split in late 1961, ostensibly over the Sino-Soviet dispute but equally over the Cuban Revolution. The pro-Moscow group led by Luiz Carlos Prestes, a man with considerable popular prestige, is known as the Partido Comunista Brasileiro (PCB). The pro-Chinese group took the name Partido Comunista do Brasil (PC do B). After the split the PCB continued to take a very moderate reformist line, accusing more radical groups of adventurism. Prestes' group insisted that there were no objective conditions for revolution in Brazil, and that basic reforms could be achieved by supporting Goulart and pushing him to the left. In general the PCB proclaimed its aim to be the destruction of feudalism and imperialism. This would be achieved through alliance with the "progressive bourgeoisie" and the achievement of a "democratic and Popular" government such as the Goulart regime to which they gave "critical" support. . . .

After the defeat of organized nationalism in the 1960 presidential elections, the nationalist movement tended to split into a revolutionary-socialist left-wing

Timothy F. Harding, "Revolution Tomorrow: The Failure of the Left in Brazil," *Studies on the Left,* IV (1964), No. 4, pp. 43–52, *passim.* Reprinted by permission.

and a pro-capitalist center. The temple of nationalism was a government institute of higher education in Rio set up under Kubitschek called the Instituto Superior de Estudos Brasileiros (ISEB). The ISEB intellectuals, including Marxists and former fascists turned "developmentists," had tried to construct a nationalist ideology to justify what Kubitschek was doing. The ISEB gravitated leftward toward socialism as its intellectuals observed that economic development without a social revolution did not bring social justice or national control of the economy. A study of the flood of nationalist literature published (and sold in large quantities) in Brazil during 1959–64 shows a steady movement to the left. . . .

Among politicians, Leonel Brizola (Goulart's brother-in-law) and Miguel Arrais, Governor of Pernambuco, had emerged by the end of the Goulart regime as twin leaders of a consciously-leftist, nationalist movement that was losing its sympathy for Goulart. Brizola, former Governor of Rio Grande do Sul, evolved from a wealthy nationalist demagogue into a self-proclaimed socialist revolutionary. As governor he rose to national prominence by expropriating the Rio Grande do Sul subsidiary of the American and Foreign Power Company. He became more of a hero when he took charge of the fight to get Goulart the Presidency after Quadros' resignation. Yet by the end of his term of office in 1962 his demagogy and sterile agitation had so discredited him in Rio Grande do Sul that his candidate to succeed him as governor was badly defeated by a more conservative figure. At the same time, Brizola had run for national deputy in Guanabara state, where he was known more by his nationalist reputation than by his administrative record. He was elected with the largest vote ever received by a national deputy in any state. He became more critical of his brother-in-law, claiming that Goulart had remained a reformist while he (Brizola) had become a revolutionary. Brizola was clearly pushing hard to become the candidate of the left for President in 1965. He published a magazine *Panfleto* which contributed to the climate of agitation before the coup.

Brizola was fast losing his national leadership of leftist nationalism to Pernambuco Governor Miguel Arrais, who was less demagogic but inspired more confidence. Arrais was the most likely choice for a leftist "unity" candidate for president, and he would stand for revolution as opposed to Goulart's status quo. His measures as Governor of Pernambuco in support of labor, peasants, and education badly scared conservatives just before the coup. Many undoubtedly supported the coup to keep Arrais from running for president. He was jailed during the coup and remains on a prison ship.*

Goulart gained both Brizola's and Arrais' support for his last-minute reforms. While many of the nationalist leaders were profiting from their agitation and the status quo, their supporters seemed increasingly aware that anti-foreign-capital campaigns were no substitute for revolution. The coup hastened the leftward movement of Brazilian nationalism. . . .

The leaderships of the various peasant movements in Brazil are another rallying point for revolution. The peasant only began to be a political force after 1959

* He subsequently took refuge in the Algerian Embassy, and later went to Paris. [Ed.]

when Francisco Julião reached national—and later international—fame as leader of the "Peasant Leagues" of the Northeast. Most peasants could not vote because they were illiterate. Most of those that could vote supported conservative candidates at the bidding of their land-owning boss. . . .

Brazilian student radicals, part of the middle class, have been the most radical element in Brazilian society in that they have been least willing to accept the stagnation and conservatism built into Brazilian government and politics. They believe that the techniques for rapid development of their country exist, the analysis of what is wrong has been made, and yet the mechanisms of politics and government that should transmit the need, desire, and urgency of change, work, instead to impede it. They feel an acute responsibility to make a revolution for the rest of the population, as if their tenuous title to the role of intellectual made them the brains of the masses. The freedom from commitment to the status quo stemming from their student status makes them intensely aware of the injustices of society and willing to act to end them. They see themselves as a revolutionary vanguard. These delusions of grandeur are combined with a romantic idea of revolutionary politics. Student meetings are filled with exaggerated posing and self-admiration. Student conferences are elaborately staged, and if someone plays a scene of agitation until he loses control of himself, the audience applauds the "pretty performance." The surprising thing, then, is that among student revolutionaries there is a real commitment to improving society as evidenced by the cultural and educational activities of the União Nacional dos Estudantes (UNE—National Student Union). One finds among these students some of the most well-informed and realistic militants of the Brazilian left. . . .

The closest thing to a union of leftist forces was achieved a few months before the coup, by the Frente de Movilizacão Popular (FMP). This was the successor to a series of national liberation movements which discredited politicians had controlled. But the FMP, with Brizola and the CGT labor command in the lead, was certainly the most radical of these fronts. It included all the major radical tendencies: labor, peasants, students, PCB, PC do B, left-wing of the PTB, the Brazilian Socialist Party and the radical Christian Democrats. However the fracturing of the left between demagogues and dedicated leaders, urban and rural masses, middle-class radicals and workers, Northeast and Central-south, and finally between reformista and revolutionaries—all these divisions prevented the mobilization of effective opposition to the rightist coup. . . . The failure of the left in Brazil continues to be a failure of leadership.

76 HALL, Some Definitions on the Left

The Left in all of Latin America means simply those who are committed to working for rapid social change, the operative word here being "rapid." For

"Portrait of a Revolution: An Interview with Barbara Hall," *The Intercollegian,* LXXXII (April, 1965), 7–9, *passim*. Reprinted by permission.

example, in a United Nations survey some years ago a plan was suggested for a ten-year program for eliminating illiteracy in such an area as Latin America. We have very reliable information which indicates that Castro eliminated virtually all illiteracy in Cuba in two years. . . .

Now no Latin American who is committed to rapid social change is content to think about a ten-year program to eliminate illiteracy, much less than ten years before medicine will be available, schools, food, and a chance for a better life. Those who were on the Left in Brazil were those who were prepared to take the risk of rapid social change (by risk, I mean the inevitable instability which comes with change). . . .

To be a little more precise, the Left Wing in Brazil represented very clear groups of people. It represented, first and foremost, a large and growing Roman Catholic Left Wing—young people and intellectuals actively working for social change, a good many priests, and at least one archbishop, who had broken rather decisively with the Catholic hierarchy's tendency to side always with the status quo. These Roman Catholics were especially active in the youth and student movements; the National Student Association of Brazil was almost completely dominated by the Roman Catholic Left.

Then there was the Communist Party of Brazil, a group very much characterized by the Khrushchev "peaceful coexistence" line, the domestic version of which in Brazil was a gradual step-by-step but rapid process of change without violence and bloodshed. In addition to this, there were certain Protestants, including the Student Christian Movement (which was very definitely a part of the Left Wing) which were active and involved as well as lots of others who weren't communists, or Catholics or Protestants, people who wore no other labels, but who were committed to change.

There was a rather strong group of intellectuals; many people involved in drama and art and music belonged to the Left in Brazil, as well as a good many professors. And there were elected representatives from each of the 13 political parties in the congress who belonged to a national organization of Left Wing politicians. There also were a few but very vocal way-out Marxists who followed the China-Mao Tse Tung line, who said that a violent revolution was the only kind you'd ever get. This was a very, very small group, but they made a good bit of noise and frightened many people very badly. . . .

Nobody can say for sure whether liberal democracy has the resources for transforming Latin America into another kind of society. It is very difficult to believe that it can when all of the U.S. aid, when what Latin American governments themselves are doing, when the great efforts at industrialization are not really helping to change the situation. . . .

Thus, when the options are posed—communism versus what the United States seems to want and what the governing oligarchies of Latin America definitely want—then the dispossessed of the land are almost forced to opt for the communist alternative. And they do this without really knowing what communism is, without fearing it particularly, because it is not an enemy they have ever suffered from. They feel strongly that what the United States is really worried about is Soviet imperialism and not hunger and disease in Latin America. They do not particularly blame Americans for this, but it isn't very helpful to Latin America.

There is a story told by one of the peasant league leaders about a landlord who came to one of his peasants out in the field and asked him if he were a communist. The peasant answered that he didn't know what communism was, but if the man would tell him he'd be glad to say whether he was one or not. So the man began to talk about communism. He said it was a dreadful thing: the communists took all of your land and all the produce from your land; you had to do forced labor, slave labor; they broke up your family; they stole your daughters away, they took your sons away; they divided husbands and wives sometimes; and communism, what with one thing and another, was really a very dreadful system. To which the peasant replied, "Well, that's exactly what we have here now, and I'm definitely not a communist; that's what I'm against." . . .

The other side of this story is that there were some of us—a good many of the Protestants and almost all the Roman Catholics—who did not trust the communists at all and were determined that communists should not be the leaders of the revolution. But there was simply no way to work for political and social change without working with the communists, and we found at many places it was perfectly possible to work with them and, indeed, we felt it was helping the cause along.

77 *RODRIGUES, An Independent Brazilian Foreign Policy*

The Second World War awoke in the Brazilian national consciousness the idea of underdevelopment. But our foreign policy, while suffering from the secondary treatment to which it had been accustomed under the policy of complete parallelism inaugurated by Lauro Müller, and reaffirmed by Nilo Peçanha, persisted in following American policy. And it continued this way, without serious reexamination. In world politics in general and in the United Nations, Brazil had no interests of her own, except in South America, where the old policy of influence and leadership prevailed. The two phases of this behavior, submission on the world scene and a policy of our own in South America, facilitated the North American political treatment of the region and made difficult the defense of our world interests.

It was especially in the administration of Juscelino Kubitschek that the purpose of national policy and consequently international policy came to be the utilization of our potentialities over the long run and the shortening of such a period, or to put it better, a policy of intensive development. It was from this that the idea arose that we should seek voluntary international cooperation.

Even before the history of Operation Pan America unfolded, one could see immediately that it limited our action to the continent, that it regionalized our

José Honório Rodrigues, "Una Política externa própria e independente," *Política Externa Independente*, No. 1 (July, 1965), 31–39, *passim*. Reprinted by permission.

policy and that it maintained the traditional line of conditioning our foreign policy on that of the United States. We would continue to be limited to a secondary role on the world scene, identified inevitably with North American foreign policy and running all the risks of its world responsibilities. We would thus lack the flexibility and autonomy to seek the necessary resources or the indispensable commercial relations for the overcoming of our difficulties.

Operation Pan America, as an economic policy for a regional bloc, eliminated all intercontinental aspects from Latin American foreign policy. One had the impression that world participation was not desired and that Latin America was regarded as an isolated part of the world. It emphasized the regionalization of our foreign policy, although it did eliminate, by progress toward continental solidarity, the old colonial remnants of our policy of securing our borders and maintaining a balance of power along the Río de la Plata. . . .

Our political option today is much more between Western orthodoxy or heresy than between East or West. This latter choice is not really at stake. We can see, without fear, the values of both, and decide, like the synthesis which we are, that the world needs more cooperation than choice. But Western orthodoxy itself accepted collaboration from heretics in the war, in which we participated, for the defense of human values, independent of politics; if they collaborate and trade with each other everywhere, in continuing coexistence, why must Brazil avoid contact with the heretics at a time when our foreign policy is an instrument for development? Only the Inquisition would think that way. The option which is important, which the Second World War imposed, is quite a different one. It is between them and us, between those who do not oppose and in fact even aid in our growth and those who discriminate against our progress by exclusion, as the European Common Market is doing now.

We are not against anyone, we are merely in favor of ourselves, as a people who aspire to economic progress and social justice.

The bases of our foreign policy confirm these principles. First, *pacifism*, which throughout our history has remained a national objective and a popular aspiration, despite 1851 and 1865–70. Violence and oppression are not traits of our national character, but conciliation is—a conciliation which seeks politically to make compatible the interests in dispute. Second, *legalism*, which means an ideology based on the idea of the superiority of a world guided by the rule of law. Third, *nonintervention*, which represented a victory in the ebb and flow of our diplomacy, and which makes conquests by force and power over weaker states impossible. Fourth, and as a consequence of this last principle, *self-determination*, for which we provided an example in 1828 when we accepted and aided the creation of the Republic of Uruguay. . . . Fifth, *anticolonialism*, which comes from the Manifesto of 1822 and from the inclusion of the clause forbidding adherence to the Empire by the Portuguese colonies in Africa, established by the Treaty of 1825. Sixth, *the right to a policy of our own*, which Dom Pedro II defended in 1862 when confronted by the crisis concerning Great Britain, with her innumerable and unjust demands, which the Visconde de Jequitinhonha, Francisco Gê Acaiaba de

Montezuma, explained as follows: "We must not embitter the questions between ourselves and England, and we must take our proper position toward that power, as the United States did in dealing with France and England." . . .

The essential goal of all Brazilian foreign policy, yesterday as well as today, has been to obtain the right to have our own orientation. . . . It was not possible for the Empire to free itself from all the injunctions and external pressures which hampered our independence in international affairs, as the Parliament felt when it condemned the concessions, the forbearance, and the weakness in the consular agreements, or the subservience and the humiliating tradition by which strong governments imposed themselves in the formulation of our foreign policy. Saldanho Marinho finally said that the fear of foreigners had determined the course of our international negotiations. "The dignity of the nation has been disregarded more than a few times." . . .

Our freedom of choice as to decision making in foreign policy has been quite limited. This led Jânio Quadros to attempt to "internationalize" our foreign policy. The change in the world picture and even the change in our position within the so-called Free World permit us a freedom of action not heretofore possible. This situation leads us to a policy of adjustment which respects hemispheric regionalism, does not devaluate international objectives, expands commerce and political relations, refuses absolute commitments, and secures the interests of representative government and of the defense of peace.

Brazil is a continental nation which must think intercontinentally, not only in her relations with the Americas, but with the whole world, including the reestablishment of our tie with Africa which Great Britain destroyed in the middle of the last century.

Brazil, since Quadros, no longer accepts, and in fact rejects the secondary role, a kind of viceroyalty, to which it was relegated by North American policy. The United States was convinced that it was imperative for her interests to isolate the Western Hemisphere from other nations, and to keep it subordinated to the royal court which was located in Washington. This modest and unrealistic position for a country such as contemporary Brazil, despite all of its shortcomings and its lack of understanding of economic nationalism, generated a resentment which the people expressed in the vote given to Jânio Quadros, and which the latter interpreted with vacillation and doubt, but in essence with wise intuition. . . .

I definitely do not believe that any truly responsible person denies the value of our alliance with the United States, particularly its economic significance, nor doubts its strategic geopolitical value. Our understanding with the United States is a legitimate tie which we must maintain for our security and development. But this does not eliminate the possibility of our having misunderstandings whenever our interests are offended or prejudiced, because we are aware of our international importance. We plead for the equality of rights, treatment and competition which we see other nations, such as Canada, Belgium and West Germany, exercising without question. . . .

The influence which we have come to have since then and the greater respect with which we are heard show that the banner of Quadros, taken up by João Goulart, cannot be lowered. Influence does not need to be proportional to power; it depends more on leadership and enlightened popular support, and Brazil can count on these today. . . .

Our new economic power and the new force of organized labor, the pressures of the nationalists, of the interest groups, of the Church, of public opinion, as well as the omissions of the political parties and the vacillations of Congress weigh in the balance of decision. But the most important pressure is popular opinion, which is not always represented in Parliament. . . .

The change in Brazilian society, with new elements involved in decision making, arouses the most profound uneasiness and the greatest anxiety among the partisans of a frozen and immobile *status quo,* which permitted them to decide the fate of the majority in the greatest secrecy and without consulting it. . . .

In the Empire and until recently in the Republic, the programs of the political parties did not deal with foreign affairs, but merely referred to our desire for peace, to the defense of our national honor and international respect, so often offended. Recently they began to recognize, in a vague and general way, international co-operation, the honoring of the principles of the United Nations, and the integration of the Pan American community. The Brazilian Labor Party, in a forward step, clearly defends the principle of nonintervention. If it fell to a nonpartisan President to adjust our foreign policy to new world conditions and to our new position, it is a President from the Labor Party who is executing it, with many vacillations but without retreat, despite all the reactions and pressures from the most backward and submissive groups. . . .

A policy which is Brazilian and independent is not a partisan matter; its inspiration comes from radical nationalism, that is from the roots of national independence, from the idea of progress, from the real sources of national conduct, and from the democratic belief that power comes from the people.

SECTION XVII

Intervention and Non-Intervention

No issue in inter-American relations has been debated longer or more bitterly than that of intervention by the United States in the affairs of Latin America. Here is a selection of cautious views on this thorny topic. Margaret Ball, who made herself a recognized expert on the OAS while a member of the Wellesley College faculty, provides a careful analysis of the legal and political problems involved. (Reading No. 78.) C. Neale Ronning, of the New School for Social Research emphasizes that legal regulations are now undergoing a process of change. (Reading No. 79.)

78   BALL, *Issue for the Americas*

Latin American opposition to intervention goes back to the era of the wars of independence, when there was a strong fear that members of the Holy Alliance might assist Spain to retain its lost colonies. This fear of European action led many Latin Americans to welcome the Monroe Doctrine when it was first enunciated. The United States would help the former Spanish colonies to resist any attempted encroachment from abroad—or so they thought.

Subsequent developments, however, markedly altered the Latin American view. . . . It soon became apparent that the Doctrine could not be invoked by the Latin Americans at will; the United States would resort to the doctrine only when a United States President considered it to be in the best interest of his country to do so. . . . The famous Roosevelt Corollary (Theodore Roosevelt) soon made Latin Americans realize that they had exchanged the danger of European incursion for that of United States intervention. . . .

Latin America . . . has been strongly opposed to intervention, whether bi-

M. Margaret Ball, "Issue for the Americas. Non-Intervention v. Human Rights and the Preservation of Democratic Institutions," *International Organization*, XV (1961), pp. 21–37, *passim*. Reprinted by permission.

lateral or multilateral. The right of the American states to determine their own form of government, and their own economic and social policies, has been regarded as well-nigh sacred. . . . It is only insofar as communism may be regarded as an outside threat to any American state that most Latin Americans have shown any enthusiasm at all for action. There has been a distinct tendency to consider that the right of self-determination ought to limit OAS action with respect to indigenous communist movements. The United States, in contrast, has been pressing for a general recognition that the installation of a communist regime in any country represents by definition foreign intervention. There has not yet been a complete meeting of minds on this matter.

The protection of human rights has been of interest to Latin American nations throughout the period since the second world war. . . . The Latin Americans have always believed strongly in democracy in principle; they have traditionally viewed it as the ideal form of government. The difficulty has been in implementing this sentiment, as dictatorships have come and gone in many, if not all, of the other American republics. . . . The Latin Americans have not always recognized the existence of a conflict, or potential conflict, between the principle of non-intervention and the protection of human rights and democratic institutions. The OAS Charter of 1948 contains the statement that representative democracy is a basic principle of the system at the same time that it indicates that every member state has the right to govern itself as it likes and to determine its own political, economic, and social policies, and provides a more sweeping condemnation of intervention than ever before. . . .

The United States has accepted the principle of non-intervention in numerous inter-American agreements, approves the protection of human rights but has declined to participate in conventions concerning this matter, and is even more firmly committed in some ways to the defense of democracy than some of its southern neighbors. Is there any conflict to be found in these diverse attitudes? *Is* there a circle to be squared? Or is the principle of non-intervention perfectly compatible with the desire to defend human rights and promote democracy in the western hemisphere? . . .

The record to date on non-intervention, human rights, and representative democracy suggests that the real issue is one of attitude rather than one of law. The incorporation of the non-intervention principle in such a multiplicity of inter-American instruments is an indication of the view of most of the Latin American countries, grounded in unhappy earlier experiences in many cases, that intervention—whether unilateral or multilateral—is bad. And although the American republics have felt so strongly about this as to decline to permit OAS action in support of human rights, it remains true, obviously, that by new international agreements the American states could open up the field to OAS action as widely as they chose.

79 RONNING, The Currents of Panamericanism Are "Rough, Muddy, and of Uncertain Direction"

In 1948 the American states* met at Bogotá to consolidate, formalize, and improve many of the institutions which had developed in this haphazard manner. Shortly after the conference the Mexican Minister of Foreign Affairs [Jaime Torres Bodet] offered a timely summary and prediction:

> After more than a century of exploration, of uncertainties, and of trials, the legal channels of Panamericanism have been decisively consolidated. What currents will flow in these channels? America will say.

A decade later one could only say that those currents were rough, muddy, and of uncertain direction. U.S. military and other assistance offered to Cuban exiles in open contradiction to conventional obligations has been only the most dramatic expression of an increasing tendency throughout the Western Hemisphere openly to disregard formerly accepted legal obligations when political expediency so requires. Foreign fishing vessels have been seized by South American governments well over a hundred miles from their shore—in waters traditionally regarded as high seas. The confiscation of billions of dollars worth of foreign-owned property is viewed by many as only a tardy arrival of justice. To others it is the crumbling of the last vestiges of order and stability.

Obviously this is not a new phenomenon. Wherever and whenever we observe the relations among states, two conflicting desires are evident: the desire for order and predictability on the one hand, and the desire for freedom of action on the other. . . .

In contemporary inter-American affairs there can be no escaping that emphasis is now upon freedom of action. . . . Many of the conflicts now troubling this hemisphere serve to remind us of the usefulness of a number of rules and practices once taken for granted. More rules, once generally accepted as obligatory, are now being questioned, ignored or given totally new interpretations by more American states than ever before.

Those who would guard the *status quo* will feel that we have fallen upon evil days and are confronted by evil men. But the American, French and Mexican Revolutions, all of them challenges to law and order, will surely deny us this easy conclusion. The solution to this difficult state of affairs will not be found in more painstaking efforts to show, on the basis of traditional sources of international law, what the rules are that states are bound to observe. Nor will it be found in moral remonstrances and logical arguments, however learned, giving the advantages of an effective legal order. There would certainly be wide agreement on

C. Neale Ronning, *Law and Politics in Inter-American Diplomacy* (New York: John Wiley and Sons, Inc., 1963), pp. 1–3, *passim*. Reprinted by permission.
* The author means the U.S. plus the twenty Latin American republics. [Ed.]

this if the question "what kind of a legal order?" or "whose legal order?" could be answered first.

We must begin by learning what we can about the economic, political and social forces which are producing these profound changes in attitudes toward so many of the traditional rules. We must also learn what we can about the economic, political and social forces which formed the sphere of application and conditioned the effectiveness of rules which at times were reasonably effective. In short we must confront the task outlined by Charles de Visscher—"one of submitting to a more realistically informed criticism the rules and practices of international law observed in their living application, and of identifying the political, economic and demographic factors that shape, sustain, and develop them, as well as those that help to distort or destroy them." . . .

We shall see how the recognition of governments, perhaps the most fundamental question in international intercourse, has been governed by two conflicting doctrines, each of which shows the stamp of economic, social and political forces which refuse to stand still. The treatment of aliens and the expropriation of their property, the doctrines of non-intervention, the control of coastal waters and the ownership of the Antarctic are some of the other questions that will be studied. For each the economic, political and social forces which condition the changing doctrines and legal interpretations will be the central theme. These complex forces are revealed in four phenomena which confront us at every turn: cold war, social revolution, anti-colonialism and nationalism.

Inter-American Relations

Alberto Lleras Camargo, now ex-President of Colombia and one of the hemisphere's most respected statesmen, delivered an optimistic address on April 29, 1954, at Bucknell University, as Secretary General of the Organization of American States. (Reading No. 80.) The first Latin American to hold this position, which had been monopolized in the past by U.S. citizens, he had served in this post since 1948 when the Pan American Union was transformed into the OAS and entrusted with additional responsibilities. He made similar statements at Caracas on June 4, 1954, at the Tenth Pan American Conference, where he stated that economic problems of the hemisphere could be solved. He admitted that "millions of words, some pleasant, some wrathful and others persuasive, had to be exchanged via the channels of the Organization before essential agreements were reached that made it impossible to differ any longer on the first principles of Pan Americanism."

This friendly interpretation was not widely held by other Latin Americans. Mariano Picón-Salas, for example, at the time of his death in December, 1964, one of the authentic and independent voices in Latin America, held a diametrically opposed view. (Reading No. 81.) As historian and essayist, he had employed his talents over the years in Chile, Mexico, Brazil, and other countries as well as his native Venezuela. The weaknesses of Pan Americanism are also emphasized by Jorge Castañeda, an official of the Mexican Foreign Office, but the following statement (Reading No. 82) is not necessarily the official view of the Mexican government. Castañeda had the collaboration of a distinguished study group assembled at the Colegio de México. This statement is part of a book in a series sponsored by the Carnegie Endowment for International Peace.

William Manger, long a member of the Pan American Union staff, presents a somber, even pessimistic, view. (Reading No. 83.) Arthur P. Whitaker, a veteran historian long a member of the University of Pennsylvania faculty, looked at the record some years ago and concluded that the Pan American movement had expired. (Reading No. 84.) A British scholar, Gordon Cornell-Smith of Hull Uni-

versity, provides a closely reasoned and frank analysis of the achievements and failures of the Organization of American States. (Reading No. 85.)

Finally, since myths still influence the minds of men, John Paddock, an anthropologist on the faculty of the University of the Americas in Mexico City, summarizes neatly some of the basic misconceptions that flourish in Latin America and the U.S. with respect to each other's history. (Reading No. 86.)

80 *LLERAS CAMARGO, The Organization of American States: An Example for the World*

The strongest and most deep-rooted of these prejudices is the notion that the American organization is the tool of North American imperialistic policy. Even among many of the citizens of this land such a thought is to be found, though perhaps expressed in other words. They believe in good faith that, in view of the material power and prestige of the United States, it would be very simple for it to adopt an inter-American policy that would permit it to exercise relative control over any situation that might arise in this hemisphere. The Russians, and most of the Europeans, have always subscribed to a similar belief. That is why they respond with such scornful incredulity when someone points to our organization as one to be emulated. When the Charter of the United Nations was being drawn up at San Francisco in 1945, and the Latin American states waged a victorious fight to preserve intact the system they and the United States had recently reaffirmed and strengthened at Chapultepec, the non-American countries could not get over their amazement. . . .

Every day, both in this country and abroad, we hear it said that the United States lacks experience in international affairs, lacks a definite foreign policy and good judgment in the management of its relations with other nations. The fact is, however, that in that section of the world in which the United States has had occasion to work out its international course over the longest period of time and under normal conditions, it has produced a genuine masterpiece. In its inter-American dealings are to be found intelligence and elasticity, self-control and tact, and the courage to promote great ideals without fear of the consequences. . . .

Even with its present imperfections, our Organization is the best experiment in international coexistence the world has ever tried. It was our Organization that first paved the way for the world associations of nations, and she who tutored those who were to propose for the entire globe a new way of international life, that at first appeared to be one of the utopic dreams of ancient philosophers.

We owe it to our Organization that imperialism has not prospered in America, and surely her patient work over more than half a century of persuasion and vigilance against the threat of violence has done more for the independence of our young republics than have any tumultuous attacks on imperialism.

Lewisburg, Pennsylvania: Bucknell University Press, 1954, pp. 7–8, pp. 15–16, *passim.* Reprinted by permission.

She has made the strong nations of America realize the necessary limitations of international action, and at the same time she has convinced the weaker ones of the tremendous power of mere words to keep in check, with their seemingly fragile barrier, armed arbitrariness and the threat of force.

She has developed the concept, through many years of effective co-operation among the members, that power must be shared by the nations if it is to endure, and that there is a duty, accompanied by an advantage, to extend and share the benefits that good fortune has heaped on one land and one group of people.

81 *PICÓN-SALAS, Pan Americanism: A South American View*

Pan-Americanism as it has operated until today is a disequal association, the unbalanced alliance of the elephant with the ants. The basis for an honest Pan-Americanism might be built upon a previous Latin American alliance, an understanding between the weak nations which, having unified their general continental policy, would come to the opulent table of arbitration to which Washington invites us with authority greater than that of mere acolytes. For the rest, the policy of the United States is no longer Pan-American, but rather ecumenical, and the ideological struggle which Yankee capitalism is now undertaking against Russia may possibly compromise us in the future. We Latin Americans do not want to let ourselves be led docilely to such a position that we cannot avoid being burned in the coals of a future conflagration. We demand our right to peace, to prosper and to grow. For, at best, we are invited to take part in another war to "defend democracy" and afterwards the colonial nations will continue to be exploited and Franco will continue to be the representative of "order" in Spain.

82 *CASTAÑEDA, The Weakness of Pan Americanism*

What is the regional "reality" of the American continent? How favorable are conditions in this continent for an authentic regional agency, both from a political and from an economic point of view? . . .

In its economic aspect, Pan Americanism has not even succeeded in establishing those basic principles of inter-American cooperation which might contribute positively to raising the standard of living of the Latin American peoples. The reason largely stems from the fact that the Pan American organs and instruments, by their very nature, do not reflect, nor are they based on, the real division of the continent into two clearly differentiated economic zones, which have funda-

Mariano Picón-Salas, "Imperialismo y buena vecindad," *Cuadernos Americanos,* XXXV (Mexico City, Septiembre-Octubre, 1947), p. 68. Reprinted by permission.

Jorge Castañeda, "Pan Americanism and Regionalism: A Mexican View," *International Organization,* X (Boston, 1956), pp. 374–388, *passim.* Reprinted by permission.

mentally opposing economic problems, interests, and aims, although their economies are complementary. . . .

Those [political] principles which are most important in the continent have not yet . . . formed bonds of solidarity sufficiently strong to create a political Pan American community. Some, such as the non-recognition of the validity of territorial conquest, the pacific settlement of disputes, or the postulate of representative democracy are common to the American peoples but not to them exclusively. . . . Other important principles, like that of non-intervention, have a negative character and their very nature, origin and importance reveal the basic political antagonism that divides the two Americas. . . .

The principle of common defense against outside forces, which by its nature might contribute to the strengthening American solidarity, has become a principle which today presents serious risks for Latin America due to the extra-continental political and military interests of its North American associate. . . . Other principles, excellent in themselves, like the international protection of democracy and human rights and the non-recognition of dictatorships imposed by violence, have not been established in America for fear that they might be used as instruments of intervention in the Latin American countries. . . .

The lack of continental political solidarity has been at the same time cause and effect of the absence of a true Pan American spirit. What has living reality in the conscience of Latin American people is the feeling and the bonds of Latin Americanism. . . . Important sectors of continental public opinion still are convinced that the permanent activity of Pan Americanism, centered in the Pan American Union and other principal bodies located in Washington, is too closely identified with the United States government, its policies and interests. . . . Pan Americanism has existed for sixty years as a system and it still has not succeeded in penetrating the conscience of our peoples. Except for some isolated incident during the Good Neighbor period, it would be difficult to verify during this long period any powerful and spontaneous public manifestation which would have lent it force and reality. . . .

The new grouping of political forces in the world has helped accentuate the artificial character of Pan Americanism.

83 *MANGER, Does the Organization of American States Have a Future?*

In recent years inter-American relations have deteriorated to one of the lowest levels in history. To find a comparable period when these relations were similarly strained and when the seeds of total disintegration were equally close to bearing fruit, it is necessary to go back nearly half a century.

Today, few of the elements that traditionally have served as the source of

William Manger, *Pan America in Crisis: The Future of the OAS* (Washington, D.C.: Public Affairs Press, 1961), pp. 2–5, 95–97, *passim.* Reprinted by permission.

strength in the international relations of the nations of the Western Hemisphere are functioning as they should. The sense of political solidarity so laboriously built up in the years from 1930 to 1950 has gradually but steadily evaporated. The spirit of cooperation has deteriorated to such an extent that little or no progress has been made in solving the all-important contemporary problems of economic development and social improvement. The unity and solidarity of the American republics has been seriously undermined and the community of American States is rapidly becoming a fiction. . . .

As an aspiration, and ideal, the inter-American regional system emerged in 1826; but its realization in the form of a system representing all the republics of the Hemisphere began only in 1890 when the First International Conference of American States met in Washington. The latest stage of its development dates from 1948, when the Charter of the Organization of American States was signed at Bogotá.

Is this latest stage the final one for the OAS? In the light of the existing situation and the course of events of the last few years, this question might well be asked, for as the OAS enters its eighth decade it is confronted by challenges greater than any it has heretofore faced. They go to the very heart of its existence as an effective international institution. On the organization's ability to meet these challenges will depend the justification for its future existence.

The OAS is faced by the challenge of mounting political tensions; tensions that began to manifest themselves in the Caribbean a decade ago and that recently have been building up at an accelerated tempo. As an institution that pretends to deal with international issues affecting the peace and security of the member states, the OAS has prided itself on it accomplishments during the past ten years. Its achievements in this area have been not without significance, especially in finding solutions to a series of minor incidents in the Caribbean area. But the tensions have tended to grow rather than to subside; their repercussions are now being felt throughout the Continent. It is not sufficient that the OAS should have been able to demonstrate a capacity to contend with the rivalries of opposing political leaders or to find temporary solutions to minor frontier incidents. Will it also be able to deal with the larger issues of peace and security that possess continental as well as inter-continental significance and are looming larger and larger on the international political horizon? . . .

The Caribbean situation is not an isolated phenomenon. Neither is it a new one. What is occurring there today is a process that has been going on for the past ten years. It is a reflection and an intensification of a basic problem that presents itself throughout the southern part of the hemisphere, the urge for economic progress and social reform and the determination to achieve them.

For the United States, the Caribbean has added significance because the events are taking place in an area of our special interest and in such close proximity to our national territory. There, also, the problem is aggravated by the deep-seated antagonisms between the so-called champions of democracy on the one hand and the forces of dictatorship on the other. Equally significant, events in the Caribbean have revealed how quickly ideologies alien to the American concept of life are prepared to take advantage of every opportunity to create even greater difficulties, and how they threaten the very foundation of the hemisphere system. . . .

The failure to find solutions to Western Hemisphere problems explains the decline and deterioration that has taken place in inter-American relations and in the prestige of the OAS during the past decade. How long can the OAS afford not to produce a constructive and effective program of economic and social action? . . .

Intervention and nonintervention, collective intervention and unilateral nonintervention must be re-examined. The Latin American emphasis on nonintervention and their determination to preserve this basic principle of the inter-American regional system is understandable. But what the Latin Americans have failed to recognize, or have conveniently ignored, is that the correlative of unilateral nonintervention is collective intervention whenever the peace and security of the Continent are threatened. Both principles originated at approximately the same time and both have followed parallel paths. . . .

The dilemma that now presents itself to the American Republics and to the inter-American regional organization is how to reconcile these two principles and make both effective. Does the continued respect for the one depend upon the effectiveness of the other? Does the failure of the principle of collective action warrant a return to unilateral action? In a situation of sufficient gravity the answer to the last question is obvious. No nation would hesitate to act when it is convinced that its national security is at stake. Article 51 of the U.N. Charter, which is the basis of the collective security treaty of Rio de Janeiro, recognizes the right of individual as well as of collective self-defense. The law of self-preservation is stronger than the principle of nonintervention. . . .

If the OAS has a future it will be found only in the spirit of the *Alianza*, in the pledge contained in President Kennedy's first State of the Union message: . . .

To our sister republics of the south, we have pledged a new alliance for progress—*Alianza para Progreso*. Our goal is a free and prosperous Latin America, realizing for all its states and all its citizens a degree of economic and social progress that matches their historic contributions of culture, intellect, and liberty.

On the effective implementation of this pledge may well depend the survival of Pan Americanism and the future of the OAS.

84 WHITAKER, *The Rise and Decline of Pan Americanism*

The present essay deals with the latest phase of the long history of the Western Hemisphere idea, from 1940 to the present. The indications are that it will also

Arthur P. Whitaker, *The Western Hemisphere Idea: Its Rise and Decline* (Ithaca, N.Y.: Cornell University Press, 1954), pp. 154, 176–177, *passim.* Reprinted by permission. For a variety of opinions on this subject, see the volume edited by Lewis Hanke, *Do the Americas Have a Common History? A Critique of the Bolton Theory* (New York: Knopf, 1964).

prove the last phase, in the sense in which we have defined the idea in these pages. This fact has been obscured by the extension that has been given to the forms of inter-American cooperation since 1940, but one must distinguish between form and substance. After 1940 the substance of the Western Hemisphere idea was lost, and its place was taken first and briefly by globalism and then by new twofold divisions of the globe, not into the traditional Eastern and Western hemispheres, but into Northern and Southern hemispheres, or, more frequently, into the communist and non-communist worlds. Both of these new-style divisions of the world grouped Western Europe with all or most of America, and thus they were in headlong conflict with the classic Western Hemisphere idea, an essential component of which was the separation of America from Europe. . . .

The idea has always found its best expression in the realm of politics and diplomacy. Whatever one may think of the results attained in that realm, they provide most of the evidence that can be adduced in support of the proposition that the peoples of America are bound together in a special relationship which sets them apart from the rest of the world. In other fields, such as the cultural, comparable evidence would be hard to find. For example, in the basic matter of language the Americas have remained divided into three major groups, English, Spanish, and Portuguese, which in this respect have closer ties with Europe than with one another. The very currents of thought which have done most to create a common American climate of opinion, such as the eighteenth-century Enlightenment and nineteenth-century positivism, were importations from Europe and in the long run strengthened trans-Atlantic as well as hemispheric ties. More broadly, despite several centuries of the common experience of development in a New World environment, the history of the Americas has so far successfully resisted the efforts of American historians to integrate it in accordance with the Western Hemisphere ideas. Save in the political realm, the record of that experience is largely one which is held together either by the common ties of the Americas with Europe or else by the covers of a book.

Though realized on a substantial scale only in the realm of politics and diplomacy, the Western Hemisphere idea has served a useful purpose. The isolationist tinge which it exhibited in the 1930's belied its earlier record. Throughout most of its history it has served the opposite purpose of promoting a limited kind of internationalism in countries where isolationism was strong, such as the United States and Argentina. For these and all the other American countries it has long provided a laboratory and proving ground for policies, institutions, and experiences that were later applied with advantage in the broader field of world affairs.

85 *CONNELL-SMITH, A Balance Sheet*

Historically, as we have seen, the inter-American system was promoted by the United States in order to secure Latin American acceptance of her own national

Gordon Connell-Smith, *The Inter-American System* (New York: Oxford University Press, 1960), pp. 317–325, *passim*. Reprinted by permission.

policy of restricting extra-continental influence in the western hemisphere. The limitation of such influence would ensure the United States the hegemony over the American continent which her leaders had long since regarded as rightfully hers. The Monroe Doctrine had staked a claim in 1823; by the end of the nineteenth century the United States was able to make it good.* The launching of the Pan American movement in the 1880s was a facet of her emergence as a world power.

But the Pan American movement was not initiated by the United States solely as a means of furthering the establishment of her hegemony in the western hemisphere. She was concerned, at the same time, to make such hegemony acceptable to the Latin Americans; so that they would not wish to seek extra-continental support against her. For this purpose, advocates of Pan Americanism appealed for 'hemispheric solidarity'. They asserted that the American republics were bound together in a special relationship setting them apart from the rest of the world and, specifically, from the powers of Europe. The United States and Latin America, they maintained, shared a system superior to that of Europe which would be threatened by an extension of the European system to the hemisphere. Moreover, they claimed that the ideal of a united hemisphere had originated in Latin America. Pan Americanism was presented as a movement fulfilling the ideals of Simón Bolívar, the most revered of Latin American figures, though the Liberator's aims had been very different from those which now motivated the policy of the United States.

The inter-American system also served to bolster the self-image of the United States, now emerging as a world power but wanting to seem to herself as well as to others to be behaving differently from the traditional great powers with their spheres of influence and empires. She wanted to believe that her association with the smaller countries of the American continent differed fundamentally from great power—small power relationships in other regions of the world; that the Monroe Doctrine had been beneficial to the countries of Latin America and was compatible with their sovereignty and self-respect. Possessed of weak neighbours in the western hemisphere, the United States chose Pan Americanism where European powers would have chosen the path of imperialism. The self-image of the United States is extremely important in any analysis of inter-American relations, and, of course, of United States foreign policy generally. It has already been suggested that Latin America has provided something of a laboratory for the development of United States foreign policy.

During the first forty or so years following the First International Conference of American States, the United States consolidated her position of hegemony in the western hemisphere. But she failed to convince the countries of Latin America that the inter-American system was beneficial to them. The Monroe Doctrine was associated with repeated interventions by the United States in Central America and the Caribbean region. Pan Americanism was regarded in Latin America as

---

* For a variety of opinions on the much discussed Monroe Doctrine, see Donald M. Dozer, ed., *The Monroe Doctrine. Its Modern Significance*, New York: Knopf, 1965.

'a cloak for Yankee imperialism' and the Pan American Union as, in effect, a colonial office. By 1928 the International Conference of American States had become a platform for voicing Latin American resentment instead of one for demonstrating hemispheric solidarity. Only far-reaching changes in the inter-American system could make it a useful instrument of United States foreign policy. This, we have seen, meant primarily acceptance of the principle of non-intervention.

In subscribing to the principle of non-intervention the United States considered she was giving up unilateral armed intervention, in return for which the inter-American system would ensure 'collective responsibility'. Given her enormous power and influence in the hemisphere, the renunciation of armed force, which seemed in any case to have outlived its usefulness, was not a considerable sacrifice viewed against the gain in goodwill it would bring. By the 1930s Latin American ill-will was causing the United States growing concern, which increased following the rise of the dictators in Europe and their attempts to penetrate Latin America. So the inter-American system became a symbol of the Good Neighbour policy and a means of attempting to draw the countries of the hemisphere together to meet the challenge of the extra-continental, Axis powers.

It is generally agreed that the inter-American system served the United States well during the Second World War. At the Meetings of Consultation of American Foreign Ministers the United States obtained general support for her policies, and, within the framework of decisions taken at these conferences, was able to make bilateral arrangements for such purposes as the use of bases and the increased production of strategic raw materials. We noted how, at the Second Meeting of Consultation, the United States obtained hemispheric acceptance of her own no-transfer principle. While not requiring any serious armed contribution from Latin America to the war effort, the United States did seek political support, especially in countering Axis subversion in the hemisphere. She was able to use the inter-American system to this end, as, for example, in establishing the Emergency Advisory Committee for Political Defense. The Second World War, as we have seen, brought a proliferation of new inter-American agencies as well as the decision to reorganize and strengthen the inter-American system.

With the establishment of the United Nations and the growing involvement of the United States in the peace settlement, the future of the inter-American system— traditionally so closely linked with the policy of isolationism—was placed in doubt. In fact, however, the inter-American system assumed a new importance in United States foreign policy. Although determined to pursue a global policy, and opposed to the concept of 'spheres of influence' in other regions of the world, the United States had no intention of relinquishing her hegemony in the western hemisphere. Condemning both the colonial empires of certain western European powers and control of eastern Europe by the Soviet Union, the United States would not accept that these were analogous with the situation in Latin America. In the western hemisphere she was able to point to the inter-American system, an old-established association of juridically equal states, now recognized as a legitimate regional grouping within the United Nations. Moreover, the Rio Treaty, based upon Article 51 of the latter document, gave the inter-American system the right to initiate action to meet armed aggression against any of its members. The United States has therefore been able to use the inter-American system to limit United Nations concern—and that of extra-continental powers—with the affairs of the western hemisphere.

Following the development of the Cold War the United States was anxious for the political support of the other members of the inter-American system. At first, when the Cold War seemed remote from the western hemisphere, this meant, above all, support in the United Nations, where the twenty-one members of the inter-American system originally formed over 40 per cent of the total membership. This support was for United States policies in other regions of the world (for example her action in Korea was endorsed in the OAS Council as well as supported within the United Nations), and also in opposition to attempts by other nations to raise embarrassing American issues in the world body. Subsequently, when the Cold War came to the western hemisphere, the United States found the inter-American system even more useful in limiting United Nations involvement with the problems it caused. The United States used the existence of the inter-American system to mask her overthrow of the Arbenz government in Guatemala; and she has succeeded to a very large extent in isolating Cuba within the hemisphere. Castro's survival has been due to extra-continental support which, regardless of any possible action by the inter-American system, the United States has not been able to prevent. It is significant that the United States based the legality of her quarantine measures against Cuba in October 1962 upon the fact that they were taken, with the support of the inter-American system, under the terms of the Rio pact. Her representative in the General Assembly said his country had received a 'mandate' from the OAS to protect the western hemisphere and would use 'all means necessary' to carry it out. Moreover, he cited the OAS resolution of 23 October as inferentially endorsing the aerial surveillance of Cuba.

On balance, it may be said that the inter-American system has served the interests of the United States in helping her to maintain a position of hegemony in the western hemisphere in a form compatible with her own traditional antipathy towards what she considers the essentially 'non-American' concepts of spheres of influence and imperialism. It has helped to give her a considerable degree of success in securing Latin America's acquiescence in her own policy of limiting extra-continental influence in the hemisphere. The United States has succeeded in marshalling a majority of Latin American governments to condemn a member of the inter-American system seeking extra-continental assistance against her on the grounds that such intervention threatened hemispheric solidarity and ideals. The existence of the inter-American system has enabled the United States to claim that her own undertakings in other regions of the world give no cause for other powers to attempt to intervene in the western hemisphere. Such intervention would not be merely against the United States, but against the inter-American system as a whole, whose members share a community of interests. . . .

As for the countries of Latin America, the most obvious way in which the inter-American system has served their interests is in establishing the principle of non-intervention, imposing some restraint upon the use of United States power as a price of inter-American co-operation. Within the inter-American system, and especially at the Inter-American Conference and the Meeting of Consultation, the United States is confronted by all the Latin American countries together. It has been observed that 'the inter-American conferences have often had all the ear-marks of a Latin American alliance against the United States,' although the same writer points out that: 'The United States has generally been able to use its influence with enough governments to prevent the "alliance" from including all or even a majority of Latin American states.' The history of the inter-American system shows, however, that when feeling on some issue has been deep and widespread among the Latin Americans at these conferences it has exerted an influence on United States policies which probably would not have been possible by individual countries through normal diplomatic exchanges.

The Latin Americans have been able to use the inter-American system with greater success, so far, to restrain the United States in the use of her political and military power than to induce her to grant them economic assistance. As we have seen, not until 1958 was there a substantial modification of United States policies on inter-American economic and social co-operation, beginning with her agreement to the Inter-American Development Bank, and followed by the Act of Bogotá and the Alliance for Progress. However, while the inter-American system is associated with the Alliance, it does not control the disbursement of funds. The trend has been for this association to become closer under Latin American pressure, but it seems extremely unlikely that the United States will relinquish the control she now exercises.

The inter-American system undoubtedly has served the interests of the countries of Latin America in bringing them together in this form of multilateral diplomacy. One great source of weakness of these states has been their limited contacts with each other. Relations between the countries of Latin America have become more intimate (if not always more friendly) within the inter-American system. It would be ironical indeed if a system conceived to promote Pan Americanism should be instrumental in fostering effective Pan Latin Americanism: Latin American solidarity rather than a truly inter-American community. Such an eventuality is perhaps remote at the present time. But on certain issues such as non-intervention and their economic condition and aspirations there has already grown up a community of interests among the Latin American members of the inter-American system.

It would seem from this brief analysis that the main disadvantage to the United States of her membership of the inter-American system lies in such curbs as it has placed upon her exercise of the enormous power she possesses in the hemisphere, while for the countries of Latin America this lies in the limitations it has imposed upon the development of extra-continental relationships which might have offset the imbalance of power between themselves and the United States. It may well be asked, however, how far membership of the inter-American system has been, in fact, responsible for these restraints and to what extent they have been imposed by external factors. Would it be feasible, for example, for the United States to invade Cuba today if she had OAS acquiescence, or even support? We noted, for example, the influence of external factors upon the development of the Good Neighbour policy. Nor can it be doubted that the most effective limitation upon Latin America's extra-continental relationships has been the unwillingness and inability—until very recently—of any non-American power seriously to challenge United States hegemony in the western hemisphere.

Clearly, the inter-American system has served the interests of the United States much more than it has those of the Latin American countries. This, of course, is only a reflection of the vast disparity of power within the hemisphere. The inter-American system has helped the United States maintain her hegemony and safeguard her interests in the hemisphere with the minimum intervention from extra-continental powers and influence.

Yet the inter-American system has never been truly isolated from international society as a whole; it has always been in some degree affected by the world environment. The extent to which its fortunes have been shaped by extra-continental factors has increased considerably since the end of the Second World War. The most important of these factors have been the establishment of the United Nations (the effects of which have already been discussed in this chapter), the development of the Cold War, and the growing division of the world into developed and economically backward countries.

One most significant result of the Cold War has been the much more intimate links which have developed between the United States and Western Europe. The North Atlantic Treaty Organization is a much closer alliance than the inter-American system, some of whose members reject the idea that it is a military alliance at all. This last point was underlined, incidentally, when Dulles suggested establishing links between the OAS and NATO in December 1957. . . .

In recent years a growing number of Latin Americans have moved nearer to the position of the Afro-Asian neutralists, rejecting the division of the world into 'Free' and 'Communist,' and regarding as more relevant to their problems a division between rich and poor nations. For, as Sr Carlos Sanz de Santamaría, subsequently appointed chairman of the Inter-American Committee on the Alliance for Progress, observed in 1960:

> Although we Ibero-Americans belong totally to the Western World, in philosophy, ethical concepts and ideals of individual freedom, our living conditions are much more like those in other areas of the world. We, unfortunately, belong to that group of countries so-called 'underdeveloped'. We are backward countries with a very low standard of living. . . .

It could be added that the vast masses of Latin Americans (Indo-Americans and not Ibero-Americans) share neither the standard of living nor the 'philosophy, ethical concepts and ideals of individual freedom' of the Western world. It is doubtful whether the countries of Latin America have ever been wholeheartedly members of the 'Free World'; but there is no doubt they feel themselves today to be among the poor. Nor can the fact that most of the poorer peoples of the world are coloured be overlooked in considering the situation within the inter-American system. . . .

86 PADDOCK, *The War of the Myths*

● **Brief formulation of the twin myths.** *Myth a:* "The English settlers of North America were many times worse than the Spanish in their treatment of the Indians. It is true that the Spanish were guilty of mistreatment, but the English carried out a campaign aimed at nothing less than extinction. Just look at the situation today— in North America hardly a trace remains of the Indians, and that trace is on reservations like wild animals in a zoo; in Hispanic America the Indians are numbered in millions. Besides, the Spanish didn't discriminate against the Indians, but rather intermarried with them, while in North America the Indians have always been discriminated against."

Myth b: "The Conquistadores were a gang of hoodlums. They came to Mexico and South America to rob, to rape, and to avoid going to jail for their past crimes at home in Spain. Whereas the English colonists were fleeing from religious persecution, the Spanish brought it to America. How much better it would have been if the English had conquered Mexico and Peru. Then the Indians would not have been enslaved, their civilization would not have been exterminated . . ." and so on.

No one could believe these stories while keeping in mind a number of obvious facts. However, many intellectually honest Latin Americans and North Americans (and, of course, Indians, Europeans, and others) do believe one or the other simply because they never have examined it critically.

● **Some historical facts.** Some of the facts (which I believe, are universally recognized as such) are these:

1. The Indian population with which the English colonists dealt was relatively small. These North American Indians were only partially an agricultural people, and their methods of food production were incapable of supporting a large population.

2. On the other hand, the Indian population of Nuclear America (that is, much of what is now Hispanic America) was very large—numbered in millions—and was fully civilized, living in cities and practicing intensive agriculture.

John Paddock, "The War of the Myths," *América Indígena,* XVIII (1958), pp. 283–289. Reprinted by permission.

3. Both the English and the Spanish settlers caused suffering, displacement, death through violence and the introduction of new diseases, and other damage to the Indian populations which came into contact with them.

4. Both Spanish and English settlers believed firmly that they were doing the Indians a favor, and carrying out God's will, by destroying Indian culture and implanting their own. There were cynical adventurers in both European groups, but the ethnocentrism of the majority, which we find so naive today, was usually sincere.

5. In spite of great drops in the Indian population of both English and Spanish colonies, few Indian groups became extinct. Some Indian groups did perish, in Spanish and in English areas.

6. The Indian population of the Americas, treated as a whole, is recovering strongly both in North America and in Latin America. Although definition of just what persons should be counted as Indians is variable, census figures show that the present Indian population of the Americas is at least 50% of that which existed in 1500 A.D., and may be 100% of the pre-Conquest figure or even more. In the United States and Canada, present Indian population is probably from 50% to 75% of the pre-Conquest figure. In Mexico, although here it is much more difficult to define the Indian, one may suggest that among the present population of over 30 million some 75% to 90% of the genes are Indian, which would make the present population figure (in these purely biological terms) much larger than the pre-Conquest one.

7. The Indian population of Mexico dropped *by millions* from 1521 to the low point, which Cook and Simpson believe to have been reached around 1650.

8. The Indian population of the English colonies dropped only by thousands, for the obvious reason that it was numbered only in thousands.

9. There are significant differences in the history of the colonization carried out: the English came for land, not for wealth; having come to live and work, they brought their own womenfolk; having the custom of working their own land, they preferred to drive the Indians off rather than enslave them. The Spanish sought wealth; when they farmed, they did it for production on large scale, not for subsistence, and for this as well as for mining they needed quantities of cheap labor.

10. When English aristocrats came to America, they brought a different outlook on farming from that of the earlier colonists, and set up (in what were to become the slave states) a system much like that of Spanish *encomenderos* and later *hacendados* in Mexico.

11. While the Spanish were interested specifically in crushing Indian civilization, the English were not.

12. While the English were interested in driving the Indians off their land, the Spanish were not.

13. Discrimination was practiced in the English colonies. There were distinctions recognized between Europeans, half-breeds, and Indians.

14. Discrimination was practiced in the Spanish colonies. There were distinguished by name as many as 32 degrees of mixture.

15. It is naive to suggest that it might have been better for the Indians, or for

Indian civilization, if the English had been the conquerors of Mexico and South America. If they had been the conquerors of those areas, they would not and could not have lived as they did in North America, where conditions were so different.

16. It is not true that the English did not practice religious persecution in their American colonies. Although they had fled from such persecution in England, they did not allow religious liberty in the colonies. Rhode Island was founded by religious refugees from Masachusetts.

17. Religious persecution was equally familiar to Spanish colonies. There were inquisitors practicing in Mexico long before the institution of the Inquisition was formally set up. The witch hunts of New England resembled the Inquisition; but the Inquisition was a much larger, more fully institutionalized, and long lasting phenomenon.

By now it is clear that what I have called myths are in fact very far removed from anything which might be called history. They are fantastically biased presentations remotely based upon history. They are in some degree *nationalist* myths, and like others of their kind they serve as rationalizations of unexplained aspects of their group's history, including events or policies which are not in accord with the group's professed philosophy.

● **Confronting the Myths with the Facts.** Some brief discussion of the historical facts listed above may be in order. First, as regards the series of statements about Indian population at the Conquest, and the subsequent decimation of that population, we may say that the facts speak for themselves. However, it may be of aid in their interpretation if we keep in mind the magnitude of the differences between North America and civilized Mesoamerica. When a few hundred Englishmen settle in an area (only a small part of North America) occupied by a few thousand Indians, the impact upon the Indians is necessarily very great. When a few hundred Spaniards land in a Mexico populated by millions of Indians, then even if Spanish and English behavior were identical, the impact is necessarily much less. Likewise, when the English bring a relatively advanced and complete culture to a land of less developed, less complete culture, the cultural impact is necessarily heavy. When the Spanish bring an advanced and complete culture, to a land of already advanced and complete culture, the impact is necessarily less overwhelming.

It is difficult to compare the population figures for North America and Mesoamerica as they were affected by the Conquest because whereas the Spanish rapidly spread throughout Mesoamerica and a part of North America the English colonists occupied only a relatively small area on the Atlantic coast of North America. However in general we are more interested in only the larger aspects of the demographic picture. Thus it is sufficient to know that the Indian population of the English colonies was of a magnitude measured only in thousands, and that of Mesoamerica included millions; to know that in both areas the Indian population fell rapidly, reached a low point, and is now recovering.

Cook and Simpson believe that the low point of Indian population in central

Mexico was reached around 1650. Several authorities think that the Indian population of the United States reached its minimum as late as around 1900. (The table of Indian population in the United States shows a low point in 1870.) What is the explanation? In Mexico, the Conquest was virtually completed within 20 years. However, in the United States there were still small frontier wars with Indians until very late in the 19th century; Arizona and Oklahoma, both having large Indian populations, were admitted as states only in 1912. Thus the population figures for Indians in the United States are affected throughout the 19th century by the addition of new states to the union. And, in the same way, the minimum Indian population is reached only after the Conquest is completed—around 1900 for the United States as against 1650 for Mexico.

The tragic decimation of Indian population in Spanish colonies was in part a consequence of violence, the near-enslavement of Indians in mines and agricultural *encomiendas,* and so on; but most of it was the result of unpremeditated factors such as disease and cultural conflicts following contact.

In North America, Indians were dispossessed in most cases through purchases and treaties. These arrangements were possible because the English (or the French or Dutch, as the case may be) believed the Indians had the right to sell their lands, while the Indians had no concept of land ownership and therefore had a quite different idea of the meaning of these treaties and "sales." Thus is produced a typical case of cultural conflict: the Indians believed that the English betrayed their contracts, and the English believed the Indians were treacherous. Yet it was usually the case that both parties had been honorable in the beginning. Obviously, neither group can be blamed for not understanding in the beginning the different culture of the other.

The interesting matter of attitudes toward miscegenation and racial differences also may be clarified by mention of historical differences. It is true that even today we do not understand properly why it is that Northern and Southern Europeans differ so much in their attitudes (at least in their *professed* ones) toward the relations of the sexes. As regards their real behavior in America, I believe it is clear that the Spaniards mixed more with the Indians than did the English. Among the significant factors lying behind this difference we may point out the one mentioned above, that the English more often had their own wives with them from the beginning. Again, in Spanish colonies there were more Indian women (and men, and children) than in the English ones. As a small minority among millions of Indians, the Spanish had more and closer contact, in urban surroundings often enough, while the North American Indians were forest dwellers. Contact thus was much reduced in North America.

Was there a difference in attitude toward the Indians as people? It has been suggested that since the Spanish were themselves already a very mixed people, with Celts, Iberians. Phoenicians, Greeks, Carthaginians, Romans, Goths, Vandals, Jews, and Moors among their ancestors they were so accustomed to the idea of mixture that, in contrast with the English, the Spanish simply paid little attention to any differences between themselves and the Indians as potential mates. This suggestion seems plausible; but it comes from a man of Spanish descent who probably overlooks the almost equally imposing list of peoples ancestral to the modern English: Celts, Iberians, Angles, Jutes, Saxons, Danes, Norsemen, Normans, Romans, probably also Greeks and Phoenicians, Jews in small numbers (and no doubt future research will disclose others).

As for differences in attitudes toward the Indian way of life we may note that while the Mesoamerican Indians had their Sahagún (and, of course, other truly humane and liberal chroniclers) among the Spanish, there arose in North America also a literature about the Indians. Sometimes this was factual, as in the work of Schoolcraft and the later ethnologists; often it was fictional, as in the works of Fenimore Cooper and Longfellow, to mention only the best known. It does appear that there is this difference: factual chronicling of Indian life appeared first in Spanish colonies, and fictional romanticizing of the Indians came along only very recently, especially with the 20th century; in the English colonies, fictional romanticizing of the Indian was well advanced before factual chronicling really began. Here again, we cannot be sure that a difference in attitude toward the Indians is the cause; it may be that the earlier growth of factual or fictional writing about the Indians was a consequence of the difference between North American and Mesoamerican Indians themselves as subjects. But once again, history comes to our aid. The Spanish were intent on destroying an Indian culture which they believed was a work of the devil; the English had no special interest in destroying Indian culture, which they believed would go on as before in lands to the west of their Atlantic Coast colonies. Thus the Spanish could see that Indian ways must be recorded at once, or lost to history; for the North Americans, the English saw no pressing need to record a way of life which they did not then perceive to be in danger of extinction.

We may note that there were no Indian governors of Spanish colonies, even though there were Indians who were educated, civilized, and accustomed to governing the same territories. Likewise, there were no Indian governors of English nor other European colonies in North America. Discrimination does not seem to be limited to either nation.

As regards the reservations of the United States, one sees that in the 1950 census, over 16% of the Indian population of that country is listed as urban. Indians are free to leave their reservations whenever they wish, and many do so. However, the reservation is necessary if the Indians are to preserve their own cultures, as some groups wish to do. Even in the protected area of a reservation, it is impossible for them to keep their way of life entirely free from outside influence.

The concept of the reservation is far from an ideal solution to the problem of dealing with the Indian; however, its existence does not seem to constitute a proof that the English settlers and their descendants were less humane than the Spanish. If Pedro de Alvarado or Nuño de Guzmán had found the idea of reservations potentially profitable, it seems very doubtful that any moral considerations would have detained him.

In one sense, the reservation is a restriction, a reduction of the Indian's freedom; this was especially true before the Indians of the United States enjoyed the rights of citizenship. However, it is true also that Indian religious practices still exist, open and unpersecuted (except by curious tourists), on the reservations. In Mexico, on the other hand, such practices are found only in the remotest areas and are subject to many kinds of persecution, the cruelest of which is the propagation of the widely diffused public opinion that they are a form of savagery and a proof of inferiority.

• **Conclusions.** Finally, it does seem justified to propose that 1) treatment of the native Americans has been ideal at no time and in no area; 2) because of important differences in geography, native cultures, native populations, and aims of the colonists, it is impossible to make an accurate evaluation of whose sins were greater; 3) the time spent in such comparisons might well be dedicated to *work* on behalf of the Indians of today, with much greater benefit to the Indians.

This is not to suggest that we turn our backs upon the past. Until we arrive at a sound factual understanding of our history, our planning for the future will continue to be defective. The first step toward comprehension of past events is to make an honest effort to distinguish between history and myth. The existence of nationalist myths seems to be related to some sense of secret guilt for the deeds of our ancestors. Those deeds cannot be undone; myth has been trying unsuccessfully to disguise them ever since men have begun to tell tales; only in the future can we do anything to balance the account, if we feel obligated to make a contribution.

United States Policy Toward Latin America

The first and fundamental fact to be learned and remembered by every student of Latin American affairs is that sharp controversy has been waged for a long time on the proper role of the U.S. in the hemisphere. Congress speaks its mind freely, as the samples given below on discussions in the House of Representatives and the Senate indicates. (Reading No. 87.)

The memorandum by Sumner Welles (Reading No. 88) provides a kind of preview of the policies put into effect by the administration of President Franklin D. Roosevelt. A trusted adviser of the president on inter-American affairs, Welles prepared in early 1933 this basis for the Good Neighbor Policy by outlining desirable action on such matters as continental defense, the principle of inter-American consultation, reciprocal trade agreements, and intervention. Assistant Secretary of States Edwin M. Martin gives an official viewpoint on the thorny and permanent problem of how to treat military governments. (Reading No. 89.)

The brilliant Mexican novelist and Marxist, Carlos Fuentes, speaks eloquently for Latin America (Reading No. 90), while Ellis Briggs, a long-time diplomat of the U.S., presents forcefully an entirely different viewpoint. (Reading No. 91.) An informed, temperate overview of the many problems involved in the relationship between Latin America and the U.S. is provided by Philip W. Quigg, Managing Editor of Foreign Affairs. (Reading No. 92.)

Most high officials of the U.S. make at some time a statement on what our policy in Latin America should be. Shortly before he was elected Vice-President, Senator Hubert Humphrey drew up his thoughtful, comprehensive declaration. (Reading No. 93.) His emphasis on the need for more education in the U.S. on Latin America and his conviction that any change in popular attitudes will come only slowly, merit careful consideration. John Bartlow Martin, an ambassador with recent experience in the hot waters of the Dominican Republic, lays bare what he believes our choices are in Latin America. (Reading No. 94.)

87 The United States Congress Discusses Latin American Affairs

A. SHOULD THE U.S. ARM LATIN AMERICA?

MR. MORSE. What does the Senator have to say about the argument we hear from the Pentagon always, no matter what administration is in power, that if we do not make these military goods available to the Latin American countries they will get them somewhere else; that if we do not sell the goods to them they will get them from England, from France, from Czechoslovakia, from Russia or from some other country in the world; and that, therefore, we had better sell them the goods and have at least that much control over the nature of the military hardware, and thus create at least a market for spare parts and repairs?

MR. GRUENING. I think the answer is to be found in a solution which we have never been willing to use; that is, so long as we are pouring millions of dollars in economic aid to these countries we have a right to exact certain reciprocal conditions from them. These were the things predicated by President Kennedy when he launched the Alianza para el Progreso. It was said that we would give help if these countries would make certain social and economic reforms. In very few cases have they done so. One of those social and economic reforms would be not to squander their substance on an arms race.

That would be the answer I would give.

Mr. President, in the 10 years since the inception of the Latin American military assistance program, we have provided over one-half billion dollars in military assistance to Latin American governments.

I ask unanimous consent that tables prepared by the AID program be printed at the conclusion of my remarks showing how much was given or loaned to Latin American countries since fiscal year 1952 for both economic and military assistance. I am asking that both tables be printed, Mr. President, because in some countries there is a disturbing contrast in the amount of economic aid given or loaned and the amount of military assistance given or loaned.

THE PRESIDING OFFICER. Without objection, it is so ordered.*

MR. GRUENING. It is interesting to note, Mr. President, that when the program of military assistance to Latin America was first instituted in 1952, total military aid that year totaled only $200,000. It has climbed—indeed soared—steadily since that time.

The figures for the intervening years are:

Congressional Record. Senate, Vol. 108 (August 2, 1962), pp. 15421ff.
* These tables are printed in the Congressional Record. Senate, Vol. 108 (August 2, 1962), Part II, p. 15426 [ed.].

Latin America Military Aid

Fiscal year

1952	$200,000
1953	11,200,000
1954	34,500,000
1955	31,800,000
1956	30,400,000
1957	43,900,000
1958	47,900,000
1959	54,000,000
1960	53,700,000
1961	91,600,000

I am informed that it is expected that $63.6 million will be the total of the military assistance to all Latin American countries in the 1962 fiscal year. For the new fiscal year, the United States is budgeting an additional $84 million in military aid.

MR. PROXMIRE. Mr. President, will the Senator yield?

MR. GRUENING. I yield with the understanding that I shall not lose my right to the floor.

MR. PROXMIRE. I congratulate the distinguished Senator from Alaska. I think he is making a very excellent, timely, and badly needed speech.

I have wondered for a long time how the United States could possibly justify the giving of military assistance to South American countries. Those countries are not going to fight the Russians. Those countries are not going to fight the Chinese. They will not be invaded by Khrushchev or by Mao.

I suppose one could say in some cases they might provide defense against Castro. Castro occupies an island country. If this country, which has the greatest Navy and the greatest Air Force in the world, cannot control the seas around Cuba, we are a lot weaker than I think, compared to a little island country with 6 million people.

Under these circumstances it seems to me that military aid to Latin America is not only a waste of money but also, as the Senator is so well stating—I think his logic is devastating—it will provide for an inevitable arms race among people whose economies are already impoverished. It would be a very dangerous as well as a very foolish policy to follow.

Is it not true that if we give substantial aid to one friendly country, judging on the basis of all our experience, we shall have to match that aid to another country?

MR. GRUENING. That has been the invariable experience.

We will be heaping Pelion upon Ossa.

Each time one country gets military aid its neighbor wants more. That is what we should understand.

MR. PROXMIRE. The Senator is stating very well how military aid has increased year after year. The trend line is steadily up, in spite of the fact that experience shows we cannot possibly justify it.

I am delighted and very grateful to the Senator from Oregon, who is of course the expert in the Senate on Latin America. The Senator is the chairman of the Sub-committee on Latin American Affairs of the Committee on Foreign Relations. I am grateful to him for speaking out as forcefully as he has in support of the Senator from Alaska.

I should like to hear those Senators who disagree with this position make their case. I have never heard it made.

MR. GRUENING. I thank the Senator from Wisconsin. I wish to say that the record is not without warnings delivered on this floor that the program of military aid to Latin America must be carefully watched.

On May 12, 1957, the distinguished senior Senator from Minnesota, our able majority whip [Mr. HUMPHREY], in his capacity as chairman of the Subcommittee on Disarmament of the Senate Committee on Foreign Relations, warned:

> The executive branch must be careful that military aid sent to Latin American nations does not promote an arms race. Nor should military aid detract from important programs of economic development and technical assistance. What we give to one nation for hemispheric defense may provoke demands by another for an equal amount of aid. The danger is particularly acute since little appears to have been done to integrate the defense functions of the separate countries. If greater attention were given the coordination of military policy and functions, it might result in a decrease in the amount Latin Amercan nations need to supply their individual establishments. Such a step might also lessen the possibility for arms competition among the several countries and, in turn, might enable more energy and resources to be channeled into constructive measures to increase living standards and develop Latin American economies.

From Latin America came words of caution also. Perhaps the most eloquent exposition was that of Eduardo Santos, a former President of Colombia and then in exile from the military dictatorship of Rojas Pinilla. Dr. Santos said:

> Against whom are we Latin Americans arming ourselves? Why are our countries ruining themselves with costly armaments which they will never be able to use . . . ? We have no reason for fighting one another; We have only reasons for drawing close to each other and living together fraternally. . . . And do we have, perhaps, a military role to play in the great international conflicts? Never. In this era of the atomic bomb with these incredibly costly armaments, with technical systems backed by billions, why are our poor countries continuing to ruin themselves with armaments which at a time of international conflict would represent absolutely nothing? Then we shall be creating armies which are insignificant in international affairs, but devastating to the internal economy of each country. Each country is being occupied by its own army.

José Figueres, while President of Cost Rica, said:

> We don't want any military support. We don't want any army. In case of aggression, our army is our moral standing and our faith in the Inter-American Treaty of

Reciprocal Assistance. The two times that we have been invaded our citizens have turned immediately into soldiers to defend democracy while the machinery of the Rio Treaty was set into motion. Any assistance we receive, we want to be directed toward education and economic development.

B. "WE HAVE THE SOVEREIGN RIGHT TO PROTECT OUR INVESTORS ABROAD"

MR. HICKENLOOPER. Mr. President, I wish to discuss for a few minutes a subject which I think is of vital importance to the United States, to our foreign policy, and to our relations with other countries. As I view it, it is the attitude of our Government toward the expropriation or seizure of American property in foreign countries. Repeated instances of expropriation have arisen, specifically, instances which occurred early this year; namely, a couple of expropriations in Brazil, some expropriations in Ceylon, some threatened expropriations in other places, and a general beginning of a wave of seizure of American property by foreign governments without adequate purpose or sufficient payment of the property. This action has aroused the indignation of many Members of Congress.

It has always been my concept that one of the duties of the U.S. Government is to protect the reasonable, fair, equitable rights of American citizens abroad. I submit that that is not being done, that it has been neglected, and that American citizens and their property are being discriminated against. Not only is their property being seized in certain countries without adequate, fair compensation, but the State Department and the administration are not exercising vigorous care or attention to see to it that the traditional protection given to their rights—not the unusual or extraordinary territorial rights, but merely the basic rights of American citizens abroad—is being afforded American citizens.

Early this year, when the Foreign Assistance Authorization Act of 1961 was before the Senate for consideration, I filed with the Committee on Foreign Relations, for the reference of the Senate, an amendment which sought to reach this situation. There had been two expropriations in Brazil. No real provision had been made to pay for the seizure of that property. Other expropriations were threatened. Bills were introduced in the legislatures of a number of countries throughout the world providing for the expropriation and seizure of foreign property under various types and kinds of alleged payment, most of which were long-term bonds of questionable value and having no certainty of convertibility. In effect, this action merely amounted to expropriation and seizure of the property.

There are other countries where unfair and inequitable tax exactions or other business requirements were placed upon American nationals doing business in those countries, requirements which were not applied to the nationals of the countries.

In many nations throughout the world the U.S. citizens were being put upon.

Congressional Record. Senate, Vol. 108 (Oct. 2, 1962), pp. 21615–21620, *passim.* For a historical perspective on this highly controversial topic, with many documents, see Marvin D. Bernstein, ed., *Foreign Investment in Latin America. Cases and Attitudes,* New York: Knopf, 1966.

They were being treated without equity as compared with the nationals of those countries. Americans were being discouraged in their business operations.

Meanwhile, there was lipservice from the U.S. Government. It was said that we were encouraging American investment abroad and were exporting American know-how. At the same time the basic interests of Americans abroad were not being protected.

The amendment to which I refer, which was considered by the Committee on Foreign Relations, provided that the United States would not attempt to control the sovereignty of any nation in the expropriation of property for public convenience as that nation saw it, or for the exercise of eminent domain, which we recognize as a sovereign power of a sovereign government. The amendment provided, in effect, that when any nation seized the property of an American citizen or imposed exactions by way of regulations or taxes upon Americans doing business abroad that were not equitably applied to all people in that country, the United States would withhold foreign aid from that country; and the President was directed to withhold foreign aid. We did not seek to dictate the sovereign rights of any country; but we reserved the right, under the amendment, to say what we would do with our money if foreign countries abused American citizens by denying them their rights.

The State Department raised all kinds of objections. They wrote memorandums; they appeared before the committee; they said, in effect, "We will protect American rights. Please do not write any such laws. Some of the countries will take offense at us and will not take our money."

The committee held a hearing, and considerable influence was brought to bear by administration sources to soften the amendment. The amendment provided that the Foreign Claims Settlement Commission of the United States, which has had a long history of surveying foreign values, has the legal machinery to determine the reasonable value of American property seized abroad. If a foreign country did not wish to accept the findings of the Foreign Claims Settlement Commission as to the facts and pay the claim in convertible currency—not in so-called bonds of questionable value or in long-deferred payments that could be subject to deception in one way or another, according to strange manipulations of foreign governments, then we would withdraw our aid. It was our view that if a foreign country wished to take American property, they should pay for it; but that if they did not want to pay for it, we would withdraw our aid. . . .

Mr. HICKENLOOPER. Mr. President, the amendment was not adopted. It was modified. It went to the House. The House further modified it. Eventually, after the conference report was adopted, we ended with a provision in the Foreign Assistance Act of 1962, section 620(e). . . .

Mr. President, I think perhaps I had better read this provision into the RECORD, so that Senators can understand just what this provision is. It is an addition to the Foreign Assistance Act of 1962. Section 620(e) of the Foreign Assistance Act of 1962 reads as follows:

(e) The President shall suspend assistance to the government of any country to which assistance is provided under this Act when the government of such country or any governmental agency or subdivision within such country on or after January 1, 1962—

(1) has nationalized or expropriated or seized ownership or control of property owned by any United States citizen or by any corporation, partnership, or association not less than 50 per centum beneficially owned by United States citizens, or

(2) has imposed or enforced discriminatory taxes or other exactions, or restrictive maintenance or operational conditions, which have the effect of nationalizing, expropriating, or otherwise seizing ownership or control of property so owned,

and such country, government agency, or government subdivision fails within a reasonable time (not more than six months after such action or after the date of enactment of this subsection, whichever is later) to take appropriate steps, which may include arbitration, to discharge its obligations under international law toward such citizen or entity, including equitable and speedy compensation for such property in convertible foreign exchange, as required by international law, or fails to take steps designed to provide relief from such taxes, exactions, or conditions, as the case may be, and such suspension shall continue until he is satisfied that appropriate steps are being taken and no other provision of this Act shall be construed to authorize the President to waive the provisions of this subsection.

That is what was written into the law by Congress.

As I stated a while ago, the ink on that act is scarcely dry; but today I am persuaded that this provision of law, which was written in by Congress, and the declaration of Congress which was made as a result of this provision, are being disregarded by the State Department, and the spirit of the law is not being put into effect. For some reason, which I do not know, this provision is being soft pedaled. . . .

Some time ago, I learned that a bill before the Honduras Legislature provided for the establishment of an agency or commission which would have the right to seize and take over foreign property in Honduras, but with no specified method of payment, except as the commission might determine, and that there would be no appeal to the courts from the action taken by the commission, or no appeal from the commission's decision. In short, the commission could do as it pleased, and could fix such payment, or even a specious payment, as it might wish to fix; and it has openly announced that its purpose is to seize American property in Honduras. The officials have stated that sometime it will get around to issuing some sort of bonds, payable at some distant time in the future, but that in the meantime Americans or American companies will lose their property.

The reason why I say I wonder how much attention is being paid by the responsible U.S. officials whose duty it is to see to it that U.S. citizens' property is given equitable treatment, is that 2 weeks ago or so I called the State Department and asked about this matter. I received a vague reply to the effect that something was being considered, but nothing was being done in Honduras.

A few days later I called and said, "I understand that the law has been passed in Honduras."

The reply was, "If it has been, we don't know anything about it."

Later I called again; and then the reply was, "We assume the law was passed, but we understand they will not be as hard on foreign property as the law might permit them to be."

On September 20, I asked the acting chairman of the Senate Foreign Relations Committee to send a letter to the State Department, because I had also heard indirectly—and I believe it to be a fact, although I cannot allege it, because I was not present when the conversations took place; but I heard it from sources which I believe to be accurate—that specific instructions had gone from our State Department, to our representatives abroad, to soft pedal this amendment, and not to emphasize it to foreign governments, because it might disturb our relationships; and our people abroad were told to be careful about what they said to foreign governments about their responsibility under this amendment.

MR. SALTONSTALL. Mr. President, will the Senator from Iowa yield again to me?

MR. HINKENLOOPER. I yield.

MR. SALTONSTALL. I point out that the property in Honduras belongs to one of the best companies in Massachusetts, the United Fruit Co. Not only does the institute or commission have the right, as I understand, to make such a decision, without the right of appeal, and to establish the amount to be paid, but I also understand that it is stated that this matter would be handled under the principles of the OAS, in order to help carry out the intention in connection with the OAS —although in my opinion it would be directly contrary to the purpose of the OAS, as I understand it.

MR. HICKENLOOPER. I agree with the Senator from Massachusetts. Furthermore, in addition to the United Fruit Co., a number of other companies are involved.

At this point I shall refer to the United Fruit Co. I know every Senator wishes to have equitable and proper treatment accorded his constituents. Furthermore, in this connection it is important to note that the United Fruit Co. has done in Honduras many things which no other company has done.

It has established schools. It has established hospitals. It has brought about the highest wage scales in the country. It has brought about better living conditions. U.S. companies have done more for the countries where they operate than the local governments have even approached doing for their own countries, but the property of the various countries is proposed to be seized under laws which we knew about, but apparently which we did nothing to attempt to stop. When I say "stop," I mean that we still recognize the right of sovereignty, but we did nothing to attempt to see that fair payment was made for the property seized. That is the point involved.

MR. MORSE. Mr. President, will the Senator yield?

MR. HICKENLOOPER. I yield.

MR. MORSE. Is it the understanding of the Senator from Iowa that the bill has already passed the Honduran Parliament?

MR. HICKENLOOPER. On last Sunday, day before yesterday, with a great deal of ceremony in Honduras, the bill was signed——

MR. MORSE. By the President?

MR. HICKENLOOPER. Signed by the President, and there was a great deal of speechmaking to the effect that they are going to take this property now and it will belong to the Hondurans. Apparently one of the major speechmakers at that time had just recently returned from Castro's Cuba and he spoke of the great day on which the land of Honduras is being returned to the Hondurans.

MR. MORSE. Mr. President, will the Senator yield for another question?

MR. HICKENLOOPER. In just a moment. On yesterday I called the State Department again and I said, "I understand the bill has been signed down there." The person to whom I spoke said, "Well, we did not know it, if it had been." I received a call at 2 o'clock in which I was told, "Well, we called the Ambassador down there and we learn it was signed yesterday."

I knew it before that. Apparently the State Department did not know about it. There is something rather mysterious about the whole thing. . . .

MR. MORSE. . . . As chairman of the Subcommittee on Latin American Affairs, I am keenly disappointed that the State Department has not taken a more adamant and persistent attitude in regard to what they knew was the plan of Honduras to enact the kind of law that was referred to by both the Senator from Iowa and the Senator from Massachusetts. The law enacted by the Honduran Parliament and signed by the President in recent days becomes meaningless so far as concerns giving any assurance to American property owners in Honduras that they will receive just compensation for property seized.

There is no question that the Government of Honduras has a sovereign power to expropriate the property of the United Fruit Co. or any other American investor in Honduras. I am not at all concerned with any controversy that may exist between the United Fruit Co. and the Honduran Government in regard to past differences.

But I am concerned with the question of U.S. sovereignty. We have the sovereign duty to protect our investors abroad. When we cooperate with our investors and when we urge them to invest in Latin American countries, as we have done time and time again, and when we have urged foreign governments to offer them such terms and conditions as will encourage them to invest in a foreign country, I say that a relationship is developed between the U.S. Government and the foreign government that imposes upon each the duty and the obligation to see to it that foreign investors, be they U.S. investors, British, Dutch, Canadian, or any other, receive fair compensation for their property when a foreign sovereign decides to seize and expropriate all property.

It is not happening in Honduras. It is as simple as that. The Senator from Iowa pointed out that it is contemplated that some script or bond or paper may be offered in payment for this property. Mr. President, there is only one compensation that means anything, and that is hard, cold American dollars. . . .

There is nothing in the Honduran law that gives the United Fruit Co. or any other investor in Honduras any assurance that it will get payment in convertible foreign exchange. . . .

I hope the Government of Honduras will take note, and that other Latin American countries will take note. I serve notice today that, although I opposed the more drastic form of the Hickenlooper amendment in committee on expropriation, next year I will support even stronger language, if we are to be faced with this kind of evasion of the purpose which, in my judgment, Honduras is on the road to committing.

We must make clear to American investors that if there is a seizure of their property they will get fair compensation. If they do not get fair compensation, we do not propose to take American tax dollars and pour them into any country by way of foreign aid, so that they will in effect get a double take—the property of American investors and the taxpayers' money.

What kind of prestige and respect does that build up for the United States in Latin American countries, or anywhere else in the world?

C. A SENATORIAL COLLOQUY ON GENERALÍSIMO TRUJILLO

MR. EASTLAND. Is it not true that Trujillo has been a friend of the United States?

MR. ELLENDER. I do not believe there is any doubt about that. I have visited the Dominican Republic on two or three occasions; I was there in 1958. As a matter of fact, it was my privilege to visit every country in South and Central America in 1958. My report filed as a result of that trip shows that I stated then, and I again state now, that there is not one country in South or Central America which, since 1952, has shown greater economic progress than the Dominican Republic.

Senators should do as I did; go there and see for themselves—go and see what that Government has done. The Dominican Republic has the finest kind of roads, excellent schools, and modern hospitals. The amount of housing has increased tremendously. All of this has been done through the prudent and wise development of the natural resources in that country.

In my humble judgment, much of the trouble which we are now experiencing in Latin America stems from the fact that quite a few of the countries in that area will not try to do what has been done in the Dominican Republic—that is, use existing resources as a means of achieving economic progress.

MR. EASTLAND. And they have done it without handouts from others.

MR. ELLENDER. That is certainly true as to the Dominican Republic. That Government has used its own resources, and the people have worked hard. I visited some of the farms there. Japanese have been brought in by the Government, as have other nationalities. Their talents have been put to good use. Evidence of

Congressional Record. Senate, Vol. 106 (Aug. 24, 1960), pp. 17405–17406, *passim.* For a historical view of dictatorship, see Hugh M. Hamill, Jr., *Dictatorship in Spanish America,* New York: Knopf, 1965.

progress is evident almost everywhere. For instance, I saw as fine a dairy there as I have ever seen, Mr. President. Let me emphasize again that all of these developments have been accomplished by the people of the Dominican Republic without gifts of money from any foreign power. The job has been done by efficiently developing the available natural resources of the country. . . .

MR. EASTLAND. Did the Senator from Louisiana find that the people there were happy and contented?

MR. ELLENDER. I saw no evidence of unrest, but I must be frank in stating that I did not go there looking for any. However, let me say that conditions in the Dominican Republic are much better than in Haiti, the next-door neighbor of the Dominican Republic. The only thing dividing Haiti from the Dominican Republic is a small chain of mountains. The two countries have about the same available natural resources. But the lack of progress in Haiti, under the present regime, is shameful, to my way of thinking. We have been supplying millions of dollars to help those people, but the progress is very slow, whereas we have not spent a dime of economic aid money in the Dominican Republic. Yet as the distinguished Senator from Mississippi has said, the people of the Dominican Republic are prosperous and are living in peace.

As I took pains to state in my report, I am not competent to comment on what, if anything, Generalissimo Trujillo may have done when he first took office. He may have had to use strong tactics to accomplish things; I frankly do not know. But I daresay that there is no country in Central America or in South America which would qualify as a democracy as the term is generally understood in the United States. Several are actually military dictatorships. . . .

MR. EASTLAND. Is it not true that the Dominican Republic has had more revolutions than any other country in the history of the world, and that Trujillo has given the country stability—something it never had before?

MR. ELLENDER. There is no question about that.

MR. EASTLAND. Is it not also true that it takes a strong arm to rule in countries of that sort and in Latin America?

MR. ELLENDER. That is certainly true in many instances. As a matter of fact, based upon my observation of conditions in the Dominican Republic as compared with conditions in some of the other countries I visited in that area, it might be said that a little of that same kind of leadership should be applied in some additional areas.

I invite Senators to visit there and see for themselves what has taken place.

I repeat that the people in the Dominican Republic are apparently happy. They have good schools, good hospitals, fine roads, and an abundance of food.

Mr. President, let me give Senators just one specific example of the kind of economic progress which has taken place there. I visited a sugar mill, Rio Haina, the largest in the world. I was dumb-founded; we have nothing like it in the Louisiana sugarcane areas. To the best of my knowledge, there is nothing like it in Florida or in any other part of the world. That sugar mill is just one of many such symbols of progress. But today there are some who wish to destroy all that.

MR. EASTLAND. If it were destroyed and if a vacuum were left, who would march in?

MR. ELLENDER. Another Castro, without a doubt. . . .

MR. EASTLAND. Is not Trujillo the foremost enemy of communism in Latin America?

MR. ELLENDER. I never met anyone there who so often and vocally professed his opposition to communism.

MR. EASTLAND. And he opposes the Communists, does he not?

MR. ELLENDER. There is no doubt about that.

MR. EASTLAND. That is the reason why Castro attempted to overthrow him, is it not?

MR. ELLENDER. I presume that is the reason.

MR. EASTLAND. In Venezuela is there democracy?

MR. ELLENDER. Not as the term is generally understood in the United States. Many governments are actually dictatorships.

MR. EASTLAND. And always have been, have they not?

MR. ELLENDER. Certainly. Until the people there are better educated, through better schools, and so forth, that condition will continue.

D. THE HOUSE OF REPRESENTATIVES' SUB-COMMITTEE ON APPROPRIATIONS
GIVES THE ALLIANCE FOR PROGRESS ADMINISTRATION A HARD TIME

MR. PASSMAN. . . .

Mr. Administrator, I find that when people are underprivileged, maybe under-clothed, underfed, having to exist on a very low standard of living, that many times they are resentful if they have those around them who are living, as we say, "high on the hog." Do you concur that they feel that way?

MR. MOSCOSO. That's right, sir.

MR. PASSMAN. How are we able to cover up the types of clambakes you have when this Development Bank meets and maybe will dissipate—even before they collected a dime or received any interest—$18,000 for whisky; the next year, up to $207,000 for their meeting, and then the next year $226,000?

How do the people who are observing these carryings-on and spending this money take it?

MR. MOSCOSO. The last one I attended was in Venezuela and President Betan-court, who is well known as a liberal and a man of the people and has the backing of the peasants and of the workers and so forth, attended every session. He was present——

MR. PASSMAN. I am talking about the people, not the ruling body. How do the

U.S. Congress. House of Representatives. *Hearings Before a Subcommittee of the Committee on Appropriations. Eighty-Eighth Congress. First Session* (Washington, D.C.: 1963), pp. 2184–2186, *passim*. Participants in this hearing were: O. E. Passman (Louisiana), Chairman of the Subcommittee; Teodoro Moscoso, Assistant Administrator for Latin America, Agency for International Development; John J. Rooney (New York); Edward F. Tennant, Controller, Agency for International Development.

people outside, without shoes on their feet and without clothes on their backs, without shelter over their heads, feel when you have a meeting there that lasts a week and you spend $226,000, and doubtlessly $25,000 of it for refreshments?

Mr. Moscoso. Mr. Chairman, in the first place, I must indicate that this is a regular yearly meeting of the Inter-American Development Bank——

Mr. Passman. It started as soon as you created the Alliance for Progress and the Inter-American Development Bank. First they spent $18,900 for a representation allowance before they had disbursed one dime out of the fund; is that not correct?

Mr. Moscoso. Yes, because——

Mr. Passman. And again before they disbursed one dime I think three of these gentlemen made a little trip to Europe—let us say they were gone 3 or 4 weeks—and they spent $12,600. I say that is actually living just a little high, especially when it is coming out of a fund that was created to alleviate poverty.

Mr. Moscoso. If you mean——

Mr. Passman. Yes; I know they got one country to commit themselves to one small loan.

Mr. Moscoso. No; what I mean to say was that nothing was spent from the social progress trust fund for the meeting.

Mr. Passman. It came out of the other fund, in the Inter-American Development Bank and the United States contributed it. It was all intended to help our friends in Latin America. Is that correct?

Mr. Moscoso. That's right, sir.

Mr. Passman. How much do you have in the aid program for representation allowance?

Mr. Tennant. $184,900.

Mr. Passman. So the amount for this 1-week clambake in Latin America——

Mr. Rooney. What do they serve? What is the menu? How could it run up this high? Do you have any such information?

Mr. Moscoso. We have a breakdown on it.

Mr. Passman. I am going to get down into it——

Mr. Rooney. I mean a real breakdown. A real breakdown.

Mr. Passman. We have even asked for sundry items.

Mr. Tennant. There is $184,900 representation allowance. There is a small item of entertainment, which is $25,000, if I remember correctly.

Mr. Rooney. $25,000 here in the United States?

Mr. Passman. To entertain dignitaries around the world, it is what amount?

Mr. Tennant. $184,900.

Mr. Passman. That is representation allowance for all aid programs, worldwide for 1 year? Not the United States?

Mr. Tennant. Not the United States; that is correct. Overseas.

Mr. Passman. There is one little representation allowance part of this $143,-000 expense account that amounted to 10 per cent in 1 week. The total amount in the entire aid program for all the world for 1 year. Is that correct.

MR. FORD. What was that, Mr. Chairman?

MR. PASSMAN. Your allowance for the first clambake they had in this Inter-American Development Bank outfit was $143,358 for a week. The representation allowance, of what they actually spent, was $17,745. That is almost 10 per cent of the total amount of the representation allowance for the entire aid program, worldwide for 1 year, for fiscal year 1963; is that correct?

MR. TENNANT. That is correct.

MR. PASSMAN. Now we have another little item, here: "Sundry expense." They are going to itemize that account for us. We complained so much last year about the representation allowance we find that the representation account for fiscal year 1963 drops substantially, but the sundry account went up in about the same proportion. Is that right?

MR. TENNANT. That is approximately correct, sir.

MR. PASSMAN. We found the representation account went down, but the sundry account went up about the same amount. We are going to look at that sundry account.

MR. ROONEY. When you get this information, Mr. Chairman, I wonder if we could have it itemized, showing how many dinners at how much a setting and how many cocktail parties at how much per head? . . .

MR. PASSMAN. There has been very little improvement made in Latin America. We know this program so far is a failure and until we recognize it as a failure because they are not doing their part, this thing will never succeed. Nobody, I believe, wants to see this phase of the program succeed more than I do. However, these people are holding back because they know they do not have to do these things in order to get our money. So far as I am concerned, I will do everything I can to try to convince them that they have misjudged the mood of the Congress and of the American people.

MR. MOSCOSO. In many instances, Mr. Chairman, the argument that is used by those who do not like us is that all we are doing is redressing something that has been done by the exploiters that have taken the oil or other natural resources out. I wish it were as simple as that.

MR. PASSMAN. These people know there never has been a country on the face of the earth as generous as the United States is. They can look on the record and see that we have given billions of dollars of the wealth of America to other nations. Yet the nations to which we have given the most aid appear to be the weakest. Your predecessor, the present Ambassador to Spain, pointed to Cuba and the sugar subsidy. It was the highest subsidized nation on the face of the earth, and look where they are. And look at Laos, as another example.

MR. MOSCOSO. In spite of the fact we have been generous you will recall that just a few years ago the Vice President of the United States suffered a great amount of indignity in Latin America because of great animosity against the United States.

MR. PASSMAN. And this animosity appears to be just as great today, notwithstanding all the aid we have given.

MR. Moscoso. I am going to quote something, Mr. Chairman, which is very true. This is from the person we quote the most in the English language.

To the noble mind, rich gifts wax poor when givers prove unkind.

Sometimes, Mr. Chairman, the style is more important than the amount we give.

MR. PASSMAN. If they are not willing to help themselves, I think we ought to come home.

MR. Moscoso. I agree with you on that. They have to help themselves. Otherwise, we should not help them.

MR. PASSMAN. They are not doing much of it.

MR. Moscoso. They are doing some, but not as much as we would like them to do.

MR. PASSMAN. Very little, comparatively.

MR. Moscoso. But it is moving ahead, Mr. Chairman.

MR. PASSMAN. Do you agree that what they are doing is very little compared to what we expected and what they promised?

MR. Moscoso. It is very little compared to what you might have expected, but knowing these people a little bit better than you, Mr. Chairman, I say this is about as fast as you are going to get them to move as of this moment. I think they are moving much faster.

MR. PASSMAN. Nations have become prosperous for literally thousands of years based upon trade. Is that right?

MR. Moscoso. That is right.

MR. PASSMAN. Giving away your wealth, hoping to cure the ills of all the other peoples of the world, is a brandnew concept in foreign policy as we think of time; is it not?

MR. Moscoso. Yes; helping the less developed countries.

MR. PASSMAN. It is a concept that is not working successfully.

As far as I am concerned, this program will fall of its own weight if we do not tighten it up.

88 WELLES, A Memorandum on Inter-American Relations, 1933

The creation and maintenance of the most cordial and intimate friendship between the United States and the other republics of the American Continent must be regarded as a keystone of our foreign policy. The erroneous interpretations given to the Monroe Doctrine over a period of many decades have constituted a constant

Charles C. Griffin, ed. "Welles to Roosevelt: A Memorandum on Inter-American Relations, 1933," *Hispanic American Historical Review*, XXXIV (1954), pp. 190–192. Reprinted by permission.

cause for apprehension and for misrepresentation of the true purposes of the Government of the United States. The Monroe Doctrine declares that the United States will not permit any non-American nation to encroach upon the political independence of any American republic; and that the United States will not consent to the acquisition in any manner of the control of additional territory in this Hemisphere by any non-American Power. These principles have until now been proclaimed solely on the authority of the United States and they will not be abandoned. But they are essentially principles of continental self-defense. And they are as vitally important to every other republic of this Hemisphere as they are to the United States itself. I would welcome their adoption by every American republic as a portion of its national policy. In that manner alone, in my opinion, can there be permanently abolished the impression which has persisted that these simple principles of self-defense can involve a threat to the sovereignty or to the national wellbeing of any republic of the Western Hemisphere. In the same spirit of mutual understanding and of coöperation for the promotion of the welfare of the American peoples, I favor the principle of consultation between the governments of the American republics whenever there arises in this Continent any question which threatens the peace and wellbeing of the American world. I believe that in such emergency there should be summoned immediately an inter-American conference, in which the American republics can determine, as individual powers bound together by a common interest, what policy best behooves them in a crisis which may be of potential danger to each of them in varying degree. The United States should take the ground that pan-American responsibilities must be accepted by all the American republics on equal terms. I would stress, in particular, the continental responsibility for the maintenance of peace in this Hemisphere, and the necessity for the perfection of the mechanism required for the carrying out of that obligation.

The lives of our citizens abroad must, of course, be protected, wherever they may be, when they are in imminent danger and the local authorities are patently unable to afford them security, but such protection by this government should never again result in armed intervention by the United States in a sister republic. I believe that the dispatch of the armed forces of the United States to any foreign soil whatsoever, save for the purpose of dealing with a temporary emergency such as that just described, should never be undertaken by the American Executive except with the consent of the American Congress.

There is no more effective means of enhancing friendship between nations than in promoting commerce between them. We cannot expect to preserve the sincere friendship of our neighbors on this Continent if we close our markets to them. We cannot enjoy the markets of the American Continent, which have as vast a potentiality for development as any in the world, unless we permit the citizens of our sister nations to trade with us. The interest of the peoples of this Continent demands that the American governments individually take without delay such action as may be necessary to abolish those barriers and restrictions which now hamper the healthy flow of commerce between their respective nations.

PERCY·LAU

89 *EDWIN M. MARTIN, U.S. Policy on Military Governments*

By tradition and conviction as well as a matter of policy, the United States opposes the overthrow of constitutional and popular democratic governments anywhere.

This is especially true in Latin America, with whose people we have such close historical ties and whose aspirations for political and economic freedom we support wholeheartedly. Moreover, under the Charter of Punta del Este the people of the Western Hemisphere have bound themselves in a joint effort for political and socio-economic development—the Alliance for Progress—within a framework of free and democratic institutions.

The deviations from these principles which we have observed in the two years since Punta del Este have caused some to question the validity of the principles of the charter and some impatient cynics to ignore the progress which has been made.

Both the impatient idealists and the defeatist cynics ignore the realities of rising nationalism; the anxieties caused by social revolution; the challenge posed by the Alliance for Progress to old value systems; the threat to the established order brought on by the new; and finally the strain which rapid social and economic change places on fragile political institutions.

In short, there is a temptation to measure current events not against historical reality and substantive progress, but against somewhat theoretical notions of the manner in which men should and do operate in a complex world.

We all have respect for motherhood and abhor sin. We may observe, however, that while motherhood has prospered, so has sin. In an increasingly nationalistic world of sovereign states, a U.S. frown doesn't deter others from committing what we consider to be political sins. And as we are pretty nationalistic ourselves and rightfully proud of our great successes, we sometimes find this fact frustrating.

Our task has only begun when we have stated our position. The real issue is how, under the conditions of the present-day world, we can assist the peoples of other sovereign nations to develop stable political institutions and help them strengthen their beliefs in these institutions so as to make them effective against brute force.

In Latin America there are very few who would argue as a matter of principle for violent overthrow of constitutional regimes. Most of those who support or accept coups d'etat would simply maintain that their particular case was surrounded by unique circumstances. This is the "yes, but" argument.

Genuine concern with an overturn of the established order, fear of left-wing extremism, frustration with incompetence in an era of great and rising expectations, and a sheer desire for power are all formidable obstacles to stable, constitutional

Edwin M. Martin, "U.S. Policy Regarding Military Governments in Latin America," *Department of State Bulletin*, XLIX, No. 1253 (Nov. 4, 1963), 698–701.

NEGRO WOMEN AT THE MARKET

government—especially in countries where the traditional method of transferring political power has been by revolution or coup d'etat. In most of Latin America there is so little experience with the benefits of political legitimacy that there is an insufficient body of opinion, civil or military, which has any reason to know its value and hence defend it.

No two countries are alike, but in general we feel that in order to enlarge their experience of legitimacy, and thus their respect for it, we must strengthen in each society the power of the educated middle class with a stake in the country, and hence in peace and order and democracy for all the people. This is in fact what the Alliance for Progress is all about—it is as much a socio-political revolution as it is an economic one.

● **The Role of the Military and the Civilian.** As societies come to have more respect for constitutional civilian governments with wide popular support, these governments will no longer be easy targets for military coups. But to tip the balance even more in favor of established civilian governments, we also must assist the military to assume the more constructive peacetime role of maintaining internal security and working on civic action programs. The latter are especially valuable in identifying them with the problems and goals of the civilian population.

Even in the United States we argue about the areas of national policy in which the military have a rightful voice. In Latin America we cannot aim to reduce them to impotence in the national life—rather it is a problem of acceptance of a mission in support of legitimate governments against subversion from extremists of both right and left, whose threat of force must be met by force. There must be military participation in the formulation of some national policies; they cannot be excluded altogether.

I should not wish this emphasis on the need for the military to acquire a new and somewhat more limited role in political life to be read as a downgrading of the real contribution they have made to political freedom and stability in many countries. Peron in Argentina, Perez Jimenez in Venezuela, and Rojas Pinilla in Colombia were all military dictators who were thrown out with the help of their own military in the 1950's. And the two worst dictators today in Latin America, it should be noted, are not military men and were able to consolidate their power only by reducing the regular military forces to impotence.

Nor are the military universal supporters of those who oppose change as represented by the programs of the Alliance. Governments controlled by the military have overseen the election to power this year in Argentina and Peru of two of the most progressive regimes either country has ever had. This year in Educador and Guatemala military regimes have announced reform programs of substantial importance.

Nevertheless, the fundamental facts remain—military coups thwart the will of the people, destroy political stability and the growth of the tradition of respect for democratic constitutions, and nurture Communist opposition to their tyranny. Moreover, the military often show little capacity for effective government, which is a political rather than military job.

● **What the United States Can Do.** Apart from our and the Alliance's vigorous long-term efforts to eliminate the political vacuums on the civilian side which invite military action, as well as our efforts to train the military in their most valuable role, what can the United States do in the case of specific threats or coups which nevertheless come?

Unless there is intervention from outside the hemisphere by the international Communist conspiracy, the use of military force involving the probability of U.S. soldiers killing the citizens of another country is not to be ordered lightly.

Nor can we, as a practical matter, create effective democracy by keeping a man in office through use of economic pressure or even military force when his own people are not willing to fight to defend him. A democracy dependent on outside physical support of this kind is a hollow shell which has no future. The people had better start over again. Moreover, once outside military support is used it may prove hard to withdraw. We have seen in this century—in Haiti, the Dominican Republic, and Nicaragua—how politically unproductive military occupations are, even when carried out with the best of intentions.

We must use our leverage to keep these new regimes as liberal and considerate of the welfare of the people as possible. In addition, we must support and strengthen the civilian components against military influences and press for new elections as soon as possible so that these countries once again may experience the benefits of democratic legitimacy. Depending upon the circumstances, our leverage is sometimes great, sometimes small.

One should not underestimate what has been accomplished by the U.S. and Alliance policies I have described. They are accomplishments that have truly enhanced the long-term prospects of the Alliance.

In Argentina the military walked up the hill a number of times to look at the green pastures of full military control and the power and perquisites that would go with it. Each time a combination of wiser heads in the military, along with more and more confident civilian leaders who were strongly buttressed by U.S. diplomatic support and aid programs, turned them back. The elections were held on schedule.

In Peru the 1-year rule of the junta was about the most respectful of civil liberties, most progressive in its policies, and quickest to give up its power peacefully in the history of Latin American military regimes. Here again the strong stand taken by the United States prior to recognition helped to secure public commitments, and followthrough, from the junta to pursue liberal policies—liberal, of course, only for a military dictatorship.

A similar story can be told of the Ecuadoran junta, which is governing through an able and representative civilian cabinet and generally without repression of civil liberties.

In every case mentioned there has been a novel and notable absence of reprisals against the leaders of the ousted regimes. The firing squads or prison guards, so characteristic of earlier political upheavals in Latin America, have been eschewed. This restraint can be credited to the progress Latin America has been making under the Alliance and to U.S. influences, brought to bear through all the means open to us, to produce moderation and a prompt return to constitutional and democratic regimes.

I fear there are some who will accuse me of having written an apologia for coups. I have not. They are to be fought with all the means we have available. Rather I would protest that I am urging the rejection of the thesis of the French philosophers that democracy can be legislated—established by constitutional fiat.

I am insisting on the Anglo-Saxon notion that democracy is a living thing which must have time and soil and sunlight in which to grow. We must do all we can to create these favorable conditions, and we can do and have done much.

But we cannot simply create the plant and give it to them; it must spring from seeds planted in indigenous soil.

90 *FUENTES, The Argument of Latin America*

South of your border, my North American friends, lies a continent in revolutionary ferment—a continent that possesses immense wealth and nevertheless lives in a misery and a desolation you have never known and barely imagine. Two hundred million persons live in Latin America. One hundred and forty million of them work virtually as serfs. Seventy million are outside the monetary economy. One hundred million are illiterate. One hundred million suffer from endemic diseases. One hundred and forty million are poorly fed.

Today, these miserable masses have decided to put an end to this situation. Latin America, for centuries nothing more than an object of historical exploitation, has decided to change. . . .

You are much given to good wishes, to what you call "wishful thinking." You have always believed that what is valid for you is valid for all men in all nations and at all times. You forget the existence of specific historical factors. You fail to realize that in reality there are two worlds, one of rich countries and one of poor countries. You fail to recognize that, of necessity, the poor countries require solutions different from yours. You have had four centuries of uninterrupted development within the capitalistic structure. We have had four centuries of underdevelopment, within a feudal structure. . . .

Latin America is a collapsed feudal castle with a cardboard capitalistic facade. This is the panorama of the historical failure of capitalism in Latin America: continuous monoproductive dependence . . . a continuous system of "latifundio" . . . continuous underdevelopment . . . continuous political stagnation . . . continuous general injustices . . . continuous dependence on foreign capital. . . .

The key question is this: How can the causes of underdevelopment in Latin America be chopped away? There is no room for doubt in the answer: stabilization

Carlos Fuentes, "The Argument of Latin America: Words for the North Americans," *Whither Latin America?* (New York: Monthly Review Press, 1963), pp. 9–24, *passim*. Reprinted by permission. For a perceptive evaluation of Fuentes, see Keith Botsford, "My Friend Fuentes," *Commentary*, XXXIX (1965), pp. 64–67.

of prices of raw materials in the short run, and economic diversification—industrialization—in the long run. But you want it to be done through peaceful evolution and the Alliance for Progress. And we think: through revolution. . . .

Revolution, yes! Don't be deceived, Americans. Open your eyes. Ask the Peruvian farmer who chews coca and eats rats if he wants fake elections or revolutions. Ask the Chilean miner who crawls through the tunnels of Lota if he believes in free enterprise or in revolution. Ask the northeast Brazilian farmer if he wants capitalism or revolution. Ask the student castrated by the Paraguayan dictator if he wants Stroessner's free press or revolution. Ask the Guatemalan farmer "freed" by Castillo Armas if he wants Alliance for Progress or revolution. Ask the Latin Americans who corrupts the press and the unions, who supports the armies and the oligarchies, who pays miserable salaries, who owns the mines and the oil wells. Ask them who gets the Alliance for Progress money, and ask what they use it for. Ask them if we believe in the free world of Franco, Salazar, Chiang Kai-shek and Ngo Dinh Diem. Ask them and they will tell you why people spat on Nixon.

Ask the men living in "misery village" in Buenos Aires, in the "favela" of Rio, in the "callampa population" of Santiago, if they are afraid of Communism. These beggars, these pariahs, will answer that they are afraid only of their present oppressors, of those who exploit them in the name of capitalism and representative democracy, and that they prefer anything that might mean a change. . . .

Do you see, Americans? The world has changed. Latin America is no longer your preserve. The world moves ahead. And you are standing on the rim. Are you going to help these inevitable revolutions or are you going to antagonize them with invasions, press campaigns, and economic aggressions? It does not matter. Revolutions are going to progress. . . .

But try to understand. Try to understand that a revolution in Latin America can affect only a handful of Yankee enterprises, but never the concrete welfare you enjoy. Try to understand that our real development, which can be achieved only through revolution, far from hurting you will help you. Do not let yourselves be fooled by this handful of enterprises and investors. Try to understand that the sooner we start our basic development, which can come only through revolution, the more buyers you will have, and we will all be closer to a planned world economy, rational and interdependent.

Understand this: Latin America is not going to be your back yard any more. We are going to enter the world.

91   *BRIGGS, The Good Neighbor Policy A Two-way Street*

Just as President Theodore Roosevelt shortly after the turn of the century added a colophon to the Monroe Doctrine, transforming it from one of *non-inter-*

From *Farewell to Foggy Bottom*, by Ellis Briggs. New York, 1964. Used by permission of David McKay Company, Inc., from pp. 179–192, *passim*.

vention by European powers to one of *intervention* by the United States, so the eager cohorts of Franklin Roosevelt invented the corollary of the Guilt Complex and added that to the Good Neighbor Policy.

The Guilt Complex involves two equally pernicious propositions. The first is that everything that *latinos* don't like about their situation—low coffee or sugar prices, galloping inflation, or the absence of a Marshall Plan for Latin America— is the fault of the United States. Wherefore each Neighbor is entitled to kick Uncle Sam's Eagle from Acapulco to Tierra del Fuego.

The second proposition, deriving from the first, is that the Underdog is Always Right. And inasmuch as Pablo Descamisado and Mario Pelado are both Underdogs, whenever they bark at some established American interest, it would be unneighborly of the United States to bark back or to try to defend that interest. . . .

Just as their Republican parents in the Hoover administration renounced armed intervention in Latin America, thus opening the way for Franklin Roosevelt and the Good Neighbor Policy, so the Republicans of 1960 assembled for the benefit of their Democratic successors practically all of the ingredients that today form that rich pudding distributed under a Democratic label.

When the Democrats took over, they quickly suppressed the Portuguese* subtitle and dreamed up *Alianza para el Progreso* instead. They earmarked one billion dollars of U.S. Treasury funds. They announced they were open for business.

Nor did the Democrats neglect to make the customary bow to the Guilt Complex. "We have not always grasped the significance," said President Kennedy in a speech in 1961 launching the *Alianza*, "of the hemisphere's common mission. . . . We have not always understood the magnitude of your problem, nor accepted our share of responsibility for the welfare of the hemisphere."

The U.S. quota for *Alianza* was upped to *three* billion dollars.

Interpreting these portents as the whistle on the most opulent gravy train since the one piloted by the Coordinator of Inter-American Affairs in World War II, the Neighbors were shortly incensed by remarks on the part of White House professors about "necessary social reforms" and "archaic tax and land-law structures." First the remedial action by Latin America, averred the professors, and then the *Alianza* handouts.

The Neighbors characterized this as intervention, and they said so in shrill, rasping voices. They intimated that if Uncle Sam expected to get his eagle back with *any* feathers left, Uncle had better stop promoting social revolution and stick to minting gold coins for Rising Expectations. . . .

The first and most important requirement is the reestablishment of *respect* as the basis for inter-American relations. There is no better formula than the Good Neighbor Policy as originally expressed in 1933:

"The policy of the neighbor who resolutely respects himself and, because he

---

* President Kubitschek developed an elaborate plan for an Operação Panamericana, designed to lead the attack on "the festering sore of underdevelopment." When President Kennedy and his advisors drew up their Alliance for Progress, they either did not know of this Brazilian initiative or chose to ignore it. [ED.]

does so, respects the rights of others . . . who respects his obligations and respects the sanctity of his agreements, in and with a world of neighbors."

That covers practically everything. Emphasize that the Good Neighbor Policy is a two-way street, and statesmen would search far indeed for a better foundation for hemispheric association.

As a first step toward regaining America self-respect, the Guilt Complex should be exorcised. We must purge ourselves of the idea that the problems besetting Latin America are the fault of the United States, or that their solution is the primary responsibility of anyone except the nations concerned. Let us recognize, albeit sadly, that some of the Neighbors may never rise far above poverty; their resources, human and material, are too meager. . . .

Viewed realistically, little of *Alianza para el Progreso* makes much sense. *Alianza* would dedicate the United States to the "principle of collective responsibility for the welfare of the people of the Americas." That means the welfare state for everybody, from the Aleuts of Alaska to the Alacalufas of Tierra del Fuego, plus those rapidly multiplying millions in between. From Nome to Ushuaia, eleven thousand miles of welfare state, and all at the expense of Uncle Sam.

Alianza ignores the fact that the bureaucracies of most undeveloped countries —disorganized, inexperienced, and frequently corrupt—are incapable of assimilating foreign aid or putting it to profitable use. It ignores the further fact that without birth control, no amount of American assistance can raise the Latin American standard of living. . . .

There is no objection to a modest and selective aid program. Unless, however, the proposed beneficiary gives honest treatment to United States citizens, the American government should decline to assist. Fair treatment should be the number one requisite for American aid. . . .

The American government should stop worrying so much about its image in foreign countries. On this issue, the *latinos* are more sophisticated than we are; they are bewildered by what seems to them to be an irrational Anglo-Saxon desire for popularity. The *respect* of the Neighbors is what the United States should seek, not their votes in an international forum, nor their signatures on even the most eloquent of inter-American resolutions. . . .

Canada should be encouraged to play a role in hemispheric affairs. The interests in Latin America of our northern neighbor are already substantial, but in terms of responsibility commensurate with ability, Canada has been coasting along, in effect enjoying the benefits of membership but paying no dues and few of the expenses. It would be naive to expect Canada to vote always with the United States, and counter-productive if that occurred, but adding the Canadian voice to hemispheric councils would strengthen the association in every particular. Canada should become a part of the inter-American system.

If Brazil should ever reach its potential, that might take some of the "curse of strength" off the United States. Brazil has the elements of a great power: area, resources, elbow-room, a sophisticated upper class, a capacity for political invention. But Brazil lacks a sense of direction, and above all discipline. Should the military establishment disintegrate, Brazil's promise of greatness could easily remain unfulfilled. It could even evaporate altogether, leaving a frightening gap in hemispheric leadership and geography.

92 *QUIGG, Advice for the United States*

Their common Hispanic culture and certain similarities in the way they [the Latin American nations] look upon life and the world around them obscure a vast indifference to one another and a marked desire to be considered unique. They look to the United States above all and secondarily to Europe, but their knowledge or awareness of other countries of South and Central America is limited largely to contacts sponsored by public or private agencies of the United States. Pan Americanism has not cut deep, and even the effort to establish a Common Market has not much strengthened the Latins' sense of involvement with one another. Though an incident in Panama or Cuba will remind them how closely their destinies are linked, it is easier to find unity in what they are against than in what they are for.

Though we may be accused with some justice of being inadequately informed about Latin America, there are some 30 North American correspondents in Mexico City; none from other Latin American countries. There are at the very least a dozen universities in the United States where one can study the history, culture, politics and economics of Latin America in some depth; there is no Latin American university offering more than the most superficial survey course in the same field. Until very recently there was no direct air or passenger-ship service between the two largest countries, Mexico and Brazil.

It is said that in the Mexican Foreign Ministry, 60 percent of the officers work on United States affairs, 20 percent on international organizational affairs, 15 percent on European affairs and 5 percent on all the rest of the world including Latin America. In some other countries the disproportion would not be quite so high, but the pattern is uniform. Similarly, the average cultivated Latin American will have made several trips to the United States and to Europe, but none to other parts of Latin America. . . .

It has been widely believed in the United States that the slow progress in Latin America has been due either to the almost insurmountable nature of its problems or to the resistance to change of its privileged classes. For parts of Latin America these explanations still have some validity, but for the major countries of Latin America—those on which all else depends—they are far from the point. What impresses a visitor to Argentina or Brazil or Mexico is that, as compared to other parts of the less developed world, the problems are so manageable, so near and yet so far from solution. . . .

Philip W. Quigg, "Latin America: A Broad-Brush Appraisal," *Foreign Affairs,* XLII (April, 1964), pp. 399–412, *passim.* Reprinted by special permission from *Foreign Affairs.* Copyright by The Council on Foreign Relations, Inc., New York.

While we must guard against applying Anglo-Saxon standards to a very different environment and culture, it is clear that until Latin America's political underdevelopment is corrected, its economic development will continue to lurch and stumble. For what is retarding development in the major Latin American countries is not so much lack of wealth and technology nor the vested interests of landed or commercial classes; it is the prevalence of corrupt and demagogic leaders, often the legacy of dictators, governing people whose cynicism about politics leads them to alternate between fatalism and violence. . . .

One senses that our responsible officials in Washington and our Foreign Service Officers in the field are being ground fine between the sensitivities of the Latin Americans and the need to state harsh truths; between their lively affection for the Latins—so generally reciprocated—and the awareness that the United States is being outrageously used; between the Latins' private respect for the United States and their public abuse of it; between American commercial interest and the national interest, which are too often assumed to be the same; between the American public's unwarranted sense of guilt about Latin America and our Congressmen's periodic outbursts of wrath. . . .

The tensions and conflicts are innumerable. What few generalizations can be drawn which will have validity for some appreciable part of this diverse area we call Latin America? After acknowledging that diversity and realizing that no policy will be relevant for all parts of Latin America, we might consider some of the following:

1. Talk more about responsible and responsive government and less about democracy.

2. Try to put our own fears of Communism in better proportion to the extent and nature of the threat. . . .

3. Distinguish more clearly in our own minds between technical and genuinely developmental aid programs, which more often than not are admirable in conception and accomplishment, and other forms of assistance which are unproductive and merely protect irresponsible governments against the day of reckoning. One reason the American people seem disillusioned with the rate of economic development in countries we have helped is that they do not know how small a proportion of our total aid has been used for development, how much to balance budgets or unsuccessfully fight inflation.

4. Avoid giving the impression that we look upon the O.A.S. merely as an instrument for fighting Communism. It has rarely been used effectively on issues of primary interest to the Latin American countries or as a means of drawing them more closely together.

5. Avoid making a fetish of consistency where circumstances in fact differ. . . .

6. Do not let our own need for resoluteness and realism become an excuse for "getting tough" or an unwillingness to discuss and act in areas of friction between us and the Latin American nations—whether it be the Panama Canal or water disputes with Mexico or the price of coffee.

7. Give the highest priority in our programs of training, education and

exchange to the search for leadership and the cultivation of a sense of individual responsibility for government.

8. Do not expect that the unwarranted abuse we are subjected to from Latin America will cease until the discrepancies between us and them—in size, power, and accomplishment—have disappeared. It will be a long time.

9. Though our "big stick" is too obvious to need to be carried, the first half of Teddy Roosevelt's dictum—to speak softly—still has great merit.

93 HUMPHREY, Latin America—The Most Critical Area in the World

Europe remains of crucial importance in our foreign policy considerations and will retain this status for the foreseeable future. But while the internal political, social and economic patterns of Europe are well determined by now, this is not the case with Latin America. The future structure of society and the external policy of Latin nations remain unanswered questions. Marxism as a guide to social development is a spent force in most European countries, but it remains a lively alternative in Latin America today. The example of Cuba suggests both the immediacy of the Marxist threat to U.S. interests and the nature of the problems which we face when Marxism is accepted as a guide to the development of a Latin American society. . . .

The emergence of a powerful Western Europe—likely to pursue a more independent foreign policy—makes hemispheric cooperation more urgent if the nations of this hemisphere are not only to solve their immediate internal problems but to play a proper role in world affairs in future decades. Although the decade of the 1960's is a crucial one for the United States and Latin America, the development of our hemispheric policy should look two or three decades ahead. We must keep in mind not only the political, economic and social problems that confront Latin America in the 1960's but also the position of the Western Hemisphere in the international relations of the 1980's and 1990's. If the hemisphere remains united, it can, with a population of 900 million people by the year 2000 and a level of economic development that its resources indicate is possible, play a major role in shaping the world of future decades, regardless of events in Asia, Europe or the Soviet Union. But neither unity within Latin America itself nor unity within the hemisphere is guaranteed. Our policy should be designed to discourage intra-hemispheric rivalry which would Balkanize the continent, as well as to prevent Communist subversion which would divide the hemisphere into an endless struggle between Communist and non-Communist states.

Our concept of hemispheric unity should not be defined in any exclusive sense that would actively discourage a greater Western European contribution to the

Hubert H. Humphrey, "U.S. Policy in Latin America," *Foreign Affairs*, LXII (July, 1964), pp. 585–601, *passim*. Reprinted by special permission from *Foreign Affairs*. Copyright by the Council on Foreign Relations, Inc., New York.

social, economic and cultural development of Latin America. Indeed, we should actively encourage Europe to expand its involvement in Latin America, both in terms of long-term development assistance and expansion of existing cultural and educational programs. But we cannot view with equanimity the separation of Latin America from the United States and Europe in favor of an exclusive association or identification with the "third world." Latin countries will and should continue to be different from both the United States and Europe, but they need not see their own future destiny in terms of the non-Western southern half of the world just because they share with the societies of Asia and Africa a less developed status. . . .

How does the United States deal with governments that have come to power through non-constitutional means? We of course cannot determine the type of governments that take office in Latin American countries. We have no choice but to work with many governments. But we should distinguish between constitutional governments pursuing progressive policies and those which shoot their way to power. We may not be able to prevent the emergence of juntas, but we can and should distinguish between dictators and democrats. In those instances when we must temporarily deal with non-constitutional governments, we should use all our levers of influence to restore constitutional government at the earliest possible time.

The problem confronting us is made even more difficult when a constitutional government is overthrown in order to meet an acknowledged Communist threat or to uproot Communist infiltration that has progressed under the protection of democratic institutions. This should not be a pretext for circumvention of constitutional procedures or for maintaining military juntas in power in violation of the constitution. . . .

In dealing with these situations we should always keep in mind the results of our policy of embracing "anti-Communist" military dictators during much of the 1950's—results dramatically illustrated when an American Vice President was nearly mobbed in Caracas in 1958.

The use of anti-Communism as a deceptive slogan in the past should not blind us to the true nature of the Communist threat in this hemisphere today. The threat is real and must be met if hemispheric unity, political democracy and socio-economic progress are to be achieved. . . .

In pursuing the political objectives of the Alliance for Progress—both the positive aim of inspiring a commitment to constitutional government and democratic institutions and the negative objective of thwarting Communist expansion—we would do well to divert more attention and resources to programs in the educational, ideological, cultural and propaganda fields. We should expand programs aimed both at the elite and at the popular classes. According to the best information available to me, approximately 3,000 Brazilians were brought to the United States during the past ten years under our various educational and cultural exchange programs. If we really appreciated the revolutionary atmosphere in Latin America today and understood the nature of the Communist appeal to younger people who will become the elite of their societies, we would raise this figure to 3,000 per year. . . .

In conclusion, I would emphasize that quite apart from the specific programs which we may support in implementing our policy in Latin America—programs of aid, trade, private investment, education or propaganda—what is equally important is our success in solving our own preeminent social problem—achieving equality for the Negro—and our attitude toward our fellow citizens in the hemisphere. In a continent where the large majority of the people are non-white, a continent that includes societies like Brazil which have developed a harmonious multi-racial society, it is hard to exaggerate the importance which people attach to our efforts to extend the benefits of modern civilization to the Negro minority in the United States, just as Latin American countries are striving to make them available to the majority of their own people.

President Kennedy is revered for opening up a new era in relations between the United States and Latin America, not primarily because he promised material assistance, but because he conveyed an understanding and respect for Latin American people, for their culture and many of their traditions. He did not regard Latin American people as inferior or expect them to see the solution to their own problems in blind imitation of the United States. It is this attitude of understanding and respect that must permeate not only our leadership, but our entire society. This will not be easy to accomplish—as most adults in this country were educated in schools where the overwhelming majority of textbooks and reference books either ignored Latin America or reflected a condescending attitude toward Latin Americans. Written chiefly by authors sympathetic to a northern European cultural inheritance, which historically has been fundamentally unsympathetic to Latin culture, these books have been all too important an influence in shaping the attitude of generations of Americans. Change in popular attitudes comes slowly. A full appreciation of the importance of Latin America will come only when our educational system begins to reflect the priority stated by President Kennedy when he described Latin America as the most critical area in the world.

94 MARTIN, We Have Several Choices in Latin America

We have several choices in Latin America.

We can become frankly imperialistic, promoting our political and economic interests to the exclusion of all other interests. Such a policy proclaims, as the Athenians did in their pride in power, that "the strong do what they can, and the weak submit." But Athens, seeking to extend its empire, dealt ever more harshly with friend and foe, betrayed its own democratic ideals, and in the end destroyed itself. Imperialism is incompatible with democracy. To embark upon a frankly imperialistic policy in Latin America would, I believe, involve us in collaboration with the most odious and authoritarian elements in that part of the world, earn

John Bartlow Martin, *Overtaken by Events: The Dominican Crisis from the Fall of Trujillo to the Civil War* (Garden City, N.Y.: Doubleday & Company, Inc., 1966), pp. 728–734, *passim*. Reprinted by permission.

us nothing but the implacable hatred of the great mass of the people there, cost us the allegiance of unnumbered millions in other parts of the world, betray our own revolution and our own ideals, cost us unimaginable billions in money and even no small number of lives, since we would surely be obliged to occupy several countries militarily, and, in the end, lead us to irretrievable disaster in our own backyard. Hardly anyone, I think, advocates this policy.

We can leave the Latin Americans to work out their own destinies with our sympathy but without our close collaboration and assistance. This would be to shirk our responsibilities to our neighbors, who look to us for help, would cost us the goodwill of millions, and would abandon the field to the Castro/Communists.

We can pursue the Kennedy policy. That, in my view, is the policy that will best advance our own interests and those of our Latin American friends. It flows fundamentally from the fact that Latin America is in revolution. Indeed, one might argue for the Kennedy policy on the most cynical of grounds: That the Czar might have averted the Russian Revolution if he had heeded the warning of the Winter Palace. I prefer to argue for the Kennedy policy not only on the ground of our own national interest but on the ground that it best upholds our ideals and best promotes the legitimate aspirations of the Latin American masses.

What, more specifically, does pursuing this policy mean?

Latin America is twenty nations—twenty-two if one counts Jamaica and Trinidad-Tobago—and to speak of a Latin American policy is perhaps impossible. Nevertheless, certain broad guidelines may be suggested.

In my view, we should actively join the forces at work for change in Latin America. We should align ourselves with the young, the students, the workers, the intellectuals, the labor leaders, *campesino* leaders, progressive churchmen, and others, who will lead the rising masses, for inevitably the future belongs to them, and by and large they are on the side of justice. . . .

In designing economic assistance programs, we should remember that the problem is not "underdeveloped nations" or "underdeveloped economies," but, rather, underdeveloped people. What the people of Latin America need is not fine public buildings, nor highways and dams alone, but better health, more food, broader opportunities, a more equitable distribution of income, and, above all, better education. I would put our heaviest emphasis on education—on conventional academic and vocational schoolroom education and on education by every shortcut available, including educational radio and television. I would hope we could undertake both sound long-range economic development projects and "political" projects, but if forced to choose between them, I would usually choose the "political" projects. They affect the people quickly and directly. A political struggle is going on in Latin America and until it is resolved sound economic development is virtually impossible anyway. . . .

We must support constitutionalism in Latin America. We must not align ourselves with dictators in the name of anti-Communism. We must seek to strengthen elected progressive regimes. They alone offer the people an alternative to communism and rightist dictatorship. This is not to say we should try to impose our system of democracy everywhere, a course both impossible and undesirable. (Mexico gets along fine with a one-party system.) Rather, we should encourage the growth of strong, independent nations with elected democratic governments of their choice. To abstain from politics would abandon the field to Castro and to local military power. It would strengthen the right. It would abandon the center entirely. It would leave the people nowhere to turn but to communism. It did in the Dominican Republic in 1965.

The Latin American masses will not wait forever. If we offer them no political standard to which they can repair, if we merely promote economic growth, if we merely protect our own nine-billion-dollar investment, if we merely announce that we are against communism, then we shall surely throw the people into the Communist complex. . . .

Finally, we must work to strengthen the OAS. The OAS has seldom faced up to its responsibilities. And in all candor we have sometimes tried to manipulate it for our own purposes. Perhaps now is the time, and the Dominican Republic the place, for the OAS to grow up—and for us to join it wholeheartedly. This entails a certain loss of sovereignty on our part and on the part of the Latin American nations. It entails renunciation or modification of the doctrine of non-intervention. True, many Latin Americans genuinely fear our intervention—and no wonder. But all too often non-intervention has become a slogan used by pontifical Latin American "elder statesmen" who have lived well in Washington for many years, making speeches at the OAS; self-serving politicians back home who raise the ancient battle cry solely for political advantage; and the Castro/Communists. Moreover, the Alliance for Progress, the OAS, and the UN imply some surrender of sovereignty. . . .

Now, the people of the United States should understand that what I advocate is not an easy policy to execute. In fact, it is the most difficult of all. It is far easier to seek stability.

Stability is tempting. It is pleasant. It is safe. It encourages foreign investment. During 1962, the year of crisis, when the Alliance first took hold and uproar commenced and I went to the Dominican Republic, foreign investors took more capital out of Latin America than they put in. They put only sixty-four million dollars into it in 1963, the year of the *coups* in Honduras and the Dominican Republic. In 1964 they invested 175 million dollars in the first nine months alone. The reasons, according to *Time*, were that Castro's influence had waned, so had fears of Communist takeovers, commodity prices rose, the United States made investment guarantees, and more governments were "moving toward stability." There can be no doubt: With stability comes fresh money. With stability are usually linked other U.S. purposes—to foster economic growth, protect the nine-billion-dollar U.S. investment in Latin America, avoid intervention in internal politics, and oppose communism.

But to seek stability means, in most of Latin America, to align ourselves with the military and the oligarchy. We could gain stability that way, for a time. But in the end, the "stable" repressive establishment will go down. And we would go down with it. Such a policy opposes history—seeks non-change in a time of revolutionary change. We cannot ride both the horses of revolution and counter-revolution.

SOURCES OF INFORMATION ON
CONTEMPORARY LATIN AMERICA

It is practically impossible to keep up with the flood of publications on Latin America in recent years. This bibliography will not attempt, therefore, to give complete or even extensive coverage, but to provide information which will help to guide the reader to sources of information and to suggest some items, largely in English, on each country.

Many of the significant publications are cited, with full bibliographical information, in the text or in the readings of this volume. A selection of other material is given below. Many other important items can be found in the reference works and periodicals listed below.

I. BIBLIOGRAPHIES

1. *Paperbacks*. The most up-to-date and comprehensive listings are by Charles J. Fleener and Ron L. Seckinger, *The Guide to Latin American Paperbacks* (Gainesville: Center for Latin American Studies, University of Florida, November 1966) and *Latin America: A Bibliography of Paperback Books* (Washington, Government Printing Office, 1967), compiled by Georgette M. Dorn of the Hispanic Foundation, Library of Congress.

2. *Current Publications*. The Hispanic Foundation of the Library of Congress prepares annually the *Handbook of Latin American Studies* (University of Florida Press), a selective and annotated guide to current publications, indispensable for the serious student. An index to the first 25 volumes is in preparation.

II. REFERENCE WORKS

3. Latin American Center, University of California, Los Angeles. This Center has prepared and published an unusual collection of guides. See the compilations by Martin H. Sable, *Master Directory for Latin America* (1965), with many addresses and much information on worldwide activities relating to Latin America; *Periodicals for Latin American Economic Development, Trade and Investment: An Annotated Bibliography* (1965); *A Guide to Latin American Studies*, 2 vols. (1967); *Latin American Urbanization: A Guide to the Literature and Organizations in the Field* (1967). The center also published Ludwig Lauerhass, *Communism in Latin America, a Bibliography: The Postwar Years* (1945–1960), (1962), and *Statistical Abstract of Latin America* (10th ed., 1966).

4. American Universities Field Staff. *A Select Bibiography: Asia, Africa, Europe and Latin America* (New York, 1961). Supplements issued about every two years. Howard F. Cline prepared the Latin American section.

5. Foreign Policy Association. *Handbook on Latin America* (New York, 1966). Much useful information in brief compass.

6. The United States Government. The Library of Congress, the National Archives, and other government agencies (Agriculture, Commerce, Mines, etc.) constitute the greatest single center in the world for information on the past and

present of Latin America. The Government Printing Office publishes much material on Latin America. The various congressional committees issue many reports, some of reference value, such as the 333-page volume issued by the Committee on Foreign Affairs of the House of Representatives, *Regional and Other Documents Concerning United States Relations with Latin America* (1966). See also the compilation by Linda Lowenstein, *Government Resources Available for Foreign Affairs Research* (1965) issued by the Office of External Research, Department of State.

The Bureau of Educational and Cultural Affairs of the Department of State issued in November 1965 a massive volume entitled *Resources Survey for Latin American Countries* (Washington: Government Printing Office, 1966). It is a record of the more than 1,200 educational, religious, business, and private organizations, and of many U.S. Government and international agencies "which seek to develop for that region the human resources essential to its educational, cultural, economic, and social progress."

7. Center for Intercultural Formation, Cuernavaca, Morelos, Mexico. Publishes a CIF Report weekly on economic, political, and social affairs in Latin America, especially as related to religious developments, and a three-volume reference work, *Latin America in Maps, Charts, Tables*, compiled by Yvan Labelle and Adriana Estrada. 3 vols. (Cuernavaca, 1963–1965). Vol. I includes "Socio-Economic Data"; Vol. II, "Socio-Religious Data (Catholicism)"; Vol. III, "Socio-Educational Data."

8. Pan American Union. Washington, D.C. The secretariat issues many reports, periodicals, and books on a variety of topics, which are listed in the current guide to its publications. A work of reference value is *América en Cifras*, which is brought up to date regularly.

9. Other Institutions.

The Inter-American Development Bank issues annually a well-edited, meaty volume, *Socio-Economic Progress in Latin America*, whose latest volume covers 1966 (Washington, 1967).

The Land Tenure Center of the University of Wisconsin has issued a number of special studies, many of which are available on request, focused on agrarian reform.

The Office for Research, Commission on Ecumenical Mission and Relations, the United Presbyterian Church in the U.S.A., published *A Factual Study of Latin America*, compiled by W. Stanley Rycroft and Myrtle M. Clemmer (New York, 1963).

The United Nations, especially its Economic Commission for Latin America, regularly issues reports and special studies of fundamental value. See its list of current publications.

III. PERIODICALS

The most up-to-date information and sometimes the best material on Latin America appears in reviews or newspapers in Latin America or elsewhere. Irene Zimmerman's *Guide to Current Latin American Periodicals: Humanities and Social Sciences* (Gainesville, Florida: Kallman Publishing Company, 1961) provides data on many. Some of the basic periodicals in English are

The Americas. A handsome, popular monthly issued by the Pan American Union. Also in Spanish and Portuguese.

Caribbean Studies. Institute of Caribbean Studies, University of Puerto Rico. Quarterly.

The Hispanic American Historical Review. Duke University Press. Quarterly.

Inter-American Economic Affairs. Edited by Simon G. Hanson. Lively and controversial. Usually critical of State Department policies. Quarterly.

Journal of Inter-American Studies. University of Miami. Quarterly.

Latin American Research Review. University of Texas Press. Three issues per year. Includes valuable review articles, such as Cole Blasier's "Studies of Social Revolution: Origins in Mexico, Bolivia, and Cuba," II, no. 3 (1967), 28–64.

South American Handbook, Forty-Third Annual Edition. Edited by Howell Davies. New York: Rand-McNally, 1967. A useful travel and commercial guide covering all of Latin America despite its title.

IV. FURTHER READINGS

GENERAL: CULTURAL ASPECTS

Anderson Imbert, Enrique. *Spanish American Literature: A History.* Detroit: Wayne University Press, 1963.

Arciniegas, Germán, ed. *The Green Continent: A Comprehensive View of Latin America by Its Leading Writers.* New York: Knopf, 1949.

Bates, Marston. *The Land and Wildlife of South America.* New York: Time, Inc., 1964.

Chase, Gilbert. *A Guide to the Music of Latin America.* Washington: Pan American Union, 1962.

Cohen, J. M., ed. *Latin American Writing Today.* Baltimore: Penguin Books, 1967.

Fitts, Dudley, ed. *Anthology of Contemporary Latin American Poetry.* New York: New Directions, 1947.

Flakoll, Darwin, and Claribel Alegría, eds. *New Voices of Hispanic America,* 1962.

Harss, Luis. *Into the Mainstream: Conversations with Latin American Writers.* New York: Harper and Row, 1967.

Heath, Dwight B., and Richard N. Adams. *Contemporary Cultures and Societies of Latin America.* New York: Random House, 1965.

Henríquez Ureña, Pedro. *Literary Currents in Hispanic America.* Cambridge, Mass.: Harvard University Press, 1945.

Hitchcock, Henry Russell. *Latin American Architecture Since 1945.* New York: Museum of Modern Art, 1955.

Hulet, Claude L., comp. *Latin American Poetry in English Translation: A Bibliography.* Washington: Pan American Union, 1965.

―――. *Latin American Prose in English Translation: A Bibliography.* Washington: Pan American Union, 1964.

Schurz, William L. *This New World: The Civilization of Latin America.* New York: Dutton, 1964.

Stabb, Martin S. *In Quest of Identity: Patterns in the Spanish American Essay of Ideas, 1890–1960.* Chapel Hill: University of North Carolina Press, 1967.

Torres-Ríoseco, Arturo. *The Epic of Latin American Literature.* Berkeley: University of Califonia Press, 1959.

GENERAL: LARGELY ECONOMIC AND POLITICAL

Adams, Richard N., and others. *Social Change in Latin America Today: Its Implications for United States Policy.* New York: Harper, 1960.

Aguilar, Luis E. *Marxism in Latin America.* New York: Knopf, 1968.

Alba, Víctor. *Alliance Without Allies: The Mythology of Progress in Latin America.* New York: Praeger, 1965.

―――. *Politics and the Labor Movement in Latin America.* New York: Praeger, 1967.

Alexander, Robert J. *Prophets of the Revolution: Profiles of Latin American Leaders.* New York: Macmillan, 1962.

————. *Organized Labor in Latin America.* New York: Free Press, 1965.

Anderson, Charles W. *Politics and Economic Change in Latin America: The Governing of Restless Nations.* Princeton: Van Nostrand, 1967.

Baerresen, Donald W., ed. *Latin American Trade Patterns.* Washington: The Brookings Institution, 1965.

Bailey, Norman A. *Latin America in World Politics.* Foreword by Ronald M. Schneider. New York: Walker, 1967.

Bernstein, Marvin. *Foreign Investment in Latin America.* New York: Knopf, 1966.

Brown, Robert T. *Transport and the Economic Integration of South America.* Washington: The Brookings Institution, 1966. A specialized monograph on the role of transport in the development of a program to foster intercontinental commerce.

Burr, Robert N. *Our Troubled Hemisphere: Perspectives on United States–Latin American Relations.* Washington: Brookings Institution, 1967.

Busey, James L. *Latin American Political Guide.* 10th ed. Colorado Springs: The Printed Page, 1966.

Considine, John J., ed. *The Church in the New Latin America.* Notre Dame: Fides Publishers, 1964.

————, ed. *Social Revolution in the New Latin America.* Notre Dame: Fides Publishers, 1965.

Dell, Sidney. *A Latin American Common Market.* New York: Oxford University Press, 1966.

Diégues, Manuel, Jr., and Bryce Wood, eds. *Social Science in Latin America.* New York: Columbia University Press, 1967.

Edelmann, Alexander T. *Latin American Government and Politics: The Dynamics of a Revolutionary Society.* New York: Dorsey, 1965.

Gerassi, John. *The Great Fear in Latin America.* New York: Collier Books, 1965.

Glade, William P. *The Latin American Economies: A Study of Their Institutional Evolution.* Princeton: Van Nostrand. To be published in 1968.

Gordon, Wendell C. *The Political Economy of Latin America.* New York: Columbia University Press, 1965.

Gunther, John. *Inside South America.* New York: Harper and Row, 1967.

Hamill, Hugh M., Jr. *Dictatorship in Spanish America.* New York: Knopf, 1965.

Hanson, Simon G. *Five Years of the Alliance for Progress.* Washington, D.C.: Inter-American Affairs Press, 1967.

Hirschman, Albert O. *Journeys Toward Progress.* New York: Twentieth Century Fund, 1963.

————, ed. *Latin American Issues: Essays and Comments.* New York: Twentieth Century Fund, 1961.

Houtart, François, and Emile Pin. *The Church and the Latin American Revolution.* New York: Sheed and Ward, 1965.

James, Preston E. *Latin America.* 3rd ed. New York: Odyssey Press, 1959.

Johnson, John J. *The Military and Society in Latin America.* Stanford: Stanford University Press, 1964.

————. *Continuity and Change in Latin America.* Edited by John J. Johnson. Stanford, Cal.: Stanford University Press, 1967.

Lambert, Jacques. *Latin America: Social Structures and Political Institutions.* Berkeley: University of California Press, 1968. Excellent synthesis, with sociological orientation.

"Latin America in the Twentieth Century," *Journal of World History,* VIII, No. 2 (1964). An entire issue, consisting of papers originally presented at a meeting at the University of Bordeaux in April 1963. Articles by Germán Arciniegas, Américo Jacobina Lacombe, Moisés González Navarro, Magnus Mörner, and Charles C. Griffin.

Lieuwen, Edwin. *Arms and Politics in Latin America.* New York: Praeger, 1960.
————. *Generals vs. Presidents: Neomilitarism in Latin America.* New York: Praeger, 1964.

Lipset, Seymour M., and A. Solari, eds. *Elites and Latin America.* New York: Oxford University Press, 1967.

Martz, John D. *The Dynamics of Change in Latin American Politics.* New York: Prentice-Hall, 1965.

Needler, Martin C., and others. *Political Systems of Latin America.* Princeton: Van Nostrand, 1964.

Pflaum, Irving Peter. *Arena of Decision: Latin American in Crisis.* Englewood Cliffs, N.J.: Prentice-Hall, 1964.

Pike, Fredrick B. *The Conflict Between Church and State in Latin America.* New York: Knopf, 1964.

Poblete Troncoso, Moisés, and Ben G. Burnett. *The Rise of the Latin American Labor Movement.* New Haven, Connecticut: College and University Press, 1960.

Romualdi, Serafino. *Presidents and Peons: Recollections of a Labor Ambassador in Latin America.* New York: Funk and Wagnalls, 1967.

Schmitt, Karl M., and David B. Burks. *Evolution or Chaos? Dynamics of Latin American Government and Politics.* New York: Praeger, 1963.

Silvert, Kalman H. *The Conflict Society: Reaction and Revolution in Latin America.* Rev. ed. New York: American Universities Field Staff, 1966.

Slater, Jerome. *The OAS and United States Foreign Policy.* Columbus: Ohio State University Press, 1967.

Tannenbaum, Frank. *Ten Keys to Latin America.* New York: Random House, 1962.

Tomasek, Robert D., ed. *Latin American Politics: Studies of the Contemporary Scene.* Garden City, New York: Doubleday, 1966.

United Nations. *The Economic Development of Latin America in the Post War Period.* New York: United Nations, 1963.

Urquidi, Víctor L. *The Challenge of Development in Latin America.* New York: Praeger, 1964.

Véliz, Claudio, ed. *Obstacles to Change in Latin America.* London: Oxford University Press, 1965.
————. *The Politics of Conformity in Latin America.* New York: Oxford University Press, 1967.

Wagley, Charles, ed. *Social Science Research on Latin America.* New York: Columbia University Press, 1964.

ARGENTINA

Alexander, Robert J. *The Perón Era.* New York: Columbia University Press, 1951.

Barager, Joseph. *Why Perón Came to Power.* New York: Knopf, 1968.

Blanksten, George I. *Perón's Argentina.* Chicago: University of California Press, 1967.

Ferrer, Aldo. *The Argentine Economy.* Berkeley: University of California Press, 1967.

Fillol, Tomás Roberto. *Social Factors in Economic Development: The Argentine Case.* Cambridge: The M.I.T. Press, 1961.

Greenup, Ruth and Leonard. *Revolution Before Breakfast: Argentina, 1941–1946.* Chapel Hill: University of North Carolina, 1947.

Kennedy, John J. *Catholicism, Nationalism and Democracy in Argentina.* Notre Dame: University of Notre Dame Press, 1958.

Peterson, Harold F. *Argentina and the United States, 1810–1910.* New York: State University of New York, 1964.

Romero, José Luis. *A History of Argentine Political Thought,* tr. by T. F. McGann. Stanford, Cal.: Stanford University Press, 1963.

Scobie, James R. *Revolution on the Pampas: A Social History of Argentine Wheat, 1860–1910.* Austin: University of Texas Press, 1964.

Taylor, Carl C. *Rural Life in Argentina.* Baton Rouge: University of Louisiana Press, 1948.

BOLIVIA

Alexander, Robert J. *The Bolivian Revolution.* New Brunswick, N.J.: Rutgers University Press, 1958. Favorable view by an American professor. For a contrary interpretation, see the work of the Bolivian exile, Alberto Ostria Gutiérrez, *The Tragedy of Bolivia: A People Crucified.* New York: Devin-Adair, 1958.

Arnade, Charles W. "Bolivia's Social Revolution, 1952–1959: A Discussion of Sources," *Journal of Inter-American Studies,* I (1959), 341–352.

Kirchoff, Herbert. *Bolivia, Its People and Scenery,* 2d ed. Buenos Aires: Guillermo Kraft, 1944. Photographs which give one the feeling of the country.

Leonard, Olen E. *Bolivia: Land, People and Institutions.* Washington: The Scarecrow Press, 1952. Sociological description, based on field work and wide use of printed material.

U.S. Army. *Area Handbook for Bolivia.* Washington: Special Operations Research Office, 1964.

Zondag, C. H. *The Bolivian Economy, 1952–1965: The Revolution and Its Aftermath.* New York: Praeger, 1967.

Zook, David H., Jr. *The Conduct of the Chaco War.* New York: Bookman Associates, 1960.

BRAZIL

Baklanoff, Eric N., ed. *New Perspectives of Brazil.* Nashville, Tenn.: Vanderbilt University Press, 1966.

Bello, José Maria. *A History of Modern Brazil, 1889–1964.* Stanford, Cal.: Stanford University Press, 1966.

Bishop, Elizabeth. *Brazil.* New York: Time, Inc., 1964.

Brazil in Pictures. Introduction by Alceu Amoroso Lima. New York: Studio Publications, 1958.

Burns, E. Bradford, ed. *A Documentary History of Brazil.* New York: Knopf, 1966.

———. *Perspectives on Brazilian History.* New York: Columbia University Press, 1967.

Castedo, Leopoldo. *The Baroque Prevalence in Brazilian Art.* New York: Charles Frank Publications, 1964.

Costa, João Cruz. *A History of Ideas in Brazil: The Development of Philosophy in Brazil and the Evolution of National History.* Berkeley: University of California Press, 1966.

Freyre, Gilberto. *Brazil, an Interpretation.* New York: Knopf, 1945.

———. *The Masters and the Slaves.* New York: Knopf, 1965.

————. *The Mansions and the Shanties: The Making of Modern Brazil.* New York: Knopf, 1963.

Furtado, Celso. *The Economic Growth of Brazil: A Survey from Colonial to Modern Times.* Berkeley: University of California Press, 1963.

————. *Diagnosis of the Brazilian Crisis.* Berkeley: University of California Press, 1965.

Griffin, William J. "Brazilian Literature in English Translation," *Review of Inter-American Bibliography,* V, Nos. 1–2 (1955), 21–37.

Guenther, Konrad. *A Naturalist in Brazil: The Flora and Fauna and the People of Brazil.* Trans. by Bernard Miall. London: Allen and Unwin, 1931.

Haring, C. H. *Empire in Brazil: A New World Experiment with Monarchy.* Cambridge, Mass.: Harvard University Press, 1958.

Havighurst, Robert, and J. Roberto Moreira. *Society and Education of Brazil.* Pittsburgh: University of Pittsburgh Press, 1965.

Horowitz, Irving Louis. "The Natural History of Revolution in Brazil: A Biography of a Book," in Gidson Sjoberg, ed., *Ethics, Politics and Social Research* (Cambridge, Mass.: Schenkman, 1967).

Johnson, Harvey L. "The Brazilian Mirror: Some Brazilian Writings in English Translation," *The Americas,* XXI (1965), No. 3, 274–294.

Mindlin, Enrique E. *Modern Architecture in Brazil.* Preface by S. Giedion (English Language Edition). New York: Reinhold, 1956.

Nabuco, Carolina. *The Life of Joaquim Nabuco.* Stanford, Cal.: Stanford University Press, 1950. Trans. and edited by Ronald Hilton.

Nash, Roy. *Conquest of Brazil.* New York: Harcourt, Brace & Co., 1927.

Normano, J. F. *Brazil: A Study of Economic Types.* Chapel Hill: University of North Carolina Press, 1935.

Pierson, Donald. *Negroes in Brazil: A Study of Race Contact at Bahia.* Chicago: University of Chicago Press, 1942.

Rodrigues, José Honório. *Brazil and Africa.* Trans. by Richard A. Mazzara and Sam Hileman. Berkeley: University of California Press, 1966.

————. *National Aspirations of Brazil.* Austin: University of Texas Press, 1966.

Wagley, Charles. *Amazon Village.* New York: Knopf, 1964.

Young, Jordan M. *The Brazilian Revolution of 1930 and the Aftermath.* New Brunswick, N.J.: Rutgers University Press, 1967.

THE CARIBBEAN ISLANDS (EXCEPT CUBA)

Abrahams, Peter. *Jamaica: An Island Mosaic.* London: Her Majesty's Stationery Office, 1957.

Anderson, Robert W. *Party Politics in Puerto Rico.* Stanford, Cal.: Stanford University Press, 1965. The author stresses that "Puerto Rican political life is conditioned by the island's preoccupation with its constitutional, political, and cultural status."

Bell, Wendell. *The Democratic Revolution in the West Indies.* Cambridge, Mass.: Schenkman Publishing Co., 1967.

Berbusse, Edward J., S.J. *The United States in Puerto Rico, 1898–1900.* Chapel Hill: University of North Carolina Press, 1966.

Blanshard, Paul. *Democracy and Empire in the Caribbean.* New York: Macmillan, 1947. Personal conclusions based on an extensive first-hand experience, 1942–1946, in Caribbean affairs as a U.S. official. Both provocative and informative, though now somewhat out of date.

Bourne, Dorothy Dulles, and James R. Bourne. *Thirty Years of Change in Puerto Rico: A Case Study of Ten Selected Rural Areas.* New York: Praeger, 1966.

The British Caribbean. London: Oxford University Press, 1957. "A brief political and economic survey," compiled by the Royal Institute of International Affairs.

Cumper, G. E., ed. *The Economy of the West Indies.* Kingston, Jamaica: Institute of Social and Economic Research, University College of the West Indies, 1960.

Developments Toward Self-Government in the Caribbean. The Hague, Netherlands: Universities Foundation for International Cooperation, 1955. A symposium covering British, Dutch, French, and U.S. territory, with selected bibliography.

De Young, Maurice. *Man and Land in the Haitian Economy.* Gainesville: University of Florida Press, 1958.

Draper, Theodore. *The Dominican Revolt: A Case Study in American Policy.* New York: Commentary, 1968.

Fermor, Patrick Leigh. *Traveller's Tree: A Journey Through the Caribbean Islands.* New York: Harper, 1950.

Goldwert, Marvin. *The Constabulary in the Dominican Republic and Nicaragua. Progeny and Legacy of United States Intervention.* Gainesville: University of Florida Press, 1962.

Goodsell, Charles T. *Administration of a Revolution: Executive Reform in Puerto Rico under Governor Tugwell, 1941–1946.* Cambridge, Mass.: Harvard University Press, 1965.

Hansen, M., and H. Wells, eds., "Puerto Rico, A Study in Democratic Development," *The Annals of the American Academy of Political and Social Science,* Vol. 285 (1953), 1–166.

Harman, Carter. *The West Indies.* New York: Time, Inc., 1963.

Hoetink, H. *The Two Variants in Caribbean Race Relations.* New York: Oxford University Press, 1967.

International Bank for Reconstruction and Development. *Surinam: Recommendations for a Ten Year Development Program.* Baltimore. Johns Hopkins University Press, 1952.

Kain, Joan. *Report on Haiti.* Washington: Federal Security Agency, Social Security Administration, Children's Bureau, 1951.

Laroche, Maximilien. *Haiti et sa littérature.* Montreal: Ageum, 1964.

Lowenthal, David. *A Study of the Development of Race Relations in the Caribbean.* London: Oxford University Press, 1966.

Manigat, Leslie. *Haiti of the Sixties: Object of International Concern.* Washington: Washington Center of Foreign Policy Research, 1964.

Masferrer, Alberto. *El minimum vital.* Guatemala: Ediciones del Gobierno de Guatemala, 1951.

Mathews, T. H., and others. *Politics and Economics in the Caribbean: A Contemporary Analysis of the Dutch, French and British Caribbean.* Río Piedras: University of Puerto Rico, Institute of Caribbean Studies, 1966.

Mintz, Sidney W. *Worker in the Cane: A Puerto Rican Life History.* New Haven: Yale University Press, 1960.

———, and Vern Carroll. "A Selective Social Science Bibliography of the Republic of Haiti," *Revista Inter-Americana de Ciencias Sociales,* II (1963), No. 3, 405–419.

Newman, Peter. *British Guiana: Problems of Cohesion in an Immigrant Society.* New York: Oxford University Press, 1964.

Oxaal, Ivan. *Black Intellectuals Come to Power: The Rise of Creole Nationalism in Trinidad and Tobago.* Cambridge, Mass.: Schenkman, 1967.

Parry, J. H., and P. M. Sherlock. *A Short History of the West Indies.* London: Macmillan and Company, Ltd., 1956. Valuable survey, emphasizing the British territories.

Revert, Eugene. *La France d'Amérique: Martinique, Guadeloupe, Guyana, Saint-Pierre et Miquelon.* Paris: Editions Maritimes et Colonials, 1955.

Rodman, Selden. *Quisqueya: A History of the Dominican Republic.* Seattle: University of Washington Press, 1964.

Rubin, Vera, ed. *Caribbean Studies: A Symposium.* Kingston, Jamaica: Institute of Social and Economic Research, University College of the West Indies, 1957. Specialized anthropological and sociological studies.

Smith, M. G. *A Framework for Caribbean Studies.* Mona, Jamaica: Extra-Mural Department, University College of the West Indies, 1955.

Springer, Hugh W. *Reflections on the Failure of the First West Indian Federation.* Cambridge, Mass.: Harvard University Press, 1962.

Swan, Michael. *British Guiana: The Land of Six Peoples.* London: Her Majesty's Stationery Office, 1957. Attractive and interesting general presentation, with much information.

U.S. Army. *Area Handbook for Panama.* Washington: Government Printing Office, 1964.

Wilgus, A. Curtis, ed. *The Caribbean.* Gainesville: University of Florida Press, 1951. 15 vols. Since 1950, the University of Florida has held annually a conference on Caribbean affairs with participants from business, government, and the academic world and has printed the proceedings. Much interesting information on a variety of matters, though expectably uneven in quality. Issued with slightly different title each year.

CENTRAL AMERICA

Castillo, Carlos M. *Growth and Integration in Central America.* New York: Praeger, 1966.

Panama: Canal Issues and Treaty Talks. Washington: The Center for Strategic Studies, Georgetown University, 1967.

Whetten, Nathan L. *Guatemala: The Land and the People.* New Haven: Yale University Press, 1961.

CHILE

Bowman, Isaiah. *Desert Trails of Atacama.* New York: American Geographical Society, 1924. Classic account of the northern desert.

Burr, Robert N. *By Reason or Force: Chile and the Balancing of Power in South America, 1850–1905.* Berkeley: University of California Press, 1965.

Ellsworth, P. T. *Chile: An Economy in Transition.* New York: Macmillan, 1945. Somewhat out-of-date statistically, this remains a fundamental volume.

Gil, Federico G. *The Political System of Chile.* Boston: Houghton Mifflin, 1966.

Halperin, Ernst. *Nationalism and Communism in Chile.* Cambridge, Mass.: M.I.T. Press, 1965.

Herrick, Bruce H. *Urban Migration and Economic Development in Chile.* Cambridge, Mass.: M.I.T. Press, 1966.

Silvert, Kalman H. *Chile.* New York: Holt, 1965.

Stevenson, John R. *The Chilean Popular Front.* Philadelphia: University of Pennsylvania Press, 1942. An evaluation of the coalition that took control in 1938, with some historical background.

Thiesenhusen, William C. *Chile's Experiments in Agrarian Reform.* Madison: University of Wisconsin Press, 1967.

COLOMBIA AND VENEZUELA

Alexander, Robert J. *Venezuelan Democratic Revolution: A Profile of the Regime of Rómulo Betancourt.* New Brunswick, N.J.: Rutgers University Press, 1964.

Fiscal Survey of Colombia. Baltimore: The Johns Hopkins University Press, 1965.

Green, G. H. "Books in English about Colombia and Venezuela," *The Library Association Record* (London, April, 1963), 156–162.

MacEoin, Gary. *Colombia and Venezuela.* New York: Time, Inc., 1965.

Martz, John D. *Acción Democrática: Evolution of a Modern Political Party in Venezuela.* Princeton, N.J.: Princeton University Press, 1966.

———. *Colombia: A Contemporary Political Survey.* Chapel Hill: University of North Carolina Press, 1962.

Parsons, J. J. *Antioqueño Colonization in Western Colombia.* Berkeley: University of California Press, 1948.

Romoli, Kathleen. *Colombia: Gateway to South America.* New York: Doubleday, Doran, 1941. Now somewhat out of date, but an interesting popular introduction and for long one of the few good books in English on Colombia.

Rourke, Thomas (D. J. Clinton). *Gómez, Tyrant of the Andes.* New York: William Morrow & Co., 1936. An attack. For a defense, see Pedro M. Arcaya, *The Gómez Regime in Venezuela* (Washington: privately printed, 1936).

Smith, T. Lynn. *Colombia: Social Structure and the Process of Development.* Gainesville: University of Florida Press, 1968.

U.S. Army. *Area Handbook for Colombia,* 2nd ed. Washington: Government Printing Office, 1964.

———. *Area Handbook for Venezuela.* Washington: Government Printing Office, 1964.

West, Robert C. *The Pacific Lowlands of Colombia.* Baton Rouge, Louisiana: 1957.

Williamson, Robert C. *El estudiante colombiano y sus actitudes: un análisis de psicología social en la Universidad Nacional.* Bogotá: Facultad de Sociología, Universidad Nacional de Colombia, 1962.

Wise, George S. *Caudillo, a Portrait of Antonio Guzmán Blanco.* New York: Colombia University Press, 1951.

Wurfel, S. W. *Foreign Enterprise in Colombia: Laws and Policies.* Chapel Hill: University of North Carolina Press, 1965.

Ybarra, T. R. *Young Man in Caracas.* New York: Ives Washburn, 1941. Amusing autobiography.

CUBA

See Fleener and Seckinger, *The Guide to Latin American Paperback Literature,* pp. 52–56, for additional titles.

Abel, Elie. *The Missile Crisis.* Philadelphia: Lippincott, 1966.

Alvarez Díaz, José, ed. *Un estudio sobre Cuba.* Miami: University of Miami Press, 1963. A compendious manual of mostly economic information, prepared by a group of Cuban exiles.

Cohen, J. M., ed. *Writers in the New Cuba.* Baltimore: Penguin Books, 1967.

Cuba Since Castro: A Bibliography. Washington: Special Operations Research Office, The American University, 1962.

Foreign Areas Studies Division. *Special Warfare Area Handbook for Cuba.* (Prepared under contract with the Department of the Army.) Washington: Special Operations Research Office, The American University, 1961.

Foreign Policy Association. *Problems of the New Cuba.* New York: 1935.

Goldenberg, Boris. *The Cuban Revolution and Latin America.* New York: Praeger, 1965.

Gray, Richard B. *José Martí, Cuban Patriot.* Gainesville: University of Florida Press, 1962.

International Bank for Reconstruction and Development. *Report on Cuba.* Washington: 1951.

Johnson, Haynes, with Manuel Artime, José Pérez San Román, Ernesto Oliva, and Enrique Ruiz Williams. *The Bay of Pigs.* New York: Norton, 1964. Based on interviews with surviving members of Brigade 2506, especially the four leaders.

Lockwood, Lee. *Castro's Cuba, Cuba's Fidel.* New York: Macmillan, 1967.

Nelson, Lowry. *Rural Cuba.* Minneapolis: University of Minnesota Press, 1950. A fundamental study by an agricultural sociologist.

Ortiz, Fernando. *Cuban Counterpoint: Tobacco and Sugar.* New York: Knopf, 1947. An informed and entertaining interpretation by a leading Cuban writer.

Phillips, R. Hart. *Cuba, Island of Paradox.* New York: McDowell, Obolensky, 1959.

Plank, John N., ed. *Cuba and the United States: Long Term Perspectives.* Washington: Brookings Institution.

Suárez, Andrés. *Cuba: Castroism and Communism, 1959–1966.* Cambridge, Mass.: M.I.T. Press, 1967.

Tetlow, Edwin. *Eye on Cuba.* New York: Harcourt Brace, 1966.

Zeitlin, Maurice, and Robert Scheer. *Cuba: Tragedy in Our Hemisphere.* New York: Grove Press, 1963.

ECUADOR

Blomberg, Rolf, ed. *Ecuador, Andean Mosaic.* Stockholm: Hugh Gebers Forlag, 1952. Excellent photographs, plus informative chapters by several hands on various aspects of Ecuadorian history and culture. Selective bibliography of works in English.

Linke, Lilo. *Ecuador, Country of Contrasts.* 3d ed. New York: Oxford University Press, 1960.

Needler, Martin C. *Anatomy of a Coup d'Etat: Ecuador, 1963.* Washington: Institute for the Comparative Study of Political Systems, 1964.

MEXICO

Ashby, Joe C. *Organized Labor and the Mexican Revolution under Lázaro Cárdenas.* Chapel Hill: University of North Carolina Press, 1967.

Cline, Howard F. *Mexico: Revolution to Evolution, 1940–1960.* London: Oxford University Press, 1963. Comprehensive, up-to-date treatment. Excellent bibliography.

———. "Mexican Community Studies," *Hispanic American Historical Review,* XXXII (Duke University Press, 1952), 212–242. Bibliographical record and analysis of this prime material for the study of contemporary Mexico.

Covarrubias, Miguel. *Mexico South: The Isthmus of Tehuantepec.* New York: Knopf, 1946. Well-illustrated socio-ethnological description.

Cronon, E. David. *Josephus Daniels in Mexico.* Madison: University of Wisconsin Press, 1960.

Dulles, John W. F. *Yesterday in Mexico: A Chronicle of the Revolution, 1919–1936.* Austin: University of Texas Press, 1961.

Ewing, Russell C., ed. *Six Faces of Mexico.* Tucson: University of Arizona Press, 1966.

Glade, William P., Jr., and Charles W. Anderson. *The Political Economy of Mexico.* Madison: University of Wisconsin Press, 1963.

Gregory, Gladys. *The Chamizal Settlement: A View from El Paso.* El Paso: Texas Western College, 1963.

Johnson, William Weber. *Mexico.* New York: Time, Inc., 1961.

Kneller, G. F. *The Education of the Mexican Nation.* New York: Columbia University Press, 1951.

Martínez, José Luis, ed. *The Modern Mexican Essay.* Trans. by H. W. Hilborn. Toronto: University of Toronto Press, 1965.

Mexican Issue, *The Texas Quarterly.* (University of Texas Press, 1959), II, No. 1. The literature, art, philosophy, and other aspects of Mexican culture today. Handsomely produced, with many illustrations.

"Mexico Today," *The Atlantic, March,* 1964, 90–154. An interesting mixture of art, history, and politics with a sampling of literature in translation.

México, cincuenta años de revolución. 4 vols. Mexico: Fondo de Cultura Económica, 1961–1962.

Meyers, Charles Nash. *Education and National Development in Mexico.* Princeton: Princeton University Press, 1965.

Millon, Robert Paul. *Mexican Marxist: Vicente Lombardo Toledano.* Chapel Hill: University of North Carolina Press, 1966.

Mosk, Sanford A. *Industrial Revolution in Mexico.* Berkeley: University of California Press, 1954. Balanced, nontechnical account, now slightly out of date.

Nicholson, Irene. *The X in Mexico: Growth Within Tradition.* New York: Doubleday, 1966.

Parkes, Henry Bamford. *A History of Mexico,* rev. ed. Boston: Houghton Mifflin Co., 1950. Still a useful work, though not a revaluation of Mexican history in the light of developments of the seventeen years since the first edition appeared.

Paz, Octavio, ed. *An Anthology of Mexican Poetry.* Trans. by Samuel Beckett. Bloomington: Indiana University Press, 1965.

Powell, J. R. *The Mexican Petroleum Industry, 1938–1950.* Berkeley: University of California Press, 1956. Analysis of the problems and production of Petroleos Mexicanos, not a study of the expropriation.

Quirk, Robert E. *An Affair of Honor: Woodrow Wilson and the Occupation of Vera Cruz.* Lexington: University of Kentucky Press, 1962.

———. *The Mexican Revolution, 1914–1915.* Bloomington: Indiana University Press, 1960.

Reyes, Alfonso. *Mexico in a Nutshell and Other Essays.* Berkeley: University of California Press, 1965.

Robinson, Cecil. *With the Ears of Strangers: The Mexican in American Literature.* Tucson: University of Arizona Press, 1963.

Romanell, Patrick. *Making of the Mexican Mind.* Lincoln: University of Nebraska Press, 1952. Sympathetic, provocative description of the intellectual scene.

Ruiz, Ramón Eduardo, *Mexico: The Challenge of Poverty and Illiteracy.* San Marino, Cal.: Huntington Library, 1963.

Schmitt, Karl. *Communism in Mexico.* Austin: University of Texas Press, 1964.

Scott, Robert. *Mexican Government in Transition.* Rev. ed. Urbana: University of Illinois Press, 1964.

Toor, Frances. *A Treasury of Mexican Folkways.* New York: Crown Publishers, 1947. A rich collection, by an experienced folklorist long a resident in Mexico.

Tucker, William P. *Government of Mexico Today.* Minneapolis: University of Minnesota Press, 1957. First comprehensive study in any language. A legalistic description, rather than an analysis of the government in actual operation.

Vaillant, George. *Aztecs of Mexico.* Garden City, New York: Doubleday & Co., 1948. The standard work.

Vernon, Raymond, ed. *Public Policy and Private Enterprise in Mexico.* Cambridge, Mass.: Harvard University Press, 1964.

Whetten, Nathan. *Rural Mexico.* Chicago: University of Chicago Press, 1948. A basic work, to be used with Eyler Simpson's *Ejido.*

Wilkie, James W. *The Mexican Revolution: Federal Expenditures and Social Change Since 1910.* Berkeley: University of California Press, 1967.

Wolf, Eric. *Sons of the Shaking Earth.* Chicago: University of Chicago Press, 1959.

PARAGUAY

Fretz, Joseph Winfield. *Pilgrims in Paraguay.* Scottsdale, Pa.: Mennonite Publishing House, 1953. On Mennonite colonization.

Krause, Annemarie Elisabeth. *Mennonite Settlement in the Paraguayan Chaco.* Chicago: University of Chicago Department of Geography, 1952.

Service, Elman R. and Helen S. *Tobatí, Paraguayan Town.* Chicago: University of Chicago Press, 1954. Anthropological study.

Ynsfran, Pablo Max, ed. *The Epic of the Chaco: Marshall Estigarribia's Memoirs of the Chaco War, 1932–1935.* Austin: University of Texas Press, 1950.

PERU

Pike, Fredrick B. "Church and State in Peru and Chile Since 1840: A Study in Contrasts," *American Historical Review,* LXXIII (1967), 30–50.

VENEZUELA

See COLOMBIA AND VENEZUELA.

Index

Numbers in bold-face type refer to pages of the Readings